TORONTO
TO 1918

The History of Canadian Cities

TORONTO
TO 1918
An Illustrated History

J.M.S. Careless

James Lorimer & Company, Publishers
and
National Museum of Man,
National Museums of Canada
Toronto 1984

To my wife, who listened,
encouraged, and always eased the way.

ISBN 0-88862-665-7 cloth

Cover design: Don Fernley
Maps: Assembly Dave Hunter

Canadian Cataloguing in Publication Data

Careless, J. M. S., 1919-
Toronto to 1918

(The History of Canadian cities series)
Co-published with the National Museum of Man, National Museums of Canada.
Bibliography: p. 212
Includes index.

1. Toronto (Ont.) — History. I. National Museum of Man (Canada). II. Title. III. Series: The History of Canadian Cities.

FC3097.4.C37 1983   971.3'541   C83-099128-X
F1059.5.T6857C37 1983

James Lorimer & Company, Publishers
Egerton Ryerson Memorial Building
35 Britain Street
Toronto, Ontario M5A 1R7

Printed and bound in Canada
6 5 4 3 2 1   84 85 86 87 88 89

Illustration Credits

City of Toronto Archives (CTA): 176 top, back flap. **CTA, James Collection:** front cover, 2, 148, 156, 159 bottom right, 160 bottom, 165, 167 top, 171, 177, 178, 184 upper left, 188 bottom, 191, 195, 196 upper left, 198, 199, backcover lower right. **CTA, Department of Public Works Collection:** 159 except bottom right, 168 bottom. **CTA Board of Education Collection:** 188 top. **Metropolitan Toronto Library Board:** 18, 20, 24, 28, 32, 34, 36, 37, 40, 44, 45 bottom, 49, 50, 53 top, 55, 61, 63, 65 top, 66 right, 67, 68, 72, 75, 79, 84, 88, 90 bottom left and upper right, 92, 93, 95, 99, 108, 110, 113 bottom right, 114, 116 left, 119, 121, 123, 127, 129, 131, 134, 135 bottom, 140 left, 142, 144, 164 top, 176 bottom, 180, 186, 189, back cover upper right. **Public Archives Canada:** 52, 53 bottom, 65 bottom, 82, 164 bottom, 167 bottom, 196 top right and bottom right. **PAC/Foreign and Commonwealth Office, United Kingdom:** 66 left, 85, 87, 90 upper left and bottom right. **Royal Ontario Museum:** 8, 12, 22, 23, 26, 42, 45 top, 47, 57, 70, 98, 106, back cover upper left. **Archives of Ontario:** 80, 103 left, 105, 135 upper right, 140 right, 160 top, 173, 182, 196 bottom left, 197. **Toronto Transit Commission:** 132, 146, 184 except upper right, 185, back cover bottom left. **Massey-Ferguson Limited:** 113 top and bottom left, 153. **Toronto Jewish Congress/Canadian Jewish Congress, Ontario Region Archives:** 158, 170. **Metropolitan Toronto Police Museum:** 145, 192. **Consumers' Gas Company Limited:** 168 top. **Art Gallery of Ontario, Toronto** (Gift of the CNE Association, 1965): 174. **Archives, Eaton's of Canada Ltd.:** 116 right. **Percy J. Robinson,** *Toronto During the French Regime* (Toronto, 1933): 10. **The Canada Newspaper Cartoonists' Association,** *Torontonians As We See 'Em* (Toronto, 1905): 151. **Freya Hahn Collection:** 135 upper left. **Mrs. Alfred A. Stanley Collection:** 162. **Ralph Greenhill Collection:** 103 right.

Table of Contents

Appendix
List of Tables

List of Maps

Foreword
The History of Canadian Cities Series

The History of Canadian Cities Series is a project of the History Division, National Museum of Man (National Museums of Canada). The project was begun in 1977 to respond to a growing demand for more popular publications to complement the already well-established scholarly publications programs of the Museum. The purpose of this series is to offer the general public a stimulating insight into Canada's urban past. Over the next several years, the Museum, in cooperation with James Lorimer and Company, plans to publish a number of volumes dealing with such varied communities as Montreal and Kingston, Halifax and Quebec City, Ottawa and Sherbrooke.

It is the hope of the National Museum of Man that the publication of these books will provide the public with information on Canadian cities in visually attractive and highly readable form. At the same time, the plan of the series is to have authors follow a similar format, and the result, it is anticipated, will be a systematic, interpretative and comprehensive account of the urban experience in many Canadian communities. Eventually, as new volumes are completed, *The History of Canadian Cities Series* will be a major step along the path to a general and comparative study of Canada's urban development.

The form for this series — the individual urban biography — is based on a desire to examine all aspects of community development and to relate the parts to a larger context. The series is also based on the belief that, while each city has a distinct personality that deserves to be discovered, the volumes must also provide analysis that will lift the narrative of a city's experience to the level where it will elucidate questions that are of concern to Canadians generally. These questions include such issues as ethnic relationships, regionalism, provincial-municipal interaction, social mobility, labour-management relationships, urban planning and general economic development.

In this volume, J. M. S. Careless details the exciting early history of Toronto from its origins through to the end of the Great War. The various steps in the city's evolution — fur-trade depot, village, port, commercial town, railway and regional hub, "nearly" national metropolis — are traced in the pleasing writing style that has graced Professor Careless's earlier works. For each period, Careless weaves together the city's economic, social and political history and describes and analyses the changing population and urban landscape.

This volume, which appears in time for Toronto's sesquicentennial celebrations, has been prepared by one of Canada's most eminent historians. Professor Careless, widely known for his many award-winning works on Canadian history, is also a well-known urban historian, and his work in this field is continued in this fine study. A companion volume to this book, *Toronto Since 1918: An Illustrated History*, by James T. Lemon, is scheduled for publication during 1984.

Professor Careless's text has been enhanced by well-selected paintings, engravings, maps and photographs. This illustrative material is not only visually enjoyable, it also plays an essential part in re-creating the past. While illustrations and maps cannot by themselves replace the written word, they can be used as a primary source in a way equivalent to more-traditional sources. The fine collection of illustrations in this volume captures images of a wide variety of situations in Toronto, allowing a later generation to better understand the forms, structures, fashions and group interactions of an earlier period.

Already published in this series:
Alan Artibise, *Winnipeg* (1977)
Max Foran, *Calgary* (1978)
Patricia Roy, *Vancouver* (1980)
John Weaver, *Hamilton* (1982)

Alan F. J. Artibise
General Editor

Acknowledgements

Virtually any scholarly work of history is a cooperative effort, even when it has nominally one author. I thus have to thank a number of individuals and the staffs of institutions who together shared sizeably in the making of this book. Taking the latter group first, I must especially acknowledge the constant aid received at the Public Archives of Canada, Archives of Ontario, City of Toronto Archives, Metropolitan Toronto Public Library, and Thomas Fisher Rare Book Library of the University of Toronto. Yet that list could be much enlarged, to include (among still more) the Library of Congress in Washington, the libraries and museums of McGill University in Montreal, those of Harvard University in Cambridge, the Royal Ontario Museum, the United Church of Canada Archives, and the Library of the Foreign and Commonwealth Office of the United Kingdom, which gave permission to use invaluable early photographs of Toronto in the 1850s.

Turning to individuals, I am grateful to my colleague at the University of Toronto, Professor James Lemon (whose study of Toronto in this series will follow on from mine), for making available to me research papers done in the Department of Geography on our common city of concern. I am no less grateful to Miss Edith Firth, a prime authority indeed on early Toronto, for her advice and expertise so cordially provided; to Mr. Stephen Otto, who kindly gave me the benefit of his inquiries into the architects of the nineteenth-century city; and to an old friend and former student, Professor Frederick Armstrong of the University of Western Ontario, himself a leading and well-published scholar on Toronto's history. In fact I owe him a particular debt, not only for generous aid throughout, but for reading and constructively criticizing my manuscript to very valuable effect. In Professor Alan Artibise of the University of Winnipeg I had an ideal series editor, fully knowledgeable and helpful, but judicious and guiding, as an editorial chief should be; and with Ted Mumford, as editor for the publisher, I had a happy and effective working partnership, which finally got the volume out.

I am also most appreciative of grants received from the National Museum of Man and of the University of Toronto's funds provided to holders of the rank of university professor, which went towards costs incurred in travel and research, typing and acquisition of illustrations.

Besides all this, I should express my thanks to my daughter Andrea Careless, now of Victoria, whose several previous years of research into economic data on the growth of Canadian cities were pursued towards my still-intended broader study of Canadian metropolitan development; yet the materials she amassed and organized that pertained to Toronto could be, and have been, applied to the present book. Here, however, I must above all acknowledge the key part played by Mrs. Gail Crawford, my research assistant, who over the past three years worked specifically on this Toronto volume. She efficiently investigated the local repositories, especially the city archives, filling in gaps in my earlier inquiries or updating them. She made initial sweeps for maps, illustrations and statistical sources, drafted the appendix tables, and typed the completed manuscript. Altogether, I could not have been more admirably assisted.

Finally, I should pay warm tribute to my graduate students at Toronto for their theses, studies and research work over two decades in seminars on Ontario regional and Canadian metropolitan history. From all they taught me, I might have made this a much fuller account of the rise of Toronto, were it not that the text space was strictly, though inevitably, confined by the requirements of an extensively illustrated study.

J. M. S. Careless
May 1984

The unsettled site of Toronto in 1793: the harbour looking west to the entrance, the main shoreline on the right, the protecting peninsula (later island) to the left.

Introduction
The Lakeland Site

A city is shaped by people, their wants and ideas, their organization and technology. Yet it is shaped as well by the location and nature of its site, the place where people gather. Thus it was with Toronto. Long before it became an urban community, long before incoming Europeans reached it, Toronto was a recognized location in wilderness America, frequented by native peoples of the surrounding Great Lakes country. For this lakeshore landing in the forests near the head of Lake Ontario gave access to an age-old Indian travel path that ran north to reach Georgian Bay on Lake Huron. In effect, this was a shortcut between the Lower and the Upper Great Lakes across the neck of the southern Ontario peninsula. And so the Toronto location had a specific significance of site: as a junction-point of land and water routes that transected the Great Lakes region. Other cities of Canada have their own distinctive site features; many similarly began as vantage points on some established course of travel. But in Toronto's case, its accessible lake harbour, low, easily traversed shoreline, and gate position on a passage through the midst of southern Ontario, were distinguishing aspects from prehistoric times — and destined to have repeated influence on its subsequent history.

"TORONTO" BEFORE URBAN OCCUPATION

The Indian way north from Toronto (which may originally have meant "Trees in the Water," though "Lake Opening" and "Place of Meeting" are other possibilities) could make use of several river entries around the landing area.[1] Mainly, however, the route ran up the valley of the Humber, across to the Holland, which flows into Lake Simcoe, and from there by other water links to Georgian Bay. The first stage of this route followed a trail some twenty-eight miles along the wooded banks of the Humber, evidently because that stream was much impeded by fallen timber and beaver dams.

The Toronto Trail or Carrying Place was thus a wearing portage. Still, in an age when long-distance travel moved by canoe, this direct path cut off many more hundreds of miles by the long way from the Lower to Upper Lakes. Even in far later days, this short land crossing would have enduring value, to be realized anew by roads and rails. But during Indian times it was a feasible way through a forest wilderness. Hence the Carrying Place at its start saw repeated transits, and shifting encampments or longer-lasting villages dotted about the landing-ground as this primitive traffic pattern went on through time without written record.

The Toronto route entered written history when French venturers probed up the St. Lawrence into the Great Lakes region from their trading base at Quebec. Étienne Brulé most probably travelled the "*passage de Toronto*," as the French came to call it, as early as 1615. The passage also figured in the warfare between the Huron Indians around Georgian Bay and the Iroquois Confederacy south of Lake Ontario, which saw the crushing of the Hurons by mid-century. Thereafter a sizeable Iroquois (Seneca) village, Teiaiagon, emerged by the Humber entry to the Toronto Trail. Here, in France's own expansion westward, explorers, fur traders and missionaries arrived to cross the passage, while French supply boats used the harbour. Moreover, fur dealers up from the English base at Albany on the Hudson visited Teiaiagon as well.[2]

In ensuing wars, which began with Indian conflict in the 1680s but became an Anglo-French imperial contest lasting to 1713, the Seneca abandoned the Teiaiagon site to the roving Mississauga; and these hunter-gatherers were not village-dwellers, although they maintained encampments and fisheries around the landing-place. Then in 1720 the French established their own post at Toronto, largely to intercept fur cargoes from north and west before they flowed on across Lake Ontario to English rivals in the expanding colony of New York. Here was a further indication of

Toronto's site significance, for that junction-point might assuredly feed trade either eastward to the St. Lawrence and Montreal, now the main French commercial base, or southward to the Mohawk-Hudson system and its British port, New York.

In any event, the first French post at Toronto, a modest storehouse closed by 1730, was merely an adjunct to a much more substantial fort at Niagara, France's bulwark against British penetration of its Great Lakes empire. Increasing British pressures, however, and by 1749 designs to strengthen the inland chain of French forts, led to the re-establishment of a post at Toronto. Fort Rouillé, or Fort Toronto, was erected there in 1751 on the shore some three miles east of the Humber (in the grounds of the present Canadian National Exhibition). It was truly a fort, with timber bastions linked by palisades, mounting four small cannons, and garrisoned by a few soldiers plus some labourers and batteaux transport men — Toronto's first little military embodiment.[3] And in 1754 imperial war returned again, although its battles took place elsewhere. In July 1759 Fort Niagara fell to British attack, whereupon the French force at Toronto burned their far weaker fort and withdrew. Two months later, the British capture of the key stronghold of Quebec spelled the end of French rule in Canada. It was already over at Toronto, leaving only blackened timber ruins in a clearing of some 300 acres.

Under British authority, fur trading revived in the Toronto area, and by the 1780s Jean Baptiste Rousseau had become the established local trader, maintaining a house and post near the Humber mouth well into the next decade. Moreover, partners in Montreal's powerful North West Company grew interested in the Toronto Passage, as potentially a less costly way to their far-flung western fur domain than via the many portages of the traditional Ottawa River route to the Upper Lakes. Nonetheless, the Toronto site still lay within the fur wilderness world — until the American Revolution loosed a transformation. While that struggle went on from 1775 to 1783, it is true that little altered. The major British inland strong points of Niagara and Detroit held firm, and the Toronto locale remained a quiet backwater. Yet the outcome of the Revolution was greatly to affect the site, which had thus stayed securely within the British Empire.

Above all, the peace of 1783 that recognized the United States drew an international boundary down the Great Lakes. Toronto again fronted on a vulnerable border, shielded only by some twenty

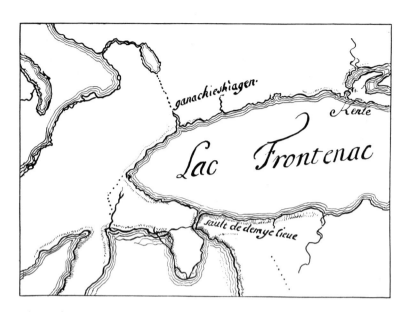

This crude map of 1674 by the French explorer Joliet marks the Toronto Passage between Lake Ontario ("Frontenac") and Georgian Bay via Lake Simcoe. An Indian village then on the route is named, as is "Kente" (Quinte), a French mission site. As well, an early reference is made to Niagara Falls: "A falls of half a league."

miles of lake. And with an unfriendly, increasingly powerful American republic opposite, that could be an uneasy position for years ahead. Yet the boundary also signified that Toronto would be part of a separate entity in America — the Canadian entity, as it evolved — and so would take shape within Canadian patterns of government and growth. The American water border might readily be crossed, certainly by the peaceful movement of goods, people and ideas; yet it could also be a dividing screen, behind which Toronto looked to British links and backing and secured its own realm to develop. Further, the political fact of the border soon led to political decisions to found a town at the Toronto site as an inland centre to sustain the British side of the lake line. In a real sense, the Revolution boundary impelled the rise of Toronto.

Beyond all this, the Revolution produced a movement of people to occupy the empty British inlands: loyal American colonials who turned northward from the vengeance of their republican foes. From 1784 these Loyalists settled on the upper St. Lawrence west to the foot of Lake Ontario where the town of Kingston now began to rise, and onward to the Bay of Quinte. Others cleared farms in the Niagara Peninsula; still others gathered near Detroit on Lake Erie shores. Their numbers grew yearly through continued influx and a vigorous birthrate. Accordingly, in 1791 the new British province of Upper Canada was erected for the 14,000 predominantly anglophone inhabitants of these areas beyond the French Canadian lands of the St. Lawrence valley — henceforth Lower Canada. And Upper Canada received a basic framework of English law and institutions, no less basic for Toronto at its core.

Settlement scarcely reached the Toronto locality until 1793. But well before, as it spread towards that site from both ends of Lake Ontario, the signs of change were plain. Several prominent figures in Montreal, including leading North West Company members, petitioned for land grants in the Toronto district, with settlement projects and trade monopolies in mind or plans to develop communications over the Toronto Passage. In response, Lord Dorchester, then British governor-in-chief at Quebec, moved to acquire Indian land rights in the vicinity. In 1787 the Toronto Purchase was effected, whereby for some £1,700 in cash and goods the Mississauga conveyed title to a fourteen-mile stretch along the lakefront, from present-day Scarborough westward past the Humber to the Etobicoke, and inland reaching back some twenty-eight miles: truly a bargain-basement deal.[4] In 1788 the Toronto Purchase was first surveyed, while Captain Gother Mann of the Royal Engineers drafted a plan for a Toronto townsite, featuring a one-mile square of city lots adjacent to the harbour entry, bordered by an open common with larger residential lots beyond. This was rather an artificial exercise in late eighteenth-century imperial town planning, yet indicated how actively Toronto was now being considered as a prime interior site for urban development. Moreover, Governor Dorchester further displayed his interest in developing Toronto when in 1791 he ordered grants there, totalling 2,400 acres, for three of his chief land petitioners.[5]

The grants were not to be completed. The creation of Upper Canada that very year produced a new government with authority over its provincial lands, and under a lieutenant-governor with ideas of his own, Colonel John Graves Simcoe. Simcoe's personal judgment that a town should be established at Toronto was not necessarily opposed to Dorchester's, but characteristically he came to it through his own strong opinions. He arrived in Upper Canada early in 1792, beginning government at Kingston, but he soon moved to Niagara, deeper in the province, to make it his provincial capital. Yet the colonel was not satisfied with "the contemptible Fortress of Niagara" under American guns across a narrow river.[6] He looked instead to more centrally located Toronto, behind the wider water reach of Lake Ontario, where a garrison and governance could be more safely based and where the Toronto Passage gave access to the whole Upper Lakes country beyond. In 1793 he arrived at that site to direct its occupation, his ship piloted into harbour by the resident fur trader, Rousseau. It was a symbolic juncture of old and new: between a fur depot enclosed in primal forests and the rise of a town in an emerging countryside.

SITE FEATURES AND TORONTO'S GROWTH

The pre-settlement era had already revealed vital geographic aspects of Toronto's site: its focal lake harbour with access to the passage inland, its location on through-traffic routes up the Great Lakes and outward via either the Hudson or the St. Lawrence, and its boundary position, set across from the mounting American presence in the continental interior. Yet other features of Toronto's physical setting became significant once the lakeland site became a town.

Clearly it had always mattered for a landing-ground at the

The Don Valley in the 1790s. Sketched probably from Governor Simcoe's homesite above the river, this view conveys the thick woods stretching inland from the shore.

Toronto site that its lakeside margin was low and fairly flat (Map 1). It was of much more consequence for a town, however, that here there was an outspread, gentle-sloping shore plain for occupation, with effective communication inward. And if there was a fairly sudden rise of fifty to seventy-five feet behind this plain (just below the present east-west artery of St. Clair Avenue, where the shoreline of long-vanished glacial Lake Iroquois sweeps up), this had still been negotiable along various stream channels by canoes in portage, and remained a problem rather than a barrier for later forms of transport. Moreover, ravines and creek beds cut deeply into the rise, in time affording easier gradients for roads or railways in the ascent from the shore level to higher plains. And from here again there were no great surface obstacles to moving on through the rolling hills that spread northward in order to reach Lake Simcoe, then Georgian Bay and the Upper Lakes.[7]

Still, the original home and continuing core of Toronto was the Shore or City Plain proper, the low waterside area that stretched some two to three miles inland and extended roughly from the Don River on the east to the Humber on the west. East of the Don, the shoreline began to rise to the Scarborough Bluffs, clay cliffs about 350 feet high, soon pinching out the plain to narrow beaches. West of the Humber, the shore similarly became less sheltered, if not as raised. But centred in between lay broad Toronto Bay or harbour, protected from the open lake and all but enclosed by a long, low, sandy peninsula cloaked with trees. Here there was plenty of room and depth of water for ships to berth by the shielded harbourside. The one drawback was that sailing vessels often had to beat out the bay's westerly facing entrance against prevailing winds. Yet the coming of steamboats in the 1820s subsequently met that difficulty, further to be solved when storms in the 1850s carved a new channel through the eastern end of the peninsula, the Eastern Gap that also created Toronto Island.

The sheltered bay and harbourfront, the low-lying expanse behind, and beyond that again, the rise to higher plains, these were the surface features that most basically affected the layout of urban Toronto, its streets and transport systems, land uses, and in due course the distribution of its business and residential districts. They also raised problems of their own. For one thing, the nearly flat Shore Plain imposed difficulties of drainage, and its churned-up masses of thick clay often made streets in the young town a succession of mud holes. For another, parts of this waterside plain initially were dank mosquito-ridden marshes, which also affected building, not to mention health, while the ground-rise behind it could block off some roads or make their development more expensive. Still further — if less material — Toronto had no particular power of natural setting, no mountain backdrop, no rugged seacoast walls or sweep of river, just a flat shore backed by low lines of inland hills. Nevertheless, in general it had a very accessible, highly usable site. And perhaps any attractiveness of setting would have to lie in the broad, shimmering lake before it, the wooded curve of Toronto Island, the spreading farm landscape that backed the town, and its rising buildings themselves.

The spread of farming was certainly vital to a young Toronto, not only to provide food supplies for the town-dwellers, but also markets for their wares in agricultural districts that emerged around it. Moreover, the fact that the whole locality lay in the midst of the generally fertile soils of future southern Ontario meant that it was excellently placed to grow with the trade of a rising agricultural community. In this regard, climate also was decidedly significant. The Great Lakes region receives ample, fairly regular rainfall, and its Lower Lakes area enjoys a longer, warmer growing season than most parts of Canada. Toronto's climate, moderate in general geographic terms, does have its own excesses: from oppressively hot and humid spells in summer to bitter, windy cold snaps in winter or too many raw, melt-and-freeze spring days. Still, it lies outside heavy-snow belts, does not face the cold extremes of northern Ontario or the prairies, and long, pleasant autumns help make up for the summertime invasions of steamy southern air, or springs that come all too reluctantly and waywardly. In short, an emerging Toronto and its surroundings not only had a sufficiently moderated, moist climate in which a considerable range of farming could flourish, but also had less-exacting needs for fuel and shelter than the great mass of Canada.

All the same, there were abundant resources for fuel and shelter in the thick forests of the area. Clearing the dense growth posed heavy tasks for incoming urban settlers of the 1790s, but felled trees provided town-building lumber from early water-driven mills on the Humber and Don, while burning the plentiful excess produced valuable potash for export. Good timber was also on hand for shipbuilding, wagons or furnishings. And quantities of wood from

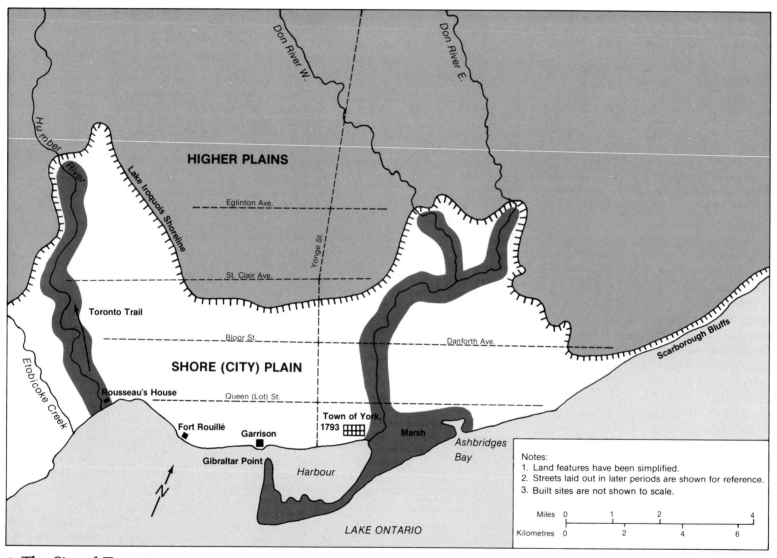

HIGHER PLAINS

Don River W.

Don River E.

Humber River

Lake Iroquois Shoreline

Eglinton Ave.

Yonge St.

St. Clair Ave.

Toronto Trail

Bloor St.

Danforth Ave.

Scarborough Bluffs

SHORE (CITY) PLAIN

Etobicoke Creek

Rousseau's House

Queen (Lot) St.

Town of York, 1793

Fort Rouillé

Garrison

Marsh

Ashbridges Bay

Gibraltar Point

Harbour

N

Notes:
1. Land features have been simplified.
2. Streets laid out in later periods are shown for reference.
3. Built sites are not shown to scale.

Miles 0 1 2 4

Kilometres 0 2 4 6

LAKE ONTARIO

1 The Site of Toronto

farther districts, gathered at the harbour, could be exported as well. Toronto, in fact, became an important lumber shipping point, though not in its early years.

Furthermore, as the pioneering phases passed away, other resources in or about the site entered into its development. Thus the sand and gravel of the vicinity, and good clay beds for brickmaking, began to furnish building materials for a rising brick-and-mortar town in the earlier nineteenth century, one no longer almost wholly shaped in wood. Not shaped in stone, however. Since bedrock here was mostly buried deep beneath clay and gravel plains, with few outcrops, building stone had largely to be shipped in; for instance, it had been brought in to adorn the aspiring Victorian city of the 1850s, by then booming with the railway age. So it was with coal, which became a growing need as local forest timber disappeared, as steamboats and locomotives switched from wood-burning in the later nineteenth century, and as steam-driven industry proliferated in Toronto around the same time. Yet water transport now brought it ample coal (and iron) via the Lakes. And in the early twentieth century, cheap hydroelectric power produced at Niagara Falls provided a whole new energy source for growth. During the same period, similarly, the opening of the Ontario mining and lumbering North made fresh raw materials available down transit routes that led to Toronto. Hence, emerging needs for energy or material supplies were largely met by the city's mounting ability to draw these to itself, thanks particularly to its position on main lines of communication.

Here we come back to location on traffic routes, conceivably the most enduring aspect of Toronto's site significance.[8] Set at the mid-front of what became heavily occupied southern Ontario, agriculturally rich and industrially powerful, the city rose to dominate this valuable heartland through a well-developed transport and communications system — that could not only deliver goods effectively by lake, road and rail, but also radiate the centre's influential press views, its political authority or financial power. Toronto was well placed, besides, to reach northward to more distant trade areas, from the time of the original Toronto Passage to that of twentieth-century mining booms. It could equally reach southward from its Ontario shore to the swelling metropolis of New York or to prosperous American states about the Great Lakes — all to provide it with traffic, markets, and sources of investment or business expertise (Map 2). To the east, the Lake Ontario–St. Lawrence transport system opened on Montreal, and Toronto remained closely linked to this major Canadian outlet from earliest days, as well as to the power, people and wealth of Britain beyond the Atlantic. To the west, by the later nineteenth century, the city could use trunk routes that led either to American mid-western centres like Chicago or to rising settlements in the northwestern Canadian prairies. At least by the First World War, Toronto had realized manifold advantages from its intersecting position on lines of continental transit across the Great Lakes basin.

Still, everything said so far simply indicates that Toronto had many potentialities if human beings grasped them under suitable conditions in history, not that anything in geographic features predetermined its rise to a great city. Its pre-settlement prelude suggests as much. While the Toronto Carrying Place and Passage had figured repeatedly in the French fur trade, the main lines of that trade had continued to run via the Ottawa route to the northwest or via the Lower Lakes route through Niagara to the Ohio and Mississippi southwest. Thus, Toronto had remained a minor post in between, fairly late to be made a French fort, and by no means having the strategic importance of Montreal as the St. Lawrence gateway to the interior, or even that of other inland forts.[9] Similarly, after the British conquest, Toronto had remained just one of a number of local trading stations along the Lake Ontario shore, any of which well might have become a small settled port once the whole region was finally populated. But then came the running of a man-made British-American boundary across the physical environment of the Great Lakes, and the consequent decision to place a defending, controlling town upon it at Toronto's site. From this point on, the various potentials of that place could come into action, once human enterprise took them up.

In sum, site factors do not necessarily ordain the emergence of a city, but do enter deeply into shaping its growth. Yet that involves as well such human factors as interests, power and work, along with innovation, expectation, and what we consider luck. Out of this amalgam comes an urban community. Out of it came the evolution of a town at Toronto to a regional, then national, Canadian metropolis.

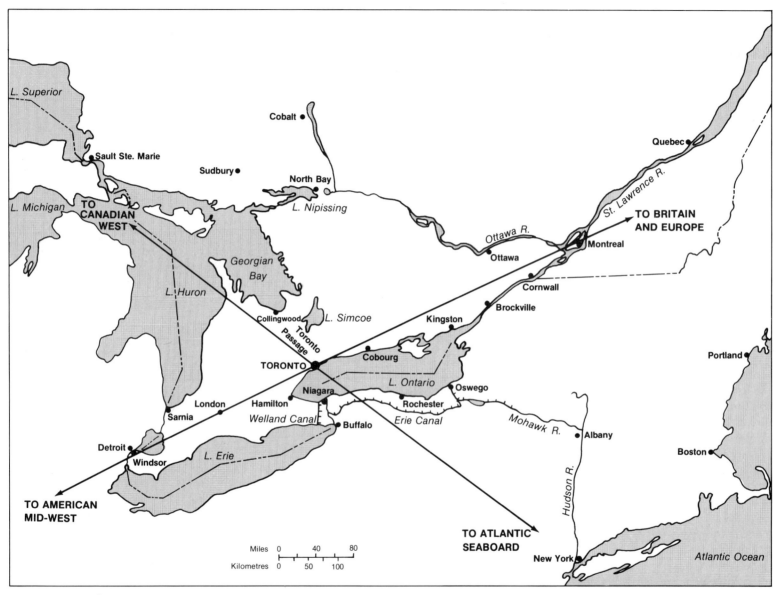

2 Location of Toronto

L. Superior

Cobalt

Quebec

Sault Ste. Marie

Sudbury

North Bay

L. Michigan

TO CANADIAN WEST

L. Nipissing

St. Lawrence R.

TO BRITAIN AND EUROPE

Georgian Bay

Ottawa R.

Montreal

L. Huron

Ottawa

Cornwall

Collingwood

L. Simcoe

Brockville

Toronto Passage

Kingston

Portland

Cobourg

TORONTO

L. Ontario

Oswego

Niagara

Rochester

London

Hamilton

Erie Canal

Sarnia

Welland Canal

Buffalo

Mohawk R.

Albany

Boston

Detroit

L. Erie

Windsor

Hudson R.

TO AMERICAN MID-WEST

TO ATLANTIC SEABOARD

Miles 0   40   80

Kilometres 0   50   100

New York

Atlantic Ocean

PATTERNS IN METROPOLITAN DEVELOPMENT

That evolution, which by the world war of 1914–18 had made Toronto second only Montreal in urban size and power in Canada, essentially comprised several main stages in metropolitan development: the process whereby a major city comes to dominate an extensive economic territory or hinterland by controlling its commerce, knitting the area into a transport network, centring many of its industrial activities, and organizing financial services for it. The hinterland territory may well contain many smaller cities and towns with their own lesser tributary districts, but all are linked to the overriding dominance of the master-city. And this metropolitan-hinterland pattern of development, equally evidenced by other leading cities in Canada or in the world beyond, is an integral feature of the whole urbanization of human society.[10]

In Toronto's case, the phases of economic metropolitan growth often overlapped or went on concurrently; but in broadest outline, they occurred most significantly in four successive stages. Firstly, in commerce, the urban community that began in 1793 built up a trading hinterland through providing its surrounding areas with marketing facilities. The initial village settlement acquired a merchant group that distributed goods to the adjacent population and received their products; as a growing port-town, it developed long-range wholesale commerce beyond merely local retail trade; and as a city by 1834 it beat rival nearby centres in thrusts for more hinterland business. Secondly, in transport, this enlarging city now linked its port and spreading commerce to a much wider regional hinterland by way of railways: beginning with the 1850s, long-distance, all-year rail routes vastly improved its land communications, far outclassing slow, seasonal early roads. Thirdly, from about the 1870s, sizeable factory industry arose in and around Toronto as a well-served transport centre, making it an increasing focus of wealth, technological headship and manufacturing supply in Ontario. And fourthly, out of capital derived in commerce, transport and industry emerged financial power, strongly displayed at least by the 1900s in big banking head offices and investment houses; a development which further tied hinterland areas, now reaching national bounds, to the credit-and-debit sway of the commanding metropolis of Toronto. By 1918 all this had taken place, even though new metropolitan growth and further hinterland extensions would scarcely cease for the city at that date.

Yet Toronto's rise did not only display these economic workings. Political factors were also highly important. The original town served as governing seat of Upper Canada; it became a capital again for some years during the union of Upper and Lower Canada in the mid-nineteenth century; and with the much broader Canadian federal union of 1867, it was made the capital of the newly created province of Ontario. The executive, parliamentary, judicial and administrative activities thus established at Toronto gave it special distinction and power even in its youngest village days. And in subsequent periods, political functions that centred in the city kept it dominant as a prime place of decision for the public and private concerns of areas well beyond it. Moreover, Toronto's role as home of prominent elite groups, as a concentration point of major ethnic and religious bodies, and in time as well as headquarters of popular movements or working-class organizations, also gave it widening social holds upon its hinterland. So did the city's influence on cultural developments, through its leading place in provincial education, publishing, professional and artistic life, and generally, over time, through its becoming a central source of information, cultivation and opinion. In evident ways, Toronto's rise to metropolitan status proceeded in much more than solely economic terms.

Accordingly, in tracing the city's growth from the beginnings in 1793 down to 1918, the basic theme can duly follow the development of the original village-capital to metropolitan existence through successive stages of major economic change; but into this there must be woven a series of other constantly related themes. These have to include political behaviour and social patterns among the urban elites and masses, population growth and ethnic composition, cultural activities, the shaping of Toronto's built environment, land uses, and its municipal life and services. Besides that, the urban community has its own internal structure of classes, families and generations. But above all, it remains externally linked with far broader realms, the complementing countryside, the region and the nation, and it responds to forces from beyond their limits also. This wider aspect, too, is bound up with the specific record of Toronto's development to be presented here: from the first settling of the tranquil lakeland site in the 1790s to the thriving Great Lakes metropolis of the young twentieth century.

Simcoe builds his base at Toronto, 1793. C. W. Jefferys's painting portrays the governor and officers supervising military construction by the Queen's Rangers.

Chapter One
The Government Village, 1793–1825

Urban places in North America did not necessarily derive from the settlement of their surrounding countrysides. Often the reverse occurred; a town was founded and frontier settlement spread about it. Notably in Canada, many major centres first began in nearly empty territory. And some came into being, as Toronto did, through specific action to establish an official base of power: to control or defend a territory and maintain government over it. It can well be noted that places as far spread as Halifax and Quebec, Toronto, Regina and Victoria, all initially took form as territorial bases of authority before significant settlement grew up outside them. Moreover, Quebec as the bastion of the seventeenth-century French Empire on the St. Lawrence, Halifax as the key to Britain's naval power in the northwestern Atlantic from the mid-eighteenth century, and Toronto as the late eighteenth-century seat of British garrison and government in the Great Lakes interior, had especially comparable roles to play. Even as raw villages in their earliest years, they shared the distinctive character of imperial bases — which from the start helped to promote their own development, and in due course that of neighbouring, supporting countrysides.

FOUNDING AN IMPERIAL BASE

On 30 July 1793, a bustling Lieutenant-Governor Simcoe landed at Toronto Bay to supervise the planting of a garrison and town. With him came his perceptive wife, Elizabeth, his staff and men of the Queen's Rangers, who were both an armed force and construction crew. Rangers sent in advance were already working on an encampment; Rousseau, the Humber River trader, and two Mississauga families were also on hand. The Simcoes chose a good spot for their portable canvas house, boated to the end of the harbour, then, as Mrs. Simcoe wrote in her diary, "walked through a grove

of fine Oaks where the Town is intended to be built." She noted that the low, wooded peninsula that sheltered the harbour broke the lake horizon and improved the view, "which indeed is very pleasing," while the waters of the bay were "beautifully clear and transparent."[1] So Toronto began, on a kind of agreeable summer outing.

Simcoe had made a preliminary visit to the site in May, and confirmed that here, assuredly, he should base control of his province of Upper Canada. Having been a distinguished British officer who had fought in the American Revolution at the head of the Loyalist Queen's Rangers, he was concerned with dangers of another American war and the need to make his colony militarily secure. The new governor combined the imperious outlook of an eighteenth-century aristocrat with the free-ranging visions of a natural optimist. He projected a whole series of towns besides Toronto for his province (all marked on a birchbark map drawn by his wife), including a future capital, London, located well inland in the southwestern reaches of Upper Canada.[2] Yet while he saw Toronto as only a temporary political headquarters, he also saw it as the essential military stronghold and naval base that would guard the border. He deemed it to be "the natural arsenal of Lake Ontario, and to afford an easy access over land to Lake Huron."[3] A fleet built in Toronto's excellent harbour could command the lake; a fort at the harbour entrance would keep off any attack. It might all be made "very strong at slight expence, and in the progress of the Country impragnable."[4] A dockyard, a sawmill to make lumber, and the town plot, these too were embraced in Simcoe's enthusiastic scheme.

But his superior, Governor-in-Chief Dorchester in Lower Canada, though he had already planned for a town at Toronto, did not agree that a place so remote from British power on the St. Lawrence could make an acceptable naval base, and for that purpose

Elizabeth Simcoe's diary and sketches vividly
record Toronto's founding years. In her late
twenties then, and of Welsh origin, she appears
above in Welsh dress. At left is her sketch
of Castle Frank, the Simcoe's Don retreat.
Its namesake, Francis Simcoe (who at age
four here had his own goat-drawn sleigh), died
at twenty-one in war in Spain. Above at left
the Garrison erected at the harbour entry, as
depicted by Mrs. Simcoe in 1796. Its powder
magazine stands below the slope.

fixed on Kingston. Simcoe thought Kingston "absolutely indefensible," open each winter to American attack across the frozen upper St. Lawrence.[5] Yet Dorchester controlled military expenditures, and refused them for Toronto. The Upper Canadian governor still did what he could there with the Queen's Rangers under his own command. He had them build a log-hut garrison by the harbour entry, beside what henceforth was to be Garrison Creek, and also constructed storehouses that might be fortified on a sandy tip of the low peninsula opposite, now grandly named Gibraltar Point. No doubt the disapproval of higher authority left Toronto's military position lamentably weak. But while its harbour might support a sizeable war fleet, the surrounding terrain was too low and too lacking in strong natural defences to provide really good protection. Nonetheless, Simcoe's own assurance, or wishful thinking, had profound consequences. Thanks to him, Toronto was launched as a garrison point, and soon as seat of government; and so could gradually become a functioning urban community, as others gathered to supply and serve its paid soldiery and officials.

The townsite itself was located further east within the harbour towards the Don River: a compact, ten-block rectangle enclosed by the present Front, George, Duke and Berkeley streets, set just below the baseline of a broader grid of concessions surveyed for farming settlement to northward. Subsequent extensions of the townsite would generally conform to the basic right-angled grid pattern thus imposed upon the landscape, of utilitarian, straight-run streets, showing small concern for any natural lies of land. At the eastern end of the town plot, near the Don, a reserve was created for government buildings; on the west, towards the Garrison, a much more extensive military reserve. And behind the town, a series of one-hundred-acre "park lots" were laid out, strips running north across the Shore Plain from the concession base line (later Queen Street, but first called Lot Street) to presently existing Bloor. These estates were intended as grants to mollify government officials unhappy at having to move from properties at Niagara to a wilderness post. Furthermore, Simcoe renamed Toronto, York, celebrated to the boom of cannon on 27 August 1793, in honour of the high-born if unspectacular British commanding-general, the Duke of York.[6]

In the next two years, a town settlement gradually took form, to become known as "Little York" in distinction from older, greater Yorks. Officials quickly sought town and park lots, though were slower to occupy them. A few more farms were opened in the vicinity, particularly up the Don. A government wharf was built, and a government sawmill on the Humber; while Isaiah Skinner, a New Jersey Loyalist, put up his own saw and grist mill on the Don. The Simcoes, too, had a house erected above the latter stream: Castle Frank, named for their small son and built of squared timbers with columned porticos of pine logs. But town-raising went on only slowly, given the dearth of actual settlers yet, and while the Rangers were busy enough on military projects. In 1794, however, William Berczy arrived, the leader of some sixty families of German emigrants who had turned from a settlement venture in New York State to Simcoe's promise of large land grants.

Berczy, a well-educated, gifted artist, now became land developer, road contractor and town builder, too. He received grants in Markham township northeast of York for his "German Company," but also employed himself and his followers for some time at the York townsite. There they cleared roadways, built Berczy's own residence and company warehouse, and put up other homes. By mid-1795 a little hamlet of log or square-hewn timber houses was clustered in the middle of the town plot, around what was to be the main east-west, central artery of King Street, thanks largely to the work of Berczy, his axemen and carpenters.[7]

Meanwhile, Simcoe had often been absent on military concerns, or touring his forest domain and ordering strategic trunk roads to be cut by the Rangers. Most significantly for York, he planned a better version of the old Toronto Trail, Yonge Street, named after Britain's secretary of war, primarily as a military link with Lake Huron. It would run north to gain the Holland River and Lake Simcoe, but not by the former Humber path, being directed instead closer to the Don and the town of York within the guarded harbour. The Rangers began hewing a road line; Berczy and his Markham settlers were contracted to work on the route. By the spring of 1796, Yonge Street was roughly useable as an ox-cart track extending thirty-three miles to a landing on the Holland, where that stream became navigable to Lake Simcoe.[8] It was a mere track indeed, full of stumps, roots and streams to ford. Still, this was another vital beginning, opening lands above York to wider settlement, and in due course to the markets of the town.

Early in 1796, moreover, the governor ordered the Rangers to erect public buildings at York. Two one-story brick structures would house the provincial legislature, which thus far had met at

Smith house in York, built 1794. Government officials might first inhabit town homes like this one — but D. W. Smith, surveyor-general, soon remade his into the more imposing Maryville Lodge.

William Berczy, artist, settlement agent, contractor, architect and pioneer builder of the Town of York.

Niagara, and provide for law courts and religious services also. In short, Simcoe was about to move the capital. He instructed the Niagara officialdom to transfer to York, "the present seat of this Government."[9] Yet while the public officers had long known of the impending move, they still delayed in facing the discomforts of a tiny bush settlement, so that the transfer actually took some two years to complete. Simcoe returned to England on leave in the fall of 1796, and there was reappointed as general in command of forces in the West Indies. And despite some later talk of Kingston, the province's capital stayed where he had left it, at York, where parliament began meeting in 1797. Thus was illustrated a principle in urban growth, as well as physics: inertia. Once started, things tend to move on in the direction set — unless deflected by some strong external force, as John Graves Simcoe had been.

In the year following his departure, there were about forty houses at York, and more under way as the officials' families continued to arrive. Apart from them, there were a few small shopkeepers and millers, contractors like Berczy, some farmers, house-building artisans, labourers and servants. In all, 241 inhabitants were enumerated at the first town meeting, held in July 1797 to elect town officers, almost four years after Simcoe had landed at Toronto Bay.[10] In one sense, this was a pretty modest achievement. In another, it was a critical head start. Through Simcoe's impetus, York had received initial advantage, another key consideration in urban development. Made garrison centre, it gained a lead in road access to the interior just because it was the command base. Ordered into being, it had equally been made a place to which Upper Canada had to look because of its role in legislative decisions or in the administering of law and land grants, not to mention its influence as the focus of imperial connections. Little York might yet be only a half-built forest hamlet, its public pretensions sneered at in older Kingston or Niagara. But it existed, with inset advantage and authority, in time to demonstrate yet another significant principle in urban growth: "Them as has, gits."

In all then, the city of Toronto needs pay respect to Simcoe, without forgetting others who shared in its foundation, from Dorchester at the inception of the idea to Berczy who worked to materialize it in town construction. Yet Dorchester, once the idea moved to implementation, did little that was positive, while Berczy as a town builder lacked Simcoe's powers over crucial policy decisions. The last-named remains pre-eminent. Once overpraised for his far-sighted vision (often wrong), he has since tended to be underrated as a caste-bound military Tory — a very partial verdict. But whatever his views, Simcoe deserves due recognition in the city that grew from his imperial base on Toronto Bay.

SETTLEMENT GROWTH AND EMERGENCE OF AN URBAN ECONOMY

The Simcoe years had produced a political headquarters. It was really the following period, from the late 1790s to the War of 1812, that saw York become a distinctly urban community, that is, with economic activities and social concerns differentiated from the rural areas that now were growing up beyond it. The rise of this town community with its own life and interests was certainly associated with the whole upsurge of settled society around the Lower Lakes. But to begin with, it was more immediately affected by the influx of officials and their families into York. The salaried and fee-receiving bureaucrats required materials and workers to build their homes and develop their estates, and their demands for goods and services were on a scale well beyond those of frontier farmers. Consequently, York could better attract storekeepers and labourers, and in addition a significant proportion of skilled craftsmen and specialized retailers. By 1812 its urban offerings included those of watchmaker, chairmaker and apothecary, hatter, tailor, hairdresser, brewer and baker, besides the general stores, mills, taverns, and blacksmith shops found also in rural hamlets.[11] The official class, then, not only put a political stamp on York; they helped energize and specialize its economic growth as well.

Economic growth brought an increasing population at the government village, from 241 in 1797 to 703 by 1812.[12] That still was small within Upper Canada in general, whose total population advanced by almost wholly rural settlement from some 14,000 in 1791 to around 90,000 in 1812.[13] Nevertheless, this farming spread necessarily impinged on York's own rise, particularly as districts around it were increasingly cleared. Numbers of settlers came in via York as an already established place, and took up land in its vicinity because it could offer them a market for produce as well as providing store supplies and a range of services. In short, town and country were starting to function in the essentially complementary, or symbiotic, relationship of service centre with hinterland. For years yet, however, the relatively thin spread of pioneer rural

Council-Office, Dec. 29, 1798.

YONGE-STREET.

NOTICE is hereby given to all persons settled, or about to settle on *YONGE-STREET*, and whose *locations* have not yet been confirmed by order of the PRESIDENT in council, that before such locations can be confirmed it will be expected that the following CONDITIONS be complied with :

First. That within *twelve months* from the time they are permitted to occupy their respective lots, they do cause to be erected thereon a good and sufficient dwelling house, of at least 16 feet by 20 in the clear, and do occupy the same in *Person*, or by a substantial *Tenant*.

Second, THAT within the same period of time, they do clear and fence *five* acres, of their respective lots, in a substantial manner.

Third, THAT within the same period of time, they do open as much of the Yonge-Street road as lies between the front of their lots and the middle of said road, amounting to one acre or thereabouts.

JOHN SMALL, C. E. C.

Regulations for settling and developing Yonge Street, 1798, issued by the Clerk of the Executive Council of Upper Canada.

settlement and the primitive state of inland communications meant that any hinterland trade remained restricted. York still lived a good deal unto itself, and from its own internal activities. But developments strongly to affect it in the long run grew, as migrants flowed into Upper Canada from the United States on through the 1790s down to 1812.

These newcomers came in the wake of the original Loyalist movement. American land-seekers pushing westward with Great Lakes frontiers brought with them a rough-and-ready pioneer individualism with small esteem for rank, and an expanding Methodism in popular religion. Broadly speaking, they filled in settlement eastward from York along Lake Ontario to Loyalist farms around the Bay of Quinte: they took up lands around the head of the lake or moved westward into the Grand and Thames valleys. More directly important for York, these post-Loyalist Americans also settled in farming townships above the town up Yonge Street, where mill-seats and little neighbourhoods began to emerge.[14] By 1812, accordingly, when war with the United States brought an abrupt end to the inflow, Upper Canada had acquired an agrarian population that was in large majority American, while the Loyalist minority among it differed more in allegiance than lifestyle. The province as a whole seemed fast becoming just another segment of the advancing American–Great Lakes world. And that marked another kind of differentiation between the Upper Canadian countryside and the small York urban centre, which remained predominantly British in make-up and convictions.

Nonetheless, the town's own economic development began to reflect the rising frontier life beyond it. York harbour attracted a growing traffic in batteaux and schooners, in part to supply its own residents, but also because it was a useful transshipment point, as crude roads extended its communications inward. Yonge Street was intermittently "improved" over the period, though remained incredibly bad by later standards. West of the town, a track was opened to Dundas and Ancaster at the head of the lake, linking there with the shore path around to Niagara and with Simcoe's Dundas Street, the route he had cut westward to the Grand and Thames. In 1799 the provincial authorities also had a road made eastward from the capital to the Bay of Quinte settlements and Kingston, in use by 1801. All these through routes could be reached from York harbour, if by rough connecting trails. At that port, accordingly, as the new nineteenth century got under way, ship-masters, shipwrights and sailors gathered; a commercial wharf was built, and flour and potash started going out, though at first irregularly. In effect, a transport pattern was forming for the town, thanks to the location of York's harbour at the centre of outreaching land lines. An official port-of-entry since 1801, its significance indeed was marked by the stone lighthouse raised on Gibraltar Point in 1808 and still standing today.

Merchants, too, began to concentrate at Little York. Rousseau, the long-established fur trader, started running a little general store once settlement took root. He formed a partnership with Thomas Barry (named first town clerk in 1797), but shortly after left the store to Barry and moved to Ancaster, where he continued to prosper.[15] Other small general storekeepers also appeared, trading in goods purchased in Kingston or Montreal. Owing to the absence of banks, the shortage of ready cash so characteristic of frontier areas, and the diversity of several accepted "currencies of account" for business transactions, local trade was mainly carried on by means of barter and credit, which often tied farmers deep in store debts and overextended the storekeepers. Then three particularly enterprising merchants arrived around the turn of the century, to gain ground by capturing much of the trade of the town elite. They were William Allan and Alexander Wood, both Scots, and Laurent Quetton de St. George, one of a group of French royalist emigrés who unsuccessfully attempted a settlement up Yonge Street.

As larger merchants with bigger and more varied stocks to furnish, these three began buying directly from Britain or New York to save on middlemen's costs. Through them, York was thus striking out for a commercial position of its own, no longer to be just a sales outlet for Kingston or Montreal businesses. Allan and Wood dealt more with British suppliers, perhaps because of their own origins and past contacts, but consequently incurred the still slow and often damaging transport of cargoes sent in via the long, rapids-impeded St. Lawrence route. St. George instead ordered largely from New York. It was near enough for goods sought there to be inspected by visiting buyers, goods that could then be forwarded by a shorter route of river, road and lake transport to arrive in a better state at York.[16] Political or tariff problems could still disadvantage shipment from New York, and since many of the items bought there were originally of British manufacture, they were often more expensive than if purchased from Britain direct. In

York in 1803, a village spreading along the shorebank, fronted by square-built wooden Georgian homes. The Don end is at the right side of the picture.

either case, however, York's commerce was shaping long-distance relationships with two external, and alternative, metropolitan sources of supply.

The physical enlargement of the town also reflected its material progress. On Simcoe's departure in 1796, his receiver-general and right-hand man, Peter Russell, carried on as administrator of the province. Because Simcoe's original town plot was fast being taken up, Russell in 1797 extended the townsite north to Lot Street and west to Peter Street, while between this planned New Town and the Old he reserved space for a jail and a courthouse, a market, hospital, school and church.[17] Only a log jail was actually erected during his administration — the rest came later — and the whole new area was slow to develop, being somewhat too ambitious for the time. Still, Russell did proceed with military construction, putting up a blockhouse at Garrison Creek and one near the eastern outskirts of the Old Town to guard the Don. Moreover, troubles with disapproving senior military officials at last were ended when another full-fledged governor, General Peter Hunter, arrived in 1799. In his alternative role of commander-in-chief of the British forces in the Canadas, Hunter ruled that York definitely would stay a garrison centre. Though its defences remained far from formidable, the would-be imperial fortress had moved a step ahead.

Under Hunter in 1803, a public market was established at its planned central location near the waterside, to which cattle and produce were brought in growing quantities on weekly market days, although for years it operated amid makeshift shelters.[18] Inns and hotels were added as well in the decade before the War of 1812. Some were little more than barrooms or small bedding-places for migrants in transit. Others, like Jordan's and Frank's, offered well-utilized ballrooms or assembly chambers, where York's first-known public theatrical performances were presented in 1809 and 1810.[19] There were hotels frequented by labourers and Garrison soldiers, by legislators attending parliament, or, as in the case of the Red Lion built around 1810 on Yonge Street north of the town, by farmers coming in to market. In the growth of its hotel trade, York was further benefiting from both its political role and enlarging economic facilities.

By 1812 that centre had not only gained sizeably in range and number of offerings, but had also considerably improved its town landscape. Board and often picket fences were replacing rough split rails, enclosing lots with cultivated gardens and orchards instead of stumps and brush. Streets were losing their ramshackle look, though their mud remained notorious: frogs, it was said, constantly chorused "knee-deep, knee-deep."[20] The town's buildings assessed in 1809 numbered 107: comprising 14 still made of logs, 11 one-storeyed square-timber houses and 27 two-storeyed, and 55 of more up-to-date frame construction, generally with one and a half storeys.[21] A number of respectably imposing Georgian wooden mansions had gone up, including the large but plain residences of Secretary William Jarvis and Judge William Dummer Powell. More handsomely designed was Peter Russell's home, produced in the late 1790s by William Berczy. A broad frame bungalow with wings, "Russell Abbey" fronted on the lakeshore in neo-classical dignity. The first brick residence in York was built in 1809 for St. George, the merchant. And the first church (Anglican, and later denominated St. James) was opened on King Street in 1807. Originally designed in stone by Berczy, costs compelled that a plain wooden building had to do instead.

Viewed from the water, Little York had thus acquired quite an attractive appearance; it stretched, half-canopied in trees, along the harbour front from near the Don towards the Garrison, but straggled out well before the western limits of the New Town were reached. The finest houses looked almost pastoral in their gardened settings, and apart from a few ship-landings with nearby storage sheds, there was no evident clustering of workplaces, for shopkeepers and craftsmen mainly carried on business within their own homes. The white or light-hued wooden residences in the forefront largely screened the lesser cottages or still crude cabins from the lake prospect. And even humbler backstreet dwellings were far less gloomy or harsh in their environment than were isolated frontier bush shanties or crowded hovels of the poor in contemporary European cities. For all its mud and straggle, York appeared a prospering small place — as indeed it was by the time of war in 1812.[22]

SOCIETY AND CULTURE IN PREWAR YORK

The officials who settled down in York from the mid-1790s, not only carried on its main political function and fostered initial economic growth, but also directed the urban society and set its cultural tone. They established long-significant families — as did English-born Thomas Ridout and William Chewett in the

The first government buildings near the Don mouth held parliaments from 1797 till burned in the American raid of 1813. Rebuilt following the war, they were abandoned after burning again in 1824.

Russell Abbey was affectionately so nicknamed by relatives of top official Peter Russell. Built in the late 1790s at the corner of later Front and Princess streets, it later became town residence of the first Catholic bishop, Alexander Macdonell.

Initially a private home, this became the Court House after the destruction of York's government buildings in the War of 1812. It was later made the "House of Industry" — the local workhouse.

York's first church, 1807, was generally just "the English Church" until dedicated to St. James in 1828. Set at the planned core of the New Town, it began in this clearing north of King.

surveyor-general's office; William Jarvis, provincial secretary for a quarter century, a New England Loyalist who had served with the Queen's Rangers in the Revolution; and Christopher Robinson, a Virginia Loyalist whose son, John Beverley Robinson, became a leading figure in the official class of the next generation. There was John Small from England, clerk of the Executive Council for nearly forty years, and, too, the Scottish army surgeon Dr. James Macaulay, whose own park-lot estate ultimately gave rise to the town's first suburb, Macaulaytown. Above all, there was Peter Russell, the Anglo-Irish administrator who emerged as one of Upper Canada's largest landowners well before his death in 1808. By laying out the New Town, extending roads, amassing properties, and making the home he shared with his sister, Elizabeth, one of the top social gathering-points in the young community, he left a strong mark on prewar Little York.

Russell had been on staff in America during the Revolution, but like most of the chief British "founding" officials who had come into Upper Canada with Simcoe, he was not of Loyalist background. In its earliest days, the town of York did contain a number of American Loyalists, some of whom continued to be prominent there. Yet unlike Kingston, York was never really a Loyalist foundation. By the time the latter started to grow, the Loyalist movement was all but over. Less than a quarter of its inhabitants as first enumerated in 1797 could also be found on Loyalist lists, and this proportion declined further as population mounted.[23] Moreover, as for the Queen's Rangers at York, though originally a Loyalist unit during the revolutionary war, it had been freshly recruited in England to accompany Simcoe to Upper Canada. Still further, after the Rangers were disbanded in 1802 (many to settle in the province), soldiers from regular British regiments formed the garrison at York. All in all, Loyalism at York became more an acclaimed attitude or an esteemed public virtue than a historic link with old colonial America, for this was truly a new town, one closely tied in its society and outlook to Britain.

Generally speaking, there was no mass British migration overseas during this era, the time of the far-reaching French Revolution during the 1790s and of the Napoleonic Wars that only ended in 1815. The relative few who did reach Upper Canada from Britain in these years were considerably drawn from the upper or middle classes: persons who came to fill military or civil posts, find a professional position, seek preferment through connections, or make their way in trade or a skilled craft. Yet their qualitative impact went well beyond their restricted numbers. Whatever their possible failings, they brought some measure of cultivation, business enterprise and specialized skills to a raw, agrarian frontier province, not to mention a general belief in a ranked, hierarchical society and conservative British institutions. And they ended up far less often on backwoods farms than in Upper Canada's incipient urban communities — particularly in its political power centre, York.

In the upper ranks of York society, well-connected or acceptably talented arrivals from the British Isles thus reinforced its dominant patterns. They often gained important places of their own, although members of the governing circles continued to come numerously from the town's already established official families. Moreover, at the apex of both the political and social elite in York stood the ruling representative of Britain's Crown — from Governors Simcoe and Hunter to Francis Gore, whose own term of office lasted right from 1806 to 1817. Amid vice-regal ceremony and Garrison parades, the social leaders of Little York, a village of clapboard houses, squared-log cabins and mud streets, firmly upheld its position as a British imperial buttress in the backwoods of America.

Among the influential British arrivals in the prewar town was the well-connected Anglo-Irishman Dr. William Warren Baldwin, who settled in York as a physician in 1802. He further became a lawyer, architect, judge and parliamentarian — as well as a wealthy landholder through managing Russell properties, which his wife inherited. The previously mentioned Scottish merchants, Allan and Wood, were made magistrates and held other posts, while the Boultons from England, lawyers, judges and politicians, grew as prominent at York as did the Baldwins. But in due course, strongminded, energetic Dr. John Strachan emerged as the most eminent of all these upper-level British immigrants. A Scottish university graduate, Strachan from 1799 taught school at Kingston and Cornwall, and also entered the Anglican ministry. In 1812 he was appointed rector at York, but when he moved there, he was already well known, since the sons of leading citizens had regularly been sent to study at his highly reputed Cornwall school.

What of the rest of society in this British-led, rank-oriented capital village? It contained an element of German origin, dating in part from William Berczy's settlers of 1797, but also drawn more widely from nearby Great Lake states. Also worthy of note were some non-Loyalist American landholders, hotel-keepers and craftsmen, such as the tanner Jesse Ketchum, later active in both politics and philanthropy. Furthermore, a few French Canadians were present, often as batteaux men, and a small number of blacks, chiefly servants, some of whom had first arrived as slaves. None of these groups, however, altered the British context of the community. Many of its early farm-settlers (like the Denisons from Yorkshire) were of British birth as well, as were varied tradesmen and labourers, including discharged soldiers. Indeed, the largest single element in early York seems to have been of English extraction, with far fewer Scots and still less Irishmen.[24] In the era before the War of 1812, the urban York community developed as manifestly distinct in its preponderantly British society and culture from the Loyalist or post-Loyalist rural areas outside it, or beyond them, from the republican American states.

The cultural context of the town was also demonstrated in religion. Anglicanism was strongly rooted there, not the Methodism or other evangelical forms of Protestantism more widely found in the countryside. No doubt the fact that the only church built in prewar York was Anglican owed much to the strength of the ruling order in the capital, which deemed the Church of England to be the official religious authority as in the English homeland; yet thus far other religious groups in York were not sufficiently numerous to set up churches on their own. Anglicanism had popular adherence as well as high-level influence in that community, expressing loyally British values in church no less than state. Moreover, when an act of 1807 established provincially supported grammar schools, Anglican clergy largely directed them, including that at York. Here the government grammar school, providing secondary education that stressed the classics, considerably improved on shaky little private ventures, especially from 1812 under the capable care of John Strachan, now schoolmaster as well as rector of York. Though this institution chiefly dealt with the children of the well-to-do, it marked a bare beginning of urban public schooling. And schooled or not, children were assuredly not left idle. In a small society with a limited labour supply, they worked (no less than their mothers) for the family unit, in homes, plots or workshops — as was often so even for the young of the estate-owning gentry.

Another important social and cultural institution appeared at York, the press. The *Upper Canada Gazette* was transferred there from Niagara in 1798, to follow the officials and the parliament. Largely a government organ, its local news, advertisements of new store stocks or reports of public meetings were nevertheless of eager interest to the capital community. A critical press with conflicting political opinions was still years away. Provincial politics in prewar York might see some passing stirs, but they scarcely shook the established regime. Accordingly, the *Gazette* sufficed until a later day of sharpening partisan discords and debate.

As for civic politics, there were none, in that the little capital had no municipal organization of its own at this stage. It is true that local institutions of a sort had come into being in 1797 when a town clerk, town wardens and other minor local officers were elected at York's first town meeting. But the powers of these officers were very restricted, as were those of town meetings themselves, which in the young province dealt largely with matters such as fence heights and straying animals. Real local power was vested in the magistrates provincially appointed for the districts, the administrative units into which Upper Canada was divided from its start; counties then were mainly just parliamentary constituencies. The district magistrates met regularly in courts of quarter session (in York's case, for the Home District) within a long-set English form of local government. The Home District magistrates levied small local taxes, looked after the jail at the district seat of York, or appointed a paid high constable and unpaid annual constables to maintain the public peace. They also supervised taverns, made fire regulations and required street upkeep by residents — along with taking a vague responsibility for the poverty-stricken or insane, directing York's public market, and doing even more. But while their broad and far-from-democratic sway extended well beyond the town, they were closely linked to it personally. The Home District magistrates named by the provincial officialdom included leading York inhabitants, in a kind of elite local directorate. Among those active in the quarter sessions of the prewar years were such York notables as William Allan (also collector of customs), Alexander Wood, William Jarvis, William Willcocks (Peter Russell's cousin) and Thomas Ridout.[25] On the whole, they gave conscientious, if conservative and constantly underfunded, administration to their town.

In a real way this paternalistic local rule by traditionally appointed authority fitted the world of prewar York. Though the system would subsequently undergo some refinements, and face strains on its capacities, it was to last without substantial questioning until the 1830s. Little York, in sum, was still a village community, and in spite of notions of grandeur it accepted habitual village controls. The role of families, close or extended, was paramount in its upper-class society, within which women from Mrs. Simcoe to Elizabeth Russell might wield conventional influence, while sons took places suitable to the family, as daughters married, with due filial obedience. In the absence of much record, it can still be presumed that those of the "generality" below endorsed similar modes of behaviour. At any rate, the populace at large was acquiescent under the customary rule of its betters, evidently satisfied to sustain them in provincial politics, to take the magistrates, the official gentry and the Anglican clergy in the places God had awarded them — and inherently suspicious of Yankee republicanism and loud noises of self-congratulating liberty from across the Lakes. York was, of course, no vibrant centre of urbane culture: an outpost on the shaggy edge of civilization still. Nonetheless, as such, it had no fixed or crowded mass of poverty and misery. Fish from the lake and game from the woods were near to hand; there was in general sufficient food, work and space for humble inhabitants.

As for the privileged group, their life was none too onerous: short work days for officials, ample time for tea or sherry with the ladies, rounds of social dinners and assemblies for both, along with rides out the breezy peninsula, or salmon-fishing and pigeon-shooting around the harbour reaches. They had "musical evenings" and a small subscription lending-library to keep in touch with fashionable works from England.[26] All the same, theirs was a narrow world of petty cliques, hemmed in by isolation and stiff social distinctions, rife with gossip as its one abiding entertainment. And so this controlling prewar York society did remain in a village state — self-centred, conformist, and by no means exciting in its ordered pace.

WARTIME SHOCKS AT YORK

By 1812 there was a good deal of unwanted excitement: the signs of approaching war with the United States. Accordingly, it might seem fortunate that the government of York had now come under the authority of General Isaac Brock, commander of British forces in Upper Canada, Governor Gore having departed for leave in England. Brock believed, with Simcoe, in the strategic value of York. He began looking to its defences; it was agreed that the naval base should be moved there from exposed Kingston, and the building of a ten-gun schooner was started in York harbour. The plans, however, to move the naval dockyard to York and erect a strong new fort to replace its inadequate, poorly kept up blockhouses had not time to be effected. War began in June; Brock died in the battle of Queenston Heights in October; and the demands of the conflict on his military successors left little possibility of achieving the designs intended for the capital. Three small batteries, a powder magazine, the earthworks of an unfinished fort, and the embodied companies of York militia — 120 men under Major William Allan who were ordered to the Garrison at the outbreak of the war — these comprised about all that could be done to strengthen York's own defences.[27]

The town's inhabitants still felt few qualms during the opening stages of the struggle, confident of Britain's protecting imperial power, even though its small forces in Canada were stretched perilously thin, depending much on Indian aid. Moreover, the early British victories at Detroit and Queenston, in which York militia played an active part, only enhanced patriotic pride, aided by the ardent eloquence of Reverend Dr. John Strachan. But the next year the war came home to York directly. On 27 April 1813 a strong American force of fourteen ships and 1,700 troops raided the town, particularly to seize the large, thirty-gun warship, the *Sir Isaac Brock*, under construction there. Landing to the west outside the harbour, the Americans overwhelmed the advanced positions held by the defending forces — in all, some 300 British regulars, a similar body of militia, and a smaller group of Indians. The invaders swept onward to the uncompleted fort. There, as they poured in, the magazine was blown up, killing numbers in a devastating blast, including the American field commander, General Zebulon Pike. The British general, Sir Roger Sheafe, retired towards Kingston from a totally untenable position, burning the *Brock* and leaving York to make what terms it could with the incensed attackers. The next few days saw looting and destruction of public property, and the burning of the Parliament Buildings by unknown hands; but there were no organized American military reprisals. In fact, reasonable terms of capitulation were reached in negotiations led by an undaunted Dr. Strachan, who thus gained a reputation as the town's resolute spokesman.[28]

The raid on York, 27 April 1813. Owen Staples's reconstruction shows the American fleet engaging shore batteries around the harbour entry, while troops land in the woods outside. The Gibraltar Point lighthouse is at the right of the picture.

Early in May the raiders departed; still, the shock was lasting. York had found how exposed it was to American dangers. Most of its public buildings had been destroyed, the landing fight had been particularly bloody, and pillagers had widely robbed the town, of even its little library. On the one hand, there was anxious criticism of the British higher command. On the other, there was fear and suspicion of American sympathizers in Upper Canada. Undoubtedly considerable disaffection existed in the countryside, where the recent American settlers felt no strong grievances against British rule, but equally no great disposition to fight for it. In the capital also, where more Americans had been congregating by the time the war began, there were those who expected an inevitable takeover by the republic, and there had been the initial, alarming breakdown of public order after the fighting at York. Almost surely, this breakdown can be attributed far more to the opportunity for plunder by lawless elements than to the expression of pro-American sympathies. Still, if the loyal citizenry did not quite

picture traitors behind every bush, they could envisage them plotting or fostering sedition. York's mood had been hardened. Pro-British loyalty had been redefined more sharply and prejudicially in anti-American terms.[29]

The rest of the war intensified these feelings. The tide of battle turned at least against any likelihood that the Americans could take Upper Canada, what with their own military setbacks and the strengthening of British regular forces. Nevertheless, a still defenceless York was again briefly seized by U.S. troops in the summer of 1813, to heighten bitterness against suspected American collaborators. At last, by July 1814, a much more defensible fort had replaced the shattered remnants of the old Garrison, and that fall, the war moved to an end. Peace was signed in December, although this news was not known at the inland capital until February of 1815. There, the chief officials consolidated power as a firmly anti-Yankee oligarchy, which soon gained leaders tested in the war — notably, young John Beverley Robinson, who had fought under Brock, and John Strachan, York's champion in the raid of 1813.

The war brought more to York than military attack and political hardening. It also brought considerable economic growth. The supply purchases of the British commissariat led to high profits and much speculation among the town merchants. The greatest returns went to the more prominent men such as Allan, St. George and Wood, but others also gained in wealth, like Jesse Ketchum or the Yorkshireman, Joseph Cawthra, who had begun with a little apothecary shop.[30] War prices soared, partly because of costly transport problems. The New York route was cut off, and that of the St. Lawrence was dangerously open to assault, especially from American ships on Lake Ontario. The resulting uprush of inflation led the magistrates to fix provision prices. Town workers at least got higher wages and full employment in the wartime boom, but it suddenly collapsed when peace returned. Prices dived as military buying ceased and "army bills," a reliable kind of British-backed paper currency, were withdrawn. Nevertheless, the boom had created a more widely based middle class, and left a small but influential moneyed group at York with expanded financial connections and expertise. The town's inhabitants, however, still only numbered 720 in 1816, since population had been almost at a standstill in the war years, with immigration virtually halted.[31] Moreover, Indians, once frequent visitors to early York, now began to disappear beyond the town's horizons — displaced to reserves on frontier fringes as their military value faded at the peace.

POSTWAR ECONOMIC DEVELOPMENTS

After the war, immigrants began coming anew to Upper Canada, but now in a growing mass movement from across the Atlantic. Henceforth the lands of the province were increasingly to be occupied by settlers from Great Britain and Ireland. From the ending of the Napoleonic conflict in 1815, the oceans lay open once more to peacetime shipping, while the people of the United Kingdom, rural and urban, were facing the harsh dislocations that accompanied the ever-spreading Industrial Revolution. The resulting flow of transatlantic migrants began for Upper Canada with only a trickle in 1815-16, but despite some fluctuations, it took an ascending curve. With population pushing out settlement again, or filling in earlier-opened districts, Upper Canada's grain and timber yields expanded,

as did their exports to Britain; and in the process, the economies of little business centres like York enlarged as well.

The full tide of overseas immigration would not be reached till the late Twenties and early Thirties. Yet even in the more immediate postwar years, it rising effects were felt in the Upper Canadian capital. The British settlers came to the province by waterways, up the St. Lawrence or inward from New York. Often they then landed at York as a central transit point, before proceeding to farming areas beyond, thereby fostering the business of its stores and inns. Some of the newcomers, in fact, remained in the town, investing new capital and skills there, though others who stayed might have had little other than their physical labour to offer. Many of the latter came ill-adapted for a life of pioneer farming. Through unpreparedness, lack of funds or sheer misfortune, some of these British immigrants failed to make a way in the countryside or never got there, adding instead to the lower ranks of the town. Here they might raise problems of urban poverty scarcely evident before, but on balance York clearly gained from its gathering numbers — from the enlarging work force, internal markets and potential enterprise they represented.

All the same, the town's economic growth did not proceed smoothly but fluctuated as did the settlement stream itself. Phases of good years and bad, wherein trade and immigration largely rose or fell together, marked the increasing influence of world business cycles on outlying Upper Canada and its capital. The very fact that long-distance trade was expanding through the mounting production of wheat and timber staples tied colonial economic life more closely to outside market conditions. A world cycle of high wartime prices had ended with the close of the Napoleonic struggle, far wider in its impact than the minor War of 1812. Readjustments that followed, adding to the derangements of the Industrial Revolution, brought recurrent periods of distress to Britain, and thus to the imperial economy on which Upper Canada now increasingly depended. As part consequence, the years 1819 and 1822 were much depressed at York, and the better times that followed were checked again by the serious British commercial slump of 1825, which only lifted slowly. Moreover, the complex workings of Britain's Corn Law of 1815 at times could all but exclude colonial grain from the British markets, until from 1822 the granting of imperial preferential duties gave it surer access.[32] This certainly benefited merchants at York, among other Upper Canadian outlets. In fact, it

Postwar York, around 1820: the newer western frontage from Peter to John streets, featuring, left to right, Cruikshank and Beikie homes, military storehouse, and Half-Way Tavern, a resort of Garrison soldiers.

promoted increasingly substantial grain exports from York harbour, despite short-term ups and downs.

The main functions of York merchants, however, lay less in the export trade than in supplying the markets of the town and its vicinity. Here again they felt the force of external economic factors, as when depressed prices for consumer goods in Britain led to their being dumped cheaply at Montreal and other ports of entry. As a result, York traders largely ceased direct purchase from British suppliers of items which they could obtain at about the same price in Montreal.[33] This effectively placed their commerce back under Montreal dominance, for while there was the alternative supply source of New York, it generally remained more expensive, especially because of increased American tariffs. Still, the postwar generation of York merchants chiefly took up ordering through Montreal houses. And in some respects this was indeed a new generation, since the three chief commercial figures of earlier days — Quetton St. George, Wood and Allan — all wound up their businesses between 1815 and 1822. William Allan nevertheless continued to be active in key official and financial circles. He became president of York's first bank, chartered in 1821, plainly because of his position as the town's leading capitalist.

The creation of this Bank of Upper Canada was undoubtedly a major economic advance for postwar York, and essentially displayed the leverage it had through being seat of government. A business group in Kingston, still by far the biggest town and trade centre in the province, had already secured an act to incorporate a bank and issue notes there; but by the time that act finally received royal assent in 1819, its terms had expired. Another very different measure was pushed on the governor (now Sir Peregrine Maitland), backed by a body of York's elite under the driving force of John Strachan, who had become a powerful executive councillor. Through fast work and successful pressure, an officially connected bank issue was incorporated at the capital instead.[34]

Now there might have been good arguments for this more solidly backed York enterprise, which had one-quarter of its stock subscribed by the government and four government directors on its board of fifteen. But it was no less the achievement of the closely interlocked York political oligarchy — soon to be dubbed the "Family Compact" — and it gave the capital a provincial bank which held a virtual monopoly, backed by government sanction, during its early formative years. Led by William Allan as president till 1835,

with directors drawn from the town's official and merchant leaders, and with large amounts of shares held by members of the ruling Compact, the Bank of Upper Canada served as a powerful agent of York's interests, facilitating trade with its notes or credits, fending off banking interventions from Montreal or elsewhere, and gradually spreading its own branches out across the province. Once more through being the governing village, York had gained special vantage and wider economic prospects.[35]

Other wider prospects were indicated by the new steamboats that appeared in growing numbers in the harbour in these postwar years, initially products of Kingston and Niagara, but in 1826 the first one was built at York — all offering greater scope to port traffic and shipping investment. The harbourside itself was building up. Already in 1816 three additional wharves were under construction.[36] Ship carpenteries, lumberyards and more storehouses followed, to give the waterfront an increasingly commercial character, as functional patterns of land use took stronger hold. Nevertheless, some of the best homes in York continued to be found on Palace or Front streets, which looked out on the harbour. There was not much residential segregation still, and there seemed plenty of room for dockside sheds and storehouses along with mansions and their gardens. In 1818, however, the strip of open land along the harbour edge was vested in perpetuity in William Allan, John Beverley Robinson and several other leading citizens, in order to preserve a public promenade in front of the town — a sign of some awareness that growth was beginning to affect York's former semi-rural scatter.[37]

Within the town also, a significant amount of new construction went on. The burned legislative chambers were rebuilt in 1819, and the next year a brick General Hospital was erected; only to be needed for the legislature when the Parliament Buildings burned down again in 1824 (Map 3, page 38). A larger Government House, a Masonic Hall, and a new jail and courthouse went up, as did a steeple for the Anglican church. Seen from the lake, York still looked somewhat rustic and unfocused as it spread out along the shore, and there were empty gaps yet between Simcoe's original plot and the New Town. But from near the Don west past Yonge Street, and from Palace and Front back to the park lots, there was a reasonably built-up area, centring around the public market south of the intersection of King and New (now Jarvis) streets. King Street traversed this urban core, and linked with the Kingston

The town market, at King and New (Jarvis) streets, was built in wood in 1820 and replaced in brick in 1831. The first public pump (1823) is in the foreground.

The Bank of Upper Canada opened in temporary quarters in 1822, but in 1825 bought land at the corner of George and Duke to erect this fine stone structure — symbolizing the growing business power of York.

John Strachan in 1818 built this leading town house, popularly called the Palace, on property originally reaching from Front to Wellington, and York to Simcoe. The photograph dates from days past its grandeur, not long before demolition in the 1890s.

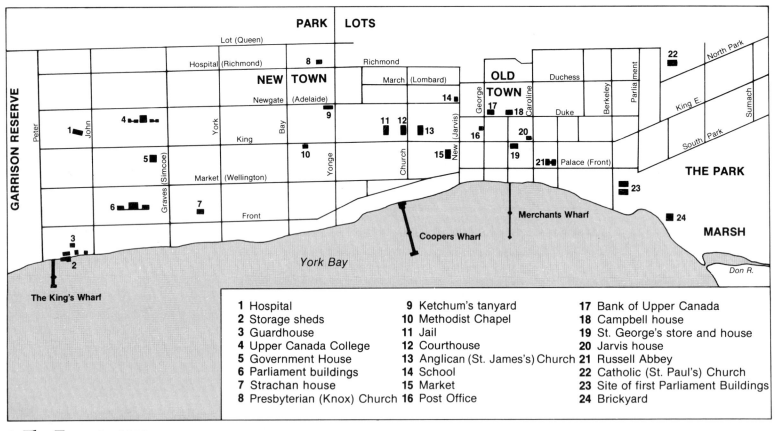

1 Hospital	**9** Ketchum's tanyard	**17** Bank of Upper Canada
2 Storage sheds	**10** Methodist Chapel	**18** Campbell house
3 Guardhouse	**11** Jail	**19** St. George's store and house
4 Upper Canada College	**12** Courthouse	**20** Jarvis house
5 Government House	**13** Anglican (St. James's) Church	**21** Russell Abbey
6 Parliament buildings	**14** School	**22** Catholic (St. Paul's) Church
7 Strachan house	**15** Market	**23** Site of first Parliament Buildings
8 Presbyterian (Knox) Church	**16** Post Office	**24** Brickyard

3 The Town to 1830

Road, over which in 1817 a stage coach first began winter service to Kingston on sleigh runners.[38] When bridges over the Don and Humber were reconstructed after the war on the Kingston and Dundas routes, they served as well to feed more business into the stores collecting along King.

Private building also proceeded; brick had become the fashion for finer residences. John Strachan put up a grand home on Front in 1818, while about 1820 Judge D'Arcy Boulton completed an elegant red-brick mansion in his park lot northward: The Grange, still standing in its classical symmetry. On his own estate further northwest, on the rise above the Shore Plain, Dr. William Baldwin

built "a very commodious house in the Country — I have called the place Spadina, the Indian word for Hill."[39] And Chief Justice Sir William Campbell in 1822 erected a graceful example of a late Georgian town house, which also survives, though moved from its original Duke Street site. Despite their formal poise, however, these gentry homes first rose in park-lot pastures or on unpaved town streets near rough sheds and simple cottages. Here there was no manicured English countryside or the terraced urban order of Jane Austen's Bath. These were urbane transfers to very different frontier surroundings. Yet they put some distinction into the York landscape, and in themselves expressed the urbanizing process under way: from village existence into full town life. By 1825 the little community had 287 private buildings to assess (compared with 139 in 1816), 132 of them one-storey houses, 107 two-storey, and 48 shops.[40] It was passing over the threshold of its rustic state — as social developments made plain as well.

IMMIGRATION AND A CHANGING URBAN SOCIETY

The postwar expansion of York's housing stock obviously reflected its rise in population, which reached more than 1,600 in 1825, by which time the provincial total stood at some 157,000.[41] The town's numbers thus were still a small fraction of the Upper Canadian whole; but they had more than doubled since 1816, while the province's population had grown only by about half.[42] Despite a shortage of statistics, one can interpret this differential growth. In prewar times, the American wave of pioneer farmers had gone overwhelmingly to open backwoods districts. But after the war, the British influx brought a significantly larger element of townsfolk, while urban attractive capacities were steadily enlarging. Hence a higher proportion of the incoming British could effectively end up in centres like York. Though natural increase played some part, the greater growth rate in that town's postwar population was essentially linked with its mounting intake of immigrants.

The lack of adequate records prevents precise statements as to how many newcomers actually settled in York, moved on or later returned; and transiency, difficult to measure, is a perennial feature in urban demography. Migrants to a new land, moreover, were often highly transient, shifting their locations as need or opportunity dictated. Nevertheless, it is beyond doubt that the British settlers, the bulk of whom landed at St. Lawrence ports of entry, came on in sizeable numbers to Upper Canada, and to York specifically,[43] so that their annual landing figures at Montreal or Quebec (mainly the latter) provide a kind of demographic barometer of the pressure moving inland, and an index also to the accretion of British migrants in Upper Canada's capital.

York's rise in population became most marked, to repeat, after 1825, for within eight years following, its numbers nearly quadrupled. Yet the impact of the annual overseas intake was already plain in the postwar town — for instance, in the problem of relief raised by the least fortunate among the arrivals. As early as 1817, the Society for the Relief of Strangers was formed at York to deal with distressed immigrants, the sick and helpless, perhaps left abandoned through the illness or death of their breadwinners.[44] For years this organization remained the main charitable agency in the community, suggesting that in this village-shaped society resident families were expected to cope with their own needs and that a growing group of migrants, not fitting into that pattern, required different treatment.

More notably, however, British newcomers to York helped expand an already emerging middle class, between the urban labouring strata and the ruling order. Within this leading segment, the associates of officialdom shared the interests of the estate-owning Family Compact, at times building up their own large, speculative landholdings. But many of the postwar middle-class arrivals from Britain looked to other means of advancement than government ties or patronage, striking out on their own in commercial or professional ventures, and often displaying an increasingly critical view of the entrenched colonial regime. Some had already derived a new and different outlook from the Reform movement now swelling in Britain. Others developed it at York, feeling the narrow confines of its existing political and social structure.

Religious connections were also influential here. Non-Anglican British immigrants to the town might well dislike the transfer of Church of England official privileges to a new country, regarding them as outmoded pretensions. And there was besides a significant leaven of Americans with Methodist or other evangelical backgrounds among the gathering middle class, for enterprising Yankees still found business opportunities in growing Canadian centres. In general, however, the rising York middle class kept its British make-up, with a large component that also held to conservative and/or Anglican persuasions. Nevertheless, it constituted a changing, dynamic factor in society. It also brought English Non-Conformists, Scots Presbyterians, Protestant Irish Methodists and Irish Catholics into increasing evidence in town — inevitably to question, though not yet to endanger, the older established order.

Some among this incoming element were to figure strongly in the York community. One such was Francis Collins, a Catholic Irish journalist who arrived in 1818, and in 1825 launched his Reform-spirited *Canadian Freeman*. There was William Draper from England, who became a leading lawyer; the Scots stationer James Lesslie, who took to reforming politics and later to radical journal-

Bridges over the Don and Humber were vital to York's east-west land links. Flimsily begun, they were not too impressive after postwar rebuilding. The Humber bridge seen here connected with Lot (Queen) Street, the Don with King.

ism; and, above all, another keenly critical Scot, William Lyon Mackenzie. Arriving at York in 1820, Mackenzie entered storekeeping, then moved onward and started a newspaper in Queenston. In 1824 he returned to York, bringing his *Colonial Advocate* with him to make it the most vehement public voice for change in Upper Canada. Urban British immigrants like these would do much to shape a less inbred and parochial York society.

Church growth also showed the more varied community that was emerging. The American-linked Methodist Episcopals, the principal Methodist body in Upper Canada, in 1818 erected a small chapel on the western outskirts of York, while the Roman Catholics began building St. Paul's Church in 1822 at the eastern edge of town.[45] A minor Presbyterian sect proceeded in 1820 to raise a little church on lands at Lot (Queen) and Yonge donated by the prosperous American tanner, Jesse Ketchum, who had his reeking tanyard in this low-price area.[46] Scots Presbyterians who held to the Church of Scotland, the state-established denomination in their homeland, continued, however, to worship at the officially recognized Anglican church for some years more. At official behest, the government-aided elementary school set up at York in 1818 was also assigned to Anglican control. As a result, this Central School became a fresh source of friction in an increasingly sectarian environment.

Furthermore, a growing concentration of Protestant Ulster Irish at York was manifested in the emergence of the Orange Order, transplanted there from Northern Ireland roots. In 1822, on July 12, the Orange festal day, John Strachan delivered a sermon to about one hundred parading Orangemen from the town and vicinity.[47] And the defence of British ties and Protestant religion fervently proclaimed by the Order attracted some non-Ulster adherents as well at York, including established middle-class citizens. But Orangeism remained more widely based in lower-class urban ranks, where its conservative loyalties offered a popular offset to any too insistent reforming forces — a fact that would give it increasingly political significance in the town.

Politically speaking, York still remained under the local rule of the Home District magistrates, who were given increased policing powers in 1817. In 1820 its growth at least gained it a seat of its own in the provincial parliament. At the election of that year, the seat was won by acclamation by John Beverley Robinson, now Upper Canada's attorney-general and the ablest member of the Tory-minded governing oligarchy. In adjoining York County, however, another prominent townsman there elected, Dr. Baldwin, began showing a remarkable readiness to talk of reform. Moreover, at the next election held in 1824, while Robinson again won the town seat, he had to face a real contest with a York storekeeper, George Duggan, an Ulster Irishman who stood against some government policies and was actively supported by Orangemen.[48] Politics were showing signs of social change; the long Orange Walk through Toronto history was already under way.

In the main, this was yet the ordered world of Little York, still dominated by the social attitudes, political and religious precepts of its ruling Compact officialdom. But the very enlarging of the newer groups in the community challenged the old stability in state, society and church. The different incoming ethnic and religious elements brought their own beliefs and biases, and there were other stirs in opinion deriving from American democratic doctrines as well as British Reform.

Consequently, times were decisively changing at York by 1825, what with Collins's *Freeman* and Mackenzie's *Advocate* launching vigorous censures of the status quo, and social and political feelings growing warmly partisan. The complacent little town was becoming a far more vibrant, interesting place. In short, Simcoe's imperial military base, Russell's clannish official village, and the postwar Compact capital now stood on the verge of a whole new stage of troubled but lively expansion.

York from the peninsula, 1828. While rather romanticized, this painting does denote the rising port town. St. James, with steeple, centres an urban shoreline, and an up-to-date steamer traverses the harbour. The advent of steam navigation enhanced the port's activities: by 1834 the new **Cobourg** *of 418 tons (owned in Toronto and with twin engines built there) was making 15 m.p.h. on its three-hour crossing to Niagara.*

Chapter Two
The Commercial Port-Town, 1825–47

The new stage did not start suddenly for York. Following depression in 1825–26, British immigration — the impetus to Upper Canadian growth in general — only began a rising sweep in 1827, when arrivals at St. Lawrence ports, which had averaged about 9,000 yearly from 1822 to 1826, increased to 16,000.[1] In 1829 almost that many landed at Quebec alone, the prime gateway, as 28,000 did in 1830.[2] Their number swelled to nearly 52,000 in 1832, continued high to 1837, then rose anew in the Forties.[3] As a result, settlement across the period greatly enlarged the Upper Canadian farm frontier, from the Ottawa Valley in the east to the Huron Tract and Lake Erie districts in the west. Agrarian expansion in turn promoted urban development; service-and-supply hamlets multiplied in the interior, providing general stores, mills and taverns. And along the older settled fronts, previously established places developed on a larger scale to furnish goods, credit and market services for the proliferating little inland centres behind them. This typified a basic feature in North American urbanization: the growth of prosperous commercial towns with the spread of hinterland settlement. In Canada it appeared in the Maritimes as well as in the St. Lawrence and Great Lakes regions, and later across the farming West. But no place gained more than York in its own day, as it rose as a trading focus for a thriving, fast-populating farm hinterland. Already an established port, the advance of rural settlement beyond it in the late 1820s and early 1830s brought on its rapid growth as a commercial town.

URBAN ECONOMY: A COMMERCIAL CENTRE TAKES OFF

The new phase for York was witnessed by an upsurge in its population. Starting in 1826 with 1,719 inhabitants, it had 2,335 by 1828, and 5,505 in 1832, by which time it had outpaced Kingston to become the largest urban community in the province.[4] Though a late starter compared with earlier centres like Niagara and Kingston, York had definitely surpassed them by the mid-1830s, essentially because it found a wider countryside to deal with as a growing commercial town. Its two older rivals were by no means as well placed to exploit new tributary areas. Niagara did have the richly fertile Niagara Peninsula around it, but this was a set-off pocket of the province. Districts beyond could be better dealt with from other locations, so that Niagara was soon outdone. As for the erstwhile commercial leader, Kingston, while it remained a significant trading entrepôt at the entry to the St. Lawrence route, the outlier of Montreal in that commerce, its own surrounding countryside was fairly early occupied and contained a good deal of rocky terrain. And Kingston, too, could not effectually expand its reach, lying as it did well to the east in Upper Canada away from the fastest-growing, fertile central and western areas. The port-town of York, instead, not only had its more central situation, but could also extend its own farm hinterland over the very road system that its role as capital had given it.

Among the roads to the hinterland, Yonge Street served York best. While the town's trade did stretch out eastward beyond the nearby Scarborough and Pickering settlements, or westward towards the head of Lake Ontario, the land routes here paralleled the lakeshores and could be tapped by competing little ports along the way. But York itself commanded Yonge Street, the highway northward. Local traffic grew particularly in this direction as the townships on either side of Yonge filled in, villages sprang up along the route to Holland Landing, and bush farms reached Lake Simcoe shores. Note that this assuredly was local traffic: Governor Simcoe's vision of re-establishing the old Toronto Passage, of reopening its access to the great northwest, was one of his many hopes that had not materialized. About the only long-range transport that moved by way of Yonge Street had come during the War of

A citified King Street, 1835. The second court house and jail (1826 and 1827) adjoin a new brick-and-stone St. James, opened in 1832. There is artistic liberty, however: the planned church tower had not yet been added in 1835.

A main corduroy road, making plain that winter sleighing would be far preferable on highways out of town. But stage coaches did negotiate these routes.

Sleigh-coach of the noted William Weller stage line. Weller ran stages to Hamilton and Montreal, and Charles Thompson those north to Holland Landing.

1812 when the North West Company made some use of this route to its western fur empire, since the way along the Lower Lakes was open to attack. In any event, the amalgamation of the North West Company with the older Hudson's Bay Company in 1821 switched the main fur transport route to Hudson Bay, closing off Canadian links with far-spread territories above the Lakes. The Toronto gateway to a huge northern and western hinterland again became a dream — though not to be forgotten. Meanwhile, at least there was Yonge Street.

Like most of the land routes of early Upper Canada, when capital and labour both were scarce, this allegedly improved road still posed fearsome challenges. "Corduroy" stretches of logs laid across swampy areas readily shifted or rotted, leaving gaps that could topple carts or break bones. Spring thaws and fall rains could make poorly drained, rutted surfaces impassable, although the winter freeze-up brought sleighing and was the best time for moving farm crops to town. Nonetheless, while mired and pot-holed, Yonge Street carried a rising traffic: by foot, on horseback, in freight wagons, and even by clumsy, lurching stage coach — which ran regularly between York and Holland Landing from 1828, and soon provided daily service.[5] Moreover, the rise in the hinterland population and the increasing demands of its little trading centres gave York merchants good reason to expand their business dealings up Yonge.

Bigger merchants with large stocks at York had regularly both retailed goods to the town market in their own shops and sold supplies wholesale to small country stores in the near vicinity. But now that the country market was growing so rapidly, wholesaling became increasingly important in its own right. New stores under new men sprang up in York from 1828, some dealing only wholesale, the chief area of expanding wealth.[6] The new men generally had good connections with Montreal or British houses, and could buy on large credits. Many themselves were recent British immigrants, like the young Scot, Isaac Buchanan, who came out in 1830. He built a major York wholesale business, which largely ordered through a partner-firm in Glasgow, and by 1836 had branches at Niagara and the rising head-of-the-lake town, Hamilton.[7] There were also Joseph and George Percival Ridout, English relatives of Surveyor General Thomas Ridout, who in 1832 began a long-lasting wholesale (and retail) hardware firm at York; and Francis Hincks from Ireland, who set up a wholesale warehouse in 1832,

though he shortly turned to banking, then to Reform journalism and an ascending political career. The bigger wholesalers handled dry goods, groceries, liquor and hardware in bulk; but smaller stores also began to specialize out of general trading: as book and stationery dealers, china merchants, druggists, drapers and iron-mongers.[8] York's commercial operations were multiplying apace.

Accordingly, the York *Courier of Upper Canada* could proclaim in 1832 that "we fairly now look on our town as a second Montreal in point of commercial and mercantile importance. Country merchants need now no longer look to Montreal for their supplies, as these can be obtained in quantity, quality and price, at York, at least equal to the Montreal markets!"[9] In actuality, some of the chief new firms were branches of big Montreal houses. Yet that helped to demonstrate that the lake port had become a sufficiently significant commercial centre to attract capital and enterprise from outside. Moreover, constant efforts were being made to bring country dealers to order their goods through York, not Montreal, which reasserted a pattern among York merchants of importing direct from Britain — and to much less extent, New York — in order to keep down costs and improve service. The imports themselves, of course, still mostly came via the St. Lawrence, and so paid trans-shipment and forwarding charges at Montreal. Nevertheless, the further mark-up of Montreal wholesalers was thus avoided, while York trade became less subject to the control and credit of its bigger rival.[10] No doubt the presence of the Bank of Upper Canada also helped York finance its own commercial enterprises. In any case, as they advanced, the Montreal branch stores either withdrew or became York-based themselves. And even the powerful Bank of Montreal withdrew after a brief attempt in 1829 to establish a branch at York. In short, York was winning a greater business sphere — and basically because of its expanding hinterland trade.

Commercial expansion was still far more evident than industrial activity in the port-town, during an era when the demands of a young farm economy for manufactures were simple and when York itself was mostly importing such factory products as were required from the potent coal-and-iron technology of Britain. Still, apart from essential saw and grist mills, the town by the early 1830s had cabinet and carriage makers, leather works, iron foundries, and plough and axe manufactories. There was a paper mill (up the Don); Knott's and Freeland's competing soap factories, begun in 1830 and 1832; and two plants that made steam engines —

The Fish Market below Front, where hotels and office blocks were appearing. Lake fishing was an important local activity, largely conducted from the peninsula. William Weller's stage service centred in the "Coffin Block" (so called from its shape), which appears to the right of the picture, at Front and Market (Wellington).

one, printing presses as well.[11] Most of these establishments were small-scale, deriving from artisans' shops, and consequently employing only a limited labour force. Yet some new ventures did point to larger investments and developments: notably the wind-driven flour mill set up in 1831-32 by two English immigrants, James Worts and his brother-in-law, William Gooderham. Their milling business led to profitable distilling and then to a variety of manufacturing, mercantile and financial operations undertaken by successor Gooderhams and Wortses. Their tall windmill near the Don, for years a commanding landmark, was actually soon replaced by steam power, as noted by the *Colonial Advocate* in 1833, which added that steam saw mills were also now "the rage" in a booming York, where water power from slow rivers had become inadequate for its needs.[12]

What capital there was available in the town, however, was invested mainly in commercial growth and related developments in transport. Improving the main land routes was difficult, given the heavy expenses involved and the dependence on the reluctant labours of adjoining property-holders as prescribed by law. Then in 1833 a group of prominent York citizens became trustees of a scheme to surface the trunk roads leading out of the town, provincially empowered to raise funds and erect toll gates, through which the outlays were ultimately to be returned. By 1835 Yonge Street, as a result, had been macadamized (surfaced with crushed, packed stone) up to the third concession line, and work was probing onward.[13] This was obviously slow and costly, and both use of the highway and complaints about it continued to increase. More noteworthy were improvements in water transit, which, after all, concerned a far wider area of traffic, opening the port of York to the world outside until each winter froze it in.

Through most of the year, larger, faster steamers brought comfortable and regular passage around Lake Ontario, so that travellers and immigrants still moved by water when they could. Bulk goods now largely went by sailing schooners, which steadily displaced the row-and-sail batteaux or Durham boats of earlier days, and dealt with Kingston, Cobourg and Port Hope, head-of-the-lake and Niagara River ports, as well as Rochester and Oswego. To handle the enlarging water traffic, more wharves and warehouses were erected along York harbour. There, dockhands and carters congregated in a rowdy work force, while steamer captains, shipowners and port officers became important adjuncts of York commerce. One in particular was steamboat owner Hugh Richardson, who put lights and buoys at the port at his own expense, and in 1833 was made a harbour commissioner with a small public grant to effect other improvements.[14]

Exports from the harbour still mainly consisted of wheat, flour and potash, with some lumber and lesser farm products for more local trade. But such exports went out from many another port along the lake. York's more significant role was as an importing and distributing centre, having the advantages of its expanding hinterland and radiating roads, its already well-provided business facilities, and its aggressive, diversifying mercantile community.[15] The lead it thus was winning as a commercial town would only hold and lengthen. It would also gain from the canal-building now under way.

In 1825 the Erie Canal had been opened from New York to Buffalo on Lake Erie, with a side-cut to Oswego on Lake Ontario completed in 1828. The Erie, affording through-water access from the Great Lakes to the Atlantic, did not immediately affect York's trading pattern; but in the long run it offered far easier contact with the markets and supplies of New York.[16] Moreover, by 1833 Upper Canada's Welland Canal across the Niagara Peninsula provided a ship route to Lake Erie and beyond, or to the Erie Canal entry at Buffalo. Meanwhile, the Lachine Canal had been built above Montreal, although the full canalization of the upper St. Lawrence route would take till 1848. All these projects promised York far better links with distant markets and supplies, and lower, competing transport rates. If the consequences for this aspiring commercial town were not immediately felt, their gradual effects and even expectations of them surely marked its growth. In hopes of improving main-line bulk transport, York's men of property invested in various canal schemes, not always well chosen in the boom-time optimism, while its Family Compact officials steered loans through the legislature for the Welland Canal especially, and ended up deeply involved as stockholders and directors in that enterprise.

The boom years, which continued till the onset of another world depression in 1837, also brought significant financial developments. In 1834 the British American Fire and Life Assurance Company was incorporated in York as a competitor of British and American firms, offering both more efficient local coverage and lower rates. Under directors who included major business figures

Jesse Ketchum's tannery at Yonge and Newgate (Adelaide). Ketchum arrived from New York State in 1799 and moved back (to Buffalo) in 1845. A Reform member of parliament from 1828 to 1834, he was also prominent in the Mechanics Institute, the Temperance Society and the Common School board.

Another early town "industry" was Peter Freeland's soap and candle works at Yonge and Front. Freeland, a Glasgow Scot, moved to York from Montreal, relocating his factory as well. In York he was active in founding the Congregational Church.

like William Allan, Isaac Buchanan, George Ridout and William Draper (already a prominent town lawyer), the company soon flourished — and survives today within a later combine.[17] Because, however, it was very much dominated by allies of the government, opponents of the Compact were led to found the rival Home District Mutual Fire Insurance Company in 1837, with directors drawn from such recognized Reformers as Dr. Baldwin (president), Francis Hincks (secretary-treasurer) and James Lesslie.[18] This enterprise also survived for years as part of the town's increasing financial services.

At the same time, both political rivalries and larger business possibilities inspired fresh banking ventures. The Bank of Upper Canada, whose branch offices now extended from Niagara to Brockville, faced constant Reform hostility as the overfed creature of a ruling Tory Compact.[19] Consequently, the Farmers Bank came into being in 1835 under a largely moderate Reform directorate, with Hincks as managing cashier. A few months later, a still more partisan-pure Reform institution, the Bank of the People, appeared as well, to which Hincks transferred his services as manager. Still further, the Commercial Bank of Kingston, which had finally been chartered in 1832, opened a York branch in 1833, as did the wealthy British-based Bank of British North America three years later. These last two banks were clearly drawn by the business concentrating at the thriving commercial town. In any event, thanks to its range of banking and insurance services, the one-time village of York had by 1837 become the largest financial centre in Upper Canada.[20]

A different development that bore on economic growth was the advance of York's press, inherently related to the town's role as provincial capital. Since political action centred there, an increasingly partisan Upper Canadian society hung on the words and doings of the key men at York, all closely reported in its newspapers, which thus acquired a widening popular hold. William Lyon Mackenzie's case revealed as much. In 1826 the office of his *Colonial Advocate* was ravaged by a mob of "well-bred" young York gentlemen connected with the leading families, in retaliation for its anti-government diatribes. The result, however, was to make Mackenzie a martyr of Reform, and enhance his paper's standing with dissatisfied elements in the countryside. Entering parliament for York County in 1828, he strengthened his popular following

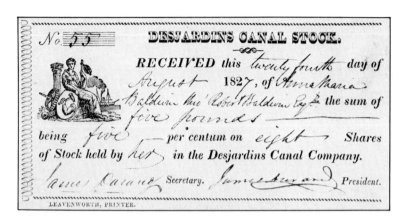

Financial aspects: the Desjardins canal project near Hamilton failed, and the Baldwins' stock (top) proved a bad investment; but the notes of the Bank of Upper Canada (bottom) stayed sound.

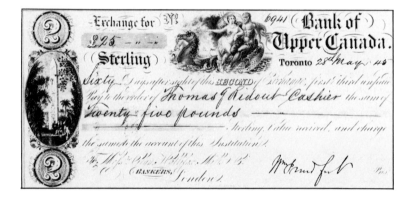

both as a Reform politician and leading capital journalist, each role interacting.

By 1834 there were seven newspapers at York: Mackenzie's *Advocate* and the official *Gazette*; the pro-government *Patriot* and *Courier*, published respectively by the Englishmen Thomas Dalton and George Gurnett; Francis Collins's *Canadian Freeman*, not as adamantly radical as the *Advocate* but still potently reformist; the *Christian Guardian*, begun in 1829 under the able editorship of a young Methodist minister of Loyalist descent, Egerton Ryerson, as the York organ for Upper Canada's main Methodist element; and the *Canadian Correspondent*, started in 1832 by William O'Grady, an Irish Catholic priest who turned political radical. The *Guardian* plainly looked to a province-wide audience, one not solely religious in interests, since the paper also voiced considerable political criticism — as the *Canadian Correspondent* decidedly did also. The fact that four of these seven newspapers were variously oriented to Reform in a town still dominated by the Tory-minded outlook of its ruling order, further demonstrated that they were appealing well beyond York — that it had indeed become a central political headquarters for the press. Yet more than this, the same journals as readily purveyed the notices and advertisements of York business to the countryside, extending its commercial communications as well as its political and social influence. In every way the town was enlarging its economic grasp, increasing its regional stature — and not the least through the dissemination of information and opinion.

THE SHAPING OF A MUNICIPAL STRUCTURE

York's vigorous growth through the earlier 1830s no less strained its established framework and raised new public needs. Furthermore, the tide of immigration did not just bring it purchasers, workers and investors, but disease and distress as well. In the summers of 1832 and 1834, cholera came with the immigrants to York, a deadly scourge ascribed to foul air or "miasmas" — not to microbes (then unknown) spread by contaminated drinking water. During the epidemic of 1832, 273 deaths were recorded; that of 1834 killed over 500, among them Francis Collins, the journalist.[21] Urgent but piecemeal efforts were made to deal with the contagion by cleaning up filth and waste, held to generate miasmas. In 1832 York for the first time got daily garbage and sewage collection,

ordered by the Home District magistrates, who also had small drains built in the dirtiest, poorest parts of town.[22] They appointed a temporary Board of Health, composed of physicians and leading citizens under Dr. W. W. Baldwin; but it lacked compelling force and funds, while the General Hospital that had finally opened in 1829 was a veritable plague pit, which sufferers dreaded to enter.[23] Hence, the epidemic of 1832 virtually ran unchecked until the colder days of autumn arrived. It harshly underlined the inadequacy of existing local government for a town which, thanks to its very expansion, faced serious shortcomings in financial and administrative powers as well as in public services.

Municipal change was in the offing. Politics had much to do with it, besides. York Reformers attacked the civic rule of the appointed district magistrates as much as the provincial rule of the Family Compact, seeking to bring both regimes under popular, representative control. Yet the established structures of authority also won support. Many anxiously loyal townsmen rallied against the appeals to American democratic models made by more radically minded advocates of Reform like William Lyon Mackenzie, preferring accepted British ways to headlong, republican-sounding proposals. In point of fact, the moderate bulk of Upper Canadian Reformers in both town and country desired less-sweeping changes still within a British colonial framework. Nevertheless, radical rhetoric roused anti-American apprehensions in York, still sensitive to its border position and memories of the War of 1812, and its attitude was shown in the provincial elections of the time.

In 1828, John Beverley Robinson again took the town seat, beating Dr. T. D. Morrison, a Radical associate of Mackenzie's. In a by-election of 1830 — after Robinson had been named chief justice — Robert Baldwin, son of Dr. Baldwin, did defeat a Compact Tory stalwart, Sheriff W. B. Jarvis. But Robert, like his father, was a firmly pro-British moderate Reformer, and his ruling-class background scarcely opened him to charges of Yankee democratic leanings. In any case, in general elections later that year, Jarvis won York, only to lose it in 1834 to James Small, another leading family offshoot become a moderate Reformer. The upshot was that York went Tory-Conservative, or at most middle-road Reform, even when Mackenzie and his left-wing allies were winning in the countryside. Of course, one might expect that the capital's gentry-officials and government retainers would take the establishment

William Lyon Mackenzie in later years: first city mayor, urban journalist and fiery hero of agrarian radicalism.

John Strachan, also in later life: warrior churchman, Compact champion, and promoter of education and economic power in young Toronto.

John Beverley Robinson: attorney-general, chief justice, and patrician Tory.

Robert Baldwin: leading Torontonian, Reform party chief and premier.

side. So would most of its commercial elite, who backed orderly rule and government aid to business, not the populist, pro-farmer militancy of Radical Reformers. Yet on evidence, too, a strong segment of the town's lesser shopkeepers and skilled artisans (those with the franchise) sustained the government cause, as largely did "loyal" immigrants, and there was no sizeable urban proletariat, whether or not it would have gone to the Radicals if it could have voted.[24]

In sum, a broad cross-section of York's political society endorsed the powers-that-be or wanted only to modify them. This may well have reflected British background traditions besides anti-American sentiments, and also a practical disbelief in vociferous Radicals who, when seated in a provincial assembly with much restricted powers, could do little more there than denounce and obstruct. At any rate, it seems clear that the town stayed pretty conservatively inclined. The presence of a faithful Reform contingent in the capital, and of such provincially significant left-wing figures there as Mackenzie, Jesse Ketchum, Dr. Morrison and the capable but devious Dr. John Rolph, could seldom alter the dominant complexion of York itself.

All the same, when it came to civic government, Tories and Conservatives as well as moderate Reformers and Radicals could be led to conclude that changes were required in the local regime at York. The elements on the right began to see the existing rule by appointed magistrates as too limited in powers and finance to supply effective services; while those to the left regarded it as corrupt and wrong in principle. The former mainly wanted a well-funded, efficient authority, but one naturally still based on reliable propertied interests. The latter sought a progressive new era of popular urban government, but naturally without increasing taxes. Despite these differences, however, both sides grew ready for a crucial step: the incorporation of York as a municipality with power over its own local concerns.

By the 1830s, in fact, the difficulties of a swelling urban centre being run by part-time magistrates, authorized merely to tax a penny on a pound of assessed property, were all too glaringly apparent. In 1827 the magistrates had had to borrow funds to pay for a new courthouse and a still inadequate new jail. By 1830 better market buildings were desperately needed, but could only be undertaken by raising another large loan.[25] The administration was continually on the edge of bankruptcy because of public needs. It had also had to establish a full-time police clerk, organize a volunteer fire company and lay some primitive sewers, all in the later Twenties, but had no funds left for major improvements, such as draining the main streets effectively. Accordingly, Henry John Boulton, Tory attorney-general, in 1830 proposed an incorporated, elected, municipal government for York with greater taxing power. Partisan debate stalled his scheme in parliament, until in 1833 a committee of Robert Baldwin, Dr. Rolph, James Small and George Ridout produced an amended draft bill that finally passed. Taking effect on 6 March 1834, it incorporated the first city in Upper Canada.[26]

Under this chartering act, the new city was to consist of five wards, bounded by Parliament Street on the east, Bathurst on the west, and extending from the lake to a line 400 yards north of Lot (Queen) Street. (See Map 7, page 126.) Beyond lay the city "liberties," in which new wards could be erected, reaching east to the Don, west to the present Dufferin Street, and north to Bloor, largely covering the Shore Plain area. Each of the five wards was annually to elect two aldermen and two common councilmen, with sizeable real-property qualifications. All adult male resident house or lot holders, being British subjects, received the civic vote. A mayor, salaried and chosen yearly by the aldermen out of their own number, would preside over and vote in the City Council, composed of both aldermen and common councilmen. That body would now take over duties formerly held by the magistrates, from dealing with public works, police, and fire prevention to controlling the market, taverns, public nuisances and the harbour, not to mention Sabbath observance and the licensing of theatrical performances. And the council could now levy taxes up to fourpence on the pound in the city, twopence in the liberties, while the municipal corporation was given increased borrowing powers. Finally — and quite significantly — the city's name was changed to Toronto, the older, more distinctive name that avoided the connotations of "Little" York.[27]

The charter of this new City of Toronto unquestionably had its failings. If a camel is a horse designed by a committee, so it had camel-like awkwardness, the results of trade-offs by contending factions. It provided elective control, but well qualified by property ownership; a mayor safeguarded from popular democracy by in-group selection, but with little real authority of his own. It left both Radicals like Mackenzie and Tories like Sheriff Jarvis considerably unhappy, and even moderates who stayed with it tended to see it as

the best of a dubious job. Above all, owing to legislative restrictions, the charter still provided insufficient sources of revenue for the enlarged municipal services that were hopefully expected from the new regime. Financial problems, quarrelling mayors and councils, public reluctance to meet the real costs of running a fast-growing city, were the vexed consequences of the incorporation act of 1834. And yet, like a camel, this municipal creation showed remarkable endurance, plodding on across the years, full of noisy grumbles but performing its tasks. A pragmatic recognition of civic responsibility, a political compromise largely between moderate Reform and Toronto Conservatism, the municipal system thus established still gave the city its own directing organization for an increasingly complex urban life.

LANDSCAPE, SOCIETY AND CULTURE IN A FRONTIER BOOM TOWN

Toronto in 1834 was beginning to look like a city. That June, its population was recorded at 9,252, though this near doubling since 1832 was partly due to the extension of its boundaries.[28] King Street, the main commercial thoroughfare, was now quite solidly built up from Caroline (Sherbourne) west to York Street, beyond Yonge. It displayed a mixture of structures that still included small wooden shops and frame houses, but consisted more and more of closed ranks of brick stores with dwelling quarters above, for both retail business and land values were steadily climbing on King. The large and handsome Chewett's Buildings were under construction at King and York, their architect a talented recent arrival from England, John Howard, who was to leave his mark on Toronto's built environment.[29] In the central King Street area, new brick market buildings had been completed in 1833, containing a public auditorium and now housing the City Hall as well. (See Map 3, page 38.) Rows of three-storey residences and stores were being promoted or erected elsewhere in this central neighbourhood, to give it an increasingly "downtown" character. On King Street at Church a new stone and brick Anglican St. James had been opened in 1832. Across Church Street from St. James was the courthouse, and north of this the second most socially significant Toronto church, St. Andrew's Presbyterian, begun by Church of Scotland adherents in 1830. A large new Methodist chapel stood a street away. And in this central section there were also major hotels like the

Bishop's Buildings at Newgate (Adelaide) and Simcoe: sizeable homes for the well-to-do. Built by 1833 (though seen here in a later photograph), these attached houses were not only indicative of the Thirties' building boom, but of a new urban pattern in residential living. The youngster at right evidently could not hold his pose.

four-storey North American, together with manufactories both large and small, since any sorting out of land uses had still not proceeded much beyond the rough distinction of a core segment from adjacent, supporting sections.

On the east of the central area of mercantile, civic and religious leadership, the original Old Town now merged into it. The Bank of Upper Canada lay here, and some imposing private mansions like that of Joseph Cawthra, a wealthy merchant. But poorer elements also tended to congregate in this section, many of them immigrants or transients, filling older, run-down little cottages on back lanes, often living in near-slum conditions. On the other side of the central area, the Macaulaytown fringe of humble homes spread into the park lots west of Yonge and above Lot. Yonge Street nearer the harbour was a rising focus of cartage, storage and workplaces. As the link between the port and the trunk route northward, it drew such concerns to its vicinity; and habitations as well were scattering up its course towards the tollgate at Bloor Street, the limit of the city liberties. North of this limit, Joseph Bloor, a prosperous local brewer, and Sheriff Jarvis (whose country seat, Rosedale, lay nearby) were planning out the future village of Yorkville.

The main thrust of development, however, was westward towards the Garrison. In the western area, fine residences fronted on the water, as they still did along the eastern shoreline. But to the west, the houses and properties tended to be larger; besides, the provincial government establishment was now centred in this section of the New Town, a prestige-factor influencing land use. Here on Front Street, three red-brick, plain but ample late-Georgian edifices had been constructed between 1829 and 1832 to house the provincial legislature and offices. Their grounds backed on those of Government House, since 1815 set in this location. East of the political complex stood John Strachan's resplendent mansion; and nearby, Henry John Boulton's stuccoed Holland House, erected in 1831 as a first attempt in Gothic Revival style at Toronto, with pointed arches and mediaeval ornamentation.[30] On Lot Street above lay Osgoode Hall, a stout brick block built by 1832 for the benchers and students of the Law Society of Upper Canada on a portion of John Beverley Robinson's estate. Beside Osgoode, broad College (later University) Avenue ran northward to the lands of the projected provincial university, for which Strachan had obtained a royal charter in 1827. Though planted and landscaped,

this road led nowhere, since chartered King's College would not be constructed at its head for another decade. West of College Avenue, however, lowlier, wooden dwellings spread unevenly along Lot Street towards another impressively wide roadway, Spadina Avenue, laid out by Dr. Baldwin below his hillcrest home. And while scarcely yet developed, both grand avenues pointed plainly to future extensions of Toronto's growth.

In many ways the new city was a frontier boom town, pushing, clamorous and cluttered, full of energy and land speculation, considerably different from the placid Little York of early years. Its older gentry families might still look to keep the lid on, but they were no less busily engaged themselves in developing and speculating, reaching after wealth and progress. And the increasingly strong and assertive business classes, the annual inundations of immigrants, the growing needs of municipal services and budgets, all testified that the stable state of official and gentry leadership was passing beyond recall. The very existence of the new, elected civic regime was further evidence. Toronto indeed had become a commercially oriented community, growing with the Upper Canada frontier, and thanks to the boom of the Thirties, no longer so greatly dependent on its old official ranks.

New cultural developments marked this larger society, improving its bare frontier plainness. In education, the failure of the provincial university to materialize was partly offset by the opening, with eighty-nine boy pupils, of publicly endowed Upper Canada College (UCC) across from Government House in 1830.[31] Governor Sir John Colborne, who had replaced Maitland, considered that a university would be premature until a fully qualified secondary school could prepare students for it, and used his still compelling authority to get his way. Directed mainly by Anglican clerics, graduates of British universities, the new institution aimed at cultivating future leaders for society. Its stress on classical studies, however, and the non-Anglican predilections of some of the city's growing middle class, fostered the appearance of private, more practically oriented academies for the sons of commerce, though age-old patterns of apprenticeship continued for professions and crafts. The old York grammar school also resumed, while primary education largely stayed with the government-supported Central School well into the 1840s. It was still generally deemed unnecessary to educate girls much beyond the primary level, though there were some private girls' schools, as well as other small

The new Parliament Buildings by J. G. Chewett, erected 1829-32, lay in a square at Front and Simcoe overlooking the water. Artistic licence again: the central portico was never added.

Upper Canada College, opened in 1830 north of the Parliament Buildings and Government House. A main school building was flanked by houses for masters and boarders.

and dubious private elementary ventures that charged little and provided less for either male or female children. The lower orders often had only church Sunday schools, which did impart some reading and writing as means to scriptural study. Toronto's educational facilities were not impressive. Yet the staffing of UCC to train a provincial elite at least planted a modest kernel of intelligentsia that would grow in years ahead.

The formation of the Literary and Philosophical Society in 1831 evinced fresh cultural stirrings, as did the Society of Artists and Amateurs, which in 1834 held an exhibition of 196 paintings at the legislature, promoted by John Howard, the architect, who was also drawing-master at UCC.[32] The tastes of the upper class still ran more to subscription balls and card parties; those of the lower to taverns for social recreation and release; while the righteous middle class largely frowned on dancing, cards and drink, and looked to church gatherings or elevating lectures as suitable social amusements. Nevertheless, the theatre also became a more regular means of public entertainment, if not of high cultural edification. Companies of American actors, travelling up the Erie canal route to Great Lakes centres, included Toronto increasingly in their tours. Moreover, instead of playing in hotel assembly rooms, they now could perform in the Theatre Royal, which acquired its own frame building at King and York in 1836. Despite its name, this was a makeshift structure that drew an unruly audience, and was continually decried by Toronto's Calvinists and Methodists, who saw theatre as mid-way between the temptations of taverns and the sins of bawdy-houses (the latter then centred on Lombard Street). All the same, the Theatre Royal provided a resident base for plays from excerpted Shakespeare to popular farces.

But for the middle class in particular, there was the Mechanics Institute. It was founded in 1830 to emulate English examples by such earnest moral uplifters as James Lesslie, and was intended primarily as a means of self-help for aspiring workers, to enable individuals to better their position through instruction in practical arts and sciences. But it soon became a middle-class institution that presented public talks in the Masonic Hall on broader philosophical and scientific topics, that ran classes on drawing or the musical arts, and that began collecting a library more suited to entertain well-to-do subscribers than meet the technical needs of artisans. Hopeful shop clerks and apprentices did attend its evening classes, yet generally most workingmen showed small interest. Nonetheless,

after a shaky start, the institute was flourishing by 1837, to be patronized by Toronto's respectability for its lecture series and social gatherings, and in time its library, which became the nucleus of the city's future Public Library.[33]

The local mechanics themselves tended to show livelier interest in collective action than individual self-help, that is, in forming trade unions of their own. Because there were no large industrial work units in this mercantile city, however, such efforts were limited to a few more-skilled, craft-conscious trades. In 1832 a printers' union had been formed; in 1833, benevolent societies among groups of building tradesmen.[34] The printers went on to set union wage levels, and in October 1836 all of them in Toronto struck when their increased rates were not accepted. William Lyon Mackenzie, one of the press owners thus affected, sounded a lot less like a friend of the people than an embattled employer defending the sanctity of the free labour market when he denounced "such an ungrateful and censurable proceeding."[35] But the strike was over in a few days, with only a general amnesty to end it. Another by journeymen tailors in November also quickly closed in failure. Evidently both the numbers and organization of labouring elements in the city were yet too weak to have much impact.

CIVIC POLITICS AND REBELLION DANGERS

Growth, thanks to the boom years, was really the basic problem that confronted the city administration inaugurated in 1834, pressing the need for better public service. Instead of decisively responding, the first municipal government became embroiled in clashes stemming from the sharp political divisions of the day. The initial civic elections of late March 1834 had produced a City Council split between twelve decided Reformers, including Mackenzie, Lesslie, Dr. Morrison and brewer John Doel, and eight staunch Tory-Conservatives, such as George Gurnett, editor of the *Courier*, George Monro, a leading wholesaler, and Colonel George T. Denison, an eminent militia officer. The fact that Reformers nevertheless won the first civic contest in this more usually Conservative community requires some explanation. At that point in 1834, local feeling against the old rule of district magistrates was more likely to hit Tory candidates at the municipal polls; Reformers, indeed, might have seemed to deserve the chance to launch a new era of civic progress. Besides, the fact that Mackenzie had recently been repeatedly and vindictively expelled from the Tory-dominated provincial assembly of the day brought him and his associates a surge of popular sympathy. At any rate, the balance did shift to Reform for Toronto's new civic regime of 1834, though only briefly as it transpired. And Mackenzie was chosen as first mayor by the council's Reform majority.[36]

From the start this regime ran into quarrels over disputed elections, during which an irate Mackenzie had Alderman George Monro forcibly ejected from the council chamber — shades of his own expulsions. Something was accomplished in establishing standing committees of council for finance, fire and water, roads, markets, police and prisons, the harbour and more; and a number of basic by-laws were passed dealing with fire or market regulations, garbage collection, Sunday observance, and so on. But few other advances were made, except in providing plank sidewalks on main streets, for besides the handicap of party strife, civic financial powers still proved inadequate to meet major needs.

The dread return of cholera in August of 1834 raised a more urgent problem. The Board of Health set up by the city corporation had scarcely more success in coping with it than had that named by the district magistrates two years before; yet it undoubtedly was hampered by its own deep factional divisions, which led to the board's recasting as a wholly Reform group. And after the disease subsided in the fall, the city government returned to heated wrangling, to wind up the year frustrated and considerably in debt. The initial Reform dominance had not had high success. Moreover, as a seasoned battler, Mackenzie did not adapt easily to presiding office, and his impetuous temperament hardly fostered concord.[37] In any event, Tories swept the civic elections of January 1835. Robert Baldwin Sullivan became mayor (a brother-in-law of Robert Baldwin, though a moderate Tory himself), while Mackenzie instead turned back to provincial politics and the fiery probing of popular grievances.

Under a solid council majority, new headway was made by the civic corporation, notably in building trunk sewers of brick under the chief streets.[38] But its deficit was thus enlarged, and attempts by this Tory council to have the city's tax base in its charter widened were held up in a provincial assembly now dominated by Mackenzie's friends. Accordingly, faced with debts from improvements while lacking an improved assessment law, a disgruntled citizenry swung back to the Reformers. They were returned

twelve to eight again on the council for 1836, which chose Dr. Morrison as mayor.[39] Whether or not Mackenzie's absence helped or the rival factions were now more chastened, this regime also made material progress, particularly in macadamizing main arteries like central King and Yonge streets. Moreover, the need to deal with growing numbers of helpless urban poor led to a civic grant for a House of Industry, which was opened the next year (under a volunteer citizens' group) to provide permanent, institutionalized poor relief on the English workhouse model.[40] Yet the hard question of municipal debt and reassessment remained unanswered. Despite its useful service, the Reform administration in turn was replaced by an all-Tory council in 1837 under George Gurnett as mayor, now one of an emergent breed of "regular" municipal politicans.

This Tory civic victory in Toronto also reflected a provincial shift; for in the election of 1836, Tories had again won control of parliament, swept on by extravagant appeals to British loyalty made by an intemperate new governor, Sir Francis Bond Head, who proved as inflammatory as Mackenzie. Still, the city did benefit from the Tory legislature. William Draper, the skilful Conservative lawyer who now sat for Toronto in the assembly, steered a measure through it by March 1837 that set up a wider system of assessment for the city, raised the maximum tax rate in its wards to one shilling sixpence on the pound, and increased its borrowing authority.[41] Hence, that spring prospects might have looked bright for Mayor Gurnett and the municipal corporation, except that, by then, a spreading world depression was making inroads at Toronto.

In consequence, the city's revenues were increasingly hit: building, street and sewer projects were cut back, and the municipal regime sank into the doldrums for months to come. All this, however, was soon overshadowed by far graver financial and political developments. Deepening depression in trade, shortages of cash and credit, led to business failures and heavy drains on the city's banks, which shook confidence in them by the summer of 1837.[42] The Reform banks were hard put to survive, though the far stronger government Bank of Upper Canada continued to meet its obligations. And many farmers who could not extend their notes in this financial turmoil were left distressed and debt-ridden, a steaming hotbed for the appeal to force which an exasperated Mackenzie and Radical comrades now worked to promote.[43] Rebellion was in view.

As the bad times worsened across the autumn, unrest deepened in the countryside. Then in November the outbreak of revolt in still more troubled Lower Canada brought Upper Canadian Radicals the signal for action. Following secret leadership meetings in Toronto, they called for armed insurgents to assemble on the capital. Governor Head had done his bubble-headed best to encourage violence by sending the troops of the Garrison off to help in Lower Canada. Hence, by early December Toronto lay open to attack — just as in 1813 — as several hundred prospective rebels collected outside the city at Montgomery's Tavern, some miles north up Yonge Street above present-day Eglinton Avenue. On the night of December 4, alarm bells rang out in Toronto when word of the massing at Montgomery's came in. Alderman John Powell, who had been scouting up Yonge Street and there been seized by a rebel party, had shot his guard with a hidden pistol, then ridden hotly for town with the news. Actually, Colonel James FitzGibbon, the veteran officer of the War of 1812 commanding Toronto's citizen militia, had already learned of the rebel gathering from other sources, and a superbly overconfident Head finally took the danger seriously. As for John Powell, he became a city hero, and a future mayor.[44]

The next day the rebel forces marched on Toronto, led by Mackenzie and Samuel Lount, a substantial North York blacksmith. They showed no clear direction, stopping to parley ineffectually with emissaries sent by Head. By nightfall their vanguard had plodded down Yonge into the city liberties to be ambushed by a picket under Sheriff Jarvis. After an excited exchange of shots, both sides fled back the way they had come. But this clash in a bush field became a turning point. The following day, December 6, the attackers did little but capture the mail coach out on Dundas Street; and many of them were already deserting in discouragement. Finally, on December 7, loyal militia who had been collecting in Toronto took the offensive. Some 900 men, with banners, two bands and, more important, several small cannon, advanced up Yonge towards Montgomery's on a crisp, sunny winter afternoon.[45] There they quickly scattered the ill-armed rebel remnants, and put cannon shots through the tavern, whereupon their enemies ran off wildly. The Yonge Street rising was over, Toronto saved from fire and sword — although, except for the few casualties in the skirmishing, it was more a comedy of errors than an epic drama. Still, the rebellion period itself was not over, and its results would be telling.

Within the city, fears and enmities led to charges against leading Reformers like Dr. Morrison, who was deeply implicated, but escaped, and James Lesslie, who was not, but still was jailed for thirteen days without warrant. Dr. John Rolph, the secret co-designer of revolt with Mackenzie,[46] successfully took off for the border before being found out; Mackenzie, too, reached the United States after a flight to the Niagara River. Now American sympathizers backed his call to free (or conquer) Canada, and their border raids which went on through 1838 cost far more in casualties and damage that the abortive original rising had done. Consequently, warlike tensions and an inevitable Tory reaction gripped the province as rebels and raiders were hunted down, suspicions ran riot, and Lount and a Yonge Street rebel comrade, Peter Matthews, were hanged at the jail in the capital in April 1838.

Nowhere was the Tory reaction more evident than in Toronto, bastion of the Family Compact and British loyalism, which now felt the alarms of 1813 sharply revived. Clearly too, the rebel movement had found few followers in the city, although some there quite likely had had no chance to join it. On balance, however, it seems evident that the possessing classes and their "respectable" supporters upheld a loyal consensus in the capital, and that the strength of any rebel sympathy lay in the hinterland. In any event, one consequence of Radical revolt was a drastic setback to the whole Reform cause in Toronto.[47] Reform papers there went out of print, while moderate party leaders like Dr. Baldwin and Robert Baldwin had publicly to disavow any links with the rebel faction. And for years to come, while Toronto necessarily served as provincial headquarters for a reviving Reform party, the city itself returned a succession of Tory or Conservative members to parliament, with only a few moderate business Liberals as exceptions to the rule.

If anything, therefore, Toronto moved decisively further right after the Rebellion of 1837. The shift showed most plainly in civic politics. Far from having any left-wing city administrations, however transitory, there would not even be a moderate Reform mayor until the 1850s. Meanwhile a string of Tory-controlled municipal governments ran Toronto, beginning with John Powell, the war hero, who proved an unimpressive mayor in 1838–40. These civic

Reaction to rebellion as envisioned by C. W. Jefferys: loyal volunteers muster at Toronto's Parliament Buildings, December 1837.

regimes often had their own contending in-group cliques, but then they did not have to fear Reform party opposition. In fact, while parties in municipal affairs might still have provided more healthy alternations, party politics as such became considered factious and unnecessary in the civic sphere. But who needed party labels when only one set of partisans ruled thereafter? Tory Toronto and Conservative civic mastery owed much to the events of 1837.[48]

THE CONSOLIDATING COMMERCIAL CITY OF THE FORTIES

Unyielding depression and border troubles that possibly threatened a new American war imposed a gloomy interlude on Upper Canada's capital, one lasting into 1840. That demographic barometer, immigrant arrivals at the port of Quebec, fell to 3,200 in 1838, rose only to 7,400 in 1839, and did not recover, to 22,000, until the year after.[49] And in the waning Thirties Toronto's civic administration stayed hard-pressed for funds, as the city's poor strained all-too-limited means of relief, and its businesses remained severely short of credit, a lack which drove more under. Ambitious projects put forward in the good times had to be abandoned, from lighting the city with gas to planning a railway north to Georgian Bay. Nevertheless, the basic commercial or municipal achievements of the preceding boom persisted, while gradually border violence was checked, tense relations with the United States were eased, and political passions lost some of their vehement heat.

A new political era, in fact, was opening. Lord Durham came out in 1838 to investigate Canadian ills. At Toronto in July he interviewed Robert Baldwin, among others, who pressed his own cherished remedy, responsible self-government on British lines. Earlier in July, Francis Hincks, by now Baldwin's close associate, had launched a newly constructive liberal paper, the Toronto *Examiner*, also dedicated to responsible rule. Under this renewed Toronto leadership, a Reform resurgence began spreading in the province, heightened by Durham's weighty Report of 1839, which endorsed responsible government, urged other reforms and condemned the old Compact's grasp on power. In the autumn of 1839, Governor-General Poulett Thomson, later Lord Sydenham, arrived to effect some of the proposals, particularly a union of the two Canadas, which could effectively develop their joint St. Lawrence waterway and commercial system. In 1840 an imperial Act of Union followed, to take effect early in 1841.

Assuredly, a different period was under way. Within the new United Province of Canada, an alliance of French and English Reformers was to obtain responsible rule before the decade closed. But whatever else transpired, not only did the former province of Upper Canada now cease to exist but Toronto also ceased to be a capital. Governor Sydenham considered that the city lay too far west in the extended Province of Canada to be its ruling seat, and chose Kingston instead. When his decision was made public, just before the United Province was proclaimed in February 1841, Kingston was gleeful at the downfall of its old rival, while Toronto was full of protests and dismay. Its press predicted ruinous declines in property values as provincial bureaucrats began to pack up for the move.[50]

And yet the change proved to have remarkably small effect. For one thing, the law courts, land agencies and some other government offices were not moved; Toronto still remained a provincial administrative centre. For another, Upper Canada did not wholly disappear, but stayed a distinctive section of the new Union — one very different from the Lower Canadian, largely French half — and although it now might be known on maps as "Canada West," the term "Upper Canada" continued in popular as well as some official use. Equally, Toronto continued to be an established focus within this section: a centre of Upper Canadian private and public elites, where the main churches, social organizations, chief newspapers and even party headquarters were still located for the western sectional community. But most important of all, Toronto by now had gained such a lead as a western urban centre, in population growth and commercial development, that the loss of its status as a capital made little serious difference to its fortunes.[51]

It also helped considerably that by the time of the move, world depression had lifted at last. With reviving export markets, imports for Toronto's hinterland correspondingly went up, and credit began to flow readily once more. By 1841, in fact, the city's commerce was on another ascending curve, to run to 1847. Enlarged wholesale, banking and insurance operations, increased harbour facilities and improved roads (especially the new plank roads), all strengthened Toronto's hold on a freshly prospering countryside. The results were displayed in more urban affluence, amenities and

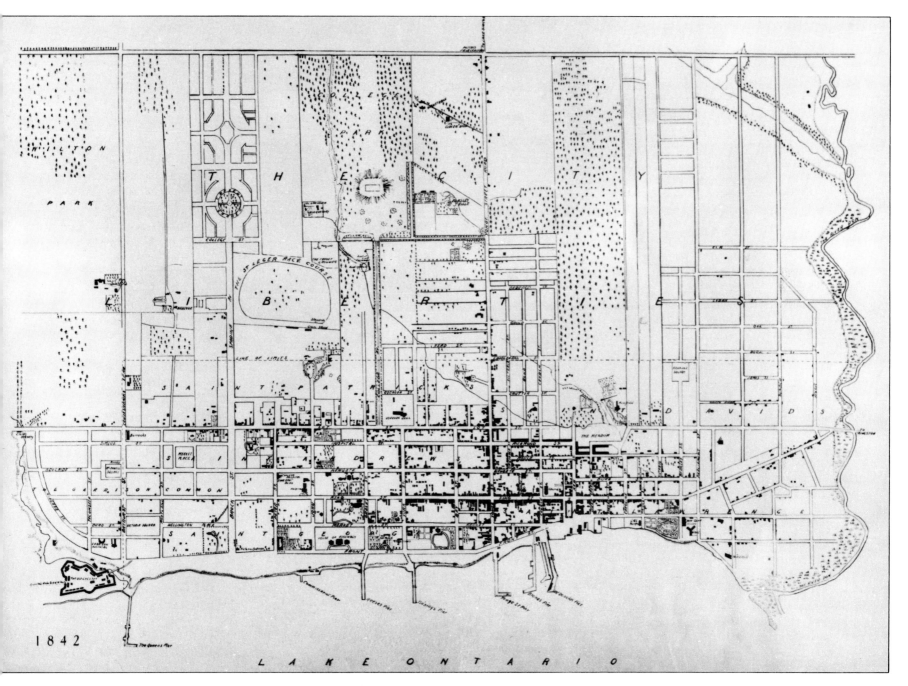

Toronto by 1842. The built-up city had already reached above Queen, especially up Yonge in the Macaulaytown area, but much vacant land remained in the "liberties" to east and west, and particularly north to the Bloor Street limit.

construction — and perhaps in the incorporation of the Board of Trade in 1845 as the city merchants' own power and pressure group.

A better-off civic government looked to developing gas and water services, pushed on by Alderman George Gurnett as a leading advocate. In 1841 it franchised Albert Furniss of the Montreal Gas Light Company to supply the city.[52] The main streets were gas lit by the next year, and the waterworks were completed the year after, although there were constant complaints about inadequate water pressure for fire-fighting.[53] The city also built its own City Hall below the central market in 1844 — more elaborately styled, with its domed cupola and "Italianate" arcaded wings, than most Toronto public structures up to that time.[54] John Howard's massive new stone city jail and his handsome classical Bank of British North America were further additions. So were the attractive Gothic Revival Anglican churches, Little Trinity and Holy Trinity, by Henry Lane, the City Hall's architect: the first out eastern King Street, the second west off Yonge above Queen (as Lot Street became in 1843). A good deal larger, however, was the impressively Gothic Roman Catholic cathedral, St. Michael's, built by William Thomas in 1845 above Queen near Church.

A pillared Methodist church on Richmond west of Yonge (1844); the stately, domed Provincial Asylum by Howard well west out Queen, begun in 1846 but not finished until 1850; more downtown rows of houses and shops; and new mansions on emerging streets to northward: these, too, were products of the flourishing Forties. Still further, the university, King's College, opened in 1843, was temporarily housed in the former Parliament Buildings until new quarters were completed on its College Avenue grounds. Generally speaking, the whole ambience of Toronto altered over these years. A shambling boom town was already becoming a respectably integrated "city in earnest" — one linked by the electric telegraph to New York and Montreal in 1847.[55] Its affluence showed in the busy docks and customs house at the port, where Toronto shipowners now controlled a substantial fleet, notably of modern steamboats. Hugh Richardson's line boasted the new *Chief Justice Robinson*, while Donald Bethune's eight vessels made him by 1845 "the largest steam boat proprietor in Canada West."[56]

Throughout the period, the city government remained firmly in Tory hands: Mayor Powell being followed by George Monro in 1841, succeeded by Henry Sherwood, then William Henry Boulton,

and back to veteran George Gurnett as mayor from 1848 to 1850. Sherwood and Boulton, besides, were not just civic politicians, but also represented Toronto in the provincial legislature. The city had been given two parliamentary seats in the new United Province; these two staunch Tories held both of them for most of the decade. They won them, for example, in 1847 despite a Baldwin Reform sweep elsewhere, which led to fully operative responsible government in the province by 1848. The Tory pair even won Toronto again in 1851.

This prevailing political response (which Charles Dickens on a visit of the early Forties termed "the wild and rabid Toryism of Toronto")[57] was not wholly the consequence of British traditionalism, anti-American attitudes and acute memories of armed raids and revolt. It stemmed also from Toronto's very demography. In the continuing British immigration, the city had still collected a high proportion of Protestant Irish and Anglican English, both elements largely inclined to Tory-Conservatism. The weight of English massed, conceivably, because many of them were already urbanized, more adapted to city needs than were rural Scottish crofters or Catholic Southern Irish cottagers, and most of them could find congenial settings in the established patterns of Toronto. The sizeable Northern Irish contingent also included numbers of town-dwellers with urban-oriented skills; but whether these and more rural Ulstermen were drawn to the city by its British-Protestant affinities may scarcely be estimated. What can be noted is that the Ulster Orange Order continued to spread in Toronto as a benevolent association and tribal shelter for incoming Northern Irish. And the vehement pro-British loyalties and biases of the Order provided a powerful underpinning for Toronto Toryism, supplying rambunctious shock troops for election campaigns, besides political links reaching well into the lower classes.

Orangemen had played a stormy part in the provincial elections of 1836, although there was not much to choose then between their cudgels and those of Radical farmers. Orangemen were central in election rioting of 1841 in Toronto, which left one man dead, and in many other public disorders for years to come.[58] In any event, the Orange Order became a prominent feature in civic life from the Thirties onward, buttressing Conservative predominance and repeatedly influencing politics. But the point to note is that this was indeed a popular, mass force that inevitably widened the base of Toronto Toryism beyond a deferential support of established

City Hall of 1844, by H. B. Lane, facing north on Front, west of Jarvis. The centre block still exists, with its Council Chamber now a city art gallery.

Lane's Holy Trinity, erected in 1847, gave Macaulaytown its own Anglican church. In 1845 a Mrs. Lambert Swale of Yorkshire, England, gave the funds for this edifice, to have its seats free "forever" for the poor. A counterpart for the Anglican poor of the eastern end of town was Little Trinity.

John Howard's monumental Provincial Asylum (1846–50), out Queen West north of the Garrison. The tall dome actually concealed a water tank for this most "modern" structure.

The dignified Bank of British North America, raised in 1845 at the corner of Yonge and Wellington, was another of the many buildings in the young city designed by Howard.

Howard, seen in old age, also made many sketches and paintings of Toronto, collected art, and built a picturesque home, Colborne Lodge, on his High Park estate west of the city. His subsequent gift of magnificent High Park to Toronto in 1873 was a present beyond price.

old-family leadership. Family Compact patrician Toryism and Orange plebian Conservatism were not the same; and truth to tell, the former was fast running out, even before the revolt of 1837.

Compact officialdom, in fact, was not just a casualty of Durham's Report and the movement to responsible government, but also succumbed to a rising business and professional class leadership with popular mass backing. Toronto politics demonstrated as much in the 1840s. Tories might rule the city, but while they yet included gentry names, they reflected changing political and social patterns that affected town and country alike. Chief Justice Robinson might yet inveigh eloquently but fruitlessly against the Canadian Union that had ended his old provincial bailiwick; John Strachan, a bishop since 1839, was still an undaunted champion of Anglican vested interests. But neither sat in governing councils any more. In the city, Mayor W. H. Boulton, MPP, was still lord of The Grange with its carriage society and fine dinners, but he had to deal with shop-owners, building contractors and Orange chieftains to function in office — in politics that were often less than gentlemanly.

In sum, while the old-family presence still persisted, particularly in social repute, both politics and society in Toronto were increasingly finding new directors. In provincial circles, William Draper (who now became a Conservative party leader) exemplified the change: acceptably a Toronto gentleman and successful lawyer, he was a postwar English immigrant, not a descendant of old official-dom. In the city community, also, there were rising figures like the Ulster Irish wholesaler, William McMaster, the biggest Toronto capitalist of the coming era, and the Scottish Liberal journalist, George Brown, whose *Globe*, founded in 1844, was to be the most influential newspaper in English-speaking Canada for some forty years ahead. Not just the capital had departed Toronto, but the former government village society; and the consolidating commer-cial city was shaping a bourgeois leadership drawn mainly from the British immigrant influx that had swelled its numbers so significantly.[59]

The immigrant tide ran on quite steadily and with no great problems down to 1847: Quebec landings reached 44,000 in 1842 and 32,000 in 1846, by which time Toronto's own population, around 11,000 in 1837, was passing the 20,000 mark.[60] The year 1847, however, brought both renewed world depression and the startling arrival of nearly 90,000 migrants at Quebec.[61] The over-

The south side of King Street looking east towards St. James, 1847. A comparison with the picture of King in the 1830s, on page 44, conveys how the city's central core had grown and consolidated since then.

whelming majority of them were impoverished, disease-stricken refugees from an Ireland devastated since 1845 by famine. Faced again with bad times and an unprecedented flood of human misery, Toronto saw its integrating span of the 1840s come swiftly to an end. Nevertheless, some other, more long-range developments promised better things instead.

In 1846 Britain had adopted free trade, removing its tariff controls over colonial commerce. The consequent ending of imperial preferential duties was a hard blow to Montreal and Kingston merchants, along with those in other centres who had been mainly engaged in sending staple Canadian exports via the St. Lawrence route to protected British markets. But Toronto had its Hudson–New York links as well, and after the initial impact of depression, stood to benefit increasingly from the newly opened state of trade. Besides, the American Drawback Acts of 1845–46 had remitted tariff charges on goods in transit between U.S. Atlantic ports and Canada, so that Toronto business could now freely use American routes to send products outward, or as freely use them to bring imports direct from Britain. Cross-lake traffic would hence develop in new volume with American towns like Buffalo and Oswego, which gave access to the New York entrepôt via the direct, efficient Erie Canal. Thanks to the lifting of trade controls, Toronto might utilize either the St. Lawrence or Erie routes with almost equal facility, could even play one off against the other, and so enhance its own trading position at a breakpoint between the rival Montreal and New York systems.[62]

In fact, the coming of imperial free trade and the new ease in trans-border commerce virtually made good Toronto's potential advantages of site as a major focus of traffic on the Lower Lakes. In the economic growth that resulted, it was to fill out its commercial metropolitan role, add railway transport, and become the business nexus of most of Upper Canada. Accordingly, the city was on the verge of another era of rapid development by the late Forties, however grey and foreboding conditions might have looked just before the approaching dawn. The commercial town that took off was now heading towards much wider control of the Ontario lakelands. A consolidated, bourgeois Toronto was soon to be caught up in eagerly welcomed change.

Even amid signs of looming trouble in 1847, there was optimism.

That May a rising young city lawyer, trained in Draper's firm, Larratt Smith, wrote cheerfully to a relative in England:

> Canada is not such a wilderness as some imagine, and when you tread the gas lit streets of Toronto, and look into as many handsome shops with full length plate glass windows as there are in Bristol or London you will not look upon us as many of your countrymen do; when you see steamers entering our noble bay as comfortable as magnificent in their internal arrangements, the bay wharves, the thousands and thousands of passengers arriving hourly from the United States and all ports, the electric Telegraph almost from one end of the Province to another every moment conveying intelligence with the rapidity of thought, you will have every reason to be proud of your country and her glorious dependencies, if you never were before, and to thank God that you were born an Englishman.[63]

What more need anyone say?

The city in 1854. Growing fast in the new era of railway building, but not yet marked by tracks along the harbour, which would line the open stretch below Front Street, to be the Esplanade. The first train from Toronto had actually run in 1853, northward about twenty miles to Aurora. The early depot and track of this Northern line lay towards the left (west) end of this scene, but are not visible here.

Chapter Three
The Railway and Regional Hub, 1847–71

Mid-Victorian Toronto saw the advent of the railway, one of the nineteenth century's greatest instruments of change, which conquered continental land space and tied together existing populated areas. From the 1850s in Canada, extending rail lines fed and supplemented waterways, enabling far greater traffic flows and fostering much bigger urban centres at focal points on transport routes. For inland regions, moreover, this new technology overcame the annual winter closing, when shipping by lake and river ceased. And rough, inadequate roads, all but unusable during spring thaws and autumn freezes, no longer dictated the timing, reach and carrying capacity of traffic by land, since now both goods and passengers could move year-round by rail, on regular journeys across wide distances. The consequences for an advancing urban place such as Toronto were powerful and pervasive. Like other leading Canadian towns, it rose as a railway city during the mid-century era, pulsing with fresh activity and building. And it did particularly well as a rail transport hub by gaining much-improved lines outward, expanding hinterland links inward, and through its own vigorous enterprise. The years down to the 1870s thus saw striking growth in Toronto as this emerging transport metropolis became a commanding centre of regional life in general. But first the city faced grave social strains at the end of the Forties: strains that would by no means vanish, even with the climbing sweep of rail prosperity.

POPULATION CHANGES AND ETHNIC STRAINS IN SOCIETY

In June of 1847 young Larratt Smith had sent a less cheery letter overseas to England, this time describing the impoverished Irish famine immigrants who then were daily flooding into Toronto on their way westward from Quebec and Montreal:

They arrive here to the extent of about 300 to 600 by any steamer. The sick are immediately sent to the hospital which has been given up to them entirely and the healthy are fed and allowed to occupy the Immigrant Sheds for 24 *hours*; at the expiration of this time, they are obliged to keep moving, their rations are stopped and if they are found begging are imprisoned at once. Means of conveyance are provided by the Corporation to take them off at once to the country, and they are accordingly carried off "willy nilly" some 16 or 20 miles, North, South, East & West and quickly put down, leaving *the country* to support them by giving them employment.... John Gamble advertised for 50 for the Vaughan plank road, and hardly were the placards out, than the Corporation bundled 500 out and set them down.... It is a great pity we have not some railroads going on, if only to give employment to these thousands of destitute Irish swarming among us. The hospitals contain over 600 and besides the sick and convalescent, we have hundreds of widows and orphans to provide for.[1]

Smith's account was more matter-of-fact than sensitive — the response of the city corporation, more concerned with controlling the problem, and passing on as much of it as possible, than with relieving the misery of the sufferers. Nevertheless, these attitudes were widespread in the Toronto of the time, confronting social needs on a scale it had never before experienced, sharing assumptions that work and settlement in the rising countryside was the ever-present remedy for want in a new land, and possessing few means of public welfare, or even private assistance, within the inundated host community itself.

The rapid spread of typhus brought with immigrants who had often sailed in "floating pesthouses" made Toronto's difficulties far more acute.[2] As in the cholera epidemics of the Thirties, a temporary Board of Health had to cope with the emerging crisis. Annually

The poor were always with them. At right, Toronto's British Colonist *of 20 August 1847 calls for aid for Irish famine immigrants in that typhus-laden year. Top, the big charitable Roman Catholic House of Providence of the 1850s reflects enlarged Catholic numbers in the city. Above, the separate charities of the Protestant majority are evinced in this 1870 ball for the Orphans' Home.*

appointed by the council, its role had been only nominal since the last epidemic in 1834, but as reorganized under Alderman George Gurnett, the board of 1847 strove its best in the face of an economy-minded civic government and a citizenry fearful of contact with infected immigrants. The General Hospital was soon overflowing with sick and dying, and the board had to seek more funds for additional quarters.[3] By September close on 30,000 immigrants had reached Toronto, more than double the previous year's arrivals for the same period.[4] By mid-October there had been 3,300 admissions to the hospital and 757 deaths there.[5] The hospital's final mortality rate was about 29 per cent — a good deal lower, at least, than the 47 per cent at Kingston.[6] Meanwhile, Torontonians who sought to care for the stricken newcomers succumbed themselves, including Dr. George Grasett, the hospital superintendent, and the Catholic bishop, Dr. Michael Power. Aside from the devastation wrought by typhus, there was also the question of its helpless leavings: whole families, wrote Sheriff W. B. Jarvis to Mayor Boulton, "lying under the shelter of fences and trees, not only on the outskirts, but within the very heart of town — human beings begging for food, having disease and famine depicted in their countenances and without a shelter to cover them."[7]

Private charity did what it could; public meetings raised money to supply relief and work to survivors. The Toronto Destitute Widow and Orphan's Society provided aid through its subscriptions, larger sums coming from such as Bishop Strachan, Chief Justice Beverley Robinson and Robert Baldwin.[8] But only the winter 1847–48 ended the typhus epidemic and the worst suffering, as the immigrant season closed down. By that time 38,560 migrants had passed through Toronto, and 1,124 persons had died there, when the city then had but some 21,000 residents.[9]

There was not to be so bitter a plague experience as this in following years. In the 1848 season, the entrants at the port of Quebec comprised less than a third of the famine wave, and no great outbreak of disease accompanied them inward. The next year, however, the older enemy, cholera, invaded again, and in Toronto killed 424.[10] In 1854 it returned anew, to carry off close to 500.[11] But it did not threaten once more till 1866, and then turned out to be a scare, not a scourge. Thereafter, advances in medicine and sanitation largely brought an end to such drastic epidemics in the city. By then, moreover, the influx of transatlantic immigrants, so often associated with the fearsome spread of contagion, had long since ceased to be an annual flood.

In sum, the mass exodus to Canada from the British Isles that rose in 1820s had sharply dwindled by the 1860s as the supply of fertile colonial wild lands ran out, and as urbanized Britain now increasingly adjusted to its industrial existence. Through the late Forties and early Fifties, however, a still deeply blighted Ireland continued to send by far the biggest numbers across to Quebec yearly: altogether some 126,000 between 1848 and a final crest in 1854.[12] And during this last sweep of the great transatlantic movement, the heavy outflow from the desolated Irish countryside, mainly from the Catholic South, added to the famine survivors of 1847 to reinforce the Irish presence in Canada. Specifically in Toronto, the Catholic Irish ingredient in the community expanded sizeably, certainly contributing to the city's growth, and to its social and ethnic tensions as well.

The provincial census of 1851–52 recorded the Irish-born as already the largest single ethnic element in Toronto. Altogether they now constituted about 11,300 in a total city population of some 30,000, over a third. The English-born residents numbered 4,958, the Scots 2,169, and there were nearly 10,000 Canadian-born of "non-French" origin, 467 of French descent, 1,405 American-born, and a scattering of "other origins," including about 50 Jews.[13] In point of fact, the Anglo-Protestant ascendancy remained firm in the city, since the great majority still were English-speaking Protestants and the Irish-born themselves included many staunchly Orange Ulstermen. But the religious census for 1851 helped to reveal more. Although Anglicanism continued to be the largest denomination in Toronto (then having 11,577 adherents, to 4,123 for Methodism and 4,544 for Presbyterianism), the Roman Catholic church stood second, with 7,940 followers, mainly comprised of Irish Catholics.[14] By 1861, in a city that had now enlarged to over 44,000, the Roman Catholic element had climbed to 12,135 and the Anglicans held a much smaller lead at 14,125, though Methodism and Presbyterianism had also increased their proportions.[15]

These mounting Catholic Irish numbers made mid-century Toronto more than a little uncomfortable. They represented a challenge to its ruling Protestant patterns and presumptions. The newcomers required, and soon obtained, more Catholic churches and clergy; and the latter pressed demands for publicly organized, state-supported Catholic separate schools. The Orange Order grew freshly vigilant against papist threats, and the ancient homeland feud of Orange and Green took on new heat, recurrently erupting in mob violence. Moreover, wider anti-Catholic sentiments in the established community reflected current Protestant reactions in Britain and America against the anti-liberal papacy of the day, while "voluntaryism" — the view that churches should be voluntary associations of faith not backed or aided by the state — was also strong among the more evangelical Protestants in the city.[16]

In consequence, Protestant and Catholic spokesmen in Toronto were drawn into sweeping doctrinal disputes. A sectarian war of newspapers broke out, to be waged recurrently through the 1850s and beyond, waged especially by a powerful Liberal *Globe* (under the resolutely voluntaryist Presbyterian, George Brown) against an ardent Irish Catholic *Mirror* and its religious allies. The dominant majority came broadly to regard the Catholic Irish as an obstreperous, discordant block, and anxious eyes were drawn to the "Catholic vote," locally or provincially. But beyond these religious and political troubles, the fact that the Irish influx largely went to swell the unpropertied element in Toronto further sharpened urban social tensions.

That the arriving Irish massed generally and for years ahead in the lower ranks of civic society was none too surprising. Those who had fled famine in 1847, and survived typhus to be dumped destitute in or out of town, were unlikely candidates for starting farms or launching city enterprises — or finding much more than day-labour for men, household or laundry work for women. From about 1850 a newly rising boom did open many pick-and-shovel jobs in urban construction, or soon in railway building. Yet even after the worst hardships had passed for the Irish arrivals of 1847, their countrymen who followed them were not much better equipped to advance economically and socially. They came mostly from a deprived, parochial rural tenantry, ill-conditioned for a starkly strange new world. The strength of their family, locality and religious ties, still helped them to cohere, to look after their own, and in time to adjust to their new environment. In all this, in fact, the experiences of the Catholic Irish were not too different from those of later disadvantaged ethnic elements who settled in

Toronto. At least they had English (though not all did) and were already British subjects — however much some of them might harbour dark memories of that fact.[17]

At any rate, the reactions of established Toronto society to the displaced Catholic Irish collecting in its midst were a good deal like those the host community would show to subsequent ethnic groups who also entered at near-bottom levels. These newcomers seemed entirely too cohesive and distinctive as they crowded into mean shanty dwellings. At one extreme, indeed, the Irish might be sentimentalized as naturally humorous and good-hearted; but at the other, the possessing order in Toronto quite readily regarded them as ignorant, feckless and a threat to lawful peace. In fact, such prejudiced opinions had some basis, given the harsh background of these immigrants and their difficult, often demoralizing, conditions of life in the urban setting. Irish names loomed on police records or among jail inmates (and certainly were so noted), especially in cases of disorderly conduct or personal assaults. Irish drunkenness in squalid little tippling shops, Irish vagrancy and illiteracy, drew the attention of the temperance advocates, moral reformers and apostles of mass public schooling who rose vigorously in the city from around the mid-century onward. At root these problems were the general troubles of a massing urban society. Yet a bottom class provided underdogs to whom social faults were regularly attributed; and in the 1850s the Catholic Irish were conspicuously represented in it in Toronto.[18]

During the same period, there was also a much smaller black migration into the city. While never numerous, blacks had been present there from the founding days of York; but in the early Fifties the drastic Fugitive Slave Law in the United States brought hundreds of refugee slaves to seek haven in Upper Canada, the final terminus of the celebrated "Underground Railroad." Many of them came on to Toronto, about as destitute as the famine Irish has been; yet the strength of local abolitionist sympathies brought them aid, particularly from the earnest Toronto Anti-Slavery Society.[19] Charity, however, cooled in time, especially after the Civil War of 1861–65 did away with slavery in the United States. Still not that numerous, some blacks moved off to farm-settlement projects; some returned to the republic after the Civil War; and others stayed on in Toronto, where colour prejudice surely helped to hold them largely at low levels. The "respectable Negro" might

Queen's Birthday celebration at Government House, 1854. Whatever the ethnic strains in mid-Victorian Toronto, its British loyalism remained fully apparent, as suggested by this early work of the Toronto painter Lucius O'Brien, then twenty-two.

aspire within much restricted limits; by contrast, the Irish immigrant experience was an open-ended exercise in upward social mobility.

As for the bigger Irish influx, it not only anticipated the heavy immigrant intakes and resulting social reactions known to the twentieth-century metropolis, but through its powerful impact on the Victorian city was also highly consequential in its own right. In Victorian Toronto, the Irish were long to form a major part of the urban masses. Working-class movements, civic politics, public education, would all be deeply affected by Catholic-Protestant divisions. So to some extent would residential location, as markedly Catholic Irish neighbourhoods emerged at the eastern and western ends of town.[20] So would public order — during Orange-Green antagonisms expressed in election clashes, at celebrations of Catholic festivals, or at Orange parades on the "Glorious Twelfth" of July. And so would the treatment of civic welfare needs, largely handled through dual Catholic and Protestant-majority services.[21] The altered population pattern of the mid-century, the Celtic-Catholic qualification on an Anglo-Protestant city, left a strong mark on its social responses also.

Nevertheless, owing to the drop in transatlantic migration over the later Fifties and much of the Sixties, mid-Victorian Toronto had some interval in which recent comers and older residents could gradually adjust to each other. At the same time, its non-immigrant, native-born element steadily expanded in proportion, almost tripling between 1851 and 1871, and constituting over half the population by the latter date.[22] Of course, many of these native-born in 1871 represented the children of earlier British immigrants. Still, while Toronto consequently retained its basic British ethnicity, it was steadily being Canadianized as well. In the later Sixties, it is true, the intake of immigrants began another rise, largely because of job opportunities in a city then entering another boom phase; but it scarcely attained its earlier levels. Notably, too, of those British who did come after 1866, the English again became the largest group. In 1869, for instance, out of some 20,000 departures from the British Isles for Canada, over 7,200 English picked Toronto for their destination compared with about 1,550 Scots and only 811 Irish.[23] Once more we cannot be sure how many of these departing actually arrived and stayed. Yet their relative ratios are significant, and they represent a continuing trend rather than special examples.

The census of 1871 showed Toronto with a total population of over 56,000: among them, in rounded numbers, 11,000 English-born, 10,300 Irish-born Catholics and Protestants, 3,200 Scots, nearly 2,000 Americans and about 29,500 Canadian-born; the remainder being mere handfuls, mainly of northern Europeans.[24] In religious affiliation, there now were about 20,600 Anglicans, 11,800 Roman Catholics, 9,600 Methodists, 8,900 Presbyterians and 1,900 Baptists, plus other small Protestant groups.[25] Plainly, this Anglo-Celtic city had remained overwhelmingly Protestant, but with a strong Catholic contingent and a continuing Anglican lead. Thus had demographic and ethnic change worked out over the whole mid-Victorian period: to strain and yet confirm the dominant patterns of the Toronto community.

URBAN ECONOMY: THE COMING OF THE RAILWAY

Population strains might have proved still sharper, had not Toronto's economy also grown so extensively over the period. Following the late-Forties' depression, prosperity returned to world commerce around 1850, backed by California gold discoveries, industrial expansion in western Europe and the eastern United States, and by generally strong demands for staple goods. In Canada a mounting inflow of British capital soon fed railway building, while in Upper Canada a veritable wheat boom arose in its more recently settled, fertile western peninsula. Still further, the Reciprocity Treaty of 1854 brought free trade with the United States for basic products like grain and lumber. Business and prices climbed swiftly, and in an increasingly inflationary but keenly optimistic era, Toronto's own economic life surged forward. One indicator, city assessments, shot from £132,359 to £186,983 just from 1850 to 1851.[26]

Aided by the American bonding system completed in 1852, the city took full advantage of its trans-lake and Erie Canal trade links. Import trade, its leading commerce, rose fivefold in value between 1849 and 1856, from some $1,200,000 to over $6,600,000 — a figure not to be surpassed till 1867.[27] Its export trade, while of lesser weight, also made it a major port in shipping grain and wood. "It seems like magic!" declared the *Globe*. "We question whether there is a town in the world which has advanced more rapidly than Toronto."[28] For the well-to-do, the good times meant opportunities for investment and development, for entrepreneurship and speculation. For poorer citizens, however, they also spelled inflating costs of living and housing, even though jobs grew more plentiful and money wages rose.

Skilled workers in particular felt prices pressing on their established craft status, and made fresh attempts at trade unionism to protect their positions, raise pay or shorten hours.[29] A series of sporadic strikes ensued, most notably by printers at the *Globe* in 1854.[30] That journal, now the strongest voice of Liberalism in the city, was no less directed by a thorough economic liberal, George Brown, who vigorously fought these assaults on the masters' freedom of contract. By and large the unionizing efforts faded out, though wage levels did go up markedly over 1853.[31] The city's industrial work force was still too limited and dispersed for unions to take firm hold. Nevertheless, some wider trades organization did subsequently appear when a branch of the British Amalgamated Society of Engineers was set up by machinists in Toronto in 1858; while in 1860 the American-based Iron Moulders laid foundations for future "international" unionism in the town.[32] And in any event, if not yet unionized or industrialized, Toronto's whole economic life was being sweepingly altered during the Fifties.

The lands beyond it were fast filling in. Frontier farm extension had met the rugged barriers of the Precambrian Shield, and intensive rural growth took over more and more. The consequences appeared in well-tilled acres that replaced stump fields, in brick and frame farmhouses instead of squared-log cabins, and in thriving villages that had been bush hamlets, now linked by improved roads, mail services and spreading newspapers to local commercial towns. As a major centre, Toronto profited increasingly from this hinterland progress, drawing on the gains of the farmsteads and lesser country places. Its own core area of trade by the early Fifties covered an Upper Canadian central zone roughly extending east to Durham County, north to around Barrie on Lake Simcoe, and west into the grainfields of Peel.[33] Further westward, the enterprising head-of-the-lake town, Hamilton, offered strenuous competition; further eastward there was Kingston still, while on the north, much of Simcoe County up to Georgian Bay was as yet little developed. Toronto's economic hinterland was hence still very much smaller than the whole Upper Canadian region. But this hinterland assuredly was flourishing, was generally well tied to its commanding city — and the advancing means of land transport, the railway, could powerfully enlarge it. And so Toronto in its fresh phase of growth turned heartily to railways.

In 1853 a line opened from Montreal to Portland, Maine, gave St. Lawrence transport an ice-free Atlantic outlet. By 1855 the Great Western (GWR) had built from the Niagara River via Hamilton to the Detroit River, connecting the American rails to New York at the one end with track westward across Michigan at the other (Map 4). But much the largest line was the Grand Trunk, chartered in 1852-53. When complete in 1860, this railway, capitalized in London but centred on Montreal, spanned United Canada, from Quebec to Montreal and Toronto, then on via Guelph to Sarnia at the foot of Lake Huron. Though enmeshed in politics and loaded with debt, the great transprovincial rail route provided all-year land transit between the Canadian interior and the St. Lawrence ports, effectively opening the "spring trade" of Toronto merchants two months earlier.[34] The city would gain abundantly from its new Grand Trunk access far to east and west. Yet other lines also came to serve it well, especially the Northern Railway, a Toronto-based venture backed by civic loans, which built to Georgian Bay on Lake Huron, thereby renewing the old Toronto Passage.

The Northern, initially named the Ontario, Simcoe and Huron, began construction in October 1851 at a gala ground-breaking ceremony on Front Street. Its track reached Barrie in 1853 and Collingwood, the newly laid-out terminal port on Georgian Bay, in 1855. The route soon began to flourish as the lands of Simcoe County were thereby opened up, and not only farm produce but lumber from huge Georgian Bay forests came down to Toronto by rail. In truth, this expanded hinterland freight traffic proved far more substantial to the city than the envisioned wealth to be won from a re-established passage to the great North West.[35] Nonetheless, Toronto business leaders looked to develop shipping services on the Upper Lakes out of Collingwood, to link one day with the western plains still ruled by the Hudson's Bay Company, and so win a vast new commercial empire for their city.[36] Meanwhile, a wide area northward had been tapped by rail into Toronto, making it a much bigger port for lumber shipments to the United States, and, by the Sixties, attracting a wheat flow down the Northern from American ports around the Upper Lakes that brought grain elevators to rise beside Toronto Bay.[37]

The same year that the Northern was completed, 1855, the Great Western Railway was extended into Toronto from Hamilton. This Toronto "branch" was largely viewed by the Hamilton-based GWR as an outthrust to tie the Toronto market into its rail

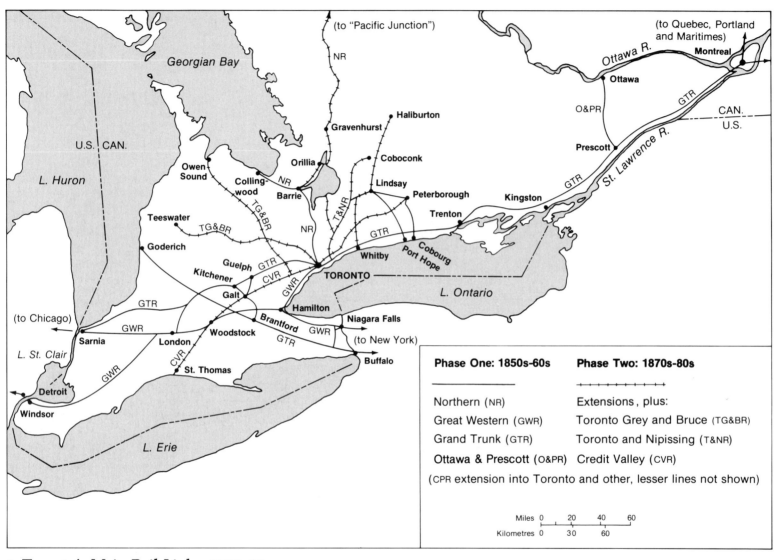

4 Toronto's Main Rail Links, 1851-86

Within the map:

(to "Pacific Junction")

(to Quebec, Portland
and Maritimes)

Georgian Bay

Montreal

Ottawa R.

NR

Ottawa

Haliburton

O&PR

GTR

CAN.
U.S.

Gravenhurst

Prescott

U.S. CAN.

L. Huron

Orillia

Coboconk

Owen
Sound

Colling-
wood

Barrie

Lindsay

St. Lawrence R.

GTR

Kingston

Teeswater

NR

T&NR

Peterborough

TG&BR

Trenton

TG&BR

NR

GTR

Goderich

Cobourg
Port Hope

Whitby

Guelph

GTR

Kitchener

CVR

GWR

L. Ontario

TORONTO

Galt

GTR

GWR

Hamilton

(to Chicago)

Brantford

GWR

Niagara Falls

Sarnia

GWR

London

Woodstock

GTR

(to New York)

L. St. Clair

CVR

Buffalo

St. Thomas

GWR

Detroit

Windsor

L. Erie

Phase One: 1850s-60s	Phase Two: 1870s-80s
Northern (NR)	Extensions, plus:
Great Western (GWR)	Toronto Grey and Bruce (TG&BR)
Grand Trunk (GTR)	Toronto and Nipissing (T&NR)
Ottawa & Prescott (O&PR)	Credit Valley (CVR)

(CPR extension into Toronto and other, lesser lines not shown)

Miles 0   20   40   60
Kilometres 0   30   60

The first locomotive on the first railroad out of Toronto, the wood-burning **Lady Elgin** was named for the wife of the then governor-general. She lifted the first sod for the Ontario Simcoe and Huron (from 1858 the Northern) on Front Street in October 1851. This engine (costing $9,000), however, proved too light for all but construction work, and was soon superseded by those from James Good's foundry on Queen Street.

Davenport Station on the Northern, a rural location now deep within Toronto. The station building was a model in its day.

system across southwestern Upper Canada. Instead, Hamilton and the whole Southwest found themselves increasingly tied into Toronto. The much larger centre, with its greater trading facilities, business resources and market demands, exercised the stronger focusing power. In effect, the fast-rising western peninsula beyond Hamilton was opened to Toronto as never before, through Woodstock and London by rail to Windsor, where train ferries crossed to Detroit and American tracks to Chicago. Furthermore, since the Great Western also joined with lines to New York, Toronto equally gained direct rail access to the giant American supply and market centre, a major supplement to the Erie Canal route.[38] No wonder the jubilant city celebrated a "Great Railway Festival" when the link to Hamilton was opened in December 1855 with a banquet and ball for 5,000 guests, held in the big new Northern Railway workshops, lavishly decorated for the occasion.[39]

The next year the Grand Trunk reached the city from Montreal, then built on westward towards Sarnia. The long Sarnia section of the line extended Toronto's traffic hinterland along a more northerly route across the broad western peninsula, on a direct course running from Toronto harbour. The track to Sarnia was not completed until 1859, by which time Canada's first railway boom had collapsed, following financial crashes in London and New York in 1857. But though depressed times lasted on into the Sixties (until the American Civil War revived market demands), the exuberant rail-building years left far more behind them than heavy loads of public debt, bankrupt schemes and strained finances — all of which certainly affected Toronto, along with other centres hit still harder.

To begin with, the city's commercial and financial growth had been strongly stimulated. Its trading activities essentially had mounted as its transport hinterland spread out by rail. Nor was this only through the wider reach of its wholesale imports. Toronto also increasingly took command of the western Upper Canada grain export trade, wresting much of it from Hamilton, for which town the building of the Grand Trunk behind it — from Toronto right to Sarnia — completed its downfall as a serious commercial rival in the 1860s.[40] Hence, still-larger Toronto mercantile houses developed in keeping with the greater scope of business. Prominent among them was that of John Macdonald, a Scot who rose with the dry-goods enterprise he began in 1849 to become a "merchant prince," whose firm occupied a city block by 1865, a capitalist-politician and ultimately a senator.[41] The Toronto Stock Exchange

began in 1852, ministering to the city's grain dealers and wholesalers, and further promoting its role as a commercial metropolis. And during the Fifties the Toronto Board of Trade became a powerful rostrum for the urban mercantile elite.[42] At the same time, the capital and expertise required in large-scale trade, or in the corporate dealings of railway companies, fostered new joint-stock financial and investment enterprises. The Bank of Toronto was founded in 1856, also serving grain and wholesale interests, with J. G. Chewett as first president, J. G. Worts as a major shareholder, and from 1862, William Gooderham as one of three successive presidents drawn from his family.[43] Insurance companies, building and loan firms multiplied as well, the most significant among the latter, the Canada Permanent Building and Savings Society, incorporated in 1855 under directors such as Chewett and Worts again.

This wave of entrepreneurship produced new prominent figures of the railway age. There was Frederick Capreol, the initial driving force behind the Northern Railway — who indeed sought to finance it by a public lottery, an idea sharply rejected by righteous mid-Victorian Toronto.[44] He subsequently lost control of the project, but it was effected under Frederic W. Cumberland, another Englishman, long influential in his adopted city as an engineer, architect and director-manager. And the Scot, Sandford Fleming, who became the Northern's chief engineer in 1857, went on thereafter to construct other lines, to survey the Canadian Pacific Railway (CPR) across the West, and pioneer the idea of Standard Time that would end the chaos of "local-time" railway schedules. Then also there was Casimir Gzowski, originally an exile from the abortive revolution of 1830 in Poland. He organized his own heavy construction company in 1853, which largely built the Toronto-Sarnia line of the Grand Trunk. In his engineering career, Gzowski later erected a massive new international bridge at Niagara, and wealthy, subsequently knighted, he long remained a leading figure in Toronto's inner circles.

Railways also laid foundations for new industrial growth. They tended to foster concentrations of industry, since the vastly improved land transport they provided invited economies of scale, whereby more could be done efficiently and cheaply by larger producing units in major places than by a host of little mills or workshops strung out across the country. This concentrating nevertheless took time. It only saw its beginnings in Toronto of the

Casimir Gzowski, with his family in the 1850s. Builder of the St. Lawrence and Atlantic, the Grand Trunk west from Toronto, and the Esplanade that brought tracks to the harbour, he also developed the heavy Toronto Rolling Mills to produce iron rails. His elegant Italianate residence stood on Bathurst.

Frederic Cumberland, Toronto entrepreneur of the railway era, managing director of the Northern, major city architect, and later member of parliament for Algoma — an early linking of Toronto interests with the Ontario north.

1860s, though ardent boosters then sought a cotton mill, a sugar refinery and a large new brewery, unsuccessfully. The change from localized patterns of merely minor manufacturing would not occur overnight; and it was risky to undertake big industrial enterprises, especially after the severe crash of 1857 cut down credit and investment funds for some years. Still, the change went forward. It was evidenced, for instance, in the fine five-floor, stone Gooderham distillery of 1859, and especially in the Toronto Rolling Mills set up by Gzowski and his partner, D. L. Macpherson, in 1857 to supply rails for their Grand Trunk contract. By the mid-Sixties the Toronto Mills near the Don's mouth turned out tons of manufactured nails as well as railway iron.[45] This was a pioneering plant of large-scale metal industry — and a clear product of the railway.

The railway, after all, was the first direct major impingement of the Industrial Revolution on Toronto. In comparison, the earlier wooden steamboats of the waterways had had far less effect, requiring merely a limited amount of machine and metal technology. Not so the locomotives, cars and iron road on land. They demanded far more from the metal trades, and so laid a broader basis for mechanized industry. On the Northern, for example, while its first small locomotive had been brought complete from Portland, the second was produced by James Good's foundry in Toronto.[46] Other engineering enterprises followed as railway work enlarged technical capacity, pointing onward to much fuller later industrialization.

But for the Toronto of the Fifties and Sixties, the most sweeping effect of railways was undoubtedly the remaking of its whole land transport system. To the north, this system had reached the rim of the Upper Great Lakes basin. To the west, its traffic now extended to the bounds of farming Upper Canada; western towns like Hamilton, Brantford or London might still control a good deal of local activity, but could not contend against the overall transport mastery of Toronto. Eastward, its one-time rival, Kingston, had declined still further. The Grand Trunk's line lay inland behind that town, but in any case, the "focusing" tendency of rail transport, to feed to and from main centres, effectively diminished Kingston's own realm. Instead, Toronto's distributing trade spread on eastward into the upper St. Lawrence area. Here, however, and in the Ottawa Valley, the commercial grasp of Montreal remained powerfully felt. But for the bulk of the region, the strategic web of tracks that now radiated southwest, west, north and east from that city's harbour made Toronto the railway hub of Upper Canada, and greatly thanks to this, the main regional business hub as well.

Toronto still had to contend with Montreal on varied fronts, while equally dealing with it as a major outlet and source of supply. The older, much bigger urban centre, with 90,000 inhabitants in 1861 to Toronto's 44,000, was at least as well served by rail and water transport, had far greater wholesaling, banking and processing facilities, and still exercised wide influence across the whole Upper Canadian business realm.[47] In the depression of the late Fifties and early Sixties, Toronto's import trade even lost some ground to Montreal's, but by the end of the decade it had regained the loss, particularly in higher-value goods.[48] Above all, Toronto consistently made use of its alternative links to New York for market and supply. It continued to play off the Erie "ditch" (down which travelled most of Upper Canada's grain crop in these years) against the St. Lawrence route, and now it had its own rail connections southward as well. Consequently, the city's businessmen and politicians fought attempts favouring Montreal interests to set preferential provincial duties on transport by way of the St. Lawrence.[49] Its Board of Trade and press generally voiced righteous free-trade principles. They opposed the placing of any barriers to the ready flow of goods to and from the United States, which might — worst of all — invite an end to the Reciprocity Treaty and the return of high American tariff rates. For reciprocity and railways had facilitated the burgeoning Lake Ontario city's access to the American seaboard, giving it a still stronger offset to either rail or water dominance from Montreal.

Toronto also had to fight the power of Montreal finance. During the stringent early Sixties, its own key Bank of Upper Canada became seriously embarrassed, in part the result of poor management and overinvestment in unrealizable land and railway assets.[50] Further damage was done when provincial government accounts were withdrawn for safety from the troubled bank in 1863. And under a sharply restrictive credit policy now really directed by the biggest Canadian bank, the Bank of Montreal, as government agent, the Bank of Upper Canada floundered more and more. In 1866 it had to close its doors. Toronto businessmen widely saw the failure as deliberately engineered. But out of it came a more aggressive enterprise founded in the city in 1867, the Canadian Bank of

Toronto Rolling Mills, 1864. The importing of steel rails by the 1870s removed the need to re-roll iron ones grown brittle in use, and so ended this early example of industrialism, luridly painted here by William Armstrong.

The Exchange Building, erected in 1855 on Wellington east of Yonge, testified to the growth of milling, transport and banking interests in the railway city. This is a notably early photograph, of 1856, by the "photographists" Armstrong, Beere and Hime.

Commerce, pushed on by the powerful wholesaler William McMaster. With McMaster as first president and John Macdonald and H. S. Howland (a leading wholesale hardware merchant) among its directors, the well-funded Commerce was soon to become Toronto's prime banking house and spread its branches widely. Moreover, between 1869 and 1871 the city's financial interests mounted a strong campaign to secure new legislation that would save note-issuing chartered banks from the sway of one paramount, government-favoured bank of issue — namely, the Bank of Montreal. They succeeded through measures now put forward by Sir Francis Hincks as minister of finance. In banking as well, then, Toronto business defended and advanced its own domain.[51]

Port activities, however, advanced far less in the urban economy. Over the period, Toronto's harbour traffic certainly enlarged to serve the expanding community, drawing ships from Kingston and Oswego, Cleveland and Chicago. Yet rail competition and the depression of the late Fifties took a heavy toll on the city's own shipping. Toronto-owned steamboats nearly disappeared; by the early Sixties steam service was virtually left to Kingston, Montreal or American-registered boats, while resident shipmasters retreated to sailing craft.[52] To an extent, this was a practical conservatism: sailing vessels still handled a major share of bulk water-carriage, and they were much less costly — and explosive — than steamers. Nevertheless, it also indicated that Toronto investments in transport had now turned chiefly to land lines inward, leaving its outward water traffic far more to other centres. This same attitude was reflected in a relative failure to improve port facilities. In 1850 the province had set up a Toronto Harbour Trust with members from the City Council and Board of Trade. Its funds were small; the needs were large.[53] Spurred by Hugh Richardson as first harbourmaster, the trust did make some progress down to 1862, rebuilding the important but decrepit Queen's Wharf and dredging the main channel entry. But by then finances were still slighter, as was public interest. Any waterfront developments thereafter rested mainly in private hands, including railways like the Northern and Grand Trunk, which built their own dock facilities. Here, too, railways had their way at the port — another sign of the triumph of rail over older transport modes.

URBAN LANDSCAPE: BUILDING THE RAILWAY CITY

The buoyant growth of the rail-construction era also promoted a major phase of urban building in Toronto, much of which survives today to mark one of its best architectural periods, thoroughly derivative in styles, but happily adapted by a set of remarkably versatile architects. Almost at the outset, in 1851, William Thomas's St. Lawrence Hall was completed to provide a first-class public auditorium. Facing north on King Street, with a new market wing behind it, the grandly classic edifice further helped to focus communal activity around the area of central King. International artists played here: the "Swedish Nightingale," Jenny Lind, in 1851, Ole Bull in 1853 and 1857, Adelina Patti in 1853 and 1860. Leading politicians drew crowds to its main chamber; and balls, lectures, performances of the current hit, *Uncle Tom's Cabin*, or gatherings of the Anti-Slavery Society kept the hall in constant use.[54] It became the civic forum of the bustling mid-Victorian community.

The erection of St. Lawrence Hall was part of considerable new construction around central King Street, largely due to the Great Fire of 7 April 1849. The fire began in a stable, then swept over ten downtown acres, from Church Street on the west to George on the east, and from King northward to Adelaide. Winds, inadequate fire equipment and faulty water supply were chiefly responsible for the blaze's spread. At length, the open ground of St. James's churchyard, a brief shower, and the arrival of troops from the Garrison to help the exhausted volunteer fire companies, enabled the conflagration to be checked. Only one life was lost, and most of the structures destroyed were of a fairly nondescript commercial and storage character.[55] Nevertheless, the north range of the market had been burned out, as had St. James's itself and the offices of the Reform *Mirror* and Conservative *Patriot*. Accordingly, St. Lawrence Hall and Market arose instead, together with large white-brick blocks of stores and a lofty new St. James Cathedral of yellow brick, built in Early English Gothic by F. W. Cumberland and his partner, Thomas Ridout, and finally opened in 1853.

Major construction proceeded elsewhere, too. The handsomely classic Normal School (by Cumberland and Ridout) was built off Yonge at Gould in 1851, a teacher-training centre for the provincial school system being zealously developed from the mid-Forties under Chief Superintendent Egerton Ryerson. A large Mechanics Institute building (by Cumberland and W. G. Storm) went up at

King Street East, south side, winter of 1856. Another early streetscape by Armstrong, Beere and Hime, it shows not only prominent stores like the Golden Lion, at left, but also a plank sidewalk and a still-unpaved, muddy thoroughfare.

St. Lawrence Hall, by William Thomas, opened on the south side of King at Jarvis, 1851. Its tall classical cupola, columns and carved stonework expressed Toronto's rising prosperity and aspirations.

St. James' Cathedral, north side of King at Church: the large new Gothic structure by Cumberland and Ridout finished in 1853. Its present spire was not added till the 1870s.

Adelaide and Church in 1854, containing a library and music hall as well as meeting rooms. In 1855 a new General Hospital was erected east off Gerrard, in "modified Old English" by William Hay (Map 5). In 1856 William Kauffman's big Rossin House replaced the Chewett Block at King and York; it was a worthily metropolitan hotel in five storeys of freestone and white brick, boasting fifteen ground-floor shops with plate-glass windows and over 180 well-appointed bedrooms, plus reception hall, ladies' parlour and gentlemen's baths.[56] The same year a long-lived major rival appeared on Front — best known as the Queen's Hotel, it would last until the Royal York was built upon its site in the 1920s.

And since Toronto again became a political capital in this era, the seat of government (periodically) of the United Province of Canada, the former Upper Canada Parliament Buildings on Front were extensively refurbished, as was the adjacent Government House. Being renewed as capital affected the now high-riding commercial and railway city only temporarily, but it does need explaining. Small-sized Kingston had proved inadequate to house the provincial political establishment, and in 1844 Montreal had taken over as government centre — until a mob burned down its Parliament Building in April 1849. Afterwards, the capital of a sectionally divided province was shifted between Toronto and Quebec, the old governing seats of Upper and Lower Canada, mainly because neither section of the Union would willingly accept a permanent capital in the other. The prickly seat-of-government problem was finally resolved by the mid-way choice of Ottawa, but the government buildings erected there were only occupied late in 1865. Thus, Toronto served as Union capital in 1849-51 and 1855-59, after which Quebec did duty until Ottawa was ready.

In any case, Toronto remained the central judicial seat for Upper Canada, and Osgoode Hall, home of the Law Society, was much rebuilt to house the leading jurists in proper style. In 1857 Cumberland and Storm provided a lordly classical portico that unified the structure, and a magnificent, vaulted library within — thus to achieve one of the finest edifices in Toronto in that day or this. And the resourceful Cumberland also designed no less a distinguished home for the provincial university in a very different mode: University College, chiefly Norman mediaeval in form and massively reared in stone by 1859, in the university's estate that headed College Avenue.

That institution had known a trying career before its splendid new building put it squarely in the landscape. In 1849 the Baldwin Reform government of the day had transformed Anglican-dominated King's College into a secular University of Toronto, leaving Bishop Strachan denouncing the new "godless university." Indeed, the indefatigable bishop secured a royal charter for a new Anglican Trinity College, whose own sizeable building, in Tudor Gothic by Kivas Tully, was erected on Queen Street in 1851. Furthermore, other denominations' colleges in Upper Canada, especially the Methodists' Victoria College at Cobourg (backed by the influential Egerton Ryerson), continued to demand shares in the provincial university endowment. Only the construction of University College, as the teaching establishment of the degree-granting University of Toronto, literally placed the non-denominational state institution on firm ground, significantly confirming public university training in Toronto. Significant, too, as marking a development that in time would see other higher educational institutions gathering about this academic focus, Roman Catholic St. Michael's College settled itself to the east of the University grounds in 1856-57.

A big Masonic Hall by Kauffman, new churches, and much residential building further marked the railway city's growth. Homes for the rich tended to be Gothic-Romantic, with pinnacles, battlements and turrets, such as William McMaster's 1860 mansion on newly stylish northern Jarvis Street or John Macdonald's "Oaklands," set in a broad estate up Avenue Road on the rise beyond Bloor. Some larger homes adopted the increasingly fashionable Italianate style, like Casimir Gzowski's out west on Bathurst, featuring round-arched windows and overhanging cornices below low-pitched roofs, though others still were more classically derived. Many smaller houses also went up for the well-to-do middle class, particularly in dignified terraces along streets adjacent to the downtown core. Admirably proportioned, if plainly built in brick, with large shuttered windows and high ceilings, these row-houses offered ample room for the families of professional men, lesser merchants and officials.

As for the lower classes, they had mainly to be content with little clapboarded or rough-cast cottages still scattered throughout the city, but more especially located towards its edges. There, at least, they had gardens and some space around them, while yet being

An 1856 view of Trinity College by Kivas Tully, opened in 1852 on Queen West beyond Garrison Creek. This was the centre of Anglican university training well into the twentieth century.

University College: original architectural drawing before construction was begun in 1857, depicting what the architect Cumberland wanted and largely achieved, and also the ungroomed "campus" then.

Osgoode Hall on Queen: a west wing and centre block had been built in the 1840s, but Cumberland and Storm remodelled the whole, 1857-60, adorning it and creating its present fine facade.

The Rossin House, by William Kauffman — Toronto's first grand-scale hotel, 1856, not yet in business, at King and York. The downtown construction boom is suggested by the excavation in the foreground.

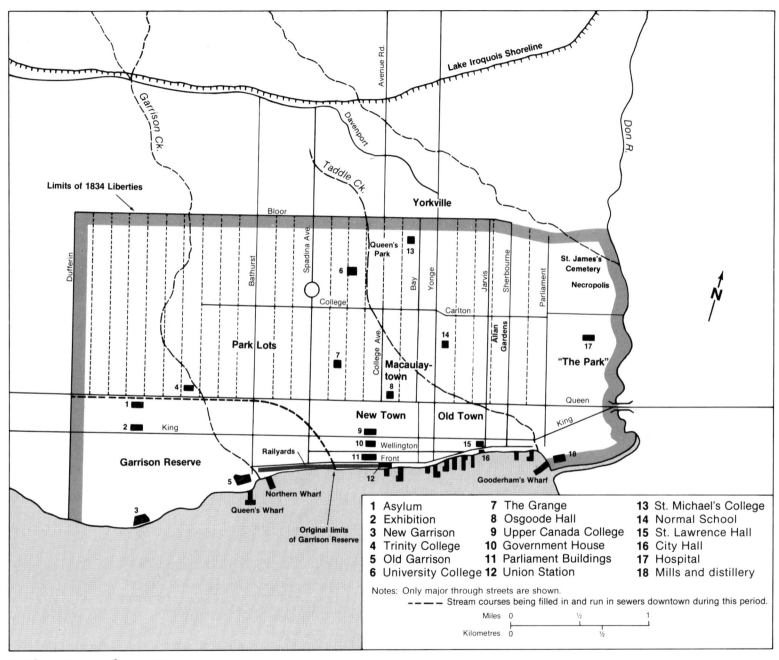

Limits of 1834 Liberties

Lake Iroquois Shoreline

Garrison Ck.

Davenport

Avenue Rd.

Don R.

Taddle Ck.

Yorkville

Bloor

Dufferin

Bathurst

Spadina Ave.

Queen's Park

13

6

Bay

Yonge

Jarvis

Sherbourne

Parliament

St. James's Cemetery

Necropolis

College

Carlton

College Ave.

Park Lots

7

14

Allan Gardens

17

"The Park"

Macaulay-town

8

Queen

4

New Town

Old Town

1

2   King

9

King

10   Wellington

15

Garrison Reserve

Railyards

11   Front

16

18

12

Gooderham's Wharf

5

Northern Wharf

3

Queen's Wharf

Original limits of Garrison Reserve

1 Asylum	7 The Grange	13 St. Michael's College
2 Exhibition	8 Osgoode Hall	14 Normal School
3 New Garrison	9 Upper Canada College	15 St. Lawrence Hall
4 Trinity College	10 Government House	16 City Hall
5 Old Garrison	11 Parliament Buildings	17 Hospital
6 University College	12 Union Station	18 Mills and distillery

Notes: Only major through streets are shown.
- - - - - Stream courses being filled in and run in sewers downtown during this period.

Miles   0   ½   1

Kilometres   0   ½

5 The City to the 1860s

The Grange, one of the city's best elite homes since the days of the Family Compact, is seen in mid-Victorian years, when ex-mayor W. H. Boulton still occupied it. In the early twentieth century it became the initial core of the present Art Gallery of Ontario, and now is admirably restored.

Mid-Victorian in-town residences for the middle class: Sherbourne Row. A similar row-house on Bond Street, last home of William Lyon Mackenzie, has been restored through the Toronto Historical Board.

A cottage in lower-class Macaulaytown. Dating from earlier days, these simple, if often well-detailed, little homes long sheltered the poor, but continually deteriorated.

within walking range of work. For Toronto still was small enough and had sufficient room available to avoid, on the whole, the close-packed, noisome tenements that disfigured urban Britain, that rose in big American centres on the seaboard, and in due course developed in Montreal. The city's poor and needy, however, were generally left to shelter where they could, in dilapidated one-storey shacks that remained from an earlier day, more frequently found still in Macaulaytown or on back streets of the Old Town area. It can only be said that the poor were not so concentrated in mid-Victorian Toronto as to make their poverty blatantly apparent in what was yet a fairly unsorted, patchwork urban territory, apart from its few considerably Catholic neighbourhoods or the Macaulaytown tract, within St. John's Ward since 1853.

That city was nevertheless expanding beyond easy walking range, especially north along the main Yonge Street artery. Here above Bloor, Yorkville was now a prosperous village of storekeepers, artisans and suburban dwellers. Horse-drawn omnibuses ran from St. Lawrence Market up Yonge to the Red Lion Hotel in Yorkville from 1849, but in 1861 the horse-powered street railway made its first appearance in Toronto on the same route, to foster more growth in the northerly direction.[57] This improved facility for internal urban transport would, in fact, promote both the wider spread of the community and the sorting-out of business and residential districts within it, aided when additional lines were soon opened on King and Queen. The consequences took time to be felt, however. Of more immediate consequence to Toronto was the effect on its built environment of the street railway's big brother, the long-distance steam railway, whose tracks now penetrated to the very heart of the city, influencing land use along their converging paths.

Obviously the railway's influence was most strongly evident where the tracks came together at the harbour front. Land was in demand along the portside, where the Northern, Great Western and Grand Trunk located station buildings, sidings and transshipment facilities, and where more warehouses, cartage firms, lumberyards (and soon industries) came to cluster around the transport lines. On the other hand, living conditions obviously depreciated around this noisy, increasingly dingy area. Those who could, left its neighbourhood, though some were slow to abandon traditional, shore-view homes. Those who stayed close to the

weedy desolation of the tracks and the drab walls of storage sheds more largely did so because they could not afford to do otherwise. Railways, then, forwarded a bleak kind of sorting-out around Toronto's once sparkling harbour. It was unplanned, in a happy-go-lucky day of faith in planless, wealth-producing "progress." But it ended in all but closing off the central lake frontage from the main mass of the town's inhabitants.

Paradoxically, one rare element of planning assisted this railway takeover along the shore. The undeveloped public promenade beside the water's edge, the open strip deeded in 1818 in trust to a leading group of York's early citizens, was in the prosperous early Fifties embodied in a grand new civic plan for an Esplanade: a landscaped walk and carriage drive to stretch along the harbour margin below Front Street on partially filled lands. In 1854 Gzowski and Company obtained a city contract for the work, but it soon transpired that this firm, which was also to build for the Grand Trunk, would obstruct water access by running that railway into Toronto right down the Esplanade. Public outcries arose, and in 1855 the City Council voted to cancel the contract, while the Grand Trunk threatened legislative sanction to build along Queen Street instead. More ferment followed, yet rail-boosting sentiment won out.[58] A provincial act of 1857 transferred the strip to the municipality, which granted the Grand Trunk right of way; and the Esplanade went ahead, with the other railroads also strung upon it.

By the Sixties the busily building city had reached the boundaries set out in its charter of 1834. Either its original wards — St. Lawrence's, St. George's, St. Andrew's, St. Patrick's and St. David's — had been extended into the city liberties, or new wards had been added — St. John's, St. James's and St. Thomas's — so that when the liberties were abolished completely by statute in 1859, there was little left of them to be taken in except for a margin on the east along the wet flats of the Don. Assuredly, most outer stretches of this civic territory still were sparsely occupied. But essentially it was already an urban domain, widely mapped out for streets and building lots, even where gardened estates, cottagers' cabbage fields or racetracks and amusement grounds as yet bordered on the built-up areas. And the city was steadily filling in westward, as well as northward towards the rise above its Shore Plain, where some of the rich found suburban refuge.[59]

To the west along the lakefront, the original Garrison Reserve

Above, towards the edge of the built-up town: Yonge Street looking north around Gerrard in the 1860s. The street rails were used by a horse-powered street railway that began service in 1861, replacing horse-drawn omnibuses like the one at left. The vehicle shown is one of four six-seaters brought into service in 1849 — Toronto's first "mass transit." To meet demand, four ten-seat omnibuses were added to the fleet the following year.

had long been dwindling, as from the mid-Thirties provincial authorities released tracts for development. Trinity College was situated on Queen just west of Garrison Creek; further west still stood the Provincial Asylum, open since 1850, itself on former Reserve land. South of the asylum gardens below Queen, the government in 1856 had turned over more Reserve land to the city for a park and exhibition ground. Here in 1858 Sandford Fleming co-designed the Crystal Palace for the annual provincial fair of "agriculture and the arts." It was virtually a commodious greenhouse, but did make Toronto a more effective exhibit centre. On the residual Garrison Reserve, a "New Fort" had been erected in 1841, west of the crumbling relic from the War of 1812. Yet enclosing fortifications for the new Garrison were never built. It remained a set of substantial but starkly plain, stone livingquarters for the military, to be later known as Stanley Barracks — a far cry from Simcoe's concept of Fortress Upper Canada.

On the west above Queen, city houses were spreading around Spadina Avenue in this era, on streets up towards Bloor initially planned by the Baldwins. But after Robert Baldwin died, his hillcrest property was sold in 1866 to James Austin, a wealthy wholesale grocer and financier of Ulster birth, who built a larger, still surviving Spadina House. Much more generally, original "park lot" gentry estates, stretching from Queen to Bloor, were increasingly being subdivided by their owners and would-be developers, Jarvises, Robinsons, Denisons, Boultons and others. Some of the park lots continued to hold large family homes with grounds. But to a great extent they were now laid out with transverse streets and ranges of building lots, just as their speculating proprietors thought best. The result was that east-west roads across a former park lot seldom met directly with those of its neighbours on either side, which still today cause main cross-town arteries through this area to take various bends, while north-south streets that once edged the estates basically run straight. Nevertheless, these almost ad-lib subdivisions often offered many small lots for lower-income homes, as was already the case in older Macaulaytown, near Yonge.[60]

East of Yonge above Queen, the same kind of subdividing and house-building went on in the park lots of this segment, eastward at least as far as Sherbourne Street. There, however, Moss Park intervened, previously the estate of banker William Allan (who had died in 1853), and now held by his son, the lawyer-politician George William Allan. Past Moss Park were mostly small fringe-cottage areas. The city's growth in this direction towards the Don continued to be slower, except for the General Hospital erected near the approaches to the river in 1855, and William Thomas's new Don Jail beyond, finally in operation in 1865. Further northward on the Don slopes were the Necropolis and St. James's new cemeteries, while beyond Bloor, Rosedale, an old Jarvis estate, was being plotted out as a high-class suburb. Otherwise there were no major changes in this eastern section down to the 1870s. Some of it had once been part of another government reserve, containing the first provincial legislative site at the foot of Parliament Street; and this district, often termed "the Park," largely a poorly drained backwater, did not readily attract boom-time speculators. Still, small cottages were spreading north of Queen from the poorer eastern reaches of the Old Town into the area later called Cabbagetown.[61]

It is all too clear that this sweep of mid-Victorian land development across Toronto took place as private enterprise, without significant public ordering or municipal design. A brief initial era of urban planning indeed had largely passed with early York: with Gother Mann's unrealized town scheme of 1788, Simcoe's Old Town plot, government reserves and park lots, and with Russell's layout for the New Town. Succeeding colonial masters had entertained more designs for land use, but public planning had essentially fallen victim to self-government and to the prevailing laissez-faire attitudes of the nineteenth century. It was scarcely to reappear in Toronto until the next century was under way. While there were a few limited attempts to plan by civic authorities, such as for the ill-fated Esplanade, and while private developers at times did plot out boulevards or crescents, physical urban growth, overall, went on uncoordinated and indiscriminantly. The cost was witnessed in confused street linkages or unrelieved, humdrum grids, made more apparent by the few exceptions like generous Spadina or landscaped College Avenue. It was seen besides in the spreading transport wilderness of the harbour front, in impressive central-district edifices mixed in with shoddy structures, and in the beginnings of upper-class, city-fleeing suburbanization.[62] These, too, were part of the landscape produced by an entrepreneurial railway city.

QUALITY OF LIFE AND SERVICES IN
THE MID-VICTORIAN CITY

And yet, amid the anarchy of get-rich individualism, surviving frontierism and incipient railway industrialism, the quality of life in this Toronto still won largely favourable opinions. William Russell, a leading correspondent of the London *Times*, visited it in the early Sixties. He observed:

> The city is so very surprising in the extent and excellence of its public edifices that I was fain to write to an American friend in New York to come up and admire what has been done in architecture under a monarchy.... Churches, cathedrals, markets, post office, colleges, schools, mechanics institute rise in imperial dignity in the city. The shops are large and well furnished with goods.... The people in the streets are well dressed, comfortable looking, well-to-do; not so tall as the people in New York, but stouter and more sturdy....[63]

Toronto, in fact, could make a good impression, at any rate along its main thoroughfare, King, lined with fashionable stores, on much of Queen, in the prosperous wholesale belt on lower Yonge, and in the emerging financial district around Wellington and Yonge, where most of the chief banking houses were congregating by the 1860s.[64] Formal streets of row-houses adjoining the central core, affluent mansions up Jarvis, Church and Bay, and well-kept smaller dwellings on many a leafy, quiet back road, all gave a substantial, ordered look to the community at large, overlying its frequent rough spots. Apparently the still conservatively cast city could avoid becoming hopelessly dishevelled by undirected development. By urban standards of the day, it was reasonably tidy and clean, and earnestly decent: a colonial town still, but by no means secluded, with real adornment, considerable wealth, and a generally thriving, solid citizenry. Nor had mass industrialism yet imposed its pace or problems on the city's life. There was time, and room, for cricket, boating and horse-racing in summer; curling, skating and sleighing in winter, often on frozen Toronto Bay.

But one particular amenity for urban living had not been produced by indiscriminate development — public parks, breathing spaces within the town for its inhabitants, above all for the less advantaged among them. In an earlier era, parks had hardly mattered, when the harbourside was easily at hand for any casual stroller, fisherman or boater, the wooded, sandy peninsula beyond gave still more rambling room, and the open countryside above the city was just a walk away. Now, however, the real countryside was more remote, while the lake frontage was being steadily taken up by rails and commerce. And the peninsula itself had decisively become an island when a great storm of 1858 cut a clear gap across its narrow eastern neck, through which ships could sail in nine feet of water. This was good for shipping access, but not for poorer citizens. They could pay to cross by ferry to the sandy strip, where hotels and amusement grounds had appeared, but the Island henceforth became increasingly a resort for those with some degree of means, where yachting and boat clubs developed, as did city-licensed private leasing.[65] Toronto began to look around for open public space within the town itself, to find that there was practically none.

Apart from the Exhibition parkland to the west — well out of the city then — there were only the limited grounds of the Parliament Buildings on Front Street, those of nearby Government House and Upper Canada College, and little else. However, in 1857, G. W. Allan had donated five acres north of his Moss Park property for the Horticultural Society of Toronto to develop gardens, and in 1862 he offered five additional acres to the city for use as the society approved. So emerged Toronto's first real in-town civic park, Allan Gardens, bordering Sherbourne and Carlton, but more through chance than any municipal initiative.[66] Queen's Park arose in a similar way. The provincial government appropriated for public purposes a sizeable eastern portion of the University's land tract, which stretched to Bloor from the head of College Avenue, and in 1859 this was passed to the city to tend.[67] In 1860 the property became Queen's Park, soon to be edged by well-to-do residences overlooking its trees and lawns, except on the western side, where the University's own buildings and grounds extended.

Along with these modest efforts to introduce public space, the city government did attempt some building regulation in the interests of fire control and safety within its ever-filling domain. It had prescribed, for instance, following the Fire of 1849, that only solid, first-class buildings could be erected in the downtown sector, a rule that led to the progressive disappearance of flimsy wooden stuctures there.[68] Lesser fires had a similar, if more random, clearing effect elsewhere. The city also retired its remaining old hand-

Winter recreation on Toronto harbour, 1853, towards the western end of town. In particular, sleigh-racing on the ice was popular among officers and the elite into the mid-century, but thereafter ice-boating increasingly replaced it.

Garden party at Sheriff W.B. Jarvis's residence, Rosedale, 1861. This Jarvis home gave its name to the fashionable new suburb of the next generation, one of the first laid out in a complex of curving streets. The guests at the party show many military uniforms, since the occasion was a prize-giving for the Fifth Militia District Rifle Association.

pumpers in 1861 in favour of steam fire-engines, already introduced, but went on largely relying on volunteer companies till 1874, and on all too undependable water mains for its fire-fighting service. In consequence, ravaging blazes continued, although fortunately did not reach the scale of 1849. It was rather in the related service to life, limb and property, police protection, that a community strong for law and order saw more significant developments.

Almost at the city's inception, full-time, paid police constables had been introduced, five being named under a high bailiff in 1835, thus making Toronto one of the first urban centres in America to found a regular police force. New York did not do so till 1844, but while it began with 400 members, Toronto by then had only 8![69] This little unit, gradually increasing and backed by part-time men for emergencies, continued under fairly casual supervision by successive high bailiffs into the 1850s. Then, however, the relative impotence of the police in riots — when troops from the Garrison had frequently to be called in — and the increase in crime in a much expanded city roused growing public disquiet. Some 5,000 persons came up on charges in 1857, for instance, over half the total charges involving drunken disorders.[70] At the same time, the ratio of policemen to citizens, 1 in 850 at the city's start, had sunk to 1 in 1,600.[71] Municipal concern and the anxiety of the respectable and propertied hence led to provincial enactments of 1858-59 that set up the Board of Police Commissioners for Toronto, consisting of the mayor, the police magistrate and a judge, with power to appoint a chief constable and recruit a larger force (paid by the City Council) as they determined.

The board went to work to build a new, trained body of over sixty men, and in this endeavour was influenced by two oddly diverse examples, the Boston police force and the Royal Irish Constabulary of Northern Ireland. From Boston they took the regular pattern of duty hours and patrol assignments. The Ulster Irish influence came largely through the newly appointed chief constable, Captain William Prince, a veteran of Britain's Crimean War of the 1850s. Prince wanted a well-drilled, semi-military formation, and chose a considerable number of men with army background, including ex-members of the Irish Constabulary. In any case, given the strong Northern Irish presence in Toronto and the influence of the Orange Order in civic affairs, it was not wholly astonishing that the Toronto force recruited a high proportion of Ulstermen. And despite a lack of due Catholic representation in this body, its

stress on disciplined efficiency did make it a much improved instrument of order for the majority of the city's residents. It still had to face the City Council, which controlled its payroll, and Prince waged constant battle with civic politicians who sought to pare down his ranks. But long before he retired in the mid-1870s, he had shaped an adequate, essentially professional force to serve Toronto's policing needs.[72]

A considerable degree of ordered security (tempered by Orange-Green clashes) was thus sustained in mid-Victorian city life. But services for its poor were far less ordered. The House of Industry, a privately run institution with some municipal and provincial funding, had been operating since 1837, and in 1848 acquired a substantial new building designed by John Howard. It dealt, however, both with "deserving" and "undeserving" poor — a favourite Victorian distinction — and so mixed attributes of a refuge for the helpless with those of a place of correction for the idle. It came to administer both inmate and outdoor relief, not to mention serving as a way station for homeless transients; yet in the main it was a poorhouse with no instructive industrial activity much beyond housework.[73] In short, it was a catch-all, as was the similar Roman Catholic House of Providence. Nevertheless, from the 1850s, more-specialized developments tended to offer at least some charitable improvements for the life of the city's poorest inhabitants. The Orphans' Home and Female Aid Society was established in 1851, largely backed by women members of Toronto's old elite families. It pointed to a new awareness of the need for child care, which brought the Boys' Home of 1861 and the Girls' Home of 1863, to provide for vagrant or abandoned children and direct them to "honest industry."[74] All these were but small institutional beginnings, but they were accompanied by increasing public support, both municipal and provincial, which by the early Seventies produced a more structured welfare system under provincial regulation.

Charitable provisions such as these were no less influenced by the rising concern among the possessing classes over the dangerous potential for lawlessness that lay in the neglected and untaught. The filling city was generating a rowdy street youth from family breakdowns among its hard-pressed poorest elements, or from their need for every bit of income, which set poor children to work not just in homes or craft shops, but as newsboys, trifle-pedlars and the like. Some indeed were homeless cast-offs, managing to keep alive by ingenuity, thievery or prostitution. All could be seen as present or future threats to moral, safe society. In response, a rising faith was placed in general public education, not only as a wholesale means of betterment but also as a community bulwark against poverty and crime.

Literacy for the masses was the great answer, to be realized through public instruction. Accordingly, the city-wide elected Public School Board, set up in 1850 with a call on civic revenues, waged a successful campaign for free schooling over the next two years, while the *Globe* proclaimed, "Educate the people and your gaols [sic — that is, jails] may be abandoned.... if we make our people intelligent they cannot fail to be prosperous; intelligence makes morality, morality industry, industry prosperity as certainly as the sun shines."[75] Under that creed, eloquently upheld by key educators like Ryerson, new "common" or public elementary schools were spread throughout Toronto's wards. The old grammar school became the first public high school (admitting girls also from 1865); and state-aided Catholic separate schools multiplied as well.[76] In 1871 compulsory schooling began, setting the course from education as an individual need to education as a social dictate — and ending the open frontier realm of childhood, or so it was intended.

At any rate, educational services had decisively advanced in the city. Not so those of health and sanitation. Civic health activities remained negligible, ruled by indifference and tight budgets.[77] A minor committee of the City Council maintained a makeshift supervision over slaughterhouses, cattle sheds, and pigs running loose, but made little headway in dealing with unsanitary dwellings, flooding cesspools and private refuse dumps. Real improvements in Toronto's public health endeavours would not come till the following era. Under the circumstances, it is almost surprising that the mid-Victorian city, aside from its earlier Fifties' epidemics, had as reasonably good a mortality and morbidity record as it did have — but again its relatively small size helped.

Moreover, there was a further problem that affected sanitary conditions, the shortcomings of the city's existing water system.[78] By the 1860s Toronto Bay was polluted well out from the shore by sewage and uncontrolled waste-dumping, even though it was the source of the pumped water supply. The bulk of the citizenry nevertheless did not have piped water, mainly because of its charges and uncertainties, and instead used water carters or private wells, even when the wells were frequently contaminated by nearby backyard privies. The "public" water supply chiefly fed fire mains and manufactories; its inadequate volume for fire fighting indeed roused more concern than its dubious quality. As a result, civic politicians waged a running battle with the municipally franchised gas and water company. In 1848, in fact, the Consumers' Gas Company was formed, headed by prominent citizens, which bought out the first gas works and in 1855 erected its own large coal-fired plant towards the eastern end of the harbour near the bottom of Parliament Street. Yet while this new private utility functioned effectively (and domestic gaslighting spread), water services remained at issue. In spite of newspaper campaigns, City Council oratory and engineering studies for larger facilities, the costs of major improvement or a municipal takeover still seemed insuperable to civic leaders and voters on through the 1860s.[79] The water company went its stumbling way, enlarging its steam-pumping equipment at the foot of Peter Street or pushing the intake pipe still further out into the bay when shortages or bad water quality became too flagrant to ignore.

More was achieved in civic draining and macadamizing streets, in paving crossings, extending plank sidewalks and putting flagstone ones in central sections.[80] The street railway helped somewhat after 1861, since by its charter it was responsible for placing pavements along its rails, for which, late in the Sixties, it took to laying cedar blocks. Yet its track also bisected streets where it ran into two muddy laneways, churned constantly by jolting wagons or spattering carriages, and pungent with manure. Such thoroughfares would not impress a later generation with the high quality of Toronto's urban existence. Still, it was acquiring a new tempo, for better or worse thrusting on to much more complex growth in city life and services.

POLITICS, CULTURE — AND REGIONAL COMMAND

The city's government over the period remained largely the preserve of a mostly Conservative coterie of lesser merchants and manufacturers, contractors and professional men. The first-rank figures in commerce and finance were seldom among them, though some prominent offspring of an older elite still appeared from time to time, such as G. W. Allan as mayor in 1855, John Beverley Robinson, Jr., in 1856, and the perennial William Henry Boulton two years later. In 1859 stirrings of municipal reform produced a mayoralty directly elected by the ratepayers, which brought to office the Reformer Adam Wilson, Baldwin's former law partner, who had led in the civic battle with the Grand Trunk over the Esplanade.[81] But though Wilson won another term in 1860, he still faced a well-established council old guard; and in 1866 the election of the mayor was once again made indirect, within the council itself. More conspicuous among Toronto's mayors of this mid-Victorian period was John George Bowes, first in office from 1851 through 1853, as a shrewd exponent of city-boosting "politics of enterprise."[82] An Irish Methodist wholesale dealer who had bought out Isaac Buchanan's Toronto business in the Forties, Bowes was active in railway promotion by the early Fifties, which helped to draw him into a notorious scandal, "The Ten Thousand Pounds Job." It was revealed in 1853 that he and Francis Hincks, then the provincial premier, had used inside knowledge to acquire and sell at a neat joint profit £10,000 of city debentures issued for the Northern Railway.[83] Yet Bowes soon regained popular acceptance in a day of flexible railway morality, and so returned to public life. Mayor anew in 1861, he was finally beaten in 1864 (largely for being insufficiently pro-Orange) by the provincial grand master of the Order, Francis Medcalf, who then held the mayoralty through 1866, and returned again in the next decade.

In spite of Bowes's passing notoriety, it would seem valid to assert that the municipal regime of this period was not blatantly involved in corruption, nor seldom even in extravagance. Rather, it was cozy, cautious and uninspired, not dynamically engaged — railways and private development drew the high-fliers. Quite evidently, however, the Loyal Orange Order operated close to the civic seats of power, and exercised its influence not only on the course of city elections but on municipal employment and contracts also. In "making it" in mid-Victorian official Toronto, one could scarcely forget that this still was a conservatively British and powerfully Protestant town.[84]

Toronto's part in the sectional politics of the Canadian Union reflected much the same pattern of Conservative predominance, from 1854 supported by a major city journal, the *Leader*. In the five Union elections after 1848, the city's two seats were won by a total of seven Conservatives to three Liberals. John G. Bowes was one such Conservative victor in 1854; John Beverley Robinson, Jr., another, both in 1857 and 1861. Yet in the election of 1857, the *Globe*'s George Brown, by then chief captain of the Upper Canada

Liberals or Reformers, gained a Toronto seat during a section-wide sweep by his newly reorganized "Clear Grit" Liberal party. In 1863 a similar Reform election sweep took both Toronto constituencies, putting into parliament wealthy John Macdonald and another city business Liberal, A. M. Smith. Still, these were the Liberal exceptions that proved the Conservative rule, and all three were anything but radical in viewpoint.

George Brown, in fact, had made his city the headquarters of an aggressive Clear Grit array dedicated to the "rights of Upper Canada": seeking representation by population in the Canadian Union, to realize the western section's greater weight of numbers, and the acquisition of the vast North West beyond the Lakes, both to serve land-hungry Upper Canadian farmers and to add a great new realm to Toronto's commercial dominance.[85] His *Globe* newspaper had now become big business, a daily by 1853, with steam-driven rotary presses, a large work force, and the widest circulation in British North America, especially throughout western Upper Canada.[86] Based on the *Globe*'s sway and his own parliamentary prowess, Brown built a party force that finally brought to terms the existing political masters of the Union, the Conservatives led by John A. Macdonald and George Étienne Cartier. Furthermore, the powerful Grit Liberal party he centred on Toronto made that city a stronger regional political focus than it had ever been before, certainly far more so than in the days of Mackenzie Reform. Undoubtedly Toronto's new railway network also helped in this regard — for example, in bringing train loads of rural Grits into town for mass Reform conventions in 1857, 1859 and 1867, each deftly managed by Brown and his urban headquarter associates.[87] By rail, press, and the bonds of party, a wide political hinterland was linked into the dominance of the Lake Ontario metropolis. And while Toronto's own preponderant local Conservatism was seldom shaken, it nonetheless became as well the centre of a Grit party empire. Thanks notably to Brown, the city thus developed its regional hold still further.

The Liberal champion and his journal in any case had a great deal in common with their own home city. Their pro-British, Protestant, anti-republican sentiments echoed strong chords in the community.[88] The *Globe*'s views on free trade, railway development and commercial policy were much as those then espoused by the influential Board of Trade, and the latter took up the former's North West campaign in 1857, calling for the annexation of the

By the mid-Victorian era, George Brown's widely read Globe *made him a wealthy Toronto figure and powerful political force: leader of the Clear Grit Liberal party and a moulder of Confederation. The* Globe's *front page is shown in the year he first entered parliament, and the year before it became a daily (on large steam-driven presses). Characteristically then, the news and editorials lay within. The left side of the page is given over to ads; the right to a record of legislative debate on railroads involving Brown himself.*

western territory to Canada. George Brown himself pressed for Toronto steamboats on the Upper Lakes, and for opening communications with the Red River settlement beyond, explicitly to enlarge the city's trading empire. In this he almost was a latter-day Simcoe, leading in recalling visions of the Toronto Passage northwestward to imperial greatness. His paper followed him: "There is no question that the merchants and other residents of Toronto are deeply interested in everything that will develop the resources of the North West route."[89]

At length, when by 1864 an all-but-equal balance of sectional forces in the provincial parliament had reduced the existing Canadian Union to deadlock, Brown also took the prime lead in bringing about a crucial coalition of parties: one that would work to recast the union in a federal form, assure the rights of Upper Canada, and incorporate the North West within a broad confederation of provinces. His approach in 1864 succeeded, the same year that the *Globe* opened imposing new premises on King Street.[90] By 1867 Confederation was achieved; and under it, the Province of Ontario came into being as old Upper Canada's successor, even as George Brown himself retired from active politics. One might reasonably suggest that his initiative not only led to the opening of the West to Canada and Toronto, but also to a fresh realization of his city's role as a political regional metropolis — for it now became the provincial capital of Ontario.

And so the first Ontario legislature met in Toronto's erstwhile Parliament Buildings in the closing days of 1867. The local citizenry (ungratefully) continued to send mainly Conservatives to both the new provincial and federal parliaments; though within four years the fall of an initial party coalition ministry in Ontario ushered in a long reign of provincial Grit Liberalism at Toronto. In any event, the city's renewal as a seat of government effectively expanded its outreach as well. Now the easternmost areas of Ontario, along the upper St. Lawrence and Ottawa, had to look politically to Toronto, whether or not they remained economically close to Montreal. More than that, if businessmen in Brockville, Cornwall or Ottawa wanted legal measures, licences or grants that lay within the quite extensive realm of provincial authority, they henceforth had to deal with the new capital. Above all, since public lands and natural resources had been allotted to the provincial sphere, timber leases up the Ottawa, the potential development of mining or forest wealth in other northerly reaches of Ontario, thereafter depended on Toronto-based authority. In essence, the creation of the new province further promoted regional focusing upon its leading city.

Again the full consequences took time to be realized, and were far from plain by 1871, when the first Ontario ministry fell from office. But by then, Toronto was well embarked on a new wave of growth, to some extent borne on by the optimistic hopes that stemmed from the achievement of Confederation (which reached to the Pacific in that year) and the creation of the new provincial realm, but far more generally responding to the flourishing state of world trade. The end of the U.S. Civil War in 1865 had checked a booming wartime market. The loss of the Reciprocity Treaty the next year — terminated by an American Congress resentful of wartime border strains with Canada and increasingly dominated by tariff protectionists — had seemed still more threatening to the city. But a new world trade revival rapidly overcame these setbacks. Toronto continued to deal actively southward, as well as eastward to Montreal; and good prices and ready markets outweighed new burdens of American tariffs on its traffic across the Great Lakes or onward to New York. Hence, along with more railway-building, another lively era of city-building developed, in full swing before the Sixties closed.

Toronto had joyfully celebrated the inauguration of Canadian federal union on 1 July 1867 — with public bonfires, ox-roasting, military drills, lake excursions, and at evening, fireworks, while Chinese lanterns lit the trees of Queen's Park in softly glowing colours.[91] Most of the city's traders and political figures of either party had pushed zealously for Confederation. The mass of its citizens were eager to believe with them that a bright new age had opened for their country and community. They also remembered less happy events in the previous summer of 1866, when raiding forces had struck into Canada across the Niagara River, the Fenians, largely composed of Irish-American Civil War veterans who thus sought to bring Ireland's wrongs home to British territory. Toronto volunteer militia had gone to meet the Fenian invaders at the little Battle of Ridgeway in June 1866; some to die there.[92] A monument to the dead, who included young University of Toronto students, would rise in Queen's Park. It seemed almost the War of 1812 again; the city's anti-American feelings were swiftly revived. But soon these feelings were caught up in a rising hope for Canadian nationalism, in pride at Confederation and aspirations for its future. This spirit was to be particularly expressed by a new group

Review of the Queen's Own Rifles Volunteers at the Normal School grounds, 1863. The Confederation years saw much military activity in Canadian cities — markedly Toronto — in days of border threats during the American Civil War, potential worries over national defence, and afterwards in the Fenian Raids and the Red River Rising. Volunteer drills and reviews like this one were typical. The new Queen's Own would serve against the Fenians and through world wars to come.

Bloor's Brewery in Rosedale ravine, as painted by Paul Kane. The recorder of western Indians did this local scene in the Yorkville area, with the Sherbourne Street blockhouse, dating from the Rebellion of 1837, on rising ground beyond.

of youthful authors who in 1868 began the Canada First Movement, chiefly centred in Toronto.

Their main literary influence would follow later, but already there had been considerable cultural development in the city through its mid-Victorian years. Increasingly Upper Canadian writers gathered there, as its publishing houses built up a long regional lead — thanks to top daily papers like the *Globe* and *Leader*, the widely read church, farm and business journals, including the *Monetary Times* from 1867. In art, Toronto-raised Paul Kane had first exhibited his graphic paintings of Plains Indians in the city in 1848, and settled his studio there from 1853, following further with canvases on the West, supported by his patron, G. W. Allan.[93] Other talented artists like George Theodore Berthon, or Frederick Verner after 1860, also established themselves in Toronto. In science, the Canadian Institute, organized in 1849 with Sandford Fleming as a leading spirit, met regularly to hear papers and foster inquiry; it was led also by University College's professor of chemistry, H. H. Croft. In the medical field, the Toronto School of Medicine, begun by Dr. John Rolph on his return from rebellion exile, became Victoria College's medical school in 1854, while Trinity College and the University further had their own schools.

In music, choral music societies were especially active, while Dr. John McCaul, president of King's College and then of University College, was tireless in organizing musical performances. Concerts at the Music Hall or at a variety of smaller halls and churches were well-patronized entertainments throughout the period. And the theatre also made a more substantial appearance at the Royal Lyceum, which had opened on King near Bay in 1848. Its success really came under John Nickinson, an English actor-manager who ran it from 1853 to 1859. He established the city's first resident stock company, and also booked touring attractions, offering everything from Shakespeare to minstrel shows. After him the Lyceum declined, but struggled on, until in 1867 it got an excellent new manager in George Holman, who brought it to a high point by the start of the Seventies, with full houses, some opera in English, and current plays from London and New York.[94]

Plainly, Toronto by 1871 was becoming much more of a cultural centre, at least in comparison with all other Ontario places. It was, besides, the home of three university institutions, of major schools in the provincial educational system; and thanks to its medical men and colleges, its senior jurists and Osgoode Hall, it offered the fullest range of professional expertise in the province. Through the city's metropolitan press, top business and political elites, leading churches and cultural associations, it was progressively tending to direct Ontario views and standards. In all these ways, Toronto had become much more than a railway hub, however important that was. It was a rising regional social determinant as well.

Toronto by 1880. On the left, Spadina Avenue runs back to Knox College (3), University College (4) appears further right in line with Knox, and the domed Northern Railway roundhouse (8) stands on the Esplanade by the harbour. Near the centre, the Northern's big grain elevator (23) dominates its wharf, the low mass of the Parliament Buildings (12) shows on Front Street above the Esplanade, with the Metropolitan Church (15), St. Patrick's (14) and others inland behind. To the right, the three-towered Union Station (16) has tall St. James's (17) behind it at one end, St. Lawrence Hall's cupola (18) beyond at the other (seen between two of the station's towers), while the Don opens at the picture's far right. Trees are still widely evident, but so is the smoke of rising industrialism.

Chapter Four
The Industrializing City, 1871–95

The later Victorian era shaped an industrial Toronto. Driven by steam-powered machinery, it featured both the economic gains of wealth-producing factories and the social problems of massing, crowding numbers. Before the period ended, the city also had electric light, telephones and electrical streetcars, while the new power of the electric motor was enlarging its productive base still further. This rising sweep of technological change stemmed out of mid-Victorian railway years; but it was only with the 1870s that its transforming influence grew sizeably evident, until, by the mid-Nineties, the results in industrialization were decisively clear.[1] Moreover, if Toronto was thereby experiencing a process widespread across later nineteenth-century Canada, it felt it with particular force and enhanced its own metropolitan role through adding large-scale manufacturing to already established commercial, transport and other functions. Population growth was one telling indication. As the city drew increasing concentrations of factory labour and service workers, its numbers rose from 56,000 in 1871 to 181,000 even by 1891[2] — and this during a long deflationary cycle in world trade and prices that lasted from 1873 through 1895 with only brief upturns. Part of Toronto's population increase was due to extensions of its civic boundaries, but these mainly annexed fringe communities that were already tied to the urban complex. In sum, if the city grew so vigorously during a lengthy period of world constraint, industrialization supplied a vital reason.

URBAN ECONOMY: THE RISE OF FACTORY INDUSTRY

Once immigration and land settlement had strongly impelled Toronto's economic growth, then came rail construction. Now it was industrialism's turn. Industrial activities rose to be a major, not a minor, aspect of the urban economy. In 1871 there were around 530 manufacturing enterprises in the city, 2,401 by 1891.[3] Their work force increased from 9,400 to 26,242 between these years; their capitalization grew over sevenfold and their annual product value more than quadrupled.[4] Beyond that, there were multiplier effects: spin-off ventures; expanding industrial demands on market, transport and financial facilities; new factory needs for fuel and producer goods; or the housing needs of a swelling labour segment. The process would go on much further after 1895, but here already was transforming change.

In examining it, one first might note that in-built advantages again applied. Manufacturing advances in the now thickly settled southern Ontario region partly centred at Toronto because of its larger amounts of capital and labour, its well-developed entrepôt structure and radiating transport network. But, as in the days of rail-building, the drive of its entrepreneurs was influential also. Even by the later 1860s their efforts to take advantage of a much widened transport hinterland had laid a basis for factory industry. In 1866, for instance, apart from the heavy Toronto Rolling Mills with 300 workers, the Jacques and Hay furniture company used 400 on largely mechanized, steam-powered production lines. The lucrative Gooderham and Worts flour mill and distillery employed 160; and there were boiler and machine foundries, sash-and-door works or shoe and clothing factories, not to mention William Davies's 300-strong packing plant — whose expanding bacon empire may well have inspired Toronto's later nickname "Hogtown."[5] Some of these firms, especially foundries, had grown out of earlier artisan workshops. Numerous small ventures still remained, and many parts of manufacturing processes as yet were carried out by handicraft, or by skilled tradesmen, rather than assembly-line labour. Moreover, little businesses particularly survived in footwear or clothing production, the latter often employing women and children under veritable sweatshop conditions. Nevertheless, even by 1871, 71 per cent of Toronto's industrial

George Gooderham, left, son of the founder of Gooderham and Worts, became its president, president of the Bank of Toronto (1882), vice-president of Manufacturers Life, and largely controlled the Toronto and Nipissing Railway. The Gooderham and Worts plant near the Don mouth, above, produced a third of the proof spirits made in Canada by the mid-Seventies. Besides milling and distilling, the firm had dairy and beef-fattening adjuncts (animals fed on mash residues), operated mills and stores in the Toronto vicinity, and held sizeable railway interests.

labour force was in factories with over 30 workers, while units with more than 50 accounted for 57 per cent of the industrial product value. Such larger units also showed the highest usage of steam power in the city's manufacturing sector.[6]

That sector continued to grow while good times lasted into the earlier Seventies, and it was only about 1874 that Toronto began to feel a spreading world recession. The growth largely followed paths already laid down in metal-working and machining, furniture and carriage production, factory-made clothing, leather goods and food-processing.[7] While woodworking plants continued active, the day of simple sawmilling was all but over at Toronto; and neither basic textile manufacturing nor basic iron-and-steel production made much new headway. Instead, the city of the Seventies exhibited a quite diversified range of relatively specialized enterprises, including machinery-building, publishing and piano-making, the last especially associated with Theodore Heintzman, an immigrant from Germany via New York whose successful factory became a leader in an enduring Toronto industry.[8]

Pianos, in truth, provide an instructive example. The manufacture of finished articles like these points to the fact that the city's industrialization was largely advancing by import replacement, not the working up of staple resource supplies.[9] Furthermore, some larger merchants spread into manufacturing to enhance their business, just as they had already taken to investing in banks and railways: in this latest case, to substitute cheaper, locally produced goods for lines they had hitherto imported. Various wholesalers branched into machinery, footwear or clothing production; the firm of Copp Clark, booksellers, became a prominent publishing house; while dry-goods handlers like Gordon Mackay and John McMurrich acquired textile mills, though not in Toronto. Exporters, such as the distillers Gooderham and Worts, grain and lumber dealers or meat-packers also made increasing investments in new industries, but it was the importers, the city's key business group, who chiefly took the lead. In any event, it would be wrong to believe that Toronto merchants did not become actively involved in manufacturing developments, even while they also kept up their interests in transport and finance.[10]

The large Gurney stove foundry established in the city in 1868, the Taylor safe works, the big printing plants of the *Globe* or its main rival, the *Leader*, all spelled additional strength for the urban economy in that its industrial eggs were not in one or a few baskets.

Toronto's range of wares could find more varied markets in spite of trade recessions than those of other centres with a narrower dependence on dominant staple industries. Its factory goods could compete across southern Ontario with similar British or American imports, through having lower transport or labour costs and already established trade connections. They even began to invade markets in Atlantic Canada, thanks to their growing scale of production, after the completion of the Intercolonial Railway in 1876 gave fuller linkage with this region.

The rising force of industrialism was also indicated in the Seventies by the spread of protectionist sentiment within Toronto's business community. A protective tariff to foster home manufactures was by no means a new idea in the city. It had been strongly urged back in 1858 by the Association for the Promotion of Canadian Industry, which that year launched its public campaign at St. Lawrence Hall, and won some noteworthy success in the increased tariff of 1859.[11] The association had again appeared on the eve of Confederation to contest — unsuccessfully this time — new lower tariff duties projected for the federal union. But while Toronto manufacturers might look to protection, the predominant business opinion in the city was not yet solidly behind it. That was evident at new gatherings of business representatives held in 1870 to discuss "united action" on tariff revision. Though prominent figures like Mackay or McMurrich favoured it, the still more weighty A. R. McMaster (William McMaster's nephew, who now ran that leading wholesale firm) wanted no burden of high duties laid on his imports; and the major capitalist J. G. Worts stood for unimpeded commerce, holding that Canada had plainly prospered under free-trade principles.[12]

A keen debate continued between high- and low-tariff advocates, argued in the city's press and in the special forum of its businessmen, the Board of Trade. The powerful *Globe*, true to George Brown's own economic liberal creed, condemned seeking an artificial prosperity for industry at the cost of consumers, primary producers and merchants alike. Yet its Conservative competitor, the *Leader*, spoke out for protection, perhaps because Conservative politicians had been considering a "national policy" of tariff protection to promote Canadian growth, but probably also because the *Leader*'s owner, James Beaty, was an important city leather manufacturer with other industrial interests as well. In any case, protectionism gained ground, particularly when world price falls after 1874 brought multiplying business failures in the city and urgent cries for government action to defend the dwindling Canadian market. By 1877, in fact, the Toronto Board of Trade had adopted protection outright, to become a determined lobby in that cause.[13] This marked a conclusive opinion shift. The weight of Toronto business went protectionist, fervent for the National Policy that was championed by the federal Conservatives in their victorious election campaign of 1878. Manufacturing interests thus triumphed in the city, and when the high tariff of 1879 was enacted, it undoubtedly stimulated many new factory ventures there. Yet increasing industrialism had moved Toronto to the National Policy — not the other way around.

All the same, factory expansion (and overexpansion) rose rapidly into the Eighties, what with the sheltering tariff rates, a world trade revival early in the decade, and hopes of broad new markets raised by the Canadian Pacific Railway, now building to open the North West. A significant aspect of Toronto's resulting industrial boom was the shifting of already established factory enterprises from smaller centres to its greater facilities and supplies. The John Inglis business came from Guelph, to set up a plant with 100 employees, particularly producing equipment for advanced steel-roller flour-milling. John Abell's implement firm arrived from Woodbridge, northwest of the city, in 1886.[14] Above all, Hart Massey moved his thriving agricultural machinery company from Newcastle, Ontario, in 1879. In 1881 he bought out the rival Toronto Mower and Reaper Company, and by 1884 occupied a four-storey factory out on King Street West, with 400 workers and heavy steam power.[15]

Transfers were further invited by municipal bonuses, tax remissions and grants in money, land or facilities. These civic aids to industrialism — widespread at the time — had been taken up in Toronto to attract new enterprises largely in the bad years of the late Seventies, when a number of foundries, engineering works and footwear firms had all gone under.[16] Never very consistent or clearly successful, and usually controversial, bonussing remained a dubious factor in the city's industrial growth. But at least the recruitment of the Massey company paid off. Its mechanical reapers and binders took repeated prizes — notably at the well-attended Toronto Industrial Exhibition, held in enlarged Exhibition Grounds on the old Garrison Reserve late each summer from 1879. The company soon widely entered farm markets across Canada, as well

as in Europe, South America and Australia. Then in 1891 Massey combined with the Harris firm of Brantford, a strong competitor that had already shaped an aggressive policy of establishing machinery-distributing depots in the Canadian West. Down to 1895 Massey-Harris absorbed a number of other related Ontario firms, while its Toronto plant by then comprised the city's largest single factory.[17]

Toronto's industrial boom slowed in renewed years of trade downturn in the mid-Eighties, picked up in better times towards the Nineties, then faced still worse world slumps until the middle of that decade. Essentially, however, its manufacturing sector continued to grow in scale and wealth. There assuredly were recurrent setbacks, or failures in worse years, along with harsh phases of labour strife and layoffs. With some exceptions, the city's footwear industry never really recovered from depression in the late Seventies, overtaken by cheaper products from Quebec.[18] Yet by and large the components of clothing, engineering and publishing strongly advanced, those of furniture, piano-making and meat-packing only somewhat less so; while agricultural machinery production soared in importance, breweries became innovative and expansive, and the heavily capitalized Gooderham and Worts distillery more than held its own.[19] Further, newer enterprises of the continuing industrial revolution appeared. The Industrial Exhibition was lit by dazzling electric arc-lamps in 1882.[20] The Bell Electric Light Company moved from London to Toronto in 1883, soon to sell equipment across the continent.[21] And the next year the Toronto Electric Light Company began lighting central streets with steam-generated electricity, then obtained a city-wide franchise in 1889.[22]

Furnaces, rubber and paper goods, carriages, chemicals and corsets, barbwire, brass fittings and track bolts, all were additional factory products of late Victorian Toronto.[23] By the early Nineties, major firms employed between 100 and 300 workers, with some 700 for Massey and over 500 for the Ontario Bolt Company.[24] Mechanized mass production had clearly become preponderant in leading industries, even at Christie Brown's big bakery. Furthermore, Toronto had not just built up its own industrial complex, but was extending it by taking over complementary outside factories, a process well exemplified by Massey-Harris. As well, firms based in Toronto were establishing subsidiary plants at suitable hinterland locations. One instance was the Polson Iron Works, founded in

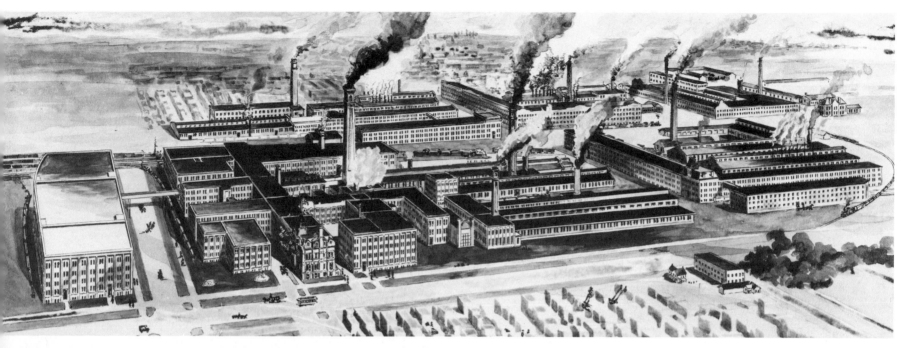

Hart Massey, left, was president of the Massey Manufacturing Company from 1870, and Massey-Harris from 1891. By 1895 he had shaped a near monopoly of the agricultural implements industry in southern Ontario, making himself the region's leading industrialist. The firm's various factories are assembled in the promotional picture above. The Toronto unit was the largest (occupying the main foreground except for the right-most block) and by itself still of impressive size. A Massey factory interior is seen at far left. Bowler hats usually denoted foremen.

The industrial Esplanade by the 1890s, towards its eastern end — a setting much changed from the view on page 70. Behind the Elias Rogers coalyard is part of the big Consumers' Gas complex. It included retort and furnace houses for producing coal gas, gas storage tanks, machine and pipe-work plants, offices, service-wagon sheds, stables, coke dumps, and still more to serve a gaslit industrial city.

1886, which operated a large marine engine and boiler factory on the Esplanade and a modern shipyard at Owen Sound on Georgian Bay. In short, Toronto had emerged as an industrial metropolis by the mid-Nineties, not only through developing its own factory base, but also by organizing increasing hinterland manufacturing under its control.

URBAN ECONOMY: DEVELOPMENTS IN COMMERCE, FINANCE AND TRANSPORT

Commercial growth accompanied industrialization, as Toronto merchants benefited from supplying city factories and distributing their products. Wholesalers still tied to old low-tariff patterns did feel the weight of protective duties after 1879; but most adjusted effectively, and on balance, demands kept up for overseas or American imports. Moreover, the railway, itself an adjunct of industrialism, spanned Canada by 1886, when the Canadian Pacific's trains ran to the West Coast, thus vastly expanding Toronto's potential trading area behind the national tariff screen. Actual settlement of the western expanses proceeded all too slowly in the continued doldrums of the waning nineteenth century. Nevertheless, Toronto as a commercial metropolis still held its valuable southern Ontario hinterland, was doing increasing wholesale business in the Maritimes, and was beginning to make sales inroads in the pioneer West.

Bad years brought mercantile failures as well to Toronto. Solidly planted major wholesalers, like A. R. McMaster, Gordon Mackay or W. H. and H. S. Howland, held their positions, however, in spite of credit strains. The efficient John Macdonald was especially successful in keeping Ontario country merchants ordering through Toronto, by adopting internally specialized departments, each with an expert buying staff, and by purchasing direct from overseas manufacturers.[25] Increasing scale and specialization were, in fact, the marks of endurance and success in wholesaling as well as industry. General wholesalers had disappeared even by 1870;[26] and many new specializations emerged thereafter, from tea or tobacco firms to fancy-goods and footwear houses.[27] By the Nineties these too were tending to consolidate in still-larger departmentalized units.

Across the period Toronto's basic import trade went on growing, despite all fluctuations. Its value of some $9 million in 1871 had doubled by 1885 (deemed a "healthy" time by the Board of Trade), and still stood close to $20 million in 1895 ("a year of quiet recovery").[28] Meanwhile, the city's export business consistently stayed smaller. This was due largely to the dwindling of both lumber exports and the old Upper Canada grain trade. By the 1880s forest frontiers had retreated far northward of Toronto, while rural southern Ontario had increasingly turned to mixed farming suited to domestic markets. Consequently, the city's commerce remained chiefly oriented to importing and distributing. And in the continued competition with Montreal for hinterland custom, it made important gains. Montreal houses had struck back in the 1860s by introducing a dread new weapon, the travelling salesman. But in the Seventies Toronto wholesalers were sending out their own host of salesmen, utilizing the railways to cover the Ontario region with "drummers" carrying samples and order forms. In the 1880s Toronto's commercial army was even invading Quebec as well as the Maritimes, and soon the West.[29] On the whole, a kind of trade apportionment developed out of the competition. Montreal remained dominant in bulky, less-differentiated goods still largely brought by ship: staple groceries, heavy iron stock and basic textiles. Toronto loomed large in higher-value commodities, in dry and fancy goods above all, and consumer products generally.[30] By the mid-Nineties Toronto business had increasingly held Montreal wholesaling to a conjunct rather than combative role in most of Ontario, while actively contending with it in regions beyond.

Retailing similarly grew in scope along with the city's massing internal market. Toronto already boasted large, well-furnished stores, the leaders lining the favoured shopping area of central King Street. Here, for instance, stood clothing and textile emporia like "The Mammoth" of Thomas Thompson or "The Golden Lion" of Walker and Son, said in the mid-Eighties to be "the finest retail clothing house in the Dominion," with nearly 100 employees.[31] Yet two newer retailers soared especially. Timothy Eaton, a Methodist Ulsterman, and Robert Simpson, a Presbyterian Scot, both moved to Toronto from storekeeping in small Ontario towns, and opened little dry-goods shops at the unfashionable corners of Queen and Yonge, in 1869 and 1872 respectively. Eaton obtained a strong line of credit from a fellow Methodist, John Macdonald — religious bonds still played an influential part in city business — and with this backing embarked on aggressive, up-to-date retailing.[32] His various steps, such as fixed prices, cash sales only, "goods satisfactory or

Timothy Eaton, "king of retail merchants," founded a retailing empire with marketing innovations such as the Eaton's mail-order catalogue. A typical page from the 1894 edition is shown at right.

Ladies' Dress Skirts.

Navy, black and brown serge, lined throughout, Empire style as cut, $3.00.

Same style in black cashmere, lined throughout, $3.50.

Same style in tweed, in brown, gray and fawn mixture, $3.50, 4.50.

Same style as cut in navy, black and brown serge, trimmed with three rows black military braid, $3.75.

Same style as cut in navy, black and brown serge, trimmed with two rows each, black military and tracing braid, $4.00.

Fine black henrietta cashmere skirts as cut, lined throughout, $5.00, 6.00.

Ladies' fine navy and black serge skirts, braid trimmed, as cut, $5.00.

When ordering costumes give bust and waist measure, also length of front of skirt.

From every part of this vast Dominion there keeps a-coming by mail orders for this thing and that. We supply thousands of families in just such a way. Why not you?

Ladies' Eton Suits.

Black and navy serge, similar style to cut, $5.50, 6.50, 7.50 and 8.50.

Also a similar style in brown, navy and black, $11.00.

White duck costumes, similar styles, $7.00, 8.00, 9.00, 10.00.

Ladies' Blazer Suits.

In black and navy serge, $7.00, 8.50, 10.00.

Linen costumes, similar style, $8.00, 10.00, 12.00, 14.00.

1614. Striped cotton, washing material, colors navy and white, black and white, and cadet and white, $4.50.

Ladies' Bathing Suits.

This style in all-wool, navy blue estamine serge, trimmed with white braid, $3.00. Same style in misses' size, $2.50.

money refunded," were not wholly new, but Eaton put them all together and was open to further changes. He particularly strove to please women customers, who bought most of the yard goods and clothing, and drew them so successfully that by 1875 his store had a staff of fourteen, including two female "sales assistants."[33] In 1883 Eaton's expanded into a new four-storey block, with elevators, on the north side of Queen.

Simpson wisely copied Eaton's procedures, while trying to improve on them: for example, by putting in a tea urn for the ladies (though Eaton's went one better with a children's nurse).[34] Simpson's store moved to larger quarters on the south side of Queen in 1881; it installed two telephones to take orders in 1885 — Eaton's only introduced one. Actually, neither suffered in this game of one-upmanship. There was plenty of trade for both, and the convenience of comparison shopping drew a flow of customers to each store, handily opposite the other at Queen and Yonge. As they grew, in fact, they increasingly became dual dominant leaders of Toronto retailing, since no competitor could hope to rival both of them.[35] Furthermore, they gradually spread out from dry goods and clothing to shoes, house furnishings, toiletries and so on, thereby developing the modern department store much further in Toronto.

Then in 1884 Eaton's launched a mail-order enterprise, followed by Simpson's on a limited scale the next year. The first thirty-two-page Eaton's catalogue was distributed free to out-of-town visitors at the Toronto Industrial Exhibition.[36] It was the start of a new commercial conquest of the hinterland by Toronto metropolitanism, ultimately to reach from Atlantic to Pacific. Relying on improved rail and postal communications, efficient service and attractive prices (now partly secured by buying direct from manufacturers), Eaton's mail-order business was able to undercut many local stores in lesser Ontario towns. Its catalogue of 1890 proclaimed, "There is absolutely nothing in the entire establishment that you cannot have precisely as if you stood in person before any counter, and at exactly the same price."[37] Such invitations to so large a stock won favour. Accordingly, in 1893 Simpson's launched an extensive mail-order campaign of its own, offering free samples.[38] The next year, after a fire, it erected a handsome new store on its site, only to lose it to another blaze in 1895. Robert Simpson promptly rebuilt in even finer style: a six-storey edifice with steel and concrete frame, electric light, elevators, and a pneumatic tube

system that delivered cash and change.[39] The giant retail store had been realized in Toronto, not only for the concentrated urban market, but for an ever-growing hinterland beyond.

The city's financial sector kept pace with commercial and industrial developments that produced expanding needs for banking, insurance and investment services. In the good times of the early Seventies (and under the favourable Banking Act of 1871), new chartered banks supplemented the city's Bank of Commerce and Bank of Toronto: the Dominion in 1871, the Imperial in 1873, presided over respectively by James Austen, the grocer-capitalist who had bought Spadina, and Henry S. Howland, a leading hardware wholesaler. Their directorates and chief shareholders were once more drawn largely from the city's mercantile elite. Meanwhile Toronto's largest bank by far, the Commerce, reached beyond its chain of Ontario branches to establish offices in Montreal and Chicago, and in 1875, New York. The highly conservative Bank of Toronto opened fewer branches, but its caution left it paying good dividends in the bleak years of the later Seventies, guided by its president, William Gooderham, who was succeeded by his son George in 1882. The big Commerce took losses, as in the collapse of an over-eager Manitoba land boom in the early Eighties; but its substantial assets, including those of President William McMaster, saw it through. On the whole, sound resources and careful direction kept most of Toronto's banks solvent during the stringent stages of the later Victorian era.[40]

The Imperial Bank, however, also essayed a gradual expansion into the West, sure that Canada's financial horizons lay here. In 1881 it opened a branch in Winnipeg, in Calgary in 1886 and Edmonton in 1891 — then the most northerly bank office in the country. The Commerce did not reach Winnipeg till 1893, but meanwhile reorganized its central position under a capable new general manager, Byron Edmund Walker, and the shrewd financial guidance of George Albertus Cox, its president from 1890. The satisfactory growth of Toronto banks was indicated by their assets as reported for 1880 and 1890. The Dominion's rose from $5.4 million to $12.4 million, the Toronto's from $6.2 to $11.7, and the Imperial's from $3.8 to $9.6 million. The Commerce still kept a commanding lead, at $21.3 million, then $22.8.[41] As Canada's second bank, it was yet far behind the first, the Bank of Montreal, with $47.7 million in assets by 1890.[42] Nonetheless, banking in Toronto had solidly advanced during an age of recurrent financial disorders, through servicing a great deal of the city's business, much of the Ontario hinterland's, and some of the emerging West's as well.

This banking was still largely commercial, financing trading credits and industrial working expenses rather than long-term investments, apart from railways. But Toronto's loan and mortgage houses also expanded, weathering the New York crash of 1873 and the tight years that followed. The Canada Permanent Mortgage Corporation remained the largest of the Toronto credit companies; its assets rose from some $3 million in 1870 to nearly $12 million by 1890.[43] The Freehold Loan and Savings, a subsidiary of the Bank of Commerce, dealt in Ontario real estate, but also followed the CPR westward to establish agencies on the prairies.[44] Trust companies emerged besides, notably the Toronto General Trust in 1882 under directors such as William Gooderham and William McMaster. Like the city's banks, its investment business was virtually controlled by an interlocking group of resident capitalists.[45] So were its insurance firms, which similarly increased in number and range, from the Confederation Life, established in 1871, and Manufacturers Life, in 1887, to new enterprises in fire, marine and farm insurance, which mobilized still more capital.

As an instrument for allocating capital, the Toronto Stock Exchange moved well beyond its original main concern with wholesale commerce. Municipal debentures, railway bonds, bank stocks and those of loan and insurance corporations were regularly traded from the Seventies.[46] This reflected the very growth of incorporated enterprises over the period, although, as yet, public joint-stock companies with shares to offer were mainly found in the sectors of finance and transportation, since private firms and partnerships still dominated commercial and industrial areas. In any case, stockbroking became an influential activity in Toronto, featuring the rising names of E. B. Osler and Henry Pellatt in the Eighties, and the young house of A. E. Ames by the early Nineties — key figures in the coming age of full-fledged corporate business power.[47] All in all, the financial segment of the urban economy developed very significantly, if not spectacularly, throughout the period.

Transport developments were similarly significant, if not spectacular. Railway promotion had revived in the city late in the 1860s, strongly pushed by an enthusiastic entrepreneur, George Laidlaw. Laidlaw envisioned inexpensive light railways to fill in Toronto's existing fan of lines into Ontario. By 1869 he had two such rail-

roads building, with impressive directorates that included William Gooderham, William McMaster and H. S. Howland: the Toronto and Nipissing to the northeast and the Toronto, Grey and Bruce northwestward. The former stretched to Coboconk in 1872, Haliburton in 1878. (See Map 4, page 78.) The latter ran to Owen Sound on Georgian Bay by 1873. In addition, the Northern Railway probed on into the woodlands of Muskoka, reaching Gravenhurst in 1875. Meanwhile, Laidlaw, "the prince of bonus hunters," promoted a further line into western Ontario, the Credit Valley, open from Toronto to St. Thomas by 1883, with other branches besides.[48] Though returns varied, the city's transport grasp was both extended and consolidated in this its second railway-building stage.

It did not do as well in rivalry with Montreal for the great railway to the Pacific. In the early Seventies, efforts by a group of capitalists centred in Toronto to obtain the charter for the transcontinental line were defeated by a Montreal-based scheme, which then collapsed in the Pacific Scandal of 1873. After the suitably punished Conservatives had regained power in 1878 (from virtuous but depression-frozen Liberals), they proposed a new Pacific rail charter. But again Toronto entrepreneurs lost to the greater wealth of Montreal, where a syndicate backed by the mighty Bank of Montreal undertook the building of the CPR. As that railway went ahead at last, Toronto's strategy was necessarily restricted to securing contact with its main line, to tap into traffic to and from the West. This "Pacific Junction" was finally achieved in 1886, when an extension of the Northern from Gravenhurst reached the newly completed transcontinental track at a point near North Bay, Ontario.[49]

Two years later, the big Grand Trunk absorbed the Northern, as it already had the Great Western in 1882. Amalgamation was impelled by too many recession years when only large systems could endure repeated deficits. The Toronto and Nipissing also fell to the Grand Trunk. The Toronto, Grey and Bruce and the Credit Valley went to the Canadian Pacific, which had itself begun invading southern Ontario. The resulting contest between two rival rail empires benefited Toronto, however. The CPR brought tracks of its own from Montreal and Ottawa into the city, running down the Don Valley to the harbour, where an agreement of 1892 gave it a right-of-way along the Esplanade and access to the docks. Subsequently, the CPR also established communications southward to Toronto from its main line, and secured links from Toronto to

The Union Station. When opened in 1873 on the waterfront, it was Canada's largest. In the Nineties an addition was built on its north side (right to Front Street), and the whole served on through the 1920s till demolished when the present station (to eastward) finally came into use.

Buffalo that connected it on to New York. Thus, the Ontario capital's role as a focus of rail traffic was further reinforced.

Water traffic and the port of Toronto did not develop so beneficially. The railways carried a mounting share of freight, increasingly restricting the port to heavy, lower-value goods, like stone and other building materials, coal and industrial iron. The removal of tolls on the American Erie Canal in 1883 (but not from Canada's Welland) gave a final blow to lumber shipments from the harbour; thereafter they came down from the Upper Lakes direct to the Erie at Buffalo.[50] On the other hand, coal imports by lake (from Pennsylvania mines) rose strongly, not only for railway, factory and gaswork use but also for heating, as in the Eighties coal took over from wood as Toronto's dominant fuel. Hence, lumberyards were widely replaced by coal dealerships along the waterfront, among them the large Elias Rogers firm, which also owned coal boats as well as mine properties.[51]

There was still a sizeable Toronto shipping fleet; and the steady displacing of square-rigged sailing vessels by fore-and-aft-rigged schooners gave more efficient bulk water-carriage, since the latter craft could be manned by smaller crews and more easily unloaded. At the same time, steamboats handled a growing amount of the remaining higher-value traffic: those owned in the city increased anew, from about 37 per cent of its total fleet in 1878 to 60 per cent in 1887.[52] Yet its steamers were mostly limited to short-range passenger transport. City shipowners were not investing greatly in long-range steam freighters, leaving these to other, mainly American, centres, although the trade of small neighbouring Lake Ontario ports did largely fall to Toronto shipping during the later Victorian years.[53] The cloud of sails along Toronto Bay, the smoke and bustle of visiting steamboats, obscured, in fact, the relative decline of the port.

Under an indolent Harbour Trust dominated by businessmen who did not want to raise expenditures, and with the waterfront almost wholly in private hands, little was done to maintain, much less improve, port functions.[54] Wharves decayed; the piling up of waste and silt, the latter evidently flowing in the Eastern Gap that had broken through in 1858, persistently reduced the harbour's deep-water capacity. The main Western Channel became dangerously narrow; ships often had to be towed to dockside. The 1870s saw the low point in deterioration, but aside from repeated dredging, the 1880s achieved little beyond starting a set of breakwaters to protect the Island, and thus the harbour, from erosion. By the Nineties there was more piecemeal work under way to improve the main entry, and plans to drain off sludges of pollution. Chiefly, however, the harbour that originally had made Toronto possible was left to laissez-faire neglect. The industrializing city had too many other prospects to give its port the attention it deserved.

POPULATION PATTERNS AND CITY EXPANSION

This later Victorian Toronto more than tripled its numbers between 1871 and 1895. Where did they come from? Natural increase and the annexation of suburban communities were only parts of the answer. A lot still turned on the intake of new residents. In regard to immigration, it was not generally as powerful a demographic factor in later nineteenth-century Canada as it had been earlier. While a varying stream of migrants continued to reach Canadian shores over the period, many were simply in transit to American destinations, and in any case, their influx was more than equalled by an exodus of Canadians to the United States: from 1861 right to 1901 Canada thus suffered a net loss in migration. But Toronto itself did manage to attract a substantial share of those who entered the country and stayed, thanks largely to its conspicuous economic growth despite world slumps — growth that promised employment, not least in rising industries. As a result, the city continued to display a high ratio of immigrants, ranging from roughly half its residents in 1871 to still about a third by the early 1890s.[55]

Relatively few Americans or continental European migrants settled in Toronto over this time, though some of the first group brought important business expertise and capital access for economic expansion. The much more numerous British arrivals (again predominantly English) offered more of the same, but also a larger amount of factory labour. By 1891, apart from the city's now substantial Canadian-born majority, nearing 100,000, there were still around 23,000 English-born, to 13,000 Irish and 6,300 Scottish, together with some 5,000 of U.S. origins and 1,500 other "foreign-born" — largely of German, Italian and Slavic backgrounds, and including a number of the Jewish faith.[56] Late Victorian Toronto remained British-Canadian to an overwhelming extent, but its ethnic variety was beginning to broaden also.

Natural increase clearly explained much of the preponderant

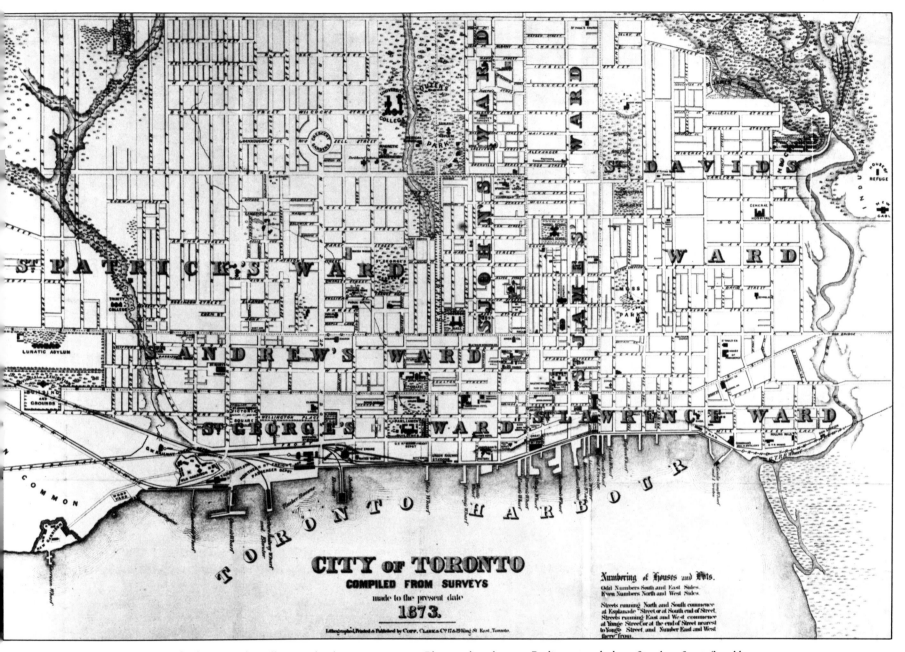

CITY of TORONTO
COMPILED FROM SURVEYS
made to the present date
1873.

Lithographed, Printed & Published by Copp, Clark & C.º 17 & 19 King St. East, Toronto.

Numbering of Houses and Lots.
Odd Numbers South and East Sides.
Even Numbers North and West Sides.

Streets running North and South commence at Esplanade Street or at South end of Street. Streets running East and West commence at Yonge Street or at the end of Street nearest to Yonge Street and Number East and West there from.

This 1873 map displays a fairly well occupied urban territory up to Bloor, at least between Parliament and about Strachan Street (by old Garrison Creek on the west). East of Parliament, the area of Cabbagetown that reached to the Don was steadily filling — often with British immigrants — as a workers' residential district above the eastern industrial area. West of Strachan Street, the creek valleys north from about the Trinity College grounds slowed development. But this western quarter, too, saw growing settlement of workers employed in industries (like Massey) around the rail lines. Well-to-do residential areas were rising northward around Queen's Park, and up Sherbourne and Jarvis near the Horticultural (Allan) Gardens.

Canadian-born segment (of mostly British stock), but there was another demographic process that also enlarged the urban population: in-migration from the countryside. In an occupied southern Ontario, where agriculture was increasingly mechanized, land values high and few good farm lots left unopened, growing numbers were disposed to move: those with inadequate capital or on poor land, surplus labourers, small town hopefuls, sons without property to inherit, and young single women. Some of these might emigrate to the U.S, others reach the pioneering West. Yet still others sought nearer opportunities in Ontario urban centres, including, above all, the factories, stores and other employments of dominant Toronto. Moreover, thanks to that city's greater scale and complexity of activities, women could increasingly find jobs there — not only in traditional domestic services, shops or manufacturing, but also, for those more qualified, in teaching or office work, since female employment (at lower pay levels) was spreading in both these enlarging sectors.

Out-migration from Toronto went on as well as intake, and transiency undoubtedly remained a regular aspect of its urban demography. Nevertheless, the consistent rise in the city's numbers shows that it was obviously gaining far more than it might have lost through transiency. Taken together, natural increase, immigration and in-migration produced a fast-multiplying city unchecked by major epidemics, for by the 1880s effective civic health measures at last were being implemented.[57] But another significant feature of this whole demographic pattern lies not in numbers but in kind, in the qualitative nature of the expanding city populace.

Unlike many other industrializing North American centres of the day, Toronto did not draw its massing work force largely from "foreign" immigrants, but almost wholly from Anglo-Canadians, motherland English and Scots, and now acclimatized Irish, all English-speaking. Although religious differences would still affect this working body, far wider ethnic and linguistic separations were absent. There was no large pool of alien newcomers to be exploited through their language and cultural difficulties, or resented for taking jobs from "proper" citizens. This is not to say that Toronto did not display its own inherited ethnic prejudices and discords. British and Protestant feelings there could still readily turn to anti-American or anti-French phobias, and repeatedly reacted to supposed popish threats to liberty in French Catholic Canada. A belief that Canada was, and was meant to be, ascendantly British and Protestant ruled a large majority of Torontonians. They volunteered readily to put down the Red River Rising of 1870 and the North West Rebellion of 1885, blamed on French Catholic trouble-making, while Toronto newspapers rose in fury to demand that the arch-rebel, Louis Riel, hang for his sins in 1885.

Within the city, rowdy sectarian clashes between Orange Protestants and Irish Catholics continued; twenty-two occurred between 1867 and 1892, chiefly centring on March 17 and July 12.[58] There also were the more serious Jubilee Riots of 1875, when Catholic religious processions celebrating a papal anniversary were attacked in the streets by Orange mobs. Nonetheless, masses of police and militia were deployed in 1875 to ensure the Catholic's right to march — violence got little sympathy from orderly, respectable Toronto — and by the early Nineties most of the steam had gone out of Orange-Green feuding. It has been observed, besides, that over the period the Orange Order largely "institutionalized" sectarian strife within bounds that both sides recognized.[59] It almost became a ritual sport for group prestige, somewhat more bruising than football without pads. Besides, the Orange Order itself, well based in the working classes, virtually operated as part of the civic establishment, providing support for local politicians, thus ensuring city jobs for the duly accredited — rather like a company union.[60]

Beyond this declining sectarian discord, the later Victorian community, all but homogeneous in linguistic terms and largely so in ethnic, displayed a high degree of confident consensus. There was wide acceptance of a brand of evangelical righteousness, a pride in churches, church-going, temperance endeavours and earnest Sunday observance, which by the Nineties brought the community the not unwelcome title of "Toronto the Good."[61] Masses as well as classes widely espoused the ardent spirit of British imperialism that swelled in the later nineteenth century, hailing the glories of Anglo-Saxondom embodied in their great world empire.[62] By no means opposed to this was the citizens' faith in a Canadian national destiny, with their town at its forefront. Altogether, a broadly cohesive city reflected its own distinctive pattern of population growth.

That spreading growth also brought boundary enlargements. The last ward created within the existing city limits was St. Stephen's in 1875, on the northwest. But by then the city was pressing

The built-up downtown, around 1875, looking south from the Metropolitan Church tower. The south side of Queen is at the fore. Towards the rear, off-centre to right, is the new Post Office (back view) at King and Toronto streets, with its curving mansard roof.

on its margins, particularly north around Yonge to Bloor, beyond which lay Yorkville, a separate unit now in little but local authority, which was backed by its inhabitants' aversion to higher city taxes.[63] Toronto, however, equally wanted a wider tax base, especially as Yorkvillians largely worked in the city and used its facilities. Annexation, debated into the 1880s, really came to turn on Yorkville's need for a larger water supply, the result of its own growth. The city, which by that time had considerably improved its water system, refused to let the suburban community tap it.[64] Faced with horrors of drought, the embattled Yorkville burghers at last surrendered. In 1883 their town became St. Paul's Ward in the city. And this first annexation led to others, all enacted by Ontario's parliament. (Changing city and ward boundaries are shown on Maps 6 and 7.)

In 1884 the village of Brockton came in on the west, as the core of St. Mark's Ward. That year St. Matthew's was set up on the east, annexing Riverside (Riverdale) in an expansion over the Don. In 1887 St. Paul's Ward was extended both east and west above Bloor, as a part of suburban Rosedale and a locality today still called the "Annex" were acquired. In 1888 Seaton Village and Sunnyside were absorbed to westward; the next year the inclusion of the town of Parkdale, a well-to-do residential retreat, completed new St. Alban's Ward in this quarter.[65] By 1893, when a strip was added along the western lakeshore road, the city stretched virtually from the Humber mouth to Ashbridges Bay beyond the Don. While land speculators' hopes played a part, this series of annexations had mainly been effected to meet the facts of population increase and of the consequent demands for greater urban integration, services and revenues.[66] Hence, Toronto's territorial expansion was both effect and cause of swelling numbers — but, in any case, was a significant aspect of its whole demographic development.

URBAN SOCIETY: CLASSES, MASSES AND ORGANIZATION

The ruling elements of later Victorian Toronto firmly sustained a faith in Christian values, imperial loyalty, hard work, and due rewards of wealth. Nor is there any need to look for hypocrisies in their creed, especially when it seemed to work so well. They also believed in free enterprise (except for necessary state aids like the tariff), a free labour market and low taxation; in short, they took their class interests seriously. Most of them took equally seriously the duty of Christian service to their church and community. It would be as wrong to deem them lacking in charity or social conscience as to overweigh their often quite practical compassion, or their readiness to take on service posts that brought desirable social distinction as well as a watch over expenditures. By and large, the Toronto elite acted like any other, in its own cause; but it did show involvement and responsibility, and subscribed to the general good in all rectitude.

This ruling elite clearly rested on personal business wealth. Though corporate forms of capitalism were present, they had not yet taken command. All the same, this was not just a crass plutocracy, where social ranking went by dollar count alone. New money needed time for mellowing; an Eaton or a Massey family would not win immediate upper-level acceptance. There were processes of social passage to be undergone, through giving the right parties (not too lavishly ostentatious) for the right guests, belonging to the right community organizations and churches (preferably Anglican or Presbyterian, though more urbane Methodism increasingly would do), displaying the right furnishings and "tasteful" art objects, and, especially, engaging in philanthropy. Moreover, shopkeepers and manufacturers, however large their operations, were not deemed as socially admirable as big wholesalers and financiers, unless, like the distillery-based Gooderhams, they had been present long enough and had acceptably diversified their business concerns.[67]

There was a continued strain of old-family gentility in upperclass society. If the proud York gentry were but a memory, Robinsons, Allans, Ridouts, Jarvises and others were still in evidence, although it helped if their scions were prominent in business or some public capacity as well. The long reign of Boultons at The Grange ended in 1875, when William Boulton's widow married Professor Goldwin Smith, formerly of Oxford and Cornell. Yet the magisterial Smith, "the Sage of The Grange," gained his own prominence as an English intellectual aristocrat, pronouncing trenchantly in journals and books on issues of the day. He represented, in fact, another leaven in the upper ranks provided by a growing intelligentsia of influential professional men. But again it helped if such city notables were manifestly successful doctors or lawyers like the legal star and leading federal Liberal, Edward Blake, or top academic statesmen like Professor Daniel Wilson, president

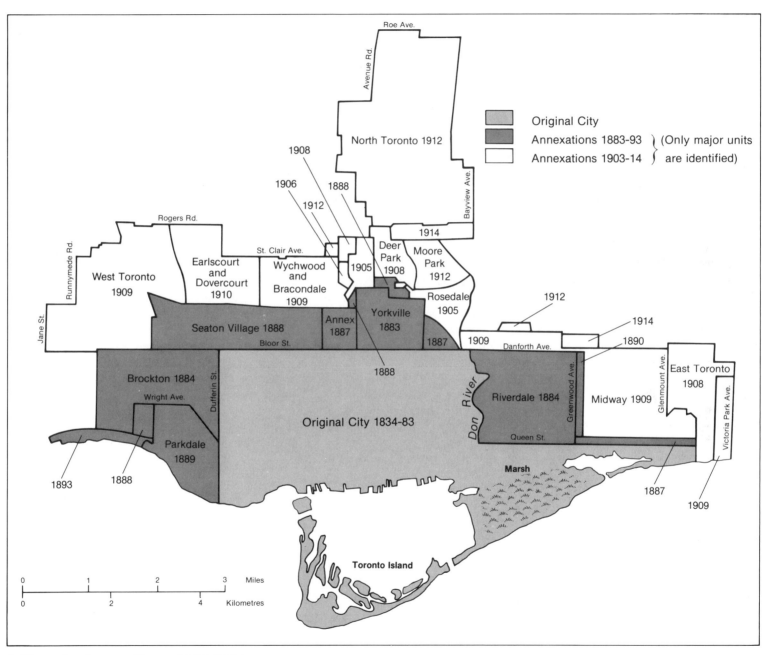

Roe Ave.

Avenue Rd.

North Toronto 1912

Bayview Ave.

Original City

Annexations 1883-93 } (Only major units

Annexations 1903-14 } are identified)

1908

1906

1912

1888

1914

Rogers Rd.

St. Clair Ave.

Runnymede Rd.

West Toronto
1909

Earlscourt
and
Dovercourt
1910

Wychwood
and
Bracondale
1909

Deer
Park
1908

Moore
Park
1912

1905

Jane St.

Rosedale
1905

1912

1914

Seaton Village 1888

Annex
1887

Yorkville
1883

1888

Bloor St.

1887

1909

Danforth Ave.

1890

Glenmount Ave.

East Toronto
1908

Brockton 1884

Dufferin St.

Riverdale 1884

Greenwood Ave.

Midway 1909

Victoria Park Ave.

Wright Ave.

Don River

Parkdale
1889

Original City 1834-83

Queen St.

1893

1888

Marsh

1887

1909

Toronto Island

0   1   2   3   Miles

0   2   4   Kilometres

6 Toronto Annexations, 1834-1914

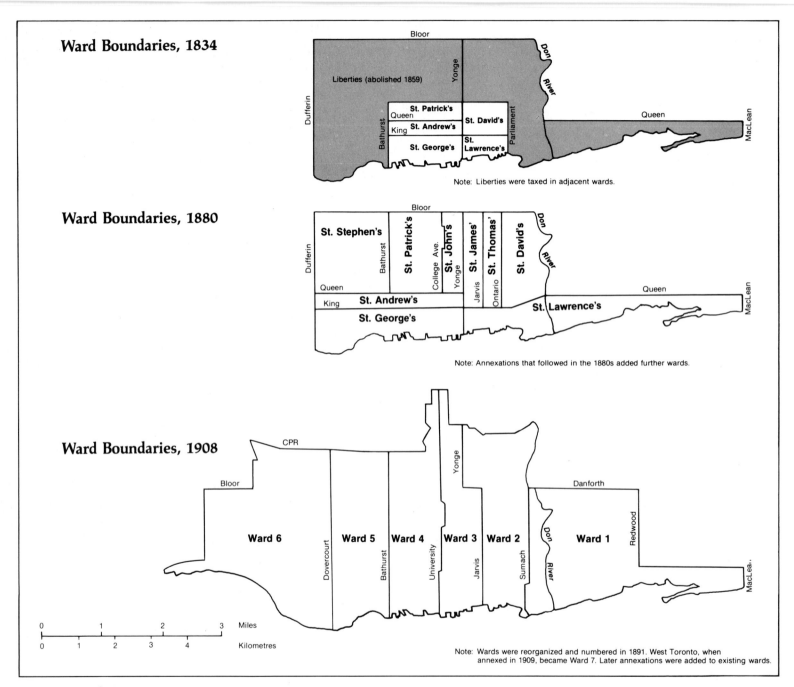

Ward Boundaries, 1834

Bloor

Liberties (abolished 1859)

Yonge

Don River

Dufferin

Queen

St. Patrick's

Bathurst

St. Andrew's

King

St. David's

Parliament

Queen

MacLean

St. George's

St. Lawrence's

Note: Liberties were taxed in adjacent wards.

Ward Boundaries, 1880

Bloor

Dufferin

St. Stephen's

Bathurst

St. Patrick's

College Ave.

St. John's

Yonge

St. James'

Jarvis

St. Thomas'

Ontario

St. David's

Don River

Queen

King

St. Andrew's

St. Lawrence's

Queen

MacLean

St. George's

Note: Annexations that followed in the 1880s added further wards.

Ward Boundaries, 1908

CPR

Yonge

Bloor

Danforth

Ward 6

Dovercourt

Ward 5

Bathurst

Ward 4

University

Ward 3

Jarvis

Ward 2

Sumach

Don River

Ward 1

Redwood

MacLean

| 0 | 1 | 2 | 3 | Miles |
| 0 | 1 | 2 | 3 | 4 | Kilometres |

Note: Wards were reorganized and numbered in 1891. West Toronto, when annexed in 1909, became Ward 7. Later annexations were added to existing wards.

7 Municipal Divisions: 1834, 1880, 1908

The British Victorian city celebrates the Queen's Diamond Jubilee, 1897. This scene on King at Yonge shows electric streetcars, which had replaced horse cars since 1894.

of University College and later of the whole university.

In any case, the urban elite was inherently business derived and oriented, led by merchant princes and banking magnates with railway entrepreneurs, big contractors and industrialists in strong association. As has been said, the economic interests of this leading element decidedly were interlocked. Socially they almost formed a new business Family Compact through intermarriages, linked investments, and church connections.[68] Of course, they were no closed circle, and their world was not that of old Compact official-dom. Still, a community does not escape its history. Though the later Victorian Toronto elite included both Liberals and Conservatives (far more of the latter) and dealt now not with a British governor but with Premier Oliver Mowat, the long-ruling Liberal master of Ontario, once a Toronto alderman in 1857, it staunchly upheld British ties, the established order and the duties of leadership in a way that would not have displeased Tory John Beverley Robinson.

The elite now was largely drawn from the generation of British immigrants that dated to the 1840s (or their children), persons who had mostly made it into the establishment from the middle classes, and there outlived many of the reforming impulses that some had felt — including the "Czar of King Street," George Brown, who appeared a fairly conservative Liberal by his death in 1880.[69] To the end of the nineteenth century and beyond, upper-rank Toronto essentially sustained a characteristic social conservatism, which is not to say that it became reactionary, opposed to further development, or to continued alterations by adjustment. The Gooderham dynasty, the McMasters, the Wortses, the Howlands and McMurrichs, and soon the Masseys and the Eatons, might maintain the predominant social tone; but they were builders as well of the much bigger industrializing city, and deeply involved in its growth and persistent change.

As for the middle classes, they remained the balance-weight of the community, largely sharing the social conservatism and values of those above them, looking, in fact, to join them, if they were sufficiently good. In the upper middle class were the households of well-to-do brokers, professionals and real estate dealers, lesser merchants and more factory owners. A few church or educational leaders, such as Chief Superintendent Ryerson, might have entry to top society, but most belonged in the level below. And in the lower middle class, smaller storekeepers and their families bulked large, as did minor contractors, craftsmen, office clerks and lower-rank teachers. Taken together, these middle classes represented sizeable economic power; politically, they were the core of the civic ratepayers' vote, and socially, the cohorts of temperance, Sabbath observance and public morality.

In social organizations, upper- and middle-class elements often readily combined: for instance, in the Mechanics Institute, in philanthropic agencies, and especially in church activities. Yet some significant insititutions were more largely upper class in emphasis, such as gentlemen's clubs, the Toronto Club being the oldest. The Albany Club became a social headquarters for affluent Conservatives; the National Club for Liberals. The distinguished Royal Canadian Yacht Club (chartered since 1854), the Toronto Cricket Club, Toronto Golf Club and Lawn Tennis Club served the social elite and upper middle-class aspirants at play. Besides these were the dining convivialities of the Board of Trade, the elevating scientific meetings of the Canadian Institute, or the various musical associations.

And finally, there were the church charitable, temperance, and mission-support groups, the Sunday schools and prayer meetings, which were a zealous part of this society and also provided valuable introductions and connections for the rising young. The Sherbourne Street Church, for example, emerged in the late Eighties and early Nineties as a very nesting-ground of wealthy Methodists, and was to be dubbed "the millionaires' church."[70] Still, dominant Anglicanism no doubt maintained a wider share of wealth behind it. And Roman Catholicism also acquired its own capitalist figures, such as Sir Frank Smith, an Irish produce merchant who became president of the Dominion Bank, the Northern Railway, the Toronto Street Railway and investment companies, as well as Conservative senator and cabinet minister.

Below the ruling classes and their allies, the masses of the city ranged from skilled tradesmen, factory or store workers, railway and port hands, carters and day labourers (plus all their families) to sweatshop denizens, the jobless, infirm and pauperized, the vagrant and disorderly. For the most disadvantaged elements, there were mainly just institutions imposed from above: church or public charities, moral uplift and temperance societies, and always poorhouses and jails. But the mass segment that was fairly regu-

The Queen's Hotel on Front Street, about 1884, with omnibus waiting. This first-class establishment drew many important visitors, among them Sir John A. Macdonald, who caucussed with Tory politicians in its Red Parlour. —which thus was deemed by honest Grits a den of party plots and patronage deals.

Well-to-do guests in the Queen's Hotel grounds, around 1880. Holland House is in the background, the "mediaeval"-styled residence built by Compact official H. J. Boulton back in 1831. Its locale, once of such fine gentry homes, was by now filling with wholesale firms close to the nearby railway stations, but the Queen's gardens remained a genteel oasis.

larly employed did have organizations that served its own needs: building and savings societies, benevolent or church associations — and, increasingly, labour unions.

Industrialization promoted unionism. In drawing lower-class family earners away from households and local workshops into mechanized, depersonalized employments, it also massed them in ever larger working units, where they could match their collective numbers against the employer's power over money and machinery. The degree of labour solidarity which thus emerged was limited by persistent traditions of individual or craft artisanry, sectarian or party ties that cut across class lines, and social conservative attitudes within the working class itself. Nevertheless, sufficient working-class consciousness did develop, together with enough determined union builders, to make Toronto a rising centre of labour organization with regional, national and international links beyond. Once more these developments did not start sharply within the 1870s. They had mid-century antecedents in recurrent collective efforts among the city's shoemakers, foundrymen and printers especially, and in the prosperous late Sixties unions seemed to be making growing headway in Toronto. Now as industrialism pushed onward in the early Seventies, so did the activities of city unions. They set up the Toronto Trades Assembly (TTA) in 1871, which the next year played a large part in sponsoring the Nine Hours Movement.[71]

This campaign to reduce the working day from ten hours to nine spread quite rapidly in urban Canada out of British and American labour backgrounds. In Toronto the printers took the lead: a well-established skilled trade in the city, whose own union there had been in continuous existence since 1844 and had become a member local of the American-based Typographical Union in 1866. In March 1872 the Toronto local struck for Nine Hours and higher wages, while the printing employers formed their own association to resist, dominated by the uncompromising, free-market Liberal, George Brown. The masters' front, however, was incomplete. James Beaty of the *Leader* adopted a pro-labour stand that was helped along by expediency: a chance to disable his old *Globe* rival, and to have his own now "run-down" paper stay open and reap circulation gains.[72] In their own cause, the printers also began the cooperative *Ontario Workman*, Toronto's first labour journal. The masters brought in non-union printers; the unionists strove to turn them away. There was fierce press talk on either side, and

charges by the masters of criminal coercion and conspiracy. At length they had striking printers arrested, whereupon the examining magistrate declared that under present law, unions were still in any case illegal combinations. It was an empty victory for Brown and his associates, for public sympathy swung strongly to the printers' union, held illegal merely for existing.

By now, mid-May, the strike nevertheless was ebbing, as was talk of a general strike for Nine Hours. The masters gave wage concessions; the printers eased their comprehensive nine-hours rule. More important, Prime Minister Sir John A. Macdonald shrewdly seized the advantage to put through a federal measure legalizing unions in conformity with existing British legislation. It did not add anything, merely confirmed what before had mainly been taken for granted; but it made Macdonald and the Conservatives self-proclaimed friends of the workingman.[73] In any event, the Nine Hours Movement had evinced the rising power of labour organization, produced a labour press and encouraged wider unionism — thanks considerably to working-class action in an industrializing Toronto.

Stirred by the mood of achievement, a key group of Toronto unionists (including J. S. Williams, editor of the *Workman*, and John Hewitt, founder of the Toronto Trades Assembly) led in erecting a national Canadian Labour Union (CLU) in 1873, which lobbied effectively for improved labour legislation. The economic recession after 1874, however, put severe strains on the union movement, and both the CLU and TTA collapsed in 1878-79. Then the recovery of the early Eighties brought a revival of labour activity in Toronto, displayed not only in fresh strikes, but also in the creation of the Toronto Trades Council in 1881 and a new national body, the Trades and Labour Congress (TLC), set up at a convention in the city in 1883. Furthermore, a powerful American organization, the Knights of Labor, entered Toronto in 1882. At its peak there, four years later, it had some fifty-three locals and nearly 5,000 members drawn from all across the labour spectrum.[74]

The Knights ideally preferred arbitration to the strike weapon, and espoused cloudily romantic rituals. But they sought to organize labour *en masse* to meet industrial capitalism, unskilled workers as well as skilled crafts. Consequently, their Toronto membership ranged from machinists, shoemakers and carpenters to streetcar drivers, dock hands and seamstresses.[75] Besides, they emphasized labour education through newspapers; their press was vigorous,

From 1879 an annual Exhibition at Toronto replaced earlier, shifting provincial fairs. It moved the Crystal Palace (enlarged) to broader grounds on the Garrison Common, and there celebrated technology as well as agriculture, exemplified by the "tower of electricity" on its prize list for 1885. By 1892, more buildings had been added, as portrayed on that year's prize list.

Street railway workers at the horse-car system's Yorkville depot, on Yonge above Bloor (till 1883, Yorkville's town hall). Men like these went through the hard-fought strike against the private streetcar company in 1886, and sought public ownership instead. The streetcar is one of the last horse-drawn vehicles, decorated to advertise the Elias Rogers company.

and talented journalists, most notably Phillips Thompson, emerged in its service. Through champions like Thompson, and printer-politician Daniel O'Donoghue, the Knights made evident progress in broadening working-class consciousness in the city. They also took to endorsing candidates acceptable to labour in civic politics. Still further, they waged a successful strike at the Massey factory in 1886, though the same year lost a bitter fight against Frank Smith's Toronto Street Railway Company.[76]

In time, the weaknesses in the Knights' own extended organization and their frequent reluctance to face confrontations led to their being supplanted by smaller, tighter, more-militant craft unions. But their legacy in expanded working-class horizons, labour writing and political action would remain highly significant in Toronto's transition to industrial society. Labour had plainly taken shape there as an enduring, influential force, a fact exemplified by strong city labour campaigns for endorsed candidates in federal, provincial and municipal elections during 1886-87.[77] Moreover, Labour Day was first celebrated in Toronto in 1886, when the Industrial Exhibition (with an eye to wider popular support) honoured the workers of the world, and a grand parade of union members marched out to the grounds to hail their mounting significance in the Canadian community.[78]

In renewed slumps of the late Eighties and early Nineties, there were few fresh working-class gains in the city. The Knights were fast fading; newer international, American-centred unions added Toronto locals only slowly. The election of E. F. (Ned) Clarke as mayor in 1888 — once a *Globe* printer arrested in 1872 — was hailed as a victory by labour, but this Orange politician who held office on through 1891 more truly symbolized a renewal of political links with Conservatism that dated back to John A. Macdonald as "the workingman's friend" of 1872. Moreover, while labour was an important component of the civic reforming groups who managed to end the unpopular old street railway monopoly in 1891, it did not succeed in its further effort to establish municipal ownership of the system.[79] Of more long-run significance, perhaps, were enlarging radical sentiments particularly among labour intellectuals, which carried some to varieties of socialism, and so to far more fundamental critiques of industrial life and relations.

Overall, when the later Victorian period drew towards a close, Toronto comprised a society controlled by a business elite and its values, increasingly stamped by industrial capitalism. Yet it was equally marked by active working-class responses and by sharper social divisions between propertied classes and wage-dependent masses, expressed as well in steadily growing residential separation.[80] Furthermore, education tended to maintain class differences, despite democratic ideals of mass schooling. Upper-class families had access to privileged schools like Upper Canada College. Middle-class children were thoroughly institutionalized into the public system, which still gave them advantages over lower-class youth. As for the latter, though education was officially compulsory, family needs and shifts often made it a come-and-go affair for them, so that poorer attendance and lower achievement continued to set them off. Nevertheless, for all this, rooted common traditions, long-fixed religious and cultural bonds, and the basic uniformities in Toronto's demography, kept the whole urban community rather less divided than those of many other major North American centres. The city on balance remained a coherent social unit, with firmly dominant patterns of outlook, standards and tastes. The results could be seen in the very urban landscape that evolved during the height of the Victorian age.

URBAN LANDSCAPE AND CULTURE: THE HIGH VICTORIAN CITY

Not just size and smoking factories distinguished Toronto's later nineteenth-century cityscape from that of earlier years. New building styles and techniques emerged as well, more concentrated central development, far better street transport and, especially, increasing land-use differences between residential, business and workplace districts. Moreover, in this expanding, changing environment, cultural life developed in keeping. The High Victorian city was both a physical fact and a state of living, each reflecting and interacting with the other.

As the Seventies began, good times saw Toronto in another building boom, which among other things produced more Italianate offices and residences, an enlarged Queen's Hotel, and a line of wholesale warehouses across the late Bishop Strachan's estate from York to Simcoe. The Metropolitan Church by Henry Langley, a stately Gothic cathedral of Methodism — which had come a long way from the frontier — went up at Queen and Church in 1872. The triple-towered Union Station opened on Front near York in 1873, and a commodious Grand Opera House in 1874 on Adelaide

POST OFFICE, TORONTO.

The Board of Trade Building, 1889, at Yonge and Front. Important for its technology, not architecture, this was Toronto's first steel-framed building. Across from it stood the more attractive — but unrevolutionary — Bank of Montreal of 1885.

The Post Office, 1873, by R. C. Windeyer. This edifice heading Toronto Street well represents the opulent Second Empire style, with its dressy mansard roof and ornate facade. It was replaced by the decidedly less attractive Mackenzie Building after the Second World War.

Government House, erected by 1871 for the new Province of Ontario, on the site of its Upper Canada predecessor on Simcoe near King. It was the lieutenant-governor's residence till 1912.

George Gooderham's mansion, 1890, at St. George and Bloor. This prime example of Romanesque style was no less detailed in its rich interior woodwork.

Metropolitan Church, 1872, by Henry Langley. This picture of his "cathedral of Methodism," at Queen and Church, also shows the spire he added to St. Patrick's Cathedral up Bond Street in the background.

off Yonge. In design, these large edifices were free-handed Victorian versions of mediaeval or Renaissance forms; the latter further developed into the Second Empire style of Napoleon III's France. Thus the Opera House and the Post Office of 1873 were built in Second Empire manner, with ornamental mansard roofs, while Presbyterian Knox College and new St. Andrew's Church, both of 1875, took mediaeval shapes.[81]

Then in the later Seventies the spread of recession slowed developments. It was not till the recovery of the early Eighties that building in Toronto began a new advance, which this time virtually lasted to the end of the period. For in spite of various economic downturns, the industrializing city had now acquired so much momentum, population increase and accumulating wealth that major construction went forward with few breaks. Sure of their city and its future, Toronto builders did not let sporadic market constraints stop them long. Beyond this, new styles and another generation of designers took hold. The rising architect, E. J. Lennox, produced his Manning Arcade of 1884, a wide-windowed office block, and in 1885 Frank Darling co-designed the Bank of Montreal at Front and Yonge, an early example of French Beaux Arts classicism in the city.

Still more significant for High Victorian Toronto was the arrival of "Richardson Romanesque" from Chicago, where H. H. Richardson had adapted an early mediaeval Italian building style to feature great round arches on thick pillars, massive walls with much carved detail, and bold, asymmetrical roof-lines. This kind of Romanesque quickly rooted itself in Toronto. New provincial Parliament Buildings were erected in the centre of Queen's Park in heavy Romanesque blocks of red sandstone, begun in 1886 and completed in 1892. The big Confederation Life Building at Yonge and Richmond (1890) had Gothic touches, but stout walls and rounded arches indicated its Romanesque origin. That origin was much clearer in the pinnacled bulk of Victoria College, opened in 1892 on the edge of Queen's Park. And the new City Hall of E. J. Lennox (designed in 1890 though not finished till 1899) brought Romanesque's finest achievement in Toronto. Set at Queen and Bay on land expropriated from Macaulaytown shacks, its clocktower soaring above the vista from the lake, this edifice was a testament in lavishly worked buff sandstone to the metropolitan dignity of the High Victorian city.

New technology also greatly affected major buildings, for instance, by introducing electric elevators, which offered far more range and speed than steam-powered or hydraulic lifts. In fact, they presaged the multi-storeyed office structure, the skyscraper — as well requiring new building techniques to give its height the necessary supporting strength. Here cast iron had pointed the way, from mid-Victorian times, supplying internal columns to uphold larger edifices, and even providing precast facades with moulded columns painted "stone" colour, as used on some remaining commercial blocks on Front. Cast iron led to stronger wrought-iron frameworks, then to the all-steel-framed building, whose outer walls were merely coverings, not ponderous supports.[82] This climactic last stage was reached in Toronto in the Board of Trade Building of 1889 at Yonge and Front. Externally, it was a seven-storeyed melange of Romanesque, Gothic and you-name-it, but its skeleton was steel. And F. M. Gouinlock's Temple Building of 1895 on Bay was a true skyscaper, ten floors high, if one still with iron framing and a largely Romanesque exterior (Map 8). Though tall buildings would not dominate the Toronto skyline till the next era, the High Victorian city had prepared their way.

Moreover, the vertical growth of offices and larger stores on expensive downtown real estate — made possible by metal framing and electric elevators even before skyscrapers fully emerged — maintained or enhanced the concentration of leading business activities within a compact core area. This central business district had sorted out its land use further by the early Nineties. While the main wholesale section remained close to the harbour and the railway stations, markedly along Front and Wellington, financial concerns were focusing around King and Bay, and the prime retail locality now centred on Yonge at Queen, where Eaton's and Simpson's ruled.[83] Electricity by then, moreover, could safely light big central buildings with incandescent "Edison" bulbs. Another achievement of electric technology also aided central concentration, once Toronto's first telephone exchange was installed in 1879. Spreading telephone lines gave downtown businesses ready access to customers, agents and dealers across wide distances, while they still could stay in close neighbourhood with related firms in their fields.

When electricity also brought much more efficient streetcar transport, it further promoted both central focusing and spatial outreach.[84] Little electric trolley cars had been in service at the annual Exhibition since 1885, carrying the public a short distance

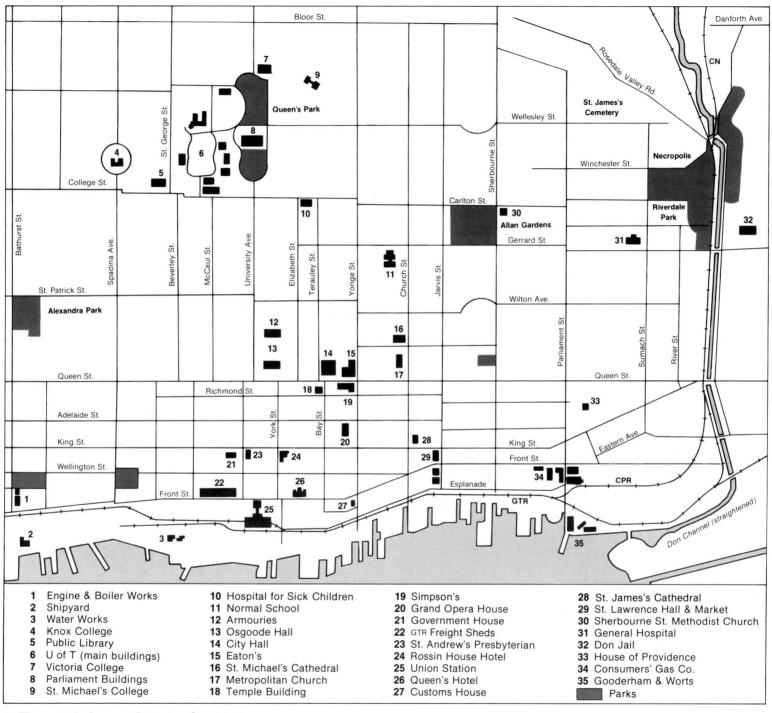

1 Engine & Boiler Works	**10** Hospital for Sick Children	**19** Simpson's	**28** St. James's Cathedral
2 Shipyard	**11** Normal School	**20** Grand Opera House	**29** St. Lawrence Hall & Market
3 Water Works	**12** Armouries	**21** Government House	**30** Sherbourne St. Methodist Church
4 Knox College	**13** Osgoode Hall	**22** GTR Freight Sheds	**31** General Hospital
5 Public Library	**14** City Hall	**23** St. Andrew's Presbyterian	**32** Don Jail
6 U of T (main buildings)	**15** Eaton's	**24** Rossin House Hotel	**33** House of Providence
7 Victoria College	**16** St. Michael's Cathedral	**25** Union Station	**34** Consumers' Gas Co.
8 Parliament Buildings	**17** Metropolitan Church	**26** Queen's Hotel	**35** Gooderham & Worts
9 St. Michael's College	**18** Temple Building	**27** Customs House	▮ Parks

8 Toronto's Inner City to the 1900s

into the grounds.[85] Six years later, one of the terms on which a new company acquired Toronto's streetcar franchise was that it would electrify the existing horse-drawn system, and this was effected between 1892 and 1894. Since, however, the full impact of the electric streetcar obviously fell in a subsequent period, it is more important here to note that the horse-car system had already put a strong imprint upon Toronto's built environment — especially as its trackage had risen from a mere six miles in 1872 to over sixty-eight by 1891.[86] Extensions and new routes were mainly products of the expansive Eighties. By 1881 the main King cross-town car line ran from the Don to the Exhibition grounds; the track on Queen was extended west to Parkdale in 1886 and across the Don eastward as far as the outlying Woodbine racetrack in 1887. To the north, the Yonge Street route pushed on through newly annexed Yorkville in 1885, while among multiplying north-south routes, the Sherbourne line crossed Bloor in 1891 to enter Rosedale, now increasingly a favoured haven for the wealthy.[87]

Streetcar transport knitted up the differentiating city, moving workers and shoppers into the central core, carrying people outward to residential districts, and opening new fringes to suburban growth beyond the basic Shore Plain. Though the street railway linked homes to workplaces, it also made for their greater spatial separation, since considerably longer journeys to work were feasible in the streetcar city than in its walking predecessor. So residential areas spread out with car lines, and suburbs with wider living space developed, mainly for the more well-to-do who could afford the regular costs of longer trips. The result was a further sorting-out in land use. Middle-class residential districts grew towards the outskirts, along with upper-class enclaves and estates, while between these reaches and the in-town business or industrial areas, predominantly lower-class neighbourhoods took shape. They were often within short range or walking distance of factories, which themselves mainly clustered either down towards the eastern end of of the harbour, near the Don mouth, or out westward, south of King, close to railway lines. In these emerging working-class districts, keen-eyed developers and contractors from the Seventies on put up lines of mass housing on small plots: narrow brick houses usually attached or semi-detached. And this spatial allocation again related to the streetcar. It occurred between high-value centrally located property and the outlying districts with their transport-added costs. Enlarged, horse-drawn, High

Victorian Toronto developed land-use patterns of social segregation to a degree unknown in the smaller walking city.[88]

The poorest quarters were generally located in deteriorating stretches of the old inner city. Slum conditions were intensifying here, as in the back-lane cottages of near-central St. John's Ward, which included old Macaulaytown, or in areas close to railyards, noisome factories and packinghouses further out to east or west. Nevertheless, tenements, crowded, cheerless hives of poverty, still generally did not arise. The bulk of working-class families continued to live on ordered streets of rented small houses, houses that some of them came to own. These rows of nestled homes, displaying plump mansard Second Empire roofs or sharp Victorian Gothic gables, may look picturesque yet — certainly to modern-day redevelopers who "restore" them.

Middle-class areas had similar if more roomy brick residences, with a stained-glass window or two, verandahs, and decorative gingerbread fretwork. Wonderfully gingerbread wooden summer homes also spread on the Island — a special world in itself. But the upper middle class, and the upper class particularly, also responded to the Romanesque urge. They erected imposing mansions with characteristic broad arches on heavy pillars, embellished stone or brickwork, and perhaps a rounded tower. George Gooderham's residence of 1890 on Bloor at St. George (now the York Club) remains an outstanding example; yet such elite homes appeared along St. George near the University, through the highly regarded Annex, along upper Jarvis and Sherbourne, and on into Rosedale.[89]

And cultural as well as material expansion went on in this physically changing city. Its upper levels acclaimed literature, art and science even when they did not understand them, for they were dutifully Improving Victorians. Besides, Toronto's enlarging wealth and audience, its already strong professional and educational components, and its advancing control of means of communication, all clearly stimulated literary, informational and artistic developments. Thus, the early Seventies in the city saw the literary upsurge of a group of young national idealists, prominent among them George Taylor Denison, already a veteran of the Fenian Raid of 1866, and William Foster, a Toronto lawyer whose pamphlet of 1871, *Canada First*, gave the movement its name. Linked with the aspiring Liberal politician, Edward Blake, and backed by Professor Goldwin Smith, the Canada Firsters founded an able journal, the *Nation*, in 1874. Thereafter, bright enthusiasm faded in the gloom of economic recession. Yet Canada First was a real expression of Toronto's own nation-building hopes, and the authors and poets it engendered left strong marks on Canadian writing.

Furthermore, this nationalist movement inspired new periodicals in the city, such as the *Canadian Monthly*, established in 1872, with Goldwin Smith as a keen contributor. This was replaced by the *Week* in 1883, which lasted till 1896 as an eminent journal of "politics, society and literature." Smith also produced his own pungent *Bystander*, voicing his scathing appraisals of sordid Canadian politics and his mounting doubts that Canada even deserved to be a nation. The citizens of Toronto read their Sage's charges while flatly rejecting his final answer, union with the United States; some, like George Denison, took up the goal of a British imperial federal union instead. More widely to the residents' tastes, however, was the work of Henry Scadding, son of Simcoe's estate manager and long the Anglican rector of Holy Trinity, whose *Toronto of Old* (1873) was a valuable record of the city's early life. His writings evoked both Toronto's pride in its past and belief in its present — feelings warmly displayed in the celebration of the fiftieth anniversary of cityhood in 1884, a glorious moment of parades and civic festival.[90]

On other levels of popular culture, John Ross Robertson's *Evening Telegram*, launched in 1876, brought mass journalism to the people. Its imperialism, sensationalism and Orange Order news marked it as a city institution for generations to come, but so did its stress on the complex local affairs of a now large community. Along with a breezily independent *Telegram*, the daily press included the Liberal *Globe* still; the *Mail*, founded as a Conservative organ in 1872 to replace a dying *Leader*; the *Empire*, another Conservative party paper, begun in 1887 but absorbed by the *Mail* in 1895; and three more independents, the *World*, started in 1880, the *News*, 1881, and the *Star*, 1893. These plentiful dailies kept up the power of the city's printing offices; their staffs produced more authors for the realm of literature. The allied domain of publishing grew also with leading firms like Copp Clark, Gage, Hunter Rose, and the Methodist Publishing Company. An illustrated press emerged besides, well exemplified in *Grip*, a light-hearted weekly of comment under J. S. Bengough from 1873 to 1892. His deft, blather-puncturing political cartoons in *Grip* were among Toronto's best achievements as a centre of opinion-making in later Victorian times.

Concern for the availability of literature led to a free Public Library.[91] By the Eighties in Toronto, the private Mechanics Institute that had provided limited reading rooms and some adult education was all but out of date. Institute lectures and exhibits had lost popular appeal. The YMCA since the 1860s had offered young men alternative interests, and the public schools supplied night classes from 1880. Yet the institute still held its large building and book collection. Urged on by Alderman John Hallam, champion of free libraries, and funded under provincial legislation, a municipal Public Library took over, opening in 1884. The central library unit was enlarged, while within four years branches were added to west, east and north. The Mechanics Institute gave way to a major civic cultural and educational institution, another lasting attainment of High Victorian Toronto.

Formal education grew also. More public and separate schools went up; kindergartens were pioneered (1883); compulsory schooling was extended; and in secondary education, Parkdale (1889) and Harbord (1892) were added to Jarvis as high schools or "collegiate institutes."[92] In 1891 august Upper Canada College moved to spacious new suburban quarters at the head of Avenue Road above St. Clair. On the university level, William McMaster gave funds for Baptist McMaster Hall, opened in 1881 on Bloor near Avenue Road, while Wycliffe College (evangelical Anglican) appeared beside Queen's Park in 1882. Wycliffe, Catholic St. Michael's and Presbyterian Knox College subsequently affiliated with the University of Toronto, while Methodist Victoria agreed to federate in 1887, but did not transfer from Cobourg for five years more. The School of Practical Science, a provincial technological institute established on the campus in 1878, was also linked with the University in 1887. Toronto's metropolitan centring of higher education was manifestly strengthened.

In a surge of post-Confederation Canadianism, the Ontario Society of Artists (OSA) was established in Toronto in 1872, the first enduring professional art association in the country. Its leaders included the distinguished watercolourist John Fraser, then Toronto partner in the well-known Notman and Fraser photographic firm of Montreal, and Lucius O'Brien, who romantically depicted rugged Canadian land masses. Toronto artists, in fact, took on national scope, evidenced in the western mountain paintings of O'Brien, Fraser and T. Mower Martin, prairie scenes by Frederick Verner, and in the whole group's role in the founding of the Royal Canadian Academy (RCA) at Ottawa in 1880. And the

THE BEAUTIES OF A ROYAL COMMISSION.

"WHEN SHALL WE THREE MEET AGAIN?"

Professor Goldwin Smith at about forty. From the 1870s nearly till his death in 1910, he was a literary mover and shaker in Toronto: ardently liberal in doctrine, but foe of set party cliques; a strenuous critic but strong backer of public causes, from workers' and farmers' rights to civic reform, from welfare needs to the advancement of the University of Toronto.

This typical Grip *cartoon of 1873 concerns the Pacific Scandal of the day, when John A. Macdonald's government was accused of taking bribes (as election funds) in awarding the charter for the Canadian Pacific Railway. Here J. S. Bengough spears the government's resultant inquiry into itself, as three John A.'s congenially deal with one another.*

Toronto Art Students League of 1886 fostered rising talents like Charles Jefferys, often found in young commercial artists' ranks. Indeed, newspaper, book-publishing and advertising work in the industrializing city attracted a growing number of draughtsmen and designers, such as Charlotte Schreiber, painter, one of the first women illustrators in Canada, and a founding member of the RCA. Furthermore, initiated by the OSA and headed by T. M. Martin in 1877, a little, provincially aided Art School in Toronto rose with the city's cultural growth to become by the Nineties the chief art-education institute in Ontario.

Developments in music were similarly linked to the High Victorian city's swelling affluence and audience, its increasingly cultivated tastes, and the professionalism all these encouraged. The Toronto Philharmonic Society was revived in 1872, after earlier sporadic existences. Under F. H. Torrington, the organist of Metroplitan Methodist Church, the Society's symphonic orchestra and its chorus of well over a hundred became very successful, so much so that Hart Massey decided to give Toronto a proper modern concert hall. Massey Hall was opened in 1894 off downtown Yonge Street: a large, austere, red-brick mass externally, but internally marked by exotic Moorish touches, and more important, excellent acoustics. The period saw as well the founding of the Toronto Choral Society, the Mendelssohn Choir and three music schools, including the predecessor of the Royal Conservatory of Music.[93]

Musical drama did not develop as significantly. Grand opera was usually imported; light opera also came from touring companies, or local amateurs. Yet theatre in general flourished, in spite of continued condemnation by Methodists and other stricter elements. "Good" theatre, in fact, had become much more desirable to upper-class society, providing as it did suitable cultural amusements and occasions to be seen. For the non-elite, while taverns still filled traditional roles in recreation, many also found escape from office and factory drabness, crowded homes and urban pressures, in the exciting glitter of theatre. Minstrel shows remained constant favourites on this popular stage, as did flimsy musical farces. Superior offerings were quite regularly available, however, from Shakespeare to recent London and New York hits. They mostly went to the Grand Opera House of 1874, a well-equipped structure seating 1,300 (and later enlarged) that supplanted a smaller, failing Royal Lyceum.[94] There were other, mainly lower-grade, rival houses, but the Grand dominated the whole period. And the upshot was that Toronto rose to be a leading theatre town on provincial and trans-border circuits.

Organized sports also developed rapidly in a built-up, regimented city craving leisure-time releases. Its needs and numbers further promoted mass spectator sport and sports business. Racetracks became big enterprises, notably the Woodbine, which from 1883 yearly ran the top-level Queen's Plate race. American baseball fast overtook English cricket; amateur and professional leagues set up from the Seventies drew heavy crowds. Still, Canadian lacrosse was even more popular. A Canadian version of rugby football took hold in the Eighties, and huge cycling meets became a virtual craze by the early Nineties. In winter, there was curling, ice-boating on the bay, or skating on large rinks, which attracted far more than hockey as yet, though intercity contests for the Stanley Cup dated from 1893. In summer, yachting and, above all, rowing reigned. The latter, marked by the prowess of the Argonaut Club founded in 1872, was crowned when Toronto's Ned Hanlan won American and British professional singles championships from 1876, and held the world title from 1880 to 1884. Victor in some 150 races, an international star, Hanlan remained a hero of High Victorian Toronto: in sports culture also, "no mean city" of its time.

URBAN POLITICS AND SERVICES

Municipal affairs were deeply affected by industrial and demographic growth, which extended the city's tasks as well as its territory, increasing calls on services and heightening problems of finance. Civic taxation rose from some $239,000 in 1861 to $937,000 by 1881; and the tax rate, since 1861 around fifteen mills on the dollar, climbed to twenty in 1878.[95] Beyond that, new political factors were entering: working-class activism, demands for efficient "business" management to restrain rising city budgets, moves to put utility monopolies in public hands, and moral designs for humanitarian progress through civic assaults on vice. All these produced concerns for municipal reform and popular action such as mid-Victorian Toronto had seldom known. Yet the later Victorian city faced public needs on a scale equally unknown in its past.

One thing, however, did not change: Toronto's lasting political preference for the Conservative party. Perhaps the federal Conservatives' commitment to the National Policy renewed that preference, but it equally appeared in provincial politics where tariff

The Metropolitan Church Bicycle Club on an outing in the 1890s. The replacement of the "penny-farthing" cycle by the equal-wheel "safety" bicycle made cycling popular for recreation as well as for sport.

The Red Jacket Rink of the Toronto Curling Club on the frozen Don in the 1870s. A carefully assembled "composite" picture of the day, when photography could not yet handle real outdoor action shots.

The touring "Gentlemen of England" play the Toronto Cricket Club, 1872, at the club grounds (now part of the University campus). In background at right appears University College, and to the left of the club pavilion, the home of Frederic Cumberland.

policy did not apply. In six federal elections between 1872 and 1896, Torontonians returned sixteen Conservatives to four Liberals; in seven Ontario contests from 1871 to 1894 they chose fifteen Conservatives to three. Municipal politics, of course, were ostensibly non-partisan; still, here too, if labels were not worn except by some resolute Labourites, Conservative ties and Orange links were widely apparent among civic politicians, whether or not some might take up civic reform.

To say the expected, any reforming thrusts took time to develop. During the Seventies, the regimes at City Hall stayed much as they had been, led by largely part-time mayors, lawyers and business worthies properly apprenticed as former aldermen, who with veteran City Council comrades kept the municipal system running reasonably well on established, restricted lines. In 1874 the mayoralty did revert to direct popular election, but this caused little change in old-guard council management,[96] not till the 1880s brought new protagonists and an altered context at last. The city by that time was feeling its problems of scale. Revived, if often uncertain, prosperity also roused a hopeful, restive climate; the Knights of Labor began shaping a working-class political front, and the urgings of moral humanitarians rose in fervour. The latter were centred in a church-based temperance movement that went back to the Forties, but by now they were more generally seeking the purification of the whole civic community. The resulting urban crusade was clearly much affected by the contemporary drive for "clean" municipal government in far more corrupt, boss-ridden American city administrations; yet if Torontonians remained acutely suspicious of U.S. power, they had often accepted American ideas. Moreover, a provincial act of 1884 gave the civic vote to widows and unmarried women with due property requirements, which likely added further weight to Toronto's moral reformism.[97]

Its first plain political manifestation came in 1884, when Alderman J. J. Withrow, a Liberal, ran for mayor and was beaten by the old-guard candidate, A. R. Boswell, by only 3 votes. Withrow tried again the next year, to lose by 145 to Alexander Manning, a rich builder-developer and ex-mayor.[98] But this still close loss only fired the forces of reform. The Manning side was charged with every sort of municipal vice: as being tools of the liquor trade (certainly well tied to Conservative local interests), promoters of brothels and depravity, dealers in bribery and graft. It was all very surprising to Manning and company, just filling their same old role, and it was

even more surprising when, in the elections of 1886, a "citizens' candidate" and political novice, William Holmes Howland, triumphed.[99] A minor insurance company president, if member of a leading family, Howland had once been a Canada Firster and a campaigner for the National Policy, but his chief claims to the mayor's office consisted of his devoted labours among the city's poor, his fervent evangelical beliefs and vigorous teetotalism.

In office Mayor Howland faced a council still dominated by old-guard forces. He failed in his temperance designs to reduce liquor outlets, failed to carry out a much-needed program of public works, and his investigations of a price-fixing coal ring and other jobbery bogged down. Nevertheless, the mayor's championing of the unsuccessful strike of 1886 by unionists against the heartily disliked monopoly of the Street Railway Company kept up public sympathy. He was viewed more as a victim of evil forces than as a failure, and hence worthy of another chance. With strong labour support as well as that of temperance faithful and civic uplifters, Howland was decisively re-elected in 1887, and this time took with him a much more favourable council. In consequence, liquor licences were cut, roads widely improved, and the city administration strengthened, while a new morality officer warred on bawdyhouses and illegal drinking-places. The authoritative mayor, however, retired at the end of the year, under personal financial and health strains; he died in 1893, not yet fifty. His successor in the mayoralty was not the reformers' candidate, Elias Rogers, the big coal merchant — whose temperance rectitude was blasted at the last moment by revelations of his involvement in a coal ring.[100] Instead, Conservative Ned Clarke won, deputy grand master of the Orange Order and publisher of the Orange *Sentinel*.[101] Still, Clarke had clear trade-union origins, and initially backed by a labour-Tory alliance, held Toronto successfully through four terms in all.

In view of this outcome, reforming Howland, emblematic as he was of High Victorian Toronto's moral fervour, might seem of merely passing note in city politics. But he was far more significant. He was a positive, directing mayor, as Clarke was also, taking the lead away from the old collegial council, which never wholly regained its clubby power. The changes Howland promoted in enlarging civic activity would only continue, as would lively issues of reform. In 1891 the streetcar franchise was wrested from the hated old company, though transferred on supposedly good terms to a hopefully better one.[102] In 1893 a spreading slump raised fresh

William Holmes Howland. His mayoralty of 1886-87 represented the first real breakthrough by forces of urban reform in the industrializing city, pointing the way to greater changes in the following generation.

cries for strong, efficient city government to end the aldermanic deals of real estate "boodlers." In 1894–95 new charges of incompetence and graft in the council brought on a major inquiry into municipal operations, which spurred demands for technical expertise and trained officials, and a remaking of the city's governing structure. The results were to follow in the next period — yet to all this Howland represented an essential transition. In short, the moral and humanitarian reformer had marked the passage to a new stage in municipal political life, embodying on one side positive civic leadership with wide popular backing, and on the other, full-time executive control of urban government services. The City Efficient was challenging laissez-faire assumptions in the industrializing municipality.

A prime question of services in the Howland years (and before and after) concerned the civic water system. Even by the 1870s the city had plainly outgrown the inadequate, polluted supply provided by the franchised water company, now retained on a contract basis while long-projected city water works were further considered.[103] In this regard, practical needs and technical or financial aspects were uppermost, not public ownership as a principle — but needs no less produced a major civic enterprise. In 1872 a Water Works Commission was voted in, to design a new system and take over the old one; in 1873 the private company accepted a purchase offer. By 1877, when the completed public utility was transferred directly to the city, homes with piped water had already increased to some 4,100 from a mere 1,375 in 1874.[104] They reached nearly 16,000 by 1883, as residents took steadily to a more ample and reliable city system, which featured new pumping equipment, more sewers, a holding reservoir north of town, and far greater fire-fighting capacities.[105] Yet the quality of the water remained in doubt: "drinkable sewage," the *Globe* called it in 1882.[106] Basic to the problem was the need for a large trunk sewer to drain the expanding system properly, together with the fact that sewage still poured into the harbour within range of the water intake. Thus, the Howland regime sought to construct a sewer east to Ashbridges Bay, only to have the voters reject its costs. A longer intake pipe to the open lake at least was built, but when this sprang leaks within the harbour in 1892, it caused brief returns to water carters and typhoid dangers.[107]

While health science exponents made scant headway on the water purity issue, they saw other decisive gains in the field of public health. Until the Eighties there were few significant changes, but then both federal and provincial incentives, as well as Toronto's own realization of the sanitary dangers in an exploding urban environment, brought the establishment of a permanent medical health officer, whose work became a vital part of civic administration. In 1883 Dr. William Canniff took up this post, a well-qualified city physician and an enthusiastic sanitary reformer. He dealt with infectious diseases, effectively checking smallpox outbreaks, though he had less success controlling diptheria. He and his staff regularly inspected schools and factories, went after bad private housing, foul privies and refuse dumps, and spread their preventive care to meat, milk and ice suppliers also.[108] They lacked much coercive power, however, and had to operate with purse-pinching aldermen who still showed laissez-faire reluctance to infringe on rights of private property. Canniff, in fact, retired from his job in 1890, frustrated by setbacks, especially regarding pure water supply.[109] Nonetheless, under him and his successor, Dr. Charles Sheard, public health services were institutionalized for a far cleaner Toronto. That the city death rate fell from 21.3 per 1,000 in 1883 to 15.18 by 1896 suggested their continuing value.[110]

For all this, hospitals in Toronto still largely functioned as refuges for the sick poor, not as key centres of medical treatment. The varying provincial or municipal grants they received came to them as charitable agencies, in which private philanthropy or religious purpose also played large roles. The large Toronto General Hospital, tight for money, was indeed reproached by the provincial inspector in 1877 for not admitting sufficient poor sufferers, but fund drives pushed by board member William Howland eased its situation.[111] Charitable motives produced the Hospital for Sick Children in 1875, founded by a group of upper-class women led by Mrs. Samuel McMaster, wife of a nephew of William McMaster.[112] In the Eighties this venture of high future importance was strongly aided by John Ross Robertson, the wealthy owner of the *Telegram*, who also raised donations through his paper for the hospital's fine new Romanesque building, opened in 1891. St. Michael's, a Catholic foundation though available to all, began in 1892, and still more small hospitals appeared and grew.

Other areas of social service saw similar growth in grant-assisted philanthropic institutions. The industrializing city responded to the human problems massed by its material development through the Houses of Industry and Providence, Boys' and Girls' Homes,

Police Constable William Leonard, 1887. A stalwart member of Toronto's police force of the period — with handcuffs at the ready.

The new electric streetcar, in summer form. Closed bodies replaced "toast-racks" of this sort for winter use. This one probably ran on the Carlton-College cross-town route west to Dovercourt Road.

and city missions, adding to them Protestant and Catholic orphanages, the Toronto Relief Society, and still more, including a city relief officer — although Goldwin Smith had to undertake to pay his salary in 1883.[113] Yet the need was great, even in good times. Roaming tramps seemed to defy social regulation. Inadequate housing was a continual bane, winter unemployment a repeated scourge. Job losses in bad years caused far more misery than any strikes — so much so that the poor might put their children in orphanages, to redeem them in better days from veritable human pawnshops.[114] Baby farming, broken families and battered wives, drunkenness, vagrancy and violent assault were still other vicious aspects of poverty on the dark side of Toronto the Good.

Towards the end of the late Victorian era, real wages did rise, while the possessing classes went on doing their uneven best with public backing to alleviate, if not eliminate, the worst features of suffering. Yet under these circumstances it seems remarkable that public order was so well sustained, in spite of brief exceptions like the Jubilee Riots of 1875. Major crime in the city was far less prevalent than sensational press reports made it appear; drunk and disorderly charges climbed sharply between 1883 and 1887 (influencing the temperance reformism of the Howland years), but then steadily declined.[115] Probably Toronto's cultural uniformities and God-fearing social controls had some bearing here, as did the Salvation Army, present from 1882. So, quite likely, did an augmented police force, watched over by a rigorous George Taylor Denison, who served as the senior police magistrate right from 1877 to 1923.

Other kinds of urban services also developed further. New parks were created in the city's extending domains, a purpose also pushed by Howland. On its western margins, John Howard, the architect, conveyed his beautifully treed and hilly estate, High Park, to Toronto in 1873, though held back part until his death in 1890; while east up the Don, broad Riverdale Park (and Zoo) was developed by the mid-Nineties. Road improvements made progress as well. The laying of cedar-block paving on major streets proceeded from the early Seventies. Macadamized gravel or merely graded earth roads stayed more numerous; but by 1884, out of 163 miles of city streets, over 44 had been cedar-surfaced, to some 52 more cheaply macadamized; and cedar paving covered Yonge Street from King to Bloor, as it did the main downtown thoroughfares.[116] This wooden pavement, much superior to rutted gravel or plain mud-holes, remained popular till about 1893, but still split and heaved, and its cracks collected noxious dirt. It was gradually to be replaced by asphalt, introduced from Trinidad in 1887, a crucial change for increasingly heavy central city traffic.[117]

The coming of the electric streetcar under the newly franchised Toronto Railway Company of 1891 also much facilitated traffic movements. With power initially from the Toronto Light Company, and then from its own steam plant on the Esplanade, the system's extending lines coped (for the time at least) with rush-hour crowds downtown, speeded street flows in most weather, and became an ever more important urban service to burgeoning Toronto. By 1895, in any event, the High Victorian city was merging into its still bigger twentieth-century successor. Policemen stood on traffic duty with stop-and-go signals as trolley cars ground by. Crossings were lit by brilliant electric arc lights, incandescent bulbs as well as gas mantles glowed from windows. Electric signs adorned theatres, and Eaton's and Simpson's advertised their latest tremendous sales to residents. Many people deplored the wearing urban pace and congestion, and those who could afford it left for summer vacations by quiet watersides, away from the clamour of the "Queen City."[118] In varied ways, a Toronto still with us had taken shape.

King Street east of Yonge in 1912, with the King Edward Hotel rising in the background.

Chapter Five
The Nearly National Metropolis, 1895–1918

Between the mid-Nineties and the First World War, Toronto neared the rank of a national metropolis, as its advancing financial power in particular confirmed a hold on hinterlands that now ranged Canada-wide. Closely involved with this advance was a new era of expanding trade, resurgent immigration, rapid western settlement, and much-enlarged resource frontiers. Linked as well were mounting supplies of cheap electric energy, continued industrial growth within the city, and far more investment in its built environment, from downtown core to radiating suburbs. Throughout the whole period Toronto, as before, was sharing developments broadly experienced in Canada. Yet once more its reponses had results of their own. After a spell of slower progress in the still-depressed mid-Nineties, its population began a new climb, reaching 208,040 in 1901, 376,538 in 1911 (with further annexations under way), then 521,893 by 1921.[1] Though its metropolitan role remained surpassed by Montreal's and was challenged somewhat within the West by the fast-rising regional metropolises of Winnipeg and Vancouver, Toronto came second only to Montreal in national scope and influence during the prewar decades. The wartime years brought it further headway, and marked, in fact, both a rounding-out of the city's past phases of evolution and an opening up towards the four-times larger Metropolitan Toronto conglomerate that was to emerge by the 1980s. Accordingly, as both conclusion and transition, the war years provide an appropriate sequel to the vigorous upthrust of the young metropolis during the early stages of the twentieth century.

URBAN ECONOMY: BUILDING FINANCIAL AND CORPORATE DOMINANCE

The years 1895–96 stayed mainly slow, but then world-trade recovery waxed into a great boom that essentially ran on till 1913.

This pervasive boom and the spread of western Canadian settlement, and thus of national markets for industrialism, were undoubtedly basic factors in Toronto's economic growth down to the First World War. Nevertheless, the leading feature of that growth was the expansion of the city's financial interests, which powerfully reinforced its metropolitan functions by adding far greater investment and policy control to its dominance over hinterlands. The agencies of Toronto finance extended operations from Atlantic to Pacific, channelling funds into western farmlands and transport, northern lumbering and mining, city utilities and urban real estate. And what this really represented was the city's massing corporate business power, rising to a national scale.

The day of the big business corporation arrived in Toronto.[2] Company boards and salaried management were supplanting personal proprietors and partners in command of major firms. Money magnates teamed with brokers and top lawyers to design heavily capitalized projects, acquire controlling stock or carry mergers, as these became more promising routes to wealth and power than manufacturing or marketing a better mousetrap. Certainly, high finance and the managerial revolution still had some distance to go in Toronto before the First World War, but their forward sweep was evident. It showed in the swelling size of the city's banks, bank clearings, loan and insurance companies, in the incorporation of big industrial, power and resource ventures, and in much proliferating stock-exchange activities. In fact, two new exchanges emerged in the city after 1896 (combined as the Standard Stock and Mining Exchange in 1899) to deal in the fruitful new field of mine investment, and there was plenty of company share trading for the older Toronto Stock Exchange as well. The very rise of corporate business towers on the downtown skyline betokened the ascent of finance.

Why this ascent? In part, it was one more exemplification of the "them as has, gits" rule. The city had already evolved leading regional financial institutions, ever since the early appearance of the Bank of Upper Canada, and particularly since mid-Victorian times. With structure, assets and expertise substantially in place, it was altogether likely that this whole funding system would rapidly expand in the new national prosperity, when credit demands soared high and investment prospects looked so inviting. Then too, Toronto's attainments in commerce, industry and transport had gathered it both capital and connections. These could be worked into a financial net that spanned the continent, its strands not only rail and postal routes, or telegraph and telephone lines, but well-established credit lines besides.

Yet there were other factors. One was the continuing initiative of Toronto business leaders; aggressive readiness to grasp opportunities was not new in an otherwise conservative community. And there was the city's ability to attract American capital, also not new. American investment as well as Yankee technology had reached Toronto business across the Lakes at least from the 1830s. But now the scale of input became decidedly new, as big U.S. corporations and entrepreneurs set up branch plants behind the Canadian tariff wall or turned increasingly to exploit untapped Canadian resources. Toronto, moreover, was both a recognized reception point on an investment path that stemmed largely from New York, and, as capital of Ontario, a crucial centre where development rights to vast provincial resource riches could be negotiated and implemented. And so American interests were drawn to this trans-border investment focus. Ties from the old days of Erie Canal traffic or the railway-building Fifties were now reconstituted in a far more weighty New York–Toronto financial axis.

There was British investment too, and with Canadian, American and overseas capital accessible for national or regional fields of development, Toronto's financial empire advanced on practically all fronts. It was most plainly evidenced in banking. Here the city's big Bank of Commerce kept to the fore, still presided over by George Albertus Cox (named a senator in 1896), with Byron Edmund Walker as general manager till Cox retired in 1907 and Walker succeeded him — to be knighted "Sir Edmund" in 1910. Both honours, incidentally, were not unrelated to the bank's close comradeship with the Liberal party, in national office from 1896 to 1911. Cox and Walker together shaped a program of expansion, tripling the Commerce's assets between 1895 and 1906.[3] In 1898 it

opened the first bank in the Yukon, during the Klondike gold rush. It dotted branches across the populating western plains, and the purchase of the Bank of British Columbia in 1901 added 7 more in that province, plus offices in San Francisco and Portland. Eastward, in 1903, the takeover of the august Halifax Banking Company brought in 20 Maritime branches, that of the Eastern Townships Bank in 1912 a large block in Quebec, while Newfoundland was invaded with an office in St. John's.[4] By the war years the Commerce was strongly represented in all the Canadian regions. It had 379 branches in 1915; notably, 181 of these were in the West, to 169 in central Canada.[5] At this time its old rival, the Bank of Montreal, had only 181 branch offices in all, though it led by far in total assets, having some $334 million worth to the Commerce's $250 million.[6]

Nonetheless, Toronto's chief bank had clearly made itself a national institution. In lesser degree the city's other chartered banks did likewise.[7] The Imperial Bank had put 48 of its 125 branches in the West by 1915. It also advanced into northern resource frontiers, to the Cobalt silver field in 1905, and to subsequent opening mine or lumber realms. The Dominion Bank, guided from 1901 to 1924 by Edmund Boyd Osler (later Sir), stayed more largely in Ontario; yet it had outspread western branches too, and greater assets than the Imperial. As for the cautious, soundly paying Bank of Toronto — still ruled over by George Gooderham down to 1905 and soon by another William Gooderham — it located one-third of its branches in the West. Moreover, in 1900 the Bank of Nova Scotia moved its general managership from Halifax to Toronto to gain a more central headquarters for expansion. This bank, second in size only to the Commerce in Toronto, added many more eastern Canadian links to the city's financial operations, and with them an extensive Caribbean business. Overall then, Toronto banking grew far beyond regional dimensions. By the First World War, it controlled 34 per cent of all banking offices in western Canada, to 33 per cent for Montreal-based houses, while its bank clearings also rose at a higher rate.[8]

Similar developments occurred in insurance and investment enterprises. Toronto indeed became the unrivalled capital of the Canadian insurance business. In 1910, for example, its fire and life insurance companies together held policies in force worth $609 million, to not quite $130 million for Montreal firms. The Canada Life Assurance Company was Toronto's leader, while Confedera-

These portraits are from **Torontonians As We See 'Em**, a project of the Canada Newspaper Cartoonists' Association, published in 1905. They show (across the top, left to right): George Albertus Cox, the canny leader of Toronto corporate finance, power behind the Bank of Commerce, Canada Life, and other investment enterprises in or far beyond the city; Edmund Boyd Osler, head of the Dominion Bank, director of the CPR and Toronto MP, 1896-1917; and Henry Pellatt, the builder of Casa Loma, knight of the brokers' ticket tape, colonel of the Queen's Own, and president of the Electrical Development Company. At left is John Craig Eaton, retail potentate, in his new car. The buildings are the firm's Toronto headquarters and Winnipeg store.

tion Life, Manufacturers Life and North American Life also stood high; and Imperial Life, established there in 1897, was rising fast. Canada Life had actually begun in Hamilton in 1847, but in 1899 moved its base to Toronto through the determined drive of the redoubtable Senator George Cox. The next year he became its president — adding to his Bank of Commerce headship — and launched the firm on widespread national expansion that reached into American and overseas markets as well.

Imperial Life, a new Cox creation, was another in a set of powerful concerns dominated by the senator and his chief associates.[9] They included the Central Canada Savings and Loan Company, which invested extensively in real estate, the wealthy National Trust, which fattened nicely on western mortgages, and Dominion Securities, which within four years of its foundation in 1901 was the biggest bond dealer in Canada. There were other major Toronto financial houses besides, but the scale and interweaving of the Cox group made them especially strong exemplars of the city's corporate finance. Cox ruled Canada Life till his death in 1914, when his son Edward replaced him. Imperial Life soon got Cox's stockbroker son-in-law, Alfred Ernest Ames, as vice-president, and son Frederick Cox as general manager — who, with his brother Herbert, was also ensconced in Central Canada Savings. A close Cox friend and fellow Methodist, Joseph Flavelle, the able manager-director and later president of the big William Davies pork-packing house, served variously on the boards of Canada Life, Imperial Life, Central Canada and the Bank of Commerce. He also presided over National Trust, which had A. E. Ames as its vice-president and by 1904 offices in Montreal, Winnipeg and Edmonton. And a Cox protégé, E. R. Wood, headed Dominion Securities and managed Central Canada Savings.

Nor were these the limits of the Cox Toronto-centred empire.[10] It stretched at least from the Crow's Nest Pass Coal Company in the Canadian West to the Sao Paulo Tramway Light and Power Company in Brazil, from which developed Brascan. It spread to other power, transport and industrial ventures. As early as 1892, Cox and the Bank of Commerce had jointly acquired over a million dollars in bonds of the Toronto Railway Company, then enfranchised to electrify the city's streetcar system. This led to growing links with William Mackenzie, the railway promoter who headed the new Toronto transit monopoly. Mackenzie himself spiralled as a utility magnate, with streetcar and electric projects from Win-

nipeg, Niagara and Saint John to Detroit, Havana and Barcelona, considerably underwritten by the Cox companies. The Commerce and the Central Canada also backed the financing of a western rail system being strung together by Mackenzie and his partner, Donald Mann, in competition with the nation-wide CPR. In 1901 this Canadian Northern line announced its intent to become a transcontinental railway, and in 1903 yet another was chartered, the Grand Trunk Pacific, on whose board Cox sat as a founding member — where Flavelle would also join him. Meanwhile, within Toronto, this time in manufacturing, the Cox coterie had linked with Massey interests to form the large Canada Cycle and Motor Company in 1899: Cox vice-president, Flavelle a director. Their CCM merged a series of bicycle firms, but by 1906 was successfully producing automobiles as well.[11]

Accordingly, if in the young century the flamboyant American-born Sir William Van Horne, engineer-builder of the CPR, was the reigning financial figure in Montreal, so Senator Cox, the astute, calm entrepreneur from Peterborough, Ontario, was the ruling embodiment of Toronto finance capital. And while Cox was still old-style in looking to personal and family aspects of control, he was new-style in building up his wealth through corporate investment, utilities and real estate, not primarily commerce or manufacturing. For money tycoons, not merchant princes or captains of industry, now led the way in Toronto. True, Joseph Flavelle, a millionaire himself by 1900,[12] had risen out of produce-dealing, but he increasingly entered into major financial undertakings, of which the National Trust was only one.

Other members of the city's new corporate elite were no less closely associated with investment control over large units of production or service: men like Edmund Walker of the Commerce, financier *par excellence*; Edmund Osler of the Dominion Bank, who emerged from stockbroking; Frederic Nicholls, managing director of the combine Canadian General Electric (CGE); or Henry Pellatt, another leading stockbroker, who had earlier got into utilities through the Toronto Electric Light Company that held the city's street-lighting franchise.[13] Finally, among still more, Zebulon Lash, Toronto's most prominent solicitor, was influential on the board of National Trust and other companies, reflecting the new significance of corporation lawyers in the city.[14] The capitalist generalship of men like these played a large part in Toronto's rise as a financial metropolis in the years before the First World War.

Assembling bicycles for Canada Cycle and Motor Co. (CCM), a Cox-Massey combine of 1899.

OTHER ECONOMIC DEVELOPMENTS

The prewar boom was finally curbed by depression in 1913, till war demands renewed the pace. And throughout the flush times, the enlargement of Toronto's commerce and industry closely accompanied that of its finance. As for commerce, retailing growth was now more apparent than wholesaling, in a city that itself constituted a rich central market for big retail firms. These largely bought direct from suppliers, not through city wholesalers, and sold direct to hinterland customers by mail order, as did Eaton's and Simpson's, or through chain store outlets of their own.[15] Moreover, the old measures of wholesale trade, the values of the city's exports and imports, had lost some of their meaning as Toronto entered increasingly into an expanding national economy.[16] Much of its merchandise fed Canadian home markets, not export fields; many of its wares now came from within the country, or if imported, arrived by rail rather than via its harbour. Yet the city's wholesale trade generally remained healthily profitable, given the much larger total volume of commerce. Furthermore, the spread of mining and mill towns in northern Ontario, from Sudbury and Sault Ste. Marie in the Nineties to Cobalt and Timmins between 1905 and 1912, produced valuable new markets for Toronto wholesaling to enter.

Nevertheless, if the city's wholesalers still did well in absolute terms, they and the merchants' traditional organ, the Board of Trade, had relatively lost weight in a financial-industrial metropolis. More noteworthy now than the Board of Trade was the Canadian Manufacturers' Association headquartered in the city, dating from 1871 but incorporated in 1902, and by then growing prodigiously.[17] Insofar as big merchandising still held high rank, its best representatives had surely become Eaton's and Simpson's. Eaton's established mail-order offices and department stores well beyond Ontario, and in 1909 set up a separate mail-order division, which got a headquarters building and factory of its own on a much enlarged Toronto store property.[18] Simpson's, reorganized after the death of its founder in 1897, also vigorously expanded with new funding and direction. Significantly, however, two of Simpson's three controlling partners were now Joseph Flavelle and A. E. Ames, and working capital came from the Bank of Commerce.[19] While Eaton's stayed under family rule, Timothy Eaton being succeeded on his death in 1907 by his son John Craig, its main rival had become another gilt-edged holding in the hands of financiers and managers.

The same trend appeared in industrial development, from CCM to CGE, a trend to strongly capitalized major units, often amalgamations, with considerably more mechanization and complexity in their operations. The effects on Toronto industry were displayed in census statistics for the period. The reported number of its manufacturing plants fell from 2,401 in 1891 to 847 in 1901, but this was rather a sign of greater concentration in larger-scale enterprises, since the number of their employees expanded across the same period from about 26,000 to more than 42,000.[20] Then in the remarkably prosperous decade from 1901 to 1911, the city's industrial units multiplied to 1,100, while their work force rose above 65,000 — and over the whole twenty-year span, their capitalization grew nearly fivefold, to reach some $145 million.[21] Moreover, the total value of Toronto's manufacturing output advanced by 243 per cent between 1890 and 1910, Montreal's by 145 per cent.[22] And a signal rise in the average productivity of Toronto plants confirmed that their increased capitalization was paying off.

In any event, manufacturing became by far the largest employer in Toronto in the prewar years, displaying its 65,000 engaged in 1911, to nearly 40,000 in commerce and finance, around 20,000 in building trades, 18,000 in domestic and personal services, with transport, the professions and government work well below in declining order.[23] Among the city industries, clothing establishments had the most employees (and a sizeable female majority).[24] Metals and machinery stood next, while printing, food processing, woodworking and furniture, leather and rubber goods, musical instruments and vehicle-making exhibited successively fewer numbers. In sum, Toronto's industrial pattern had now greatly altered in character since the preceding period that established it, although it had markedly expanded and added newer components like electrical supplies, elevators and automobiles. More important was the fact that the city's manufacturing sector was still further outdistancing those of other Ontario centres. By 1911 Toronto employed 27 per cent of the province's industrial force, compared to 10 per cent back in 1881,[25] since to its older advantages as a transport and commercial entrepôt had now been added its primacy in financing large corporate enterprises.

Important, too, was advancing electrical technology in factories, applying adaptable electric motors to do away with the restrictive clutter of belt-driven steam machinery. But the growing demands for efficient, mass electric power for manufacturing, lighting and street railways required the developing of some great new energy source, such as the hydroelectric potential of Niagara Falls. In 1903 the Electrical Development Company, set up by Mackenzie, Nicholls and Pellatt, secured extensive Niagara power and transmission rights from the Ontario Liberal government. They constructed a magnificent generating plant at the Falls, which by 1907 was delivering power to Toronto.[26] Their projected total electric monopoly, however, met hot opposition in the City Council and from a "cheap public power" movement, strong across southern Ontario.[27] Accordingly, a new Conservative provincial regime in 1906 erected a public power-transmission authority, an Ontario Hydro-Electric Power Commission that would construct its own lines and sell low-cost hydroelectricity to municipalities. In Toronto the City Council contracted with the commission for delivery in 1908, organizing the Toronto Hydro-Electric System to build its own civic utility.[28] Commission power finally reached the city in May 1911. Though the Mackenzie interests still held a large part in power generation at Niagara, the low public transmission rates, providing electric energy from a seemingly unlimited supply, became one more impelling factor in the city's economic expansion.

In transport, Toronto's railroad services continued to expand as well. Mackenzie and Mann moved their Canadian Northern headquarters there in 1899, to work on extending their prairie rail system eastward, and later, westward to the Pacific. By 1906 Canadian Northern track ran from Toronto past Parry Sound. The remaining gap to the Lakehead was closed by 1914; the next year this Toronto-based railway was open to Vancouver. The CPR in 1908 also completed a direct link between Toronto and Sudbury on its main line. By 1915 the Ontario capital not only had these routes to the lands above it (plus the original Northern line up to North Bay) but access to the Grand Trunk Pacific besides, completed that year as a transcontinental. Still further, the provincial government's own colonization railway, the Temiskaming and Northern Ontario (TNO) begun in 1902, pushed on into northeastern Ontario from North Bay, opening up new resource areas to Toronto. Thus, in the Cobalt silver boom of 1905–10, prospectors and suppli-

ers could reach the mining camps by direct train from the city. The TNO built on to Cochrane in 1908 to intersect with the National Transcontinental coming from Quebec, the eastern half of the new Grand Trunk Pacific route. In consequence, Toronto's ability to tap the North was further enlarged. Even by 1909 over 90 per cent of northern Ontario's trade flowed mainly to that centre, to less than 10 per cent for Montreal.[29] And these land transport gains abetted more investment northward.

Toronto's water-borne transport, however, faced incessant problems: inadequate financing, the competition both from railways and other major lake ports, a restricted, ineffective harbour board, and beyond that, undirected private control of almost all the waterfront. Certainly, the port kept busy over the period, but even much of its basic coal trade had now diverted to rail.[30] Moreover, Toronto shipowners remained slow to invest in expensive, specialized, steel lake freighters. They left them largely to outside lines, and clung to older, cheaper vessels crammed indiscriminately with freight. As for port improvements, they went on only piecemeal: breakwaters to check erosion of the Island, piers to protect the eastern entrance, undertaken in 1901, and a deeper western entrance dredged south of the old channel, finally completed between 1908 and 1911 thanks to federal government funds.[31]

At length, by 1910, the growing realization that only well-funded public management could reverse laissez-faire neglect and spur port development roused a campaign for a comprehensive civic harbour authority. Pushed by the Board of Trade and the press (as the *Telegram* decried "docks that cannot be reached and a 1,300-acre swamp"),[32] the City Council won the voters' approval for a Toronto Harbour Commission, established by federal act in 1911. The new commission, with unrestricted borrowing rights and the power to expropriate, sell or lease waterfront lands, set up its plans in 1912, and within two years owned 95 per cent of the harbourside property.[33] It took up rebuilding and increasing dock facilities, deepening and protecting the harbour, and rationalizing shore land-uses. Depression, then war, slowed down its work, which was still far from removing the drab, depressing tangle around the port. But at least an impressive start was made, as public interest at last gained ground after a century of private exploitation and abuse of Mrs. Simcoe's "beautiful clear" bay.

Public hydroelectric power reaches Toronto, 1911, and "Niagara Falls" cascades down City Hall for the celebration.

POPULATION TRENDS: ETHNIC GROWTH
AND CIVIC ENLARGEMENT

Still more impressive was the impact of immigration on the prewar city. In the good times from the late Nineties onward, immigrants again flowed abundantly into Canada, to farm the "last, best West," work on resource frontiers or build up urban centres. The years 1901–11 especially showed a large net balance of population intake over exodus, the decade before having been burdened by depression in its first half, while that following soon brought world war to check immigration. Accordingly, the first twentieth-century decade saw Toronto's own growth particularly affected by the incoming tide: indirectly, through the overall expansion of Canadian numbers and activities; directly, through the substantial addition of new producers and consumers to the city itself. At the same time, the surging young metropolis attracted a continued influx from Ontario rural areas and lesser towns; in fact, in-migration, natural increase and boundary extensions all played parts as well as immigration in Toronto's rapid prewar population rise. Yet the upsweep in transatlantic migration had a special significance, since this now produced a mounting element of non-English-speaking ethnic residents in the city's midst — no longer sparse handfuls, but forming a whole new feature in its demographic pattern.

The main mass of immigrants who entered the community in this era were still drawn from the British Isles, again preponderantly from England.[34] But streams of continental European newcomers, long running to the United States, by 1900 had begun to find more Canadian destinations as well — among them, the workplaces and construction jobs of thriving Toronto. This growing foreign presence in the city was reflected in the decline of its overwhelming Anglo-Celtic majority from 91.7 per cent in 1901 to 86.4 in 1911.[35] By 1921 this was down to 85.3 per cent, to fall through successive decades as other immigrant groups arrived. Hence, though the prewar years scarcely upset the predominant pattern, they did mark an advancing, different demographic trend: away from the homogeneity of the nineteenth-century British Canadian city towards the ethnic pluralism of the modern metropolitan community.

Even by 1911, the census for that year indicated there were over 30,000 foreign-born in Toronto,[36] the bulk of them readily apparent from language and cultural differences, and their residential clustering in low-rent, near-central neighbourhoods. A smaller segment of the non-British newcomers, Americans by birth, were far less perceivable by trait or residence, and quickly assimilable, too; while any Asian-born then constituted a mere 0.3 per cent of the total urban populace.[37] But the main, continental European segment of the "strangers within our gates" (so termed in a classic study of 1909 by J. S. Woodsworth) included Austro-Hungarian and Italian nationals, and diverse former subjects of Imperial Russia. Many of the last were Jews, as were others drawn from Central Europe. The Jewish community in Toronto, in sum, now stood at more than 18,000, having grown sixfold since 1901.[38] The Italian community thus far was much smaller, at about 4,000; yet it had also multiplied over four times across the decade.[39] Moreover, the Germanic and various Slavic communities together were not inconsiderable, though far more fractionalized. In that regard, even the Jewish and Italian groups were not at all as homogeneous as appeared from outside.

The established community saw problems of public welfare and cultural dislocation stemming from these strangers, who were largely poor, unskilled villagers in origin. They had alien customs, conversed together incomprehensibly, crowded into run-down inner areas, most notably "the Ward" (in once St. John's Ward) west of Yonge and above Queen. (See Map 9, page 181.) They collected in its low-rent housing both from economic necessity and desire for familiar neighbours: approximately 10,000 foreigners lived in the Ward even by 1907.[40] There the established order might feel an unassimilable slum ghetto was developing, generating immorality and crime as well as fiscal and sanitary ills. High-coloured articles on Ward conditions became a staple of the city press. City churches set up missions to these handy heathens. In part the missions provided needed welfare and help in adjustment to a new country, but they also sought to convert Jews and foreign Christians to acceptable (majority) Christian faiths — with no great success.[41]

The foreigners themselves, however, sought chiefly to survive in their own identities, and to make economic headway in a difficult but materially promising environment.[42] They did both. While learning the language and ways of Toronto, they worked as they could: women quite generally in garment sweatshops, needle trades and laundries; men often in road work, building construction or door-to-door peddling. From peddling some rose to operate little family stores, usually in their own ethnic communities, where immigrant boardinghouses and eating places also brought income. Some newcomers with artisan or entrepreneurial skills built up their own modest businesses; others bossed ethnic labour gangs; and still others put hard-gleaned earnings into small house properties as landlords, or dealt in shipping more home-country migrants out to jobs or back to the old land. By the First World War, in consequence, not only a middle class, but ethnic notables of some influence and affluence, were becoming evident inside this new society. Without in the main losing their own cultural and religious patterns, the strangers had rooted themselves, become far less strange in the process, and laid a basis for the subsequent growth of their communities within Toronto.

Despite the long-term importance of this emerging ethnic variety, the British arrivals did much more to make prewar Toronto again an immigrant city, although they did not loom as anything so visibly different. Most of the British migrants, who arrived from about 1897 on, came from a highly urbanized and industrialized homeland.[43] They moved with little noticeable disruption into factories, stores, services and dwellings across the city, although many did tend to settle in newer-developing neighbourhoods, such as around Gerrard or Danforth east of the Don, or in other extending districts beyond the older built-up core. Some working-class newcomers helped add radical sentiments brought from their British trade-union backgrounds, but much more widely Toronto's strong imperialist feelings were reinforced. The city warmly upheld the unity of the Empire in the South African War of 1899–1902, recruiting volunteer troops to fight and die on distant sunburnt plains. Again in 1914 Toronto went determinedly into the Great War overseas, with recent British arrivals forming a high proportion of the early units that were raised locally. Red-coated public school cadet corps, black mourning banners at the death of the revered Victoria, profuse Union Jacks for the coronations of Edward VII and George V, were further public testimony to the paramount British heritage of the prewar community.

In any event, the British migrants served to make Toronto — in the short run — less Canadian than it had been. The 1911 census, for example, showed that since 1901 the city's proportion of native-born inhabitants had fallen to 63 per cent, or around 205,100; the British-born risen to 28 per cent, or about 91,000.[44] Among this latter group, there were twice as many English as Scots and Irish combined, while there now were fewer citizens of Irish birth than

The Wolfishes, a Jewish family, outside their Elizabeth Street store, 1913.

Winter in the Ward. The rear of Centre Avenue, 1912.

A Macedonian boarding house on King East, 1911.

Italian labourers at work on a retaining wall on Dundas. Often such migrants went into construction gangs, intending to stay in Canada only temporarily. Yet many of these "sojourners" in time became residents.

Arriving British immigrant families cross a footbridge at Union Station around 1910. Less distinctive as newcomers, the British were by far the most numerous entrants to settle in Toronto in the prewar period.

Parliament Buildings in Queen's Park decorated to welcome "Heroes of Paardeberg" returning from South Africa. The battle of Paardeberg, 1900, was the "first major overseas engagement ever fought by Canadian troops serving officially as such."

Turnout at Yonge below Richmond for a parade of troops in 1900, during the South African War. The troops are behind this zealous crowd.

residents of Jewish origin in Toronto. The religious census of 1911 showed corresponding patterns. The Anglican church came first, in rounded numbers having some 101,000 adherents, while Roman Catholicism had fallen to fourth place, with 43,000. Presbyterians and Methodists stood second and third with 65,000 and 63,000. Interesting again, though, the Jewish faith was now sixth largest, coming behind the Baptists.[45]

Census figures revealed still more about the city's demographic growth over the young century years. In sex ratios, for example, there was a total female preponderance over male of about one per cent in the population of 1911, a margin that had actually fallen from some 3 per cent in 1891, since immigration, as usual, had initially brought in higher proportions of male venturers.[46] But breaking the sex ratios down for the main component demographic groups revealed something else. While the British-born immigrants by 1911 displayed a male preponderance of 8 per cent, and the foreign of 12 (indicating the larger number of young male transients or temporary "sojourners" among them), the Canadian-born majority element itself showed a female predominance of over 7 per cent.[47] This last fact surely reflected the continuing feminization of employment amid the established community — increased jobs for women in offices, stores, modernized factories, telephone service or education — and was no doubt related to in-migration from the countryside as well. Wartime industrial needs would later enlarge the working roles of women in Toronto much further.

And in general, after registering only around a 15 per cent increase between 1891 and 1901, the city's total population shot up by over 80 per cent from 1901 to 1911, to go on climbing till the depression of 1913 and the coming of war.[48] These swelling numbers consequently sent Toronto flooding beyond its existing limits, and led to a big new set of suburban annexations. They began in 1903 with minor additions both north of Yorkville and bordering Humber Bay. (See Map 6, page 125.) Then in 1905 the bulk of Rosedale and lands northward up Avenue Road to above St. Clair Avenue were taken in. To this, the rest of the old Annex west of Avenue Road was added the next year, while 1908 saw the Deer Park estate included, again thrusting Toronto centrally north around Yonge beyond St. Clair. To the east, in 1908-9 Midway, East Toronto and Balmy Beach entered as the city advanced out the Danforth and Queen routes, carrying it far past the Don and Riverdale to the eastern lake beaches. To the west, in 1909-10 the annexing of Wychwood, Bracondale, Earlscourt, Dovercourt and West Toronto pushed the civic borders to the village of Swansea and the Humber Valley, where once the Toronto Trail had run. Still further, in 1912, the inclusion of Moore Park, a northward offshoot of Rosedale, and North Toronto, by now a sizeable municipality in its own right, produced a total new area more than half the size of the original city limits of 1834.[49]

Two other small annexations in 1914 completed the process. It left a civic territory that stretched between Jane Street on the west, Victoria Park Avenue on the east, and Roe on the north. The whole area roughly formed an inverted "T", in which the cross bar reached from the lake to well above St. Clair in its western half, above Danforth in its eastern, while the stem ran on north past Eglinton, past the vanished Montgomery's Tavern of 1837, and on up main-route Yonge Street to the incipient residential districts of Lawrence Park and the Bedford Estate. This much-expanded domain had now spread far beyond the original Shore Plain to the higher grounds above; and outside it still newer suburban communities of "Greater Toronto" were steadily rising by the First World War. Altogether, here was a powerful demonstration, and consequence, of the city's rapid demographic growth in the prewar years.

SOCIAL PATTERNS IN A HIGH-FLYING METROPOLIS

The elite of this fast-growing society differed more in degree than kind from their Victorian predecessors. They had more money; their scope and expectations were greater. In the previous era, for all the city's advances, a sluggish world economy had still restricted its horizons, and it had known gruelling phases, too. But after 1895 the good times that rolled to 1913 were only briefly marked by downturns. Prime Minister Laurier had proclaimed the new twentieth century would belong to Canada; if so, Toronto's leaders meant to have their share of it. However much western boosters might tout the marvels of their Winnipegs or Vancouvers, Toronto's opulent saw how much they themselves controlled and might hope to control. Beyond that, the taxes on their fortunes were still minimal; the graduated income tax would not be introduced as a

Among others, a suburban radial line went east along Kingston Road to Scarborough by 1904, and one westward from Sunnyside to Port Credit by 1905. They were swift and sure, compared to primitive "automobiling" on the unpaved rural roads of the prewar era. And while growing in number, automobiles then largely remained rich men's symbols, though some became express delivery vehicles within the city. For internal transport, however, the electric streetcar was the key to public movement. The cars grew in size and had trailers added. They ran out to new amusement grounds at easternmost Scarborough Beach and to the western beaches at Sunnyside; their traffic more than tripled between 1900 and 1910.[87] Streetcars, moreover, served Toronto's sports facilities, theatres, museums, libraries and colleges. The city's cultural as well as material environment owed much to them.

POLITICAL ASPECTS: URBAN SERVICES, REFORM AND PLANNING

The very importance of streetcar service also thrust it into civic political life. One episode was close to comedy: the great fight to gain Sunday streetcars that climaxed in a city plebiscite of 1897.[88] Yet the issue hit at a firm-set institution, Toronto's closed and righteous Sabbath. The franchised Toronto Railway Company (TRC) led by William Mackenzie was more than willing to have its cars used seven days a week, while many politicians and businessmen were quite ready to see Sunday activities enlarged. A mass of bicyclists desired good Sunday access to parks and sportsgrounds by the TRC; and labour, too, widely wanted to get the most of its one full day for recreation. Some workers, however, feared that efforts for shorter hours would be set back by a more open Sunday. More forceful still was opposition to Sabbath desecration — especially among Methodists — which brought clergymen and capitalists to join with labour figures such as Jimmy Simpson in passionate resistance. At a grand rally in Allan Gardens, they sang out, "Rally to the Standard, boys, against our City's foe! For the cause of Sabbath rest we'll strike another blow."[89] Nevertheless, the ensuing plebiscite voted narrowly in favour of Sunday cars. Moral reformers deplored the victory of secularism and sin, but more likely the outcome was at base a response to urbanism, to the leisure needs of a new large city. Nor was Toronto Sabbatarianism finished. In 1912, spurred by a militant Lord's Day Alliance, it at

least succeeded in closing winter toboggan slides in the city parks on Sundays.[90]

The opening decades of the twentieth century raised other streetcar issues, on which the TRC found scant support.[91] Service problems — delayed and crowded cars, or too many uncomfortable old ones — were inevitable complaints as the company struggled to keep up with ever-growing traffic. Yet its profits did not fail to keep up, and it was known as a hard employer, prone to strikes and remorseless strikebreaking. The TRC did build more cars and improved downtown routes to relieve congestion. The City Council, however, chiefly wanted "new lines," extensions out to the widening urban limits. On this the company stood by its franchise of 1891, good for thirty years, insisting that it need only serve to the city limits of that date. Mackenzie himself got into the developing surburban radials, but this meant extra fares where (and if) these lines met with city tracks.[92] The city fathers repeatedly took the company to court for inadequate service. Some of them talked of expropriation, and citizen meetings urged public ownership. In 1907 the civic case for new lines even went to the judges of the imperial Privy Council, where its ultimate defeat contributed to a decision of 1910 to build city-owned routes to extend streetcar service.[93] In 1912 the first of these Civic Car Lines was opened on Gerrard East; on St. Clair and on Danforth the next year. An actual attempt to buy out the TRC in 1914 was then halted by the outbreak of the war: the commitment seemed too large. But it was pretty clear that the company franchise would not be renewed on its expiry in 1921. And meanwhile, the city was learning how to operate its own transport utility. Already by 1914 some 21 per cent of its population lived beyond the limits of the old private service.[94] Significantly, too, a report of 1915 indicated that working-class districts now provided the "greater proportion" of streetcar users of the expanded transit system.[95]

Fire and water service also made significant progress, thanks largely to a disaster, the Great Fire of April 1904, that devastated nearly twenty acres in the downtown warehouse district at a cost of over $10 million.[96] No lives or dwellings were lost in this night conflagration, but more than 5,000 workers were left temporarily jobless. Breaking out in a neckware manufactory (perhaps from defective wiring), the fire centred around Bay Street between Wellington and Front. Though the buildings here were of solid masonry, their inflammable stores, wooden inner construction and

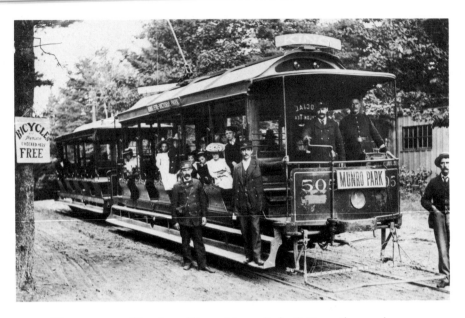

The streetcar out King Street West to Munro Park, 1900, another popular recreation ground.

Workers laying a streetcar intersection on Queen Street West at Roncesvalles, about 1910.

A group of streetcar-track workers operating out of the Front Street shops, photographed in 1905.

Rush-hour crowding on Queen: the kind of congestion which did not help the franchised company's reputation.

Yonge St. North from King

The streetcar city in full flower. Yonge Street north from King, 1910. "Autos" and carts are evident, but the trolleycar clearly dominates — as do overhead wires.

Ruins after the fire of 1904 on Wellington west of Bay, in the heart of the wholesale district.

unprotected elevator shafts produced exploding blazes that leaped streets under a driving wind. At their fullest extent, flames raced from Melinda near King down to the tracks on the Esplanade, east nearly to the Customs House on Yonge, west almost to the Queen's Hotel on Front. Toronto's now well-organized, full-time fire department put some 200 firemen, steam pumpers, water tower and ladder trucks to use, plus men and equipment arriving by train from as far as London and Buffalo. But all too typically, water pressure proved as inadequate as were fire-proofing measures. At length, a wind shift and some better-protected buildings enabled the firemen to stop the spread. Afterwards — in the good times — recovery and rebuilding moved on remarkably fast. Yet the city also adopted far broader building regulations; much reconstruction was done in steel-reinforced concrete; and a new high-pressure water system was approved by public vote for the downtown area, finished in 1909.

Along with the high pressure system, other improvements in water supply were effected by 1910 through a major scheme originally designed in 1896.[97] Water was now taken well out in a still-pure lake, passed through a modern filtration plant on the Island, then pumped by tunnel under the bay to enlarged reservoir facilities. A sewage disposal plant was opened by the Scarborough Bluffs, remote from the city intake line. The trunk sewer thus was achieved; only storm drains henceforth flowed into the harbour. By 1912, accordingly, the typhoid death rate in Toronto was below 0.2 per thousand, less than any comparable North American centre.[98] Moreover, under an active health administration, well exemplified by Dr. Charles Hastings as medical officer, the city took up extensive powers over privy pits, unhealthy boardinghouses, and indeed any premises from 1916.[99] Sanitary reform was far from all-embracing, but public controls were steadily extended over once-sacrosanct private property rights. If Toronto sanitation was not perfect, an annual death rate that continued to fall from 15.18 per thousand in 1896 to 11.2 in 1914 said something of obvious value.[100]

Hospitals played their part also. There were six general hospitals by the First World War, ten specialized ones.[101] In particular, the Toronto General Hospital moved in 1913 from its overcrowded old quarters into fine new buildings by Darling and Pearson at the corner of University and College, replacing a tract of "Ward" slums.

The city met the price of the site, and the province promised substantially larger grants from 1905. But a great part of the funds for the ultimate 670-bed complex costing $3,450,000 came from wealthy Toronto philanthropists. Joseph Flavelle, who had joined the hospital's board in 1902, vigorously directed the fund-raising. Among others, the Massey, Eaton and Gooderham families, Cox, Walker, Osler and Lash made major contributions, and at the end Flavelle added to his own in paying off a $250,000 deficit.[102] The citizens gained a first-rate health facility, the University a teaching hospital soon of world quality, and the metropolis a further centring of scientific expertise and professional training. In sum total, Toronto hospitals by the war had truly evolved from charitable shelters to curative institutions for all, supported by paying patients, and provincial and municipal aid, yet still with care for needy cases.

What this indicates is a real advance in public betterment, but by no means the attainment of some just welfare society. As late as 1900, a number of homeless elderly were still being committed to jail in Toronto, their crimes consisting of infirmity and absence of family support; the true crime being the lack of sufficient space in refuge agencies.[103] One of three new wings opened in 1898 at the House of Industry did provide more room for aged inmates, yet it was soon filled to capacity. The shelter and relief needs of working-age people were no doubt eased by the prosperous times of the new century. Yet, leaving aside the damage still done by seasonal layoffs, it has been estimated that most male manual workers in Toronto then earned less than enough to support a family adequately, requiring wives and children to work as well, with effects upon the household unit that could readily show up in city welfare problems.[104] Excessive infant mortality was a further woe, at length reduced through the institution of public health nurses in 1908 and the compulsory pasteurization of milk in 1914. Another initiative in welfare, however, was taken in combatting juvenile deliquency and child abuse through Toronto's municipally assisted Children's Aid Society.

Reflecting conservative concerns for social order, humane sentiments of the social gospel, and newer ideas on childhood as a life stage of its own, the Children's Aid Society (begun in 1891) became an influential welfare instrument in Toronto from the mid-Nineties onward, with J. J. Kelso as its guiding spirit.[105] It sought to

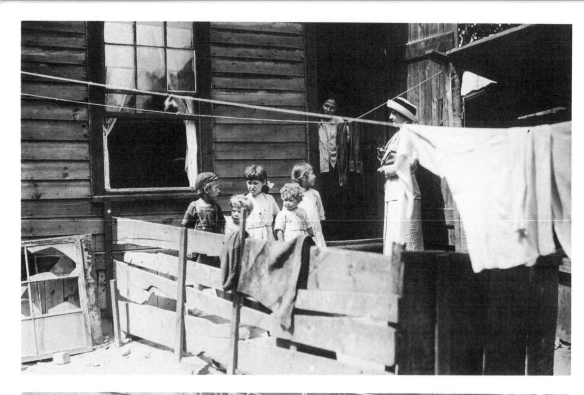

The visit of the public health nurse, in 1913 here, was an indication of the "attack on slums."

Sewers come to the Ward — another reflection of improving public health standards. This excavation is on Elizabeth Street, 1910.

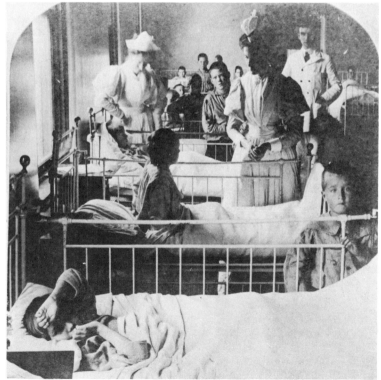

The most obvious sign of the broadening of medical facilities in this era was the opening in 1913 of the Toronto General Hospital, above — one of the prewar city's finest achievements. Fronting on College Street, with University Avenue (old College Avenue) at the right, it marked the development of a growing hospital complex in the area. At left is the convalescent ward of the Sick Children's Hospital in 1902, within its building just to the east on College Street.

sustain the family unit, seen as the very basis of society, by improving the home environment; but in dealing with neglect and cruelty, it widely took to foster homes. The Society's own shelter, besides, housed both dependent children and delinquents. As a typical result of covering so much, these quarters became overcrowded, so that the city cut its grants in 1901 because of undesirably congested conditions! Nevertheless, the Society held to its claim, "It is wiser and less expensive to save children than to punish criminals."[106] This stress on child saving as sound policy as well as social compassion led on to a separate juvenile court in Toronto by 1912, probation officers, family visitors, and volunteer aides, the Big Brothers and Big Sisters, given some training at the University's new Department of Social Services.[107] Apart from other accomplishments, the city's social service thus grew more professionalized, largely thanks to the impetus of the child welfare movement ardently espoused by Kelso.

From waterworks to welfare, these urban services demanded far more in city finance and administration, as did asphalting roads, running civic power lines, enlarging park facilities and the police force, or expanding the annual Exhibition that drew close to a million visitors by 1912.[108] Toronto's government was now big business; the city's debt, steady at about $12 million through the 1890s, was $60 million by 1914.[109] Municipal expenditure seemed almost out of hand, given its restricted revenue base in property taxes, while politicians' promises of retrenchment looked empty, given constantly increasing commitments. Consequently, rate-burdened businessmen raised stronger calls for management on "business principles." But this was only one of the springs of the urban reform movement that welled up anew.[110] Another, flowing chiefly from the intelligentsia, had both aesthetic and social-engineering aims. It sought to realize the City Beautiful concept, which looked to planned arteries adorned by handsome buildings and parks, to erase degenerative slums, and to establish an effective urban physical plant under an expert bureaucracy. The plush Guild of Civic Art, dating from 1897, stressed spatial plans, with many "garden-city" features. The University social scientist S. Morley Wickett also led from 1902 in urging municipal control of the city's "utility base" under trained professional administrators.[111]

Nor was this all. Older moral reformism swelled again to cleanse Toronto of boodling politicians allegedly mired in dirty deals or sold to liquor interests. Labour leaders still fought private monopolies and urged democratic public ownership. Newspapers like the *World* championed the ordinary citizen against big interests, and John Ross Robertson of the *Telegram* invoked true civic spirit against urban vice and blight.[112] This medley of causes often overlapped and at times evinced cross-purposes. But generally it represented responses to problems of power in an increasingly collectivized urban polity. Whether or not idealist rhetoric had much meaning for the practical running of a complicated urban political mechanism, manifest results were to be left on the civic power structure: governmental changes that sought to combine efficiency and democracy, the inception of planning controls on unbridled laissez-faire development, a quite professional municipal civil service, and potent public enterprises like the Toronto Hydro, Civic Car Lines and Harbour Commission. The collectivist state was taking over in Canada and its provinces, and not least in Toronto itself.

This trend in the city was displayed even as the period opened, when stark evidence of aldermanic bribe-taking from a judicial inquiry late in 1894 roused demands for stronger executive authority.[113] Both an elitist citizens' reform committee and union leaders pressed for a city-wide Board of Control above council; politicians agreed, if it were elected by the council from its own numbers. In 1896 this board of four was implemented, the first in Canada. In 1904 the controllers became directly elected by citizenry, viewed as a further step in democratic urban reform. Otherwise, beneath the executive of mayor and Board of Control, the older pattern of a council of aldermen elected by wards persisted. Wards had been numbered and considerably amalgamated since 1891, and these bigger wards were largely just extended northward during the series of annexations made in the new century.[114] (See Map 7, page 126.) The design was partly to sustain "good government" efficiency by keeping general interests paramount over local ward issues and parochial ward politicos, but it also assured broader mixes of ward residents, thereby effectively reducing the weight of the working-class municipal voters.

Despite these structural changes and the preachings of reformers, urban politics in prewar Toronto kept much of its former character. There still were political in-groups linked with Conservative and Orange machinery, lawyers and contractors steering land-lot schemes, merchants and manufacturers keenly

The state of a residential road: Muddy York still in 1912. Such roadways, however, were no longer evident in paved downtown Toronto, only towards the fringes. Moreover, the first paved highway outward, to Hamilton, was in process within two years.

The city police had its mounted constables, like the one above left, posed around 1900, and its men on foot wore similar British "bobby" uniforms. Then in 1912 the first motorcycle squad was formed. As shown above, its members did not receive uniforms till the experiment was judged a success. The first motorized police (at left) came in 1912 — but the first parking ticket in 1907. And the first motor fire truck entered service in 1911.

guarding business interests — and not very many labour represen-tatives. Ward Three (now containing "the Ward") also witnessed the colourful reign of the machine politician, Dr. Beatty Nesbitt, as boss of its rising immigrant ethnic vote.[115] The mayors of the period generally remained safely substantial worthies with regular backgrounds as aldermen and most often strong Conservative ties. The majority of them were prosperous lawyers, though they included "the People's Bob," Robert Fleming, a Liberal real estate broker (mayor in 1896–97, as he had been in 1892–93), Joseph Oliver (1908–9), a lumber dealer, and Horatio Hocken (1912–14), once a printer-unionist, who had risen to control his own press company but stayed sensitive to reform issues.[116]

In provincial and federal politics, moreover, prewar Toronto by no means lost its Conservative identification. The Ontario Conser-vative Whitney regime of 1905–14, with its cheap hydroelectric program, new grants to the General Hospital and University, proved in many ways much more favourably disposed to the city's interests than previous Liberal provincial governments had been. And while in federal affairs the long rule of Sir Wilfrid Laurier at Ottawa had enhanced Liberal links in Toronto, Laurier's pursuit of a new reciprocity agreement with the United States in 1911 caused an outright revolt among some of his leading party supporters in the city. The National Policy of protection had become an enduring article of faith for its Board of Trade and Canadian Manufacturers' Association, but far more than city industrialists took alarm at the thought of American goods flooding the Canadian market through reciprocity. In particular, the "Toronto Eighteen," a pre-eminent group of Liberals, came out with a manifesto against the proposal; their number including Walker of the Commerce, E. R. Wood of Dominion Securities, J. C. Eaton, president of Eaton's, W.T. White, managing director of National Trust, and Zebulon Lash, now vice-president of the Canadian Northern. When the Conservative government of Robert Borden took over in Ottawa that year, Toronto's dominant interests snuggled to it in reinforced devotion.

Nonetheless, whatever the enduring aspects of the city's political life, the collectivist changes across the period decidedly had impact. Even by lip service, civic politicians had to acknowledge urban reform, and many not only endorsed, but pushed, the practical extensions of civic authority — that is, the growth of public enter-prises so obviously wanted by the voters.[117] The municipal rulers spent funds on large projects directly authorized by ballot, and some that were not; they accepted executive management and interventions into private rights to degrees that would have startled their forebears. But most of all, they helped revive public planning through establishing some real designs for land-use, absent almost since the colonial days of Little York.

The move towards planning and spatial control was first effec-tively expressed in "non-residential restrictions," provincially enacted at the city's request in 1904, to enable it to specify location and land use for stores, manufactories, laundries and so forth; and thereafter extended to cover a wide range of other items, from hospitals to dance halls, gas stations to stables and junk shops.[118] This was a highly practical response to the problems of congested urban living, but it soon covered large areas of the city, and led onward to restrictions for residential areas as well. By 1912, accord-ingly, Toronto was prohibiting tenement or apartment houses in most of the latter areas; in fact, zoning was taking form, though not yet explicit.[119] At the same time, more widely general planning schemes emerged, largely deriving from the aesthetic reformism of the Guild of Civic Art. In 1909 they produced a full-size city plan, with new diagonal main arteries, an enlarged park system and waterfront amenities. This was followed by a plan from the coun-cil's Civic Improvement Committee in 1911, a municipal scheme which stressed efficient routes for streetcars, railways and private traffic, but also proposed developing parks, waterfront and a civic centre.[120]

Neither plan saw action, though they did produce University Avenue (the former College Avenue) as a grand roadway. Besides, they led to the City and Suburbs Act of 1912, which required further subdivisions within five miles of the city to be publicly approved, and established a City Surveyor's Office to administer the measure. In consequence, the city gained planning control over land and new street layouts for the first time.[121] And official plan-ning in Toronto took off from here. The urban tract in general was still marked by arrays of poles and overhead electric wires, uneven route development and cluttered locales. But a major civic break had been made into the future. Until depression — and much beyond that, war — rose abruptly in the way.

THE WAR YEARS: SEQUEL AND TRANSITION

From 1914 to 1918 Toronto deeply experienced the carnage of world war, even though remote from battlegrounds. Some 70,000 of its men — a seventh of national enlistments — went into the forces, the weight of its younger male adult population.[122] One in seven did not return, and of those that did, many were so badly wounded that their lives were shattered. The strains on families at home were bitter as well. Never had the city faced human loss and heartbreak on such a scale, or for so long. When it was over, there was pride no less than mourning, and perhaps the assurance of having come through a cruel testing. But the breezy, unlimited optimism of the bright new century was gone forever. An age had closed for a now-maturing metropolitan city.

The outbreak of war with Germany in August 1914 was assuredly greeted with patriotic fervour and renewed optimism. Young men thronged to volunteer at the University Avenue Armouries and other recruiting stations, to get in on a heroic venture overseas before it ended, or at least to escape from the unemployment of the depression since 1913. From 1915, however, when Canadian troops were increasingly committed to the trenches of Europe, the full demands of a murderous, stalemated conflict hit home to Toronto. Not just the casualty lists steadily mounted, but numbers of returning wounded: the old General Hospital and the former Bishop Strachan's School were taken over on a growing list of military hospitals.[123] More columns of soldiers marched to Union Station, the Exhibition held troop depots, the University officers in training. And flying fields were established around the suburbs to provide men for the new warfare of the air, making Toronto the chief aviation centre in Canada.[124] Army recruiting drew increasingly on family men rather than the original young single floaters of 1914, but over 1916 the supply of volunteers began to run short. Hence, the next year most Torontonians grimly approved the national government's adoption of conscription, to share the real costs of patriotism equitably. But the troops departing, the casualty lists arriving, paced their very life. At least they found a popular, responsive wartime civic leader in "Tommy" Church, mayor from 1915 right through 1921. He was there whenever the soldiers left; he knew the men and their next-of-kin to an amazing degree.[125] At last an end came. In November 1918 the signing of an armistice was heralded in the city by factory whistles, church bells, bonfires, and sheer release of emotion. The four-year agony was over.

War had meant a draining emigration, not to be stopped till the troops poured home. Meanwhile, immigration into Toronto had come to a virtual standstill, though in-migration to its war factories rose, and women, above all, entered urban employment in greater numbers. They replaced men in many former jobs, but also filled new places in munition plants, equipment factories and much more. Yet demands for labour still increased, and in due course impelled workers generally to larger and more active union organization.[126] All this did not occur at once; large-scale war production took time to be required and organized, while there was unused capacity left by prewar depression first to be taken up. In fact, a slump lasted well on into 1915, and only by 1916 had the turn-around clearly taken place.

In the subsequent wartime boom, propelled by demands for munitions, the urban economy grew rapidly again and jobs became plentiful. But at the same time, inflation sent living costs upwards over 50 per cent between 1915 and 1919, while food alone climbed by nearly 75 per cent.[127] Housing was heavily overcrowded, thanks to high rents and little new building.[128] Labour strife rose as well, as did outcries against rapacious war profiteers, or demands for government controls on food and basic goods, instituted to some extent in 1917–18 (but following Prohibition, in 1916). Toronto grew feverish, displaying hot suspicions of conspiring foreigners and "socialists" no less than exploiting capitalists or unpatriotic squanderers. Optimism was dead indeed.

Nevertheless, significant economic gains did come out of the city's wartime years. Its investment interests advanced in size and scope. For example, the assets of the Bank of Commerce stood at $467 million by 1919, compared with $537 million for the Bank of Montreal, further reducing the older rival's lead.[129] Toronto's retail trading empires similarly extended, while its transport system was used to the utmost — even though the Canadian Northern Railway, financially strained in the 1913–14 depression and hit by high construction costs, went into crisis, and in 1917 was taken over by the federal government. Yet Toronto manufacturing was especially stimulated. An aircraft industry emerged, mainly in air frames but with engine components; and overall, war production considerably expanded factories, shipyards and power facilities.

New war plants themselves would be mostly as short-lived as the munitions they turned out. Still, the large factories required to fill huge shell contracts, the precision skills demanded, fostered both broader industrial organization and higher technical capacity in

Toronto was a major recruiting and initial training centre during the Great War. Military tents dotted the University campus in 1915 — which then settled down as an officers' school.

Troop train leaving Union Station, 1916. Altogether 70,000 Torontonians served.

On the home front, some Toronto women took up rifle practice, though those who went overseas mainly did so as nurses and nursing aides.

Far more women went into the city's war factories, as here milling shell caps at the Russell Motor Car works.

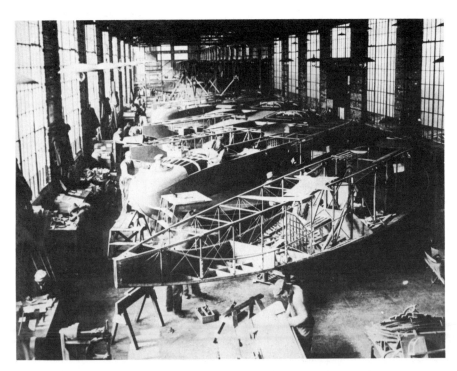

War plants poured out aircraft also. This assembly line at the Canadian Aeroplane Co. produced seaplanes.

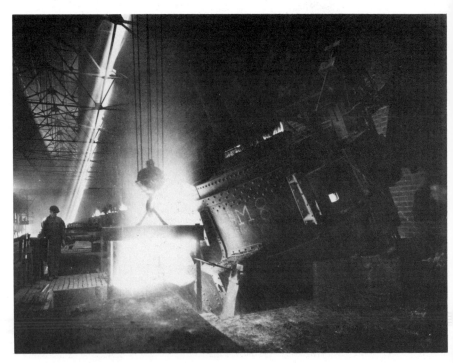

War demands raised heavier industries as well, exemplified in this pouring of steel at British Forgings Ltd., near the waterfront.

Toronto's citizens could let loose at the Armistice, 11 November 1918, in happy hordes like these on King Street.

Toronto. A strong case in point is that of the Imperial Munitions Board (IMB), set up in Canada in 1915 to supply the British government and headed by Joseph Flavelle. He created a network of shell, machining and aircraft plants, with contracts out across the country, but with expertise and management centred in Toronto: "the biggest business that had ever existed in Canada, indeed by mid-1917 the biggest business in North America."[130] Though Flavelle would be more remembered as a pork packer who purveyed bad bacon to soldiers — a sensational press story amply discredited — he was a powerful force in wartime Toronto.[131] If anyone then earned his title it was portly Sir Joseph of the IMB.

By the close of 1918, when the blood-letting had passed, though war's disruptions had not, the chief desire was a swift return to normal. It would not happen, even though many other older patterns of life resumed, and former issues put by in the great ordeal were brushed off for the postwar era. For what was normal — 1913, or 1910, or 1900? Too much had gone on changing, both because of and in spite of the war. For Toronto, it had assuredly meant transition from a bygone youth. Ahead lay a metropolis that counted its residents in millions, not thousands, and was interconnected with a widespread complex of suburban towns. Automobiles would sweepingly refashion its built environment; aircraft, electronic media and new modes of service industry extend still broader hinterland links; social welfare needs and massive civic investment heavily pattern its municipal policies. And the collectivized community, increasingly regulated and regulating, would face far bigger issues of reconciling the claims of mass urban democracy with those of local neighbourhoods or growing ethnic pluralisms.

None of this, of course, was wholly new by the end of 1918. Toronto's population then was nearing the half million mark, and the nucleus of ethnic variety was set firmly in its midst. Its automotive traffic was now expanding fast; the war had engendered the development of aircraft and technological service industries; and the problems of big urban government's relations with citizen-responsive rule had plainly come into view. The war years had been prologue no less than epilogue, as the metropolis moved on towards national primacy. From Simcoe to Jimmy Simpson, Berczy to Joseph Flavelle, was a very long way. Yet 1918 still marked only an end to the beginnings of what human action would do to transform a Lake Ontario locality into a world-scale city.

Looking up the financial mainline, Bay Street, in 1912. At the top of the picture are the Temple Building, Toronto's first real skyscraper, by this date already outclassed, and the City Hall's Romanesque tower, itself being hemmed in by other rising structures.

Aerial view of the heart of the city about 1917. In the foreground, at the foot of the central Yonge Street artery, is the Board of Trade Building's curved front; to the left, across Yonge, the Bank of Montreal. Up Yonge, the major skyscapers rise, including the tallest, the Royal Bank. Just north of it on the east side is the Confederation Life Building. At the top towards the left is the City Hall tower; just below the City Hall, the Temple Building on Bay, and to the right of the City Hall the mass of Eaton's and Simpson's. Down Bay from the Temple Building are banks, insurance headquarters and newspaper offices.

Appendix
Statistical Tables

TABLE I
The Growth of Manufacturing in Toronto, 1871-1921

Year	Population	Number of Firms	Number of Employees	Yearly Payroll ($)	Value of Articles Produced ($)
1871	56,092	530[1]	9,400	2,690,993	13,686,093
1881	86,415	932	13,245	3,876,909	19,562,981
1891	181,216	2,401	26,242	9,638,537	44,963,922
1901	208,040	847	42,515	15,505,466	58,415,498
1911	376,538	1,100	65,274	36,064,815	154,306,948
1921	521,893	—	185,443	205,486,690	—

[1] Table LIV, which provided aggregates for cities, did not provide a category for number of firms in 1871. This figure was arrived at, therefore, by extracting for Toronto individual industries listed by city in Tables XXVIII-LIII of vol. 3 of published *Census* for 1871. Note also that after 1891 the census only counted employees in firms with more than five workers. This might explain somewhat the drop in units at 1901 — but was no less part of the rise of larger-scale plants, as growth in work force numbers makes plain. See Spelt, *Urban Development*, pp. 155-59. See also chapter 4, note 3, p. 208.

Source: *Census of Canada*, 1871-1921.

TABLE IV
Population Growth in Central Canadian Cities, 1851-1921

Year	Toronto	Hamilton	Ottawa	London	Kingston	Montreal City
1851	30,775	14,112	7,760	7,035	11,627	57,715
1861	44,821	19,096	14,669	11,555	13,743	90,323
1871	56,092	26,880	24,141	18,000	12,407	115,000
1881	86,415	36,661	31,307	26,266	14,091	155,238
1891	181,215	48,959	44,154	31,977	19,263	219,616
1901	208,040	52,634	59,928	37,976	17,961	267,730
1911	376,538	81,969	87,062	46,300	18,874	470,480
1921	521,893	114,151	93,740	53,838	24,104	618,506

Note: *Census of 1911*, vol. 1, p. 554, Table XIV, provides figures for 1871-1911 period sometimes at variance with totals provided in other volumes. With the exception of Kingston, 1911 compilations cite larger population totals, but Toronto's here are consistent with those in Tables I and III.

Source: *Census of Canada*, 1851-1921.

TABLE II
Males/Females in Toronto's Population, 1831-1921

Year	Males	Females	Total Population
1831	2,362	1,607	3,969
1841	6,941	7,308	14,249
1851	15,176	15,599	30,775
1861	21,677	23,144	44,821
1871	27,539	28,553	56,092
1881	41,917	44,498	86,415
1891	69,521	74,502	144,023[1]
1901	72,864	83,234	156,098[2]
1911	161,842	165,911	327,753[3]
1921	250,944	270,949	521,893

[1] This was revised to 181,216 in 1901 and subsequent censuses. See chapter 4, note 3, p. 208.
[2] Obviously incomplete figure; total too low for entire city.
[3] The same as above — incomplete. Better ratios shown on p. 426 in vol. 2, *Census of 1911*.

Source: *Census of Canada*, 1871-1921.

TABLE III
Toronto as a Percentage of Ontario Population, 1831-1921

Year	Toronto Population	Ontario Population	Percentage
1831	3,939	236,702	1.6
1841	14,249	455,668	3
1851	30,775	952,004	3
1861	44,821	1,396,091	3
1871	56,092	1,620,851	3.5
1881	86,415	1,923,229	4.5
1891	181,216[1]	2,144,321	8.6
1901	208,040	2,182,947	9.5
1911	376,538	2,523,274	14.9
1921	521,593	2,933,662	17.8

[1] City figure here for 1891 is as revised in 1901.

Source: *Census of Canada*, 1851-1921.

TABLE V
Population Growth in Toronto, 1801-1921[1]

Year	City Population	Numerical Change	Percent Change
1801	681	—	—
1811	1,324	643	94.4
1821[2]	1,559	235	17.7
1831[3]	3,969	2,410	154.6
1841	14,249	10,280	259
1851	30,775	16,526	116
1861	44,821	14,046	45.6
1871	56,092	11,271	25.1
1881	86,415	30,323	54.1
1891	181,216	94,801	109.7
1901	208,040	26,824	14.8
1911	376,538	168,498	80.9
1921	521,893	145,355	38.6

[1] The existent city, not including adjacent suburbs, is covered through this table.
[2] TPL, Minutes of Town Meetings (1801-31 figures).
[3] *Census of Canada*, 1871-1921. *Census of 1871*, vol. 4, substantiates Minutes figures of 1831 and those of 1841-61 in TCA's Statistical Book.

Source: *Census of Canada*, 1851-1921.

TABLE VI
Birthplace of Toronto's Population, 1851-1921

Year	Canadian-Born n	%	British-Born n	%	Foreign-Born n	%	Total
1851	10,423	34	18,432	60	1,920	6	30,775
1861	19,385	43	22,788	51	2,648	6	44,821
1871	28,578	51	24,927	44	2,587	5	56,092
1881	51,489	60	30,469	35	4,457	5	86,415
1891	93,162	65	43,039	30	7,831	5	144,023*
1901	113,972	73	33,338	21	8,476	6	155,786*
1911	205,439	63	91,378	28	30,936	9	327,753*
1921	324,768	62	149,184	29	47,941	9	521,893

* The table bases again gave lower city totals than these figures.

Source: *Census of Canada*, 1851-1921.

TABLE VII
Major Religious Affiliations of Toronto's Population, 1841-1921

Religion	1841 n	%	1851 n	%	1861 n	%	1871 n	%	1881 n	%	1891 n	%	1901 n	%	1911 n	%	1921 n	%
Church of England	6,754	47	11,577	37	14,125	32	20,668	37	30,913	36	46,084	32	46,442	30	101,856	32	92,328	31
Roman Catholic	2,401	17	7,940	25	12,135	27	11,881	21	15,716	18	21,830	15	23,699	15	43,080	14	41,908	14
Methodist: All Types	1,929	14	4,123	13	6,999	16	9,586	17	16,357	19	32,505	23	35,130	23	63,084	20	43,004	15
Church of Scotland	1,503	11	1,061	3	2,893	6	1,268	2.3	45	.005	27,449	19	30,812	20	65,339	21	58,779	20
Presbyterian	483	3	4,483	14	3,711	8	7,714	14	14,567	17								
Baptist	430	3	948	3	1,288	3	1,953	4	3,667	4	6,909	5	3,148	5	17,548	6	12,734	4
Lutheran	—		40	.13	167	.4	343	.6	494	.6	728	.5	833	.5	2,525	.8	1,008	.3
Jewish	3	.02	57	.18	153	.3	157	.2	534	.6	1,425	.10	3,038	2	6,719	2	31,468	11
Congregational	404	3	646	2	826	2	1,186	2	2,018	2.3	3,102	2.2	2,613	2	3,453	1	1,792	1
Other	342	2	900	3	2,524	6	1,336	2	2,104	2.4	3,991	3	5,383	3	13,249	4	11,882	4
Totals	14,249		30,775		44,821		56,092		86,415		144,023		156,098		316,853		294,903	

Note: Censuses of 1901, 1911 and 1921 show increasing fragmentation of population in religious persuasions, and totals bear no relation to actual population of Toronto but presumably reflect only those who participated in this part of the census. That of 1891 shows the "low" total, later revised to 181,216.

Sources: ICA, Statistical Book of the City of Toronto; *Census of Canada*, 1861-1921.

TABLE VIII
Ethnic Origins of Toronto's Population, 1851-1921

Group	1851 n	1851 %	1861 n	1861 %	1871 n	1871 %	1881[1] n	1881[1] %	1901 n	1901 %	1911 n	1911 %	1921 n	1921 %
Asian	—	—	—	—	—	—	10	.01	219	.1	1,111	.3	2,149	.4
British	29,793	96.8	41,738	93.1	53,603	95.6	80,750	93.4	190,788	91.7	· 325,173	86.4	445,230	85.3
French	467	1.5	501	1.1	572	1	1,230	1.4	3,015	1.5	4,886	1.3	8,350	1.6
German	113	.3	336	.7	985	1.8	2,049	2.4	6,028	3	9,775	2.6	4,689	.9
Netherlanders	—	—			62	.1	163	.19	737	.4	1,639	.4	3,961	.8
Italian	—	—	22	.04	34	.06	104	.12	1,054	.5	4,617	1.2	8,217	1.6
Jewish	—	—	156	.3	11	.01	124	.14	3,090	1.5	18,237	4.8	34,619	6.6
Polish	—	—	23	.05	81	.1	132	.15			700	.2	2,380	.5
Russian	—	—							142	.07	693	.2	1,332	.3
Scandinavian[2]	—	—	7	.01	20	.03	89	.10	253	.12	1,079	.3	1,844	.4
Ukrainian	—	—	—	—	—	—	—	—	—	—	—	—	1,149	.2
Others	402	1.31	2,038	5	724	1.3	1,764	2.1	2,714	1.3	8,628	2.3	7,973	1.5
Totals	30,775	100	44,821	100	56,092	100	86,415	100	208,040	100	376,538	100	521,893	100

[1] 1891 census figures not relevant. Breakdown then gave: natives 32,534; natives with a foreign father 60,628; foreign-born 50,861. Total: 144,023 — the smaller figure again.
[2] Includes Norway, Sweden, Denmark, Finland, Iceland.

Source: *Census of Canada*, 1851-1921.

TABLE IX
Age Composition of Toronto's Population, 1831-1921

Year	Population	Under 16	Over 16
1831	3,969	1,905	2,064
1841	14,249	6,348	7,901

Year	Population	0-15	15-40	40-60	60+	Not Given
1851	30,775	11,885	14,365	3,722	634	169
1861	44,821	16,144	21,072	6,010	1,399	196
1871[1]	56,092	21,478	24,887	7,798	1,911	18

Year	Population	0-14	15-44	45-64	65+	Not Given
1881	86,415	28,339	45,436	10,132	2,387	121
1891	159,288	59,008	78,026	17,597	4,038	619
1901	234,441[2]	55,041	85,592	87,472	6,316	290
1921	521,893	139,757	274,215	86,537	20,482	902

[1] 1871 listed its categories as: 0-16; 16-41; 41-61; 61+.
[2] 1911 did not provide age breakdown for the general population.

Source: *Census of Canada*, 1851-1921. Population totals here do not always correspond to figures in Table V, etc. — again data base variants.

TABLE X
Value of Building Permits Issued
in City of Toronto, 1901-14

Year	Value of Permits ($)
1901	3,568,883
1902	3,854,903
1903	4,356,457
1904	5,900,000
1905	10,347,910
1906	13,160,396
1907	14,225,800
1908	11,795,436
1909	18,139,000
1910	21,127,000
1911	24,374,539[1]
1912	27,401,761
1913	27,038,624
1914	20,858,443

[1] In 1906-11 Toronto was the most active of all Canadian cities in building (*Labour Gazette*, May 1910).

Sources: *Canadian Finance*, *Labour Gazette*, and *Monetary Times Annual Review*.

TABLE XI
Bank Clearings in Toronto, 1895-1918

Year	Value of Clearings ($)
1895	306,239,000
1900	513,629,628
1905	1,047,490,701
1910	1,593,954,254
1914	2,013,055,664
1918	3,379,864,506

Source: *Monetary Times Annual Review*, 1919, vol. 62, p. 54.

TABLE XII
City of Toronto Assessments, 1834-1921

Year	Population	Assessed Totals
1834	9,254	£3,450[1]
1841	14,249	£81,610
1851	30,775	£186,983
1861	44,821	$1,600,000
1871	56,092	$29,600,000
1881	86,415	$53,379,634
1891	181,216	$132,402,383
1901	208,040	$128,271,583[2]
1911	376,538	$309,147,053
1921	521,893	$697,418,435

[1] 1834 includes Statute Labour £1,014.

[2] 1901. There is no explanation in either source as to why figure is lower.

Sources: TCA, Statistical Book of the City of Toronto for 1834–51 especially; TCA, City Council Minutes Appendices for 1861-1921. Where possible, revised totals ascertained after Court of Revision had considered appeals have been used. These figures were often lower than those cited in TCA's Statistical Book, which were before revisions took place.

TABLE XIII
City of Toronto Mayors, 1934-1921

1834	William Lyon Mackenzie
1835	Robert Baldwin Sullivan
1836	Thomas D. Morrison
1837	George Gurnett
1838-40	John Powell
1841	George Monro
1842-44	Henry Sherwood
1845-47	William Henry Boulton
1848-50	George Gurnett
1851-53	John George Bowes
1854	Joshua George Beard
1855	George William Allan
1856	John Beverley Robinson
1857	John Hutchison
1858	William Henry Boulton
1858	David Breakenridge Read
1859-60	Adam Wilson
1861-63	John George Bowes
1864-66	Francis H. Medcalf
1867-68	James E. Smith
1869-70	Samuel Bickerton Harman
1871-72	Joseph Sheard
1873	Alexander Manning
1874-75	Francis H. Medcalf
1876-78	Angus Morrison
1879-80	James Beaty Jr.
1881-82	William B. McMurrich
1883-84	Arthur R. Boswell
1885	Alexander Manning
1886-87	William H. Howland
1888-91	Edward F. Clarke
1892-93	Robert J. Fleming
1894-95	Warring Kennedy
1896-97	Robert J. Fleming
1897-99	John Shaw
1900	Ernest A. Macdonald
1901-2	Oliver Aikin Howland
1903-5	Thomas Urquhart
1906-7	Emerson Coatsworth
1908-9	Joseph Oliver
1910-12	George R. Geary
1912-14	Horatio C. Hocken
1915-21	Thomas Langton Church

Sources: TCA, City of Toronto Municipal Handbook; Victor Russell, *Mayors of Toronto, 1834-99* (Erin, Ont., 1982).

Notes

Abbreviations

CHR   *Canadian Historical Review*
DCB   *Dictionary of Canadian Biography*
OH   *Ontario History*
PAC   Public Archives of Canada
PAO   Public Archives of Ontario
TCA   Toronto City Archives
TPL   Metropolitan Toronto Public Library
UHR   *Urban History Review*

INTRODUCTION

1 Percy J. Robinson, *Toronto During the French Regime, 1615–1793* (Toronto, 1933; reprinted 1965), pp. 1–3, 6–9, 221–25.

2 Ibid., pp. 14–42, 46–50.

3 Ibid., pp. 100–27.

4 Jacob Spelt, *Toronto* (Toronto, 1973), p. 17. As the purchase terms were too informally drawn, a deed of conveyance was renegotiated in 1805. See Anthony Hall, "The Red Man's Burden: Land, Law and the Lord in Upper Canada" (Ph.D. thesis, University of Toronto, 1984).

5 Robinson, *Toronto During the French Regime*, pp. 175–76.

6 E. A. Cruickshank, ed., *The Simcoe Papers*, 5 vols. (Toronto, 1912–31), 1: 339 (Simcoe to Clarke, 1793).

7 Spelt, *Toronto*, pp. 4–8. See for following environmental aspects.

8 Ibid., pp. 12–16.

9 Ibid., pp. 14, 18.

10 J. M. S. Careless, "Metropolis and Region: The Interplay Between City and Region in Canadian History," *UHR* 78, no. 3 (1979): 108–18.

CHAPTER ONE

1 M. Q. Innis, ed., *Mrs. Simcoe's Diary* (Toronto, 1965), p. 101.

2 Ibid., map illustration, following p. 92.

3 Cruikshank, ed., *Simcoe Papers*, 1: 144 (Simcoe to Dundas, 1792).

4 E. G. Firth, ed., *The Town of York, 1793–1815* (Toronto, 1962), p.4. (Simcoe to Clarke, 1793).

5 Cruikshank, *Simcoe Papers*, 2: 57 (Simcoe to Dundas, 1793).

6 Ibid., 2: 46 (General Order, 26 August 1793).

7 John André, *William Berczy, Co-Founder of Toronto* (Toronto, 1967), pp. 36–40.

8 Firth, *1793–1815*, p. 27.

9 Cruikshank, *Simcoe Papers*, 4: 202 (Circular Letter, 28 February 1796).

10 Firth, *1793–1815*, p. lxxvii.

11 Ibid., pp. 114–41.

12 Ibid., p. lxxvii.

13 In absence of records, figures are best choices between estimates that range from a clearly low 10,000 for 1791 to a probably high 100,000 for 1812.

14 Jacob Spelt, *The Urban Development in South-Central Ontario* (Assen, 1955), pp. 27, 29–30.

15 Firth, *1793–1815*, p. iv.

16 Ibid., pp. lv–lviii.

17 Ibid., p. xxxix.

18 Proclamation of Peter Hunter, 3 November 1803, quoted in Henry Scadding, *Toronto of Old*, ed. F. H. Armstrong (Toronto, 1966), p. 15.

19 Mary Shortt, "From Douglas to the Black Crook: A History of Toronto Theatre, 1809–1874" (M.A. thesis, Toronto, 1977), pp. 1–4.

20 John Mitchell, *The Settlement of York County* (n.p., n.d., 1950?), p. 14.

21 Firth, *1793–1815*, p. lxxvi.

22 E. W. Hounsom, *Toronto in 1810* (Toronto, 1970), pp. 28–34. See throughout for prewar-built environment.

23 Firth, *1793–1815*, p. lxxviii.

24 Ibid.

25 Ibid., p. xlix.

26 Ibid., p. lxxxiii.

27 Ibid., p. xlvi.

28 Charles W. Humphries, "The Capture of York," *OH* 51, no. 1 (1959): 2–12.

29 Ibid., pp. 13–21.

30 Firth, *1793-1815*, p. lxxxviii.

31 E. G. Firth, *The Town of York, 1815-1834* (Toronto, 1966) p. lxxxii.

32 T. W. Acheson, "York Commerce in the 1820's," *CHR* 50, no. 4 (1969): 415-16.

33 Firth, *1815-34*, pp. xxv-xxvi.

34 G. M. Craig, *Upper Canada: The Formative Years* (Toronto, 1963), pp. 161-62.

35 Firth, *1815-34*, pp. xxx-xxxi.

36 G. P. de T. Glazebrook, *The Story of Toronto* (Toronto, 1971), p. 54.

37 Ibid., p. 59.

38 E. C. Guillet, *Early Life in Upper Canada* (Toronto, 1933), p. 553.

39 R. M. Baldwin and J. Baldwin, *The Great Experiment* (Don Mills, 1969), p. 106.

40 Firth, *1814-34*, p. lxxxii.

41 Ibid., *Census of Canada, 1870-71*, vol. 4 (Ottawa, 1876), p. 86.

42 Provincial rate is calculated in regression from censuses of 1824 and 1825 (pp. 83-86 in above *Census* volume), weighed with estimates for 1812 and 1820.

43 See H. I. Cowan, *British Emigration to British North America* (Toronto, 1928; reprinted 1961); Craig, *Upper Canada*, pp. 124-31; and R. L. Jones, *History of Agriculture in Ontario* (Toronto, 1946; reprinted 1977), pp. 50-62.

44 Firth, *1815-34*, p. lxv.

45 Ibid., pp. liv-lix.

46 Scadding, *Toronto of Old*, pp. 221, 279-80.

47 C. J. Houston and W. J. Smyth, *The Sash Canada Wore* (Toronto, 1980), p. 18.

48 Firth, *1815-34*, p. xxxvii.

CHAPTER TWO

1 H. C. Pentland, *Labour and Capital in Canada, 1650-1860* (Toronto, 1981), Table III, p. 82.

2 Cowan, *British Emigration*, Appendix B, p. 289.

3 Ibid.

4 Firth, *1815-34*, p. lxxxii.

5 G. P. de T. Glazebrook, *History of Transportation in Canada* (Toronto, 1938), p. 142.

6 Firth, *1815-34*, pp. xxvi-xxvii.

7 Douglas McCalla, *The Upper Canada Trade, 1834-1872: A Study of the Buchanans' Business* (Toronto, 1979), pp. 20-28.

8 Firth, *1815-34*, pp. xxvii-xxviii.

9 *Courier of Upper Canada* (York), 29 September 1832.

10 Firth, *1815-34*, pp. xxvi-xxvii; F. H. Armstrong, "Toronto in Transition: The Emergence of a City, 1828-1838" (Ph.D. thesis, Toronto 1965), pp. 378-82.

11 Firth, *1815-34*, pp. xxxii, 66, 80; George Walton, *York Commercial Directory* (York, 1833).

12 *Colonial Advocate* (York), 4 July 1833.

13 Armstrong, "Toronto," pp. 418-19.

14 F. H. Armstrong, "Hugh Richardson," *DCB* (Toronto, 1976), 9: 657.

15 Armstrong, "Toronto," p. 406.

16 Firth, *1815-34*, p. xxvii.

17 Armstrong, "Toronto," p. 482. The firm is now in the Royal Insurance Group.

18 Ibid., pp. 482-83.

19 Ibid., p. 455.

20 Ibid., pp. 458, 468, 471.

21 Geoffrey Bilson, *A Darkened House: Cholera in Nineteenth Century Canada* (Toronto, 1980), pp. 57, 86.

22 Firth, *1815-34*, p. lxiv.

23 Ibid.

24 Paul Romney, "Voters under the Microscope: A Quantitative Meditation on the Toronto Parliamentary Poll Book of 1836" (Paper given at Canadian Historical Association, 1983), p. 37 and throughout.

25 Firth, *1815-34*, p. lxx.

26 Ibid., pp. lxxiv-lxxvii.

27 Armstrong, "Toronto," pp. 84-97.

28 Firth, *1815-34*, p. lxxxii.

29 Armstrong, "Toronto," p. 24. See pages 14-44 for cityscape of 1834.

30 Eric Arthur, *Toronto, No Mean City* (Toronto, 1964), p. 40.

31 Firth, *1815-34*, p. xlix.

32 Arthur, *No Mean City*, p. 248; Graham MacInnes, *Canadian Art* (Toronto, 1950), p. 28.

33 J. R. Robertson, *Landmarks of Toronto*, 6 vols. (Toronto, 1894-1914), 3: 756; E. C. Guillet, *Toronto from Trading Post to Great City* (Toronto, 1934), pp. 362-63.

34 Firth, *1815-34*, pp. xxxiii-xxxiv.

35 Armstrong, "Toronto," pp. 487-89.

36 Ibid., pp. 106-7.

37 Ibid., pp. 118-32, 149-56, 171-73. See also P. Romney, "William Lyon Mackenzie as Mayor of Toronto", *CHR* 56, no. 4 (1975): 416-36.

38 Armstrong, "Toronto," pp. 192-96, 201-6; TCA, Journals of Council, 23 June 1835.

39 *Courier of Upper Canada*, 14 January 1836.

40 TCA, Minutes of Council, 19 January 1837; R. B. Splane, *Social Welfare in Ontario, 1791-1893* (Toronto, 1965), pp. 70-73.

41 Armstrong, "Toronto," pp. 236-37; TCA, Journals of Council, 12 January 1838.

42 Craig, *Upper Canada*, p. 243.

43 Ibid., pp. 244-47.

44 Armstrong, "Toronto," pp. 272-73.

45 G. F. G. Stanley, *Canada's Soldiers, 1604-1954* (Toronto, 1954), pp. 202-3.

46 J. M. S. Careless, "James Lesslie," *DCB* (Toronto, 1982), 11: 517.

47 Armstrong, "Toronto," pp. 261, 274-75.

48 Ibid., pp. 276-79.

49 Cowan, *British Emigration,* Appendix B, p. 289.

50 *Patriot* (Toronto), 9 and 12 February 1841; B. D. Dyster, "Toronto 1840-1860" (Ph.D. thesis, Toronto, 1970), pp. 9-12.

51 J. M. S. Careless, *The Union of the Canadas, 1841-1857* (Toronto, 1967), p. 28.

52 J. E. Middleton, *The Municipality of Toronto,* 3 vols. (Toronto, 1923), 1: 228.

53 TCA, Report of the Committee on Fire, Gas and Water, 1847.

54 Arthur, *No Mean City,* p. 79.

55 R. H. Bonnycastle, *The Canadas in 1841,* 2 vols. (London, 1842), 1: 107-8.

56 Quoted in Peter Baskerville, "Donald Bethune's Steamboat Business," *OH* 67, no. 3 (1975): 141.

57 Quoted in Middleton, *Municipality of Toronto,* 2: 679 (Dickens to John Foster, 1842).

58 *Patriot,* 3 April 1841.

59 G. Brown, *Toronto City and Home District Directory* (Toronto, 1846).

60 Cowan, *British Emigration,* Appendix B; Dyster, "Toronto 1840-1860," pp. 36-37.

61 Dyster, "Toronto 1840-1860," pp. 36-37.

62 Spelt, *Urban Development,* pp. 78-79; Dyster, "Toronto 1840-1860," pp. 23-24.

63 M. L. Smith, ed., *Young Mr. Smith in Upper Canada* (Toronto, 1980), pp. 110-11.

CHAPTER THREE

1 Smith, *Young Mr. Smith,* pp. 11-12.

2 Norman Macdonald, *Canada: Immigration and Colonization, 1841-1903* (Toronto, 1966), p. 61.

3 Heather MacDougall, "Health Is Wealth: Development of Public Health Activity in Toronto, 1834-1890" (Ph.D. thesis, Toronto, 1981), pp. 59-64.

4 *British Colonist* (Toronto), 7 September 1847.

5 Ibid., 2 November 1847.

6 Ibid.

7 PAO, Toronto City Council Papers, 1834-96, Jarvis to Boulton, 20 August 1847.

8 *British Colonist,* 31 August 1847.

9 Ibid., 8 February 1848.

10 Ibid., October 23, 1849; Bilson, *Darkened House,* p. 128

11 MacDougall, "Health Is Wealth," p. 74.

12 Cowan, *British Emigration,* Appendix B, p. 289.

13 *Census of the Canadas, 1851-52* (Quebec, 1853), vol. 1, pp. 30-31.

14 Ibid., pp. 66-67.

15 *Census of the Canadas, 1860-61* (Quebec, 1864), vol. 1, pp. 256-57.

16 J. M. S. Careless, *Brown of the Globe* (Toronto, 1959), vol. 1, pp. 123-38; Dyster, "Toronto, 1840-1860," pp. 361-67, 372, 449-59.

17 M. W. Nicolson, "The Other Toronto: Irish Catholics in a Victorian City, 1850-1900," to be published in R. F. Harney, ed., "*Meeting-Place: Peoples and Neighbourhoods of Toronto*" (Toronto, expected 1984).

18 Ibid., pp. 23-26.

19 I. C. Pemberton, "The Anti-Slavery Society of Canada" (M.A. thesis, Toronto, 1967), especially pp. 17-75, 113-39.

20 Nicolson, "The Other Toronto," pp. 24-27.

21 Ibid., pp. 32-38.

22 See Table VI.

23 G. W. Quinn, "Impact of European Immigration Upon the Elementary Schools of Central Toronto 1815-1915" (M.A. thesis, Toronto, 1968), Tables 5, 6.

24 *Census of Canada, 1870-71* (Ottawa, 1873), vol. 1, pp. 350-51.

25 Ibid., pp. 114-17.

26 Dyster, "Toronto, 1840-1860," p. 20.

27 C. C. Taylor, *Toronto "Called Back" from 1886 to 1850* (Toronto, 1886), Tables of Trade, p. 236.

28 *Globe* (Toronto), 5 February 1853.

29 Pentland, *Labour and Capital,* pp. 187-88.

30 *Globe,* 2 July 1853, 6 June 1854. See also S. F. Zerker, *The Rise and Fall of the Toronto Typographical Union* (Toronto, 1982), pp. 31-37, 44-47; and G. S. Kealey, *Toronto Workers Respond to Industrial Capitalism, 1867-1892* (Toronto, 1980), for other skilled trades reactions in the 1850s; e.g., shoemakers (pp. 38-39) and tailors' strike of 1852 (pp. 39-40).

31 Unskilled labour rates rose 40 per cent, e.g., largely due to railway demands: W. T. Easterbrook and H. G. J. Aitken, *Canadian Economic History* (Toronto, 1956), p. 311.

32 Kealey, *Toronto Workers,* pp. 66, 77.

33 Based on examination of shipment notices, market reports and store advertisements in Toronto press for 1850-51, plus hinterland transport services recorded, e.g., in W. H. Smith, *Canada Past, Present and Future,* 2 vols. (Toronto, 1851).

34 *Globe,* 19 March 1860.

35 Spelt, *Toronto,* pp. 24-31.

36 Careless, *Brown,* 1: 229-33.

37 Spelt, *Urban Development,* pp. 121-22.

38 Ibid., pp. 100-1.

39 *Globe*, 21 December 1855.

40 Spelt, *Urban Development*, p. 124. D. McCalla, "The Decline of Hamilton as a Wholesale Centre," *OH* 65, no. 4 (1973): 250-51.

41 Michael Bliss, "John Macdonald," *DCB*, 11: 551-52.

42 D. McCalla, "The Commercial Politics of the Toronto Board of Trade, 1850-1860," *CHR* 50, no. 1, (1969): 51-67.

43 Dyster, "Toronto, 1840-1860," pp. 277-79. See also for insurance and loan companies, pages 280-92.

44 R. D. Smith, "The Northern Railway: Its Origins and Construction," *OH* 48, no. 1 (1956): 26-27.

45 *Globe*, 12 February 1866. Note Gzowski and Macpherson also pushed the abortive cotton mill project: see TCA, Minutes of City Council, 1861, Appendix 27; 1864, Appendix 105.

46 R. D. Smith, "The Northern Railway," pp. 31-32.

47 Gene Allen, "Competition and Consolidation in the Toronto Wholesale Trade" (Research paper, University of Toronto, 1862), pp. 9-11.

48 Province of Canada, *Sessional Papers*, 1860, 1861, Tables of Trade; Dominion of Canada, *Sessional Papers*, 1870, 1871, Tables of Trade.

49 McCalla, "Board of Trade," pp. 58-59.

50 Dyster, "Toronto, 1840-1860," pp. 271-76.

51 D. C. Masters, "Toronto vs. Montreal: The Struggle for Financial Hegemony, 1860-75," *CHR* 12, no. 2 (1944): 133-46.

52 Malcolm Davidson, "The Port of Toronto, 1850-1860" (Research paper, University of Toronto, 1982), pp. 31-36.

53 TCA, Statutes specially relating to the City of Toronto, pp. 243-47.

54 Robertson, *Landmarks*, 3: 322-45.

55 F. H. Armstrong, "The First Great Fire of Toronto," *OH* 53, no. 1 (1961): 201-21.

56 See *Globe*, "Pictorial Supplement," 13 December 1856, for descriptions of these buildings. See also Arthur, *No Mean City*, for buildings named below.

57 L. H. Pursley, *Street Railways in Toronto* (Los Angeles, 1958), pp. 5-7.

58 PAC, Pamphlet 1016, *Esplanade Contract*, Public letter, 1855, pp. 1-8.

59 For the following account of this expansion of the Fifies and Sixties, see ibid., especially pp. 164-69; P. G. Goheen, *Victorian Toronto, 1850-1900* (Chicago, 1970), especially pp. 53-54, 81-90, 115-55. See also Spelt, *Toronto*, pp. 41-47; Robertson, *Landmarks*; and W. C. F. Caverhill, *Toronto City Directory, 1859-60* (Toronto, n.d.).

60 Dyster, "Toronto, 1840-1860," pp. 157, 168-69.

61 Spelt, *Toronto*, pp. 42-43.

62 Goheen, *Victorian Toronto*, pp. 125-27.

63 Quoted in Taylor, *Toronto "Called Back,"* p. 161.

64 Spelt, *Toronto*, p. 47.

65 The city received Crown licence to occupy the land for leasing in 1848, though did not gain complete control and begin letting private lots until 1867.

66 Glazebrook, *Story of Toronto*, p. 120.

67 Ibid., pp. 120-21.

68 Armstrong, "Rebuilding of Toronto," pp. 248-49.

69 J. C. E. Williams, "The Growth of the Toronto Police Force, 1793-1875" (Research paper, University of Toronto, 1981), p. 9.

70 J. Scadding and J. C. Dent, *Toronto, Past and Present* (Toronto, 1884), p. 213.

71 Williams, "Growth," p. 12; TCA, Council Minutes, 2 April 1855.

72 Williams, "Growth," pp. 24-28, 31-34, 38-40.

73 Splane, *Social Welfare*, pp. 72-73, 75, 76-77, 80.

74 Ibid., pp. 223-24, 226-27.

75 *Globe*, 11 December 1851.

76 H. M. Cochrane, ed., *Centennial Story: The Board of Education for the City of Toronto* (Toronto, 1950), pp. 35-38, 42-43, 57-58, 143; Quinn, "Impact," pp. 32-35.

77 MacDougall, "Health Is Wealth," pp. 77-84, 97-106, 120-25.

78 TCA, Proceedings of the Standing Committee on Fire, Water and Gas in Connection with the Supply of Water to the City, 1854.

79 Middleton, *Municipality of Toronto*, 1: 261.

80 TCA, Public Works Department, "Outline History of the Roads in Toronto."

81 Dyster, "Toronto, 1840-1860," pp. 343-44.

82 Ibid., pp. 236-37.

83 Ibid., pp. 345-50.

84 Ibid., throughout, but especially pp. 454-59.

85 Careless, *Brown*, 1: 229, 233, 236-37.

86 Ibid., 1: 177; 2: 5, 41, 68.

87 Ibid., 1: 234-36, 314-22; 2: 247-51.

88 D. C. Masters, *The Rise of Toronto, 1850-1890* (Toronto, 1947), p. 80.

89 *Globe* 1 August 1856.

90 Careless, *Brown*, 2: 161.

91 *Leader* (Toronto), 2 July 1867.

92 C. S. Stacey, "Fenianism and the Rise of National Feeling in Canada at the Time of Confederation," *CHR* 12, no. 3 (1931): 250-52; G. T. Denison, *The Fenian Raid on Fort Erie* (Toronto, 1866), Appendix B.

93 Kane did 100 pictures for Allan by 1856 for $20,000. See *DCB*, 10: 392.

94 Shortt, "From Douglas to the Black Crook."

CHAPTER FOUR

1 Goheen, *Victorian Toronto*, pp. 154-55, 201-6, 219-22. Goheen effectively closes this period of industrialization at 1899. I prefer to end it at 1895, to distinguish a new phase emerging thereafter which brought a

high cycle of world prosperity, the settling of a new western Canadian hinterland, and the rise of financial metropolitanism in Toronto on a scale not witnessed in the phase preceding, stamped as that was much more by industrial developments. Of course the city's industrial growth by no means failed to move onward after 1895, and in this respect the choice of 1899, 1900 or 1914 would equally not mark an end.

2 See Table V. Remember that census records may evince discrepancies. The census of 1891 gives 144,023 for Toronto's total population (1: 370) but the 1891 count was revised in the census of 1901 to 181,216 (1: 22). The revised figure also relates better to the city's own assessment count for 1891, 167,439 (TCA, Statistical Book), and covered annexed areas.

3 See Table I. Again one must warn about discrepancies. Goheen (p. 66) gives 497 industrial units for 1871 (taken from *Census of 1871*, 3: 290–445); Kealey (*Toronto Workers*, p. 32) lists 561. But here both record variants and questions of evaluation arise — e.g., should 8 "painters and glaziers" then employing 36 men and 3 boys in Toronto (*Census of 1871*, 3: 376) be included under manufacturing firms? Accordingly, my total comes best to 530.

4 See Table I.

5 *Globe*, 12 February 1866. See also Michael Bliss, *A Canadian Millionaire . . . Sir Joseph Flavelle, Bart, 1858–1938* (Toronto, 1978), p. 52.

6 Kealey, *Toronto Workers*, pp. 25, 27, 30.

7 Ibid., pp. 24–30.

8 *Encyclopedia of Music in Canada* (Toronto, 1981), pp. 423–24.

9 J. M. Gilmour, *Spatial Evolution of Manufacturing: Southern Ontario, 1851–1891* (Toronto, 1972), pp. 32–34, 89–90, 99–100, 110–11; Jane Jacobs, *The Economy of Cities* (Toronto, 1970), pp. 146–62; Taylor, *Toronto "Called Back,"* p. 247.

10 Gene Allen, "Merchants and Manufacturers in Toronto, 1865–1900" (Research paper, York University, 1979), pp. 15–18, 35–36, 40–68, 84–90.

11 Masters, *Rise of Toronto*, p. 63.

12 Ibid., p. 106.

13 *Monetary Times* (Toronto), 2 February 1877.

14 J. E. MacNab, "Toronto's Industrial Growth to 1891," *OH* 47, no. 2 (1955): 74.

15 Ibid., p. 73.

16 Kealey, *Toronto Workers*, pp. 30–31.

17 MacNab, "Toronto's Industrial Growth," p. 73; Masters, *Rise of Toronto*, p. 175.

18 Kealey, *Toronto Workers*, p. 30.

19 Ibid., p. 32.

20 Telephones, too, were stringing wires and poles by then.

21 MacNab, "Toronto's Industrial Growth," p. 75.

22 Carlie Oreskovich, *Sir Henry Pellatt: The King of Casa Loma* (Toronto, 1982), pp. 52–53.

23 Taylor, *Toronto "Called Back,"* pp. 249–53, 402–7.

24 Kealey, *Toronto Workers*, p. 317.

25 Taylor, *Toronto "Called Back,"* pp. 324–25; *Globe*, 16 May 1885.

26 Allen, "Competition and Consolidation," p. 24.

27 Ibid., pp. 35–39, 45.

28 *Toronto Board of Trade, Annual Report, 1886* (Toronto, 1887), p. 10; *Board of Trade Report for 1895* (Toronto, 1896), pp. 10, 45; Taylor, *Toronto "Called Back,"* p. 236.

29 Allen, "Competition and Consolidation," p. 43; *Monetary Times*, 5 September 1890.

30 Allen, "Competition and Consolidation," p. 33.

31 Taylor, *Toronto "Called Back,"* p. 310.

32 Bliss, *Flavelle*, p. 63.

33 Brenda K. Newell, "Toronto's Retail Trade, 1869–1914" (Research paper, University of Toronto, 1981), p. 6.

34 Ibid., pp. 5–8.

35 Bliss, *Flavelle*, p. 63.

36 Newell, "Toronto's Retail Trade," p. 7.

37 Ibid., p. 14.

38 Ibid., p. 16.

39 Bliss, *Flavelle*, pp. 63–64.

40 On banking growth, see R. C. McIvor, *Canadian Banking and Fiscal Development* (Toronto, 1958); E. P. Neufeld, *Money and Banking in Canada* (Toronto, 1964); Victor Ross, *A History of the Canadian Bank of Commerce*, 2 vols. (Toronto, 1920–22).

41 *Monetary Times*, 30 July 1880; 25 July 1890.

42 Masters, *Rise of Toronto*, p. 181.

43 Ibid., pp. 122, 183.

44 Ibid., p. 182.

45 For membership on boards of directors of Toronto banks, finance and insurance companies, see yearly Toronto City Directories for the period.

46 *Globe*, 24 January 1877; 4 May 1885.

47 See chapter 5.

48 T. F. McIlwraith, "George Laidlaw," *DCB* (1972), 10: 481–83.

49 R. M. Stamp, "J. D. Edgar and the Pacific Junction Railway," *OH* 55, no. 3 (1963): 119–30.

50 Masters, *Rise of Toronto*, p. 173.

51 Paul Marsden, "The Development of Toronto Harbour, 1850–1911" (Research paper, University of Toronto, 1982), pp. 22–23, 26.

52 Ibid., pp. 8, 24.

53 Ibid., pp. 28, 30.

54 See F. N. Mellen, "The Development of the Toronto Waterfront during the Railway Expansion Era, 1850–1912" (Ph.D. thesis, Toronto, 1976).

55 Goheen, *Victorian Toronto*, p. 77.

56 See Table VI. *Census of 1891*, 1: 348–49.

Skills Tested by Reading Test Questions	
Information and Ideas	Close reading, citing textual evidence, determining central ideas and themes
Summarizing	Understanding relationships, interpreting words and phrases in context
Rhetoric	Analyzing word choice, assessing overall text structure, assessing part-whole relationships, analyzing point of view, determining purpose, analyzing arguments
Synthesis	Analyzing multiple texts, analyzing quantitative information

THE PSAT WRITING & LANGUAGE TEST

The PSAT Writing & Language Test will focus on your ability to revise and edit text from a range of content areas.

PSAT Writing & Language Test Overview	
Timing	35 minutes
Questions	44 passage-based multiple-choice questions
Passages	4 single passages with 11 questions each
Passage Length	400–450 words per passage

The PSAT Writing & Language Test will contain four single passages, one from each of the following subject areas: Careers, Humanities, History/Social Studies, and Science.

Writing & Language Passage Types	
Careers	Hot topics in "major fields of work" such as information technology and healthcare
Humanities	Arts and letters
History/Social Studies	Discussion of historical or social sciences topics such as anthropology, communication studies, economics, education, human geography, law, linguistics, political science, psychology, and sociology
Science	Exploration of concepts, findings, and discoveries in the natural sciences including Earth science, biology, chemistry, and physics

Passages will also vary in the "type" of text. A passage can be an argument, an informative or explanatory text, or a nonfiction narrative.

Writing & Language Passage Text Type Distribution	
Argument	1–2 passages
Informative/Explanatory Text	1–2 passages
Nonfiction Narrative	1 passage

Some passages and/or questions will refer to one or more informational graphics that represent data. Questions associated with these graphical representations will ask you to revise and edit the passage based on the data presented in the graphic.

The most prevalent question format on the PSAT Writing & Language Test will ask you to choose the best of three alternatives to an underlined portion of the passage or to decide that the current version is the best option. You will be asked to improve the development, organization, and diction in the passages to ensure they conform to conventional standards of English grammar, usage, and style.

Skills Tested by Writing & Language Test Questions	
Expression of Ideas (24 questions)	Development, organization, and effective language use
Standard English Conventions (20 questions)	Sentence structure, conventions of usage, and conventions of punctuation

TEST-TAKING STRATEGIES

You have already learned about the overall structure of the PSAT as well as the structure of the three tests it entails: Reading, Writing & Language, and Math. The strategies outlined in this section can be applied to any of these tests.

The PSAT is different from the tests you are used to taking in school. The good news is that you can use the PSAT's particular structure to your advantage.

For example, on a test given in school, you probably go through the questions in order. You spend more time on the harder questions than on the easier ones because harder questions are usually worth more points. You probably often show your work because your teacher tells you that how you approach a question is as important as getting the correct answer.

This approach is not optimal for the PSAT. On the PSAT, you benefit from moving around within a section if you come across tough questions because the harder questions are usually worth the same number of points as the easier questions (with the exception of the Math Test's Extended Thinking question). It doesn't matter how you arrive at the correct answer—only that you bubble in the correct answer choice.

STRATEGY #1: TRIAGING THE TEST

You do not need to complete questions on the PSAT in order. Every student has different strengths and should attack the test with those strengths in mind. Your main objective on the PSAT should be to score as many points as you can. While approaching questions out of order may seem coun-terintuitive, it is a surefire way to achieve your best score.

Just remember, you can skip around within each section, but you cannot work on a section other than the one you've been instructed to work on.

To triage the test effectively, do the following:

- First, work through all the easy questions that you can do quickly. Skip questions that are hard or time-consuming

- For the Reading and Writing & Language Tests, start with the passage you find most manage-able and work toward the one you find most challenging. You do not need to go in order

- Second, work through the questions that are doable but time-consuming

- Third, work through the hard questions

- If you run out of time, pick a Letter of the Day for remaining questions

A Letter of the Day is an answer choice letter (A, B, C, or D) that you choose before Test Day to select for questions you guess on.

STRATEGY #2: ELIMINATION

Even though there is no wrong-answer penalty on the PSAT, Elimination is still a crucial strategy. If you can determine that one or more answer choices are definitely incorrect, you can increase your chances of getting the right answer by paring the selection down.

To eliminate answer choices, do the following:

- Read each answer choice

- Cross out the answer choices that are incorrect

- Remember: There is no wrong-answer penalty, so take your best guess

STRATEGY #3: GUESSING

Each question on the PSAT has four answer choices and no wrong-answer penalty. That means if you have no idea how to approach a question, you have a 25 percent chance of randomly choosing the correct answer. Even though there's a 75 percent chance of selecting the incorrect answer, you won't lose any points for doing so. The worst that can happen on the PSAT is that you'll earn zero points on a question, which means you should *always* at least take a guess, even when you have no idea what to do.

When guessing on a question, do the following:

- Always try to strategically eliminate answer choices before guessing

- If you run out of time, or have no idea what a question is asking, pick a Letter of the Day

COMMON TESTING MYTHS

Since its inception in 1971, the PSAT/NMSQT has gone through various revisions, but it has always been an integral part of helping high school students qualify for various scholarships. As a result of its significance and the changes it has undergone, a number of rumors and myths have circulated about the exam. In this section, we'll dispel some of the most common ones. As always, you can find the most up-to-date information about the PSAT at the College Board website (https://www.collegeboard.org/psat-nmsqt/).

Myth: **Colleges use PSAT scores to make admissions decisions.**

Fact: Nothing could be further from the truth. When you take the PSAT, your scores are provided to a variety of organizations, including the National Merit Scholarship Corporation, that offer scholarships based on students' needs, merits, and backgrounds. Colleges can opt to receive lists of high-scoring PSAT students to target them with advertising. In short, a great score on the PSAT can help you get noticed by top colleges, but a terrible score won't have an adverse impact on your admissions decision.

Myth: **There is a wrong-answer penalty on the PSAT to discourage guessing.**

Fact: While this statement was true a few years ago, it is no longer true. Older versions of the PSAT had a wrong-answer penalty so that students who guessed on questions would not have an advantage over students who left questions blank. This penalty has been removed; make sure you never leave a PSAT question blank!

Myth: **Answer choice C is most likely to be the correct answer.**

Fact: This rumor has roots in human psychology. Apparently, when people such as high school teachers, for example, design an exam, they have a slight bias toward answer choice C when assigning correct answers. While humans do write PSAT questions, a computer randomizes the distribution of correct choices; statistically, therefore, each answer choice is equally likely to be the correct answer.

Myth: **The PSAT is just like the SAT.**

Fact: The PSAT is a valuable tool to help you prepare for the SAT. However, there are important differences between the two exams. First, the PSAT is shorter than the SAT in terms of timing and the number of questions. Second, the PSAT does not include an essay section. Third, the PSAT does not test more complex topics such as imaginary numbers or trigonometry. Finally, you'll take the PSAT at your high school and not an established testing center. Most students find that their PSAT experience helps get them ready for the SAT, but remember that taking the PSAT should form only a small part of your SAT preparation.

Myth: **The PSAT is just like another test in school.**

Fact: While the PSAT covers some of the same content as your high school math, literature, and English classes, it also presents concepts in ways that are fundamentally different. While you might be able to solve a math problem in a number of different ways on an algebra test, the PSAT places a heavy emphasis on working through questions as quickly and efficiently as possible.

Myth: **You have to get all the questions right to get a perfect score.**

Fact: Many students have reported missing several questions on the PSAT and being pleasantly surprised to receive perfect scores. Their experience is not atypical: Usually, you can miss a few questions and still get a coveted perfect score. The makers of the PSAT use a technique called scaling to ensure that a PSAT score conveys the same information from year to year, so you might be able to miss a couple more questions on a slightly harder PSAT exam and miss fewer questions on an easier PSAT exam and get the same scores. Keep a positive attitude throughout the PSAT, and in many cases, your scores will pleasantly surprise you.

Myth: **You can't prepare for the PSAT.**

Fact: You've already proven this myth false by buying this book. While the PSAT is designed to fairly test students, regardless of preparation, you can gain a huge advantage by familiarizing yourself with the structure and content of the exam. By working through the questions and practice tests available to you, you'll ensure that nothing on the PSAT catches you by surprise and that you do everything you can to maximize your score. Your Kaplan resources help you structure this practice in the most efficient way possible, and provide you with helpful strategies and tips as well.

HOW TO USE THIS BOOK

WELCOME TO KAPLAN!

Congratulations on taking this important step in your college admission process! By studying with Kaplan, you'll maximize your score on the PSAT, a major factor in your overall college application.

Our experience shows that the greatest PSAT score increases result from active engagement in the preparation process. Kaplan will give you direction, focus your preparation, and teach you the specific skills and effective test-taking strategies you need to know for the PSAT. We will help you achieve your top performance on Test Day, but your effort is crucial. The more you invest in preparing for the PSAT, the greater your chances of achieving your target score and getting into your top-choice college.

Are you registered for the PSAT? Kaplan cannot register you for the official PSAT. If you have not already registered for the upcoming PSAT, talk to your high school guidance counselor or visit the College Board's website at www.collegeboard.org to register online and for information on registration deadlines, test sites, accommodations for students with disabilities, and fees.

The PSAT is administered on only two days in mid-October. Therefore, students should be registered well in advance of the test dates. Your high school guidance counselor may also have more information about registering for the PSAT. Homeschooled students can contact the guidance office of a local high school to make arrangements to take the exam at that school.

PRACTICE TESTS

Kaplan's practice tests are just like the actual PSAT. By taking a practice exam you will prepare yourself for the actual Test Day experience. One of your practice tests is included in this book and the other one can be accessed online. See the Digital Resources section to learn how to access your online practice test.

EXTRA PRACTICE

You need to reinforce what you learn in each chapter by practicing the Kaplan methods and strategies. At the top of each extra practice assignment there is a list of required and recommended questions. The required questions are the ones that will help prepare you the most for Test Day.

SMARTPOINTS

Each chapter contains a breakdown of SmartPoints. By studying the information released by the College Board, Kaplan has been able to determine how often certain topics are likely to show up on the PSAT, and therefore how many points these topics are worth on Test Day. If you master a given topic, you can expect to earn the corresponding number of SmartPoints on Test Day.

PSAT EXTRA MATERIALS

The chapters that are in this book will help you answer the most questions on Test Day. However, there is additional content that will be covered on the PSAT. We have provided 16 additional chapters online to help you prepare for Test Day. See the note below on Digital Resources to learn how to access these extra materials.

DIGITAL RESOURCES

Register Your Online Companion

To access your online companion:

1. Go to kaptest.com/booksonline.

2. Follow the on-screen instructions. Have this book available.

Join a Live Online Event

Kaplan's PSAT Live Online sessions are interactive, instructor-led prep lessons that you can participate in from anywhere you have Internet access.

PSAT Live Online sessions are held in our state-of-the-art visual classroom: Actual lessons in real time, just like a physical classroom experience. Interact with your teacher using audio, chat, whiteboards, polling, and screen-sharing functionality. And just like courses at Kaplan centers, PSAT Live Online sessions are led by top Kaplan instructors.

To register for a PSAT Live Online event:

1. Once you've signed in to your student home page, open your syllabus.

2. In the Syllabus window, go to the Live Online Registration menu option.

3. Click on the link. A separate window will appear with registration instructions.

PSAT Live Online events are scheduled to take place throughout the year. Please check the registration page with dates and times.

PSAT Practice Test

Your PSAT/NMSQT online companion includes a full-length practice test. We recommend you complete this practice test after having gone through the contents of the book. After completing the practice test, you'll receive a detailed online score report. Use this to help you focus and review over the sections in the book that pertain to your greatest areas of improvement.

Extra Materials

Your PSAT/NMSQT online companion includes 16 extra chapters that you can use to prepare for the PSAT. If you have additional time to study, it is recommended that you access these chapters and use them to help you prepare for the PSAT.

Math

Heart
of Algebra

IN THIS UNIT, YOU WILL LEARN:

1. The Kaplan Method for Math

2. How to solve linear equations and inequalities

3. How to graph linear equations and inequalities

4. Strategies for efficiently solving systems of linear equations

5. Strategies for translating word problems into math

CHAPTER 1

The Kaplan Method for Math & Linear Equations

CHAPTER OBJECTIVES

By the end of this chapter, you will be able to:

1. Apply the Kaplan Method for Math to Heart of Algebra questions

2. Recognize, simplify, and solve linear equations efficiently

3. Translate complex word problems into equations

4. Interpret the most commonly tested types of linear graphs

SMARTPOINTS

Point Value	SmartPoint Category
Point Builder	Kaplan Method for Math
110 Points	Linear Equations

THE KAPLAN METHOD FOR MATH

Because the PSAT is a standardized test, students who approach each question in a consistent way will be rewarded on Test Day. Applying the same basic steps to every math question—whether it asks you about geometry, algebra, or even trigonometry—will help you avoid minor mistakes as well as tempting wrong answer choices.

Use the Kaplan Method for Math for every math question on the PSAT. Its steps are applicable to every situation and reflect the best test-taking practices.

The Kaplan Method for Math has three steps:

Step 1: Read the question, identifying and organizing important information as you go

Step 2: Choose the best strategy to answer the question

Step 3: Check that you answered the *right* question

Let's examine each of these steps in more detail.

Step 1: Read the question, identifying and organizing important information as you go

This means:

- **What information am I given?** Take a few seconds to jot down the information you are given and try to group similar items together.

- **Separate the question from the context.** Word problems may include information that is unnecessary for solving the question. Feel free to discard any unnecessary information.

- **How are the answer choices different?** Reading answer choices carefully can help you spot the most efficient way to solve a PSAT math question. Noting, for example, whether answer choices are all decimals you can put in your calculator or simplified fractions can save you precious time while you decide how to solve.

- **Should I label or draw a diagram?** If the question describes a shape or figure but doesn't provide one, sketch a diagram so you can see the shape or figure and add notes to it. If a figure is provided, take a few seconds to label it with information from the question.

> ✔ **Expert Tip**
>
> Don't assume you understand a question as soon as you see it. Many students see an equation and immediately begin solving. Solving math questions without carefully reading can take you down the wrong path on Test Day.

Step 2: Choose the best strategy to answer the question

- **Look for patterns.** Every PSAT math question can be solved in a variety of ways, but not all strategies are created equal! To finish all of the questions, you'll need to solve questions as *efficiently* as possible. If you find yourself about to do time-consuming math, take a minute to look for time-saving shortcuts.

- **Pick numbers or use straightforward math.** While you can always solve a PSAT math question with what you've learned in school, doing so won't always be the fastest way. On questions that describe relationships between numbers (like percentages) but don't actually use numbers, you can often save time on Test Day by using techniques like Picking Numbers instead of straightforward math.

> ✔ **Expert Tip**
>
> Remember, the PSAT won't give you any extra points for solving a question the hard way.

Step 3: Check that you answered the *right* question

- When you get the final answer, **resist the urge to immediately bubble in the answer.** Take a moment to:

  - Review the question stem

  - Check units of measurement

  - Double-check your work

- The PSAT will often ask you for quantities like $x + 1$ or the product of x and y. **Be careful on these questions!** They often include tempting answer choices that correspond to the values of x or y individually. There's no partial credit on the PSAT, so take a moment at the end of every question to make sure you're answering the right question.

LINEAR EQUATIONS

Linear equations and linear graphs are some of the most common elements on the PSAT Math Test. They can be used to model relationships and changes like those concerning time, temperature, or population.

The graphs of these equations are as important as the equations themselves. The graphs you will see most are either linear or lines of best fit. A sample graph is shown:

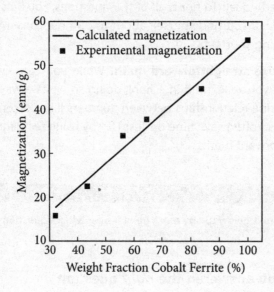

When working with a graph like this, you may not know anything about magnetization or cobalt ferrite, but you do see a graph with a straight line on it. That straight line is your clue that you're dealing with a linear equation.

Being able to work with, understand, and interpret linear equations will make up a substantial part of your Math score. In this chapter, we will explore all of those scenarios so you'll be ready to tackle linear equations in whatever form you encounter them on the test.

Many students inadvertently switch on "math autopilot" when solving linear equations, automatically running through the same set of steps on every equation without looking for the best way to solve the question. On the PSAT, however, every second counts. You will want to use the *most* efficient strategy for solving questions. Take a look at the following example:

1. $\dfrac{1}{2}(3x + 17) = \dfrac{1}{6}(8x - 10)$

    Which value of x satisfies the equation above?

    A) −61

    B) −55

    C) −42

    D) −35

Let's work through this example step-by-step to use the Kaplan Method for Math and demonstrate the expert thinking that can help you get through this question quickly on Test Day. The following table shows Kaplan's strategic thinking on the left, along with suggested math scratchwork on the right. Keeping your notes organized is critical for success on the PSAT, so take the time now to practice setting up well-organized scratchwork.

Strategic Thinking	Math Scratchwork
Step 1: Read the question, identifying and organizing important information as you go *What are you actually being asked to do here?* This question is straightforward: You're being asked to solve the equation and find the correct value of *x*.	$\frac{1}{2}(3x+17)=\frac{1}{6}(8x-10)$
Step 2: Choose the best strategy to answer the question *Should you distribute those fractions through first, or is there a faster way to solve?* By multiplying both sides of the equation by 6, you make the equation much simpler: Finish by using the distributive property and collecting like terms.	$3(3x+17)=8x-10$ $9x+51=8x-10$
Step 3: Check that you answered the *right* question Now you have an answer: *x* = −61. Ask yourself: *"Did I answer the right question?"* In this case, you solved for *x*, the correct quantity. You can confidently select (A).	$x=-61$

You could have approached a question like this in many ways, but remember, the goal is to get the correct answer quickly. The faster you solve algebraic equations, the more time you'll be able to devote to challenging questions, setting you up to earn more points on Test Day.

✔ **Remember**

As you practice, always ask yourself: "Is there a faster way to solve this question?" Use the Answers & Explanations at the back of this book to check!

When solving an equation, always keep in mind the fundamental principles of equality: Because both sides of an equation are equal, you need to do the same thing to both sides so that equality is preserved. Try solving another linear equation for extra practice:

2. $2(x + 3) = 17$

What value of x satisfies the equation shown?

A) $\dfrac{5}{2}$

B) $\dfrac{7}{2}$

C) $\dfrac{9}{2}$

D) $\dfrac{11}{2}$

Use the Kaplan Method for Math to solve this question, working through it step-by-step. The following table shows Kaplan's strategic thinking on the left, along with suggested math scratchwork on the right.

Strategic Thinking	Math Scratchwork
Step 1: Read the question, identifying and organizing important information as you go *What are you actually being asked to do here?* This looks similar to the first question. It's asking you to solve the equation and find the correct value of x.	$2(x + 3) = 17$
Step 2: Choose the best strategy to answer the question *What's the fastest way to solve this?* It doesn't look like there are many options. Use principles of equality and do the same thing to both sides until x is by itself. First, distribute the 2. Continue by collecting like terms and proceed to isolate x.	$2x + 6 = 17$ $2x = 11$
Step 3: Check that you answered the *right* question Ask yourself, *"Did I answer the right question?"* and check the question stem one last time before bubbling. As requested, you've solved for x. Choice (D) is correct.	$x = \dfrac{11}{2}$

Be aware of the fact that you didn't end up with an integer value for x. The PSAT may challenge you by designing questions so that the answer is in a form you do not expect. If you get an answer in an unusual form, don't be dissuaded. Fractions and decimals are often correct on the PSAT!

Looking carefully at how the PSAT uses fractions and decimals can guide your strategy in solving linear equations. The presence of fractions in the answer choices likely means you'll need to rely on techniques for combining and simplifying fractions to get to the right answer. Seeing decimals in the answer choices, on the other hand, likely indicates that you can rely on your calculator and save time on Test Day.

Try to determine the best strategy for solving the next question.

3. $\dfrac{8}{7}\left(x - \dfrac{101}{220}\right) + 4\left(x + \dfrac{8}{9}\right) = 38$

   Which approximate value of x satisfies the equation shown?

   A)   4.29

   B)   4.65

   C)   6.6

   D)   6.8

Use the Kaplan Method for Math to solve this question, working through it step-by-step. The following table shows Kaplan's strategic thinking on the left, along with suggested math scratchwork on the right.

Strategic Thinking	Math Scratchwork
Step 1: Read the question, identifying and organizing important information as you go *What are you being asked to do here?* Notice a pattern? Again, the question is asking you to solve for *x*.	$\dfrac{8}{7}\left(x - \dfrac{101}{220}\right) + 4\left(x + \dfrac{8}{9}\right) = 38$

Step 2: Choose the best strategy to answer the question	
How can you quickly solve this problem?	
Clearing the fraction outside the parentheses is a smart move. Multiply both sides by 7.	$8\left(x - \dfrac{101}{220}\right) + 28\left(x + \dfrac{8}{9}\right) = 266$
What do you notice about the answer choices? How are they different from the answers in the last problem?	
That's right, the presence of decimals means your calculator will be a great asset here. Don't worry about common denominators. Divide the fractions. Because the answer choices are only written to two decimal places, write your intermediate steps to two places as well.	$8(x - 0.46) + 28(x + 0.89) = 266$
Now distribute the terms outside the parentheses and collect the *x* terms. Finally, divide through.	$8x - 3.68 + 28x + 24.92 = 266$ $36x = 244.76$
Step 3: Check that you answered the *right* question	$x = 6.8$
Double-check the question stem. Choice (D) is correct.	

Notice in the previous question that careful use of your calculator can eliminate the need to complete time-consuming tasks by hand. Be conscious of the format of the answer choices—decimal answers are a great clue that you can use your calculator.

> ✔ **Note**
>
> Many graphing calculators have a built-in function that will let you input and solve algebraic equations like the one above. Consider learning how to use it ahead of Test Day by reading the instruction manual or searching online.

LINEAR WORD PROBLEMS (REAL-WORLD SCENARIOS)

Another way linear equations can be made complicated is for them to be disguised in "real-world" word problems, where it's up to you to extract and solve an equation. When you're solving these problems, you may run into trouble translating English into math. The following table shows some of the most common phrases and mathematical equivalents you're likely to see on the PSAT.

Word Problems Translation Table	
English	**Math**
equals, is, equivalent to, was, will be, has, costs, adds up to, the same as, as much as	=
times, of, multiplied by, product of, twice, double, by	×
divided by, per, out of, each, ratio	÷
plus, added to, and, sum, combined, total, increased by	+
minus, subtracted from, smaller than, less than, fewer, decreased by, difference between	−
a number, how much, how many, what	*x, n,* etc.

Linear word problems are made more difficult by complex phrasing and extraneous information. Don't get frustrated—word problems can be broken down in predictable ways. To keep you organized on Test Day, use the **Kaplan Strategy for Translating English into Math:**

- **Define any variables, choosing letters that make sense.**
- **Break sentences into short phrases.**
- **Translate each phrase into a mathematical expression.**
- **Put the expressions together to form an equation.**

Let's apply this to a straightforward example: Colin's age is three less than twice Jim's age.

- **Define any variables, choosing letters that make sense:** We'll choose C for Colin's age and J for Jim's age.

- **Break sentences into short phrases:** The information about Colin and the information about Jim seem like separate phrases.

- **Translate each phrase into a mathematical expression:** Colin's age = C; 3 less than twice Jim's age = $2J - 3$.

- **Put the expressions together to form an equation:** Combine the results to get $C = 2J - 3$.

This strategy fits into the larger framework of the Kaplan Method for Math: When you get to **Step 2: Choose the best strategy to answer the question** and are trying to solve a word problem as efficiently as possible, switch over to this strategy to move forward quickly.

The Kaplan Strategy for Translating English into Math works every time. Apply it here to a test-like example:

4. The number k can be determined in the following way: Multiply m by 2, add $3n$ to the result, and subtract $(4m - 5n)$ from this sum. What is the value of k in terms of m and n?

    A) $-2m - 3n$

    B) $-2m + 2n$

    C) $-2m + 8n$

    D) $6m - 2n$

Use the Kaplan Method for Math to solve this question, working through it step by step. The following table shows Kaplan's strategic thinking on the left, along with suggested math scratchwork on the right.

Strategic Thinking	Math Scratchwork
Step 1: Read the question, identifying and organizing important information as you go *What are you being asked to do here?* The question is asking you to solve for k in terms of m and n. You're looking for what comes after $k =$.	
Step 2: Choose the best strategy to answer the question *Where should you start to tackle this? Can you systematically translate from English into math?* Go through each component of the **Kaplan Strategy for Translating English into Math.** *Do you need to choose variables?* No, the variables are already defined for you. *How can you logically break this question down?* Phrases about k and phrases about m and n are reasonable choices.	

What should you do next with your natural-language phrases? Go ahead and translate:	$k =$
"k can be determined" *What math operation is the best match for the verb "determined"?*	
"Multiply m by 2, add 3n to the result" *Any tricks here? Seems straightforward.*	$2m + 3n$
"Subtract (4m − 5n)" *Where should this come in the expression? Remember to work in order.*	$-(4m - 5n)$
Combine the results.	$k = 2m + 3n - (4m - 5n)$
This doesn't look like an exact match for the answer choices. Can you simplify?	
Distribute the negative through and combine like terms.	$k = 2m + 3n - 4m + 5n$
Step 3: Check that you answered the *right* question Perfect! Now you have an exact match for (C).	$k = -2m + 8n$

LINEAR GRAPHS

Working with equations algebraically is only half the battle. The PSAT will also expect you to work with graphs of linear equations, which means using lines in slope-intercept form and point-slope form.

One of the most important quantities you'll be working with when graphing a linear equation is the slope. Slope is given by the following equations: $m = \frac{(y_2 - y_1)}{(x_2 - x_1)}$, $m = \frac{rise}{run}$, and $m = \frac{\Delta y}{\Delta x}$, where (x_1, y_1) and (x_2, y_2) are coordinates of points on the line and Δy is the change in the y direction and Δx is the change in the x direction.

One of the most common forms of a linear equation is *slope-intercept form*, which is used to describe the graph of a straight line. The formula is quickly recognizable: $y = mx + b$. The variables y and x represent a point on the graph through which the line passes, while m tells us what the slope of the line is and b represents the point at which the line intersects the y-axis.

Remember: A line with a positive slope runs up and to the right ("uphill"), and a line with a negative slope runs down and to the right ("downhill"). In the following figure, lines *n* and *l* have positive and negative slopes, respectively.

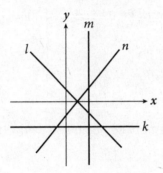

Occasionally, you will encounter a line with a slope of 0—meaning it does not rise or fall from left to right. These lines are easy to spot because they are horizontal and are parallel to the *x*-axis (line *k* in the figure shown). Lines that are parallel to the *y*-axis, like line *m* in the figure, have slopes that are "undefined." The lines themselves exist, but their slopes cannot be calculated numerically.

The slope of a graph can also tell you valuable information about the rate of change of numbers and variables associated with the line. A positive slope signifies an increase in a variable, while a negative slope indicates a decrease. *Large* numerical values for slope indicate rapid change, while *small* numerical values point to more gradual changes. Imagine the balance in your checking account is *B*, and it changes with the number of days that go by, *D*. Several proposed models are listed here. Think about how each one would impact your life.

$B = 100D + 75$

$B = 0.25D + 75$

$B = -100D + 75$

$B = -0.25D + 75$

Notice, the *y*-intercept didn't change at all. The first equation probably looks pretty good! The second equation isn't as great. An extra quarter a day isn't going to do much for you. The third equation would quickly drive you into bankruptcy, while the fourth equation might be cause for concern after a while.

The *y*-intercept, on the other hand, is much less significant, typically representing the initial condition in a number of models—that is, where the model begins. In the checking account example, the beginning balance was $75 in all four models.

Look at the following question to see how the PSAT may test your ability to match a linear equation with its graph.

5. Which of the following answer choices shows the graph of the line $y = 4x + 7$?

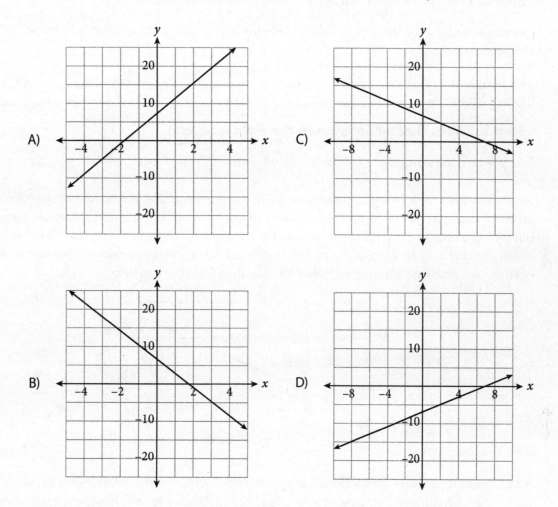

Approach this question with the Kaplan Method for Math. Because there isn't any scratchwork required for a problem like this, only the column containing Kaplan's strategic thinking is included. Try to ask yourself similar questions as you work through problems like this on Test Day.

Strategic Thinking
Step 1: Read the question, identifying and organizing important information as you go
What are you being asked to do here?
This question is asking you to match the linear equation to the appropriate graph.

Step 2: Choose the best strategy to answer the question

What is the fastest way to solve this? Should you use your graphing calculator, or can you eliminate some answer choices quickly?

Notice that the graphs are vastly different. You're looking for a graph that slopes up and to the right (positive slope) and has a *y*-intercept of +7. Only one of the graphs matches those criteria.

Step 3: Check that you answered the *right* question

Only (A) has a graph with a positive slope and a positive *y*-intercept.

Some questions are a little more challenging. They're usually similar in structure to the "checking account" equation described earlier, but they can involve more complicated scenarios. This next question requires you to choose the best model for a given "real-world" situation. See if you can match the graph to an appropriate model. Watch out! It's a science crossover question, so you'll need to be particularly careful to separate the question from the context.

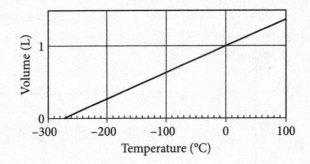

6. Jacques Charles was a French scientist who discovered the relationship between the temperature and volume of a gas. Specifically, Charles found that gases expand when heated. This relationship was formalized in Charles's Law, which illustrates a linear relationship between temperature and volume in gases. The graph here shows the volume of a sample of gas as it is cooled. If *T* is the temperature of the gas and *V* is the volume, which of the following gives a line that, when plotted, could produce the graph shown?

   A) $V = 0.004T + 100$

   B) $V = 0.004T$

   C) $V = 0.004T + 1$

   D) $V = 0.004T - 0.25$

> ✔ **Notes**
>
> Remember to use the *y*-coordinate to find the *y*-intercept. The *x*-coordinate at that point will always be zero!

While you may enjoy learning history with your math, you don't need to waste time digesting extraneous information. The following table shows the strategic thinking that can help you solve this question. No scratchwork is necessary.

Strategic Thinking

Step 1: Read the question, identifying and organizing important information as you go

Take another look at the question. Which part tells you exactly what you need to do?

Only the last two sentences describe the graph. They are underlined here:

6. Jacques Charles was a French scientist who discovered the relationship between the temperature and volume of a gas. Specifically, Charles found that gases expand when heated. This relationship was formalized in Charles's Law, which illustrates a linear relationship between temperature and volume in gases. <u>The graph here shows the volume of a sample of gas as it is cooled. If T is the temperature of the gas in °C and V is the volume in liters, which of the following gives a line that, when plotted, could produce the graph shown?</u>

What are you being asked to do here?

Match the graph to the equation. Because V is on the y-axis and T is on the x-axis, the standard $y = mx + b$ equation should resemble $V = mT + b$. All you need to do now is figure out the slope and y-intercept.

Step 2: Choose the best strategy to answer the question

Should you plot each of the lines in the answer choices on your calculator? Is that the most efficient use of time?

Probably not. Notice that the answer choices describe very different lines.

What part is different in each answer choice?

In this case, each option has a different y-intercept. To solve this complicated question, all you need to do is find the y-intercept of the graph and match it to an answer choice.

Where is the y-axis in the graph?

Notice the unusual orientation of the graph. The y-axis will always be at $x = 0$, but it does not have to be located at the far left of the graph. In this graph, the y-axis is offset and is located in the middle of the right side of the graph. In this case, the line intersects the y-axis at the point (0, 1). Therefore, you know you're looking for a line that has a y-intercept of 1.

Step 3: Check that you answered the *right* question

Which answer choice has a y-intercept of 1?

You can safely eliminate every answer choice except (C), the correct answer.

While scatterplots will be described in more detail in subsequent chapters, this next question shows that the principles covered here for graphing linear equations can be equally applied to the line of best fit on a scatterplot. See what you can conclude from the slope and *y*-intercept of the equation of the best-fit line. Note that this question is an example of a very complex word problem—don't be intimidated! If you can tackle this problem, you'll be able to handle the most onerous PSAT word problems.

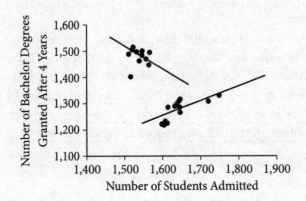

7. A university admissions department compiled data that were collected on students over a 25-year period. The department was particularly interested in how many students admitted in a given year graduated four years later with a degree. It noted that the number of students admitted showed a regular and consistent increase over the 25-year period. These data are plotted in the graph shown. Halfway through the data collection period, the general college enacted a policy that would allow students to take a year-long break during their studies. The college wants to model the relationship between the number of students admitted and the number of degrees attained in four years with a line of best fit before and after the policy change. Which of the following describes the best estimate for *m*, the slope of this line, before the change and after the change?

A) Before: $m = -1$, after: $m = 0$

B) Before: $m = 1$, after: $m = -\dfrac{1}{2}$

C) Before: $m = -1$, after: $m = \dfrac{3}{4}$

D) Before: $m = \dfrac{3}{4}$, after: $m = 0$

Use the Kaplan Method for Math to make short work of a question like this. The following table shows the strategic thinking that can help you solve even a complex problem.

Strategic Thinking
Step 1: Read the question, identifying and organizing important information as you go *Simplify greatly. What are you being asked to do here? Can the answer choices help? Ultimately, what do you need to calculate in this question?* In this case, the question is asking you to find the slope before and after the policy change. Because the number of students admitted increased over time, you know that data before the policy change are on the left side of the graph and data after the policy change are on the right side.
Step 2: Choose the best strategy to answer the question *How can you solve this efficiently? Do you notice any differences between the answer choices that would result in vastly different slopes? Do the signs tell you anything?* Because the line of best fit for the data collected before the policy change slopes down and to the right, you're looking for a negative slope. That eliminates B and D. Because the line of best fit for the data collected after the policy change slopes up and to the right, you know you need a positive slope. That eliminates A.
Step 3: Check that you answered the *right* question *Do you need to worry about the actual numerical value of the slope?* Because only one answer choice remains that describes the slopes of both lines correctly, you can confidently choose (C) without worrying about the numbers here.

Notice that even complicated-looking questions involving linear graphs often boil down to the same basic concepts of slope and *y*-intercept. Master those ideas and you'll be able to handle any linear graph you'll see on the PSAT.

Now you'll have a chance to try a few more test-like questions. Use the scaffolding as needed to guide you through the question and get the right answer.

Some guidance is provided, but you'll need to fill in the missing parts of explanations or the step-by-step math to get to the correct answer. Don't worry—after going through the examples at the beginning of this chapter, these questions should be completely doable. If you find yourself struggling, however, review the worked examples in this chapter and the additional questions further.

8.   Ms. Walser's class had 18 students. She used three equally weighted tests to determine their final grades. The class average for the first test was 92, and the class average for the second test was 77. If the overall class average was 84, what was the average score for the third test?

   A)   74.3

   B)   77

   C)   83

   D)   84.3

The following table can help you structure your thinking as you go about solving this problem. The Kaplan strategic thinking is provided, as are bits of structured scratchwork. If you're not sure how to approach a question like this, start at the top and work your way down.

Strategic Thinking	Math Scratchwork
Step 1: *What are you actually solving for here?* You're solving for the average of the third test. *If the tests are equally weighted, what does that tell you about the number of students?* The number of students is extraneous information. Since the tests are equally weighted, just divide by 3 to calculate the final average.	
Step 2: Use the Kaplan Strategy for Translating English into Math to get through this word problem quickly. *Can you give the variables names that make sense? Careful, T would give you trouble with Test Two and Test Three. Could you start at the beginning of the alphabet?*	Average of Test One = _____ Average of Test Two = _____ Average of Test Three = _____ Overall Average = _____

How can you logically break this question apart into shorter sentences?	On Test One the class scored an average of _____. On Test _____ the class scored an average of 77. The class's _____ average was 84.
Is it possible to translate each phrase into a math expression? Because you don't have a score for the third test, what should you do? Leave it as a variable?	_____ = 92 _____ = 77 _____ = __ _____ = 84
Almost there. Can you put all the pieces together? How can you use the average of the three scores to solve for the third test score?	
Remember that the average is equal to the sum of terms divided by the number of terms.	(___+___+___)/3=___
Test 3 should remain a variable because it is the quantity being solved for.	
After you've plugged everything in, can you rearrange the equation to get the score on Test Three?	
Step 3: Check your work. Does the variable you solved for correspond to the score on Test Three?	_____ = _____

✔ **Notes**

$$\text{Average} = \frac{\text{Sum of terms}}{\text{Number of terms}}$$

Here's another test-like example to try with this method:

9. A box of candies contains only chocolates, licorice sticks, peppermints, and gummy bears. If $\frac{1}{4}$ of the candies are chocolates, $\frac{1}{6}$ of the candies are gummy bears, $\frac{1}{3}$ are peppermints, and 9 are licorice sticks, what is the product of the number of peppermints and the number of chocolates?

   A) 12

   B) 36

   C) 72

   D) 108

The following table can help you structure your thinking as you go about solving this problem. The Kaplan strategic thinking is provided, as are bits of structured scratchwork. If you're not sure how to approach a question like this, start at the top and work your way down.

Strategic Thinking	Math Scratchwork
Step 1: *What is this question asking you to find?* In this case, you want the product of peppermints and chocolates. That means you'll need both of those quantities.	
Step 2: *How can you effectively translate this English into math?* Use the Kaplan Strategy for Translating English into Math. *Can you think of a variable to correspond to the total number of candies in the box?* *Be careful! Because chocolates, gummy bears, and peppermints are all defined in terms of the total number of chocolates, do they need their own variables?* *How can each candy be written as a fraction of b?* Break the question down into shorter phrases and translate into math. *Almost there. What should all of these candies add up to? Think about what variable they're all a fraction of.* At this point, solve for the number of candies in the box.	Total Candies = _____ $\dfrac{1}{4}b =$ _____ ___ $b =$ _____ ___ $b =$ _____ $9 =$ _____ $\dfrac{1}{4}b +$ ___$b +$ ___$b + 9 =$ ____ $b =$ _____
Step 3: *Did I answer the right question?* Careful! Don't bubble in what you just solved for! You're looking for the product of chocolates and peppermints. *Can you use your fractions to get these candies individually?* Now multiply these candies together to get the final answer.	chocolates $= \dfrac{1}{4}b =$ _____ peppermints $=$ ___ $b =$ _____ product = _____

Now that you've seen the variety of ways in which the PSAT can test you on linear equations, try the following questions to check your understanding. Give yourself 3.5 minutes to tackle the following three questions. Make sure you use the Kaplan Method for Math on every question. Remember, you'll need to emphasize speed and efficiency in addition to simply getting the correct answer.

10. Ibrahim has a contract for a cell phone plan that includes the following rates: The plan has a fixed cost of $50 a month, a data plan that provides 2 GB of data for free and $8 for each GB of data after that, and a text message plan that costs $0.10 per text message sent. Which of the following equations represents the amount of money in dollars that Ibrahim will spend as long as he uses at least 2 GB of data? (Assume d = dollars, g = number of GB of data used, and t = number of text messages sent.)

A) $d = 50 + 8g + 0.1t$

B) $d = 50 + (8g - 2) + 0.1t$

C) $d = 50 + 8(g - 2) + 0.1t$

D) $d = 5{,}000 + 800g + 10t$

11. If $3(n-2)=6$, then what does $\dfrac{(n-2)}{(n+2)}$ equal?

12. A certain gym sells two membership packages. The first package, the die-hard package, costs $250 for 6 months of unlimited use. The second package, the personal package, costs $130 initially plus $4 each day the member visits. How many visits would a person need to use for each package to cost the same amount over a 6-month period?

A) 2

B) 30

C) 96

D) 120

Answers & Explanations for this chapter begin on page 397.

Step 3: Check that you answered the *right* question

Which answer choice matches the difference you found?

If you came up with (A), you're absolutely right.

8. Given $2x + 5y = 49$ and $5x + 3y = 94$, what is the product of x and y?

Larger numbers don't make this question any different; just be careful with the arithmetic. Again, the following table can help you structure your thinking as you go about solving this problem. The Kaplan strategic thinking is provided, as are bits of structured scratchwork. If you're not sure how to approach a question like this, start at the top and work your way down.

Strategic Thinking	Math Scratchwork
Step 1: Read the question, identifying and organizing important information as you go *What are you being asked to do here?* You're asked to find the product of *x* and *y*.	

Step 2: Choose the best strategy to answer the question	
What's the quickest route to the answer?	
You have coefficients on all four variable terms and large constants on the right sides of the equations, so combination will likely be faster than substitution.	$2x + 5y = 49$ $5x + 3y = 94$
How do you cancel out one of the variables?	
Although you can often get away with manipulating only one equation, you'll need to adjust both here. The *x* coefficients are 2 and 5. No integer will multiply by 2 to get 5 and vice versa, but what about multiplying both equations by numbers that will get you a common multiple on both *x* terms? Don't forget to make one of them negative.	____(____ + ____ = ____) ____(____ + ____ = ____)
What is the next step?	
Carry out combination as usual, being especially careful with the larger numbers.	
What's the value of y?	
Straightforward algebra from your combined equations gets you this.	$y =$ ____
How about x?	
Plug your *y* value back into one of the original equations and solve for *x*:	$x =$ ____
Lastly, multiply *x* and *y* together:	$xy =$ ____ × ____ = ____
Step 3: Check that you answered the *right* question	
What is the product of x *and* y*?*	$xy =$ ____
If your answer is 51, you're correct.	

Now that you've seen the variety of ways in which the PSAT can test you on systems of linear equations, try the following questions to check your understanding. Give yourself 4.5 minutes to tackle the following three questions.

$$8x + 4y = 17$$

$$\frac{1}{5}x + zy = \frac{1}{2}$$

9. In the system of linear equations shown, z is a constant. If the system has no solution, what is the value of z?

A) $\dfrac{1}{10}$

B) $\dfrac{1}{4}$

C) 8

D) 10

10. If x and y are both integers such that $x + 6 = 17$ and $y + 9 = 12$, what is the value of $x + y$?

11. Sixty people attended a concert. Children's tickets sold for $8, and adults' tickets sold for $12. If $624 was collected in ticket money, what is the product of the number of children and the number of adults who attended the concert?

A) 275

B) 779

C) 864

D) 900

Answers & Explanations for this chapter begin on page 409.

EXTRA PRACTICE

Required	Recommended
Questions 1, 2, 3, 5, 6, 7, 8, 9	Question 4

1. Guests at a wedding had two meal choices, chicken or vegetarian. The catering company charges $12.75 for each chicken dish and $9.50 for each vegetarian dish. If 62 people attended the wedding and the catering bill was $725.25, which of the following systems of equations could be used to find the number of people who ordered chicken, c, and the number of people who ordered vegetarian, v, assuming everyone ordered a meal?

A) $\begin{cases} c + v = 725.25 \\ 12.75c + 9.5v = 62 \end{cases}$

B) $\begin{cases} c + v = 62 \\ 12.75c + 9.5v = \dfrac{725.25}{2} \end{cases}$

C) $\begin{cases} c + v = 62 \\ 12.75c + 9.5v = 725.25 \end{cases}$

D) $\begin{cases} c + v = 62 \\ 12.75c + 9.5v = 725.25 \times 2 \end{cases}$

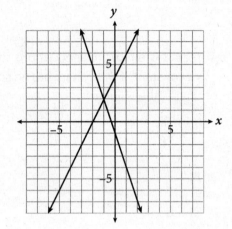

3. If (x, y) is the solution to the system of equations graphed in the figure, what is $x + y$?

A) –2

B) –1

C) 1

D) 4

$$2x - 4y = 14$$
$$5x + 4y = 21$$

2. What is the y-coordinate of the solution to the system of equations shown?

A) –1

B) 0

C) $\dfrac{7}{3}$

D) 5

$$2x + 3y = 8 - y$$
$$x - 6y = 10$$

4. If (x, y) is a solution to the system of equations shown here, what is $x - y$?

A) $-\dfrac{3}{4}$

B) $\dfrac{19}{4}$

C) $\dfrac{11}{2}$

D) $\dfrac{25}{4}$

5. A television set costs $25 less than twice the cost of a radio. If the television and radio together cost $200, how much more does the television cost than the radio?

A) $50

B) $75

C) $100

D) $125

6. Two turkey burgers and a bottle of water cost $3.25. If three turkey burgers and a bottle of water cost $4.50, what is the cost of two bottles of water?

A) $0.75

B) $1.25

C) $1.50

D) $3.00

$$3x - 4y = 10$$
$$6x + wy = 16$$

7. For which of the following values of w will the system of equations above have no solution?

A) −8

B) −4

C) 4

D) 8

$$\frac{1}{2}x - \frac{2}{3}y = c$$
$$6x - 8y = -1$$

8. If the system of linear equations shown has infinitely many solutions, and c is a constant, what is the value of c?

A) $-\dfrac{1}{2}$

B) $-\dfrac{1}{12}$

C) 2

D) 12

9. At a certain restaurant, there are 25 tables, and each table has either 2 or 4 chairs. If a total of 86 chairs accompany the 25 tables, how many tables have exactly 4 chairs?

A) 12

B) 15

C) 18

D) 21

Problem Solving & Data Analysis

IN THIS UNIT, YOU WILL LEARN:

1. The Kaplan Method for Math: Extended Thinking

2. How to use rates, ratios, proportions, and percentages to answer questions

3. Strategies for interpreting and extracting information from scatterplots and two-way tables

4. Techniques for analyzing simple and complex data sets

CHAPTER 3

Introduction to Problem Solving

CHAPTER OBJECTIVES

By the end of this section, you will be able to:

1. Use the Kaplan Method for Math: Extended Thinking to answer Problem Solving questions effectively

2. Solve multistep problems involving rates, ratios, and proportions

3. Use appropriate formulas to find percentages and single or multiple percent changes

SMARTPOINTS

Point Value	SmartPoint Category
Point Builder	Kaplan Method for Math: Extended Thinking
100 Points	Rates, Ratios, Proportions, & Percentages

The new PSAT contains multiple-choice and grid-in questions, as well as a new type of question: the Extended Thinking question. Extended Thinking questions have multiple parts and require more analysis and planning than multiple-choice questions. To help you answer these questions effectively, use the Kaplan Method for Math: Extended Thinking.

KAPLAN METHOD FOR MATH: EXTENDED THINKING

Step 1: Read the first part of the question, looking for clues

Step 2: Identify and organize the information you need

Step 3: Based on what you know, plan your steps to navigate the first part

Step 4: Solve, step-by-step, checking units as you go

Step 5: Did I answer the *right* question?

Step 6: Repeat for remaining questions, incorporating results from the previous parts

The next few pages will walk you through each step in more detail.

Step 1. Read the first part of the question, looking for clues

- **Focus all your energy here** instead of diluting it over the whole question; solving an Extended Thinking question in pieces is far simpler. Further, you'll need the results from earlier parts to solve subsequent ones. Don't even consider the later parts of the question until you've solved the first part.

- **Watch for hints** about what you'll need to use or how to solve. Underlining key quantities is often helpful for separating what you need from extraneous prose.

Step 2. Identify and organize the information you need

If you think this sounds like the Kaplan Method for Math, you're absolutely right. You'll use some of those same skills. The difference: The Extended Thinking question is just more involved with multiple pieces.

- **What information am I given?** Jot down key notes, and group related quantities to develop your strategy.

- **What am I solving for?** This is your target. As you work your way through subsequent steps, keep your target at the front of your mind. This will help you avoid unnecessary extra steps (and subsequent time loss). You'll sometimes need to tackle these problems from both ends, so always keep your goal in mind.

> ✔ **Expert Tip**
>
> Many students freeze up when they encounter a problem with multiple steps and seemingly massive amounts of information. Don't worry! Take each piece one at a time, and you won't be intimidated.

Step 3. Based on what you know, plan your steps to navigate the first part

- **What pieces am I missing?** Many students become frustrated when faced with a roadblock such as missing information, but it's an easy fix. Sometimes you'll need to do an intermediate calculation to elucidate the missing piece or pieces of the puzzle.

Step 4. Solve, step-by-step, checking units as you go

- **Work quickly but carefully**, just as you've done on other PSAT math questions.

Step 5. Did I answer the *right* question?

- As is the case with the Kaplan Method for Math, **make sure your final answer is the requested answer**.
- Review the first part of the question.
- Double-check your units and your work.

Step 6. Repeat for remaining sections, incorporating results from the previous parts

- Now take your results from the first part and think critically about how they fit into the subsequent parts.

When you've finished, congratulate yourself for persevering through such a challenging task. The Extended Thinking questions are the toughest on the PSAT. If you can ace these questions, you'll be poised for a great score on Test Day. Don't worry if the Kaplan Method seems complicated; we'll walk through an example shortly.

> ✔ **Expert Tip**
>
> As these questions take substantially more time, consider saving the Extended Thinking questions for last.

RATES, MEASUREMENT, & UNIT CONVERSIONS

By now, you've become adept at using algebra to answer many PSAT math questions, which is great, because you'll need those algebraic skills to answer questions involving rates. You're likely already familiar with many different rates—kilometers per hour, meters per second, and even miles per gallon—all are considered rates.

A fundamental equation involved with rates is "Distance = Rate × Time" (a.k.a. the DIRT equation—Distance Is Rate × Time). If you have two of the three components of the equation, you can easily find the third. An upcoming Extended Thinking example demonstrates this nicely.

You'll notice units of measurement are important for rate questions (and others that require a unit conversion) and, therefore, also an opportunity to fall for trap answers if you're not careful. How do you avoid this? Use the factor-label method. The factor-label method is a simple yet powerful way to ensure you're doing your calculations correctly and getting an answer with the requested units.

For example, suppose you're asked how many cups are in two gallons. First, identify your starting quantity's units (gallons) and then identify the end quantity's units (cups). The next step is to piece together a path of relationships that will convert gallons into cups, cancelling out units as you go. Keep in mind that you will often have multiple stepping stones between your starting and ending quantities, so don't panic if you can't get directly from gallons to cups.

What English volume relationships do you know? A gallon is the same as 4 quarts, every quart contains 2 pints, and a pint equals 2 cups. And there you have it! Your map from gallons to cups is complete. The last step is to put it together as a giant multiplication problem. Each relationship, called a conversion factor, is written as a fraction. The basic rules of fraction multiplication apply, so you can cancel a unit that appears in both the numerator and denominator.

> ✔ **Notes**
>
> The PSAT will not require you to memorize conversions for conventional imperial units. If the test asks you to convert miles into inches, for example, you will be provided with enough conversion factors to solve the problem.

Follow along as we convert from gallons to quarts to pints to cups:

$$\frac{2 \text{ gallons}}{1} \times \frac{4 \text{ quarts}}{1 \text{ gallon}} \times \frac{2 \text{ pints}}{1 \text{ quart}} \times \frac{2 \text{ cups}}{1 \text{ pint}} = (2 \times 4 \times 2 \times 2) \text{ cups} = 32 \text{ cups}$$

The DIRT equation is actually a variation of this process. Suppose you travel at 60 mph for 5 hours. You would calculate the distance traveled with $d = rt = \frac{60 \text{ mi}}{1 \text{ h}} \times 5 \text{ h} = 300 \text{ mi}$. The hour units cancel out, leaving you with miles, which you know is a distance. This built-in check is a great way to ensure your math is correct. If your units are off, check your steps for mistakes along the way. The PSAT will never ask you for a quantity like miles^4 or gallons^3, so if you end up with funky units like that, you've made an error somewhere in your work.

> ✔ **Notes**
>
> When using the factor-label method, don't be afraid to flip fractions and rates to make your units cancel out as needed.

The following question demonstrates the factor-label method in a test-like question.

1. A homeowner wants to buy 81 square feet of grass for his yard, but the vendor he uses only sells grass by the square yard. How many square yards of grass does the homeowner need? (1 yd = 3 ft)

   A) 9

   B) 27

   C) 243

   D) 729

Use the Kaplan Method for Math to solve this question, working through it step-by-step. The following table shows Kaplan's strategic thinking on the left, along with suggested math scratchwork on the right.

Strategic Thinking	Math Scratchwork
Step 1: Read the question, identifying and organizing important information as you go *What are you being asked to find? What information does the question stem supply?* You're asked how many square yards of grass the homeowner needs. You know he needs 81 square feet of grass.	81 ft^2 grass needed
Step 2: Choose the best strategy to answer the question *How do you convert from square feet to square yards?* The factor-label method will be the quickest path to the correct answer. *What are the starting and ending quantity units? Which conversion factors are needed?* You're starting in square feet and need to convert to square yards. You know that 1 yd = 3 ft, but be careful: 1 yd^2 is not the same as 3 ft^2. Consider each feet-to-yards conversion separately. You'll need to multiply by your conversion factor twice. Remember your rules for exponents: To cancel out ft^2, you'll need to divide by ft^2.	starting qty: 81 ft^2 end qty: ? yd^2 $\dfrac{81 \text{ ft}^2}{1} \times \dfrac{1 \text{ yd}}{3 \text{ ft}} \times \dfrac{1 \text{ yd}}{3 \text{ ft}} = \dfrac{81}{9} \text{ yd}^2$ $= 9 \text{ yd}^2$
Step 3: Check that you answered the *right* question *How many square yards of grass should the homeowner buy?* You've correctly converted from square feet to square yards to get the correct answer, (A).	9 yd^2

> **✔ Notes**
>
> The conversion from feet to yards is not the same as the conversion from square feet to square yards (or cubic feet to cubic yards). Trap answers will often use incorrect conversion factors. Be particularly careful when dealing with area or volume conversions that have multiple dimensions.

Next, you'll walk through a test-like Extended Thinking question that involves rates. Follow along with the Kaplan Method for Math: Extended Thinking, and think about how knowledge of rates is used to get to the answer.

Remember, even though the Extended Thinking question has multiple parts, you'll rely on the same math skills you'd use in a simple multiple-choice question to solve each part. If you find that there are missing pieces or missing quantities, use techniques such as the factor-label method to bridge the gap.

Think of solving an Extended Thinking question as building a three-dimensional puzzle. You collect all the relevant pieces and then arrange and assemble them to make the foundation, akin to using information in the first part of the question to map a route to its answer. Just as the top part of a 3D puzzle is built on the foundation, the second part of an Extended Thinking question builds on a key piece of information from the first part. Once you've secured this key piece, the process for solving the second part is exactly the same.

Next, you'll see an example of a typical Extended Thinking question:

Three business professionals are traveling to New York City for a conference. Mr. Black is taking a train from Philadelphia that leaves at 7:00 AM ET, Ms. Weiss is driving in from Newark at 6:15 AM ET, and Dr. Grey plans to catch a plane from Chicago that departs at 8:30 AM CT (one hour behind ET).

2. With traffic, Ms. Weiss averages a speed of 25 mph for the length of her 20-mile commute. Mr. Black's train will get to NYC, a 100-mile journey, at 8:15 AM ET. How much longer, in minutes, will Mr. Black travel than Ms. Weiss?

3. Dr. Grey's flight is delayed 45 minutes. If the plane flies at 332 mph for the 830-mile flight, how many hours after Ms. Weiss arrives will Dr. Grey arrive? Round your answer to the nearest tenth of an hour.

Use the Kaplan Method for Math: Extended Thinking to solve this question, working through it step-by-step. The following table shows Kaplan's strategic thinking on the left, along with suggested math scratchwork on the right.

Strategic Thinking	Math Scratchwork
Step 1: Read the first part of the question, looking for clues *What information are you given?* You know the travel start times of the three colleagues, as well as Ms. Weiss's speed and commute length and Mr. Black's commute length and arrival time.	*departure times:* *B: 7:00 AM ET* *W: 6:15 AM ET* *G: 8:30 AM CT* *W: 25 mph, 20 mi traveled* *B: 100 mi traveled, arrives at 8:15 ET*
Step 2: Identify and organize the information you need *What do you need to find for part 1? Of the information given, what will help answer the question? What can you dismiss?* You're asked to find the time between Ms. Weiss and Mr. Black's arrivals. Because part 1 asks only about Mr. Black and Ms. Weiss, you can disregard any information about Dr. Grey for now. To answer part 1, you need Mr. Black and Ms. Weiss's travel times. *What about Mr. Black's speed?* Part 1 asks for the difference in arrival times. Because you're given Mr. Black's travel time, finding his speed is not necessary.	*B travel time: ?* *W travel time: ?* *disregard G for now*
Step 3: Based on what you know, plan your steps to navigate the first part *How do you find Mr. Black's travel time? What about Ms. Weiss's?* Finding Mr. Black's travel time is straightforward; just take the difference between his departure and arrival times. You can use the DIRT equation to find Ms. Weiss's travel time.	*B: start @ 7:00 AM, arrive @ 8:15 AM* *W: d = rt*

Step 4: Solve, step-by-step, checking units as you go	
What is Mr. Black's travel time? What's Ms. Weiss's?	B: 7:00 AM – 8:15 AM = 1 h 15 min = 75 min
You know it took Mr. Black 75 min.	
For Ms. Weiss, plug her given speed (rate) and distance traveled into the DIRT equation, then solve for *t*.	W: 20 mi = 25 mi/h x *t* $t = \dfrac{20}{25} h = 0.8 h = 48$ min
How much longer did Mr. Black spend traveling?	
Take the difference in travel times, ensuring your answer is in the units requested (minutes).	75 min – 48 min = 27 min
Step 5: Did I answer the *right* question?	
Did you find the value requested?	
Mr. Black will travel 27 minutes longer than Ms. Weiss.	

✔ Notes

You might be given extra information on questions like these. If you don't need it to get to the answer, then don't worry about it.

Now on to Step 6: Repeat for remaining questions. Kaplan's strategic thinking is on the left, along with suggested math scratchwork on the right.

Strategic Thinking	Math Scratchwork
Step 1: Read the second part of the question, looking for clues	
What does this part give you?	
From the intro, you know Dr. Grey's flight was supposed to depart at 8:30 AM CT. Part 2 tells you there is a 45-minute delay, as well as Dr. Grey's speed and distance traveled. You found Ms. Weiss's travel time in part 1.	8:30 AM CT planned start, delayed 45 min plane speed: 332 mi/h distance covered: 830 mi W travel: 48 min

Step 2: Identify and organize the information you need *What does part 2 ask you to find?* You need to determine how many hours separate the arrival times of Ms. Weiss and Dr. Grey.	W arrival: **?** G arrival: **?**
Step 3: Based on what you know, plan your steps to navigate the second part *What calculations will yield Dr. Grey's travel time?* Dr. Grey's transit time is not provided, so you'll need to find it. You're given Dr. Grey's speed and distance, so you can use the DIRT equation to find his time in transit. Then add this time to his start time, taking the delay and time zone change into account.	G travel time: **?** $d = rt$ +45 min (delay), +1 h (time zone)
Step 4: Solve, step-by-step, checking units as you go *How long is Dr. Grey's flight?* Plug the rate and distance into the DIRT equation and solve for time. *What effect do the delay and time zone change have on his arrival time?* Add 45 minutes to the initial start time to account for the delay, and then add 2 h 30 min flight time. Add another hour for the time zone change. *At what time did Ms. Weiss arrive in New York? How many hours before Dr. Grey's arrival is this?* Add 48 minutes to Ms. Weiss's start time to yield her arrival time. Lastly, find the difference between the two colleagues' arrival times.	$d = rt$ 830 mi = 332 mi/h x t t = 2.5 h (2 h 30 min) G: 8:30 AM → 9:15 AM (delay) + 2 h 30 min flt = 11:45 AM CT → 12:45 PM ET W: 6:15 AM ET + 48 min = 7:03 AM ET 7:03 AM ET vs. 12:45 PM ET: diff = 5 h 42 min
Step 5: Did I answer the *right* question? *How far apart are Ms. Weiss and Dr. Grey's arrival times?* Adjust your answer so it's in the requested format.	5 h 42 min = $5\frac{42}{60}$ h = 5.7 h

As you saw, using the Kaplan Method for Math: Extended Thinking makes an intimidating question far more straightforward. You'll have a chance to try it yourself later in this chapter.

RATIOS AND PROPORTIONS

Ratios and proportions are ubiquitous in everyday life. Whether it's making a double batch of meatballs or calculating the odds of winning the lottery, you'll find that ratios and proportions are invaluable in myriad situations.

A ratio is a way of comparing one quantity to another. When writing ratios, you can compare part of a group to another part of that group, or you can compare a part to the whole group. Suppose you have a bowl of apples and oranges. You can write ratios that compare apples to oranges (part to part), apples to total fruit (part to whole), and oranges to total fruit (part to whole).

You can also combine ratios. If you have two ratios, a:b and b:c, you can derive a:c by finding a common multiple. Take a look at the following table to see this in action.

a	:	b	:	c
3	:	4		
		3	:	5
9	:	12		
		12	:	20
9	:			20

What's a common multiple of the b terms? The number 12 is a good choice because it's the smallest possible value, which will reduce the need to simplify later. Where do you go from there? Multiply each ratio by the factor (use 3 for a:b and 4 for b:c) that will get you to $b = 12$.

The ratio a:c equals 9:20. Notice we didn't merely say a:c is 3:5; this would be incorrect on Test Day (and likely a wrong-answer trap!).

Proportions are simply two ratios set equal to each other. They are an efficient way to solve certain problems, but you must exercise caution when setting them up. Watching the units of each piece of the proportion will help you with this. Sometimes the PSAT will ask you to determine whether certain proportions are equivalent—check this by cross-multiplying. You'll get results that are much easier to compare.

If $\dfrac{a}{b} = \dfrac{c}{d}$, then: $ad = bc$, $\dfrac{a}{c} = \dfrac{b}{d}$, $\dfrac{d}{b} = \dfrac{c}{a}$, $\dfrac{b}{a} = \dfrac{d}{c}$, BUT $\dfrac{a}{d} \neq \dfrac{c}{b}$

Each derived ratio shown except the last one is simply a manipulation of the first, so all except the last are correct. You can verify this via cross-multiplication ($ad = bc$), then dividing both sides by a variable from each side (d and c, a and b, etc. but not a and d or b and c).

Alternatively, pick numerical values for a, b, c, and d; then simplify and confirm the two sides of the equation are equal. For example, take the two equivalent fractions $\dfrac{2}{3}$ and $\dfrac{6}{9}$ ($a = 2, b = 3, c = 6, d = 9$). Cross-multiplication gives $2 \times 9 = 3 \times 6$, which is a true statement. Dividing a and b by c and d gives $\dfrac{2}{6} = \dfrac{3}{9}$, also true, and so on. However, attempting to equate $\dfrac{a}{d}\left(\dfrac{2}{9}\right)$ and $\dfrac{b}{c}\left(\dfrac{3}{6}\right)$ will not work.

Let's take a look at a test-like question that involves ratios:

4. A researcher is optimizing solvent conditions for a chemical reaction. The conventional protocols use either 7 parts dioxane (an organic solvent) and 3 parts water or 5 parts water and 2 parts methanol. The researcher wants to see what happens when she uses dioxane and methanol without deviating from the given protocols. What ratio of methanol to dioxane should she use?

   A)   35:6

   B)   7:2

   C)   2:7

   D)   6:35

Use the Kaplan Method for Math: Extended Thinking to solve this question, working through it step-by-step. The following table shows Kaplan's strategic thinking on the left, along with suggested math scratchwork on the right.

Strategic Thinking	Math Scratchwork
Step 1: Read the question, identifying and organizing important information as you go *What are you being asked to find? What do you know?*	
You need the ratio of methanol to dioxane. You're given two ratios: dioxane to water and water to methanol.	D:W = 7:3 W:M = 5:2

Step 2: Choose the best strategy to answer the question	
How can you directly compare methanol to dioxane? What's a common multiple of the two water components?	
The two given ratios both contain water, but the water components are not identical. However, they share a common multiple: 15. Multiply each ratio by the factor that will make the water part equal 15.	D:W = 7:3 W:M = 5:2 *common multiple: 5 x 3 = 15* (7:3) x 5 = 35:15 (5:2) x 3 = 15:6
What does the combined ratio look like?	
Merging the two ratios lets you compare dioxane to methanol directly.	D:W:M = 35:15:6 D:M = 35:6
Step 3: Check that you answered the *right* question	
Did you find the ratio requested?	
The question asks for methanol to dioxane, so flip your ratio, and you're done. Watch out for trap answer A. You aren't looking for dioxane to methanol.	M:D = 6:35

✔ Notes

Beware of trap answers that contain incorrect ratios! Always confirm that you've found the one requested.

PERCENTAGES

Percentages aren't just for test grades; you'll find them frequently throughout life—discount pricing in stores, income tax brackets, and stock price trackers all use percents in some form. It's critical that you know how to use them correctly, especially on Test Day.

Suppose you have a bag containing 10 blue marbles and 15 pink marbles, and you're asked what

percent of the marbles are pink. You can determine this easily by using the formula $\% = \dfrac{\text{Part}}{\text{Whole}} \times 100\%$.

Plug 15 in for the part and 10 + 15 (= 25) for the whole, then compute to get $\dfrac{15}{25} \times 100\% = 60\%$

pink marbles.

Another easy way to solve many percent problems is to use the following statement: (blank) percent of (blank) is (blank). Translating from English into math, you obtain (blank)% × (blank) = (blank). As you saw with the DIRT equation in the rates section, knowledge of any two will unlock the third.

You might also be asked to determine the percent change in a given situation. Fortunately, you can find this easily using a variant of the percentage three-part formula:

$$\text{Percent increase or decrease} = \frac{(\text{Amount of increase or decrease})}{(\text{Original amount})} \times 100\%$$

✔ Notes

The percent three-part formula requires the percent component to be in decimal form. Remember to move the decimal point appropriately before using.

Sometimes more than one change will occur. Be especially careful here, as it can be tempting to take a "shortcut" by just adding two percent changes together (which will almost always lead to an incorrect answer). We'll demonstrate this in an upcoming problem.

Following is a test-like question involving percentages.

5. Ethanol is almost always mixed with gasoline to reduce automobile emissions. Most tanks of gasoline are 15% ethanol by volume. An oil company tries decreasing the ethanol content to 6% to lower the cost of gas. If a car with a 14-gallon tank is filled with the 15% blend, and a second car with a 10-gallon tank is filled with the 6% blend, how many times more ethanol is in the first car than in the second car?

A) 1.5

B) 2.5

C) 3.5

D) 4.0

Use the Kaplan Method for Math: Extended Thinking to solve this question, working through it step-by-step. The following table shows Kaplan's strategic thinking on the left, along with suggested math scratchwork on the right.

Strategic Thinking	Math Scratchwork
Step 1: Read the question, identifying and organizing important information as you go *What do you need to find? What helpful information is provided?* You need to find how many times more ethanol is in the 15% tank. The question supplies information about a 14-gallon tank and a 10-gallon tank, each containing a different ethanol/gasoline blend.	14 gal tank: 15% ethanol 10 gal tank: 6% ethanol

Step 2: Choose the best strategy to answer the question	
Which equation will get you closer to the answer?	_____% of _____ is _____
Straightforward math with the percent three-part formula works well here. You can use it for both tanks.	
How much ethanol is in the 14-gallon tank? How much ethanol is in the 10-gallon tank?	
Plug the appropriate values into the percent three-part formula. Remember to move the decimal points of your percents to get their decimal forms.	0.15×14 gal $= 2.1$ gal 0.06×10 gal $= 0.6$ gal
How many times more ethanol is in the larger tank?	
Set up an equation to show 0.6 times a number equals 2.1. Solving for Z gives 3.5; that is, the larger tank contains 3.5 times more ethanol than the smaller one.	0.6 gal $\times Z = 2.1$ gal $Z = 2.1$ gal$/0.6$ gal $= 3.5$
Step 3: Check that you answered the *right* question	
Did you find the correct comparison of the tanks?	
The question asks for how many times more ethanol is in the 14-gallon tank, which is what you found. You did it: 3.5 matches (C).	

✔ **Notes**

Resist the urge to merely take the difference between the two ethanol quantities. Make sure you're answering the question posed.

Here's an example of an Extended Thinking question that tests your percentage expertise.

A bank normally offers a compound annual interest rate of 0.25% on any savings account with a minimum balance of $5,000. The bank is currently offering college students a higher rate—0.42%—with a $1,000 minimum balance. Assume the average balances are kept constant at the required minima (e.g., all interest is withdrawn) for the following.

6. How much more interest does the regular account earn after three years than the student account?

7. What is the minimum balance a student would need to maintain to earn the same amount of interest as would be earned by saving money in the regular account? Round your answer to the nearest dollar.

Use the Kaplan Method for Math: Extended Thinking to solve this question, working through it step-by-step. The following table shows Kaplan's strategic thinking on the left, along with suggested math scratchwork on the right.

✔ **Notes**

Percent implies dividing by 100. For example, $15\% = \dfrac{15}{100} = 0.15$.

Strategic Thinking	Math Scratchwork
Step 1: Read the first part of the question, looking for clues *What information do part 1 and the intro give you?* The intro provides information on two account types.	regular acct: 0.25%, $5,000 min student acct: 0.42%, $1,000 min
Step 2: Identify and organize the information you need *What does part 1 ask you to find? What will get you to the answer to part 1?* You need to find how much more interest the $5,000 account will have after three years.	difference in interest: ?
Step 3: Based on what you know, plan your steps to navigate the first part *What pieces needed to find the answer are missing? How do you find the difference in interest?* You'll need the amount of interest that each account accrues after three years. Use the three-part percentage formula to find annual interest, then find the interest after three years, then take the difference.	reg. int. = ? stu. int. = ? reg. int. x 3 = ? stu. int. x 3 = ? reg. – stu. = ? (blank)% of (blank) is (blank)
Step 4: Solve, step-by-step, checking units as you go *How much interest does each account earn after one year? After three years?* Plug in appropriate values. Remember to adjust the decimal point on the percents appropriately. Triple the interest amounts to get the total accrued interest after three years. *What's the difference in interest earned?* Subtract.	0.0025 x $5,000 = $12.50 0.0042 x $1,000 = $4.20 $12.50 x 3 = $37.50 $4.20 x 3 = $12.60 $37.50 – $12.60 = $24.90

Step 5: Did I answer the *right* question?	
What is part 1 asking?	
You've found how much more interest the regular account makes after three years, so you're done with part 1.	24.9

✔ **Note**

Disregard the 0 in the hundredths place when gridding in your answer.

Part 1 is complete. Now on to Step 6: Repeat for remaining sections. Kaplan's strategic thinking is on the left, along with suggested math scratchwork on the right.

Strategic Thinking	Math Scratchwork
Step 1: Read the second part of the question, looking for clues	
What new information do you have?	
No new information here, but some pieces from part 1 might be useful.	
Step 2: Identify and organize the information you need	
What does part 2 ask you to find? Is there any information from part 1 that will help?	
Part 2 asks for the student account balance that will yield the same interest as a regular account at the minimum balance. You know the interest rates for a regular account and a student account at their respective minimum balances. You also know the interest earned annually (from part 1).	reg. acct: 0.25%, $12.50/yr stu. acct: 0.42%, $4.20/yr
Step 3: Based on what you know, plan your steps to navigate the second part	
How can you determine when the two accounts will earn the same interest? Will algebra work here?	
To answer part 2, you'll need to find when annual student interest equals annual regular interest. Set up equations with interest earned as a function of the account balance, one for each account. You already know what the regular account makes in interest annually, so it's just a matter of finding when the student equation equals that value.	$y = mx + b$

Step 4: Solve, step-by-step, checking units as you go

When does the student account earn $12.50 in interest per year?

Plug 12.5 in for your dependent variable, then solve for *x*.

reg.: $y = 0.0025x$

$12.5 = 0.0025 \times 5,000$

stu.: $y = 0.0042x$

$12.5 = 0.0042x$
$x = 2,976.19$

Step 5: Did I answer the *right* question?

Did I provide what was requested?

Part 2 asks for the balance a student account needs to make the same interest as a regular account. Round to the nearest dollar, and you're done!

2976

✔ **Notes**

It's tempting to incorporate the minimum balances into your equations, but remember what you need to find: interest. The minima aren't relevant here.

Now you'll have a chance to try a few test-like problems in a scaffolded way. See if you can fill in the missing pieces and solve for the correct answer without a full explanation.

We've provided some guidance, but you'll need to fill in the missing parts of explanations or the step-by-step math to get to the correct answer. Don't worry—after going through the worked examples at the beginning of this section, you should find these problems are completely doable.

8. Fuel efficiency is a measure of how many miles a car can go using a specified amount of fuel. It can change depending on the speed driven and how often the driver brakes and then accelerates, as well as other factors. Jack is taking a road trip. If he travels 180 miles at 40 mpg and then another 105 miles at 35 mpg, how much fuel has his car consumed?

    A) 1.5 gal

    B) 3.0 gal

    C) 4.5 gal

    D) 7.5 gal

The following table can help you structure your thinking as you go about solving this problem. The Kaplan strategic thinking is provided, as are bits of structured scratchwork. If you're not sure how to approach a question like this, start at the top and work your way down.

Strategic Thinking	Math Scratchwork
Step 1: Read the question, identifying and organizing important information as you go *What are you being asked to find here? What information is presented?* You need to find the amount of fuel Jack's car consumed. The question provides information about two legs of Jack's trip.	___ mi @ ___ mpg ___ mi @ ___ mpg

Step 2: Choose the best strategy to answer the question *What hint does the unit "miles per gallon" give you? Is there a standard equation you can use?* The unit mpg is a rate, so straightforward math using the DIRT equation is appropriate. *Which variable do I need to find?* 180 mi is clearly a distance, and 40 miles per gallon is your rate. Therefore, you need to find the time. Don't forget your units. Repeat for the second leg. *Are you finished?* The ultimate goal is to find the total fuel consumption. Add the two gallon figures together.	___ = ___ × ___ Leg 1: _____ = _____ × t t = _____ Leg 2: _____ = _____ × t t = _____ _____ + _____ = _____
Step 3: Check that you answered the *right* question *How much fuel did Jack's car consume?* If your answer is (D), you're correct!	fuel consumed: ___ gal

✔ Expert Tip

Sometimes your distance or time units won't look like those you're used to (e.g., miles, minutes, etc.). Don't let this deter you. If you have a rate, you can use the DIRT equation.

Here's another test-like example to try using this method:

9. Financial advisers are often hired to manage people's retirement accounts by shifting how money is invested in stocks and bonds. During a particularly volatile stock market period, a financial adviser makes a number of changes to a client's stock allocation. She first decreases this allocation by 25%, then increases it by 10%, then increases it an additional 50%. What is the approximate net percent increase in this client's stock allocation?

A) 20%

B) 24%

C) 30%

D) 35%

The Kaplan strategic thinking is provided, as are bits of structured scratchwork. If you're not sure how to approach a question like this, start at the top and work your way down.

Strategic Thinking	Math Scratchwork
Step 1: Read the question, identifying and organizing important information as you go *What is the question asking? What information will help you find the answer?* You need to find the net percent change in this client's stock allocation. The question provides a series of percent changes that this allocation undergoes.	start → _____ → _____ → _____ → end
Step 2: Choose the best strategy to answer the question *What kind of question is this? What's a good starting point for calculations?* This is a percent change problem. You aren't given a concrete starting point, so pick a starting number that's easy to use with percents, and get ready for a series of three-part percent formula calculations. *How many shares are left after each change?* Plug in the starting share count and the new percent, then solve for the new share count. Using the percent left in your calculation instead of the percent change will save you a step. When you compute the second and third changes, remember to use the final share count from the previous calculation, not the original number of shares. *Am I finished?* You found the final stock share count, now you need to find the percent change.	assume ___ shares @ start after –25%: _____% × _____ = _____ shares left: _____ after +10%: _____% × _____ = _____ shares left: _____ after +50%: _____% × _____ = _____ shares left: _____ _____ × 100% = _____
Step 3: Check that you answered the *right* question *What is the net percent change in stock allocation?* If you chose (B), you're correct.	net change: _____%

Now try your hand at an Extended Thinking question.

An artist is creating a rectangular tile mosaic. Her desired pattern uses 5 green tiles for every 3 blue tiles per square foot of mosaic.

10. If the artist's entire mosaic is 12 feet by 18 feet, how many more green tiles than blue will she need?

11. The artist discovers her tile vendor has a very limited supply of green tiles, so she alters her design so that it requires 2 green tiles for every 3 blue tiles. She also decides to add red tiles to her mosaic. How many red tiles will the artist need to make the ratio of red tiles to green tiles 3:4?

The following table can help you structure your thinking as you go about solving this problem. The Kaplan strategic thinking is provided, as are bits of structured scratchwork. If you're not sure how to approach a question like this, start at the top and work your way down.

Strategic Thinking	Math Scratchwork
Step 1: Read the first part of the question, looking for clues *What information do part 1 and the intro provide?* Included are the size of the mosaic and the ratio of green to blue tiles.	green:blue → ___:___ mosaic dimensions: ___×___
Step 2: Identify and organize the information you need *What does part 1 ask you to find?* You must find how many more green tiles than blue tiles the artist will use.	diff. between green & blue: ?
Step 3: Based on what you know, plan your steps to navigate the first part *What's missing? What calculations will get you the tile counts? How are the mosaic dimensions important?* You're missing the number of green tiles and blue tiles, as well as the number of times the pattern appears in the mosaic. You know the pattern appears once per square foot of mosaic, so finding the mosaic area will tell you how many times the pattern repeats. Multiply this number by the tile ratio to find how many of each color the artist needs, then take the difference.	# green tiles: ? # blue tiles: ? # pattern appearances: ? A = ? A × green:blue = # green: # blue

Step 4: Solve, step-by-step, checking units as you go	
What's the area of the mosaic?	$A = \underline{\quad} \times \underline{\quad} = \underline{\quad}$
Use the rectangle area formula to find the mosaic area (and the number of times the pattern repeats).	
How many green tiles and blue tiles will the artist require? How many more green will she need?	
Multiply the area by each number in the tile ratio, and then take the difference.	green: $\underline{\quad} \times \underline{\quad} = \underline{\quad}$ blue: $\underline{\quad} \times \underline{\quad} = \underline{\quad}$ $\underline{\quad}$ green $- \underline{\quad}$ blue $= \underline{\quad}$
Step 5: Did I answer the *right* question?	difference: $\underline{\quad}$
Did I find the difference requested?	
If you came up with 432 more green tiles, great job! You're correct.	

Now repeat for the other part. Once again, Kaplan strategic thinking is provided, as are bits of structured scratchwork. If you're not sure how to approach the second part, start at the top and work your way down.

Strategic Thinking	Math Scratchwork
Step 1: Read the second part of the question, looking for clues	
What's new in part 2?	
You know the new ratio of green to blue tiles and what the ratio of red to green tiles should be, as well as the area of the mosaic (from part 1).	green:blue $\rightarrow \underline{\quad} : \underline{\quad}$ red:green $\rightarrow \underline{\quad} : \underline{\quad}$ area: $\underline{\quad}$
Step 2: Identify and organize the information you need	
What is needed to solve this part?	
You need to find how many red tiles are required to make the ratio of red to green 3:4.	# red tiles: ?

Step 3: Based on what you know, plan your steps to navigate the second part *Anything missing? How does the new green:blue ratio affect the green tile count?* The ratios here are different, so you'll need new tile counts for green and red (blue stays constant). First, find the adjusted number of green tiles needed. Then determine the number of red tiles needed to satisfy the given ratio using a proportion that compares red to green.	# green tiles: ? #red tiles: ?
Step 4: Solve, step-by-step, checking units as you go *Given the new green:blue ratio, how many green tiles are now needed?* Multiply the number of pattern appearances from part 1 by the green tile component of the adjusted ratio. *What red tile count will satisfy the desired red:green ratio? Could a proportion be useful?* Set up a proportion using the red:green ratio and the new green tile count to find the number of red tiles required. Be careful when setting it up.	# green: ____ x ____ = $\dfrac{red}{green} : \dfrac{?}{?} = \dfrac{?}{?} \rightarrow$ ____ = ____ ____ = ____
Step 5: Did I answer the *right* question? *What is part 2 asking?* Did you get 324 red tiles? If so, congrats! You're correct.	___ red tiles

You've just completed your first Extended Thinking question. Way to go! Now it's time to see how much you've learned with a quiz.

Now that you've seen the variety of ways in which the PSAT can test you on ratios, rates, and percentages, try the following questions to check your understanding. Give yourself 5 minutes to tackle the following four questions. Make sure you use the Kaplan Method for Math as often as you can (as well as the Kaplan Method for Math: Extended Thinking when necessary). Remember, you want to emphasize speed and efficiency in addition to simply getting the correct answer.

12. An engineer is monitoring construction of a 75-foot escalator. The difference in height between the two floors being connected was originally noted as 40 feet, but due to a calculation error, this figure must be reduced by 25%. The angle between the escalator and the floor must not change in order to comply with the building code. What is the change in length in feet between the original escalator measurement and its corrected value?

A) 18.75

B) 25

C) 56.25

D) 100

13. Grocery stores often sell larger quantities of certain foods at reduced prices so that customers ultimately get more food for less money. Suppose an 8 oz. can of pineapple sells for $0.72 and a 20 oz. can costs $1.10. How much more (in cents) does the 8 oz. can cost per ounce than the 20 oz. can?

Questions 14 and 15 refer to the following information.

An electronics store is having a Black Friday Blowout sale: All items are 40% off, and the first 50 customers will receive an additional 25% off the reduced prices.

14. Two people purchase a home theater system that normally costs $2,200. The first person is one of the first 50 customers. The second person arrives much later in the day. How much more does the first customer save than the second customer?

15. In addition to price reductions, the store is offering to pay part of the sales tax on customers' purchases: Instead of paying the regular 6.35% sales tax, customers pay only half this rate. Assuming the same conditions from part 1 and that you are among the first 50 in the store, what is the total difference in price between the reduced price (with reduced tax) and the full price with standard tax? Round your answer to the nearest dollar.

Answers & Explanations for this chapter begin on page 417.

EXTRA PRACTICE

Required	Recommended
Questions 5, 6, 9, 10, 11, 14, 25, 26	Questions 1, 2, 3, 4, 7, 8, 12, 13, 15, 16, 17, 18, 19, 20, 21, 22, 23, 24, 27, 28, 29, 30

1. During fairly heavy traffic, the number of cars that can safely pass through a stoplight during a left turn signal is directly proportional to the length of time in seconds that the signal is green. If 9 cars can safely pass through a light that lasts 36 seconds, how many cars can safely pass through a light that lasts 24 seconds?

   A) 4

   B) 6

   C) 7

   D) 8

2. A cybercafé is a place that provides internet access to the public, usually for a fee, along with snacks and drinks. Suppose a cybercafé charges a base rate of $25 to join for a year, an additional $0.30 per visit for the first 50 visits, and $0.10 for every visit after that. How much does the cybercafé charge for a year in which 72 visits are made?

   A) $32.20

   B) $36.60

   C) $42.20

   D) $46.60

3. A high school's Environment Club receives a certain amount of money from the school to host an all-day Going Green Teach-in. The club budgets 40% for a guest speaker, 25% for educational materials, 20% to rent a hotel conference room, and the remainder for lunch. If the club plans to spend $225 on lunch for the participants, how much does it plan to spend on the guest speaker?

   A) $375

   B) $450

   C) $525

   D) $600

Bead Content of Necklace

4. A certain necklace is made up of beads of the following colors: red, blue, orange, indigo, silver, and clear. The necklace contains 120 beads. According to the pie chart shown, how many beads of the necklace are not blue?

   A) 20

   B) 24

   C) 80

   D) 96

5. The average college student reads prose text written in English at a rate of about 5 words per second. If the pages of Jorge's world history textbook contain an average of 500 words per page, how long will it take him to read a 45-page chapter?

A) 50 minutes

B) 1 hour, 15 minutes

C) 1 hour, 25 minutes

D) 1 hour, 40 minutes

6. Most of the world uses the metric system of measurements. The United States uses the standard system, also called the English system. Luca is from a country that uses the metric system and is visiting his cousin Drew in the United States. He gives Drew a family recipe for bread. The recipe is for one loaf and calls for 180 milliliters of milk. Drew wants to make 5 loaves. If 1 U.S. cup equals 236.588 milliliters, how many cups of milk will Drew need?

A) $\frac{3}{4}$

B) $1\frac{1}{3}$

C) $3\frac{4}{5}$

D) $6\frac{1}{2}$

7. For every 4,000 snowblowers produced by a snowblower factory, exactly 8 are defective. At this rate, how many snowblowers were produced during a period in which exactly 18 snowblowers were defective?

A) 6,000

B) 9,000

C) 12,000

D) 18,000

8. The Occupational Safety and Health Act (OSHA) was passed in 1970 to "assure safe and healthful working conditions." Its provisions cover all non-farm employers. Some small businesses, however, are exempt from certain reporting and inspection requirements if they have fewer than 10 employees. A certain city has 2,625 businesses in its jurisdiction and has a ratio of 5:2 of businesses that are exempt from inspections to those that are not exempt. Of the businesses that were required to have inspections, 12% had safety violations and were required to address the deficiencies. How many covered businesses did not have to address any OSHA safety issues?

A) 90

B) 315

C) 660

D) 2,310

9. Carmen is a traffic engineer. The city she works for recently added a number of new intersections with stoplights and wants to redesign the traffic system. The distance between the new intersections increases as one moves down Main Street. Carmen has been given the task of determining the length of the green lights at the intersections along Main Street, according to the following guidelines:

- The length of each green light should be greater than or equal to 8 seconds but less than or equal to 30 seconds.

- Each green light should be at least 25% longer than the one at the intersection before it.

- The length of each green light must be a whole second.

Which list of light lengths meets the city guidelines and includes as many intersections as possible?

A) 8, 12, 16, 20, 25, 30

B) 8, 10, 13, 17, 22, 28

C) 8, 10, 12.5, 16, 20, 25

D) 8, 10, 12, 15, 18, 22, 27

10. According to data provided by The College Board, the cost of tuition and fees for a private nonprofit four-year college in 1988 was approximately $15,800 (in 2013 dollars). In 2013, the cost of tuition and fees at the same type of college was approximately $30,100. If the cost of education experiences the same total percent increase over the next 25 years, approximately how much will tuition and fees at a private nonprofit four-year college cost (in 2013 dollars)?

A) $44,400

B) $45,800

C) $57,300

D) $66,200

11. A radiology center administers magnetic resonance images (MRIs) to check for abnormalities in a patient's body. One MRI scan typically produces about 3.6 gigabits of data. Every night, for 8 hours, the hospital backs up the files of the scans on a secure remote server. The hospital computers can upload the images at a rate of 2 megabits per second. What is the maximum number of MRI scans that the hospital can upload to the remote server each night? [1 gigabit = 1,024 megabits]

A) 15

B) 16

C) 56

D) 202

12. An average consumer car can travel 120 miles per hour under controlled conditions. An average race car can travel 210 miles per hour. How many more miles can the race car travel in 30 seconds than the consumer car?

A) $\dfrac{3}{4}$

B) 1

C) $\dfrac{3}{2}$

D) 45

The following table shows the product of each step.

1	2	3
$3x^3 \times 2x^2 = 6x^5$	$3x^3 \times x = 3x^4$	$3x^3 \times -17 = -51x^3$
4	**5**	**6**
$5x \times 2x^2 = 10x^3$	$5x \times x = 5x^2$	$5x \times -17 = -85x$

All that's left to do now is write out the expression and combine any like terms.

$$6x^5 + 3x^4 - 51x^3 + 10x^3 + 5x^2 - 85x$$

$$6x^5 + 3x^4 - 41x^3 + 5x^2 - 85x$$

Although it is relatively straightforward to add, subtract, and multiply polynomials, dividing polynomial expressions requires a different, more involved process: polynomial long division. Polynomial long division is just like regular long division except, as the name suggests, you use polynomials in place of numbers. The procedure is still the same.

Let's say we want to divide $x^3 + 3x + 7$ by $x + 4$. We can set this up just like a long division problem.

$$x + 4 \overline{)\, x^3 + 0x^2 + 3x + 7}$$

You'll notice that even though the larger polynomial does not have an x^2 term, we wrote one in so we don't lose track of things. You know $0x^2$ is, of course, equal to 0, so adding this placeholder term doesn't change the value of the polynomial. Start by dividing the first term of the dividend by the first term of the divisor to get x^2. Now multiply the entire divisor by x^2 and subtract this product from the dividend.

$$
\begin{array}{r}
x^2 \\
x + 4 \overline{)\, x^3 + 0x^2 + 3x + 7} \\
-\ (x^3 + 4x^2) \\
\hline
-4x^2 + 3x + 7
\end{array}
$$

Continue by dividing the next term, $-4x^2$, by the first term of the divisor. Next, multiply the quotient, $-4x$, by the entire divisor and subtract.

$$\begin{array}{r}
x^2 - 4x \\
x + 4 \overline{)\, x^3 + 0x^2 + 3x + 7} \\
-\ \underline{(x^3 + 4x^2)} \\
-4x^2 + 3x + 7 \\
\underline{-(-4x^2 - 16x)} \\
19x + 7
\end{array}$$

Finally, repeat this process with the $19x + 7$.

$$\begin{array}{r}
x^2 - 4x + 19 \\
x + 4 \overline{)\, x^3 + 0x^2 + 3x + 7} \\
-\ \underline{(x^3 + 4x^2)} \\
-4x^2 + 3x + 7 \\
\underline{-(-4x^2 - 16x)} \\
19x + 7 \\
\underline{-(19x + 76)} \\
-69
\end{array}$$

When all is said and done, the quotient is $x^2 - 4x + 19$ with a remainder of -69; the remainder is put over the divisor in a separate term. Thus, the final answer is $x^2 - 4x + 19 - \dfrac{69}{x + 4}$. This is a topic many students tend to forget as soon as math class is over, so make sure to dust off those cobwebs by trying out the problem in the practice section.

> ✔ **Note**
>
> You can use polynomial long division to determine whether a binomial is a factor of a polynomial. If the remainder in the example had been 0, then $x + 4$ would have been a factor of the polynomial $x^3 + 3x + 7$.

RATIONAL EXPRESSIONS

A rational expression is simply a ratio (or fraction) of polynomials. In other words, it is a fraction with a polynomial as the numerator and another polynomial as the denominator. The rules that govern fractions and polynomials also govern rational expressions, so if you know these well, you'll be in good shape when you encounter one on Test Day.

There are a few important tidbits to remember about rational expressions; these are summarized here. They are also true for rational equations.

- For an expression to be rational, the numerator and denominator must both be polynomials.

- Like polynomials, rational expressions are also designated certain degrees based on the term with the highest variable exponent sum. For instance, the expression $\dfrac{1 - 2x}{3x^2 + 3}$ has a first-degree numerator and a second-degree denominator.

- Because rational expressions by definition can have polynomial denominators, they will often be undefined for certain values. For example, the expression $\frac{x-4}{x+2}$ is defined for all values of x except –2. This is because when $x = -2$, the denominator of the expression is 0, which would make the expression undefined.

- Factors in a rational expression can be cancelled when simplifying, but under no circumstances can you do the same with individual terms. Consider, for instance, the expression $\frac{x^2 - x - 6}{x^2 + 5x + 6}$.

  Many students will attempt to cancel the x^2, x, and 6 terms to give $\frac{1-1-1}{1+5+1} = \frac{-1}{7}$, which is *never* correct. Don't even think about trying this on Test Day.

- Like fractions, rational expressions can be proper or improper. A proper rational expression has a lower-degree numerator than denominator $\left(\text{e.g., } \frac{1-x}{x^2+3}\right)$, and an improper one has a higher-degree numerator than denominator $\left(\text{e.g., } \frac{1-x}{x^2+3}\right)$. The latter can be simplified using polynomial long division.

✔ Note

For those who are curious, the correct way to simplify $\frac{x^2 - x - 6}{x^2 + 5x + 6}$ is to factor, which you'll learn about in chapter 6. For now, know that this equals $\frac{(x+2)(x-3)}{(x+2)(x+3)}$. Cancel the **x + 2** factors to get $\frac{(x-3)}{(x+3)}$.

---

7. If $\dfrac{(x-3)^2}{16} - \dfrac{(x+2)^2}{25} = 0$, what does $x + 5$ equal?

   A)   8

   B)   12

   C) $\dfrac{107}{9}$

   D)   28

✔ Note

Terms that are being multiplied or divided can be cancelled, but terms that are being added or subtracted cannot.

Use the Kaplan Method for Math to solve this question, working through it step-by-step. The following table shows Kaplan's strategic thinking on the left, along with suggested math scratchwork on the right.

Strategic Thinking	Math Scratchwork
Step 1: Read the question, identifying and organizing important information as you go *What's the ultimate goal for this question?* You're asked for the value of *x*.	
Step 2: Choose the best strategy to answer the question *What is the best first step to take?* You might think to expand the binomial numerators, but this will be costly time-wise. In addition, you would need to produce a common denominator to subtract the two fractions. Neither would be pleasant. *What's a quicker route to x?* You could plug the answer choices in for *x* to find which one works, but there's an even faster way: Use your knowledge of rational expression manipulation. You have a 0 on the other side of the equation, so move the second expression to the other side to make a proportion. *Is there a way to simplify the fractions before cross-multiplying the proportion? What do you notice about the numerators and denominators?* The numerators and denominators are perfect squares. Therefore, you can eliminate the exponent in the numerator by taking the square root of both sides. Now you can easily cross-multiply to get a more friendly-looking equation. *What remaining steps do you need to complete to find x?* Distribute the coefficients outside the parentheses on both sides. Then combine like terms and isolate *x*. Solving for *x* gives 23, and adding 5 gives you 28, which is (D).	$$\frac{(x-3)^2}{16} - \frac{(x+2)^2}{25} = 0$$ $$\frac{(x-3)^2}{16} = \frac{(x+2)^2}{25}$$ $$\sqrt{\frac{(x-3)^2}{16}} = \sqrt{\frac{(x+2)^2}{25}}$$ $$\frac{\sqrt{(x-3)^2}}{\sqrt{16}} = \frac{\sqrt{(x+2)^2}}{\sqrt{25}}$$ $$\frac{x-3}{4} = \frac{x+2}{5}$$ $5(x-3) = 4(x+2)$ $5x - 15 = 4x + 8$ $x = 23$ $x + 5 = 28$

Strategic Thinking	Math Scratchwork
Step 3: Check that you answered the *right* question *Did you find x + 5?* You've found $x+5$, so your work for this question is done. The correct answer is (D).	

> ✔ **Note**
>
> Extraneous solutions are solutions that cause the entire expression to become undefined. Look out for zeros in denominators and negatives under square roots.

This polynomial equation had one solution that was an integer. However, you may be given problems with complicated solutions. Furthermore, it is important to know that a rational equation can have what are called **extraneous solutions**. Extraneous solutions are numbers that are found algebraically but do not solve the original problem. For example, you may find a value for a variable that would cause a 0 to be in the denominator, which makes the entire expression undefined. Plug the solutions that you find back into the original expression/equation to make sure that a 0 is not created in the denominator.

MODELING REAL-WORLD APPLICATIONS USING POLYNOMIAL, RADICAL, AND RATIONAL EQUATIONS

Sometimes the testmakers want you to test your simplifying prowess by converting an expression into a "useful" form, as standard form is not always the most practical for use.

Let's say you and your friends want to enjoy a brisk fall day by going apple picking. To go apple picking, you must rent a basket for $20, and you'll be charged an additional $0.35 for each apple you pick. On top of that, a 9% sales tax will be added to your final bill. We could represent this scenario with the following equation:

$$c = 1.09 \times (0.35a + 20)$$

In this situation, c is the cost of your picking experience and a is the number of apples you pick. You'll notice the 1.09 out in front of the parentheses ensures that sales tax is applied to your entire purchase, not just the apples or the rental. Now suppose you're asked to determine the true price of each additional apple; that is, how much more money will one extra apple cost you? We can't get that by just glancing at the equation, but distributing the 1.09 will help. When we do this, we arrive at a different equation for the same apple-picking experience:

$$c = 0.3815a + 21.8$$

Although this equation isn't as elegant or intuitive as our initial equation, it is much more useful for answering the question at hand. Now we can see how sales tax affects our fixed costs (basket rental) and our variable costs (each additional apple). The only term that matters here is the one that depends on the number of apples: Each additional apple will cost about $0.38 when tax is included.

Try the more challenging example below.

8. Two twins, Jenny and Megan, have separate savings accounts created by their parents. Each girl received $5,000 to invest in a savings account of her choosing. Jenny picked a savings account that has an interest rate of 2% that compounds monthly, and Megan picked a savings account with an interest rate of 5% that compounds yearly. If $A = P\left(1+\dfrac{r}{n}\right)^{nt}$, where A is the final account balance, P is the initial balance, r is the interest rate in decimal form, n is the number of compoundings per year, and t is the amount of time in years, what is the difference between Jenny and Megan's account balances after two years?

A) $149.08

B) $155.81

C) $308.62

D) $322.71

Use the Kaplan Method for Math to solve this question, working through it step-by-step. The following table shows Kaplan's strategic thinking on the left, along with suggested math scratchwork on the right.

Strategic Thinking	Math Scratchwork
Step 1: Read the question, identifying and organizing important information as you go *What are you being asked to do here?* You must identify the difference in the balances of the two different savings accounts after two years.	

Step 2: Choose the best strategy to answer the question

Where can you start?

Focus on the relevant information. Make sure that you convert the interest rates to decimal form, and take care not to mix up your variables. Subscripts are helpful in keeping them straight.

$$A = P\left(1+\frac{r}{n}\right)^{nt}$$

$P = 5,000$

Jenny's rate (r_j): 2% = 0.02
   # compoundings (n_j): 12
Megan's rate (r_m): 5% = 0.05
   # compoundings (n_m): 1
years (t): 1

How can you determine each account's balance?

Plug in the values you know and solve for each balance after two years. Note that although $\frac{0.02}{12}$ is written rounded, you should not round until the very end.

Jenny

$$A_j = P\left(1+\frac{r_j}{n_j}\right)^{n_j t}$$

$$A_j = 5,000\left(1+\frac{0.02}{12}\right)^{12\times 2}$$

$A_j = 5,000(1+0.00167)^{24}$

$A_j = 5,000(1.00167)^{24}$

$A_j = 5,203.88$

What's the next step after finding the two balances?

Take the difference between the two balances to get to the answer.

Megan

$$A_m = P\left(1+\frac{r_m}{n_m}\right)^{n_m t}$$

$$A_m = 5,000\left(1+\frac{0.05}{1}\right)^{1\times 2}$$

$A_m = 5,000(1 + 0.05)^2$

$A_m = 5,000(1.05)^2$

$A_m = 5,512.50$

diff. = $5,512.50 - 5,203.88 = 308.62$

Step 3: Check that you answered the *right* question

What's the difference between the two balances?

Choice (C) is the correct answer.

SOLVING A FORMULA OR EQUATION FOR A GIVEN VARIABLE

If you've ever taken a chemistry or physics course, you probably noticed that many real-world situations can't be represented by beautiful linear equations. There are frequently radicals, exponents, and fractions galore. Furthermore, these equations can seem to lack a logical arrangement. For example, the root-mean-square velocity for particles in a gas can be described by the following equation:

$$v = \sqrt{\left(\frac{3kT}{m}\right)}$$

In this equation, v represents the root-mean-square velocity, k is the Boltzmann constant, T is the temperature in degrees Kelvin, and m is the mass of one molecule of the gas. It's a great equation if you have k, T, and m and are looking for v. However, if you're looking for a different quantity, having that unknown buried among others (and under a radical to boot) can be unnerving, but unearthing it is easier than it appears. Let's say we're given v, k, and m but need to find T. First, square both sides to eliminate the radical to yield $v^2 = \dfrac{3kT}{m}$. Next, isolate T by multiplying both sides by m and dividing by $3k$: $\dfrac{mv^2}{3k} = T$.

At this point, you can plug in the values of m, v, and k to solve for T. Sometimes the PSAT will have you do just that: Solve for the numerical value of a variable of interest. In other situations, you'll need to rearrange an equation so that a different variable is isolated. The same rules of algebra you've used all along apply. The difference: You're manipulating solely variables.

Now you'll have a chance to try a few more test-like questions. Some guidance is provided, but you'll need to fill in the missing parts of explanations or the step-by-step math to get to the correct answer. Don't worry—after going through the examples at the beginning of this chapter, these questions should be completely doable. If you're still struggling, review the worked examples in this chapter.

9. A plasma is a gas composed of positively charged atom nuclei and negatively charged electrons. When a plasma is at equilibrium, the density of charge oscillates (shifts back and forth) at what is called the plasma frequency, -which can be found using the following formula:

$$\omega_p = \sqrt{\frac{ne^2}{m_e \varepsilon_0}}$$

where n is the number of electrons present, e is electric charge, m_e is the mass of a single electron, and ε_0 is permittivity of free space. Which of the following expressions correctly shows the electric charge in terms of the other variables?

A) $\sqrt{\dfrac{\omega_p^2 m_e \varepsilon_0}{n}}$

B) $\sqrt{\dfrac{\omega_p^2}{n m_e \varepsilon_0}}$

C) $\dfrac{\omega_p^2 m_e \varepsilon_0}{n}$

D) $\dfrac{ne^2}{\omega_p^2 m_e}$

Strategic thinking follows, as well as bits of scratchwork. If you aren't sure where to start, answer the questions in italics and fill in the blanks in the table as you work from top to bottom.

Strategic Thinking	Math Scratchwork
Step 1: Read the question, identifying and organizing important information as you go *What are you being asked to do here?* You need to identify the expression equal to *e*. Translation: Solve the given equation for *e*.	

PRACTICE

Step 2: Choose the best strategy to answer the question	$\omega_p = \sqrt{\dfrac{ne^2}{m_e \varepsilon_0}}$
There are several variables and unusual symbols. How should this be solved?	____ = ____
Don't let the strange Greek letters intimidate you; just treat them as you would "normal" variables. Start by undoing the radical so you can get to what's underneath, then isolate the correct variable. Related note: Don't panic if you've never heard of "permittivity of free space." If you don't need it to answer the question, don't sweat it.	____ = ____ ____ = ____ ____ = ____
Step 3: Check that you answered the *right* question *Did you solve for the right term?* Did you get (A)? If so, you're absolutely correct.	Answer: ____

✔ **Note**

Beware of look-alike variables; it's easy to mistake ε_0 for e in this question. Make sure you keep them straight in your scratchwork.

10. What is the value of the remainder when $6x^3 - 4x^2 + 3$ is divided by $x - 1$?

Use the following scaffolding as your map through the question. Strategic thinking is on the left, and bits of scratchwork are on the right. If you aren't sure where to start, answer the questions in italics and fill in the blanks in the table as you work from top to bottom.

Strategic Thinking	Math Scratchwork
Step 1: Read the question, identifying and organizing important information as you go *What are you being asked to do here?* You need to divide the first polynomial by the second.	
Step 2: Choose the best strategy to answer the question *Can anything be factored out of the first polynomial?* Possibly, but it would likely take time you don't have. Polynomial long division will prevent wasted time. Fill in the blanks on the right to get to the answer.	$$\begin{array}{r} \\ \underline{\smash{\big)}} \\ -(\ -\ ) \\ \overline{} \\ -(\ -\ ) \\ \overline{} \\ -(\ -\ ) \\ \end{array}$$ Remainder: ———
Step 3: Check that you answered the *right* question *What's the remainder of this division problem?* If your answer is 5, congrats! You're correct.	Answer: _____

11. Which of the following is the correct simplification of $\dfrac{\sqrt{3x^2y^3}}{4\sqrt{5xy^3}}$?

   A) $\dfrac{\sqrt{15}}{20}$

   B) $\dfrac{\sqrt{15x}}{20}$

   C) $\dfrac{y\sqrt{15x}}{20}$

   D) $\dfrac{xy^2\sqrt{15x}}{40}$

Use the scaffolding below as your map through the question. Strategic thinking is on the left, and bits of scratchwork are on the right. If you aren't sure where to start, answer the questions in italics and fill in the blanks in the table as you work from top to bottom.

Strategic Thinking	Math Scratchwork
Step 1: Read the question, identifying and organizing important information as you go *What is the question asking?* You need to correctly simplify the given expression.	
Step 2: Choose the best strategy to answer the question *There's no real equation. What route should you take?* Use your exponent and radical rules to get to the answer. You can remove squares from under the radical now, but there's a faster route: Split the numerator's radical terms so each is under a separate radical; repeat with the denominator. Doing this makes cancelling easier and lessens the chance of making a careless error. *What do you do after cancelling?* Rationalize the denominator.	$$\dfrac{\sqrt{3x^2y^3}}{4\sqrt{5xy^3}}$$ $$\dfrac{\sqrt{}\times\sqrt{}\times\sqrt{}}{\underline{}\times\sqrt{}\times\sqrt{}\times\sqrt{}}$$ $$=\dfrac{\sqrt{}\times\sqrt{}}{\underline{}\times\sqrt{}}$$ $$\dfrac{\sqrt{}\times\sqrt{}}{\underline{}\times\sqrt{}}\times\dfrac{\sqrt{}}{\sqrt{}}$$ $$=\dfrac{\sqrt{}\times\sqrt{}\times\sqrt{}}{\underline{}\times\sqrt{}\times\sqrt{}}$$ $$=\dfrac{\sqrt{}}{\underline{}\times\sqrt{}}$$
Step 3: Check that you answered the *right* question *Did you simplify fully and properly?* Did you get (B)? If so, you're absolutely correct.	Answer: _____

Now that you've seen the variety of ways in which the PSAT can test you on the topics in this chapter, try the following questions to check your understanding. Give yourself 3.5 minutes to tackle the following three questions. Make sure you use the Kaplan Method for PSAT Math as often as you can. Remember, you want to emphasize speed and efficiency in addition to simply getting the correct answer.

12. The electromagnetic spectrum encompasses all types of light, both visible and invisible. A light's wavelength is inversely proportional to its damage capability and can be found using the equation $c = \lambda v$, where c is the speed of light in a vacuum in meters per second 3×10^9 (m/s), λ (lambda) is wavelength in meters, and v (nu) is frequency in reciprocal seconds (s^{-1}). Suppose environmental scientists are scanning for ozone layer depletion and discovered an unusually high concentration of ultraviolet light near Los Angeles. If this light has a wavelength of 150 nanometers (1 m = 1×10^9 nm), what is its frequency in s^{-1}?

A) 2×10^7

B) 3×10^7

C) 2×10^{16}

D) 3×10^{16}

13. Which of the following expressions is equal to $\dfrac{2 - \sqrt{3}}{2 + \sqrt{3}}$?

A) $7 - 4\sqrt{3}$

B) 1

C) 7

D) $7 + 4\sqrt{3}$

14. If $n^3 = -8$, what is the value of $\dfrac{(n^2)^3}{\frac{1}{n^2}}$?

Answers & Explanations are provided on page 431.

EXTRA PRACTICE

Required	Recommended
Questions 3, 5, 7, 8, 10, 11, 14, 16	Questions 1, 2, 4, 6, 9, 12, 13, 15, 17, 18

1. Which of the following is equivalent to the expression $\dfrac{9^4 \times 3^2}{9^5}$?

    A) 0

    B) 1

    C) 3

    D) 9

2. Which of the following is the reduced form of $\dfrac{2x + 6y}{10x - 16}$?

    A) $\dfrac{x + 3y}{5x - 8}$

    B) $\dfrac{x + 6y}{5x - 16}$

    C) $\dfrac{1}{5} - \dfrac{3y}{8}$

    D) $\dfrac{1 + 3y}{-3}$

3. What is the resulting coefficient of x after multiplying $-x + 4$ by $x - 5$?

    A) –9

    B) –1

    C) 1

    D) 9

4. What is the difference when $\dfrac{3x + 1}{x + 3}$ is subtracted from $\dfrac{4x - 9}{x + 3}$?

    A) $\dfrac{-x + 10}{x + 3}$

    B) $\dfrac{x - 10}{x + 3}$

    C) $\dfrac{x - 8}{x + 3}$

    D) $\dfrac{x - 8}{2x + 6}$

5. Which of the following is equivalent to the expression above?

    $$\dfrac{3}{k^{\frac{2}{5}}}$$

    A) $\sqrt[5]{\dfrac{k^2}{3}}$

    B) $3\sqrt{k^5}$

    C) $3\sqrt[5]{k^2}$

    D) $\sqrt{3k^5}$

6. The expression $\dfrac{x^{\frac{3}{2}}}{\sqrt{x}}$ is equivalent to which of the following?

    A) $\sqrt{x}$

    B) 1

    C) x

    D) x^3

7. What is the quotient of $\dfrac{8x^2 + 14x + 3}{4x + 1}$?

   A) $2x + 1$

   B) $2x + 3$

   C) $4x + 3$

   D) $4x + 7$

$$v = \sqrt[3]{\dfrac{P}{0.02}}$$

8. The power generated by a windmill is related to the velocity of the wind by the equation shown above, where P is the power in watts and v is the wind velocity in miles per hour. What is the wind velocity when the windmill is generating 160 watts of power?

   A) 20 mph

   B) 32 mph

   C) 64 mph

   D) 89 mph

9. If $M = 12x^2 + 4x - 7$ and $N = 5x^2 - x + 8$, then which of the following equals $M - N$?

   A) $7x^2 + 3x + 1$

   B) $7x^2 + 5x + 1$

   C) $7x^2 + 3x - 15$

   D) $7x^2 + 5x - 15$

10. The value of $6x + 5$ is how much more than the value of $6x - 1$?

   A) 4

   B) 6

   C) $6x - 4$

   D) $6x + 6$

$$t = 2\pi\sqrt{\dfrac{L}{32}}$$

11. The period of a pendulum is the amount of time that it takes for the pendulum to swing back and forth to complete one full cycle. The period t in seconds depends on the length L of the pendulum in feet and is defined by the equation above. Which equation defines the length of the pendulum in terms of its period?

   A) $L = \dfrac{8t^2}{\pi^2}$

   B) $L = \dfrac{\pi^2 t^2}{8}$

   C) $L = \dfrac{8t^2}{\pi}$

   D) $L = \dfrac{16t^2}{\pi}$

12. Which of the following represents $9^{\frac{3}{2}}$ as an integer?

   A) 3

   B) 9

   C) 27

   D) 81

13. When a liquid leaks onto a level surface, it generally spreads out equally in all directions, so the puddle is usually in the shape of a circle. When a hazardous chemical leaks like this, it is important to know how long it has been leaking to determine the possible risk to nearby water sources, vegetation, animals, and people. For a certain chemical, the equation $d = 1.25\sqrt{m-1}$, where d represents the diameter of the puddle in inches, can be used to find the number of minutes, $m \geq 1$, that have passed since the leak began. If the diameter of a puddle created by a leak is 3 feet, about how many minutes has the liquid been leaking?

A) 8

B) 15

C) 830

D) 2,026

14. If $x > 1$, which of the following must be true?

A) $\dfrac{\sqrt{x}}{x} - 1 < 0$

B) $\dfrac{x}{\sqrt{x}} < 1$

C) $2\sqrt{x} < x$

D) $\sqrt{x} + x > x^2$

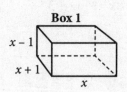

Box 1

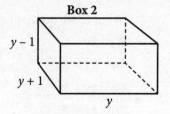

Box 2

15. The length of Box 2 (y) shown above is twice the length of Box 1 (x). Which expression shows the difference in the volumes of the two boxes?

A) $2x^3 - 2x$

B) $7x^3 - x$

C) $7x^3 - 2x$

D) $8x^3 - 2x$

16. For all a and b, what is the product of $(a - b)^2$ and $(a + b)$?

A) $a^2 - b^2$

B) $a^3 - b^3$

C) $a^3 - ab^2 + a^2b - b^3$

D) $a^3 - a^2b - ab^2 + b^3$

17. If $A = 25x^2 + 10x - 45$ and $B = -12x^2 - 32x + 24$, what is $\dfrac{3}{5}A + \dfrac{1}{2}B$?

A) $2x^2 - 6x - 3$

B) $2x^2 - 6x + 20$

C) $9x^2 - 10x - 15$

D) $21x^2 + 22x - 39$

18. If $x > 4$ and $\dfrac{18}{\sqrt{x-4}} = 6$, what is the value of x?

CHAPTER 5

Functions
&
Function Notation

CHAPTER OBJECTIVES

By the end of this section, you will be able to:

1. Use function notation to answer questions containing equations, tables, and/or graphs

2. Interpret functions and functional statements that represent real-world scenarios

3. Combine functions properly using basic operations and compute compositions of functions correctly

4. Determine if a function is increasing, decreasing, or constant and correctly apply transformations to a given function or functions

SMARTPOINTS

Point Value	SmartPoint Category
70 points	Functions

FUNCTIONS & FUNCTION NOTATION

Functions act as rules that transform inputs into outputs, and they differ from equations in that each input must have only one corresponding output. For example, imagine a robot: Every time you give it an apple, it promptly cuts that apple into three slices. The following table summarizes the first few inputs and their corresponding outputs.

Domain x: # apples given to robot	Range $f(x)$: # slices returned by robot
0	0
1	3
2	6
3	9

From the table you see that the output will always be triple the input, and you can express that relationship as the function $f(x) = 3x$ (read "f of x equals three x").

PSAT questions, especially those involving real-world situations, might ask you to derive the equation of a function, so you'll need to be familiar with the standard forms. Following, for instance, is the standard form of a linear function:

$$f(x) = kx + f(0)$$

The input, or **domain**, is the value represented by x. Sometimes the domain will be constrained by the question (e.g., x must be an integer). Other times, the domain could be defined by real-world conditions. For example, if x represents the time elapsed since the start of a race, the domain would need to exclude negative numbers. The output, or **range**, is the result of what you plug into the function and is represented by $f(x)$. The initial condition or **y-intercept** is represented by $f(0)$—the value of the function at the very beginning. If you think this looks familiar, you're absolutely right! It's just a dressed-up version of the standard $y = mx + b$ you've already seen. Take a look at the following table for a translation:

Linear Function Piece	What It Represents	Slope-Intercept Counterpart
$f(x)$	dependent variable or output	y
k	rate of change, slope	m
$f(0)$	y-intercept or initial quantity in a word problem	b

As you might have guessed, an exponential equation has a standard function notation as well. Here we've used g in place of f for visual clarity. Know that the letter used to represent a function (f, g, h, etc.) is sometimes arbitrarily chosen.

$$g(x) = g(0)(1+r)^x$$

Analogous to the linear standard function form, $g(x)$ has replaced y, and $g(0)$ has replaced $f(0)$. Recognizing that function notation is a variation of something you already know will go a long way toward reducing nerves on Test Day. You should also note that graphing functions is a straight-forward process: In the examples above, just set the side on the right equal to y and enter into your graphing calculator.

> ✔ **Note**
>
> A quick way to determine whether an equation is a function is to conduct the vertical line test: If a vertical line passes through the graph of the equation more than once at any time, the equation is not a function.

Following is an example of a test-like functions question.

1. If $f(x) = x^2 - x$ for all $x \le -1$ and $f(x) = 0$ for all $x > -1$, which of the following could not be a value of $f(x)$?

   A) −4

   B) 0

   C) $\dfrac{7}{13}$

   D) 2

Use the Kaplan Method for Math to solve this question, working through it step-by-step. The following table shows Kaplan's strategic thinking on the left, along with suggested math scratchwork on the right.

Strategic Thinking	Math Scratchwork
Step 1: Read the question, identifying and organizing important information as you go *What is the question asking you to do?* The question is asking for the answer choice that could *not* be in the range of this function.	
Step 2: Choose the best strategy to answer the question *How can you determine which of the four choices is not part of the range?* You'll need to examine each piece of the domain individually to learn more. First, summarize each piece of the domain description. *Can you use the domain information to eliminate any answer choices? What happens when x > −1?* Because the range is 0 when $x > -1$, you can eliminate B. *Would your knowledge of number properties be helpful for the second domain component?* Absolutely. Because the range $x^2 - x$ only applies when $x \le -1$, you only need to consider what happens when a negative number less than −1 is substituted for x. No matter what number you use, your output will always be positive. Eliminate C and D.	domain $x \le -1$: range $= x^2 - x$ domain $x > -1$: range $= 0$ (negative)^2 − negative ⟶ positive + positive ⟶ positive
Step 3: Check that you answered the *right* question *Which value will never be in the range of this function?* The only remaining choice is (A).	$f(x) \ge 0$

Once broken into simpler pieces, this function question became much easier. Read on for more information about other ways the PSAT can test your knowledge of functions.

✔ **Notes**

You might be tempted to plug the answer choices in and solve for x, but this will cost you valuable time. While Backsolving can be a strategy of last resort on problems like this, it takes far too long. Use it only if you can't approach the problem in any other way. The PSAT will reward you for knowing the quickest way to answer the question, which in this case involves knowing number properties.

GRAPHICAL & TABULAR FUNCTION INTERPRETATION

The ability to interpret the graphs of functions will serve you well on Test Day (as well in real life . . . even outside of math class!). Better yet, to interpret graphs of functions, you'll need to utilize the same skills you use to interpret "regular" equations on the coordinate plate, so this material shouldn't be completely foreign.

You know from the first part of this chapter that a function is merely a dressed-up equation, so translating from function to "regular" notation or vice versa is a straightforward process. Consider the following brief example.

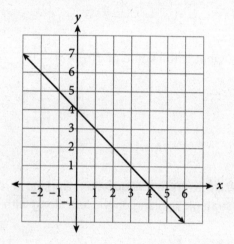

Suppose you're asked to find the value of x for which $f(x) = 6$. Because $f(x)$ represents the output value, or range, translate this as "When does the y value equal 6?" To answer the question, find 6 on the y-axis, then trace over to the function (the line). Read the corresponding x value: It's –2, so when $f(x) = 6$, x must be –2.

The PSAT might also present functions in the form of tables. These may or may not have an equation associated with them, but regardless, you'll need to be adept at extracting the information necessary to answer questions. Most of the time the table will have just two columns, one for the domain and another for the range.

✔ Notes

Remember: A value of $f(x)$ corresponds to where you are on the y-axis. A value of x corresponds to a location on the x-axis.

Now try a test-like example on the next page.

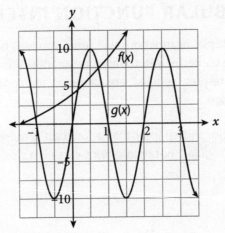

2. In the figure shown, what is the value of $f(0) + g\left(\dfrac{1}{2}\right)$?

   A) −4

   B) 6

   C) 10

   D) 14

Use the Kaplan Method for Math to solve this question, working through it step-by-step. The following table shows Kaplan's strategic thinking on the left, along with suggested math scratchwork on the right.

✔ **Notes**

Watch your axis scales; like scatterplot questions, questions involving graphs of functions often contain trap answers waiting for students who misread the axes.

Strategic Thinking	Math Scratchwork
Step 1: Read the question, identifying and organizing important information as you go *What is the question asking you to find?* You're asked to determine the value of $f(0) + g\left(\dfrac{1}{2}\right)$. In other words, you need to find the *y*-value of function *f* when *x* = 0 and the *y*-value of function *g* when $x = \dfrac{1}{2}$, then add those values together.	

Step 2: Choose the best strategy to answer the question

How can you find f(0)?

Graph interpretation will get you to the answer in little time; just consider the expression piecewise. Start with $f(x)$. Locate the spot on $f(x)$ where $x = 0$. At that point, $f(x)$ has a y-value of 4. Therefore, $f(0) = 4$.

What about $g\left(\dfrac{1}{2}\right)$?

Repeat the previous process for $g(x)$ when $x = \dfrac{1}{2}$; at this x value, $y = 10$. In function notation, $g\left(\dfrac{1}{2}\right) = 10$.

What's the sum of the two values?

The hard part is over; now just add the values together:

$$f(0) + g\left(\frac{1}{2}\right) = 4 + 10 = 14$$

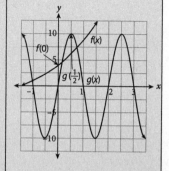

Step 3: Check that you answered the *right* question

Did you answer the question posed?

You found $f(0) + g\left(\dfrac{1}{2}\right)$, which matches (D). You're finished!

$$f(0) + g(\frac{1}{2}) = 4 + 10$$
$$= 14$$

Of course, this question would have been much simpler if the graph had labeled the points or given you an equation to plug values into, but then it wouldn't be testing you on functions. Your ability to figure out what functions questions are actually asking you for is key to making these problems a breeze on Test Day.

Following is a sample functions question involving a table of values. Notice that for each value for "game," there is only one corresponding value for "number of students." Once you recognize that relationship, you know that a given table must be a function.

Game	Number of students
1	5
2	11
3	21
4	35
5	53
6	75
7	101
8	131

3. West Valley High School is keeping track of how many students show up to the home football games wearing face paint in the school colors. To encourage participation, there is a prize giveaway at each game. As the prizes get more exciting, participation begins to increase. If j represents the game number and $f(j)$ represents the number of students in face paint at game j, which of the following functions best describes the information in the table?

A) $f(j) = j + 4$

B) $f(j) = 2j + 5$

C) $f(j) = \dfrac{1}{2}j^2 + 7$

D) $f(j) = 2j^2 + 3$

Use the Kaplan Method for Math to solve this question, working through it step-by-step. The following table shows Kaplan's strategic thinking on the left, along with suggested math scratchwork on the right.

Strategic Thinking	Math Scratchwork
Step 1: Read the question, identifying and organizing important information as you go *What is the question asking you?* The question is asking which function accurately depicts the relationship between the game number and how many students show up in face paint.	

Step 2: Choose the best strategy to answer the question	
What information does the question stem provide?	
The question stem tells you what *f* and *j* represent and provides a table relating the two variables.	f = number of students j = the game number
Can you eliminate any obviously incorrect answers right away?	
Choices A & B are linear functions. Since the number of students does not increase by a constant amount, we can safely eliminate these choices.	A and B disagree w/table
How can you best evaluate the remaining answer choices?	
Try plugging a pair of data points from the table into the remaining choices. The point (8, 131) invalidates C, so eliminate it.	
There's only one answer choice left. Am I done?	use (8, 131)
	$C: 131 = \dfrac{1}{2} \times 8^2 + 7$
You know D must be correct, but plug in (8, 131) to confirm.	$131 = \dfrac{1}{2} \times 64 + 7$ $131 = 32 + 7$ $131 \neq 39$ $D: 131 = 2 \times 8^2 + 3$ $131 = 2 \times 64 + 3$ $131 = 128 + 3$ $131 = 131$
Step 3: Check that you answered the *right* question	
Did you provide what the question asked for?	
The only function that fits all the entries in the table is (D).	

As you saw, you won't always have to plug points into each answer choice; you can often reduce your work by knocking out blatantly incorrect answers first. This is crucial for saving time on the PSAT and quickly getting to the correct answer.

✔ **Notes**

When you only have a single answer choice remaining, it isn't necessary to evaluate it. If you've done your math correctly up until that point, you know it has to be correct. However, if you are at all worried that you might have made a mistake earlier, check the remaining answer to validate your math.

REAL-WORLD APPLICATION OF FUNCTIONS

Because functions are equations, you have a great deal of flexibility in working with them. For example, order of operations (PEMDAS) and the basic rules of algebra apply to functions just as they do to equations.

For example, suppose a homeowner wants to determine the cost of installing a certain amount of carpet in her living room. In prose, this would quickly become awkward to handle, as a description would need to account for the cost per square foot, fixed installation fee, and sales tax to get the final cost. However, you can easily express this as a function.

Suppose that, in the homeowner example, carpet costs $0.86 per square foot, the installer charges a $29 installation fee, and sales tax on the total cost is 7%. Using your algebra and function knowledge, you can describe this situation in which the cost, c, is a function of square footage, f: $c = 1.07(0.86f + 29)$. In function notation, this becomes $c(f) = 1.07(0.86f + 29)$, where $c(f)$ is short-hand for "cost as a function of square footage." The following table summarizes the origin of each piece of the function.

English	Overall cost	Square footage	Material cost	Installation fee	Sales tax
Math	c	f	$0.86f$	29	1.07

> ✔ **Notes**
>
> Why does a 7% tax translate to 1.07? Using 0.07 would only provide the sales tax due. Because the function is meant to express the total cost, 1.07 is used to retain the carpet cost and installation fee while introducing the sales tax. Think of it as 100% (the original price) + the 7% sales tax on top. In decimal form, $1 + 0.07 = 1.07$.

This test-like question will test your ability to write a function and use it to solve a problem.

4. A country club allows its members to host private parties. The price is a function of a number of variables. First, members are charged a fixed fee of $1,000 during the peak season (spring, summer, fall) and $500 during the winter months. Members must also pay a certain additional amount for each attendee: $150 per guest in the peak season and $120 per guest in the winter. An administrative fee of 20% of the headcount cost is added to account for logistics, and a 6% sales tax is added to the final bill. How much would a member save by holding a party for 85 guests in winter instead of spring? Round your answer to the nearest dollar.

A word problem like this is a great time to reach for the Kaplan Strategy for Translating English into Math. The following table shows Kaplan's strategic thinking on the left, along with suggested math scratchwork on the right.

Strategic Thinking	Math Scratchwork
Step 1: Read the question, identifying and organizing important information as you go *What do you need to find?* You're asked to find the difference in cost between a winter and spring party for 85 people.	
Step 2: Choose the best strategy to answer the question *How do you sort through all the words?* Use the Kaplan Strategy for Translating English into Math to extract what you need. *What variables need to be defined?* You have a cost, c, which is a function of guests, g, in attendance outside the winter months. In winter the cost is w, which is also a function of guests. *What other information is provided?* The question provides several numbers; break it apart to get each numerical piece by itself. *What math pieces can I get from the small phrases?*	c = cost of party (peak/spring) w = cost of party (winter) g = guests $\$150$ per guest (peak) $\$120$ per guest (winter) $\$1,000$ rental fee (peak) $\$500$ rental fee (winter) 20% admin. cost on headcount 6% sales tax on entire cost
Examine the question carefully to ensure the right figures are being combined. This is an easy place to inadvertently switch a peak season figure with one from winter.	fixed fees: 1,000 (peak), 500 (winter) headcount cost: $150g$ (peak), $120g$ (winter) fee: $(1 + 0.2) \times$ headcount cost tax: $(1 + 0.06) \times$ total price

What function represents the total cost during the peak season?	
Put the pieces together to get your function. Remember to add 1 onto your percents so you're calculating the total cost and not the administrative charge or tax alone.	$c(g) = 1.06(1.2(150g) + 1,000)$ $\quad = 1.06(180g + 1,000)$ $\quad = 190.8g + 1,060$
What function represents the total cost during the winter season?	
Repeat the same process, but make sure not to confuse any quantities.	$w(g) = 1.06(1.2(120g) + 500)$ $\quad = 1.06(144g + 530)$ $\quad = 152.64g + 530$
How much will the party for 85 people cost in spring?	
Plug 85 into the appropriate function.	$c(85) = 190.8 \times 85 + 1060$ $\quad = 16,218 + 1060$
How much would the same party cost in the winter?	$\quad = 17,278$
Plug 85 into the appropriate function.	$w(85) = 152.64 \times 85 + 530$ $\quad = 12,974.4 + 530$
How can you find the amount of savings?	$\quad = 13,504.4$
Subtract the winter costs from peak costs.	$c(85) - w(85) = 3,773.6$
Step 3: Check that you answered the *right* question	
How much will you save on your party if you hold it in winter?	3774
Round your answer to the nearest dollar.	

✔ **Notes**

On Test Day it would take considerable time to write out everything in this scratchwork column verbatim; use good judgment when doing scratchwork, and abbreviate when you can. For clarity, we've included more than the average student would write.

Now you're ready to become a wedding planner! Notice that even with a high-difficulty word problem, the Kaplan Strategy for Translating English into Math gets the job done. You also should have noticed how function notation can help keep your scratchwork clear and organized.

MULTIPLE FUNCTIONS

There are several ways in which the PSAT might ask you to juggle multiple functions simultaneously. Fortunately, the rules governing what to do are easy to understand. To start, we'll look at how to combine functions. This technique simply involves adding, subtracting, multiplying, and/or dividing the functions in play. Check out the following table for a synopsis of how to combine functions with the four basic operations (and make them look less intimidating).

When you see . . .	. . . convert it to:
$(f + g)(x)$	$f(x) + g(x)$
$(f - g)(x)$	$f(x) - g(x)$
$(fg)(x)$	$f(x) \times g(x)$
$\left(\dfrac{f}{g}\right)(x)$	$\dfrac{f(x)}{g(x)}$

You'll have a chance to solve a problem involving combined functions shortly.

A more challenging type of function combination you're apt to see is a **composition of functions** or **nested functions**. Questions involving a composition of functions require you to find the range of a function at a given value and plug that range into the domain of another function to get the final solution. A composition of functions would be written as $f(g(x))$, (*f* of *g* of *x*), or $(f \circ g)(x)$ (*f* follows *g*(*x*)). Remember PEMDAS. To tackle these questions, start with the innermost parentheses and work your way out. A hypothetical situation follows.

> ✔ **Notes**
>
> You might see a composition of functions written as $(f \circ g)(x)$. Just remember that it's the same as $(f(g(x))$, and solve as you would normally, working from the inside outward.

If $f(x) = 8x$ and $g(x) = x + 3$, find the value of $f(g(1))$. Your steps are as follows:

1. Determine $g(1)$, the innermost function when $x = 1$.

2. By substituting 1 in for x in $g(x)$, you can quickly see that $g(1) = 4$. Now use substitution. If $g(1) = 4$, then you can plug in a 4 every time you see a $g(1)$. Rewrite $f(g(1))$ as $f(4)$.

3. Find $f(4)$, the outer function when $x = 4$. Substituting 4 in for x in function f, we quickly realize that our final answer must be 32.

Don't let the weird-looking notation unnerve you; it only looks confusing. Start at the inside and work your way outward to tackle these function questions. After you've solved for an inner function, use substitution to see what value to plug into the outer function. Read on for an example question involving a composition of functions and how to correctly answer it.

> ✔ **Notes**
>
> Note that $f(g(x))$ does *not* equal $g(f(x))$! Not only is interchanging these incorrect, but this practice might also lead you to a trap answer on Test Day.

5. Given that $f(m) = 2m + 1$ and $g(m) = \dfrac{m+2}{3}$, what is the distance between $(g - f)(10)$ and $(fg)(1)$ on a number line?

   A) −20

   B) −14

   C) 14

   D) 20

Appearances can be deceiving; at first glance, this looks tough, but the following table will clarify anything confusing. Kaplan's strategic thinking is on the left, along with suggested math scratchwork on the right.

Strategic Thinking	Math Scratchwork
Step 1: Read the question, identifying and organizing important information as you go *What do you ultimately need to find?* You're asked for the distance between $(g - f)(10)$ and $(fg)(1)$ on a number line.	
Step 2: Choose the best strategy to answer the question *Is there an answer choice that you can eliminate before solving the problem?*	
In this case, there are two! The question is asking for a distance; because distances are always positive, eliminate A and B.	*distance* → answer > 0

What are the individual values of (g − f)(10) and (fg)(1)?	$(g-f)(10)=g(10)-f(10)$
Start by rewriting the functions to reflect the steps required, then evaluate each function at the specified values. As you can see, this problem requires quite a bit of work. Make sure you keep your work clear and organized.	$(fg)(1)=f(1)\times g(1)$ $g(10)=\dfrac{10+2}{3}=\dfrac{12}{3}=4$ $f(10)=2\times 10+1=20+1$ $\qquad\qquad =21$ $(g-f)(10)=g(10)-f(10)$ $\qquad\qquad =4-21=-17$ $g(1)=\dfrac{1+2}{3}=\dfrac{3}{3}=1$ $f(1)=2\times 1+1=2+1=3$ $(fg)(1)=f(1)\times g(1)=3\times 1=3$
Step 3: Check that you answered the _right_ question _What is the distance between the two expressions?_ The question is asking for the distance between the two numbers: −17 is 17 units to the left of zero on a number line, and 3 is 3 units to the right. Therefore, the distance between them is 20, (D).	$\lvert -17 \rvert + \lvert 3 \rvert = 20$

Let's look at a sample test-like question involving a composition of functions.

6. Given $f(x)=x^2+17$ and $g(x)=\dfrac{3x}{x+1}$, where $x\neq -1$, find $g(f(3))$.

    A) $\dfrac{26}{9}$

    B) $\dfrac{299}{16}$

    C) 26

    D) $\dfrac{113}{4}$

Use the Kaplan Method for Math to solve this question, working through it step-by-step. The following table shows Kaplan's strategic thinking on the left, along with suggested math scratchwork on the right.

Strategic Thinking	Math Scratchwork
Step 1: Read the question, identifying and organizing important information as you go *What are you asked to find?* The question is asking for the solution of $g(f(3))$.	
Step 2: Choose the best strategy to answer the question *What is the first step in this calculation?* You have a composition of functions, so start with the inner-most set of parentheses. Substitute 3 for x in f. Next, simplify using order of operations until you get a single value for $f(3)$. *How do you use f(3) to solve for g(f(3))?* You know $f(3) = 26$, so substitute 26 wherever you see $f(3)$ to yield $g(26)$. In other words, plug in the first "output" as the new "input" of the second function. *The answer choices do not include $\frac{78}{27}$, however. How can you simplify this expression?* Both 78 and 27 are multiples of 3, so you can reduce to $\frac{26}{9}$.	$f(3) = x^2 + 17$ $\quad\quad = (3)^2 + 17$ $\quad\quad = 9 + 17$ $f(3) = 26$ $g(26) = \dfrac{3(26)}{26+1}$ $\quad\quad = \dfrac{78}{27}$ $\dfrac{78}{27} = \dfrac{26}{9}$
Step 3: Check that you answered the *right* question *Which value corresponds to the expression in the question stem?* The fraction $\frac{26}{9}$ matches (A).	

As you saw, handling multiple functions in the same question or equation is only slightly more involved than manipulating a single function.

RELATIONSHIPS BETWEEN FUNCTION VARIABLES AND FUNCTION TRANSFORMATIONS

When describing a graph of a function or an interval (a specific segment) of a function, the trend of the relationship between the x and y values while reading the graph from left to right is often important.

Three terms you are sure to see in higher-difficulty function questions are **increasing**, **decreasing**, and **constant**. Let's look carefully at what these terms mean and how they apply to PSAT questions.

- **Increasing** functions have *y* values that *increase* as the corresponding *x* values increase.

- **Decreasing** functions have *y* values that *decrease* as the corresponding *x* values increase.

- **Constant** functions have *y* values that *stay the same* as the *x* values increase.

The PSAT can ask about function trends in a variety of ways. The most basic would be to examine a function's interval and determine if it's increasing, decreasing, or constant. Tougher questions might ask you to identify the trend and then explain what it means in the context of a real-life situation presented in the question, or to identify the effect a transformation would have on the trend of a function.

A function transformation occurs when a change is made to the function's equation or graph. Transformations include translations (moving a graph up/down, left/right), reflections (flips about an axis or other line), and expansions/compressions (stretching or squashing horizontally or vertically). How do you know which is occurring? The following table provides some rules for guidance when altering a hypothetical function $f(x)$.

Algebraic Change	Corresponding Graphical Change	Graph	Algebraic Change	Corresponding Graphical Change	Graph
$f(x)$	N/A—original function		$f(x + a)$	$f(x)$ moves left *a* units	
$f(x) + a$	$f(x)$ moves up *a* units		$f(x - a)$	$f(x)$ moves right *a* units	
$f(x) - a$	$f(x)$ moves down *a* units		$-f(x)$	$f(x)$ reflected over the *x*-axis (top-to-bottom)	

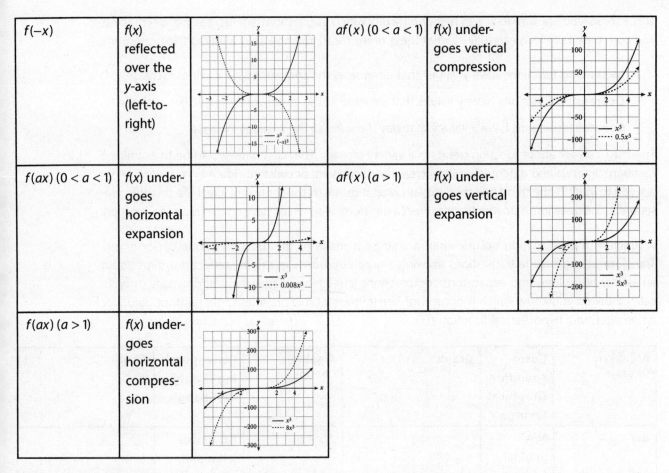

$f(-x)$	$f(x)$ reflected over the y-axis (left-to-right)		$af(x)\ (0 < a < 1)$	$f(x)$ undergoes vertical compression	
$f(ax)\ (0 < a < 1)$	$f(x)$ undergoes horizontal expansion		$af(x)\ (a > 1)$	$f(x)$ undergoes vertical expansion	
$f(ax)\ (a > 1)$	$f(x)$ undergoes horizontal compression				

If you forget what a particular transformation looks like, you can always plug in a few values for x and plot the points to determine the effect on the function's graph.

✔ **Expert Tip**

Adding or subtracting inside the parentheses of a function will always effect a horizontal change (e.g., shift left/right, horizontal reflection); if the alteration is outside, you're looking at a vertical change.

A function transformation question for you to try follows.

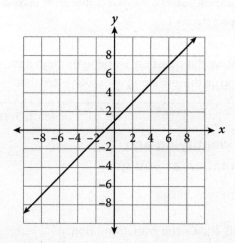

7. The graph above represents the function $f(x)$. Which of the following choices corresponds to $f(x-2)-5$?

A)

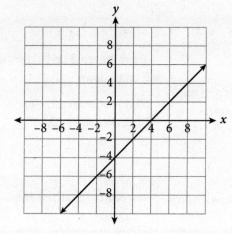

C)

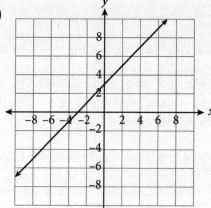

B)

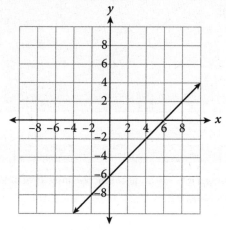

D)

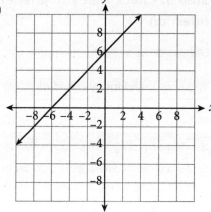

Use the Kaplan Method for Math to solve this question, working through it step-by-step. The following table shows Kaplan's strategic thinking on the left, along with suggested math scratchwork on the right.

Strategic Thinking	Math Scratchwork
Step 1: Read the question, identifying and organizing important information as you go *What are you asked to do here?* You must determine which graph shows the transformation specified in the question stem.	
Step 2: Choose the best strategy to answer the question *How do you begin solving?* First, determine what the transformation is. Next, identify a couple points on the initial function and apply the transformation "instructions" to them. The *y*-intercept is a good choice here. *On which graph are the transformed points?* Determine which answer's graph contains your new coordinates.	graph moves 2 units right and 5 units down (0, 1) becomes (2, –4) (1, 2) becomes (3, –3) new points fall on the graph of (B)
Step 3: Check that you answered the *right* question *Did you answer the question posed?* The only matching graph is (B).	

Now you'll have a chance to try a few test-like problems in a scaffolded way. See if you can fill in the missing pieces and solve for the correct answer without a full explanation.

We've provided some guidance, but you'll need to fill in the missing parts of explanations or the step-by-step math to get to the correct answer. Don't worry—after going through the worked examples at the beginning of this section, these problems should be completely doable.

8. Scientists are modeling population trends and have noticed that when a certain bacterial population changes, the change is based on a linear function of the amount of time elapsed in seconds. When $t = 21$ seconds, the population is 8 colonies, and when $t = 35$ seconds, the population is 10 colonies. Which of the following best describes $f(t)$?

   A) $\frac{1}{3}t + 1$

   B) $\frac{1}{5}t + 3$

   C) $\frac{1}{7}t + 5$

   D) $7(t - 5)$

The following table can help you structure your thinking as you go about solving this problem. The Kaplan strategic thinking is provided, as are bits of structured scratchwork. If you're not sure how to approach a question like this, start at the top and work your way down.

Strategic Thinking	Math Scratchwork
Step 1: Read the question, identifying and organizing important information as you go *What are you being asked to find?* You need to find the function that describes the population increase observed.	$f(t) = ?$

Step 2: Choose the best strategy to answer the question *How can you rewrite the information in function notation?* Start with the first time-population point pair, then repeat for the second. *Can you eliminate any obviously incorrect answers?* One of the choices will give negative populations early on. Eliminate this one. *How do you find which of the remaining choices is correct?* Notice that all of the answer choices have different slopes. If you can find the slope of your linear function, you'll have your answer.	$f(21) =$ ____ $f(\_\_\_) =$ ____ in choice ___ , negative colonies eliminate slope: $m = \dfrac{y_2 - y_1}{x_2 - x_1} =$ _____ $=$ ___ matches choice _____
Step 3: Check that you answered the *right* question *Which function accurately reflects the data?* If you picked (C), you were right! You can check by plugging one or both of your points into this equation.	

✔ Expert Tip

This is another question where it's easy to fall prey to math autopilot and do extra work (and use extra time). Don't let this happen to you! Only do what you need to do to zero in on the correct choice.

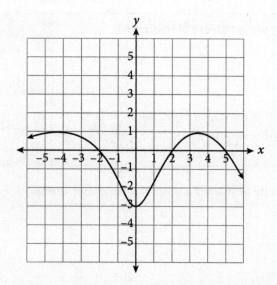

9. The figure shows the of graph $r(x)$. What is one value of x for which $r(x) = 0$?

The following table can help you structure your thinking as you go about solving this problem. The Kaplan strategic thinking is provided, as are bits of structured scratchwork. If you're not sure how to approach a question like this, start at the top and work your way down.

Strategic Thinking	Math Scratchwork
Step 1: Read the question, identifying and organizing important information as you go *What is your task for this question?* You need to find a value of x where $r(x) = 0$.	 $r(x) = 0$ at $x = ?$
Step 2: Choose the best strategy to answer the question *What information does the question provide? What does "$r(x) = 0$" mean graphically?* You have a graph of the function $r(x)$; you must determine where $y = 0$ on the function $r(x)$.	 when $r(x) = 0, y = $ _____ when $y = 0, x = $ _____, _____, _____

Step 3: Check that you answered the *right* question

Where does r(x) = 0?

Did you get –2, 2, and 5? If so, you're right. Because Grid-ins answers can only be positive, choose either 2 or 5. Both answers are correct.

Way to go! You just correctly answered a graphical functions question.

Now that you've seen the variety of ways in which the PSAT can test you on functions and their graphs, try the following questions to check your understanding. Give yourself 3.5 minutes to tackle the following three questions. Make sure you use the Kaplan Method for Math as often as you can. Remember, you want to emphasize speed and efficiency in addition to simply getting the correct answer.

10. For the two functions $f(x)$ and $g(x)$, tables of values follow. What is the value of $f(g(1))$?

x	$f(x)$
–2	8
–1	6
0	4
1	2

x	$g(x)$
–1	–4
1	0
2	2
4	6

A) 0

B) 2

C) 4

D) 6

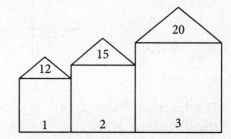

11. A construction company plans to build a long row of houses, each with a certain number of brown shingles on its roof. The number of brown shingles on a house's roof, $f(h)$, is a function of its house number, h. The first few houses are shown here. If only brown shingles are used, how many shingles will the seventh house have?

A) 7

B) 27

C) 46

D) 60

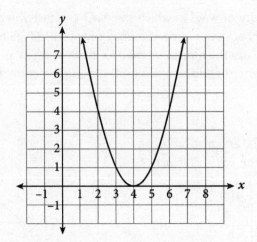

12. The function $f(x) = (x-4)^2$ is shown here. Which of the following correctly depicts the transformation $g(x) = (-x+2)+3$?

A)

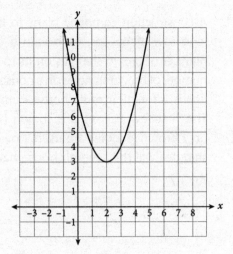

C)

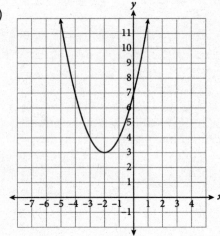

B)

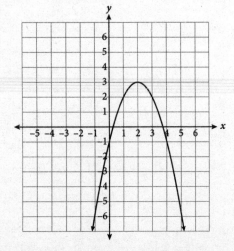

D)

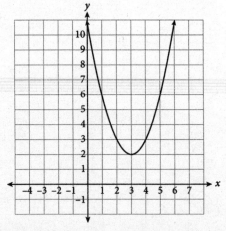

Answers & Explanations for this chapter begin on page 440.

EXTRA PRACTICE

Required	Recommended
Questions 2, 3, 4, 8, 9, 10, 11, 15	Questions 1, 5, 6, 7, 12, 13, 14

1. Which set of ordered pairs could represent part of a function?

   A) [(–4, –4), (–2, –2), (0, 0), (–2, 2), (–4, 4)]

   B) [(–4, –2), (–2, 0), (0, 2), (2, 0), (4, –2)]

   C) [(–2, 0), (0, –2), (2, 0), (0, 2), (4, 2)]

   D) [(–2, –4), (–2, –2), (–2, 0), (–2, 2), (–2, 4)]

2. An ecosystem is a network in which all living and nonliving things are connected. Components of an ecosystem are interdependent, meaning that a change in one component affects all other elements of the ecosystem. Biologists often study changes in ecosystems to predict other changes. A biologist studying the birth rate of a certain fish uses the function $b(n)$ to analyze the fish's effect on other parts of the ecosystem, where n is the number of eggs laid by the fish over a given period of time. Which of the following lists could represent a portion of the domain for the biologist's function?

   A) {... –1,500, –1,000, –500, 0, 500, 1,000, 1,500...}

   B) {–1,500, –1,000, –500, 0, 500, 1,000, 1,500}

   C) {0, 0.25, 0.5, 0.75, 1, 1.25, 1.5...}

   D) {0, 500, 1,000, 1,500, 2,000...}

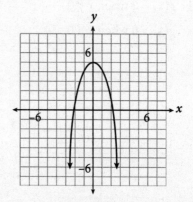

3. The graph of $f(x)$ is shown here. Which of the following represents the domain and range of the function?

   A) Domain: $f(x) \geq 5$; Range: all real numbers

   B) Domain: $f(x) \leq 5$; Range: all real numbers

   C) Domain: all real numbers; Range: $f(x) \geq 5$

   D) Domain: all real numbers; Range: $f(x) \leq 5$

4. If $h(x) = 3x - 1$, what is the value of $h(5) - h(2)$?

   A) 3

   B) 8

   C) 9

   D) 14

✔ **Remember**

Arrows at the end of a function mean that the function continues infinitely, well beyond what is depicted in the graph.

5. If $g(x) = \dfrac{2}{5}x + 3$, which of the following statements is always true?

A) $g(x) < 0$

B) $g(x) > 0$

C) $g(x) < 0$ when $x < 0$

D) $g(x) > 0$ when $x > 0$

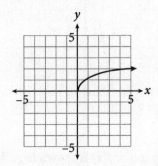

6. The figure shown represents the function $q(x) = \sqrt{x}$. Which statement about the function is not true?

A) $q(0) = 0$

B) $q(2) = 4$

C) The range of $q(x)$ is $y \geq 0$.

D) The domain of $q(x)$ is $x \geq 0$.

7. A function is defined by the equation $f(x) = \dfrac{2}{5}x - 7$. For what value of x does $f(x) = 5$?

A) -5

B) 2

C) 9

D) 30

8. Tyree is dropping old pennies into a jar that contains a cleaning solution. As he adds more pennies, the height of the solution in the jar changes based on the number of pennies he adds. The figure shows this relationship after 50 pennies have been dropped in the jar. If the height of the solution in the jar was 5 inches before any pennies were added, which of the following linear functions represents the relationship between the number of pennies and the height of the solution in the jar?

A) $h(p) = 0.7p + 5$

B) $h(p) = 0.7p + 8.5$

C) $h(p) = 0.07p + 5$

D) $h(p) = 0.07p + 8.5$

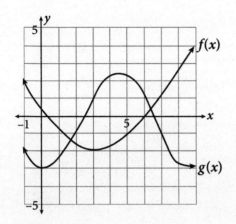

9. In the figure shown, what is the value of
$f(3) - g(3)$?

A) −3

B) 0

C) 3

D) 6

x	g(x)
−2	1
0	2
1	3
4	2
6	1

x	h(x)
−2	4
−1	2
0	0
1	−2
2	−4

10. Several values for the functions $g(x)$ and
$h(x)$ are shown in the tables. What is the
value of $g(h(-2))$?

A) −2

B) 0

C) 2

D) 3

11. If $f(x) = -4x + 1$ and $g(x) = \sqrt{x} + 2.5$,
what is the value of $(f \circ g)\left(\dfrac{1}{4}\right)$?

A) −11

B) 0

C) 2.5

D) 3

12. If the graph of $R(x)$ passes through the
point (−2, 6), through which point does
the graph of $-R(x + 5) + 1$ pass?

A) (−7, −5)

B) (3, −5)

C) (3, 7)

D) (7, 7)

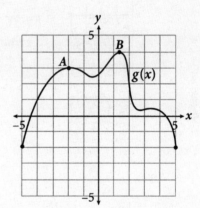

13. The graph of $g(x)$ is shown in the figure.
If $k(x) = -g(x) - 1$, which of the following
statements is true?

A) The range of $k(x)$ is $-5 \le y \le 1$.

B) The minimum value of $k(x)$ is −4.

C) The coordinates of point A on the
function $k(x)$ are (2, 0).

D) The graph of $k(x)$ is increasing between $x = 0$ and $x = 1$.

14. If $f(x) = -x + 5$ and $g(x) = x^2$, which of the following is not in the range of $f(g(x))$?

    A) −11

    B) 0

    C) 1

    D) 9

$$c(t) = -0.05t^2 + 2t + 2$$

15. Doctors use the function shown to calculate the concentration, in parts per million, of a certain drug in a patient's bloodstream after t hours. How many more parts per million of the drug are in the bloodstream after 20 hours than after 10 hours?

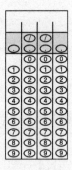

CHAPTER 6

Quadratic Equations

CHAPTER OBJECTIVES

By the end of this section, you will be able to:

1. Solve quadratic equations via algebra, graphing, or the quadratic formula

2. Sketch the graph of a given quadratic equation

3. Identify how various components of a quadratic equation are significant to its graph or a real-world scenario

SMARTPOINTS

Point Value	SmartPoint Category
50 Points	Quadratics

INTRODUCTION TO QUADRATIC EQUATIONS

A quadratic equation or expression is simply one that contains a squared variable (x^2) as the highest-order term (also called highest-powered term). In standard form, a quadratic equation is written as $ax^2 + bx + c = 0$, where a, b, and c are constants. However, quadratics can be written in a variety of other forms as well, such as these:

$$x^2 - 9 = 0 \qquad 2r^2 - 8r + 10 = 4 \qquad 2(x-3)^2 = 8 \qquad (x-2)(x+3) = 6$$

> **Note**
>
> At first glance, the last equation might not look like a quadratic, but it is; it's merely masquerading as a product of binomials. You'll learn a strategy for unveiling its x^2 term shortly.

All quadratic equations will have 0, 1, or 2 real solutions. When you are asked to find the solutions of a quadratic, all you need to do is equate the variable to a constant. Solutions might also be called roots, x-intercepts, or zeroes.

Before you can solve, however, there is a step you must always complete: **Set the equation equal to 0**. In other words, move everything to one side of the equation so that 0 is the only thing left on the other side. Once your quadratic equation is equal to 0, you can take one of three routes to determine how many solutions it has: **algebra**, **graphing**, or the **quadratic formula**. Read on for more information about these three techniques.

SOLVING QUADRATICS ALGEBRAICALLY

Algebra is often the most efficient way to work through quadratics, so getting comfortable with it is critical. We'll start with a technique that is highly useful for manipulating quadratics: FOIL. **FOIL is essential for putting a quadratic into standard form.**

> ✔ **Expert Tip**
>
> If you're really stuck on the algebra in a quadratics question, Picking Numbers can often help. Just remember that it might take more time than the algebra route, so use good judgment if you're in a bind—and remember that you can always skip the question and revisit it later.

FOIL

Whenever you see a pair of binomials on the PSAT, your default algebra strategy should be FOIL, which stands for First, Outer, Inner, Last. This acronym helps ensure that you don't forget any terms when distributing. You multiply the first terms in each binomial together, then repeat with the outer, inner, and last terms. Then you add the four products together, combining like terms as needed. Here is a generic scheme for the FOIL procedure:

$$(a + b)(c + d) = ac + bc + ad + bd$$

(Binomial 1)(Binomial 2) = First + Outer + Inner + Last

It is often tempting to FOIL in your head, but this is risky: It is very easy to lose a negative sign or switch a pair of coefficients (and arrive at a trap answer). Show *all* of your work when using FOIL.

Factoring

Factoring, also known as reverse-FOIL, allows you to go from a quadratic to a product of two binomials. This is a very powerful tool; once you have a binomial pair, you're a few short algebraic steps away from the solution(s). The factoring process is demonstrated in the following table:

Step	Scratchwork
Starting point. Notice a, the coefficient in front of x^2, is equal to 1, a great condition for factoring!	$x^2 + 5x + 6 = 0 \longrightarrow (x \pm ?)(x \pm ?) = 0$
1. What are the factors of c? Remember to include negatives.	factors of 6: 1 & 6, −1 & −6, 2 & 3, −2 & −3
2. Which factor pair, when added, equals b, the coefficient in front of x?	$2 + 3 = 5$
3. Write as a product of binomials.	$(x + 2)(x + 3) = 0$
4. Split the product of binomials into two equations set equal to 0.	$x + 2 = 0, \ x + 3 = 0$
5. Solve each equation.	$x = -2, \ x = -3$

Factoring is easiest when a is 1, so whenever possible, try to simplify your expression so that is the case. In addition, if you see nice-looking numbers (integers, simple fractions) in your answer choices, this is a clue that factoring is possible. If you're ever not sure that you've done your factoring correctly, go ahead and FOIL to check your work. You should get the expression you started with.

> ✔ **Note**
>
> Sometimes the two factors you choose for your binomials will be identical. In this case, the quadratic will have only one real solution (because the two solutions are identical).

Completing the Square

For more difficult quadratics, you'll need to turn to a more advanced strategy: completing the square. In this process you'll create a perfect square trinomial, which has the form $(x + h)^2 = k$, where h

and k are constants. This route takes some practice to master but will pay dividends when you sail through the most challenging quadratic questions on Test Day. The following table illustrates the procedure along with a corresponding example.

Step	Scratchwork
Starting point.	$x^2 + 6x - 7 = 0$
1. Move the constant to the opposite side.	$x^2 + 6x = 7$
2. Divide b by 2, then square the quotient.	$b = 6;\ \left(\dfrac{b}{2}\right)^2 = \left(\dfrac{6}{2}\right)^2 = (3)^2 = 9$
3. Add the number from the previous step to both sides of the equation, then factor.	$x^2 + 6x + 9 = 7 + 9 \rightarrow (x+3)(x+3) = 16 \rightarrow (x+3)^2 = 16$
4. Take the square root of both sides.	$\sqrt{(x+3)^2} = \pm\sqrt{16} \rightarrow x + 3 = \pm 4$
5. Split the equation in two and solve.	$x + 3 = 4,\ x + 3 = -4 \rightarrow x = 1,\ x = -7$

A note about completing the square: a needs to be 1 to use this process. You can divide the first term by a to convert the coefficient to 1, but if you start getting strange-looking fractions, it may be easier to use the quadratic formula instead.

Grouping

Although less commonly seen than other strategies, grouping is useful with the more challenging quadratics, especially those with a values greater than 1. You'll need two x terms to use this route. The goal of grouping is to identify the greatest common factor (GCF) of the first two terms, repeat for the second two terms, then finally combine the two GCFs into a separate binomial. Check out the following example if this seems murky.

Step	Scratchwork
Starting point.	$2x^2 - 7x - 15 = 0$
1. You need to split the x term in two; the sum of the new terms' coefficients must equal b, and their product must equal ac.	$a \times c = 2 \times -15 = -30, b = -7$ new x-term coefficients : 3 and -10 $2x^2 - 10x + 3x - 15 = 0$
2. What's the GCF of the first pair of terms?	GCF of $2x^2$ and $-10x$: $2x$
3. Factor out the GCFs.	$2x^2 - 10x + 3x - 15 = 0 \rightarrow$ $2x(x-5) + 3(x-5) = 0$

4. Factor out the newly formed binomial and combine the GCFs into another.	$2x(x-5)+3(x-5)=0 \rightarrow (2x+3)(x-5)=0$
5. Split into two equations and solve as usual.	$2x+3=0$, $x-5=0 \rightarrow x=-\dfrac{3}{2}$, $x=5$

Straightforward Math

Sometimes you can get away with not having to FOIL or factor extensively, but you need to be able to spot patterns or trends. When you're missing an x term or constant, that's a good clue that straightforward math will work. Don't resort to complex techniques when some easy simplification will get the job done. Equations similar to the following examples are highly likely to appear on the PSAT.

No Middle Term	No Last Term	Squared Binomial	
$x^2 - 9 = 0$	$x^2 - 9x = 0$	$(x-3)^2 = 9$	
$x^2 = 9$	$x(x-9) = 0$	$(x-3) = \pm\sqrt{9}$	
$x = \pm 3$	$x = 0, 9$	$(x-3) = \pm 3$	
		$x - 3 = 3$	$x - 3 = -3$
		$x = 6$	$x = 0$

✔ **Expert Tip**

You can also factor $x^2 - 9$ to get $(x + 3)(x - 3)$; this is called a difference of squares. Note that this only works when the terms are being subtracted.

Quadratic Formula

The quadratic formula can be used to solve any quadratic equation. However, because the math can often get complicated, use this as a last resort or when you need to find exact (e.g., not rounded; fractions and/or radicals intact) solutions.

The quadratic formula that follows outputs solutions to a quadratic equation, given values of a, b, and c from the equation of a parabola in standard form.

$$x = \frac{-b \pm \sqrt{b^2 - 4ac}}{2a}$$

The $\pm$ operator indicates you will use two equations to solve to get all potential solutions, so remember to compute both.

The expression under the radical ($b^2 - 4ac$) is called the discriminant, and its sign determines the number of real solutions. If this quantity is positive, there are two distinct real solutions; if it is equal to zero, there is just one distinct solution; and if it's negative, then there are no real solutions.

> ✔ **Note**
>
> Being flexible on Test Day and familiar with your strengths is essential; you can then choose the path to an answer that's fastest for you.

On the next few pages, you'll get to try applying some of these strategies to test-like PSAT problems.

1. Which of the following is an equivalent form of the expression $(x - 4)(x + 2)$?

   A) $x^2 - 8x - 2$

   B) $x^2 - 2x - 8$

   C) $x^2 + 2x - 8$

   D) $x^2 - 2x + 8$

Use the Kaplan Method for Math to solve this question, working through it step-by-step. The following table shows Kaplan's strategic thinking on the left, along with suggested math scratchwork on the right.

Strategic Thinking	Math Scratchwork
Step 1: Read the question, identifying and organizing important information as you go *What is the question asking you to find?* You're asked to identify the quadratic expression equivalent to $(x - 4)(x + 2)$.	
Step 2: Choose the best strategy to answer the question *Are you presented with anything familiar in the question stem? How about in the answer choices? What's the best route to the answer?* You have binomials in the stem and standard form quadratics in the answer choices, so FOIL is the quickest route. Follow the standard FOIL procedure, then simplify.	$(x - 4)(x + 2)$ $(x)(x) + (-4)(x) + (2)(x) + (-4)(2)$ First + Outer + Inner + Last $x^2 + (-2x) + (-8)$ $x^2 - 2x - 8$

Step 3: Check that you answered the *right* question

Did you answer the question?

You correctly expanded the quadratic using FOIL and got an exact match for (B), the correct answer.

✔ Expert Tip

Although you could use the Picking Numbers strategy here, remember you've only got a few seconds to get through questions like this. FOIL is much faster and should be your preferred method on Test Day.

Although it's technically not a quadratic expression, the expression in the following question provides a chance to practice the strategies you've learned in this section.

2. Which of the following is equivalent to $\dfrac{x^2 - 4x + 4}{2x^2 + 4x - 16}$?

A) $\dfrac{1}{2}$

B) $\dfrac{x^2 - 4x + 4}{x^2 + 2x - 8}$

C) $-\dfrac{(2 - x)}{2(x + 4)}$

D) $\dfrac{(2 - x)}{2(x + 4)}$

Use the Kaplan Method for Math to solve this question, working through it step-by-step. The following table shows Kaplan's strategic thinking on the left, along with suggested math scratchwork on the right.

Strategic Thinking	Math Scratchwork
Step 1: Read the question, identifying and organizing important information as you go *What are you being asked to do here?* You need to identify an expression that's equivalent to the one in the question stem.	

Step 2: Choose the best strategy to answer the question	
What familiar pieces do you see?	
There are a few x^2 terms, so you should be thinking about quadratics and factoring. Also, whenever you're given a fraction, think about ways to cancel terms out.	$$\dfrac{x^2 - 4x + 4}{x^2 + 2x - 8}$$
What should be done first?	
Examine the numerator first. It's an example of a perfect square, so it's easy to factor. The denominator is a bit more involved. Factor out the 2 to get 1 for the x^2 coefficient, then factor the quadratic as usual.	$$\dfrac{(x-2)(x-2)}{2(x+4)(x-2)}$$ $$\dfrac{(x-2)}{2(x+4)}$$
The answer doesn't match any of the choices. Did I make a mistake?	
Not necessarily. In this case, you'll notice your choice is very close to (C); all you need to do is factor a –1 out of your answer's numerator to get the whole expression to match.	$$\dfrac{(-1)(-x+2)}{2(x+4)}$$ $$\dfrac{(-1)(2-x)}{2(x+4)}$$ $$-\dfrac{(2-x)}{2(x+4)}$$
Step 3: Check that you answered the *right* question	
Did you answer the question?	
The expression is now in simplest form, so you're done. Choice (C) is correct.	

✔ **Expert Tip**

Something seemingly trivial like a negative sign can separate your answer from the correct answer. If you've checked your math for errors but found none, look for ways to alter your answer's appearance so that it matches an answer choice. When in doubt, Pick Numbers and plug a few test cases into your expression and the answer choices to find a match.

3. What is an approximate value of x^2 that satisfies the equation $4x^2 + 24x = -8$?

A) $-3 - \sqrt{7}$

B) $-3 + \sqrt{7}$

C) 16

D) $16 + 6\sqrt{7}$

Radicals everywhere. Don't panic. You can use the Kaplan Method for Math to tackle this problem efficiently on Test Day. The following table shows Kaplan's strategic thinking on the left, along with suggested math scratchwork on the right.

Strategic Thinking	Math Scratchwork
Step 1: Read the question, identifying and organizing important information as you go *What are you being asked to do?* The question asks for a solution for the given equation. First find the *x*-value. Then square it.	
Step 2: Choose the best strategy to answer the question *What math strategy would be good to use?* The equation is a quadratic, so think about factoring. Remember to first put it in standard form.	$4x^2 + 24x + 8 = 0$
How can you make factoring easier here? Divide both sides of the equation by 4 to get an x^2 coefficient of 1.	$x^2 + 6x + 2 = 0$
The number 2 does not have factors that add up to 6. What can you do besides factoring? You only have three terms with no perfect squares, so grouping and square rooting are out. Try completing the square instead.	$x^2 + 6x = -2$
Be careful! You're looking for x^2 here! Make sure you square your values. FOIL each expression to get the possible answers.	$\left(\dfrac{b}{2}\right)^2 = \left(\dfrac{6}{2}\right)^2 = 3^2 = 9$

| Now that you have two possible values of x, what should you do next?

Identify the solution that is among the answer choices. | $x^2+6x+9=-2+9$
$(x+3)^2=7$
$(x+3)=\sqrt{7}\quad(x+3)=-\sqrt{7}$
$x=\sqrt{7}-3\quad x=-\sqrt{7}-3$

$x^2=(\sqrt{7}-3)^2$
$\quad=(\sqrt{7}-3)(\sqrt{7}-3)$
$x^2=(\sqrt{7})(\sqrt{7})+(\sqrt{7})(-3)$
$\quad+(-3)(\sqrt{7})+(-3)(-3)$
$x^2=7-3\sqrt{7}-3\sqrt{7}+9$
$x^2=16-6\sqrt{7}$

or

$x^2=(-\sqrt{7}-3)^2$
$\quad=(-\sqrt{7}-3)(-\sqrt{7}-3)$
$x^2=(-\sqrt{7})(-\sqrt{7})+(-\sqrt{7})(-3)$
$\quad+(-3)(-\sqrt{7})+(-3)(-3)$
$x^2=7+3\sqrt{7}+3\sqrt{7}+9$
$x^2=16+6\sqrt{7}$ |
| **Step 3: Check that you answered the *right* question**

Did you answer the question?

One of your solutions is an exact match for (D), the correct answer. | |

✔ Note

A common mistake students make when faced with an expression like $(\sqrt{7}-3)^2$ is to just square $\sqrt{7}$ and 3, then add them together. This is never correct and will likely lead to a trap answer. Take the time to use the proper route: FOIL.

CONNECTIONS BETWEEN QUADRATICS AND PARABOLAS

A quadratic function is simply a quadratic equation set equal to y or $f(x)$ instead of 0. To solve one of these, you would follow the same procedure as before: Substitute 0 for y or $f(x)$, then solve using one of the three methods demonstrated (algebra, graphing, quadratic formula). Consider the graphical connection: When you set $y = 0$, you're really solving for x-intercepts.

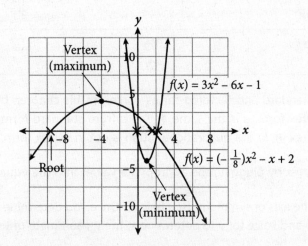

All quadratic functions will graph as parabolas (U-shaped), opening up or down. To determine whether a parabola will open up or down, examine the a value in your function's equation. If a is positive, the parabola will open upward; if a is negative, it will open downward. Take a look at the examples to see this graphically.

Like quadratic equations, quadratic functions will have zero, one, or two real solutions, corresponding to the number of times a parabola crosses the x-axis. As you saw with previous examples, graphing is a powerful way to determine the number of solutions a quadratic function has. The three possibilities are shown here.

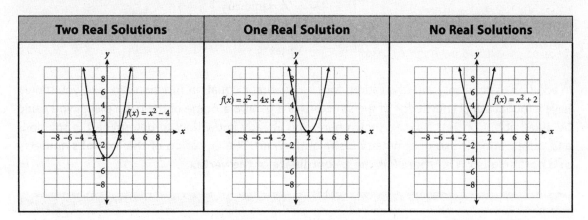

Two Real Solutions	One Real Solution	No Real Solutions

There are three forms that a quadratic function can take: standard, factored, and vertex. Each is provided in the following table along with some helpful properties of each form.

Standard	Factored	Vertex
$y = ax^2 + bx + c$	$y = a(x - m)(x - n)$	$y = a(x - h)^2 + k$
y-intercept: c	Solutions are m and n	Vertex is (h, k)
In real-world contexts, starting quantity is c		Min/max function value (vertex) is k
Format used to solve via quadratic formula		

You've already seen standard and factored forms earlier in this chapter, but vertex form might be new to you. In vertex form, a is the same as the a from standard form, and h and k are the coordinates of the vertex (h, k). If a quadratic function is not in vertex form, you can still find the x-coordinate of the vertex by plugging the appropriate values into the equation $h = \dfrac{-b}{2a}$, which is also the equation for the axis of symmetry (see below). Once you determine h, plug this value into the quadratic function and solve for y to determine k, the y-coordinate of the vertex.

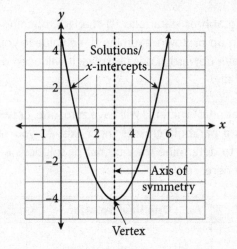

In addition to familiarity with the various forms a quadratic equation/function can take, you should have a foundational knowledge of the structure of a parabola. Some of the basic pieces you could be asked about on Test Day are shown here. You already know how to determine the solutions and vertex, and the axis of symmetry is straightforward. **The equation of the axis of symmetry of a parabola is $x = h$, where k is the x-coordinate of the vertex.**

✔ **Note**

The formula for a parabola's axis of symmetry is easy to remember: It's the quadratic formula without the radical component. If the x-intercepts are rational numbers, you can also determine the axis of symmetry by finding the midpoint, the point exactly halfway between.

Take some time to explore the questions on the next several pages to test your new wealth of quadratic knowledge.

A question like this next one could arise in either the calculator or the non-calculator section. Think critically about how you'd solve it in either case.

4. Will $f(x) = \dfrac{5}{2}x - 2$ intersect $f(x) = \dfrac{1}{2}x^2 + 2x - 3$?

    A)   Yes, only at the vertex of the parabola

    B)   Yes, once on each side of the vertex

    C)   Yes, twice to the right of the vertex

    D)   No, it will not intersect

The following table shows Kaplan's strategic thinking on the left, along with suggested math scratch-work on the right. Because this question could occur in either the calculator or the non-calculator section, graphical and algebraic approaches to solving this question are included.

Strategic Thinking	Math Scratchwork
Step 1: Read the question, identifying and organizing important information as you go *You're given a standard quadratic, but what else is there?* Other provided information includes a line in slope-intercept form. The vertex is not even mentioned.	$f(x) = \dfrac{1}{2}x^2 + 2x - 3$ $f(x) = \dfrac{5}{2}x - 2$
Step 2: Choose the best strategy to answer the question *What should you find first, the vertex or the intersection points?* Because the equations may not even intersect, ignore the vertex for now. You can always find it later, if need be. *How can you discover whether these intersect without graphing?* Recall from our discussion of equations and lines in other chapters: You can simply set these equal to one another! Set the equations equal to each other and combine all of your terms on one side to get a quadratic in standard form. Factor to find solutions: *Your quadratic has two solutions; what does this mean?*	$\dfrac{5}{2}x - 2 = \dfrac{1}{2}x^2 + 2x - 3$ $0 = \dfrac{1}{2}x^2 - \dfrac{1}{2}x - 1$ $0 = \dfrac{1}{2}(x^2 - x - 2)$ $0 = (x^2 - x - 2)$ $0 = (x + 1)(x - 2)$

The two functions intersect at two points.	$x = -1$ and $x = 2$
Can you eliminate any answer choices?	
A and D.	
How can you determine where the vertex of the parabola is?	
Use the formulas for h and k. Putting a parabola in standard form into vertex form is too time-consuming for the PSAT.	$h = \dfrac{-b}{2a} = \dfrac{-2}{2(1/2)} = \dfrac{-2}{1} = -2$
	$k = f(-2) = \dfrac{1}{2}(-2)^2 + 2(-2) - 3$
	$\quad = \dfrac{1}{2}(4) - 4 - 3$
	$\quad = 2 - 7 = -5$
	Vertex: $(-2, -5)$
Where are the points of intersection with respect to the vertex?	
To the right. The correct answer is (C).	
How can your calculator make this question much easier?	
You can simply graph the equations and visually estimate the vertex and intersection points. Enter the equations on your calculator to see what you can ascertain. Make sure you carefully set an appropriate window. Upon further investigation, it is clear that there are two intersection points to the right of the vertex, which matches (C).	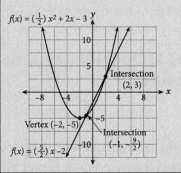
Step 3: Check that you answered the *right* question	
In either method you saw that the line intersects at two locations to the right of the vertex, which is what the problem asked for.	

In one final type of quadratic-related question, you may be asked to match a function to a graph or vice versa. The following is an example of this type of question; unfortunately, it is not likely to appear in the calculator section of the test.

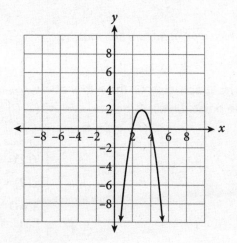

5. Which of the following represents the function shown?

   A) $f(x) = -(x-3)^2 + 2$

   B) $f(x) = -2(x-3)^2 + 2$

   C) $f(x) = -2(x+3)^2 + 2$

   D) $f(x) = -(x+3)^2 + 2$

Use the Kaplan Method for Math to work through this problem step-by-step. The following table shows Kaplan's strategic thinking on the left, along with suggested math scratchwork on the right.

Strategic Thinking	Math Scratchwork
Step 1: Read the question, identifying and organizing important information as you go *While it is clear that you're given a parabola, what do you notice about the answer choices? What do you ultimately need to find?* They represent functions in vertex form. Your task is to determine which matches the graph.	

Step 2: Choose the best strategy to answer the question

Use what you know about vertex form to systematically eliminate choices. What is the vertex of the function in the plot?

(3, 2).

Which choices can you eliminate?

C and D.

How might you determine which remaining function matches without using a calculator?

Check a few key points. The graph crosses the *x*-axis at *x* = 2 and *x* = 4. Check those points first.

vertex = (3,2)

key points:
(2, 0) and (4,0).

Choice A:
$$f(2) = -(2-3)^2 + 2$$
$$f(2) = -1 + 2 = 1$$
$$1 \neq 0$$
Eliminate A.

Choice B:
$$f(2) = -(2-3)^2 + 2$$
$$f(2) = -2 + 2 = 0$$
$$0 = 0$$

Step 3: Check that you answered the *right* question

Did you successfully match the graph to a function?

You bet. Choice (B) must be the correct answer.

GRAPHING QUADRATICS ON A CALCULATOR

At this point, you've become quite an expert at working with quadratics on paper. In this part, we'll explore how you can use your calculator to efficiently graph quadratics. Calculators can be great time-savers *when you're allowed to use them*.

Graphing

All quadratics can be solved by graphing. That said, you might ask why you should bother learning all the aforementioned algebra gymnastics. There are a few reasons why graphing shouldn't be the first option you turn to:

- Remember, there's a non-calculator section of the PSAT; graphing isn't an option here.

- Graphing is often slower because entering complex equations and then zooming to trace the graph(s) can be tedious.

- It is easy to accidentally mistype when you're being timed—a misplaced parenthesis or negative sign will likely lead to a trap answer choice.

However, if you have complicated algebra ahead (e.g., fractional coefficients), decimals in the answer choices, or time-consuming obstacles to overcome, graphing can be a viable alternative to solving quadratics algebraically. A set of straightforward steps for graphing on a calculator follows:

1. Manipulate your equation so that it equals 0.

2. Substitute $y =$ or $f(x) =$ for the 0.

3. Enter the function into your calculator.

4. Trace the graph to approximate the x-intercepts (usually the answer choices will be sufficiently different to warrant approximation over an exact value) or use your calculator's built-in capability to find the x-intercepts exactly.

Graphing on the TI-83/84

While on the home screen, press [**Y=**]. Then enter your function to be graphed. Press [**GRAPH**] and allow the function to plot. If you can't see everything or want to ensure there isn't something hiding, consider pressing [**WINDOW**] to set your own manual parameters or hitting [**ZOOM**] to quickly zoom in and out, among other quick options. If you want to simply investigate your graph, press [**TRACE**] and use the right and left arrow keys to move around on the graph. If you type in any x-value and press [**ENTER**], the y-value will be returned on screen.

Determining Solutions on the TI-83

Once you have your graph on screen, you're ready to find solutions. Press [2ND] [TRACE] to pull up the CALC menu, which has options for finding points of interest. Select option 2: ZERO by highlighting and pressing [ENTER]. You will be taken back to the graph. Use the arrow keys to move to the left of where the *x*-intercept (zero) is you want to calculate. Once you are just to the left of only the zero you are interested in, press [ENTER]—this is called the Left Bound. Next, move to the right of that zero only, careful not to go past any others, and press [ENTER]—this is called the Right Bound. Finally, the calculator will ask you to "Guess," so move left or right to approximately where the zero is you want to get the value for and press [ENTER].

Because you've already set your quadratic equation equal to zero, you know the zeros that your calculator returns will be the solutions to the overall equation.

> ✔ **Note**
>
> Take the time to get comfortable with your calculator functions regardless of what calculator you have. You can find great instructions and even video demonstrations on the Internet.

Next, you'll get to try a sample test-like problem that could be solved via graphing or the quadratic formula. Choose wisely. In almost every case, graphing will be faster, but familiarize yourself with the quadratic formula approach in case you encounter a problem like this in the non-calculator section.

6. Which are the real values of *x* that satisfy $3x^2 + 2x + 4 = 5x$?

   A) 3 and –2

   B) $\dfrac{3}{5}$ and $-\dfrac{2}{5}$

   C) 0

   D) No real solutions

Use the Kaplan Method for Math to solve this question, working through it step-by-step. The following table shows Kaplan's strategic thinking on the left, along with suggested math scratchwork on the right.

Strategic Thinking	Math Scratchwork
Step 1: Read the question, identifying and organizing important information as you go *What do you need to do to answer the question?* You need to identify the values of *x* that satisfy the given equation.	

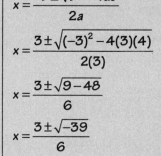

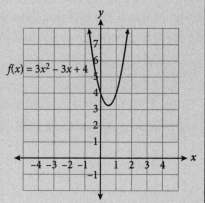

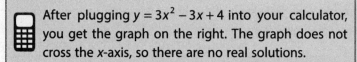

Step 2: Choose the best strategy to answer the question

What tools can you use?

With quadratics, you have a few options: solve algebraically, graphically, or via quadratic formula.

What is the first step?

Set the quadratic equal to 0.

Which path is the most efficient?

Solving algebraically is not wise, as this equation does not look easy to factor.

Graphing and the quadratic formula will be quicker.

$$3x^2 + 2x + 4 = 5x$$
$$\underline{-5x \qquad -5x}$$
$$3x^2 - 3x + 4 = 0$$

Graphical Approach

After plugging $y = 3x^2 - 3x + 4$ into your calculator, you get the graph on the right. The graph does not cross the x-axis, so there are no real solutions.

Quadratic Formula (Non-calculator) Approach

Plug in your coefficients and constants appropriately. You'll notice that the discriminant will be negative, meaning there are no real solutions.

Don't worry about calculating the actual complex solutions—that's beyond the scope of this problem.

$$x = \frac{-b \pm \sqrt{b^2 - 4ac}}{2a}$$

$$x = \frac{3 \pm \sqrt{(-3)^2 - 4(3)(4)}}{2(3)}$$

$$x = \frac{3 \pm \sqrt{9 - 48}}{6}$$

$$x = \frac{3 \pm \sqrt{-39}}{6}$$

Step 3: Check that you answered the *right* question

Did the problem ask for just the solutions?

This equation has no real solutions, which is (D).

> ✔ **Note**
>
> Don't worry if graphing is still somewhat foreign to you; the next section has more examples to get you comfortable with this route.

Nicely done! Take a look at another example.

7. The equation $\frac{1}{3}(3x^2 + kx - 9) = 9$ is satisfied when $x = 4$ and when $x = -3$. What is the value of $2k$?

   A) -6

   B) -3

   C) $-\frac{1}{3}$

   D) 3

Although this question is tougher than others you've seen in this chapter, use the Kaplan Method for Math and you'll find the correct answer. The following table shows Kaplan's strategic thinking on the left, along with suggested math scratchwork on the right.

Strategic Thinking	Math Scratchwork
Step 1: Read the question, identifying and organizing important information as you go *What do you ultimately need to find?* You're asked to find the value of $2k$.	
Step 2: Choose the best strategy to answer the question *What do you notice about the format of the equation?* The equation is not in standard form. However, you are given solutions, meaning you should know what binomials make up this quadratic. *Where should you start?* Distributing the $\frac{1}{3}$ won't give nasty fractions, so that won't cost you a lot of time. Set the equation equal to 0. *What's the quickest way forward? How do the given solutions fit in?*	$\frac{1}{3}(3x^2 + kx - 9) = 9$ $x^2 + \frac{1}{3}kx - 12 = 0$

CHAPTER 8

Citing Textual Evidence and Determining Central Ideas & Themes

 ## CHAPTER OBJECTIVES

By the end of this chapter, you will be able to:

1. Locate appropriate textual evidence to support the answer to a previous question

2. Summarize the passage or key information and ideas within the passage

3. Identify central ideas and themes of a passage to answer questions about central ideas and themes

SMARTPOINTS

Point Value	SmartPoint Category
15 Points	Global
65 Points	Command of Evidence

GLOBAL QUESTIONS

Global questions require you to both identify explicit and determine implicit central ideas or themes in a text. If you pay attention to the big picture—the author's main idea and purpose—while reading PSAT Reading passages, you will be able to answer Global questions with little to no rereading of the passage. To understand fully the central ideas and themes of a passage, you must synthesize the different points the author makes with his or her thesis statement, which you should underline when Passage Mapping.

Global questions may also ask you to choose a correct summary of the passage as a whole or key information and ideas within the passage. When presented with this type of Global question, you can use your Passage Map, which is essentially a brief summary of what you have read.

> ✔ **On Test Day**
>
> The italicized portion at the beginning of a PSAT Reading passage can be very helpful in determining the author's central ideas and themes. Make sure you take the time on Test Day to read this information—it orients you to the passage.

You can recognize Global questions because they typically do not reference line numbers or even individual paragraphs. To confidently answer Global questions, you need to not only identify the central idea or theme of the passage but also avoid choosing answers that summarize secondary or supplementary points.

Do note there is a slight difference between nonfiction and fiction passages. Science and History/ Social Studies passages are nonfiction and will have a definite central idea and thesis statement; U.S. and World Literature passages are fiction and will have a central theme but no thesis statement.

> ✔ **Remember**
>
> History/Social Studies and Science passages on the PSAT Reading Test are just well-written essays or article excerpts. You can normally find the thesis statement of a well-written piece at the end of the introductory paragraph.

COMMAND OF EVIDENCE QUESTIONS

To answer Command of Evidence questions effectively, do the following:

- When you see a question asking you to choose the best evidence to support your answer to the previous question, review how you selected that answer

- Avoid answers that provide evidence for incorrect answers to the previous question

- The correct answer will support why the previous question's answer is correct

Command of Evidence questions ask that you cite the textual evidence that best supports a given claim or point. The given claim or point will be the correct answer choice to the previous question. Then, you will choose one of the four excerpts from the passage as the best evidence or support for that answer.

The first step to approaching a Command of Evidence question is to make sure you approached the previous question—no matter its type—correctly. If you answer the question preceding a Command of Evidence question incorrectly, you have a smaller chance of selecting the correct answer.

> ✔ **Remember**
>
> There is no wrong answer penalty on the PSAT, so even if you have no idea of how to approach a question, take your best guess and move on.

Let's look at the following example of a test-like U.S. and World Literature passage and question set. After the mapped passage, the left column contains questions similar to those you'll see on the Reading Test on Test Day. The column on the right features the strategic thinking a test expert employs when approaching the passage and questions presented. Pay attention to how a test expert varies his or her approach to the different question types.

Questions 1-3 are based on the following passage.

The following, adapted from an English novel published in 1907, describes the family environment and early childhood of Rickie Elliot, a boy with a mild physical disability.

suburbs

Rickie doesn't like suburbs

Some people spend their lives in a suburb, and not for any urgent reason. This had been the fate of Rickie. He had opened his eyes to filmy heavens,
Line and taken his first walk on asphalt. He had seen
5 civilization as a row of semi-detached villas, and society as a state in which men do not know the men who live next door. He had himself become part of the gray monotony that surrounds all cities. There was no necessity for this—it was only rather
10 convenient to his father.

physical description of Rickie's father

Mr. Elliot was a barrister. In appearance he resembled his son, being weakly and lame, with hollow little cheeks, a broad white band of forehead, and stiff impoverished hair. His voice, which he did not trans-
15 mit, was very suave, with a fine command of cynical intonation. By altering it ever so little he could make people wince, especially if they were simple or poor. Nor did he transmit his eyes. Their peculiar flatness, as if the soul looked through dirty windowpanes, the

20 unkindness of them, the cowardice, the fear in them, were to trouble the world no longer.

Rickie's mother?

He married a girl whose voice was beautiful. There was no caress in it yet all who heard it were soothed, as though the world held some unexpect-
25 ed blessing. She called to her dogs one night over invisible waters, and he, a tourist up on the bridge, thought "that is extraordinarily adequate." In time he discovered that her figure, face, and thoughts were adequate also, and as she was not impossible
30 socially, he married her. "I have taken a plunge," he told his family. The family, hostile at first, had not a word to say when the woman was introduced to them; and his sister declared that the plunge had been taken from the opposite bank.

Mr. E's feelings abt. marriage

35 Things only went right for a little time. Though beautiful without and within, Mrs. Elliot had not the gift of making her home beautiful; and one day, when she bought a carpet for the dining room that

family's opinion

Mrs. E =
not a home-
maker

parents
lived in
separate
houses

clashed, he laughed gently, said he "really couldn't,"
40 and departed. Departure is perhaps too strong
a word. In Mrs. Elliot's mouth it became, "My
husband has to sleep more in town." He often came
down to see them, nearly always unexpectedly, and
occasionally they went to see him. "Father's house,"
45 as Rickie called it, only had three rooms, but these
were full of books and pictures and flowers; and
the flowers, instead of being squashed down into
the vases as they were in mummy's house, rose
gracefully from frames of lead which lay coiled

50 at the bottom, as doubtless the sea serpent has to
lie, coiled at the bottom of the sea. Once he was
let to lift a frame out—only once, for he dropped
some water on a creton.* "I think he's going to have
taste," said Mr. Elliot languidly. "It is quite possible,"
55 his wife replied. She had not taken off her hat
and gloves, nor even pulled up her veil. Mr. Elliot
laughed, and soon afterwards another lady came in,
and they went away.

*here, a piece of furniture covered with a cotton
fabric

Questions	Strategic Thinking
1. Mr. Elliot is described as being A) monotonous and opportunistic. B) superficial and condescending. C) tasteful and classy. D) weak and generous.	**Step 1: Read actively** *Read the passage and notes provided.* **Step 2: Examine the question stem** *What kind of question is this?* A Global question. *How do you know?* It asks about the description of a character mentioned throughout the passage. **Step 3: Predict and answer** *What is the general characterization of Mr. Elliot?* Negative. *Which answer choice contains two negative adjectives that reflect Mr. Elliot's personality?* Choice (B)

Questions	Strategic Thinking
2. According to the passage, the family's life in the suburbs is described as A) an impersonal and unfortunate situation chosen to accommodate Mr. Elliot. B) a dull environment from which Mr. Elliot wanted to escape. C) an impoverished but friendly upbringing for Rickie. D) oppressive to Mrs. Elliot, but something she endured in order to please her husband.	**Step 1: Read actively** *Read the passage and notes provided.* **Step 2: Examine the question stem** *What kind of question is this?* A Detail question. *How do you know?* "According to the passage." **Step 3: Predict and answer** *In what part of the passage does the author mention the suburbs?* The first paragraph. *What is Rickie's attitude toward the suburbs?* Negative. *Why does the family live in the suburbs?* Because it's "convenient" (line 10) for Mr. Elliot. *What answer choice matches this?* Choice (A)
3. Which choice provides the best evidence for the answer to the previous question? A) Lines 1-2 ("Some . . . reason") B) Lines 3-7 ("He had opened . . . next door") C) Lines 7-8 ("He had himself . . . cities") D) Lines 9-10 ("There was . . . father")	**Step 1: Read actively** *Read the passage and notes provided.* **Step 2: Examine the question stem** *What kind of question is this?* A Command of Evidence question. *How do you know?* The question stem's wording. **Step 3: Predict and answer** *Where did you find the answer to the previous question?* The first paragraph. *Who insists that the family live in the suburbs?* Mr. Elliot. *What answer choice matches this?* Choice (D)

You have now seen how to answer both Global and Command of Evidence questions.

Look at the test-like Science passage that follows. There are three questions associated with it. Part of the passage has been mapped already. Your first step is to complete the Passage Map. Then, use the Kaplan Method for Reading Comprehension and the strategies discussed in this chapter to answer the questions. Strategic thinking questions have been included to guide you—some of the answers have been filled in, but you will have to fill in the answers to others.

Use your answers to the strategic thinking questions to select the correct answer, just as you will on Test Day.

Questions 4-6 are based on the following passage.

Paleontology is the study of life from prehistoric or geological times through the use of fossils. The following is adapted from a magazine article written by a paleontologist for a general interest magazine.

water-made
rocks = lots
of info

fossils from
water-made
rocks; lots
of info but
ignored

3 of most
common
water-made
rocks

shale

sandstone

limestone

Of the thousands of different kinds of rocks on Earth's surface, the <u>sedimentary</u>, or "water-made," rocks hold the most information for paleontologists and other fossil collectors, since water plays such an important role in the making of fossils. Because water-made rocks are common and fossils are easy to find and extract in many locations, many people overlook these fascinating objects. This is quite a shame since fossils can act as windows into the past for the informed observer.

Sandstone, limestone, and shale are three of the most common water-made rocks, and they all can play a role in fossil creation. <u>Shale</u> is composed of mud—often distinct layers that have dried together—and is usually formed by erosion from landmasses. By contrast, sandstone and limestone often come from the ocean bottom. <u>Sandstone</u> is made up of grains of sand that, with the help of water, have adhered to one another over time, often trapping and fossilizing simple sea creatures and plants in the process. <u>Limestone</u> is a more complex category. Sometimes, the lime that occurs naturally in water settles to the bottom of a body of water and hardens into rock. Of more interest to fossil hunters is the limestone that forms when the shells of water animals, like crab or shrimp, pile up on the bottom of a body of water and eventually become a layer of stone. Limestone formed through such accretion is actually a composite of myriad fossilized shells.

Unlike the slow but inevitable creation of fossilized limestone on the ocean floor, the creation of fossils in shale requires a rather incredible sequence of circumstances. Consider the fossilized footprint of a dinosaur. It starts when a dinosaur steps in semisoft mud. In mud that is too soft, the footprint will simply disappear as the mud levels out, while mud that is too dry will not take a print at all. Under the right circumstances, however, the print will be captured in the drying dirt when the sun comes out. In the meantime, the print can easily be ruined or obscured by the tracks of other animals or even the delicate touch of a fallen leaf or branch. If the print somehow survives these dangers, a reasonably dry environment will eventually harden the mud to form rock. Incredibly, many such fragile offerings have been produced through this process and found by paleontologists.

Fossils in any form of sedimentary rock act as a vital source of information about animals, insects, and plants from long ago. Many parts of Earth's surface are dominated by metamorphic or volcanic rocks rather than sedimentary rocks, and so have a dearth of fossils. Such places, blank slates to the paleontologist, serve to remind us of the gift of the water-made rock and our good fortune in having so much of it on our planet.

Questions	Strategic Thinking
4. Throughout the passage, the author advocates that A) fossil collecting is an ideal hobby suitable for many people. B) fossils found in limestone and shale are more useful to paleontologists than those found in sandstone. C) few people are qualified to understand the story told by Earth's record. D) knowledge about Earth's geological history is important.	**Step 1: Read actively** *Read the passage and the notes provided for the first half. Then, Passage Map the remainder of the passage on your own.* **Step 2: Examine the question stem** *What kind of question is this?* A Global question. *How do you know?* "Throughout the passage" and no line numbers. **Step 3: Predict and answer** *What is the central idea of the passage?* Fossils are very helpful in understanding Earth. *Which answer choice matches this?* _____
5. The author notes in lines 21-22 that limestone is a "more complex category" because A) it is formed in both landmasses and on the ocean floor. B) fossils formed in limestone require a very particular process. C) many of its forms are of little interest to paleontologists. D) it can be formed through a variety of processes.	**Step 1: Read actively** *Read the passage and the notes provided for the first half. Then, Passage Map the remainder of the passage on your own.* **Step 2: Examine the question stem** *What kind of question is this?* A Detail question. *How do you know?* The line reference and quotation. **Step 3: Predict and answer** *Read around the cited lines. Why does the author note that limestone is a "more complex category"?* _____ _____ *What answer choice matches this?* _____

Questions	Strategic Thinking
6. Which choice provides the best evidence for the answer to the previous question? A) Lines 16-17 ("By contrast . . . bottom") B) Lines 24-28 ("Of . . . stone") C) Lines 28-29 ("Limestone . . . shells") D) Lines 47-49 ("Fossils . . . ago")	**Step 1: Read actively** *Read the passage and the notes provided for the first half. Then, Passage Map the remainder of the passage on your own.* **Step 2: Examine the question stem** *What kind of question is this? _____* *_____* *How do you know? _____* *_____* **Step 3: Predict and answer** *Where did you find the answer to the previous question? _____* *What answer choice matches this? _____*

Now, use the strategies you learned about in this chapter to answer questions for a History/Social Studies passage. Give yourself 5 minutes to read and map the passage and answer the questions.

Questions 7-9 are based on the following passage.

This passage, about the decline of the Norse colonies that once existed in Greenland, is from a comprehensive research report examining this anthropological mystery.

In 1721, the Norwegian missionary Hans Egede discovered that the two known Norse settlements on Greenland were completely deserted. Ever since, the
Line reasons behind the decline and eventual disappearance
5 of these people have been greatly debated. Greenland, established by the charismatic outlaw Eric the Red in about 986 CE, was a colony of Norway by 1000, complete with a church hierarchy and trading community. After several relatively prosperous centuries, the colony had
10 fallen on hard times and was not heard from in Europe, but it wasn't until Egede's discovery that the complete downfall of the settlement was confirmed.

Throughout the nineteenth century, researchers attributed the demise of the Norse colonies to war
15 between the colonies and Inuit groups. This is based largely on evidence from the work *Description of Greenland*, written by Norse settler Ivar Bardarson around 1364, which describes strained relationships between the Norse settlers and the Inuits who had recently come
20 to Greenland. However, because there is no archeological evidence of a war or a massacre, and the extensive body of Inuit oral history tells of no such event, modern scholars give little credence to these theories.

New theories about the reason for the decline of the
25 Norse colonies are being proposed partially because the amount of information available is rapidly increasing. Advances in paleoclimatology, for example, have increased the breadth and clarity of our picture of the region. Most notably, recent analyses of the central
30 Greenland ice core, coupled with data obtained from plant material and sea sediments, have indicated severe climate changes in the region that some are now calling a "mini ice age." Such studies point toward a particularly warm period for Greenland that occurred between the
35 years 800 and 1300, which was then followed—unfortunately for those inhabiting even the most temperate

portions of the island—by a steady decline in overall temperatures that lasted for nearly 600 years. The rise and fall of the Norse colonies in Greenland, not surpris-
40 ingly, roughly mirrors this climate-based chronology. Researchers have also found useful data in a most surprising place—fly remains. The insect, not native to the island, was brought over inadvertently on Norse ships. Flies survived in the warm and less than sanitary
45 conditions of the Norse dwellings and barns and died out when these were no longer inhabited. By carbon dating the fly remains, researchers have tracked the occupation of the settlements and confirmed that the human population began to decline around 1350.

50 Changing economic conditions likely also conspired against the settlers. The colonies had founded a moderately successful trading economy based on exporting whale ivory, especially important given their need for the imported wood and iron that were in short supply
55 on the island. Unfortunately, inexpensive and plentiful Asian and African elephant ivory flooded the European market during the fourteenth century, destroying Greenland's standing in the European economy. At the same time, the trading fleet of the German Hanseatic
60 League supplanted the previously dominant Norwegian shipping fleets. Since the German merchants had little interest in the Norse colonists, Greenland soon found itself visited by fewer and fewer ships each year until its inhabitants were completely isolated by 1480.

65 Cultural and sociologic factors may have also contributed to the demise of the Norse settlements. The Inuit tribes, while recent immigrants to Greenland, had come from nearby areas to the west and had time-tested strategies to cope with the severe environ-
70 ment. The Norse settlers, however, seem to have viewed themselves as fundamentally European and did not adopt Inuit techniques. Inuit apparel, for example, was

far more appropriate for the cold, damp environment;
the remains from even the last surviving Norse settle-
75 ments indicate a costume that was undeniably European
in design. Likewise, the Norse settlers failed to adopt
Inuit hunting techniques and tools, such as the toggle
harpoon, which made it possible to capture calorie-rich
seal meat. Instead, the Norse relied on the farming styles
80 that had been so successful for their European ancestors,
albeit in a radically different climate. It seems likely that
this stubborn cultural inflexibility prevented the Norse
civilization in Greenland from adapting to increasingly
severe environmental and economic conditions.

7. The main purpose of the passage is to

   A) explain possible theories explaining a
      historical event.

   B) refute a commonly held belief about a
      group of people.

   C) chronicle the conflict between immi-
      grant settlers and a country's indigenous
      people.

   D) analyze the motivations behind a num-
      ber of conflicting explanations.

8. The author implies that, during the period
   in which the Norse settlements were initially
   founded, the climate in the region was

   A) uncharacteristically mild.

   B) typically inhospitable.

   C) unusually harsh.

   D) increasingly cold.

9. Which choice provides the best evidence for
   the answer to the previous question?

   A) Lines 29-32 ("Most notably . . . region")

   B) Lines 33-35 ("Such studies . . . 1300")

   C) Lines 35-38 ("Which was . . . 600 years")

   D) Lines 38-40 ("The rise . . . chronology")

Answers & Explanations for this chapter begin on
page 466.

EXTRA PRACTICE

Required	Recommended
Questions 3, 4, 5, 6, 9	Questions 1, 2, 7, 8

Questions 1-9 are based on the following passage.

In the following excerpt from a novella, Rosemary, an elderly woman, reminisces about her childhood as she waits for her grandson to wake up.

Rosemary sat at her kitchen table, working a crossword puzzle. Crosswords were nice; they filled the time, and kept the mind active. She needed just one word to complete this morning's puzzle; the clue was "a Swiss river," and the first of its three letters was "A." Unfortunately, Rosemary had no idea what the name of the river was, and could not look it up. Her atlas was on her desk, and the desk was in the guest room, currently being occupied by her grandson Victor. Looking up over the tops of her bifocals, Rosemary glanced at the kitchen clock: It was almost 10 AM. *Land sakes!* Did the boy intend to sleep all day? She noticed that the arthritis in her wrist was throbbing, and put down her pen. At 87 years of age, she was glad she could still write at all. She had decided long ago that growing old was like slowly turning to stone; you couldn't take anything for granted. She stood up slowly, painfully, and started walking to the guest room.

The trip, though only a distance of about 25 feet, seemed to take a long while. Late in her ninth decade now, Rosemary often experienced an expanded sense of time, with present and past tense intermingling in her mind. One minute she was padding in her slippers across the living room carpet, the next she was back on the farm where she'd grown up, a sturdy little girl treading the path behind the barn just before dawn. In her mind's eye, she could still pick her way among the stones in the darkness, more than 70 years later. . . . Rosemary arrived at the door to the guest room. It stood slightly ajar, and she peered through the opening. Victor lay sleeping on his side, his arms bent, his expression slightly pained. *Get up, lazy bones,* she wanted to say. Even in childhood, Rosemary had never slept past 4 AM; there were too many chores to do. How different things were for Victor's generation! Her youngest grandson behaved as if he had never done a chore in his life. Twenty-one years old, he had driven down to Florida to visit Rosemary in his shiny new car, a gift from his doting parents. Victor would finish college soon, and his future appeared bright—if he ever got out of bed, that is.

Something Victor had said last night over dinner had disturbed her. Now what was it? Oh yes; he had been talking about one of his college courses—a "gut," he had called it. When she had asked him to explain the term, Victor had said it was a course that you took simply because it was easy to pass. Rosemary, who had not even had a high school education, found the term repellent. If she had been allowed to continue her studies, she would never have taken a "gut" . . . The memory flooded back then, still painful as an open wound all these years later. It was the first day of high school. She had graduated from grammar school the previous year, but her father had forbidden her to go on to high school that fall, saying she was needed on the farm. After much tearful pleading, she had gotten him to promise that next year, she could start high school. She had endured a whole year of chores instead of books, with animals and rough farmhands for company instead of people her own age. Now, at last, the glorious day was at hand. She had put on her best dress (she owned two), her heart racing in anticipation.

But her father was waiting for her as she came downstairs.

"Where do you think you're going?" he asked.

70 "To high school, Papa."

"No you're not. Take that thing off and get back to work."

"But Papa, you promised!"

"Do as I say!" he thundered.

75 There was no arguing with Papa when he spoke that way. Tearfully, she had trudged upstairs to change clothes. Rosemary still wondered what her life would have been like if her father had not been waiting at the bottom of the stairs that day, or if

80 somehow she had found the strength to defy him. . . .

Suddenly, Victor stirred, without waking, and mumbled something unintelligible. Jarred from her reverie, Rosemary stared at Victor. She wondered if he were having a nightmare.

1. Rosemary's attitude toward the physical afflictions of old age can best be described as one of

   A) acceptance.

   B) sadness.

   C) resentment.

   D) anxiety.

2. Rosemary's walk to the guest room in lines 21-28 reveals that she

   A) feels nostalgia for her family.

   B) is anxious about Victor.

   C) is determined to conquer her ailments.

   D) has an elastic perception of time.

3. Rosemary's memory of the day she finally prepared to start high school indicates that she had

   A) anticipated her father's command to stay home.

   B) hesitated over her choice of clothes.

   C) done especially well in grammar school.

   D) strongly desired to continue her education.

4. Which choice provides the best support for the answer to the previous question?

   A) Lines 10-13 ("Looking up . . . day")

   B) Lines 47-51 ("When she . . . repellent")

   C) Lines 59-60 ("After much . . . high school")

   D) Lines 81-84 ("Suddenly . . . nightmare")

5. The author includes Rosemary's thoughts regarding her grandson in lines 38-43 ("Her youngest . . . that is") in order to

   A) emphasize Rosemary's dislike of her grandson.

   B) demonstrate that Rosemary's grandson does not appreciate how fortunate he is.

   C) set up a juxtaposition between Rosemary's grandson's opportunities with Rosemary's own struggles.

   D) explain why Rosemary is waiting for him to get out of bed.

6. Which choice provides the best evidence for the answer to the previous question?

   A) Lines 1-3 ("Rosemary sat . . . active")

   B) Lines 34-38 ("Get up . . . generation")

   C) Lines 51-53 ("If . . . 'gut'")

   D) Lines 64-66 ("She had . . . anticipation")

7. As used in line 27, "sturdy" most nearly means

   A) stoic.

   B) physically strong.

   C) capable.

   D) flighty.

8. "If he ever got out of bed" in line 43 suggests that Rosemary thinks Victor

   A) lacks a sense of humor.

   B) is ashamed of what he said last night.

   C) is promising but undisciplined.

   D) works himself to exhaustion.

9. The passage as a whole is most concerned with

   A) Rosemary's affectionate concern for Victor.

   B) Rosemary's struggle to suppress painful memories.

   C) the abusive treatment Rosemary suffered at the hands of her father.

   D) the interplay in Rosemary's mind between past and present.

CHAPTER 9

Inferring Relationships and Vocab-in-Context Questions

CHAPTER OBJECTIVES

By the end of this chapter, you will be able to:

1. Identify explicitly stated cause-and-effect, compare-and-contrast, and sequenced relationships in a passage

2. Determine implicit cause-and-effect, compare-and-contrast, and sequenced relationships in a passage

3. Interpret words and phrases in context to answer test-like questions

SMARTPOINTS

Point Value	SmartPoint Category
65 Points	Inference
65 Points	Vocab-in-Context

INFERENCE QUESTIONS: EXPLICIT RELATIONSHIPS

Before we jump into the specifics about inferring relationships—explicit and implicit—let's look at different kinds of relationships that can exist in a PSAT Reading passage.

Relationship questions ask about how two events, characters, or ideas are connected. The three most common relationship types are:

1. **Cause-and-Effect** relationships require you to identify an action or condition that brings about a predictable result. You can identify cause-and-effect relationships by the keywords *caused by*, *results in*, *because*, and *therefore*.

2. **Compare-and-Contrast** relationships highlight the similarities or differences between two items. Common compare-and-contrast keywords are *similar*, *different*, *despite*, and *like*.

3. **Sequential** relationships describe the chronology, or order, in which the items are arranged or occur. Keywords include *first*, *second*, *following*, and *after*.

Some Inference questions about relationships will ask about explicit relationships. Questions about explicit relationships will provide one part of the relationship and ask you to find the other part. In an Explicit Relationship question, the wording of the correct answer will be very similar to the wording of the passage.

> ✔ **Remember**
>
> **Don't forget Step 2 of the Kaplan Method for Reading Comprehension: Examine the question stem.**

INFERENCE QUESTIONS: IMPLICIT RELATIONSHIPS

Questions about implicit relationships, like those about explicit relationships, ask you to identify how items are connected. However, unlike explicit relationship questions, an implicit relationship question requires you to find a connection that may not be directly stated in the passage.

When answering implicit relationship questions, describe the relationship being tested in your own words by using keywords like *because*, *although*, and *in order to*.

> ✔ **Expert Tip**
>
> **Eliminating answer choices that are clearly wrong will help you answer even the toughest implicit relationship questions correctly.**

VOCAB-IN-CONTEXT QUESTIONS

Vocab-in-Context questions require you to deduce the meaning of a word or phrase by using the context in which the word or phrase appears. You can recognize Vocab-in-Context questions because the wording of the question stem is often like this: "As used in line 7, 'clairvoyant' most nearly means...."

Remember to use the Kaplan Strategy for Vocab-in-Context questions:

- Pretend the word is a blank in the sentence
- Predict what word could be substituted for the blank
- Select the answer choice that best matches your prediction

Let's look at the following example of a test-like, primary source History/Social Studies passage and question set. After the mapped passage, the left column contains questions similar to those you'll see on the Reading Test on Test Day. The column on the right features the strategic thinking a test expert employs when approaching the passage and questions presented. Pay attention to how a test expert varies his or her approach to the different question types.

Questions 1-3 are based on the following passage.

The following excerpt is from a speech delivered in 1873 by Susan B. Anthony, a leader in the women's rights movement of the nineteenth century.

Friends and fellow-citizens: I stand before you tonight under indictment for the alleged crime of having voted at the last Presidential election, without having a lawful right to vote. It shall be
5 my work this evening to prove to you that in thus voting, I not only committed no crime, but, instead, simply exercised my citizen's rights, guaranteed to me and all United States citizens by the National Constitution, beyond the power of any State to
10 deny.

The preamble of the Federal Constitution says: "We, the people of the United States, in order to form a more perfect union, establish justice, insure domestic tranquillity, provide for the common de-
15 fense, promote the general welfare, and secure the blessings of liberty to ourselves and our posterity, do ordain and establish this Constitution for the United States of America."

It was we, the people; not we, the white male
20 citizens; nor yet we, the male citizens; but we, the

accused

argue

no crime

right

background = Const.

defines "the people"

whole people, who formed the Union. And we
formed it, not to give the blessings of liberty, but
to secure them; not to the half of ourselves and
the half of our posterity, but to the whole people—
25 women as well as men. And it is a downright
mockery to talk to women of their enjoyment of the
blessings of liberty while they are denied the use of
the only means of securing them provided by this
democratic-republican government—the ballot.

30   For any State to make sex a qualification that
must ever result in the disfranchisement* of
one entire half of the people is a violation of the
supreme law of the land. By it the blessings of
liberty are forever withheld from women and their
35 female posterity. To them this government had no
just powers derived from the consent of the gov-
erned. To them this government is not a democracy.
It is not a republic. It is an odious aristocracy; a
hateful oligarchy of sex; this oligarchy of sex, which

40 makes father, brothers, husband, sons, the oligarchs
over the mother and sisters, the wife and daughters of every household—which ordains all men
sovereigns, all women subjects, carries dissension,
discord and rebellion into every home of the na-
45 tion. Webster, Worcester and Bouvier all define a
citizen to be a person in the United States, entitled
to vote and hold office.

The one question left to be settled now is: Are
women persons? And I hardly believe any of our
50 opponents will have the hardihood to say they are
not. Being persons, then, women are citizens; and
no State has a right to make any law, or to enforce
any old law, that shall abridge their privileges or
immunities. Hence, every discrimination against
55 women in the constitutions and laws of the several
States is today null and void, precisely as is every
one against African Americans.

disfranchisement: to deprive of the right to vote

Margin notes (left):

secure, not give, liberty

liberty requires voting

laws break the law

if women can't vote, not democ

Margin notes (right):

trouble everywhere

citizen = person voting

??

women = person?

person = citizen

women = voting

Questions	Strategic Thinking

1. In line 7, "exercised" most nearly means
 	
  A) used.
 	
  B) practiced.
 	
  C) angered.
 	
  D) trained.
	Step 1: Read actively
	
	Read the passage and notes provided.
	
	Step 2: Examine the question stem
	
	What kind of question is this? Vocab-in-Context.
	
	How do you know? The question uses the phrase "most nearly means."
	
	Step 3: Predict and answer
	
	Pretend "exercised" is blank in the sentence from the passage. What word or phrase can you substitute for the blank? Acted within.
	
	Which answer choice matches your prediction? Choice (A)

Questions	Strategic Thinking
2. The author suggests that without the lawful right to vote, women A) can still hold elected office. B) cannot be considered citizens. C) can still receive the blessings of liberty. D) cannot consent to be governed.	**Step 1: Read actively** *Read the passage and notes provided.* **Step 2: Examine the question stem** *What kind of question is this?* An Inference question asking about an implicit relationship. *How do you know?* By using the word "suggests," the question stem describes a "cause," so the correct answer must describe an effect. **Step 3: Predict and answer** *Which paragraph discusses the results of "disfranchisement"?* Paragraph 4. *What is the cause of women not being able to vote, according to the passage?* Government has no "just powers derived from the consent . . ." (line 36). *Which answer choice best matches this?* Choice (D)

Questions	Strategic Thinking
3. Based on the passage, which of the following is necessary to secure the blessings of liberty? A) A republic B) The ballot C) A constitution D) The people	**Step 1: Read actively** *Read the passage and notes provided.* **Step 2: Examine the question stem** *What kind of question is this?* An Inference question asking about an explicit relationship. *How do you know?* The specificity of the question stem and answers. **Step 3: Predict and answer** *Where in the passage does the author discuss this relationship?* The last sentence of the third paragraph. *What question describes this relationship?* What has to happen to secure liberty? *Which answer choice best matches this?* Choice (B)

You have now seen how to approach these question types on Test Day.

Look at the test-like U.S. and World Literature passage that follows. There are three questions associated with it—one of each kind reviewed in this chapter. Part of the passage has been mapped already. Your first step is to complete the Passage Map. Then, use the Kaplan Method for Reading Comprehension and the strategies discussed in this chapter to answer the questions. Strategic thinking questions have been included to guide you—some of the answers have been filled in, but you will have to fill in the answers to others.

Use your answers to the strategic thinking questions to select the correct answer, just as you will on Test Day.

Questions 4-6 are based on the following passage.

> ✔ **Note**
>
> PSAT Passages often use primary source material, which means the language can be antiquated to modern readers. Don't let that distract you from making a passage map focusing on the main ideas.

James Weldon Johnson was a poet, diplomat, composer, and historian of African American culture who wrote around the turn of the twentieth century. In this narrative passage, Johnson recalls his first experience of hearing ragtime jazz.

Music

Line

good player

New kind of music

good

RTM

When I had somewhat collected my senses, I
realized that in a large back room into which the
main room opened, there was a young fellow sing-
ing a song, accompanied on the piano by a short,
5 thickset young man. After each verse, he did some
dance steps, which brought forth great applause and
a shower of small coins at his feet. After the singer
had responded to a rousing encore, the stout man at
the piano began to run his fingers up and down the
10 keyboard. This he did in a manner which indicated
that he was a master of a good deal of technique.
Then he began to play; and such playing! I stopped
talking to listen. It was music of a kind I had never
heard before. It was music that demanded physi-
15 cal response, patting of the feet, drumming of the
fingers, or nodding of the head in time with the
beat. The dissonant harmonies, the audacious reso-
lutions, often consisting of an abrupt jump from
one key to another, the intricate rhythms in which
20 the accents fell in the most unexpected places, but
in which the beat was never lost, produced a most
curious effect . . .

This was rag-time music, then a novelty in New
York, and just growing to be a rage, which has not

history

25 yet subsided. It was originated in the questionable
resorts about Memphis and St. Louis by black
piano players who knew no more of the theory of
music than they did of the theory of the universe,
but were guided by natural musical instinct and
30 talent. It made its way to Chicago, where it was
popular some time before it reached New York.
These players often improvised simple and, at
times, vulgar words to fit the melodies. This was the
beginning of the rag-time song. . . .

35 American musicians, instead of investigating
rag-time, attempt to ignore it, or dismiss it with
a contemptuous word. But that has always been
the course of scholasticism in every branch of
art. Whatever new thing the *people* like is pooh-
40 poohed; whatever is *popular* is spoken of as not
worth the while. The fact is, nothing great or
enduring, especially in music, has ever sprung
full-fledged and unprecedented from the brain of
any master; the best that he gives to the world he
45 gathers from the hearts of the people, and runs
it through the alembic* of his genius. In spite of
the bans which musicians and music teachers
have placed upon it, the people still demand and

enjoy rag-time. One thing cannot be denied; it is
50 music which possesses at least one strong element
of greatness: it appeals universally; not only the
American, but the English, the French, and even
the German people find delight in it. In fact, there
is not a corner of the civilized world in which it is
55 not known, and this proves its originality; for if it
were an imitation, the people of Europe, anyhow,
would not have found it a novelty. . . .

I became so interested in both the music and
the player that I left the table where I was sitting,
60 and made my way through the hall into the back
room, where I could see as well as hear. I talked to
the piano player between the musical numbers and
found out that he was just a natural musician, never
having taken a lesson in his life. Not only could he
65 play almost anything he heard, but he could ac-

company singers in songs he had never heard. He
had, by ear alone, composed some pieces, several
of which he played over for me; each of them was
properly proportioned and balanced. I began to
70 wonder what this man with such a lavish natural
endowment would have done had he been trained.
Perhaps he wouldn't have done anything at all; he
might have become, at best, a mediocre imitator of
the great masters in what they have already done
75 to a finish, or one of the modern innovators who
strive after originality by seeing how cleverly they
can dodge about through the rules of harmony and
at the same time avoid melody. It is certain that
he would not have been so delightful as he was in
80 rag-time.

alembic: scientific apparatus used in the process
of distillation

Questions	Strategic Thinking
4. In line 19, "intricate" most nearly means A) innate. B) elaborate. C) complex. D) ornate.	**Step 1: Read actively** *Read the passage and the notes provided for the first half. Then, Passage Map the remainder of the passage on your own.* **Step 2: Examine the question stem** *What kind of question is this?* Vocab-in-Context. *How do you know?* The question uses the phrase "most nearly means." **Step 3: Predict and answer** *Pretend "intricate" is blank in the sentence from the passage. What word or phrase can you substitute for the blank?* Complicated. *Which answer choice matches your prediction?* ___

Questions	Strategic Thinking
5. According to the author, the "most curious effect," lines 21-22, was most likely the result of A) tension between surprising and familiar elements. B) conflicts between scholastic and popular music. C) differences between natural and trained techniques. D) contrast between simple and lavish melodies.	**Step 1: Read actively** *Read the passage and the notes provided for the first half. Then, Passage Map the remainder of the passage on your own.* **Step 2: Examine the question stem** *What kind of question is this?* An Inference question about an implicit relationship. *How do you know?* The words "most likely" in the question stem indicate that this is an Inference question. The question stem describes an effect and asks for the cause. **Step 3: Predict and answer** *What was the cause of the "curious effect"?* _____ *Which answer choice best matches this?* _____

Questions	Strategic Thinking
6. Based on the passage, which choice best describes the reason for the author's opinion that the piano player was "a natural musician," line 63? A) He might have become a mediocre imitator. B) He could play and compose by ear. C) He cleverly dodged the rules of harmony. D) He was a master of technique.	**Step 1: Read actively** *Read the passage and the notes provided for the first half. Then, Passage Map the remainder of the passage on your own.* **Step 2: Examine the question stem** *What kind of question is this? An Inference question asking about an explicit relationship.* *How do you know?* _____ _____ _____ **Step 3: Predict and answer** *Why does the author think the piano player was a "natural musician"?* _____ *Which answer choice best matches this?* _____

Now, use the strategies you learned in this chapter to answer questions about a Science passage. Give yourself 6 minutes to read and map the passage and answer the questions.

Questions 7-10 are based on the following passage.

This passage, about infant language acquisition, was adapted from a research paper that explores early childhood development.

For an infant just beginning to interact with the surrounding world, it is imperative that he quickly become proficient in his native language.
Line While developing a vocabulary and the ability to
5 communicate using it are obviously important steps in this process, an infant must first be able to learn from the various streams of audible communication around him. To that end, during the course of even the first few months of development, an infant will begin to
10 absorb the rhythmic patterns and sequences of sounds that characterize his language, and will begin to differentiate between the meanings of various pitch and stress changes.

However, it is important to recognize that such
15 learning does not take place in a vacuum. Infants must confront these language acquisition challenges in an environment where, quite frequently, several streams of communication or noise are occurring simultaneously. In other words, infants must not only learn how to seg-
20 ment individual speech streams into their component words, but they must also be able to distinguish between concurrent streams of sound.

Consider, for example, an infant being spoken to by his mother. Before he can learn from the nuances of
25 his mother's speech, he must first separate that speech from the sounds of the dishwasher, the family dog, the bus stopping on the street outside, and, quite possibly, background noise in the form of speech: a newscaster on the television down the hall or siblings playing in an
30 adjacent room.

How exactly do infants wade through such a murky conglomeration of audible stimuli? While most in-fants are capable of separating out two different voices despite the presence of additional, competing streams of
35 sound, this capability is predicated upon several specific conditions.

First, infants are better able to learn from a particular speech stream when that voice is louder than any of the competing streams of background speech; when two
40 voices are of equal amplitude, infants typically dem-onstrate little preference for one stream over the other. Most likely, equally loud competing voice streams, for the infant, become combined into a single stream that necessarily contains unfamiliar patterns and sounds that
45 can quite easily induce confusion. Secondly, an infant is more likely to attend to a particular voice stream if it is perceived as more familiar than another stream. When an infant, for example, is presented with a voice stream spoken by his mother and a background stream
50 delivered by an unfamiliar voice, usually he can eas-ily separate out her voice from the distraction of the background stream. By using these simple yet important cues an infant can become quite adept at concentrating on a single stream of communication and, therefore,
55 capable of more quickly learning the invaluable charac-teristics and rules of his native language.

7. According to the information in paragraph 5, whether an infant is able to distinguish a certain voice depends partially on whether that voice is

   A) noncompetitive.

   B) in a vacuum.

   C) nuanced.

   D) familiar.

8. As used in line 35, "predicated upon" most nearly means

   A) predicted by.

   B) expressed by.

   C) replaced by.

   D) influenced by.

9. Based on the passage, which choice best describes the relationship between language acquisition and distinct speech streams?

   A) Acquiring language helps an infant to distinguish speech streams.

   B) Acquiring language requires an infant to distinguish speech streams.

   C) Distinguishing speech streams improves an infant's capacity for language acquisition.

   D) Distinguishing speech streams reduces an infant's capacity for language acquisition.

10. As used in line 46, "attend to" most nearly means

   A) care for.

   B) participate in.

   C) listen to.

   D) cope with.

Answers & Explanations for this chapter begin on page 473.

EXTRA PRACTICE

Required	Recommended
Questions 1, 3, 4, 5, 6	Questions 2, 7, 8, 9

Questions 1-9 are based on the following passage.

This passage is an excerpt adapted from the novel You Can't Go Home Again *by Thomas Wolfe. (©1934, 1937, 1938, 1939, 1940 by Maxwell Perkins as Executor of the Estate of Thomas Wolfe. Reprinted by permission of HarperCollins Publishers.)*

It was late afternoon and the shadows were slant-ing swiftly eastward when George Webber came to his senses somewhere in the wilds of the upper
Line Bronx. . . . All he could remember was that suddenly
5 he felt hungry and stopped and looked about him and realized where he was. His dazed look gave way to one of amazement and incredulity, and his mouth began to stretch into a broad grin. In his hand he still held the rectangular slip of crisp yellow paper. . . .

10 It was a check for five hundred dollars. His book had been accepted, and this was an advance against his royalties.

So he was happier than he had ever been in all his life. Fame, at last, was knocking at his door and
15 wooing him with her sweet blandishments. . . . The next weeks and months were filled with the excite-ment of the impending event. The book would not be published till the fall, but meanwhile there was much work to do. Foxhall Edwards had made some
20 suggestions for cutting and revising the manuscript, and, although George at first objected, he surprised himself in the end by agreeing with Edwards. . . .

George had called his novel *Home to Our Mountains,* and in it he had packed everything he
25 knew about his home town in Old Catawba. . . . He had distilled every line of it out of his own experi-ence of life. And, now that the issue was decided, he sometimes trembled when he thought that it would only be a matter of months before the whole
30 world knew what he had written. He loathed the thought of giving pain to anyone, and that he might do so had never occurred to him until now. . . . Of course it was fiction, but it was made as all

honest fiction must be, from the stuff of human
35 life. Some people might recognize themselves and be offended, and then what would he do? Would he have to go around in smoked glasses and false whiskers? He comforted himself with the hope that his characterizations were not so true as, in another
40 mood, he liked to think they were, and he thought that perhaps no one would notice anything.

Rodney's Magazine, too, had become interested in the young author and was going to publish a story, a chapter from the book. . . . This news added
45 immensely to his excitement. He was eager to see his name in print, and in the happy interval of expectancy he felt like a kind of universal Don Juan, for he literally loved everybody—his fellow instruc-tors at the school, his drab students, the little shop-
50 keepers in all the stores, even the nameless hordes that thronged the streets. *Rodney's,* of course, was the greatest and finest publishing house in all the world, and Foxhall Edwards was the greatest editor and the finest man that ever was. George had liked
55 him instinctively from the first, and now, like an old and intimate friend, he was calling him Fox. George knew that Fox believed in him, and the editor's faith and confidence . . . restored his self-respect and charged him with energy for new work.

60 Already his next novel was begun and was beginning to take shape within him. . . . He dreaded the prospect of buckling down in earnest to write it, for he knew the agony of it. . . . While the fury of creation was upon him, it meant sixty cigarettes a
65 day, twenty cups of coffee, meals snatched anyhow and anywhere and at whatever time of day or night

he happened to remember he was hungry. It meant sleeplessness, and miles of walking to bring on the physical fatigue without which he could not sleep,
70 then nightmares, nerves, and exhaustion in the morning. As he said to Fox:

"There are better ways to write a book, but this, God help me, is mine, and you'll have to learn to put up with it."

75 When *Rodney's Magazine* came out with the story, George fully expected convulsions of the earth, falling meteors, suspension of traffic in the streets, and a general strike. But nothing happened. A few of his friends mentioned it, but that was all.
80 For several days he felt let down, but then his common sense reassured him that people couldn't really tell much about a new author from a short piece in a magazine. The book would show them who he was and what he could do. . . . He could afford
85 to wait a little longer for the fame which he was certain would soon be his.

1. Through describing George Webber's experiences, what central idea does the author establish about life as a writer?

   A) Like most professions, work as a writer eventually settles into predictable routine that usually requires hardly any exhaustive effort to maintain.

   B) A young author's big break—such as getting your first book published—is a complex experience that can have the writer at the mercy of the full range of human emotions.

   C) A young author's big break is usually the final hurdle one must overcome to bask in the fame and money that being a successful author brings.

   D) A traditional marker of success such as getting one's first book published does not always lead to a long career as an author—in fact, many young authors never again publish.

2. Throughout the passage, George Webber is described as

   A) a young author who is hungry for the fame, recognition, and wealth that a career as a fiction writer could potentially provide.

   B) a young author who is wary of the corrupting influences of fame, recognition, and wealth.

   C) a seasoned writer who has grown tired of the literary and publishing worlds.

   D) a nonfiction author who chronicles life in small-town America.

3. George's new book, *Home to Our Mountains*, is described as

   A) a memoir about George's time growing up in his home town, Old Catawba.

   B) a novel that was inspired by George's time growing up in his hometown, Old Catawba.

   C) a novel based on life in a small town George once visited.

   D) set in a small town, most of the details of which were invented by George to suit the purposes of his story.

4. Which choice provides the best support for the answer to the previous question?

   A) Lines 10-12 ("His . . . royalties")

   B) Lines 17-22 ("The . . . Edwards")

   C) Lines 23-27 ("George . . . life")

   D) Lines 75-79 ("When . . . all")

5. As used in line 7, "incredulity" most nearly means

   A) nonbelief.

   B) repudiation.

   C) conviction.

   D) fatigue.

6. Based on lines 27-41 ("And, now . . . notice anything"), what can the reader infer about the details of George's soon-to-be-released novel?

   A) George's experiences in Old Catawba informed his writing only sparingly, providing inspiration for bland details such as time and place.

   B) George based most of the novel's contents on experiences he had after he left his hometown, even though the novel is set in a town like Old Catawba.

   C) Most of the novel is based on real events, and the characters on real people, from the time of George's childhood in Old Catawba.

   D) George looked beyond Old Catawba when he sought inspiration for the novel.

7. When writing a new work, George

   A) has a different creative process for every work he creates.

   B) has a creative process that is arduous and difficult, but he relishes the opportunity to produce something new.

   C) has learned how to control his creative periods, resulting in pleasantly predictable experiences when he writes new work.

   D) has a creative process that takes a heavy toll on his mind and body and is not necessarily something he looks forward to.

8. Which choice provides the best support for the answer to the previous question?

   A) Lines 1-6 ("It . . . was")

   B) Lines 60-71 ("Already . . . morning")

   C) Lines 75-78 ("When . . . strike")

   D) Lines 83-86 ("The . . . his")

9. As used in line 63, "fury" most nearly means

   A) indignation.

   B) agitation.

   C) serenity.

   D) animosity.

CHAPTER 10

Rhetoric

 ## CHAPTER OBJECTIVES

By the end of this chapter, you will be able to:

1. Determine the author's purpose in a given passage

2. Determine the author's point of view in a given passage

3. Determine why the author used a certain word or phrase in a given passage

SMARTPOINTS

Point Value	SmartPoint Category
65 Points	Rhetoric

RHETORIC QUESTIONS: ANALYZING PURPOSE

Some analyzing purpose questions ask about the purpose of the passage as a whole. Every author has a reason for writing. To identify that reason—or purpose—ask these two questions:

- Why did the author write this passage?

- What does the author want me to think about this topic?

Your answers will tell you the author's purpose.

Other analyzing purpose questions will ask you to identify the purpose of part of a passage, usually one or more paragraphs. To answer this type of question, read around the cited portion, review your Passage Map, and ask yourself these two questions:

- What job is this section performing?

- How does this section help achieve the author's purpose?

Answering these questions allows you to determine the purpose of that portion of the passage.

> ✔ **Remember**
>
> **Everything an author includes in a passage is there to help achieve the author's purpose in writing.**

RHETORIC QUESTIONS: ANALYZING POINT OF VIEW

Rhetoric questions that ask you to analyze point of view require you to establish the author's perspective and how that perspective affects the content and the style of the passage. That is, you need to figure out not only what the author says, but also how the author says it. Your Passage Map will help you determine the author's point of view.

When answering these types of questions, ask yourself:

- Is the author's tone positive, negative, or neutral?

- Does the author want things to change or stay the same?

- Is the author speaking to supporters or opponents?

> ✔ **Expert Tip**
>
> **As you study, practice asking these questions on every passage you encounter. The author is always trying to tell you something, so the more accustomed you are to asking these questions, the easier it will be for you to determine the author's point of view.**

RHETORIC QUESTIONS: ANALYZING WORD CHOICE

Rhetoric questions about analyzing word choice ask about a particular word or phrase and how it affects your understanding of the author's purpose and point of view.

While these questions do focus on a word or phrase, do not confuse them with Vocab-in-Context questions. Vocab-in-Context questions ask about the meaning of a word or phrase; analyzing word choice questions ask about the function of a word or phrase within the passage. That is, why did the author use this word or phrase?

If you want to review Vocab-in-Context questions, turn to chapter 9.

To answer analyzing word choice questions, ask what the function of the cited word or phrase is. Common functions of words or phrases include

- Setting a mood
- Conveying an emotion
- Building to a conclusion
- Calling to action
- Stating an opinion

✔ **Remember**

Correct answers to analyzing word choice questions will always be in line with the author's overall purpose.

Let's look at the following example of a test-like Science passage and question set. After the mapped passage, the left column contains questions similar to those you'll see on the Reading Test on Test Day. The column on the right features the strategic thinking a test expert employs when approaching the passage and questions presented. Pay attention to how a test expert varies his or her approach to the different question types.

Questions 1-3 are based on the following passage.

The following passage about evolutionary science was excerpted from the writings of a well-known biologist.

evolution

questions

GBS opin-
ion

Mod sci=
perfection
no
improve
yes

There is something intrinsically fascinating about the idea of evolution. What principles govern the evolution of species? And what does evolution
Line tell us about the place of *Homo sapiens* in the grand
5 order of things? The writer George Bernard Shaw held that a mystical guiding force impels life to evolve toward eventual perfection. Modern scientists may not believe in this guiding force or in the possibility of perfection, but many would agree that
10 life has been improving itself through evolution for billions of years. (Note that this conveniently makes *Homo sapiens*, a very recent product of evolution, one of the newest and most improved versions of life.) In the view of these scientists, constant
15 competition among species is the engine that drives the process of evolution and propels life upward. In order to win one day's struggle and live to fight another day, a species always has to adapt, be a little faster, a little stronger, and a little smarter than its
20 competitors and its predecessors.

Author PoV

competition
drives pro-
cess

No less an eminence than Charles Darwin put
forth the idea that species were in constant competition with each other. To Darwin, nature was a

25 surface covered with thousands of sharp wedges,
all packed together and jostling for the same space.
Those wedges that fared best moved toward the
center of the surface, improving their position by
knocking other wedges away with violent blows.

30 The standard example that textbooks give of such
competitive wedging is the interaction between the
brachiopods and the clams. Clams were long held
to be ancient undersea competitors with brachiopods due to the fact that the two species inhabited
the same ecological niche. Clams are abundant

35 today, whereas brachiopods (dominant in ancient
times) are not. Modern clams are also physiologi-
cally more complex than brachiopods are. The
standard interpretation of these facts is that the
clams' physiology was an evolutionary improve-

40 ment that gave them the ability to "knock away"
the brachiopods.

In recent years, however, the prominent naturalists Stephen Jay Gould and C. Brad Calloway have
challenged the validity of this example as well as the

45 model it was meant to support. Gould and Calloway found that over most of geological time, clams
and brachiopods went their separate ways. Never
did the population of brachiopods dip as that of the
clams rose, or vice versa. In fact, the two popula-

50 tions often grew simultaneously, which belies the
notion that they were fighting fiercely over the same
narrow turf and resources. That there are so many
more clams than brachiopods today seems rather

to be a consequence of mass dyings that occurred
55 in the Permian period. Whatever caused the mass
dyings—some scientists theorize that either there
were massive ecological or geological changes, or a
comet crashed down from the heavens—clams were
simply able to weather the storm much better than
60 the brachiopods.

Out of these observations, Gould and Calloway
drew a number of far-reaching conclusions.
For instance, they suggested that direct competition
between species was far less frequent than Darwin
65 thought. Perhaps nature was really a very large
surface on which there were very few wedges, and
the wedges consequently did not bang incessantly
against each other. Perhaps the problem facing
these wedges was rather that the surface continually
70 altered its shape, and they had to struggle indepen-
dently to stay in a good position on the surface as
it changed. In this alternate model, competition
between species is not the impetus for evolutionary
adaptation—changes in the environment (geologi-
75 cal and climatic variations) are.

So where does that leave Homo sapiens if evolution is a response to sudden, unpredictable, and
sweeping changes in the environment rather than
the result of a perpetual struggle? No longer are we
80 the kings of the mountain who clawed our way
to the top by advancing beyond other species. We
are instead those who took to the mountains when
floods began to rage below and then discovered
that living high up has its definite advantages . . . so
85 long as our mountain doesn't decide to turn into a
volcano.

Marginal notes (left): CD theory =comp improves position; example; brachi vs clam; more clams = clams win; G&C question evidence and theory; brachi and clams separate; no comp

Marginal notes (right): bad luck for brach; clams lucky not better; G&C conclusions; less comp; big space; wedge vs new situations; question re: humans; dramatic lang.; skeptical re: humans

Questions	Strategic Thinking
1. The main purpose of the second and third paragraphs is to A) question a standard theory in light of new scientific research. B) provide an example of how evolutionary science has changed its focus. C) highlight the difference between theoretical thinking and empirical data. D) argue for caution before accepting a new scientific theory.	**Step 1: Read actively** *Read the passage and notes provided.* **Step 2: Examine the question stem** *What kind of question is this?* A Rhetoric question asking you to analyze the purpose of part of the passage, specifically paragraphs 2–3. *How do you know?* The question uses the phrase "main purpose of." **Step 3: Predict and answer** *Review the Passage Map for the cited paragraphs. What is the author trying to accomplish with these paragraphs?* Predict: Question Darwin's theory after Gould and Calloway's discoveries. *Which answer choice matches your prediction?* Choice (A)

Questions	Strategic Thinking
2. The stance the author takes in the passage toward *"Homo sapiens"* is best described as A) a skeptic questioning a cherished belief. B) an advocate seeking recognition for a new idea. C) a philosopher outlining an ethical position. D) a scientist presenting evidence for a hypothesis.	**Step 1: Read actively** *Read the passage and notes provided.* **Step 2: Examine the question stem** *What kind of question is this?* A Rhetoric question in which you are asked to analyze point of view. *How do you know?* The question stem asks about the author's "stance". **Step 3: Predict and answer** *Which paragraph(s) mention(s) "Homo sapiens"?* The first and last paragraphs. *What does the author conclude about* Homo sapiens? Predict: Not "the kings of the mountain" anymore (line 80). *Is this positive, negative, or neutral in tone?* Negative. *Which answer choice best matches this?* Choice (A)
3. The author's use of the phrase "No less an eminence than Charles Darwin" in line 21 is primarily meant to convey A) Darwin's age when he developed his ideas about evolution. B) the author's skepticism toward Darwin's ideas about evolution. C) Darwin's importance to the field of evolutionary science. D) the author's respect for Darwin's historical significance.	**Step 1: Read actively** *Read the passage and notes provided.* **Step 2: Examine the question stem** *What kind of question is this?* An analyzing word choice question. *How do you know?* The question stem asks about the purpose of a phrase. **Step 3: Predict and answer** *Read around the cited lines. What is the author letting you know about Darwin?* Predict: He is very important in the history of evolutionary science. *Which answer choice best matches this?* Choice (C)

You have now seen how to approach these question types on Test Day.

Look at the test-like U.S. and World Literature passage that follows. Part of the passage has been mapped already. Your first step is to complete the Passage Map. Then, use the Kaplan Method for Reading Comprehension and the strategies discussed in this chapter to answer the questions. Strategic thinking questions have been included to guide you—some of the answers have been filled in, but you will have to fill in the answers to others.

Use your answers to the strategic thinking questions to select the correct answer, just as you will on Test Day.

Questions 4-6 are based on the following passage.

The following is adapted from two excerpts from a 1926 diary of a resident of Moscow, Russia. At that time, Russia, as part of the Soviet Union, was ruled by a dictatorial government and was experiencing a severe economic depression.

going to a play

memory

misses plays

emotions small concerns

real concern danger

small concerns gone

Late afternoon, blustery and gray.

It has been many years since I have attended a performance of a play. My black fox fur is quite tat-
Line tered, but I have spent the last two evenings before
5 the fire mending it. Before the children were born, we went to the theater at least once a week. I wished later, during the upheaval, that we had not given it up. Once it was gone, truly gone, I missed it so.

I did not expect to be this nervous. It's as if I've
10 never been to a proper theater, and I can scarcely remember a time when I've so fussed over the state of my hair. I'm wondering if I will remember how to behave. In truth, the cause of my nervous condition is this feeling that the whole of Moscow has
15 contrived to engage in a rebellious act. Will we be putting ourselves in danger tonight? It's hard to believe we will not. Perhaps only a handful of people will attend.

Later the same night, very cold.
20 I certainly had no need to fret over the con-
dition of my fox fur. Others even attended the performance with tattered bits of sweaters wrapped around their necks, but people were not judged for the state of their clothing. Triumph Square was

25 abuzz with energy and anticipation. Once among the throng, all of my fears of punishment evapo-
rated. Moscow was united tonight in support of its theater. The play was by Gogol and of course I've seen it many times, but never like this. The direc-
30 tor was a man whose name I had almost forgotten, Vsevolod Meyerhold. The pace of the show was breathtaking. I found that I could scarcely keep up—it's very lucky I'm familiar with the script. The audience was quite bowled over. At the curtain call,
35 much of the audience rose to their feet. The roar of the crowd was a mix of jeering and applause. I was so overwhelmed with emotion, I found myself on my feet clapping loudly—until I realized that the figures on stage for the curtain call were only
40 papier-mâché* dummies, rather than the actors from the performance. I even felt momentarily foolish for being taken in by the ruse. I wonder if this was why others in the crowd were scoffing, or if they were indeed unhappy with the entire
45 production. I did not stop to ask anyone—the paper tomorrow morning will tell me. I rushed home, not bothered by the cold.

*a material made of paper pulp and glue

Questions	Strategic Thinking
4. The main rhetorical effect of the question in lines 15-16 ("Will . . . tonight?") is to A) reveal the narrator's concern that she will be unprepared for the cold. B) emphasize how important proper etiquette is when attending the theater. C) convey the narrator's fear of large crowds. D) express the narrator's understanding of the threat posed by the government.	**Step 1: Read actively** *Read the passage and the notes provided for the first half. Then, Passage Map the remainder of the passage on your own.* **Step 2: Examine the question stem** *What kind of question is this?* A Rhetoric question about word choice. *How do you know?* The question asks about the "main rhetorical effect" of a phrase from the passage. **Step 3: Predict and answer** *How can you paraphrase the quotation from the question stem?* Will they be punished just for going? *Which answer choice matches your prediction?* ____
5. The stance the narrator takes in the passage can be best described as A) a political dissident protesting injustice. B) a theater critic reviewing a performance. C) an art historian recounting an episode in the development of Russian theater. D) an individual citizen participating in an act of collective bravery.	**Step 1: Read actively** *Read the passage and the notes provided for the first half. Then, Passage Map the remainder of the passage on your own.* **Step 2: Examine the question stem** *What kind of question is this?* A Rhetoric question about point of view. *How do you know?* The question asks about the narrator's stance. **Step 3: Predict and answer** *What is the narrator's recurring tone?* _____ _____ *Which answer choice best matches this?* _____

Questions	Strategic Thinking
6. The main purpose of the second paragraph, lines 20-47, is to A) describe the narrator's ordinary worries to contrast them with the gravity of her actual fears. B) portray a character's activities to emphasize her love of theater. C) offer insight into a character to show how thoughts can influence actions. D) present a list of concerns to show how small troubles may lead to larger problems.	**Step 1: Read actively** *Read the passage and the notes provided for the first half. Then, Passage Map the remainder of the passage on your own.* **Step 2: Examine the question stem** *What kind of question is this?* A Rhetoric question about analyzing the purpose of part of the passage. *How do you know?* _____ _____ _____ **Step 3: Predict and answer** *Look at your Passage Map. What was the overall purpose of the second paragraph?* _____ _____ _____ *Which answer choice best matches this?* ____

Now, use the strategies you learned about in this chapter to answer questions about a History / Social Studies passage. Give yourself 6 minutes to read and map the passage and answer the questions.

Questions 7-9 are based on the following passage.

The following passage is excerpted from a popular journal of archeology.

About fifty miles west of Stonehenge, buried in the peat bogs of the Somerset flatlands in southwestern England, lies the oldest road known
Line to humanity. Dubbed the "Sweet Track" after its
5 discoverer, Raymond Sweet, this painstakingly constructed 1,800-meter road dates back to the early Neolithic period, some 6,000 years ago. Thanks primarily to the overlying layer of acidic peat, which has kept the wood moist, inhibited the growth of
10 decay bacteria, and discouraged the curiosity of animal life, the road is remarkably well-preserved. Examination of its remains has provided extensive information about the people who constructed it.

The design of the Sweet Track indicates that its
15 builders possessed extraordinary engineering skills. In constructing the road, they first hammered pegs into the soil in the form of upright Xs. Single rails were slid beneath the pegs, so that the rails rested firmly on the soft surface of the bog. Then planks
20 were placed in the V-shaped space formed by the upper arms of the pegs. This method of construction—allowing the underlying rail to distribute the weight of the plank above and thereby prevent the pegs from sinking into the marsh—is remarkably
25 sophisticated, testifying to a surprisingly advanced level of technology.

Furthermore, to procure the materials for the road, several different species of tree had to be felled, debarked, and split. This suggests that the
30 builders possessed high-quality tools, and that they knew the differing properties of various roundwoods. It appears also that the builders were privy to the finer points of lumbering, maximizing the amount of wood extracted from a given tree by

35 slicing logs of large diameter radially and logs of small diameter tangentially.

Studies of the Sweet Track further indicate a high level of social organization among its builders. This is supported by the observation that the road
40 seems to have been completed in a very short time; tree-ring analysis confirms that the components of the Sweet Track were probably all felled within a single year. Moreover, the fact that such an involved engineering effort could be orchestrated in the first
45 place hints at a complex social structure.

Finally, excavation of the Sweet Track has provided evidence that the people who built it comprised a community devoted to land cultivation. It appears that the road was built to serve as a
50 footpath linking two islands—islands that provided a source of timber, cropland, and pastures for the community that settled the hills to the south. Furthermore, the quality of the pegs indicates that the workers knew enough to fell trees in such a way
55 as to encourage the rapid growth of long, straight, rodlike shoots from the remaining stumps, to be used as pegs. This method is called coppicing, and its practice by the settlers is the earliest known example of woodland management.

60 Undoubtedly, the discovery of the Sweet Track in 1970 added much to our knowledge of Neolithic technology. But while study of the remains has revealed unexpectedly high levels of engineering and social organization, it must be remembered that the
65 Sweet Track represents the work of a single isolated community. One must be careful not to extrapolate sweeping generalizations from the achievements of such a small sample of Neolithic humanity.

7. The purpose of paragraphs 2 through 5 is to

   A) offer historical background to show how various cultures evolve along similar paths.

   B) present various interpretations of the findings to show how different aspects of a society contribute its development.

   C) provide specific examples to illustrate the range of information gathered from a discovery.

   D) outline a social structure to frame a discussion of different contemporaneous societies.

8. The point of view the author expresses in the passage can best be described as that of

   A) a scientist presenting research in defense of a hypothesis.

   B) a sociologist exploring alternative interpretations of an ancient civilization's progress.

   C) an anthropologist proposing a theory to explain a unique cultural phenomenon.

   D) an archeologist reporting on specific findings used to support conclusions about a particular society.

9. In the context of the passage, the author's use of the phrase "But while . . ." in line 62 is primarily meant to convey the idea that

   A) despite evidence to the contrary, the Sweet Track represents the pinnacle of Neolithic achievement.

   B) because the people who built Sweet Track isolated themselves, they may not have had the most advanced Neolithic tools.

   C) although the builders of the Sweet Track possessed advanced skills, other Neolithic societies, perhaps, did not.

   D) as a result of the Sweet Track discovery, extrapolations about Neolithic humanity generally cannot be made.

Answers & Explanations for this chapter begin on page 480.

EXTRA PRACTICE

Required	Recommended
Questions 2, 3, 5, 6, 9	Questions 1, 4, 7, 8, 10

Questions 1-10 are based on the following passage.

The following passage is adapted from a psychologist's discussion of the development of the human brain.

Although the brain comprises only 2 percent of the human body's average weight, the billions of neurons and trillions of synaptic connections
Line that are the human brain constitute a truly impres-
5 sive organ. In terms of what it can do, the human brain is in some ways unable to match the brain functioning of "lower" animals; in other ways, its capabilities are quite unrivaled. Salmon, caribou, and migrating birds, for example, have naviga-
10 tional abilities unparalleled in our own species, and even dogs and cats have senses of hearing and smell known only, in human form, to comic book superheroes. Yet no other animal on the planet can communicate, solve problems, or think abstractly
15 about itself and the future as we do. While these relative strengths and weaknesses can be attributed to the unique and complex structure of the human brain, neuroscientists also have traced these charac-teristics to the human brain's remarkable flexibility,
20 or what researchers call plasticity.

Encased in a hard, protective skull that by the age of two is already 80 percent of its eventual adult size, the human brain has little room for size expan-sion even while the rest of the body, especially dur-
25 ing adolescence, is experiencing significant changes in physical appearance. The first few years of a child's life are a time of rapid brain growth. At birth, each neuron in the cerebral cortex has an estimated 2,500 synapses; by age three, this number blossoms
30 to 15,000 synapses per neuron. The average adult, however, has about half that number of synapses. Nevertheless, the human brain's plasticity allows for marked capacity changes because of usage, practice, and experience throughout one's life. This idea that
35 the human brain continues to develop and, some

might say, improve over the course of one's life is a relatively new concept. Neuroscientists, even after brain size was no longer considered a direct determiner of brain capacity, once believed that the
40 basic structure and abilities of the adult brain are developed early in life and not subject to change. But, as early as 1890, psychologist William James suggested that "organic matter, especially nervous tissue, seems endowed with a very extraordinary
45 degree of plasticity." However, this idea went largely ignored for many years. Then, several provocative experiments dramatically complicated conventional thinking about the human brain.

In the 1920s, researcher Karl Lashley provided
50 evidence of changes in the neural pathways of rhe-sus monkeys. By the 1960s, researchers began to ex-plore cases in which older adults who had suffered massive strokes were able to regain functioning, demonstrating that the brain was much more mal-
55 leable than previously believed. Modern researchers have also found evidence that the brain is able to rewire itself following damage. One of these experi-ments, for example, examined the various effects an enriched environment, in this case an "amusement
60 park" for rats, could have on brain development. Researchers kept one group of rats in an empty cage, devoid of any stimulus, while another group lived in a cage filled with ladders, platforms, boxes, and other toys. Over the course of the experiment,
65 researchers used magnetic resonance imaging technology to observe the brain development of the two groups. Those rats that lived in the enriched environment full of stimuli developed heavier, thicker brains with more neurons and synaptic
70 connections—the cellular activity by which the

brain functions—than those that were deprived. Such results were then found to be even more noticeable in humans. Whereas it was once believed that the brain's physical structure was permanent,
75 this experiment and other contemporary findings show that the brain continues to create new neural pathways and alter existing ones in order to adapt to new experiences, learn new information, and create new memories. As we gain new experiences,
80 some connections are strengthened while others are eliminated in a process called "synaptic pruning." Frequently used neurons develop stronger connections; those rarely (or never) used eventually die. By developing new connections and pruning away
85 weak ones, the brain is able to adapt to the changing environment, thus confirming an essential point: one's life experiences and environment not only mold the brain's particular architecture but can also continue to expand its capacity to
90 function.

1. What is the author's central idea in this passage?

   A) The brain's capability to grow and develop is greatly limited after childhood.

   B) The science of studying the brain has come a long way in the past century.

   C) The human brain is remarkably flexible and is able to develop new synapses and pathways well into adulthood.

   D) Despite many decades of studying brain development and dynamics, scientists are no closer to unlocking the brain's secrets than they were a hundred years ago.

2. According to the passage, which choice best describes the number of synapses per neuron of a three-year-old, compared to that of an average adult?

   A) Three-year-olds have twice as many synapses per neuron as the average adult.

   B) Three-year-olds have half as many synapses per neuron as the average adult.

   C) Three-year-olds and adults tend to have about the same number of synapses per neuron.

   D) Scientists are unable to tell how many synapses per neuron people have.

3. Which choice provides the best evidence for the answer to the previous question?

   A) Lines 21-26 ("Encased in . . . physical appearance")

   B) Lines 27-31 ("At birth . . . number of synapses")

   C) Lines 51-55 ("By the 1960s . . . previously believed")

   D) Lines 79-83 ("As we gain . . . eventually die")

4. As used in line 17, "complex" most nearly means

   A) messy.

   B) intricate.

   C) unknowable.

   D) challenging.

5. Based on lines 57-73 ("One of these experiments . . . noticeable in humans"), the reader can conclude that

  A) experiments with rats tell us little about the human brain.

  B) scientists were mistaken in their hypothesis that an enriched environment would affect brain growth.

  C) surprisingly, environments devoid of enrichment actually boost brain growth.

  D) an enriched environment abundant in stimuli positively impacts the development of brains in rats as well as humans.

6. As used in line 33, "marked" most nearly means

  A) pronounced.

  B) modest.

  C) infinitesimal.

  D) eye-catching.

7. Which choice best describes the scientific consensus on brain flexibility and development beyond childhood?

  A) No one suspected the brain's ability to develop and grow throughout a person's life until the past fifty years.

  B) Scientists have been convinced of the brain's flexibility for a very long time, but the experiments to prove this flexibility were only recently developed.

  C) The brain's flexibility was hypothesized more than a century ago, but the concept did not gain proof until later in the twentieth century.

  D) Few scientists are convinced that the human brain retains any elasticity beyond childhood.

8. Which choice provides the best evidence for the answer to the previous question?

  A) Lines 15-20 ("While these . . . plasticity")

  B) Lines 37-48 ("Neuroscientists . . . human brain")

  C) Lines 61-67 ("Researchers . . . two groups")

  D) Lines 84-90 ("By developing . . . function")

9. As used in line 59, "enriched" most nearly means

  A) wealthy.

  B) enhanced.

  C) streamlined.

  D) clean.

10. As used in line 88, "architecture" most nearly means

  A) silhouette.

  B) façade.

  C) edifice.

  D) configuration.

CHAPTER 11

Synthesis

CHAPTER OBJECTIVES

By the end of this chapter, you will be able to:

1. Apply the Kaplan Strategy for Paired Passages to History and Science paired passages and question sets

2. Synthesize, compare, and contrast information from two different but related passages

3. Analyze quantitative information and infographics and combine information from infographics and text

4. Use the Kaplan Method for Infographics to answer questions about charts and graphs.

SMARTPOINTS

Point Value	SmartPoint Category
20 Points	Synthesis
Point Builder	The Kaplan Method for Infographics

PAIRED PASSAGES

There will be exactly one set of Paired Passages on the PSAT Reading Test. These passages will be either History/Social Studies passages or Science passages.

The Kaplan Strategy for Paired Passages helps you attack each pair you face by dividing and conquering, rather than processing two different passages with 9–10 questions all at once:

- Read Passage 1 then answer its questions
- Read Passage 2 then answer its questions
- Answer questions about both passages

By reading Passage 1 and answering its questions before moving on to Passage 2, you avoid falling into wrong answer traps that reference the text of Passage 2. Furthermore, by addressing each passage individually, you will have a better sense of the central idea and purpose of both passages, and this will help you answer questions that ask you to synthesize information.

> ✔ Remember
>
> **Even though the individual passages are shorter in a Paired Passage set, you should still Passage Map both of them.**

Questions in a Paired Passage set that ask about only one of the passages will be no different from questions you've seen and answered about single passages. Use the same methods and strategies you've been using to answer these questions.

Other questions in a Paired Passage set will ask you questions about both passages. You may be asked to identify similarities or differences between the passages or how the author of one passage may respond to a point made by the author of the other passage.

THE KAPLAN METHOD FOR INFOGRAPHICS

The PSAT Reading Test will contain one or more passages and/or questions that include one or more infographics. Each infographic will convey or expand on information from or related to the passage.

The Kaplan Method for Infographics consists of three steps:

Step 1: Read the question

Step 2: Examine the infographic

Step 3: Predict and answer

Let's take a closer look at each step.

> ✔ **Expert Tip**
>
> Expert test takers consider infographics as part of the corresponding passages, so they make sure to take notes on the infographic as part of their Passage Map.

Step 1: Read the question

Assess the question stem for information that will help you zero in on the specific parts of the infographic that apply to the question.

Step 2: Examine the infographic

Make sure to:

- Circle parts of the infographic that relate directly to the question
- Identify units of measurement, labels, and titles

> ✔ **Expert Tip**
>
> For more data-heavy infographics, you should also make note of any present variables or categories, trends in the data, or relationships between variables.

Step 3: Predict and answer

Just like Step 3 of the Kaplan Method for Reading Comprehension, do not look at the answer choices until you've used the infographic to make a prediction.

Let's look at the following example of an abbreviated History/Social Studies Paired Passage set. After the mapped passage, the left column contains questions similar to those you'll see on the Reading Test on Test Day. The column on the right features the strategic thinking a test expert employs when approaching the passage and questions presented.

Questions 1-3 are based on the following passages and supplementary material.

Passage 1

obesity

Researchers have consistently proven obesity to be a leading risk factor for several diseases, including diabetes, hypertension, coronary heart disease,
Line and many types of cancer. Disturbingly, obesity
rising rates= bad
5 is on the rise. From 1960 to 2000, the obesity rate rose from 13.3 to 30.9 percent of the population and jumped nearly 75 percent from 1991 to 2001 alone. As the prevalence of obesity increases, so too do the economic consequences of the condi-
costs
10 tion. Missed work and the escalating expense of health care are part of the hundred-billion-dollar-plus total cost of obesity that affects the nation's economy. Intensified government efforts to address
gov. should fix it
obesity and its consequences would benefit not
15 only the nation's economy, but also the well-being of its citizens.

Passage 2

stats scary

The United States of America is getting fatter. Statistics show that obesity rates more than doubled from 1960 to 2000. However, advocates who cite
20 such statistics and demand government action ignore existing initiatives. The U.S. government
what gov is doing
has responded to the obesity epidemic by creating many programs aimed at obesity awareness, prevention, and control. In addition, its healthcare
25 system continues to improve and respond to the needs of the obese population. Statistics describing
too many stats= bad
rising obesity rates are alarmist and neglect existing antiobesity efforts, as well as the nonquantitative factors that affect health. Fighting obesity is a noble
30 objective, but the overzealous use of statistics contributes to an incomplete and ultimately inaccurate portrayal of the situation.

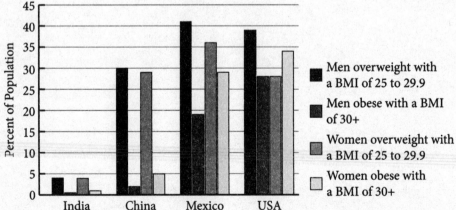

Overweight and Obesity in Adults

Questions	Strategic Thinking
1. One difference between responses described in the passages is that, unlike the author of Passage 1, the author of Passage 2 A) suggests that new government efforts to combat obesity would be largely ineffective. B) recommends conducting additional research before intensifying government efforts. C) cites existing programs and improved healthcare that already address the problem. D) questions the statistics indicating obesity is a problem that needs addressing.	**Step 1: Read actively** *Read the passage and notes provided.* **Step 2: Examine the question stem** *What is this question asking you to do? Describe one of the differences between the opinions of the authors of the two passages.* **Step 3: Predict and answer** *Review your Passage Map. How do the authors' opinions differ?* Author 1 says combatting obesity is the government's job. Author 2 says the government already has programs to this effect. *Which answer choice matches your prediction?* Choice (C)
2. Are the benefits of addressing the consequences of obesity described in Passage 1 consistent with the main conclusion drawn by the author of Passage 2? A) Yes, because the conclusion suggests that addressing obesity has societal value. B) Yes, because the conclusion implies that government is best suited to pursue such goals. C) No, because the conclusion offers alternative benefits associated with a different approach. D) No, because the conclusion focuses mainly on the use of statistics to evaluate the problem.	**Step 1: Read actively** *Read the passage and notes provided.* **Step 2: Examine the question stem** *What is this question asking you to do? Compare part of one passage with the conclusion of another passage.* **Step 3: Predict and answer** *What is the conclusion in Passage 2?* Fighting obesity is good, and statistics can be misleading. *Which part of the conclusion matches with the benefits mentioned in Passage 1?* Fighting obesity is good for citizens. *Which answer choice best matches this?* Choice (A)

Questions	Strategic Thinking
3. Based on the information in Passage 2 and the chart, it can be reasonably inferred that A) obesity rates for U.S. women are increasing more rapidly than are the rates for U.S. men. B) in the United States, the proportion of overweight men to overweight women suggests that existing initiatives are more effective for women. C) the statistics displayed in the graph suggest a serious problem, but don't present a complete picture. D) governments in other countries have spent too much time fighting obesity.	**Step 1: Read the question** *Assess the question for information on what part of the infographic to focus on.* **Step 2: Examine the infographic** *What are the units of measurement, labels, or titles?* The units on the y-axis are population percentages. The labels on the x-axis are four countries: India, China, Mexico, and USA. The key also provides labels for the four different categories: men and women who are overweight and obese. The title of the chart is "Overweight and Obesity in Adults." **Step 3: Predict and answer** *The question stem does not point you to the part of the chart you need to focus on. Evaluate each answer choice.* Choice A is incorrect because the chart does not display time, so it's impossible to know if the rates are increasing more rapidly. Choice B is incorrect—the percentage of overweight men and women in the United States is almost identical. Choice D is incorrect because it is way outside the scope of the passage. *What is the answer?* Choice (C)

Look at the abbreviated History/Social Studies Paired Passage set that follows. Part of the passage set has been mapped already. Your first step is to complete the Passage Map. Then, use the Kaplan Method for Reading Comprehension and the strategies discussed in this chapter to answer the questions. Strategic thinking questions have been included to guide you—some of the answers have been filled in, but you will have to fill in the answers to others.

Use your answers to the questions to select the correct answer, just as you will on Test Day.

Questions 4-6 are based on the following passages and supplementary material.

Passage 1

reform
campaigns

$$ = bad

In the United States, we should make it an ⬭urgent priority⬭ to reform the process of campaigning for elective office. The vast sums necessary
Line to mount credible presidential and congressio-
5 nal campaigns are especially detrimental. They threaten to limit the pool of candidates to the very wealthy and also give disproportionate influence to lobbyists and other special interests. We should also change the length of such campaigns. In the

too long

10 United Kingdom, campaigns for parliamentary elections last for weeks; in the ⬭United States⬭ the process lasts for well over a year. Finally, the two major parties should establish norms for campaign advertising, with the goal of sharply curtailing

be nice

15 "attack ads."

Passage 2

American elections would be more democratic if candidates were required to debate and if everyone eligible to vote was required to do so. Under the present system, a candidate with the advantages of
20 incumbency or widespread name recognition is free to sidestep an opponent's challenge to debate. This puts the opponent at a disadvantage and compromises the goals of our two-party system. Debates needn't play the determining role in elections, but
25 they should be an important factor as the public evaluates candidates' positions on issues. Of course, a well-informed public is irrelevant if people don't vote. Many foreign countries have a far higher election turnout than we do in the United States. We
30 should consider legislation requiring people to vote in national elections. Citizenship has its privileges, but it also involves responsibilities.

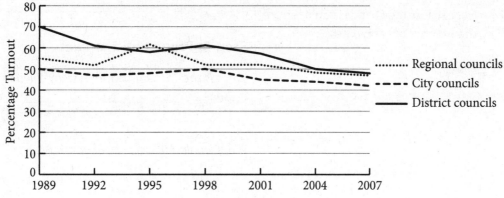

Voter Turnout at Selected Local Elections

.... Regional councils
– – – City councils
——— District councils

Questions	Strategic Thinking
4. The arguments presented in Passage 1 and Passage 2 share what element? A) Recommendation of changes to campaign finance rules B) Citation of supporting evidence from foreign countries C) Recommendation of a mix of voluntary and required actions D) Support of an expanded debate schedule	**Step 1: Read actively** *Read the passage set and the notes provided for the first passage. Then, Passage Map the remainder of the passage set on your own.* **Step 2: Examine the question stem** *What is this question asking you to do? Find an argumentative element shared by both passages.* **Step 3: Predict and answer** *What element do both authors employ when making their arguments? Passage 1 cites United Kingdom affairs while Passage 2 describes the election turnout in foreign countries.* *What answer matches this? _____*
5. Is the author of Passage 1 likely to agree with the changes to the current debate system as presented in Passage 2? A) Yes, because the changes could increase voter turnout. B) Yes, because the changes could reduce the influence of lobbyists. C) No, because the changes could increase the length of election campaigns. D) No, because the changes could reduce the number of candidates.	**Step 1: Read actively** *Read the passage set and the notes provided for the first passage. Then, Passage Map the remainder of the passage set on your own.* **Step 2: Examine the question stem** *What is this question asking you to do? _____* *_____* *_____* **Step 3: Predict and answer** *What is the "current debate system" cited in Passage 2? _____* *_____* *What would Author 1 say about that? _____* *_____* *Which answer choice best matches this? _____*

Questions	Strategic Thinking
6. Based on the information in Passage 2 and the graphic, which answer choice, if true, would weaken the argument made by the author of Passage 2?	**Step 1: Read the question**
	Assess the question for information on what part of the infographic to focus on.
A) The graph shows voter turnout in the United States.	
	Step 2: Examine the infographic
B) The graph shows voter turnout after campaign reforms have been enacted.	*What are the units of measurement, labels, or titles?*
C) The graph shows voter turnout in the European Union.	_____
	_____
D) The graph shows voter turnout after laws requiring citizens to vote were repealed.	**Step 3: Predict and answer**
	What trend do you notice in the graph?
	_____
	What reason for this trend goes against the argument of Passage 2?
	_____
	Which answer choice matches this? ____

Now, use the strategies you learned about in this chapter to answer questions for a Science Paired Passage set. Give yourself 6 minutes to read and map the passages and answer the questions.

Questions 7-9 are based on the following passages and supplementary material.

The infringement of one species on the habitat of another can cause serious biological and environmental damage, especially when this infringement is caused by human intervention. To what extent should we work to prevent this? The following passages address differing aspects of this issue.

Passage 1

A plant or animal species is considered invasive when it spreads to an area where it does not naturally occur, causing economic or environmental harm.
Line Biologists have long recognized that invasive species
5 can present problems for native ecosystems, but recent developments have intensified their concern. In May 2002, hundreds of invasive northern snakehead fish were found in a Maryland pond, having been spawned by a pair of fish released by a man who had bought
10 them at a live fish market. Unlike native fish, which have natural predators to keep their populations in check, snakeheads, which evolved in Asia, can destroy ecosystems where they have no natural predators by eating huge amounts of smaller fish and plant life. Their ability
15 to survive for up to four days out of water and to "walk" with their fins on land for short distances has made their potential spread especially worrisome.

Measures that have been taken to contain the spread of invasive fish include banning the importation or pos-
20 session of snakeheads, draining ponds or lakes where they have been found, poisoning ponds with herbicides and pesticides, and inspecting pet stores to make sure they are not illegally selling the fish. The United States, however, does not appear to be acting swiftly enough
25 either to prevent the further spread of invasive fish or, more generally, to minimize other plant or animal invasions in the future. Although laws are now in place to prevent the introduction and spread of invasive species, they were slow to be enacted, despite ample evidence
30 from Australia and elsewhere that nonnative animals can cause severe and irreversible environmental harm.

The number of scientists and environmentalists who recognize invasive species as a serious environmental problem, however, is increasing. If scientists, govern-
35 ment officials, and the general population work together and make it a priority to identify and prevent the spread of invasive species in the early stages where containment or eradication is still feasible, we may at least be able to minimize the unwelcome impact of exotic species on
40 native ecosystems.

Passage 2

Lately, much attention has been focused on the snakehead fish and other invasive species. Environmentalists issue dire warnings about the disappearing
Line habitats of native species and suggest that ecological
45 disaster will follow if we do not take immediate action to contain exotic plant and animal invasions whenever and wherever they are perceived as a threat. While they are surely right that the uncontrolled spread of nonnative plants and animals may have undesirable
50 consequences for the ecosystem, they seem to forget that the environmental concerns raised by invasive species must be weighed against many other environmental issues competing for adequate funding. The discovery of snakehead fish in Maryland, for instance, was highly
55 publicized and prompted a great expenditure of time and resources to eradicate them, and the spread of carp in the Great Lakes has likewise been addressed at great cost. While these fish do pose very real problems, pollution, deforestation, and a host of other environmental
60 problems are at least as worthy of funding. The fact that invasive species are currently a "hot topic" in the media does not mean they should overshadow larger environmental issues, even if discussion of the larger issues has become more mundane. Containing invasive species
65 is a worthwhile goal, but it is not the only worthwhile environmental goal.

Scientific evidence is lacking about what containment measures work and about how serious the threat posed by various invasive species actually is. Recently,
70 the discovery of a single snakehead fish in one lake prompted officials to drain and refill the lake at a cost of more than $10,000, yet no additional snakeheads were even found there. Instead of taking drastic and expensive measures every time a potential problem
75 is reported, we should strive for a balance between environmental protection and economic responsibility. Scientific data can be valuable because they alert us to an issue we should watch closely, but simply identifying an environmental threat does not mean we should
80 automatically give it priority over other important issues. Instead, scientific data should be treated as just that—data that allow us to make informed and balanced policy decisions after reflecting on the consequences of various courses of action.

	Annual Spending in $1,000		
Year	2010	2011	2012
Environmental Protection Agency	$6,663,000	$6,848,000	$6,071,000
National Invasive Species Council	$2,207,000	$2,238,000	$2,221,000
Total	$8,870,000	$9,086,000	$8,292,000

7. One difference between the assessment of environmental issues described in the two passages is that unlike the author of Passage 1, the author of Passage 2

A) minimizes the risk associated with invasive species.

B) considers invasive species as only one of a number of environmental concerns.

C) questions whether scientific data have a role when larger economic or environmental issues are concerned.

D) argues that the legislative response to the threat posed by invasive species has been rapid and effective.

8. The authors of Passage 1 and Passage 2 would most likely agree on which of the following statements?

A) Greater expenditures to reduce the impact of invasive species are justified.

B) The economic benefits of environmental protection must be weighed against the severity of the environmental threat.

C) Effective use of the media can increase public awareness of mundane environmental issues.

D) Efforts by scientists and environmentalists to contain environmental damage are worth continuing.

9. Based on the information in Passage 1 and the graphic, it can be reasonably inferred that the author considers spending by the National Invasive Species Council to be

A) continually overshadowed by spending on other environmental issues.

B) an important part of a coalition working to prevent the spread of invasive species.

C) less effective than the EPA in combatting invasive species.

D) most effective when the Council works in partnership with the EPA.

Answers and Explanations for this chapter begin on page 487.

EXTRA PRACTICE

Required	Recommended
Questions 1, 2, 6, 9, 10	Questions 3, 4, 5, 7, 8

Questions 1-10 are based on the following two passages.

Passage 1

In 1984, great fanfare and optimism accompanied the funding of an ecosystem research project
called "Biosphere 2." The project's mission was to
Line create an airlock-sealed habitat that could support
5 a human crew for several years without contact
with or resources from the outside world. Less
than a decade later, however, enthusiasm for the
project had almost entirely eroded after serious
questions were raised about adherence to that
10 mission.

The problems that hampered expectations for
the project from the start involved the construction
of the Biosphere itself. Shaping bodies of water to
have waves and tidal changes posed troublesome
15 issues. During the mission, unforeseen difficulties
included overstocked fish dying and clogging filtration systems. Unanticipated condensation made
the "desert" too wet. Populations of greenhouse
ants and cockroaches exploded. Morning glories
20 overran the "rainforest," blocking out other plants.
These issues did not draw media fire, however, until
it was revealed that the project team had allowed
an injured member to leave and return, carrying
new material inside. Although the administra-
25 tors claimed the only new supplies brought in
were plastic bags, other sources accused mission
members of bringing food and other items. More
criticism was raised when it was learned that the
project had been pumping oxygen inside, to make
30 up for a failure in the balance of the system that
resulted in the amount of oxygen steadily declining. This scrutiny only intensified when these same
administrators denied having tampered with the
project. As an unfortunate result, doubts regarding
35 the integrity of all the scientific data generated by
the project hampered the perceived value of the
overall project.

Passage 2

An amazing undertaking, despite its ultimate
failure, Biosphere 2 was a colossal Arizona-desert
40 space-age ark devoted to exploration and ex-
perimentation. As promised by its promoters,
Biosphere 2 inhabitants would produce all their
own food and oxygen and recycle their own waste.
However, despite currying the initial favor of media
45 sources, the project became riddled with controversy. The story of its start is an awkward page of
scientific history but also incidentally a chronicle of
the metamorphosis of media relations from auspi-
cious beginnings to recriminating endings.

50 Promoters of Biosphere 2 were not shy about putting the project into the public eye and on the radar
of the scientific community. In July 1987, SBV and
The Institute of Ecotechnics held the First International Workshop on Closed Ecological Systems in
55 conjunction with the Royal Society in London. This
workshop brought together for the first time pio-
neers in the field from Russia, NASA, and Europe's
biological life support programs. The architectural-
engineering team of Allen, Augustine, Hawes, and
60 Dempster authored the preliminary Biosphere 2 designs. In addition, Biosphere 2 was from the beginning consistently propped up by the press. Biosphere
2 came to be regarded as an indicator of the possibility of human habitation in space. Even as many
65 scientists worked to temper such lofty goals, the media dubbed Biosphere 2 the most exciting scientific
project undertaken since the moon landing. But, in
the aftermath, the project's first crew emerged from
a supposed two-year isolation only to be greeted by
70 a swirl of negative attention and controversy. The
publications that had trumpeted the project quickly
reversed direction. Frustrated with Biosphere 2's
failures, the project's financiers fired their management team and, in a reversal of their own, lashed out
75 at the same press they had once courted.

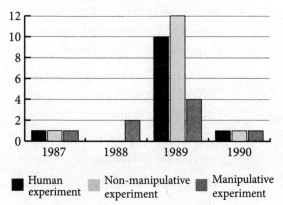

# of Publications from
Biosphere 2 Center Research

Human experiment | Non-manipulative experiment | Manipulative experiment

1. The author of Passage 1 would most likely describe the statement in lines 41-49 as a

   A) fair assessment of the project's results.

   B) clear example of the media hype surrounding the project.

   C) misleading statement regarding the project's outcome.

   D) compelling argument requiring a new review of the project.

2. Which choice provides the best evidence for the answer to the previous question?

   A) Lines 1-3 ("In 1984 . . . Bisophere 2")

   B) Lines 15-17 ("During . . . systems")

   C) Lines 27-32 ("More criticism . . . declining")

   D) Lines 34-37 ("As an . . . project")

3. As used in line 19, "exploded" most nearly means

   A) burst.

   B) increased.

   C) destroyed.

   D) opened.

4. The author of Passage 1 supports his claim about the Biosphere 2 project with

   A) hypothetical scenarios.

   B) analogous situations.

   C) supporting details.

   D) comparative analyses.

5. The main structure used in the second paragraph of Passage 1 can best be described as

   A) cause-and-effect.

   B) sequential.

   C) compare-and-contrast.

   D) continuation.

6. Passage 1 and Passage 2 differ mainly in that

   A) Passage 1 describes problems with Biosphere 2, while Passage 2 suggests possible solutions to those problems.

   B) Passage 1 relies on press reports for the basis of its argument, while Passage 2 provides internal documents to refute those claims.

   C) Passage 1 strikes a balance between initial optimism and subsequent pessimism, while Passage 2 remains neutral throughout.

   D) Passage 1 focuses on the internal causes of the problems with Biosphere 2, while Passage 2 focuses on how external perceptions of the project changed.

7. The author of Passage 1 would most likely agree with which of the following statements?

   A) The Biosphere 2 project was doomed to fail despite the fanfare it generated.

   B) The questions about how the project was conducted limit the usefulness of its results.

   C) The project deserves to be reevaluated given the potential value of its scientific data.

   D) The problems associated with Biosphere 2 were directly caused by media bias.

8. As used in line 65, "temper" most nearly means

   A) anger.

   B) strengthen.

   C) calm.

   D) anneal.

9. According to the chart, which of the following was the most consistently published research based on Biosphere 2?

   A) Human experiments

   B) Non-manipulative experiments

   C) Manipulative experiments

   D) None of the above

10. When read together, Passage 1 and Passage 2

    A) provide an overview of how the project was perceived and specific reasons for those perceptions.

    B) agree on the key issues raised, but differ in their assessment of the impact of those issues.

    C) offer contrasting opinions on a controversial undertaking.

    D) demonstrate how both the media and administrators may hamper exciting scientific discoveries.

PART THREE

Writing

Writing & Language— Expression of Ideas

IN THIS UNIT, YOU WILL LEARN:

1. The Kaplan Method for Writing & Language
2. Effective passage organization
3. Effective passage development
4. Effective language use

CHAPTER 12

The Kaplan Methods for Writing & Language and Infographics

CHAPTER OBJECTIVES

By the end of this chapter, you will be able to:

1. Identify issues in a passage and select the correct answer by applying the Kaplan Method for Writing & Language

2. Identify and analyze quantitative information and infographics

3. Synthesize information from infographics and text

SMARTPOINTS

Point Value	SmartPoint Category
Point Builder	The Kaplan Method for Writing & Language
Point Builder	The Kaplan Method for Infographics

THE KAPLAN METHOD FOR WRITING & LANGUAGE

The Kaplan Method for Writing & Language is the method you will use to boost your score on the Writing & Language Test. By understanding what the question is looking for, how it relates to the passage, and what questions you should ask yourself on Test Day, you will maximize the number of points you earn. Use the Kaplan Method for Writing & Language for every PSAT Writing & Language Test passage and question you encounter, whether practicing, completing your homework, working on a Practice Test, or taking the actual exam on Test Day.

The Kaplan Method for Writing & Language has three steps:

Step 1: Read the passage and identify the issue

- If there's an infographic, apply the Kaplan Method for Infographics

Step 2: Eliminate answer choices that do not address the issue

Step 3: Plug in the remaining answer choices and select the most correct, concise, and relevant one

> ✔ **On Test Day**
>
> The PSAT will expect you to be able to recognize errors in organization, pronouns, agreement, comparisons, development, sentence structure, modifiers, verbs, wordiness, style, tone, and syntax.

Let's take a closer look at each step.

Step 1: Read the passage and identify the issue

This means:

- Rather than reading the whole passage and then answering all of the questions, you can answer questions as you read, because they are mostly embedded in the text itself.

- When you see a number, stop reading and look at the question. If you can answer it with what you've read so far, do so. If you need more information, keep reading for context until you can answer it.

Step 2: Eliminate answer choices that do not address the issue

Eliminating answer choices that do not address the issue:

- Increases your odds of getting the correct answer by removing obviously incorrect answer choices.

Step 3: Plug in the remaining answer choices and select the most correct, concise, and relevant one

Correct, concise, and relevant means that the answer choice you select:

- Makes sense when read with the correction
- Is as short as possible while retaining the information in the text
- Relates well to the passage overall

> ✔ **Remember**
>
> There is no wrong answer penalty on the PSAT. When in doubt, eliminate what you can and then guess. You won't lose points for guessing.

Answer choices should not:

- Change the intended meaning of the original sentence, paragraph, or passage

- Introduce new grammatical errors even if the answer choice in question resolves the initial issue in the passage

> ✔ **On Test Day**
>
> If you have to guess, eliminate answer choices that are clearly wrong and then choose the shortest one—the PSAT rewards students who know how to be concise.

APPLYING THE KAPLAN METHOD FOR WRITING & LANGUAGE

You will see four Writing & Language passages on Test Day, each of which will have 11 questions. When you encounter a Writing & Language question, use the Kaplan Method asking yourself a series of strategic thinking questions.

By asking these strategic thinking questions, you will be able to select the correct answer choice more easily and efficiently. Pausing to ask questions may seem like it takes a lot of time, but it actually saves you time by preventing you from weighing the four answer choices against each other. Better to ask questions that lead you directly to the correct answer than to debate which of four answers seems the least incorrect.

Let's look at the following example of the Kaplan Method for Writing & Language in action in a short test-like passage. The left column contains text and a question similar to what you'll see on the Writing & Language Test on Test Day. The column on the right features the strategic thinking a test expert employs when approaching the passage and question presented.

Question	Strategic Thinking
Interest in developing wind power as an alternative renewable energy source has increased in recent years. In the eastern United States, exposed summits or ridge crests in the Appalachian Mountains have high wind power potential, and **1** <u>numerous wind power projects are being proposed by power companies.</u> While generally supportive of energy development from renewable sources, the U.S. Fish & Wildlife Service, state wildlife agencies, nongovernmental organizations, and the public are concerned about potential impacts of wind power development on wildlife.	**Step 1: Read the passage and identify the issue** *Can you identify a grammatical issue?* No, the underlined phrase is grammatically correct. *When there is no apparent grammatical issue, check style, tone, and syntax. Are there any style, tone, or syntax errors?* The sentence is written in the passive voice: The subject—"power companies"—comes after the object: "wind power projects."
1. A) NO CHANGE B) numerous wind power projects have been proposed. C) numerous wind power projects will be proposed. D) power companies have proposed numerous wind power projects.	**Step 2: Eliminate answer choices that do not address the issue** *What answer choice(s) can you eliminate, then?* Choices B and C, because they just change the verb tense, rather than address the error. **Step 3: Plug in the remaining answer choices and select the most correct, concise, and relevant one** *So, what is the answer?* Choice (D), because it puts the subject of the sentence—"power companies"—before the object.

THE KAPLAN METHOD FOR INFOGRAPHICS

The PSAT Writing & Language Test will contain one or more passages and/or questions that include one or more infographics. Each infographic will convey or expand on information from the passage.

The Kaplan Method for Infographics has three steps:

> Step 1: Read the question
> Step 2: Examine the infographic
> Step 3: Predict and answer

Let's examine these steps a bit more closely.

Step 1: Read the question

Assess the question stem for information that will help you zero in on the specific parts of the infographic that apply to the question

Step 2: Examine the infographic

Make sure to:

- Circle parts of the infographic that relate directly to the question

- Identify units of measurement, labels, and titles

✔ **Expert Tip**

For more data-heavy infographics, you should also make note of any present variables or categories, trends in the data, or relationships between variables.

Step 3: Predict and answer

Just like Step 3 of the Kaplan Method for Reading Comprehension, do not look at the answer choices until you've used the infographic to make a prediction. Even though the Kaplan Method for Writing & Language does not ask you to predict before you peek, make sure to do so when presented with an infographic question on the PSAT Writing & Language Test.

APPLYING THE KAPLAN METHOD FOR INFOGRAPHICS

No matter how many infographics you see on the Writing & Language Test on Test Day, make sure you use the Kaplan Method for Infographics for each one so that you maximize your score by answering the associated questions correctly.

PSAT experts ask themselves the questions outlined in the previous section as well as other questions that are more specific to the infographic and the passage it accompanies. Remember, infographics range in format—there can be tables, graphs, charts, and so on—so be flexible when you ask yourself these critical-thinking questions.

As always, asking questions and taking time to assess the given information before answering the test question will increase your chances of selecting the correct answer.

Let's look at how to apply the Kaplan Method for Infographics. This infographic would either represent data described in the passage or present new data that expand on what the passage is about.

The left column contains an infographic similar to the ones you'll see on the Writing & Language Test on Test Day. The column on the right features the strategic thinking a test expert employs when approaching the question and infographic presented.

Question	Strategic Thinking

Reduction of Flying Animals in the Appalachians

Species	2007	2008	2009	2010
Kestrel	415	383	320	268
Bat	543	421	267	233
Eagle	58	45	34	33
Hawk	196	138	85	85

2. Assume that from 2007 to 2010, the number of wind power projects in the Appalachians increased. According to the table, then, wind power projects

A) lowered the bat and bird populations.

B) increased the bat and bird populations.

C) had no effect on bat and bird populations.

D) cannot be determined.

Step 1: Read the question

Assess the question for information on what part of the infographic to focus on.

What information in the question stem corresponds to the infographic? The years 2007 to 2010.

Step 2: Examine the infographic

What are the units of measurement, labels, or titles?

The units in the table are numbers. They aren't labeled, so you'll need to look for context. Since the numbers go down, and the title of the graph is "Reduction of Flying Animals in the Appalachians," you can conclude that these must be populations. Don't blindly make assumptions.

Step 3: Predict and answer

Now that you understand the table, read the question. Based on the question, what parts of the table do you need to look at? The number of each species as the years progress.

Which answer choice best describes the table? Choice (A)

You have seen what kinds of strategic thinking questions PSAT experts ask themselves when they encounter Writing & Language test questions.

Look at the Writing & Language passage excerpt below. There are three questions associated with it. Use the Kaplan Method for Writing & Language to answer the questions. But remember to look at the guiding questions that have been laid out for you—some of the answers have been filled in, but you will have to fill in the answers to others.

Use your answers to the strategic thinking questions to select the correct answer, just as you will on Test Day.

During their seasonal migration, there are ③ large numbers migrating the mountainous landforms used for wind power. Wind power development could potentially impact populations of several species. Baseline information on nocturnally migrating birds and bats has been collected at some wind power development sites in the Appalachians, generally within a single season. However, a stronger scientific basis is critically needed to assess and mitigate risks at a regional scale.

The United States Geological Survey (USGS) is studying the distribution and flight patterns of birds and bats that migrate at night. Researchers analyze weather surveillance radar data (NEXRAD) to allow for a broad view of spring and fall migration through the Appalachians and ④ assessing the response of migrant birds to mountain ridges and other prominent landforms. Although NEXRAD data ⑤ provide information on the broad-scale spatial and temporal patterns of nocturnal migration through the region, the devices generally do not detect bird or bat targets within the altitudinal zone potentially occupied by wind turbines. Therefore, researchers are using two complementary ground-based techniques—acoustic detection and portable radar sampling—to obtain site-specific information on the abundance and flight characteristics of nocturnal migrants in lower airspace.

Questions	Strategic Thinking
3. A) NO CHANGE B) large amounts C) innumerable birds and bats D) birds and bats	**Step 1: Read the passage and identify the issue** *Can you identify a grammatical issue?* There's a modifier issue—as written, the sentence states that large numbers are migrating, not the actual birds and bats. **Step 2: Eliminate answer choices that do not address the issue** *What answer choice(s) can you eliminate?* _____ **Step 3: Plug in the remaining answer choices and select the most correct, concise, and relevant one** *Do any of the remaining answer choices change the original meaning? Which one(s)?* _____ _____ *What is the answer?* _____
4. A) NO CHANGE B) to assess C) assessed D) are assessors	**Step 1: Read the passage and identify the issue** *What is the grammatical issue?* _____ _____ **Step 2: Eliminate answer choices that do not address the issue** *What answer choice(s) can you eliminate?* _____ **Step 3: Plug in the remaining answer choices and select the most correct, concise, and relevant one** *Which answer choice corrects the error?* _____

5. A)   NO CHANGE
    B)   provides
    C)   has provided
    D)   will provide

Step 1: Read the passage and identify the issue

What part of speech is underlined? _____
_____

Does it agree with its subject in person and number? _____

Step 2: Eliminate answer choices that do not address the issue

What answer choice(s) can you eliminate?
_____

Step 3: Plug in the remaining answer choices and select the most correct, concise, and relevant one

What is the correct answer?
_____

Now, try a test-like Writing & Language passage and infographic on your own. Give yourself 5 minutes to read the passage and answer the questions.

Questions 6-14 are based on the following passage.

BUSINESS ENTITIES

In the business sector of New York City, giant corporations conduct their business in colossal towers. But what about the individual who wants to operate a business without being subject to the whims of corporate shareholders? How can such an individual realize her dreams to own a business, perhaps not equal in size to large corporations but at least their rival in ambition? **6** Life goes on, for the eager entrepreneur has two options.

For the confident entrepreneur looking to succeed on her own, there is *sole proprietorship*. In a sole proprietorship, there is one owner who is "solely" responsible for the business and any decisions regarding **7** it's operation. Of course, as with all choices in life, **8** this does not come without its share of disadvantages. Sole proprietorships aren't seen as separate **9** from their owners, so credit may be a problem, especially if you don't have a lot of financial assets on hand. You're fine if the business is lucrative, but if not, sole proprietorships can be a scary proposition since being the only boss also means taking on any and all debt that your business incurs.

If our entrepreneur is lucky enough to have a group of like-minded acquaintances with **10** who to start her company, she and her associates might instead opt to form a partnership. A partnership sacrifices some of the operational freedom that comes with a sole proprietorship, as you now have a bunch of "friends" to convince before you can have things your way on any business decisions that need to be **11** made however these same individuals will also be chipping in on expenses and sharing responsibility for any debt that the business may incur.

6. A) NO CHANGE
   B) Never fear,
   C) Don't worry,
   D) In fact,

7. A) NO CHANGE
   B) their
   C) its
   D) its'

8. A) NO CHANGE
   B) sole proprietorship
   C) business
   D) this operation

9. A) NO CHANGE
   B) with
   C) between
   D) by

10. A) NO CHANGE
    B) who's
    C) whose
    D) whom

11. A) NO CHANGE
    B) made, however
    C) made; however,
    D) made, however,

⑫ <u>Profits are shared with your partners</u> on payday, but the extra support they can provide if the business struggles helps to make up for that. **⑬** <u>Partnerships, however, are less lucrative for the individual than sole proprietorships.</u>

While the partnership seems to alleviate many of the problems that plague the sole proprietorship, it does have its share of disadvantages. In a sole proprietorship, the business could be sold if you, the owner, desire it, but a partnership requires consent from your partners before **⑭** <u>this</u> can take place. Moreover, unlike corporations, which come with limited liability for their shareholders, if the business runs deeply into debt, you are still responsible for your complete share of the debt, even if you do have others to share that debt with. When viewed in this light, the "evil corporations" surrounding us may be a necessary evil indeed.

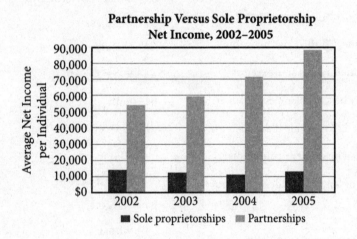

Partnership Versus Sole Proprietorship Net Income, 2002–2005

12. A) NO CHANGE
    B) You will share profits with your partners
    C) Profits will be shared with your partners
    D) Partners will share your profits

13. Which choice best reflects the data in the graph?
    A) NO CHANGE
    B) Sole proprietorships, however, are more lucrative for the individual than partnerships.
    C) Partnerships, however, have a lower net income per person than sole proprietorships.
    D) Partnerships are also more lucrative for the individual than are sole proprietorships.

14. A) NO CHANGE
    B) this partnership
    C) this consent
    D) this sale

Answers & Explanations for this chapter begin on page 494.

EXTRA PRACTICE

Required	Recommended
Questions 2, 3, 7, 8, 10	Questions 1, 4, 5, 6, 9, 11

Questions 1-11 are based on the following passage.

The North American Suburb

The North American suburb is an architectural and civic phenomenon distinct from suburban areas in any other part of the world. It was **1** a counterreaction to the need, especially keen after World War II, to "get away" from the city and all the noise, pollution, and general nastiness that went along with it. Cities were where the factories were, and the factories before modern pollution and safety standards were horrific things to behold. Of those who could **2** get out, many did.

Suburban communities, however, were not **3** sufficient by themselves to support life. The people who lived in them needed to work, shop, and socialize, and most of the active part of their lives remained fixed in urban centers. **4** Paradoxically, suburbs were clustered around their parent cities, with the suburban inhabitants avoiding the city center.

1. A) NO CHANGE
   B) an avoidance of
   C) a response to
   D) an intensifier of

2. A) NO CHANGE
   B) get out many did.
   C) get out . . . many did.
   D) get out; many did.

3. A) NO CHANGE
   B) self-sufficient.
   C) entirely sufficient by themselves to support life.
   D) sufficiently able to adequately support life by themselves.

4. A) NO CHANGE
   B) Therefore, suburbs were unnecessarily far from their parent cities, hampering suburban inhabitants' intent to commute to the city for work and play.
   C) Therefore, suburbs were clustered around their parent cities, with suburban inhabitants commuting daily to the city center for work and play.
   D) Suburbs therefore developed the amenities needed for suburbanites who were unwilling to ever go back into the city.

All this seems perfectly logical and inevitable. The suburb should be the ambiguous halfway point between city and country—away from the noise, congestion, and pollution but not so far away that there's no access to culture, to income, to all the exciting **5** pitfalls of urban life. In reality, though, few suburbs have actually approached this ideal. Moreover, the structure of the **6** modern suburb, while offering a respite from city pollution, has created health and environmental risks of its own.

Suburban zoning laws **7** have forced the separation of living and commercial spaces. As such, the city dweller's fond experience of walking down the block to the neighborhood cafe may be rare or entirely alien to a suburbanite. Should a suburb dweller, on a Saturday morning, desire a change of scenery and a cup of coffee, she must get in her car and drive some distance. **8** Come to think of it, nearly everything aside from the other houses and the occasional neighborhood park requires an automobile trip. All of this driving comes at the cost of pollution and a lack of daily exercise. Surely, we must begin to balance the appeal and freedom of the car with ecological and civic responsibility.

5. A) NO CHANGE
   B) drawbacks
   C) perils
   D) benefits

6. A) NO CHANGE
   B) modern suburb while offering a respite from city pollution has created
   C) modern suburb (while offering a respite from city pollution) has created
   D) modern suburb; while offering a respite from city pollution; has created

7. A) NO CHANGE
   B) has
   C) having
   D) had

8. A) NO CHANGE
   B) As fate would have it, nearly everything
   C) Contrary to popular belief, nearly everything
   D) In fact, nearly everything

[1] Some have charged that America doesn't need any more of these bland developments, that these projects line construction companies' pockets without contributing much to the value and diversity of American culture. [2] **9** I, however, think that the problem of suburbs can be described as one of degree rather than kind. [3] We don't need to abandon suburbs altogether; we instead need to more knowingly pursue

9. A) NO CHANGE

    B) I, however, believe that the problem of the suburbs should be described as one of degree rather than kind.

    C) I, however, see the problem of suburbs as one of degree rather than kind.

    D) I, however, think that one can see the problem of suburbs as one of degree rather than kind.

that ideal of the best of city and country. [4] Suburbs could be fascinating and beautiful places; we need only exercise our power to determine the nature of the places in which we live. 10 11

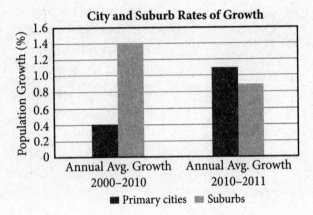

City and Suburb Rates of Growth

10. Which answer choice best describes the data in the graph as it relates to the passage?

A) Despite the growing awareness of the shortcomings of suburban living, America's suburban population continues to grow faster than that of the country's primary cities.

B) It also seems that Americans' opinions of the suburbs are quantifiably changing—from 2010 to 2011, population growth in cities outstripped growth in the suburbs.

C) Suburbs may have their naysayers, but the fact remains that it is hard to detect any change in where Americans are settling.

D) Contrary to continued positive perceptions of the suburbs, population growth swung back in favor of primary cities in the early twenty-first century.

11. What is the best placement for the sentence featured in the answer to the previous question?

A) After sentence 1

B) After sentence 2

C) Before sentence 4

D) After sentence 4

Writing & Language— Standard English Conventions

IN THIS UNIT, YOU WILL LEARN:

1. Conventions of punctuation

2. Proper sentence structure

3. Conventions of usage

CHAPTER 13

Conventions
of Punctuation

CHAPTER OBJECTIVES

By the end of this chapter, you will be able to:

1. Recognize and correct inappropriate uses of punctuation within and at the end of sentences

2. Identify and correct inappropriate uses of possessive nouns

3. Recognize and omit unnecessary punctuation

SMARTPOINTS

Point Value	SmartPoint Category
40 Points	Punctuation

END-OF-SENTENCE AND WITHIN-SENTENCE PUNCTUATION

The PSAT Writing & Language Test will require you to identify and correct inappropriate use of ending punctuation that deviates from the intent implied by the context. You will also have to identify and correct inappropriate colons, semicolons, and dashes when used to indicate breaks in thought within a sentence.

You can recognize Punctuation questions because the underlined portion of the text will include a punctuation mark. The answer choices to the question will move that punctuation mark around or replace it with another punctuation mark.

Use **commas** to:

- Separate independent clauses connected by a FANBOYS conjunction (*For, And, Nor, But, Or, Yet, So*)

- Separate an introductory phrase from the rest of the sentence

- Set off three or more items in a series or list

When you see an underlined **comma**, ask:

- Can the comma be replaced by a **period** or a **semicolon**?

Use **semicolons** to:

- Join two independent clauses when a FANBOYS conjunction is not present

- Separate items in a series or list if those items already include commas

Use **colons** to:

- Introduce and/or emphasize a short phrase, quotation, explanation, example, or list

Use **dashes** to:

- Indicate a hesitation or a break in thought

When you see an underlined **colon** or **dash**, ask:

- Has the author shifted gears by introducing or explaining something or breaking his or her thought process?

Let's look at the following example of the Kaplan Method for Writing & Language in action in a short test-like passage. The left column contains text and a question similar to what you'll see on the Writing & Language Test on Test Day. The column on the right features the strategic thinking a test expert employs when approaching the passage and question presented.

Question	Strategic Thinking

San Francisco's cable cars get their name from the long, heavy cable that runs beneath the streets along which the cars travel. This cable system resembles a giant laundry clothesline with a pulley at each end. Electricity turns the wheels of the **1** <u>pulleys, they</u> in turn make the cable move. Under its floor, each car has a powerful claw. The claw grips the cable when the car is ready to move, and it releases the cable when the car needs to stop. The cars themselves are not powered and don't generate any locomotion. Instead, they simply cling to the cable, which pulls them up and down San Francisco's steep hills.
 	
1. Which of the following is LEAST acceptable?
  A) NO CHANGE
  B) pulleys; they
  C) pulleys, and they
  D) pulleys. They
	Step 1: Read the passage and identify the issue
	
	What punctuation does the underlined segment include? A comma.
	
	Can the comma be replaced by a period or semicolon? Yes, because the two clauses the comma connects are both independent.
	
	Step 2: Eliminate answer choices that do not address the issue
	
	What kind of question is this? The question asks for the LEAST acceptable answer. Choices B, C, and D all correct the error, so they can be eliminated.
	
	Step 3: Plug in the remaining answer choices and select the most correct, concise, and relevant one
	
	What is the answer? Choice (A)

POSSESSIVE NOUNS AND PRONOUNS

Possessive nouns and pronouns indicate who or what possesses another noun or pronoun. Each follows different rules, and the PSAT will test both. These questions require you to identify both the singular and plural forms.

You can spot errors in possessive noun and pronoun construction by looking for:

- Two nouns in a row
- Context clues
- Pronouns with apostrophes
- Words that sound alike

Possessive Nouns		
Singular	sister's	My oldest *sister's* soccer game is on Saturday.
Plural	sisters'	My two older *sisters'* soccer games are on Saturday.

Questions about possessive pronouns often require you to watch out for contractions and sound-alike words.

Possessive Pronouns and Words to Watch Out For	
Its = possessive	It's = it is
Their = possessive	There = location/place
Whose = possessive	Who's = who is/who has

Let's look at the following example of the Kaplan Method for Writing & Language in action in a short test-like passage. The left column contains text and a question similar to what you'll see on the Writing & Language Test on Test Day. The column on the right features the strategic thinking a test expert employs when approaching the passage and question presented.

Question	Strategic Thinking
In 1928, bacteriologist Dr. Alexander Fleming observed that a spot of mold had contaminated one of the glass plates on which he was growing a colony of bacteria. Instead of discarding the plate immediately, he noticed that bacteria were flourishing everywhere on the plate except in the ②molds' vicinity. He decided to culture the mold and found that a broth filtered from it inhibited the growth of several species of bacteria. Nine years later, a team of scientists led by Howard Florey and Ernst Chain isolated the active antibacterial agent in Fleming's broth: penicillin. Florey and Chain went on to demonstrate that penicillin could cure bacterial infections in mice and in humans. Penicillin became a "miracle drug." 2. A) NO CHANGE B) mold C) molds D) mold's	**Step 1: Read the passage and identify the issue** *Are there any clues that suggest a grammatical issue?* Yes, an apostrophe is underlined. *What's the issue?* "Mold" should be singular, so the singular possessive is needed here. **Step 2: Eliminate answer choices that do not address the issue** *What answer choice(s) can you eliminate, then?* Choices B and C, because they are both nouns and therefore cannot modify another noun. **Step 3: Plug in the remaining answer choices and select the most correct, concise, and relevant one** *What is the answer?* Choice (D) because it properly forms a singular possessive and correctly modifies the noun "vicinity."

NONRESTRICTIVE/PARENTHETICAL ELEMENTS AND UNNECESSARY PUNCTUATION

Use **commas**, **dashes**, or **parentheses** to set off parenthetical or nonrestrictive information in a sentence.

> ### ✔ Definition
>
> Parenthetical or nonrestrictive information includes words or phrases that aren't essential to the sentence structure or content. Sometimes, however, this information is explanatory.

The PSAT will also ask you to recognize instances of unnecessary punctuation, particularly **commas**.

Do not use a comma to:

- Separate a subject from its predicate

- Separate a verb from its object or its subject, or a preposition from its object

- Set off restrictive elements

- Precede a dependent clause that comes after an independent clause

- Separate adjectives that work together to modify a noun

> ### ✔ Expert Tip
>
> To determine if information is nonessential, read the sentence without the information. If the sentence still makes sense without the omitted words, then those words need to be set off with punctuation.

Let's look at the following example of the Kaplan Method for Writing & Language in action in a short test-like passage. The left column contains text and a question similar to what you'll see on the Writing & Language Test on Test Day. The column on the right features the strategic thinking a test expert employs when approaching the passage and question presented.

Question	Strategic Thinking

Question

American ③ author, Raymond Carver, once said that everything we write is in some way autobiographical. This observation applies particularly to Carver's own work. In his seven books of short stories, Carver wrote almost exclusively about the working-class environment in which he grew up, portraying a neglected section of the American people with honesty and clarity. Born in the blue-collar town of Yakima, Washington, Carver was raised in a house where Zane Gray westerns and the local newspaper constituted the world of literature. After graduating from high school with Ds in English, he held a variety of jobs, ranging from scrubbing floors in a hospital to assembling bicycles at the local Sears. Few would have predicted that he would become a master of the short-story form, a literary figure mentioned in the same breath as Hemingway and Chekhov. And yet, it was in these humble surroundings that Carver found the inspiration for his unique narrative style: a plainspoken voice that enabled him to express the fears and aspirations of ordinary people.

3. A)   NO CHANGE
    B)   author, Raymond Carver once,
    C)   author Raymond Carver once
    D)   author Raymond Carver, once

Strategic Thinking

Step 1: Read the passage and identify the issue

What clue is in the underlined section? Commas setting off "Raymond Carter."

What do those commas tell you? That if you delete the information within the commas, the sentence must still make sense logically.

Does the sentence still make sense? No, because "American author once said . . ." doesn't make sense. The sentence needs the information that is currently set off by commas.

Step 2: Eliminate answer choices that do not address the issue

What answer choice(s) can you eliminate, then? Any answer with commas—B and D.

Step 3: Plug in the remaining answer choices and select the most correct, concise, and relevant one

What is the answer? Choice (C), because it removes the commas around the necessary information.

You have seen the ways in which the PSAT tests you on Punctuation in Writing & Language passages and the way a PSAT expert approaches these types of questions.

Look at the Writing & Language passage excerpt that follows. There are four questions associated with it. Use the Kaplan Method for Writing & Language to answer the questions. Remember to look at the strategic thinking questions that have been laid out for you—some of the answers have been filled in, but you will have to fill in the answers to others.

Use your answers to the strategic thinking questions to select the correct answer, just as you will on Test Day.

The Sistine Chapel

One shudders to contemplate Michelangelo's reaction if he were to gaze up today at the famous frescoes* he painted on the ceiling of the Sistine Chapel over four centuries ago. A practical man, he would no doubt be unsurprised by the effects of time and environment on his masterpiece. He would be philosophical about the damage wrought by mineral salts left behind when rainwater leaked through the roof. The layers of dirt and soot from coal braziers that heated the chapel and from candles and incense burned during religious functions would—prior to their removal during restoration—likely have been taken in stride as **4** well, however, he would be appalled at the ravages recently inflicted on his work by restorers.

The Vatican restoration team reveled in inducing a jarringly colorful transformation in the frescoes with special cleaning solvents and computerized analysis equipment. However, this effect was **5** not as they claimed achieved merely by removing the dirt and animal glue (employed by earlier restorers to revive muted colors) from the frescoes; they removed Michelangelo's final touches as well. Gone from the ceiling is the quality of suppressed anger and thunderous pessimism so often commented on by admiring scholars. That quality was not an artifact of grime, not a misleading monochrome imposed on the ceiling by time, for Michelangelo himself applied a veil of glaze to the frescoes to darken them after he had deemed his work too bright. The master would have felt compelled to add a few more layers of glaze had the ceiling radiated forth as it does now. The solvents of the restorers, in addition to stripping away the shadows, reacted chemically with Michelangelo's pigments to produce hues the painter never beheld.

Of course, the restorers left open an avenue for the reversal of their progress toward color and brightness. Since the layers of animal glue were no longer there to serve as protection, the atmospheric pollutants from the city of Rome gained direct access to the frescoes. Significant darkening was already noticed in some of the restored work a mere four years after **6** it's completion. It remains to be seen whether the measure introduced to arrest this process—an extensive climate-control **7** system—will itself have any long-term effect on the chapel's ceiling.

fresco: a style of painting on plaster using water-based pigments

Questions	Strategic Thinking
4. A) NO CHANGE B) well; however C) well. However D) well. However,	**Step 1: Read the passage and identify the issue** *What is the punctuation issue?* There is a comma joining two independent clauses. *How can you fix this?* Properly join the clauses or separate them into two sentences. **Step 2: Eliminate answer choices that do not address the issue** *What answer choice(s) can you eliminate?* Choices B and C fail to include the appropriate punctuation after the word "however." **Step 3: Plug in the remaining answer choices and select the most correct, concise, and relevant one** *What is the answer?* _____

Questions	Strategic Thinking
5. A) NO CHANGE B) not as they claimed, achieved C) not, as they claimed achieved D) not, as they claimed, achieved	**Step 1: Read the passage and identify the issue** *What is the grammatical issue?* There is missing punctuation—the sentence is confusing as written. *What part of the underlined segment is nonessential?* "As they claimed." **Step 2: Eliminate answer choices that do not address the issue** *What answer choice(s) can you eliminate?* _____ **Step 3: Plug in the remaining answer choices and select the most correct, concise, and relevant one** *What is the correct answer?* _____
6. A) NO CHANGE B) its C) their D) it is	**Step 1: Read the passage and identify the issue** *What is the grammatical issue?* "It's" means "it is," which doesn't make sense in context. *What should "it's" be replaced with?* _____ **Step 2: Eliminate answer choices that do not address the issue** *What answer choice(s) can you eliminate?* _____ **Step 3: Plug in the remaining answer choices and select the most correct, concise, and relevant one** *What is the answer?* _____

Questions	Strategic Thinking
7. A) NO CHANGE B) system will C) system, will D) system, and will	**Step 1: Read the passage and identify the issue** *What is the grammatical issue?* _____ _____ **Step 2: Eliminate answer choices that do not address the issue** *What answer choice(s) can you eliminate?* _____ **Step 3: Plug in the remaining answer choices and select the most correct, concise, and relevant one** *What is the correct answer?* _____

Now, try a test-like Writing & Language passage on your own. Give yourself 5 minutes to read the passage and answer the questions.

Questions 8-15 are based on the following passage.

MUSEUMS

City museums are places where people can learn about various cultures by studying objects of particular historical or artistic value. The increasingly popular "design museums" that are opening today perform quite a different function. Unlike most city 8 museums the design museum displays and assesses objects that are readily available to the general public. These museums place everyday household items under 9 spotlights. Breaking down the barriers between commerce and creative invention.

Critics have argued that design museums are often manipulated to serve as advertisements for new industrial technology. Their 10 role however is not simply a matter of merchandising—it is the honoring of 11 impressive, innovative products. The difference between the window of a department store and the showcase in a design museum is that the first tries to sell you something, while the second informs you of the success of the attempt.

One advantage that the design museum has over other civic museums is that design museums are places where people feel familiar with the exhibits. Unlike the average art gallery patron, a design 12 museums visitors rarely feel intimidated or disoriented. This is partly because design museums clearly illustrate how and why mass-produced consumer objects work and look as they 13 do, and show how design contributes to the quality of our lives. For example, an exhibit involving a particular design of chair would not simply explain how it functions as a chair. It would also demonstrate how its various features combine to produce an artistic effect or redefine our manner

8. A) NO CHANGE
    B) museums; the
    C) museums: the
    D) museums, the

9. A) NO CHANGE
    B) spotlights; breaking
    C) spotlights, breaking
    D) spotlights breaking

10. A) NO CHANGE
    B) role; however, is
    C) role, however is
    D) role, however, is

11. A) NO CHANGE
    B) impressive innovative
    C) impressive, and innovative
    D) impressively innovative

12. A) NO CHANGE
    B) museums' visitors
    C) museum's visitors
    D) museum visitor's

13. A) NO CHANGE
    B) do and show
    C) do: show
    D) do—show

of performing the basic act of being seated. Thus, the purpose of such an exhibit would be to present these concepts in novel **14** ways and to challenge, stimulate, and inform the viewer. An art gallery exhibit, on the other hand, would provide very little information about the chair and charge the visitor with understanding the exhibit on some abstract level.

Within the past decade, several new design museums have opened their doors. Each of these museums has responded in totally original ways to the public's growing interest in the field. London's Design Museum, for instance, displays a collection of mass-produced objects ranging from Zippo lighters to electric typewriters to a show of Norwegian sardine-tin labels. The options open to curators of design museums seem far less rigorous, conventionalized, and preprogrammed than those open to curators in charge of public galleries of paintings and sculpture. **15** Societies humorous aspects are better represented in the display of postmodern playthings or quirky Japanese vacuum cleaners in pastel colors than in an exhibition of Impressionist landscapes.

14. A) NO CHANGE
    B) ways to challenge,
    C) ways; to challenge,
    D) ways—to challenge,

15. A) NO CHANGE
    B) Society's
    C) Societys'
    D) Societie's

Answers & Explanations for this chapter begin on page 499.

EXTRA PRACTICE

Required	Recommended
Questions 2, 5, 7, 9, 11	Questions 1, 3, 4, 6, 8, 10

Questions 1-11 are based on the following passage.

The Modern Professional

Despite the honor accorded them by society and the usually substantial monetary rewards they enjoy for their work, many modern professionals **1** complain and they feel demoralized. They don't command the respect of the public or enjoy special privileges as members of exclusive groups to the extent that professionals once did. This decline in the **2** profession's status is difficult for them to bear because, they vehemently **3** maintain, the knowledge and unique skills of professionals are as vital and indispensable to society as they have ever been.

Originally, being a professional meant practicing in one of the "learned professions," a category that included only law, theology, university scholarship, and (eventually) medicine **4** —long considered a practical art. Members of these groups distinguished themselves from the rest of society by their possession of certain special knowledge that brought with it power and abilities most others could not even fully fathom. **5** Aspirants, to a profession, were required not only to devote themselves to a demanding life of learning but also to adhere to a specifically tailored system of ethics to prevent the misuse of professional powers. The special deference and privileges these professionals received were their reward for using their knowledge in the service of others rather than of themselves.

1. A) NO CHANGE
   B) complain; they
   C) complain, and they
   D) complain that they

2. A) NO CHANGE
   B) professional
   C) professions'
   D) professions

3. A) NO CHANGE
   B) maintain the
   C) maintain. The
   D) maintain; the

4. A) NO CHANGE
   B) — considered a practical art
   C) —for a long while considered to be a practical art
   D) OMIT the underlined portion.

5. A) NO CHANGE
   B) Aspirants to a profession were
   C) Aspirants to a profession, were
   D) Aspirants, to a profession were

6 Because many of today's professionals would argue that this description still applies to them, the truth of the matter is that the professional scene has changed quite a bit since the days of the "learned professions." When the members of the professions began to organize themselves in the nineteenth century, establishing work standards and policing themselves to prevent the government from cleaning house for them, they proclaimed that they were doing this for the good of the public. The professional associations 7 that emerged from this structuring proved to be, however, far more advantageous to the professionals than to the general 8 populace. The associations began to function as 9 lobbies, and interest groups.

A further consequence of this organizing was that the elevated position of the professional gradually eroded as members of other occupations 10 jumped on the bandwagon. When just about any group could organize itself and call itself a profession, the concept of the professional as the possessor of special knowledge and abilities didn't seem to be as valid. Thus, many professions have had to struggle to 11 sustain and preserve the notion that their members provide a critical service to society that no one else can.

6. A) NO CHANGE
   B) As a result
   C) In addition
   D) Although

7. A) NO CHANGE
   B) who
   C) whom
   D) when

8. A) NO CHANGE
   B) populace because the
   C) populace, and the
   D) populace; the

9. A) NO CHANGE
   B) lobbies and, interest groups.
   C) lobbies and interest groups.
   D) lobbies, interest groups.

10. Which choice most effectively maintains the tone and style of the passage as a whole?
    A) NO CHANGE
    B) claimed professional status
    C) joined in on the fun
    D) stated their wishes to be seen professionally

11. A) NO CHANGE
    B) sustain, and preserve
    C) preserve and sustain
    D) sustain

CHAPTER 14

Conventions of Usage

CHAPTER OBJECTIVES

By the end of this chapter, you will be able to:

1. Recognize and correct errors in pronoun clarity, grammatical agreement, and logical comparison

2. Distinguish among commonly confused possessive determiners, contractions, and adverbs

3. Recognize and correct incorrectly constructed idioms and frequently misused words

SMARTPOINTS

Point Value	SmartPoint Category
40 Points	Usage

PRONOUNS

A pronoun is ambiguous if its antecedent is either missing or unclear. On the PSAT, you must be able to recognize either situation and make the appropriate correction. When you see an underlined pronoun, make sure you can find the specific noun to which it refers.

MISSING ANTECEDENT

- When the flight arrived, *they* told the passengers to stay seated until the plane reached the gate. (The pronoun "they" does not have an antecedent in this sentence.)

- When the flight arrived, *the flight crew* told the passengers to stay seated until the plane reached the gate. (Replacing the pronoun with a specific noun clarifies the meaning.)

UNCLEAR ANTECEDENT

- Martha asked Mia to drive Samantha to the airport because *she* was running late. (The pronoun "she" could refer to any of the three people mentioned in the sentence.)

- Because Martha was running late, she asked Mia to drive Samantha to the airport. (By rearranging the sentence, the pronoun "she" unambiguously refers to Martha.)

> ✔ **Definition**
>
> The **antecedent** is the noun that the pronoun replaces or stands in for in another part of the sentence. To identify the **antecedent** of a pronoun, check the nouns near the pronoun. Substitute those nouns in for the pronoun to see which one makes sense.

AGREEMENT

Pronoun-Antecedent Agreement

Pronouns must agree with their antecedents not only in person and number but also in gender. Only third-person pronouns make a distinction based on gender.

Gender	Example
Feminine	Because Yvonne had a question, *she* raised her hand.
Masculine	Since *he* had lots of homework, Justin started working right away.
Neuter	The rain started slowly, but then *it* became a downpour.
Unspecified	If a traveler is lost, *he* or *she* should ask for directions.

Pronoun-Case Agreement

There are three pronoun cases:

- Subjective case: The pronoun is used as the subject.
- Objective case: The pronoun is used as the object of a verb or a preposition.
- Possessive case: The pronoun expresses ownership.

Subjective Case	I, you, she, he, it, we, you, they, who
Objective Case	me, you, her, him, it, us, you, them, whom
Possessive Case	my, mine, your, yours, his, her, hers, its, our, ours, their, theirs, whose

> ✔ **Expert Tip**
>
> When there are two pronouns or a noun and a pronoun in a compound structure, drop the other noun to confirm which case to use. For example: *Tom and me walk into town.* Would you say, "Me walk into town?" No, you would say, "I walk into town." Therefore, the correct case is subjective and the original sentence should read *Tom and I walk into town.*

> ✔ **Remember**
>
> Use "who" when you would use "he" or "she." Use "whom" when you would use "him" or "her."

Subject-Verb Agreement

A verb must agree with its subject noun in person and number.

- Singular: A **stamp sticks** to an envelope.
- Plural: **Stamps stick** to envelopes.

The noun closest to a verb may not be its subject: *The **chair** with the cabriole legs **is** an antique.* The noun closest to the verb in this sentence ("is," which is singular) is "legs," which is plural. However, the verb's subject is "chair," so the sentence is correct as written.

Only the conjunction *and* forms a compound subject requiring a plural verb form.

- Danny **and** Jared **are** in the fencing club.
- **Either** Danny or Jared **is** in the fencing club.
- **Neither** Danny nor Jared **is** in the fencing club.

Noun-Number Agreement

Related nouns must be consistent in number.

- *Students* applying for college must submit their *applications* on time. (The sentence refers to multiple students, and they all must submit applications.)

FREQUENTLY CONFUSED WORDS

The English language contains many pairs of words that sound alike but are spelled differently and have different meanings.

ACCEPT/EXCEPT: To *accept* is to take or receive something that is offered: *Dad said he would accept my apology for putting a dent in his new car, but then he grounded me for two weeks.* To *except* is to leave out or exclude: *The soldier was excepted from combat duty because he had poor field vision.* Except is usually used as a preposition meaning, "with the exception of, excluding": *When the receptionist found out that everyone except him had received a raise, he demanded a salary increase as well.*

AFFECT/EFFECT: To *affect* is to have an influence on something: *Al refused to let the rain affect his plans for a picnic, so he sat under an umbrella and ate potato salad.* To *effect* is to bring something about or cause something to happen: *The young activist received an award for effecting a change in her community.* An *effect* is an influence or a result: *The newspaper article about homeless animals had such an effect on Richard that he brought home three kittens from the shelter.* Most often, *affect* is used in its verb form, and *effect* is used in its noun form.

AFFLICT/INFLICT: To *afflict* is to torment or distress someone or something. It usually appears as a passive verb: *Jeff is afflicted with severe migraine headaches.* To *inflict* is to impose punishment or suffering on someone or something: *No one dared displease the king, for he was known to inflict severe punishments on those who upset him.*

ALLUSION/ILLUSION: An *allusion* is an indirect reference to something, a hint: *I remarked that Sally's boyfriend was unusual looking; this allusion to his prominent tattoos did not please Sally.* An *illusion* is a false, misleading, or deceptive appearance: *A magician creates the illusion that something has disappeared by hiding it faster than the eye can follow it.*

EMIGRATE/IMMIGRATE: To *emigrate* is to leave one country for another country, and is usually used with the preposition *from: Many people emigrated from Europe in search of better living conditions.* To *immigrate* is to enter a country to take up permanent residence there, and is usually used with the preposition *to: They immigrated to North America because land was plentiful.*

EMINENT/IMMINENT: Someone who is *eminent* is prominent or outstanding: *The eminent archeologist Dr. Wong has identified the artifact as prehistoric in origin.* Something that is *imminent* is likely to happen soon, or is impending: *After being warned that the hurricane's arrival was imminent, beachfront residents left their homes immediately.*

LAY/LIE: To *lay* is to place or put something down, and this verb usually does have a "something"—a direct object—following it: *Before she begins her pictures, Emily lays all of her pencils, brushes, and paints on her worktable to avoid interruptions while she draws and paints.* One form, *laid*, serves as the simple past and the past participle of *lay*. To *lie* is to recline, to be in a lying position or at rest. This verb never takes a direct object: you do not lie anything down. The simple past form of *lie* is *lay*; the past participle is *lain*. Notice that the past form of *lie* is identical with the present form of *lay*. This coincidence complicates the task of distinguishing the related meanings of *lay* and *lie*: *Having laid the picnic cloth under the sycamore, they lay in the shady grass all last Sunday afternoon.*

LEAVE/LET: To *leave* is to depart, or to allow something to remain behind after departing, or to allow something to remain as it is. One irregular verb form, *left*, serves as the simple past and the past participle: *I boarded my plane and it left, leaving my baggage behind in Chicago.* When *leave* is used in the third sense—to allow something to remain as it is—and followed by *alone*, this verb does overlap with *let*: *If parents leave* (or *let*) *a baby with a new toy alone, she will understand it as quickly as if they demonstrated how the toy works.* To *let* is to allow, or to rent out. These are the verb's core meanings, but it also combines with several different prepositions to produce various specific senses. *Let* is irregular. One form serves as present, past, and past participle. *The French border police would not let the Dutch tourist pass without a passport.*

RAISE/RISE: To *raise* is to lift up, or to cause to rise or grow, and it usually has a direct object: you *raise* dumbbells, roof beams, tomato plants, children. *Raise* is a completely regular verb. *The trade tariff on imported leather goods raised the prices of Italian shoes.* To *rise* is to get up, to go up, to be built up. This verb never takes a direct object: you do not *rise* something. The past and past participle forms are irregular; *rose* is the simple past, *risen* the past participle. *Long-distance commuters must rise early and return home late.*

SET/SIT: The difference between *set* and *sit* is very similar to the difference between *lay* and *lie* and between *raise* and *rise*. To *set* is to put or place something, to settle or arrange it. But *set* takes on other specific meanings when it combines with several different prepositions. *Set* is an irregular verb in that one form serves as present, past, and past participle. *Set* usually takes a direct object: you *set* a ladder against the fence, a value on family heirlooms, a date for the family reunion: *The professor set the students' chairs in a semicircle in order to promote open discussion.* To *sit* is to take a seat or to be in a seated position, to rest somewhere, or to occupy a place. This verb does not usually take a direct object, although you can say: *The usher sat us in the center seats of the third row from the stage.* The irregular form *sat* serves as past and past participle. Usually, no direct object follows this verb. *The beach house sits on a hill at some distance from the shoreline.*

Other pairs of words do not sound alike at all but have similar meanings that are often confused.

AMONG/BETWEEN: The preposition *among* refers to collective arrangements; that is, use it when referring to three or more people or items. *The soccer team shared a whole case of water among themselves. Between* is also a preposition but is used in the presence of only two people or items: *Amy and Tonia split the tasks between them.*

AMOUNT/NUMBER: *Amount* is used in reference to mass nouns (also known as uncountable nouns): *The amount of bravery displayed was awe-inspiring. Number* is used in reference to countable nouns: *The recipe calls for a specific number of chocolate chips.*

FEWER/LESS: *Fewer* should be used when referring to countable objects and concepts: *Diana's yard has fewer squirrels than mine. Less* should be used only with a grammatically singular noun: *Diana's yard has less wildlife than mine.* One common misuse of *less* is a sign you probably encounter frequently at the supermarket: The *10 items or less* sign should actually be *10 items or fewer*, because the items are countable.

MANY/MUCH: *Many* modifies things that can be counted, such as plural nouns: *Samantha has many awards in her collection. Much*, on the other hand, modifies things that cannot be counted, often singular nouns: *Jim has much more money than I do.*

The PSAT will also test your ability to correctly use and identify possessive pronouns, contractions, and adverbs.

ITS/IT'S: *Its* is a possessive pronoun like *his* and *hers*: *The rare book would be worth more if its cover weren't ripped. It's* is a contraction that can mean *it is*, *it has*, or *it was*: *It's been a long time since I last saw you.*

THEIR/THEY'RE/THERE: *Their* is a possessive form of the pronoun *they*: *The players respected their coach. They're* is a contraction of *they are*: *The students say they're planning to attend college. There* is used to introduce a sentence or indicate a location: *There was no water in the well when we arrived there.*

THEIRS/THERE'S: *Theirs* is the possessive plural form of the pronoun *they*: *The careless bikers admitted the fault was theirs. There's* is a contraction of *there is* or *there has*: *There's been a lot of rain this summer.*

WHOSE/WHO'S: *Whose* is a possessive pronoun used to refer to people or things: *Whose phone is ringing? Who's* is a contraction of *who is* or *who has*: *Who's planning to join us for dinner?*

COMPARISONS

The PSAT will test your ability to recognize and correct improper comparisons. There are three rules governing correct comparisons:

1. Compare Logical Things

   The **price of tea** has risen sharply, while **coffee** has remained the same.

   This sentence incorrectly compares *the price of tea* to *coffee*. The sentence should read: *The* **price of tea** *has risen sharply, while the* **price of coffee** *has remained the same.*

2. Use Parallel Structure

*I prefer **hiking** rather than **to read**.*

This sentence uses the gerund verb form (*hiking*) then switches to the infinitive verb form (*to read*). To correct the sentence, make sure the verb forms are consistent: *I prefer **to hike** rather than **to read**.*

3. Structure Comparisons Correctly

*Some students are **better** in Reading **than** they are in Math.*
*Other students are **as** good in Math **as** they are in Reading.*

Both of these sentences are correctly structured: the first with the use of *better . . . than*, and the second with the use of *as . . . as*.

When comparing like things, adjectives must match the number of items being compared. When comparing two items or people, use the comparative form of the adjective. When comparing three or more items or people, use the superlative form.

Comparative	Superlative
Use when comparing two items.	Use when comparing three or more items.
better	best
more	most
newer	newest
older	oldest
shorter	shortest
taller	tallest
worse	worst
younger	youngest

IDIOMS

An **idiom** is a combination of words that must be used together to convey either a figurative or literal meaning. Idioms are tested in four ways on the PSAT:

1. Proper Preposition Usage in Context

*The three finalists will compete **for** the grand prize: an all-inclusive cruise to Bali.*
*Roger will compete **against** Rafael in the final round of the tournament.*
*I will compete **with** Deborah in the synchronized swimming competition.*

2. Verb Forms

   *The architect likes **to draft** floor plans.*
   *The architect enjoys **drafting** floor plans.*

3. Idiomatic Expressions

   Idiomatic expressions refer to words or phrases that must be used together to be correct.

   *Simone will **either** continue sleeping **or** get up and get ready for school.*
   ***Neither** the principal **nor** the teachers will tolerate tardiness.*
   *This fall, Shari is playing **not only** soccer, **but also** field hockey.*

4. Implicit Double Negatives

   Some words imply a negative and therefore cannot be paired with an explicit negative.

   *Janet **cannot hardly** wait for summer vacation.*

   This sentence is incorrect as written. It should read: *Janet **can hardly** wait for summer vacation.*

Frequently Tested Prepositions	Idiomatic Expressions	Words That Can't Be Paired with Negative Words
at	as . . . as	barely
by	between . . . and	hardly
for	both . . . and	scarcely
of	either . . . or	
on	just as . . . so too	
to	neither . . . nor	
with	not only . . . but also	

Let's look at the following Writing & Language passage and questions. After the passage, there are two columns. The left column contains test-like questions. The column on the right features the strategic thinking a test expert employs when approaching the passage and questions presented.

Questions 1-4 are based on the following passage.

Woolly Mammoth

There is likely no animal that better captures the public's imagination of the prehistoric Ice Age than the woolly mammoth. Although remains of many mammoths have been discovered over the years, none have been found better preserved than the "Jarkov Mammoth" found on Siberia's Taimyr Peninsula in 1997. Soon after a 9-year-old boy out playing in the snowy hills first spotted the remains, scientists descended on the site. Then, after battling weeks of frigid weather and approximately 20,000 years' worth of dense frost coating the entire body of the mammoth, the assembled team finally completed a successful excavation. Important for numerous scientific reasons, the Jarkov Mammoth, in particular, **1** <u>have</u> helped scientists settle a debate that has been raging for many years concerning the possible reasons behind the sudden extinction of these ancient giants.

Woolly mammoths roamed the cold northern plains of the globe for much of the last 2 million years, including most of the Ice Age that began roughly 70,000 years ago. Then, quite suddenly, 10,000 years ago, a time that corresponds with the end of the Ice Age, the mammoths disappeared. Scientific theories explaining this rapid extinction ranged **2** <u>from thoughts of</u> meteor showers pelting Earth to massive volcanic eruptions. Today, however, partially through evidence taken from the Jarkov Mammoth, it is generally agreed that these creatures died out from a combination of changing climate, hunting pressures from humans, and probably even disease. In fact, scientists consider it likely that the rising temperatures accompanying the end of the Ice Age worked against the evolutionary adaptations made by the mammoths, including their signature woolly coats of dense fur. Indeed, the demise of the Jarkov Mammoth seems to have involved a deep patch of mud, perhaps a sign that these behemoths were unaccustomed to treading on increasingly softer ground.

Having adapted to the cold and snow that blanketed much of Earth during the Ice Age, the mammoth kept its enormous body at an optimal temperature with a covering of long, thick, dark black hair and layer of underfur. Typically, these herbivorous precursors to the modern-day elephant were about 12 feet long, 10 feet tall at the shoulders, and weighed nearly 6,000 pounds. The long, distinctively curved tusks of the mammoth were used for protection by all members of the species and specifically by the males to assert their dominance, much the same way **3** <u>they</u> utilize their own shorter, straighter toothy appendages. For a woolly mammoth living in the Ice Age, these tusks were particularly important **4** <u>for digging</u> through layers of ice in search of grass and other plant food. Although the eventual melting of these layers would seem to ease this search, the sudden change in climate apparently proved too much for the woolly mammoth to overcome.

Questions	Strategic Thinking

1. A) NO CHANGE
   B) had
   C) has
   D) having
	Step 1: Read the passage and identify the issue
	
	What is the grammatical issue? Subject-verb agreement.
	
	What part of speech is underlined? A third person plural verb.
	
	What is its subject? The Jarkov Mammoth.
	
	What is the subject's person and number? Third person singular.
	
	Step 2: Eliminate answer choices that do not address the issue
	
	What answer choice(s) can you eliminate? Choice A because the subject and verb do not match. Choice B because the tense changes. Choice D because it creates a run-on.
	
	Step 3: Plug in the remaining answer choices and select the most correct, concise, and relevant one
	
	What is the correct answer? Choice (C)

| 2. A) NO CHANGE
B) from thoughts about
C) from ideas of
D) from | **Step 1: Read the passage and identify the issue**

What is the issue? Comparisons.

As written, what is being compared? "Thoughts of" and "eruptions."

What is logically being compared? "Meteor showers" and "volcanic eruptions."

Step 2: Eliminate answer choices that do not address the issue

What answer choice(s) can you eliminate? Choices B and C because they don't correct the comparison error.

Step 3: Plug in the remaining answer choices and select the most correct, concise, and relevant one

What is the correct answer? Choice (D) |
| 3. A) NO CHANGE
B) today's elephants
C) woolly mammoths
D) scientists | **Step 1: Read the passage and identify the issue**

What is the issue? The pronoun's antecedent is not clear.

How do you know? The paragraph talks about both mammoths and elephants.

Step 2: Eliminate answer choices that do not address the issue

What answer choice(s) can you eliminate? Choice C because the writer is making a distinction between mammoths and something else. Choice D because scientists don't have "toothy appendages."

Step 3: Plug in the remaining answer choices and select the most correct, concise, and relevant one

What is the answer? Choice (B) |

4. A) NO CHANGE
    B) to dig
    C) at digging
    D) from digging

Step 1: Read the passage and identify the issue

What is the issue? The underlined portion is an idiomatic phrase with a preposition.

Step 2: Eliminate answer choices that do not address the issue

What answer choice(s) can you eliminate? Choices B, C, and D because none of them are grammatically correct in context.

Step 3: Plug in the remaining answer choices and select the most correct, concise, and relevant one

What is the answer? Choice (A)

You have seen the ways in which the PSAT tests you on Usage in Writing & Language passages and the way a PSAT expert approaches these types of questions.

Look at the Writing & Language passage excerpt that follows. There are four questions associated with it. Use the Kaplan Method for Writing & Language to answer the questions. Remember to look at the strategic thinking questions that have been laid out for you—some of the answers have been filled in, but you will have to fill in the answers to others.

Use your answers to the strategic thinking questions to select the correct answer, just as you will on Test Day.

Questions 5-8 are based on the following passage.

Hudson River School

The first truly American art movement was formed by a group of landscape painters that emerged in the early nineteenth century, called the Hudson River School. The first works in this style were created by Thomas Cole, Thomas Doughty, and Asher Durand, a trio of painters who worked during the 1820s in the Hudson River Valley and surrounding locations. Heavily influenced by European romanticism, these painters set out to convey the remoteness and splendor of the American wilderness. The strongly nationalistic tone of their paintings caught the spirit of the times, and within a generation, the movement had mushroomed to include landscape painters from all over the United States. Canvases celebrating such typically American scenes as Niagara Falls, Boston Harbor, and the expansion of the railroad into rural Pennsylvania **5** was greeted with enormous popular acclaim.

One factor contributing to the success of the Hudson River School was the rapid growth of American nationalism in the early nineteenth century. The War of 1812 had given the United States a new sense of pride in its identity, and as the nation continued to grow, there was a desire to compete with Europe on both economic and cultural grounds. The vast panoramas of the Hudson River School fit the bill perfectly **6** while providing a new movement in art that was unmistakably American in origin. The Hudson River School also arrived at a time when writers in the United States were turning their attention to the wilderness as a unique aspect of their nationality. The Hudson River School painters profited from this nostalgia because they effectively represented the continent the way it used to be. The view that the American character was formed by the frontier experience was widely held, and many **7** <u>of them</u> wrote about their concerns regarding an increasingly urbanized country.

In keeping with this nationalistic spirit, even the painting style of the Hudson River School exhibited a strong sense of American identity. Although many of the artists studied in Europe, their paintings show a desire to be free of European artistic rules. Regarding the natural landscape as a direct manifestation of God, the Hudson River School painters attempted to record what they saw as accurately as possible. Unlike European painters, who brought to their canvases the styles and techniques of centuries, the Hudson River School **8** <u>painters</u> sought neither to embellish nor to idealize their scenes, portraying nature with the objectivity and attention to detail of naturalists.

Questions	Strategic Thinking

5. A) NO CHANGE
   B) is
   C) are
   D) were
	Step 1: Read the passage and identify the issue
	
	What is the issue? Subject-verb agreement.
	
	What is the subject of the underlined verb? Canvases.
	
	Should the underlined verb be singular or plural? Plural.
	
	Step 2: Eliminate answer choices that do not address the issue
	
	What answer choice(s) can you eliminate? Choices A and B because they feature singular verbs.
	
	Step 3: Plug in the remaining answer choices and select the most correct, concise, and relevant one
	
	What is the answer? _____

6. A)   NO CHANGE
   B)   by providing
   C)   in providing
   D)   only providing

Step 1: Read the passage and identify the issue

What is the grammatical issue? Preposition usage.

How can you determine which preposition is correct? By carefully reading the sentence to identify what meaning the preposition needs to convey.

Step 2: Eliminate answer choices that do not address the issue

What answer choice(s) can you eliminate?

_____

Step 3: Plug in the remaining answer choices and select the most correct, concise, and relevant one

What is the correct answer? _____

7. A)   NO CHANGE
   B)   painters
   C)   writers
   D)   Europeans

Step 1: Read the passage and identify the issue

What is the issue? Pronoun ambiguity.

How can you identify the correct antecedent? By rereading enough of the passage to be able to determine who "were concerned."

Step 2: Eliminate answer choices that do not address the issue

What answer choice(s) can you eliminate?

_____

Step 3: Plug in the remaining answer choices and select the most correct, concise, and relevant one

What is the answer? _____

8. A) NO CHANGE
   B) canvases
   C) styles
   D) techniques

Step 1: Read the passage and identify the issue

What is the grammatical issue? Comparing like things.

What are the "painters" in the underlined portion being compared to? _____
_____
_____

Step 2: Eliminate answer choices that do not address the issue

What answer choice(s) can you eliminate?
_____

Step 3: Plug in the remaining answer choices and select the most correct, concise, and relevant one

What is the answer? _____

Now, try a test-like Writing & Language passage on your own. Give yourself 5 minutes to read the passage and answer the questions.

Questions 9-16 are based on the following passage.

1929 Stock Market Crash

On October 29, 1929, the stock market crashed in one of the
9 most worst financial panics in American history. The ensuing
economic meltdown, known as the Great Depression, left Americans
thinking about what went wrong and how to ensure that it would never
happen again. To this day, economists study the speculative boom of the
Roaring '20s, the crash, and the Great Depression, trying to find patterns that can be applied to today's economy.

After World War I, America, having proven itself a world power,
began to reap the benefits of new technologies and investments opening
everywhere. Mass production made all types of new gadgets, such as
10 vacuum cleaners and automobiles, available to more Americans
because of cheaper prices. The same was true of stocks and bonds.
Throughout the 1920s, many Americans, not just the rich, played the
stock market. Laws of the day made this investment possible by requiring
only 10 percent, or a "margin," of an investment to be paid immediately,
with the rest payable over time. If something went wrong, however, the
investor would have to pay back the balance of **11** their loan.

Economists of the time worried about how much investing was
being done by people who could not **12** hardly afford the losses if the
market crashed, but government policy of the day called for noninterven-
tion into business matters. Economists, nonetheless, sought a way to wean
the people away from margin investing, but no laws were implemented
for fear of causing a panic. As long as the stock prices continued to go
up and investors continued to benefit, no one was willing to take action.

9. A) NO CHANGE
   B) most worse
   C) worst
   D) more worse

10. A) NO CHANGE
    B) the vacuum cleaner and automobiles
    C) the vacuum cleaner and automobiles
    D) vacuum cleaners or automobiles

11. A) NO CHANGE
    B) the
    C) her
    D) his

12. A) NO CHANGE
    B) barely afford
    C) scarcely afford
    D) afford

History has taught us, however, that markets are cyclic in nature, and eventually even the strongest bull market* will begin to fail.

In this case, (13) it came in 1929. The year was filled with nervous tension as investors (14) which had bought a great quantity of stock on credit sought a way out of a market that was declining. Finally, on October 29, the pressure (15) in everyone trying to sell stock became too much, and the market began a downward spiral from which there would be no easy recovery.

The lessons of 1929 have taught investors that the stock market is no game. Laws have been passed that significantly reduce margin investing. In addition, many safeguards have been implemented to stem financial panic when the (16) market starts to decline. Although the economy will always have high and low points, the hope is that by moderating people's behavior, the raw panic that allowed the crash of '29 and the Great Depression to occur can be prevented.

    * bull market: a successful market with confident investors

13. A) NO CHANGE
    B) the bull market
    C) the failure
    D) the cycle

14. A) NO CHANGE
    B) who
    C) whom
    D) those of whom who

15. A) NO CHANGE
    B) when
    C) on
    D) of

16. A) NO CHANGE
    B) markets starts
    C) market start
    D) market started

Answers & Explanations for this chapter begin on page 504.

EXTRA PRACTICE

Required	Recommended
Questions 1, 2, 5, 8, 10	Questions 3, 4, 6, 7, 9, 11

Questions 1-11 are based on the following passage.

Violence in Children's Entertainment

[1] In recent years, many parents have expressed concern that the atmosphere of violence ❶ propagated by the American entertainment industry may be having a harmful effect on their children. [2] Certainly these parents are correct that ❷ violent acts such as murder, have become the pervasive theme of everything from feature films to television cartoons. [3] But is this kind of depravity altogether new to the world of the ❸ child. [4] Haven't parents for centuries been exposing their children to fairy tales that are at least as gory and violent? ▧4

1. A) NO CHANGE
    B) secreted
    C) populated
    D) advocated

2. A) NO CHANGE
    B) violent acts; such as murder; have become
    C) violent acts, such as murder have become
    D) violent acts, such as murder, have become

3. A) NO CHANGE
    B) child?
    C) child!
    D) child;

4. For the sake of cohesion of this paragraph, sentence 2 should be placed
    A) where it is now.
    B) before sentence 1.
    C) after sentence 3.
    D) after sentence 4.

5 Consider, for example, the tale of "Little Red Riding Hood," a story of murder and mayhem that has been told to children—and repeated by them—for at least 300 years. In the earliest known version of the tale, both Granny and Little Red are devoured. **6** Little Red is engaged in one of the most terrifying conversations in all literature when the wolf, having already eaten dear old Granny, says: "But, Granny, what large eyes . . . what sharp teeth . . . what big claws you have." Even Charles Dickens, an author whose own fictional world was hardly free of brutality against children, confessed that he deplored "the

5. A) NO CHANGE

   B) Consider, for example, the tale of "Little Red Riding Hood," a story of murder and mayhem.

   C) Consider, for example, the tale of "Little Red Riding Hood."

   D) Consider, for example, the tale of "Little Red Riding Hood," a story told to children—and repeated by them—for at least 300 years.

6. A) NO CHANGE

   B) Little Red is engaged in one of the most terrifying conversations in all literature when the wolf says to her

   C) The wolf, having already eaten dear old Granny, engages Little Red in one of the most terrifying conversations in all literature

   D) The wolf, having already eaten dear old Granny, says to Little Red

cruelty and treachery of that dissembling wolf who ate [Little Red's] grandmother without making any impression on his appetite, and then ate her [Little Red], after making a ferocious joke about his teeth."

7 Believe it or not, but the version where both Grandmother and Little Red are eaten was not the worst version of the tale circulating in Charles Dickens's time. In other parts of the world, children heard an even more horrifying story that concluded with the wolf collecting the grandmother's blood in bottles.

7. A) NO CHANGE

B) Yet that was not the worst version of the tale circulating in Dickens's time.

C) Yet the version where both Grandmother and Little Red are eaten was not the worst version of the tale circulating in Dickens's time.

D) Believe it or not, that was not the worst version of the tale circulating in Dickens's time.

8 One theory suggests that fairy tales represent an attempt to deal with realistic threats in **9** <u>fantastic</u> terms. Living conditions for most families from Elizabethan times to the early nineteenth century made it impossible to shelter children from many of the harsher aspects of adult life. Families lived in cramped quarters that precluded **10** <u>any form of privacy. While prevailing notions</u> of criminal justice required

8. Which choice most effectively establishes the central idea of the paragraph?

A) So why did the writers and tellers of fairy tales continually gloss over unsavory stories, avoiding themes of homicide, maiming, and lunacy?

B) So why did Dickens continue to study—and mimic—the fairy tales he claimed to dislike?

C) Theories for why fairy tales continually revisit these themes are hard to find.

D) So why did the writers and tellers of fairy tales continually produce such unsavory stories, with their thinly veiled themes of homicide, maiming, and lunacy?

9. A) NO CHANGE

B) caustic

C) existent

D) plausible

10. A) NO CHANGE

B) any form of privacy, while prevailing notions

C) any form of privacy while prevailing notions

D) any form of privacy; while prevailing notions

that punishment—whether flogging or imprisonment in stocks or even hanging or disembowelment—be conducted as a public spectacle. Fairy tales distanced this grisly reality by placing it in a context of unreal fantasies. But at the same time, the tales made children aware of dangers and wary of evil temptations. **11**

11. Which choice most effectively concludes the paragraph and the passage?

A) Indeed, fairy tales of old could do little to protect a child from the harshness of life and, at best, could only serve as a brief escape from the drudgery and danger that typified reality for most people.

B) Thus, the fictionalized violence of fairy tales was simply the ancestor of the American entertainment industry.

C) Far from harming children, then, the fictionalized violence of fairy tales—as deplorable as it may seem in principle—was possibly one of the things that prepared children for survival in a violent world.

D) Far from harming children, then, the fictionalized violence of fairy tales—as deplorable as it may seem in principle—is comparable to the film industry's violence today, in that it seems to have little effect on raising healthy children.

PART FOUR

Practice Test

PSAT PRACTICE TEST ANSWER SHEET

Remove (or photocopy) this answer sheet and use it to complete the test. See the answer key following the test when finished.

Start with number 1 for each section. If a section has fewer questions than answer spaces, leave the extra spaces blank.

SECTION 1

1. Ⓐ Ⓑ Ⓒ Ⓓ	13. Ⓐ Ⓑ Ⓒ Ⓓ	25. Ⓐ Ⓑ Ⓒ Ⓓ	37. Ⓐ Ⓑ Ⓒ Ⓓ
2. Ⓐ Ⓑ Ⓒ Ⓓ	14. Ⓐ Ⓑ Ⓒ Ⓓ	26. Ⓐ Ⓑ Ⓒ Ⓓ	38. Ⓐ Ⓑ Ⓒ Ⓓ
3. Ⓐ Ⓑ Ⓒ Ⓓ	15. Ⓐ Ⓑ Ⓒ Ⓓ	27. Ⓐ Ⓑ Ⓒ Ⓓ	39. Ⓐ Ⓑ Ⓒ Ⓓ
4. Ⓐ Ⓑ Ⓒ Ⓓ	16. Ⓐ Ⓑ Ⓒ Ⓓ	28. Ⓐ Ⓑ Ⓒ Ⓓ	40. Ⓐ Ⓑ Ⓒ Ⓓ
5. Ⓐ Ⓑ Ⓒ Ⓓ	17. Ⓐ Ⓑ Ⓒ Ⓓ	29. Ⓐ Ⓑ Ⓒ Ⓓ	41. Ⓐ Ⓑ Ⓒ Ⓓ
6. Ⓐ Ⓑ Ⓒ Ⓓ	18. Ⓐ Ⓑ Ⓒ Ⓓ	30. Ⓐ Ⓑ Ⓒ Ⓓ	42. Ⓐ Ⓑ Ⓒ Ⓓ
7. Ⓐ Ⓑ Ⓒ Ⓓ	19. Ⓐ Ⓑ Ⓒ Ⓓ	31. Ⓐ Ⓑ Ⓒ Ⓓ	43. Ⓐ Ⓑ Ⓒ Ⓓ
8. Ⓐ Ⓑ Ⓒ Ⓓ	20. Ⓐ Ⓑ Ⓒ Ⓓ	32. Ⓐ Ⓑ Ⓒ Ⓓ	44. Ⓐ Ⓑ Ⓒ Ⓓ
9. Ⓐ Ⓑ Ⓒ Ⓓ	21. Ⓐ Ⓑ Ⓒ Ⓓ	33. Ⓐ Ⓑ Ⓒ Ⓓ	45. Ⓐ Ⓑ Ⓒ Ⓓ
10. Ⓐ Ⓑ Ⓒ Ⓓ	22. Ⓐ Ⓑ Ⓒ Ⓓ	34. Ⓐ Ⓑ Ⓒ Ⓓ	46. Ⓐ Ⓑ Ⓒ Ⓓ
11. Ⓐ Ⓑ Ⓒ Ⓓ	23. Ⓐ Ⓑ Ⓒ Ⓓ	35. Ⓐ Ⓑ Ⓒ Ⓓ	47. Ⓐ Ⓑ Ⓒ Ⓓ
12. Ⓐ Ⓑ Ⓒ Ⓓ	24. Ⓐ Ⓑ Ⓒ Ⓓ	36. Ⓐ Ⓑ Ⓒ Ⓓ	

right in Section 1

wrong in Section 1

SECTION 2

1. Ⓐ Ⓑ Ⓒ Ⓓ	12. Ⓐ Ⓑ Ⓒ Ⓓ	23. Ⓐ Ⓑ Ⓒ Ⓓ	34. Ⓐ Ⓑ Ⓒ Ⓓ
2. Ⓐ Ⓑ Ⓒ Ⓓ	13. Ⓐ Ⓑ Ⓒ Ⓓ	24. Ⓐ Ⓑ Ⓒ Ⓓ	35. Ⓐ Ⓑ Ⓒ Ⓓ
3. Ⓐ Ⓑ Ⓒ Ⓓ	14. Ⓐ Ⓑ Ⓒ Ⓓ	25. Ⓐ Ⓑ Ⓒ Ⓓ	36. Ⓐ Ⓑ Ⓒ Ⓓ
4. Ⓐ Ⓑ Ⓒ Ⓓ	15. Ⓐ Ⓑ Ⓒ Ⓓ	26. Ⓐ Ⓑ Ⓒ Ⓓ	37. Ⓐ Ⓑ Ⓒ Ⓓ
5. Ⓐ Ⓑ Ⓒ Ⓓ	16. Ⓐ Ⓑ Ⓒ Ⓓ	27. Ⓐ Ⓑ Ⓒ Ⓓ	38. Ⓐ Ⓑ Ⓒ Ⓓ
6. Ⓐ Ⓑ Ⓒ Ⓓ	17. Ⓐ Ⓑ Ⓒ Ⓓ	28. Ⓐ Ⓑ Ⓒ Ⓓ	39. Ⓐ Ⓑ Ⓒ Ⓓ
7. Ⓐ Ⓑ Ⓒ Ⓓ	18. Ⓐ Ⓑ Ⓒ Ⓓ	29. Ⓐ Ⓑ Ⓒ Ⓓ	40. Ⓐ Ⓑ Ⓒ Ⓓ
8. Ⓐ Ⓑ Ⓒ Ⓓ	19. Ⓐ Ⓑ Ⓒ Ⓓ	30. Ⓐ Ⓑ Ⓒ Ⓓ	41. Ⓐ Ⓑ Ⓒ Ⓓ
9. Ⓐ Ⓑ Ⓒ Ⓓ	20. Ⓐ Ⓑ Ⓒ Ⓓ	31. Ⓐ Ⓑ Ⓒ Ⓓ	42. Ⓐ Ⓑ Ⓒ Ⓓ
10. Ⓐ Ⓑ Ⓒ Ⓓ	21. Ⓐ Ⓑ Ⓒ Ⓓ	32. Ⓐ Ⓑ Ⓒ Ⓓ	43. Ⓐ Ⓑ Ⓒ Ⓓ
11. Ⓐ Ⓑ Ⓒ Ⓓ	22. Ⓐ Ⓑ Ⓒ Ⓓ	33. Ⓐ Ⓑ Ⓒ Ⓓ	44. Ⓐ Ⓑ Ⓒ Ⓓ

right in Section 2

wrong in Section 2

SECTION 3

1. Ⓐ Ⓑ Ⓒ Ⓓ
2. Ⓐ Ⓑ Ⓒ Ⓓ
3. Ⓐ Ⓑ Ⓒ Ⓓ
4. Ⓐ Ⓑ Ⓒ Ⓓ

5. Ⓐ Ⓑ Ⓒ Ⓓ
6. Ⓐ Ⓑ Ⓒ Ⓓ
7. Ⓐ Ⓑ Ⓒ Ⓓ
8. Ⓐ Ⓑ Ⓒ Ⓓ

9. Ⓐ Ⓑ Ⓒ Ⓓ
10. Ⓐ Ⓑ Ⓒ Ⓓ
11. Ⓐ Ⓑ Ⓒ Ⓓ
12. Ⓐ Ⓑ Ⓒ Ⓓ

13. Ⓐ Ⓑ Ⓒ Ⓓ

right in Section 3

wrong in Section 3

14. 15. 16. 17.

SECTION 4

1. Ⓐ Ⓑ Ⓒ Ⓓ
2. Ⓐ Ⓑ Ⓒ Ⓓ
3. Ⓐ Ⓑ Ⓒ Ⓓ
4. Ⓐ Ⓑ Ⓒ Ⓓ
5. Ⓐ Ⓑ Ⓒ Ⓓ
6. Ⓐ Ⓑ Ⓒ Ⓓ
7. Ⓐ Ⓑ Ⓒ Ⓓ

8. Ⓐ Ⓑ Ⓒ Ⓓ
9. Ⓐ Ⓑ Ⓒ Ⓓ
10. Ⓐ Ⓑ Ⓒ Ⓓ
11. Ⓐ Ⓑ Ⓒ Ⓓ
12. Ⓐ Ⓑ Ⓒ Ⓓ
13. Ⓐ Ⓑ Ⓒ Ⓓ
14. Ⓐ Ⓑ Ⓒ Ⓓ

15. Ⓐ Ⓑ Ⓒ Ⓓ
16. Ⓐ Ⓑ Ⓒ Ⓓ
17. Ⓐ Ⓑ Ⓒ Ⓓ
18. Ⓐ Ⓑ Ⓒ Ⓓ
19. Ⓐ Ⓑ Ⓒ Ⓓ
20. Ⓐ Ⓑ Ⓒ Ⓓ
21. Ⓐ Ⓑ Ⓒ Ⓓ

22. Ⓐ Ⓑ Ⓒ Ⓓ
23. Ⓐ Ⓑ Ⓒ Ⓓ
24. Ⓐ Ⓑ Ⓒ Ⓓ
25. Ⓐ Ⓑ Ⓒ Ⓓ
26. Ⓐ Ⓑ Ⓒ Ⓓ
27. Ⓐ Ⓑ Ⓒ Ⓓ

right in Section 4

wrong in Section 4

28. 29. 30. 31.

READING TEST

60 Minutes—47 Questions

Turn to Section 1 of your answer sheet to answer the questions in this section.

Directions: Each passage or pair of passages below is followed by a number of questions. After reading each passage or pair, choose the best answer to each question based on what is stated or implied in the passage or passages and in any accompanying graphics (such as a table or graph).

Questions 1-9 are based on the following passage.

This passage is adapted from "Metamorphosis" by Franz Kafka, a famous story that combines elements of fantasy and reality. This excerpt begins with the protagonist realizing he has literally turned into a giant, beetle-like insect.

One morning, when Gregor Samsa woke from troubled dreams, he found himself transformed in his bed into a horrible vermin. He lay on his armor-
Line like back, and if he lifted his head a little he could
(5) see his brown belly, slightly domed and divided by arches into stiff sections. The bedding was hardly able to cover it and seemed ready to slide off any moment. His many legs, pitifully thin compared with the size of the rest of him, waved about help-
(10) lessly as he looked.

"What's happened to me?" he thought. It wasn't a dream. His room, a proper human room although a little too small, lay peacefully between its four familiar walls. A collection of textile samples lay
(15) spread out on the table—Samsa was a travelling salesman—and above it there hung a picture that he had recently cut out of an illustrated magazine and housed in a nice, gilded frame. It showed a lady fitted out with a fur hat and fur boa who sat upright,
(20) raising a heavy fur muff that covered the whole of her lower arm towards the viewer.

Gregor then turned to look out the window at the dull weather. Drops of rain could be heard hitting the pane, which made him feel quite sad. "How
(25) about if I sleep a little bit longer and forget all this nonsense," he thought, but that was something he was unable to do because he was used to sleeping on his right, and in his present state couldn't get into

that position. However hard he threw himself onto
(30) his right, he always rolled back to where he was. He must have tried it a hundred times, shut his eyes so that he wouldn't have to look at the floundering legs, and only stopped when he began to feel a mild, dull pain there that he had never felt before.

(35) He thought, "What a strenuous career it is that I've chosen! Travelling day in and day out. Doing business like this takes much more effort than doing your own business at home, and on top of that there's the curse of travelling, worries about making
(40) train connections, bad and irregular food, contact with different people all the time so that you can never get to know anyone or become friendly with them." He felt a slight itch up on his belly; pushed himself slowly up on his back towards the headboard
(45) so that he could lift his head better; found where the itch was, and saw that it was covered with lots of little white spots which he didn't know what to make of; and when he tried to feel the place with one of his legs he drew it quickly back because as soon as he
(50) touched it he was overcome by a cold shudder.

He slid back into his former position. "Getting up early all the time," he thought, "it makes you stupid. You've got to get enough sleep. Other travelling salesmen live a life of luxury. For instance, whenever
(55) I go back to the guest house during the morning to copy out the contract, these gentlemen are always still sitting there eating their breakfasts. I ought to just try that with my boss; I'd get kicked out on the spot. But who knows, maybe that would be the best
(60) thing for me. If I didn't have my parents to think about I'd have given in my notice a long time ago, I'd have gone up to the boss and told him just what I think, tell him everything I would, let him know

GO ON TO THE NEXT PAGE

just what I feel. He'd fall right off his desk! And it's a
(65) funny sort of business to be sitting up there at your
desk, talking down at your subordinates from up
there, especially when you have to go right up close
because the boss is hard of hearing. Well, there's
still some hope; once I've got the money together to
(70) pay off my parents' debt to him—another five or six
years I suppose—that's definitely what I'll do. That's
when I'll make the big change. First of all though,
I've got to get up, my train leaves at five."

1. According to the passage, Gregor initially
   believes his transformation is a

   A) curse.

   B) disease.

   C) nightmare.

   D) hoax.

2. As used in line 12, "proper" most nearly means

   A) called for by rules or conventions.

   B) showing politeness.

   C) naturally belonging or peculiar to.

   D) suitably appropriate.

3. The passage most strongly suggests which of the
   following about Gregor's attitude toward his
   profession?

   A) He is resentful.

   B) He is diligent.

   C) He is depressed.

   D) He is eager to please.

4. Which choice provides the best evidence for the
   answer to the previous question?

   A) Lines 14-18 ("A collection . . . gilded frame")

   B) Lines 22-24 ("Gregor then turned . . . quite
      sad")

   C) Lines 53-59 ("Other . . . the spot")

   D) Lines 59-64 ("But who knows . . . I feel")

5. What central idea does the excerpt communicate
   through Gregor's experiences?

   A) Imagination is a dangerous thing.

   B) People are fearful of change.

   C) Dreams become our reality.

   D) Man is a slave to work.

6. The passage most strongly suggests that which of
   the following is true of Gregor?

   A) He feels a strong sense of duty toward his
      family.

   B) He is unable to cope with change.

   C) He excels in his profession.

   D) He is fearful about his transformation.

7. Which choice provides the best evidence for the
   answer to the previous question?

   A) Lines 11-14 ("What's happened . . . familiar
      walls")

   B) Lines 22-24 ("Gregor then turned . . . quite
      sad")

   C) Lines 36-43 ("Doing business . . . with
      them")

   D) Lines 68-71 ("Well, there's still . . . what I'll
      do")

8. As used in line 32, "floundering" most nearly means

   A) thrashing.

   B) painful.

   C) pitiful.

   D) trembling.

GO ON TO THE NEXT PAGE ⟶

9. The main rhetorical effect of the final sentence of the excerpt ("First of all though, I've got to get up, my train leaves at five") is to

A) provide a resolution to the conflict Gregor faces.

B) foreshadow the conflict between Gregor and his boss.

C) illustrate Gregor's resilience and ability to move on.

D) emphasize Gregor's extreme sense of duty.

Questions 10-18 are based on the following passage.

This passage is adapted from Hillary Rodham Clinton's speech titled "Women's Rights Are Human Rights," addressed to the U.N. Fourth World Conference on Women in 1995.

If there is one message that echoes forth from this conference, it is that human rights are women's rights. . . . And women's rights are human rights.

Line
(5) Let us not forget that among those rights are the right to speak freely and the right to be heard.

Women must enjoy the right to participate fully in the social and political lives of their countries if we want freedom and democracy to thrive and endure.

It is indefensible that many women in nongov-
(10) ernmental organizations who wished to participate in this conference have not been able to attend—or have been prohibited from fully taking part.

Let me be clear. Freedom means the right of people to assemble, organize, and debate openly. It
(15) means respecting the views of those who may disagree with the views of their governments. It means not taking citizens away from their loved ones and jailing them, mistreating them, or denying them their freedom or dignity because of the peaceful
(20) expression of their ideas and opinions.

In my country, we recently celebrated the seventy-fifth anniversary of women's suffrage. It took one hundred and fifty years after the signing of our Declaration of Independence for women to

(25) win the right to vote. It took seventy-two years of organized struggle on the part of many courageous women and men.

It was one of America's most divisive philosophical wars. But it was also a bloodless war. Suffrage was
(30) achieved without a shot fired.

We have also been reminded, in V-J Day observances last weekend, of the good that comes when men and women join together to combat the forces of tyranny and build a better world.

(35) We have seen peace prevail in most places for a half century. We have avoided another world war. But we have not solved older, deeply-rooted problems that continue to diminish the potential of half the world's population.

(40) Now it is time to act on behalf of women everywhere.

If we take bold steps to better the lives of women, we will be taking bold steps to better the lives of children and families too. Families rely on mothers and wives for emotional support and care; families
(45) rely on women for labor in the home; and increasingly, families rely on women for income needed to raise healthy children and care for other relatives.

As long as discrimination and inequities remain so commonplace around the world—as long as
(50) girls and women are valued less, fed less, fed last, overworked, underpaid, not schooled and subjected to violence in and out of their homes—the potential of the human family to create a peaceful, prosperous world will not be realized.

(55) Let this conference be our—and the world's—call to action.

And let us heed the call so that we can create a world in which every woman is treated with respect and dignity, every boy and girl is loved and cared for
(60) equally, and every family has the hope of a strong and stable future.

GO ON TO THE NEXT PAGE

10. What is the primary purpose of the passage?

   A) To chastise those who have prevented women from attending the conference

   B) To argue that women continue to experience discrimination

   C) To explain that human rights are of more concern than women's rights

   D) To encourage people to think of women's rights as an issue important to all

11. Which choice provides the best evidence for the answer to the previous question?

   A) Lines 4-5 ("Let us . . . be heard")

   B) Lines 9-12 ("It is indefensible . . . taking part")

   C) Lines 37-39 ("But we have . . . population")

   D) Lines 43-47 ("Families . . . other relatives")

12. As used in line 28, "divisive" most nearly means

   A) conflict-producing.

   B) carefully-watched.

   C) multi-purpose.

   D) time-consuming.

13. Based on the speech, with which statement would Clinton most likely agree?

   A) More men should be the primary caregivers of their children in order to provide career opportunities for women.

   B) Women do not need the support and cooperation of men as they work toward equality.

   C) Solutions for global problems would be found faster if women had more access to power.

   D) The American movement for women's suffrage should have been violent in order to achieve success more quickly.

14. Which choice provides the best evidence for the answer to the previous question?

   A) Lines 6-8 ("Women . . . endure")

   B) Lines 29-30 ("Suffrage . . . shot fired")

   C) Lines 43-47 ("Families . . . relatives")

   D) Lines 48-54 ("As long . . . realized")

15. As used in line 26, "organized" most nearly means

   A) arranged.

   B) cooperative.

   C) hierarchical.

   D) patient.

16. Which claim does Clinton make in her speech?

   A) The conference itself is a model of nondiscrimination toward women.

   B) Democracy cannot prosper unless women can participate fully in it.

   C) Women's rights are restricted globally by the demands on them as parents.

   D) Women are being forced to provide income for their families as a result of sexism.

17. Clinton uses the example of V-J Day observations to support the argument that

   A) campaigns succeed when they are nonviolent.

   B) historical wrongs against women must be corrected.

   C) many tragedies could have been avoided with more female participation.

   D) cooperation between men and women leads to positive developments.

GO ON TO THE NEXT PAGE ⟹

18. The fifth paragraph can be described as

   A) a distillation of the author's main argument.

   B) an acknowledgment of a counterargument.

   C) a veiled criticism of a group.

   D) a defense against an accusation.

Questions 19-28 are based on the following passages and supplementary material.

Passage 1

Europe was a coffee-drinking continent before it became a tea-drinking one. Tea was grown in China, thousands of miles away. The opening of trade routes with the Far East in the fifteenth and sixteenth cen-
(5) turies gave Europeans their first taste of tea.

Line   However, it was an unpromising start for the beverage, because shipments arrived stale, and European tea drinkers miscalculated the steeping time and measurements. This was a far cry from the Chinese
(10) preparation techniques, known as a "tea ceremony," which had strict steps and called for steeping in iron pots at precise temperatures and pouring into porcelain bowls.

China had a monopoly on the tea trade and kept
(15) their tea cultivation techniques secret. Yet as worldwide demand grew, tea caught on in Europe. Some proprietors touted tea as a cure for maladies. Several European tea companies formed, including the English East India Company. In 1669, it imported
(20) 143.5 pounds of tea—very little compared to the 32 million pounds that were imported by 1834.

Europeans looked for ways to circumvent China's monopoly, but their attempts to grow the tea plant (Latin name *Camellia sinensis*) failed. Some plants
(25) perished in transit from the East. But most often the growing climate wasn't right, not even in the equatorial colonies that the British, Dutch, and French controlled. In 1763, the French Academy of Sciences gave up, declaring the tea plant unique to China
(30) and unable to be grown anywhere else. Swedish and English botanists grew tea in botanical gardens, but this was not enough to meet demand.

After trial and error with a plant variety discovered in the Assam district of India, the British
(35) managed to establish a source to meet the growing demands of British tea drinkers. In May 1838, the first batch of India-grown tea shipped to London. The harvest was a mere 350 pounds and arrived in November. It sold for between 16 and 34 shillings
(40) per pound. Perfecting production methods took many years, but ultimately, India became the world's largest tea-producing country. By the early 1900s, annual production of India tea exceeded 350 million pounds. This voluminous source was a major factor
(45) in tea becoming the staple of European households that it is today.

Passage 2

In Europe, there's a long tradition of taking afternoon tea. Tea time, typically four o'clock, means not just enjoying a beverage, but taking time out to
(50) gather and socialize. The occasion is not identical across Europe, though; just about every culture has its own way of doing things.

In France, for example, black tea is served with sugar, milk, or lemon and is almost always accom-
(55) panied by a pastry. Rather than sweet pastries, the French prefer the savory kind, such as the *gougère*, or puff pastry, infused with cheese.

Germans, by contrast, put a layer of slowly melting candy at the bottom of their teacup and top the
(60) tea with cream. German tea culture is strongest in the eastern part of the country, and during the week tea is served with cookies, while on the weekend or for special events, cakes are served. The Germans think of tea as a good cure for headaches and stress.

(65) Russia also has a unique tea culture, rooted in the formalism of its aristocratic classes. Loose leaf black tea is served in a glass held by a *podstakannik*, an ornate holder with a handle typically made from silver or chrome—though sometimes it may be gold-
(70) plated. Brewed separately, the tea is then diluted with boiled water and served strong. The strength of the tea is seen as a measure of the host's hospitality. Traditionally, tea is taken by the entire family and served after a large meal with jams and pastries.

(75)   Great Britain has a rich tradition of its own. Prior to the introduction of tea into Britain, the English

GO ON TO THE NEXT PAGE

had two main meals, breakfast and a second, dinner-like meal called "tea," which was held around noon. However, during the middle of the eighteenth

(80) century, dinner shifted to an evening meal at a late hour; it was then called "high tea." That meant the necessary introduction of an afternoon snack to tide one over, and "low tea" or "tea time" was introduced by British royalty. In present-day Britain, your

(85) afternoon tea might be served with scones and jam, small sandwiches, and cookies (called "biscuits"), depending on whether you're in Ireland, England, or Scotland.

Wherever they are and however they take it,

(90) Europeans know the value of savoring an afternoon cup of tea.

Average Annual Tea Consumption
(Pounds Per Person)

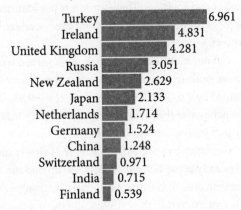

Turkey	6.961
Ireland	4.831
United Kingdom	4.281
Russia	3.051
New Zealand	2.629
Japan	2.133
Netherlands	1.714
Germany	1.524
China	1.248
Switzerland	0.971
India	0.715
Finland	0.539

Data from Euromonitor International and World Bank.

19. It can be reasonably inferred, based on Passage 1, that

A) European nations tried to grow tea in their colonies.

B) European tea growers never learned Chinese cultivation techniques.

C) Europeans' purpose in opening trade routes with the Far East was to gain access to tea.

D) Europeans believed tea was ineffective as a treatment against illness.

20. Which choice provides the best evidence for the answer to the previous question?

A) Lines 6-9 ("However . . . measurements")

B) Lines 16-17 ("Some . . . maladies")

C) Lines 25-28 ("But . . . French controlled")

D) Lines 38-40 ("The harvest . . . per pound")

21. It is reasonable to infer, based on Passage 2, that

A) serving tea is an important part of hosting guests in Russia.

B) Germans generally avoid medicine for stress.

C) drinking tea in modern Britain is confined to the upper classes.

D) the usual hour for drinking tea varies across Europe.

22. Which choice provides the best evidence for the answer to the previous question?

A) Lines 48-50 ("Tea time . . . socialize")

B) Lines 63-64 ("The Germans . . . stress")

C) Lines 71-72 ("The strength . . . hospitality")

D) Lines 81-84 ("That meant . . . royalty")

23. As used in line 22 of Passage 1, "circumvent" most nearly means

A) destroy.

B) get around.

C) ignore.

D) compete with.

24. As used in line 66 of Passage 2, "aristocratic" most nearly means

    A) culinary.

    B) political.

    C) rigid.

    D) noble.

25. Which statement is the most effective comparison of the two passages' purposes?

    A) Passage 1's purpose is to describe the early history of tea in Europe, while Passage 2's purpose is to compare European cultural practices relating to tea.

    B) Passage 1's purpose is to argue against the Chinese monopoly of tea, while Passage 2's purpose is to argue that Europeans perfected the art of tea drinking.

    C) Passage 1's purpose is to express admiration for the difficult task of tea cultivation, while Passage 2's purpose is to celebrate the rituals surrounding tea.

    D) Passage 1's purpose is to compare Chinese and European relationships with tea, while Passage 2's purpose is to describe the diffusion of tea culture in Europe.

26. Compared with France's tradition of tea-drinking, having tea in Germany

    A) is more formal.

    B) involves sweeter food.

    C) requires greater solitude.

    D) is more of a meal than a snack.

27. It can be inferred from Passage 1 and the graphic that

    A) English botanical gardens helped make the United Kingdom one of the highest tea-consuming countries in the world.

    B) if the French Academy of Sciences hadn't given up growing tea in 1763, France would be one of the highest tea-consuming countries in the world.

    C) Britain's success at growing tea in India in the 1800s helped make the United Kingdom one of the highest tea-consuming nations in the world.

    D) China's production of tea would be higher if Britain hadn't discovered a way to grow tea in India in the 1800s.

28. Both passages support which generalization about tea?

    A) Tea drinking in Europe is less ritualized than in China.

    B) Coffee was once more popular in Europe than tea was.

    C) India grows a great deal of tea.

    D) Tea is a staple of European households.

Question 29-38 are based on the following passage.

At long last, paleontologists have solved a century-old mystery, piecing together information discovered by scientists from different times and
Line places.
(5)   The mystery began when, in 1911, German paleontologist Ernst Stromer discovered the first evidence of dinosaurs having lived in Egypt. Stromer, who expected to encounter fossils of early mammals, instead found bones that dated back to the Creta-
(10) ceous period, some 97 to 112 million years prior. His finding consisted of three large bones, which he preserved and transported back to Germany for examination. After careful consideration, he announced that he had discovered a new genus of

GO ON TO THE NEXT PAGE

(15) sauropod, or a large, four-legged herbivore with a long neck. He called the genus Aegyptosaurus, which is Greek for Egyptian lizard. One of these Aegyptosaurs, he claimed, was the Spinosaurus. Tragically, the fossils that supported his claim were
(20) destroyed during a raid on Munich by the Royal Air Force during World War II. The scientific world was left with Stromer's notes and sketches, but no hard evidence that the Spinosaurus ever existed.

It was not until 2008, when a cardboard box of
(25) bones was delivered to paleontologist Nizar Ibrahim by a nomad in Morocco's Sahara desert, that a clue to solving the mystery was revealed. Intrigued, Ibrahim took the bones to a university in Casablanca for further study. One specific bone struck him as in-
(30) teresting, as it contained a red line coursing through it. The following year, Ibrahim and his colleagues at Italy's Milan Natural History Museum were look-ing at bones that resembled the ones delivered the year before. An important clue was hidden in the
(35) cross-section they were examining, as it contained the same red line Ibrahim had seen in Morocco. Against all odds, the Italians were studying bones that belonged to the very same skeleton as the bones Ibrahim received in the desert. Together, these bones
(40) make up the partial skeleton of the very first Spino-saurus that humans have been able to discover since Stromer's fossils were destroyed.

Ibrahim and his colleagues published a study describing the features of the dinosaur, which point
(45) to the Spinosaurus being the first known swimming dinosaur. At 36 feet long, this particular Spinosaurus had long front legs and short back legs, each with a paddle-shaped foot and claws that suggest a carnivo-rous diet. These features made the dinosaur a deft
(50) swimmer and excellent hunter, able to prey on large river fish.

Scientists also discovered several aquatic adapta-tions that made the Spinosaurus unique compared to dinosaurs that lived on land but ate fish. Similar
(55) to a crocodile, the Spinosaurus had a long snout, with nostrils positioned so that the dinosaur could breathe while part of its head was submerged in water. Unlike predatory land dinosaurs, the Spino-saurus had powerful front legs. The weight of these
(60) legs would have made walking upright like a Tyran-nosaurus Rex impossible, but in water, their strong

legs gave the Spinosaur the power it needed to swim quickly and hunt fiercely. Most notable, though, was the discovery of the Spinosaur's massive sail. Made
(65) up of dorsal spines, the sail was mostly meant for display and did not serve a purpose of its own.

Ibrahim and his fellow researchers used both modern digital modeling programs and Stromer's basic sketches to create and mount a life-size replica
(70) of the Spinosaurus skeleton. The sketches gave them a starting point, and by arranging and rearranging the excavated fossils they had in their possession, they were able to use technology to piece together hypothetical bone structures until the mystery of
(75) this semiaquatic dinosaur finally emerged from the murky depths of the past.

29. Which of the following best summarizes the central idea of this passage?

A) Paleontologists were able to identify a new species of dinosaur after overcoming a series of obstacles.

B) Most dinosaur fossils are found in pieces and must be reconstructed using the latest technology.

C) The first evidence of the Spinosaurus was uncovered by German paleontologist Ernst Stromer.

D) Fossils of an aquatic dinosaur called the Spinosaurus were first found in Egypt in the early twentieth century.

30. Based on the information in the passage, the author would most likely agree that

A) aquatic dinosaurs were more vicious than dinosaurs that lived on land.

B) too much emphasis is placed on creating realistic models of ancient dinosaurs.

C) most mysteries presented by randomly found fossils are unlikely to be solved.

D) the study of fossils and ancient life provides important scientific insights.

GO ON TO THE NEXT PAGE ⟶

31. Which choice provides the best evidence for the answer to the previous question?

    A) Lines 13-16 ("After careful . . . long neck")

    B) Lines 18-23 ("Tragically, . . . ever existed")

    C) Lines 43-46 ("Ibrahim . . . swimming dinosaur")

    D) Lines 70-76 ("The sketches . . . past")

32. As used in line 37, the phrase "against all odds" most nearly means

    A) by contrast.

    B) at the exact same time.

    C) to their dismay.

    D) despite low probability.

33. The author uses the phrases "deft swimmer" and "excellent hunter" in lines 49-50 is to

    A) produce a clear visual image of the Spinosaurus.

    B) show how the Spinosaurus searched for prey.

    C) create an impression of a graceful but powerful animal.

    D) emphasize the differences between aquatic and land dinosaurs.

34. The information presented in the passage strongly suggests that Ibrahim

    A) chose to go into the field of paleontology after reading Stromer's work.

    B) was familiar with Stromer's work when he found the fossils with the red lines.

    C) did not have the proper training to solve the mystery of the Spinosaurus on his own.

    D) went on to study other aquatic dinosaurs after completing his research on the Spinosaurus.

35. Which choice provides the best evidence for the answer to the previous question?

    A) Lines 24-27 ("It was . . . revealed")

    B) Lines 43-46 ("Ibrahim . . . swimming dinosaur")

    C) Lines 52-54 ("Scientists . . . ate fish")

    D) Lines 67-70 ("Ibrahim and his fellow researchers . . . skeleton")

36. As used in line 74, "hypothetical" most nearly means

    A) imaginary.

    B) actual.

    C) possible.

    D) interesting.

37. Based on the information in the passage, which statement best describes the relationship between Stromer's and Ibrahim's work with fossils?

    A) Stromer's work was dependent on Ibrahim's work.

    B) Stromer's work was contradicted by Ibrahim's work.

    C) Ibrahim's work built on Stromer's work.

    D) Ibrahim's work copied Stromer's work.

38. Which of the following is most similar to the methods used by Ibrahim to create a life-size replica of the Spinosaurus?

    A) An architect using computer software and drawings to create a scale model of a building

    B) A student building a model rocket from a kit in order to demonstrate propulsion

    C) A doctor using a microscope to study microorganisms unable to be seen with the naked eye

    D) A marine biologist creating an artificial reef in an aquarium to study fish

GO ON TO THE NEXT PAGE ➡

Questions 39-47 are based on the following passage and supplementary material.

Today's technology and resources enable people to educate themselves on any topic imaginable, and human health is one of particular interest to all. *Line* From diet fads to exercise trends, sleep studies to (5) nutrition supplements, people strive to adopt healthier lifestyles. And while some people may associate diets and gym memberships with sheer enjoyment, most of the population tends to think of personal healthcare as a necessary but time-consuming, (10) energy-draining, less-than-fun aspect of daily life.

Yet for centuries, or perhaps for as long as conscious life has existed, sneaking suspicion has suggested that fun, or more accurately, *funniness*, is essential to human health. Finally, in recent years (15) this notion, often phrased in the adage, "Laughter is the best medicine," has materialized into scientific evidence.

When a person laughs, a chemical reaction in the brain produces hormones called endorphins. Other (20) known endorphin-producing activities include exercise, physical pain, and certain food choices, but laughter's appearance on this list has drawn increasing empirical interest. Endorphins function as natural opiates for the human body, causing what (25) are more commonly referred to as "good feelings." A boost of endorphins can thwart lethargy and promote the mental energy and positivity necessary to accomplish challenging tasks. Furthermore, recent data reveal that the laughter-induced endorphins are (30) therapeutic and stress reducing.

This stress reduction alone indicates significant implications regarding the role of laughter in personal health. However, humor seems to address many other medical conditions as well. One study (35) from Loma Linda University in California found that the act of laughing induced immediate and significant effects on senior adults' memory capacities. This result was in addition to declines in the patients' cortisol, or stress hormone, measurements. (40) Another university study found that a mere quarter hour of laughter burns up to 40 calories. Pain tolerance, one group of Oxford researchers noticed, is also strengthened by laughter—probably due to the release of those same endorphins already described.

(45) And a group of Maryland scientists discovered that those who laugh more frequently seem to have stronger protection against heart disease, the illness that takes more lives annually than any other in America.

(50) Already from these reputable studies, empirical data indicates that laughter's health benefits include heart disease prevention, good physical exertion, memory retention, anxiety remedy, and pain resilience—not to mention laughter's more self-evident (55) effects on social and psychological wellness. Many believe that these findings are only the beginning; these studies pave the way for more research with even stronger evidence regarding the powerful healing and preventative properties of laughter. As (60) is true for most fields of science, far more can be learned.

As for how laughter is achieved, these studies used various methods to provoke or measure laughter or humor. Some used comedy films or television (65) clips; others chose humor-gauging questionnaires and social- or group-laughter scenarios. Such variance suggests that the means by which people incorporate laughter into their daily routine matters less than the fact that they do incorporate it. (70) However, it should be said that humor shared in uplifting community probably offers greater benefits than that found on a screen.

Time-pressed millennials might, in the interest of wellness, choose isolated exercise instead of social- (75) or fun-oriented leisure activities. However, this growing pool of evidence exposes the reality that amusement, too, can powerfully nourish the health of both mind and body. Humor is no less relevant to well-being than a kale smoothie or track workout. (80) But, then, some combination of the three might be most enjoyable (and, of course, beneficial) of all.

GO ON TO THE NEXT PAGE ⟹

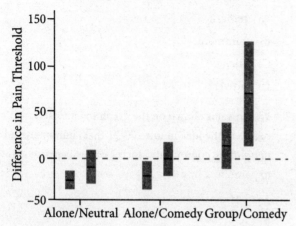

Laughter and Its Effect on Pain

Adapted from I.M. Dunbar, et al., "Social Laughter Is Correlated with an Elevated Pain Threshold." © 2011 by The Royal Society of Biological Sciences.

39. The author would probably characterize the study findings mentioned in the passage as

A) irrelevant.

B) very promising.

C) inconclusive.

D) mildly interesting.

40. Which choice provides the best evidence for the answer to the previous question?

A) Lines 4-6 ("From diet . . . lifestyles")

B) Lines 14-17 ("Finally, . . . evidence")

C) Lines 18-19 ("When a person . . . endor-phins")

D) Lines 66-69 ("Such variance . . . incorporate it")

41. Based on the passage, which statement best explains the relationship between endorphin production and mental outlook?

A) Increasing a person's amount of endorphins encourages a positive state of mind.

B) The act of laughing produces endorphins, which can offer a person protection against heart disease.

C) Research indicates that chemical reactions in the brain produce endorphins.

D) If a person has more endorphins, he or she has a difficult time tolerating pain.

42. As used in line 50, "reputable" most nearly means

A) honorable.

B) distinguished.

C) celebrated.

D) credible.

43. Which of the following statements can you best conclude from the passage?

A) Laughing alone or in the company of others benefits people's health equally.

B) There is reason for optimism about future research into laughter's health benefits.

C) Public support for the idea that laughter is healthy is somewhat limited.

D) Physical exercise is sufficient to maintain and improve mental health.

GO ON TO THE NEXT PAGE

44. Which choice provides the best evidence for the answer to the previous question?

    A) Lines 11-14 ("Yet for centuries, . . . health")

    B) Lines 31-34 ("This stress . . . well")

    C) Lines 55-59 ("Many believe . . . of laughter")

    D) Lines 78-81 ("Humor is . . . of all")

45. Which reason best explains why the author chose to discuss the function of endorphins in lines 23-25 ("Endorphins . . . good feelings")?

    A) To reach a wider audience without a background in physiology

    B) To support the claim that laughter affects an individual's mental state

    C) To show that laughter is one of several endorphin-producing activities

    D) To demonstrate why scientists have an interest in studying laughter

46. As used in line 15, "adage" most nearly means

    A) remark.

    B) comment.

    C) cliché.

    D) proverb.

47. Which value shown on the graph most closely relates to the idea in lines 70-71 that "humor shared in uplifting community" increases resilience to pain?

    A) −25

    B) 0

    C) 20

    D) 75

WRITING AND LANGUAGE TEST

35 Minutes—44 Questions

Turn to Section 2 of your answer sheet to answer the questions in this section.

Directions: Each passage below is accompanied by a number of questions. For some questions, you will consider how the passage might be revised to improve the expression of ideas. For other questions, you will consider how the passage might be edited to correct errors in sentence structure, usage, or punctuation. A passage or a question may be accompanied by one or more graphics (such as a table or graph) that you will consider as you make revising and editing decisions.

Some questions will direct you to an underlined portion of a passage. Other questions will direct you to a location in a passage or ask you to think about the passage as a whole.

After reading each passage, choose the answer to each question that most effectively improves the quality of writing in the passage or that makes the passage conform to the conventions of standard written English. Many questions include a "NO CHANGE" option. Choose that option if you think the best choice is to leave the relevant portion of the passage as it is.

Questions 1–11 are based on the following passage.

From Here to the Stars

Gene Kranz hadn't slept in ages. ❶ The flight director, pacing between rows of monitors in NASA's Mission Control Center, an impossible problem weighing heavy in his weary mind: Three astronauts were operating a crippled spacecraft nearly 200,000 miles from Earth. And time was running out.

Kranz was no stranger to ❷ issues. After losing his father at an early age, Kranz turned to the stars for guidance—and found inspiration. His high school thesis was about the possibility of ❸ space travel; an idea that prompted Kranz to set a path for the stars. Kranz pursued a degree in aeronautical engineering after high school graduation. Until the Wright brothers had pioneered powered, controlled flight only half a century earlier, aviation milestones like breaking the sound barrier and World War II changed the future of flight. Aeronautical engineering

1. A) NO CHANGE
    B) The flight director paced
    C) The pacing flight director
    D) The flight director pacing

2. A) NO CHANGE
    B) adversity
    C) deadlines
    D) maladies

3. A) NO CHANGE
    B) space travel: an idea
    C) space travel, an idea
    D) space travel. An idea

GO ON TO THE NEXT PAGE ➡

required a thorough understanding of ❹ physics—like lift and drag on wings—as well as proficiency in mathematics to determine maximum weight on an aircraft. After graduating from Saint Louis University's Parks College of Engineering, Aviation, and Technology, Kranz piloted jets for the Air Force Reserve before performing research and development on missiles and rockets. Kranz later joined NASA and directed the successful *Apollo 11* mission to the moon in 1969.

[5] One year later, the mood had drastically altered in the Mission Control Center. There were no cheers, no celebratory pats on the back or teary-eyed congratulations. Coffee and adrenaline fueled the scientists and engineers communicating with the astronauts on *Apollo 13*. ❻ Kranz was easy to spot among the avalanche of moving bodies and shifting papers.

4. A) NO CHANGE
    B) physics; like lift and drag on wings, as well as proficiency
    C) physics like lift and drag on wings, as well as proficiency
    D) physics: like lift and drag on wings—as well as proficiency

5. Which sentence most effectively establishes the main idea of the paragraph?
    A) Without his unusual vest, no one would have noticed Kranz in the crowd.
    B) Kranz stood out as a pillar of strength in the chaos of the command center.
    C) During the *Apollo 11* mission, Kranz earned the badges of honor that now adorned his vest.
    D) Kranz possessed more years of experience than anyone in the control center.

6. A) NO CHANGE
    B) Among the avalanche of moving bodies and shifting papers, it is easy to spot Kranz.
    C) Kranz easily spotted the avalanche of moving bodies and shifting papers.
    D) Kranz is easy to spot among the avalanche of moving bodies and shifting papers.

GO ON TO THE NEXT PAGE ⟹

He was dressed, as ever, in his signature handmade vest. **7**

Kranz's wife, Marta, had begun making vests at his request in the early '60s. **8** <u>Their was</u> power in a uniform, something Kranz understood from his years serving overseas. The vests served not as an authoritative mark or **9** <u>sartorial</u> flair, but a defining symbol for his team to rally behind. During the effort to save the *Apollo 13* crew, Kranz wore his white vest around the clock like perspiration-mottled battle armor.

10 <u>Among</u> meetings and calculations, Kranz and the NASA staff hatched a wild plan. By using the gravitational force of the moon, **11** <u>it</u> could slingshot the injured spacecraft back on an earthbound course. It was a long shot, of course, but also their best and only one. And, due to the tireless efforts of support staff on earth and the intrepid spirit of the *Apollo 13* crew, it worked. Six days after takeoff, all three astronauts splashed down safely in the Pacific Ocean.

7. Which sentence provides effective evidence to support the main focus of the paragraph?

A) The engineers looked to the calm man in the homemade vest.

B) Many of the men in the Mission Control Center had lengthy military careers.

C) Kranz's thoughts returned to the many tribulations he had experienced.

D) Several engineers joined together as a bastion of calm in a sea of uncertainty.

8. A) NO CHANGE
   B) They're was
   C) There was
   D) They were

9. A) NO CHANGE
   B) sanguine
   C) military
   D) martial

10. A) NO CHANGE
    B) In spite of
    C) Amid
    D) Between

11. A) NO CHANGE
    B) he
    C) they
    D) one

GO ON TO THE NEXT PAGE

Questions 12-22 are based on the following passage.

The UK and the Euro

[1] The United Kingdom is a longstanding member of the European Union (EU), a multinational political organization and economic world leader **12** elected over the course of the past half-century. [2] However, there is one key feature of the EU in which the UK does not **13** participate; the monetary union known as the Eurozone, consisting of countries that share the euro as currency. **14** [3] While the nation's public opinion has remained generally supportive of that decision, evidence suggests that the euro's benefits for the UK might, in fact, outweigh the risks. [4] When the EU first implemented the euro in 1999, intending to strengthen collective economy across the union, Britain was permitted exclusion and continued using the pound instead. [5] This, UK leaders hoped, would shield Britain from financial dangers that the euro might suffer. Proponents for avoiding the euro point **15** to faltering economies in the Eurozone region throughout the Eurozone. To join a massive, multinational economy would involve surrendering taxable wealth from one's own region to aid impoverished countries that may be some thousands of miles away. If a few economies in the Eurozone suffer, all of the participating nations suffer, too. Other proponents point to details of financial policy such as interest rates and territory responsibilities, fearing loss of agency and political traction. **16**

12. A) NO CHANGE
    B) determined
    C) advanced
    D) built

13. A) NO CHANGE
    B) participate: the monetary
    C) participate, the monetary
    D) participate. The monetary

14. To present the ideas of this paragraph in logical order, the most appropriate place for sentence 3 to appear is

    A) where it is now.
    B) after sentence 1.
    C) after sentence 4.
    D) after sentence 5.

15. Which choice best completes the sentence?

    A) to faltering economies in the Eurozone region throughout the Eurozone.
    B) to faltering economies throughout the Eurozone.
    C) to faltering economies in most if not all Eurozone countries.
    D) to faltering economies in Eurozone countries throughout Europe.

GO ON TO THE NEXT PAGE

But complications loom: the UK's current EU status may be untenable. In recent years, EU leaders seem to intend to transition all members ❶⑦ <u>toward the Eurozone, for many reasons,</u> this action appears necessary for protecting nations involved and ensuring the monetary union's long-term success. These conditions may potentially force the UK to choose either the security of its multidecade EU membership, or the pound and all it entails for Britain's economy. Enjoying both may not remain possible. `18`

16. Which statement most clearly communicates the main claim of the paragraph on the previous page?

A) The UK's taxable wealth would decrease if it assisted impoverished countries.

B) Economic independence from impoverished countries would still be possible.

C) The UK would take on significant economic risk if it adopted the euro as its currency.

D) Euro adoption would require subsequent economic assistance on the UK's behalf.

17. A) NO CHANGE

B) toward the Eurozone. For many reasons,

C) toward the Eurozone, for many reasons.

D) toward the Eurozone. For many reasons.

18. Which choice best summarizes details that support the main claim in this paragraph?

A) The UK wants to maintain the pound as its currency.

B) All EU members may soon have to accept the euro.

C) The UK faces a difficult decision regarding its EU membership.

D) All member nations want to ensure the success of the EU.

GO ON TO THE NEXT PAGE

[1] Regarding Britain's intent to be protected from the Eurozone's economic dangers, this hope never quite materialized. [2] The UK saw economic downturns of its own during the euro's problematic years thus far. [3] Many families in the UK still struggle to pay their bills in the face of higher than normal unemployment rates. [4] It seems that regardless of shared currency, the economies of Britain and its Eurozone neighbors are too closely **⑲** <u>intertwined</u> for one to remain unscathed by another's crises. **20**

Perhaps this question of economic security has been the wrong one. Due to Britain's location and long-standing trade relationships with its neighbors, economies will persist to be somewhat reliant on each other, euro or not. **㉑** <u>Furthermore,</u> political security, power, and protection bear more significance for the future. If the UK hopes to maintain and expand its influential presence in world leadership, its association and close involvement with greater Europe is invaluable. Considering that the euro probably offers a lower risk margin than many have supposed, the benefits of euro adoption: **㉒** <u>to secure EU membership and strengthen its cause,</u> bid Britain carefully reconsider.

Questions 23-33 are based on the following passage.

Coffee: The Buzz on Beans

Americans love coffee. **㉓** <u>Some</u> days you can find a coffee shop in nearly every American city. But this wasn't always true. How did coffee, which was first grown in Africa over five hundred years ago, come to America?

The coffee plant, from which makers get the "cherries" that **㉔** <u>is dried and roasted</u> into what we call beans, first appeared in the East-African country Ethiopia, in the province of Kaffa. From there, it spread to the Arabian Peninsula, where the coffeehouse, or *qahveh khaneh* in Arabic, was very popular. Like spices and cloth, coffee was traded internationally as

---

19. A) NO CHANGE
    B) disparate
    C) identical
    D) relevant

20. Which sentence is least relevant to the central idea of this paragraph?
    A) Sentence 1
    B) Sentence 2
    C) Sentence 3
    D) Sentence 4

21. A) NO CHANGE
    B) Or,
    C) Also,
    D) However,

22. A) NO CHANGE
    B) —to secure EU membership and strengthen its cause—
    C) : to secure EU membership and strengthen its cause—
    D) ; to secure EU membership and strengthen its cause,

23. A) NO CHANGE
    B) Many
    C) The
    D) These

24. A) NO CHANGE
    B) are being dried and roasted
    C) are dried and roasted
    D) is being dried and roasted

GO ON TO THE NEXT PAGE ⟶

European explorers reached far lands and **25** establishing shipping routes. The first European coffeehouse opened in Venice, Italy, in 1683, and around that time London **26** displayed over three hundred coffeehouses.

There is no record of coffee being amongst the cargo of the *Mayflower*, which reached the New World in 1620. It was not until 1668 that the first written reference to coffee in America was made. A beverage was being made from roasted beans and flavored with sugar or honey, and cinnamon. Coffee was then described in the New England colony's official records of 1670. In 1683, William Penn, who lived in a settlement on the Delaware River, wrote of buying supplies of coffee in a **27** New York market, he paid eighteen shillings and nine pence per pound. **28**

25. A) NO CHANGE
    B) established
    C) having established
    D) was establishing

26. A) NO CHANGE
    B) bragged
    C) highlighted
    D) boasted

27. A) NO CHANGE
    B) New York market and William Penn
    C) New York market so he paid
    D) New York market, paying

28. Which choice most effectively establishes a summative concluding sentence for the paragraph?

    A) Coffee's appearance in the historical record shows it was becoming more and more established in the New World.

    B) The colonies probably used more tea than coffee since there are records of it being imported from England.

    C) William Penn founded Pennsylvania Colony, which became the state of Pennsylvania after the Revolutionary War with England ended.

    D) The Mayflower did carry a number of items that the colonists needed for settlement, including animals and tools.

GO ON TO THE NEXT PAGE

Coffeehouses like those in Europe were soon established in American colonies, and as America expanded westward, coffee consumption grew. In their settlement days, **29** Chicago St. Louis and New Orleans each had famous coffeehouses. By the mid-twentieth century, coffeehouses were abundant. In places like New York and San Francisco, they became **30** confused with counterculture, as a place where intellectuals and artists gathered to share ideas. In American homes, coffee was a social lubricant, bringing people together to socialize as afternoon tea had done in English society. With the invention of the electric coffee pot, it became a common courtesy to ask a guest if she wanted "coffee or tea?" **31**

29. A) NO CHANGE
    B) Chicago, St. Louis, and New Orleans
    C) Chicago, St. Louis, and, New Orleans
    D) Chicago St. Louis and, New Orleans

30. A) NO CHANGE
    B) related
    C) associated
    D) coupled

31. Which choice most effectively establishes the main topic of the paragraph?
    A) There were many coffee shops in New York and in Chicago.
    B) Electric coffee machines changed how people entertained at home.
    C) Over time, coffee became a part of everyday American life.
    D) People went to coffehouses to discuss major issues.

GO ON TO THE NEXT PAGE

However, by the 1950s, U.S. manufacturing did to coffee what it had done to **32** other foods; produced it cheaply, mass-marketed it, and lowered the quality. Coffee was roasted and ground in manufacturing plants and freeze-dried for a long storage life, which compromised its flavor. An "evangelism" began to bring back the original bracing, dark-roasted taste of coffee, and spread to the rest of the world. **33** In every major city of the world, now travelers around the world, expect to be able to grab an uplifting, fresh, and delicious cup of coffee—and they can.

32. A) NO CHANGE
    B) other foods produced
    C) other foods, produced
    D) other foods: produced

33. A) NO CHANGE
    B) Now travelers, in every major city of the world, around the world expect to be able to grab an uplifting, fresh, and delicious cup of coffee—and they can.
    C) Now in every major city of the world, travelers around the world expect to be able to grab an uplifting, fresh, and delicious cup of coffee—and they can.
    D) Now travelers around the world expect to be able to grab an uplifting, fresh, and delicious cup of coffee in every major city of the world—and they can.

GO ON TO THE NEXT PAGE

Questions 34-44 are based on the following passage.

Predicting Nature's Light Show

One of the most beautiful of nature's displays is the aurora borealis, commonly known as the Northern Lights. As ③④ their informal name suggests, the best place to view this phenomenon ③⑤ is the north. How far north one needs to be to witness auroras depends not on conditions here on Earth, but on the sun. ③⑥

As with hurricane season on Earth, the sun ③⑦ observes a cycle of storm activity, called the solar cycle, which lasts approximately 11 years. Also referred to as the sunspot cycle, this period is caused by the amount of magnetic flux that rises to the surface of the sun, causing sunspots, or areas of intense magnetic activity. The magnetic energy is sometimes so great it causes a storm that explodes away from the sun's surface in a solar flare.

34. A) NO CHANGE
    B) an
    C) its
    D) that

35. A) NO CHANGE
    B) is in North America.
    C) is above the Arctic Circle.
    D) is in the Northern Hemisphere.

36. Which of the following would most strengthen the passage's introduction?

    A) A statement about the Kp Index and other necessary tracking tools scientists use

    B) A mention that the National Oceanic and Atmospheric Administration monitors solar flares

    C) An explanation about why conditions on the sun rather than on Earth affect the Northern Lights

    D) A statement that scientists can predict the best time and location to see the Northern Lights by studying the sun

37. A) NO CHANGE
    B) experiences
    C) perceives
    D) witnesses

GO ON TO THE NEXT PAGE

38 These powerful magnetic storms eject high-speed electrons and protons into space. Called a coronal mass ejection, this ejection is far more powerful than the hot gases the sun constantly emits. The speed at which the atoms are shot away from the sun is almost triple that of a normal solar wind. It takes this shot of energy one to three days to arrive at Earth's upper atmosphere. Once it arrives, it is captured by Earth's own magnetic field. It is this newly captured energy that causes the Northern Lights.

39 Scientists and interested amateurs in the Northern Hemisphere **40** use tools readily available to all in order to predict the likelihood of seeing auroras in their location at a specific time. One such tool is the Kp Index, a number that determines the potential visibility of an aurora. The Kp Index measures the energy added to Earth's magnetic field from the sun on a scale of 0-9, with 1 representing a solar calm and 5 or more indicating a magnetic storm, or solar flare. The magnetic fluctuations are measured in three-hour intervals (12 AM to 3 AM, 3 AM to 6 AM, and so on) so that deviations can be factored in and accurate data can be presented.

Magnetometers, tools that measure the strength of Earth's magnetic field, are located around the world. When the energy from solar flares reaches Earth, the strength and direction of the energy **41** is recorded by these tools and analyzed by scientists at the National Oceanic and Atmospheric Administration, who calculate the difference between the average strength of the magnetic field and spikes due to solar flares. They plot this information on the Kp Index and **42** update the public with information on viewing the auroras as well as other impacts solar flares may have on life on Earth.

38. What fact is omitted from this paragraph that would help support the author's claims?

A) The speed of normal solar wind

B) The strength of Earth's magnetic field

C) The temperature of normal solar wind

D) The definition of coronal mass ejection

39. A) NO CHANGE

B) Interested scientists and amateurs

C) Scientists and amateurs interested

D) Scientists interested and amateurs

40. A) NO CHANGE

B) use tools for prediction

C) use specific tools to predict

D) use all tools readily available to predict

41. A) NO CHANGE

B) are

C) will be

D) has been

42. A) NO CHANGE

B) update aurora viewing information

C) update information on viewing the auroras

D) update aurora viewing information for the public

GO ON TO THE NEXT PAGE

43 <u>While</u> solar flares can sometimes have negative effects on our communications systems and weather patterns, the most common effect is also the most enchanting: a beautiful light show.

Potential Visibility of an Aurora

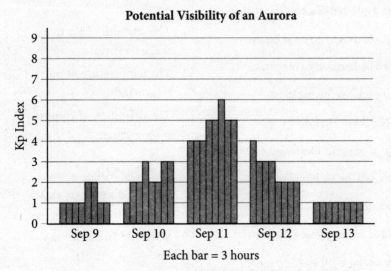

Each bar = 3 hours

Data from National Oceanic and Atmospheric Administration.

43. A) NO CHANGE

   B) However,

   C) Since

   D) Whereas

44. Using the graphic and the information in the passage, identify the complete time period when a solar flare took place.

   A) 3 PM to 6 PM on September 11

   B) 12 AM on September 11 to 3 AM on September 12

   C) 9 AM on September 10 to 12 PM on September 12

   D) 9 AM on September 11 to 12 AM on September 12

MATH TEST

25 Minutes—17 Questions

NO-CALCULATOR SECTION

Turn to Section 3 of your answer sheet to answer the questions in this section.

Directions: For this section, solve each problem and decide which is the best of the choices given. Fill in the corresponding oval on the answer sheet. You may use any available space for scratch work.

Notes:

1. Calculator use is NOT permitted.
2. All numbers used are real numbers.
3. All figures used are necessary to solving the problems that they accompany. All figures are drawn to scale EXCEPT when it is stated that a specific figure is not drawn to scale.
4. Unless stated otherwise, the domain of any function f is assumed to be the set of all real numbers x, for which $f(x)$ is a real number.

Information:

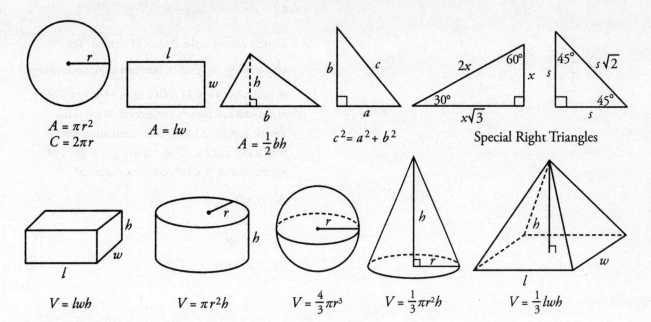

$A = \pi r^2$
$C = 2\pi r$

$A = lw$

$A = \frac{1}{2}bh$

$c^2 = a^2 + b^2$

Special Right Triangles

$V = lwh$

$V = \pi r^2 h$

$V = \frac{4}{3}\pi r^3$

$V = \frac{1}{3}\pi r^2 h$

$V = \frac{1}{3}lwh$

The sum of the degree measures of the angles in a triangle is 180.

The number of degrees of arc in a circle is 360.

The number of radians of arc in a cirlce is 2π.

GO ON TO THE NEXT PAGE

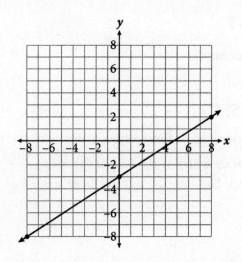

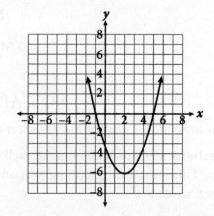

1. What is the average rate of change for the line graphed in the figure above?

   A) $\dfrac{3}{5}$

   B) $\dfrac{5}{8}$

   C) $\dfrac{8}{5}$

   D) $\dfrac{5}{3}$

2. Which of the following could be the factored form of the equation graphed in the figure above?

   A) $y = \dfrac{1}{5}(x - 2)(x + 6)$

   B) $y = \dfrac{1}{5}(x + 2)(x - 6)$

   C) $y = \dfrac{2}{3}(x - 1)(x + 5)$

   D) $y = \dfrac{2}{3}(x + 1)(x - 5)$

3. Kinetic energy is the energy of motion. The equation $E_K = \dfrac{1}{2}mv^2$ represents the kinetic energy in joules of an object with a mass of m kg traveling at a speed of v meters per second. What is the kinetic energy in joules of an unmanned aircraft with a mass of 2×10^3 kg traveling at a speed of approximately 3×10^3 meters per second?

   A) 9×5^9

   B) 9×10^8

   C) 9×10^9

   D) 1.8×10^{10}

GO ON TO THE NEXT PAGE ⟹

$$\frac{3(k-1)+5}{2} = \frac{17-(8+k)}{4}$$

4. In the equation above, what is the value of k?

    A) $\dfrac{9}{13}$

    B) $\dfrac{5}{7}$

    C) $\dfrac{8}{7}$

    D) $\dfrac{8}{5}$

5. An environmental protection group had its members sign a pledge to try to reduce the amount of garbage they throw out by 3% each year. On the year that the pledge was signed, each person threw out an average of 1,800 pounds of garbage. Which exponential function could be used to model the average amount of garbage each person who signed the pledge should throw out each year after signing the pledge?

    A) $y = 0.97 \times 1{,}800^t$

    B) $y = 1{,}800 \times t^{0.97}$

    C) $y = 1{,}800 \times 1.97^t$

    D) $y = 1{,}800 \times 0.97^t$

$$\frac{6x+2}{x+5} - \frac{3x-8}{x+5}$$

6. Which of the following is equivalent to the expression above?

    A) $\dfrac{3x-6}{x+5}$

    B) $\dfrac{3x+10}{x+5}$

    C) $\dfrac{3x-6}{2x+10}$

    D) $\dfrac{3x+10}{2x+10}$

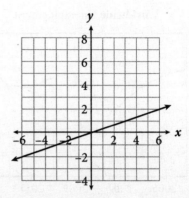

7. If the equation of the line shown in the figure above is written in the form $\dfrac{y}{x} = m$, which of following could be the value of m?

    A) -3

    B) $-\dfrac{1}{3}$

    C) $\dfrac{1}{3}$

    D) 3

8. If $4x^2 + 7x + 1$ is multiplied by $3x + 5$, what is the coefficient of x in the resulting polynomial?

    A) 3

    B) 12

    C) 35

    D) 38

GO ON TO THE NEXT PAGE

Worldwide Unemployment

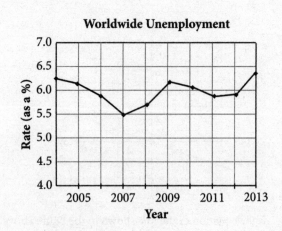

9. The figure above shows worldwide unemployment rates from 2004 to 2013. Which of the following statements is true?

A) The graph is decreasing everywhere.

B) The graph is increasing from 2007 to 2010.

C) The graph is decreasing from 2004 to 2007 and from 2009 to 2011.

D) The graph is increasing from 2007 to 2010 and decreasing from 2011 to 2013.

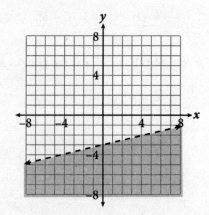

10. The solution to which inequality is represented in the graph above?

A) $\frac{1}{4}x - y > 3$

B) $\frac{1}{4}x - y < 3$

C) $\frac{1}{4}x + y > -3$

D) $\frac{1}{4}x + y < -3$

$$\begin{cases} \frac{1}{3}x + \frac{2}{3}y = -8 \\ ax + 6y = 15 \end{cases}$$

11. If the system of linear equations above has no solution, and a is a constant, what is the value of a?

A) $-\frac{1}{3}$

B) $\frac{1}{3}$

C) $\frac{3}{2}$

D) 3

GO ON TO THE NEXT PAGE

12. A taxi in the city charges $3.00 for the first $\frac{1}{4}$ mile, plus $0.25 for each additional $\frac{1}{8}$ mile. Eric plans to spend no more than $20 on a taxi ride around the city. Which inequality represents the number of miles, m, that Eric could travel without exceeding his limit?

A) $2.5 + 2m \leq 20$

B) $3 + 0.25m \leq 20$

C) $3 + 2m \leq 20$

D) $12 + 2m \leq 20$

13. A projectile is any moving object that is thrown near the Earth's surface. The path of the projectile is called the trajectory and can be modeled by a quadratic equation, assuming the only force acting on the motion is gravity (no friction). If a projectile is launched from a platform 8 feet above the ground with an initial velocity of 64 feet per second, then its trajectory can be modeled by the equation $h = -16t^2 + 64t + 8$, where h represents the height of the projectile t seconds after it was launched. Based on this model, what is the maximum height in feet that the projectile will reach?

A) 72

B) 80

C) 92

D) 108

GO ON TO THE NEXT PAGE

Directions: For questions 14-17, solve the problem and enter your answer in the grid, as described below, on the answer sheet.

1. Although not required, it is suggested that you write your answer in the boxes at the top of the columns to help you fill in the circles accurately. You will receive credit only if the circles are filled in correctly.

2. Mark no more than one circle in any column.

3. No question has a negative answer.

4. Some problems may have more than one correct answer. In such cases, grid only one answer.

5. **Mixed numbers** such as $3\frac{1}{2}$ must be gridded as 3.5 or $\frac{7}{2}$. (If $3\frac{1}{2}$ is entered into the grid as ⬛, it will be interpreted as $\frac{31}{2}$, not $3\frac{1}{2}$).

6. **Decimal answers:** If you obtain a decimal answer with more digits than the grid can accommodate, it may be either rounded or truncated, but it must fill the entire grid.

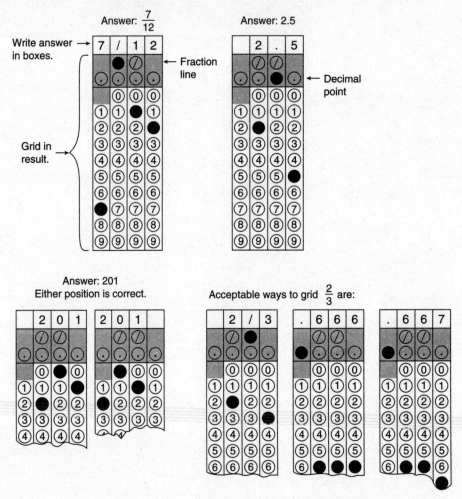

14. If $\dfrac{3}{4}x + \dfrac{5}{6}y = 12$, what is the value of $9x + 10y$?

15. How many degrees does the minute hand of an analogue clock rotate from 3:20 PM to 3:45 PM?

$$\dfrac{3x^{\frac{3}{2}}(16x^2)^3}{8x^{-\frac{1}{2}}}$$

16. What is the exponent on x when the expression above is written in simplest form?

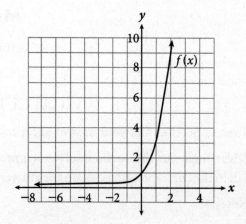

17. An exponential function $f(x)$ is shown in the figure above. What is the exact value of $f(-4)$?

IF YOU FINISH BEFORE TIME IS CALLED, YOU MAY CHECK YOUR WORK ON THIS SECTION ONLY. DO NOT TURN TO ANY OTHER SECTION IN THE TEST.   STOP

MATH TEST

45 Minutes—31 Questions

CALCULATOR SECTION

Turn to Section 4 of your answer sheet to answer the questions in this section.

Directions: For this section, solve each problem and decide which is the best of the choices given. Fill in the corresponding oval on the answer sheet. You may use any available space for scratch work.

Notes:

1. Calculator use is permitted.
2. All numbers used are real numbers.
3. All figures used are necessary to solving the problems that they accompany. All figures are drawn to scale EXCEPT when it is stated that a specific figure is not drawn to scale.
4. Unless stated otherwise, the domain of any function f is assumed to be the set of all real numbers x, for which $f(x)$ is a real number.

Information:

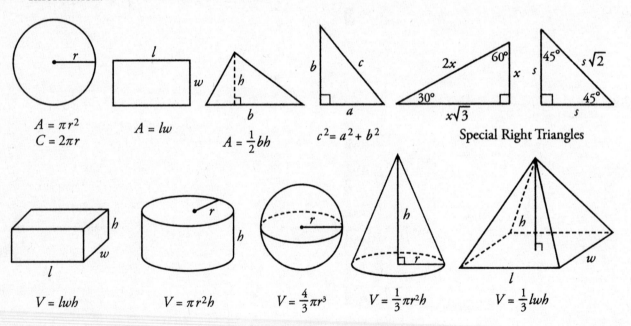

$A = \pi r^2$
$C = 2\pi r$

$A = lw$

$A = \frac{1}{2}bh$

$c^2 = a^2 + b^2$

Special Right Triangles

$V = lwh$

$V = \pi r^2 h$

$V = \frac{4}{3}\pi r^3$

$V = \frac{1}{3}\pi r^2 h$

$V = \frac{1}{3}lwh$

The sum of the degree measures of the angles in a triangle is 180.

The number of degrees of arc in a circle is 360.

The number of radians of arc in a cirlce is 2π.

GO ON TO THE NEXT PAGE ⇨

1. A home improvement store that sells carpeting charges a flat installation fee and a certain amount per square foot of carpet ordered. If the total cost for f square feet is given by the function $C(f) = 3.29f + 199$, then the value 3.29 best represents which of the following?

   A) The installation fee

   B) The cost of one square foot of carpet

   C) The number of square feet of carpet ordered

   D) The total cost not including the installation fee

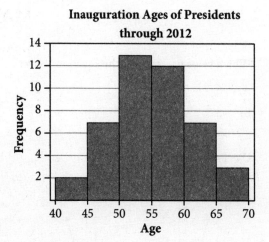

Inauguration Ages of Presidents through 2012

2. The United States Constitution requires that any candidate for the presidency be at least 35 years of age, although no president to date has been that young. The figure above shows the distribution of the ages of the presidents through 2012 at the time they were inaugurated. Based on the information shown, which of the following statements is true?

   A) The shape of the data is skewed to the left, so the mean age of the presidents is greater than the median.

   B) The shape of the data is fairly symmetric, so the mean age of the presidents is approximately equal to the median.

   C) The data has no clear shape, so it is impossible to make a reliable statement comparing the mean and the median.

   D) The same number of 55-or-older presidents have been inaugurated as ones who were younger than 55, so the mean age is exactly 55.

GO ON TO THE NEXT PAGE

$$\frac{1}{3}(5x - 8) = 3x + 4$$

3. Which value of *x* satisfies the equation above?

A) –5

B) –3

C) –1

D) 1

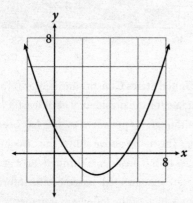

4. The following quadratic equations are all representations of the graph shown above. Which equation could you use to find the minimum value of the function, without doing any additional work?

A) $y = \frac{3}{8}(x - 3)^2 - \frac{3}{2}$

B) $y = \frac{3}{8}(x - 1)(x - 5)$

C) $y - \frac{15}{8} = \frac{3}{8}x^2 - \frac{9}{4}x$

D) $y = \frac{3}{8}x^2 - \frac{9}{4}x + \frac{15}{8}$

5. The Farmers' Market sells apples by the basket. The market charges \$3.00 for the basket itself, plus \$1.97 per pound of apples. A 6% sales tax is also applied to the entire purchase. Which equation represents the total cost of *p* pounds of apples at the Farmers' Market?

A) $c = (1.97 + 0.06p) + 3$

B) $c = 1.06(1.97p) + 3$

C) $c = 1.06(1.97 + 3)p$

D) $c = 1.06(1.97p + 3)$

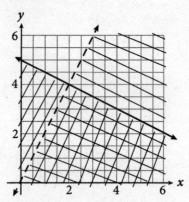

6. Which of the following is a solution to the system of inequalities shown in the figure above?

A) (1, 5)

B) (2, 6)

C) (4, 1)

D) (5, 4)

GO ON TO THE NEXT PAGE ⟩

7. Marion is a city planner. The city she works for recently purchased new property on which they plan to build administrative offices. Marion has been given the task of sizing the lots for new buildings, using the following guidelines:

   • The square footage of each lot should be greater than or equal to 3,000 square feet, but less than or equal to 15,000 square feet.

   • Each lot size should be at least 30% greater in area than the size before it.

   • To simplify tax assessment calculations, the square footage of each lot must be a multiple of 1,000 square feet.

   Which list of lot sizes meets the city guidelines and includes as many lots as possible?

   A) 3,000; 5,000; 10,000; 15,000

   B) 3,000; 4,500; 6,000; 7,500; 10,000; 15,000

   C) 3,000; 4,000; 6,000; 8,000; 11,000; 15,000

   D) 3,000; 3,900; 5,100; 6,600; 8,600; 11,200; 14,600

8. One function of the Environmental Protection Agency (EPA) is to reduce air pollution. After implementing several pollution reduction programs in a certain city, EPA calculated that the air pollution should decrease by approximately 8% each year. What kind of function could be used to model the amount of air pollution in this city over the next several years, assuming no other significant changes?

   A) A linear function

   B) A quadratic function

   C) A polynomial function

   D) An exponential function

9. Escape velocity is the speed that a traveling object needs to break free of a planet or moon's gravitational field without additional propulsion (for example, without using fuel). The formula used to calculate escape velocity is $v = \sqrt{\dfrac{2Gm}{r}}$, where G represents the universal gravitational constant, m is the mass of the body from which the object is escaping, and r is the distance between the object and the body's center of gravity. Which equation represents the value of r in terms of v, G, and m?

   A) $r = \dfrac{2Gm}{v^2}$

   B) $r = \dfrac{4G^2m^2}{v^2}$

   C) $r = \sqrt{\dfrac{2Gm}{v}}$

   D) $r = \sqrt{\dfrac{v}{2Gm}}$

10. A movie rental kiosk dispenses DVDs and Blu-rays. DVDs cost $2.00 per night and Blu-rays cost $3.50 per night. Between 5 PM and 9 PM on Saturday, the kiosk dispensed 209 movies and collected $562.00. Solving which system of equations would yield the number of DVDs, d, and the number of Blu-rays, b, that the kiosk dispensed during the 4-hour period?

   A) $\begin{cases} d + b = 209 \\ 2d + 3.5b = \dfrac{562}{4} \end{cases}$

   B) $\begin{cases} d + b = 562 \\ 2d + 3.5b = 209 \end{cases}$

   C) $\begin{cases} d + b = 562 \\ 2d + 3.5b = 209 \times 4 \end{cases}$

   D) $\begin{cases} d + b = 209 \\ 2d + 3.5b = 562 \end{cases}$

GO ON TO THE NEXT PAGE

11. The United States Senate has two voting members for each of the 50 states. The 113th Congress had a 4:1 male-to-female ratio in the Senate. Forty-five of the male senators were Republican. Only 20 percent of the female senators were Republican. How many senators in the 113th Congress were Republican?

   A) 20
   B) 49
   C) 55
   D) 65

12. According to the *Project on Student Debt* prepared by The Institute for College Access and Success, 7 out of 10 students graduating in 2012 from a four-year college in the United States had student loan debt. The average amount borrowed per student was $29,400, which is up from $18,750 in 2004. If student debt experiences the same total percent increase over the next eight years, approximately how much will a college student graduating in 2020 owe, assuming she takes out student loans to pay for her education?

   A) $40,100
   B) $44,300
   C) $46,100
   D) $48,200

13. Annalisa has 10 beanbags to throw in a game. She gets 7 points if a beanbag lands in the smaller basket and 3 points if it lands in the larger basket. If she gets b beanbags into the larger basket and the rest into the smaller basket, which expression represents her total score?

   A) $3b$
   B) $3b + 7$
   C) $30 + 4b$
   D) $70 - 4b$

GO ON TO THE NEXT PAGE ⟶

Getting to the Answer: First, solve the second equation for x to get $x = 3y - 11$, and then substitute this equation into the first equation to find y.

$$2x + 4y = 13$$
$$2(3y - 11) + 4y = 13$$
$$6y - 22 + 4y = 13$$
$$10y - 22 = 13$$
$$10y = 35$$
$$y = \frac{7}{2}$$

Now, substitute the result into $x = 3y - 11$ and simplify to find x:

$$x = 3\left(\frac{7}{2}\right) - 11$$
$$= \frac{21}{2} - 11$$
$$= -\frac{1}{2}$$

The question asks for the sum, so add x and y to get $-\frac{1}{2} + \frac{7}{2} = \frac{6}{2} = 3$.

17. C
Difficulty: Medium

Category: Problem Solving and Data Analysis / Statistics and Probability

Strategic Advice: The keyword in the answer choices is "consistently," which relates to how spread out a player's scores are. Standard deviation, not mean, is a measure of spread so you can eliminate choice A right away.

Getting to the Answer: A lower standard deviation indicates scores that are less spread out and therefore more consistent. Likewise, a higher standard deviation indicates scores that are more spread out and therefore less consistent. Notice the opposite nature of this relationship: lower standard deviation = more consistent; higher standard deviation = less consistent. Choice (C) is correct because the standard deviation of Mae's scores is the lowest, which means she bowled the most consistently.

18. B
Difficulty: Medium

Category: Passport to Advanced Math / Quadratics

Strategic Advice: Notice the structure of the equation. The expression on the left side of the equation is the square of a quantity, so start by taking the square root of both sides.

Getting to the Answer: After taking the square roots, solve the resulting equations. Remember, $4^2 = 16$ and $(-4)^2 = 16$, so there will be *two* equations to solve.

$$(x + 3)^2 = 16$$
$$\sqrt{(x + 3)^2} = \sqrt{16}$$
$$x + 3 = \pm 4$$
$$x + 3 = 4 \rightarrow x = 1$$
$$x + 3 = -4 \rightarrow x = -7$$

19. C
Difficulty: Medium

Category: Problem Solving and Data Analysis / Rates, Ratios, Proportions, and Percentages

Strategic Advice: Pay careful attention to the units. You need to convert all of the dimensions to inches, and then set up and solve a proportion.

Getting to the Answer: The real statue's height is $305 \times 12 = 3,660 + 6 = 3,666$ inches; the length of the nose on the real statue is $4 \times 12 = 48 + 6 = 54$ inches; the height of the model statue is 26 inches; the length of the nose on the model is unknown.

$$\frac{3,666}{54} = \frac{26}{x}$$
$$3,666x = 26(54)$$
$$3,666x = 1,404$$
$$x = \frac{1,404}{3,666} = \frac{18}{47}$$

20. B

Difficulty: Medium

Category: Passport to Advanced Math / Functions

Strategic Advice: When evaluating a function, substitute the value inside the parentheses for *x* in the equation.

Getting to the Answer: Evaluate the function at *x* = 6 and at *x* = 2, and then subtract the second output from the first. Note that this is not the same as first subtracting 6 − 2 and then evaluating the function at *x* = 4.

$$f(6) = 3(6) + 5 = 18 + 5 = 23$$

$$f(2) = 3(2) + 5 = 6 + 5 = 11$$

$$f(6) - f(2) = 23 - 11 = 12$$

21. A

Difficulty: Medium

Category: Problem Solving and Data Analysis / Scatterplots

Strategic Advice: Examine the graph, paying careful attention to units and labels. Here, the years increase by 2 for each grid line and the number of owls by 25.

Getting to the Answer: The average change per year is the same as the slope of the line of best fit. Find the slope of the line of best fit using the slope formula, $m = \dfrac{y_2 - y_1}{x_2 - x_1}$, and any two points that lie on (or very close to) the line. Using the two endpoints of the data, (1994, 1,200) and (2014, 700), the average change per year is $\dfrac{700 - 1,200}{2014 - 1994} = \dfrac{-500}{20} = -25$.

Pay careful attention to the sign of the answer—the number of owls is decreasing, so the rate of change is negative.

22. D

Difficulty: Medium

Category: Passport to Advanced Math / Quadratics

Strategic Advice: The solution to a system of equations is the point(s) where their graphs intersect. You could solve this question algebraically, one system at a time, but this is not time efficient. Instead, graph each pair of equations in your graphing calculator and look for the graphs that intersect at *x* = −4 and *x* = 2.

Getting to the Answer: The graphs of the equations in A and B don't intersect at all, so you can eliminate them right away. The graphs in C intersect, but both points of intersection have a positive *x*-coordinate. This means (D) must be correct. The graph looks like:

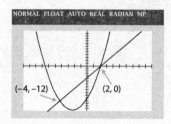

23. C

Difficulty: Medium

Category: Problem Solving and Data Analysis / Statistics and Probability

Strategic Advice: Read the question, identifying parts of the graphic you need—the question asks about litters of 7 or more pups, so you'll only use the heights of the bars for 7, 8, and 9 pups.

Getting to the Answer: Start by finding the percent of the mice in the study that had a litter of 7 or more pups. Of the 200 mice in the sample, 25 + 14 + 5 = 44 had a litter of 7 or more pups. This is $\dfrac{44}{200} = \dfrac{22}{100} = 22\%$ of the mice in the study. Given the same general conditions (such as living in the same geographic region), you would expect approximately the same results, so multiply the number of female mice in the whole population by the percent you found: 35,000 × 0.22 = 7,700.

24. C

Difficulty: Medium

Category: Heart of Algebra / Linear Equations

Strategic Advice: You'll need to interpret the information given in the question to write two ordered pairs. Then you can use the ordered pairs to find the slope and the y-intercept of the linear model.

Getting to the Answer: In an ordered pair, the independent variable is always written first. Here, the heart rate depends on the amount of exercise, so the ordered pairs should be written in the form (time, heart rate). They are (8, 90) and (20, 117). Use these points in the slope formula, $m = \dfrac{y_2 - y_1}{x_2 - x_1}$, to find that $m = \dfrac{117 - 90}{20 - 8} = \dfrac{27}{12} = 2.25$. Then, substitute the slope (2.25) and either of the points into slope-intercept form and simply to find the y-intercept:

$$90 = 2.25(8) + b$$
$$90 = 18 + b$$
$$72 = b$$

Finally, write the equation using the slope and the y-intercept that you found to get $r = 2.25t + 72$. Note that the only choice with a slope of 2.25 is (C), so you could have eliminated the other three choices before finding the y-intercept and saved yourself a bit of time.

25. B
Difficulty: Hard

Category: Passport to Advanced Math / Functions

Strategic Advice: Transformations that are grouped with the x in a function shift the graph horizontally and, therefore, affect the x-coordinates of points on the graph. Transformations that are not grouped with the x shift the graph vertically and, therefore, affect the y-coordinates of points on the graph. Remember, horizontal shifts are always backward of what they look like.

Getting to the Answer: Start with $(x + 3)$. This shifts the graph left 3, so subtract 3 from the x-coordinate of the given point: $(5, 1) \rightarrow (5 - 3, 1) = (2, 1)$. Next, apply the negative in front of f, which is not grouped with the x, so it makes the y-coordinate negative: $(2, 1) \rightarrow (2, -1)$. Finally, -2 is not grouped with x, so subtract 2 from the y-coordinate: $(2, -1 - 2) \rightarrow (2, -3)$.

26. C
Difficulty: Hard

Category: Problem Solving and Data Analysis / Rates, Ratios, Proportions, and Percentages

Strategic Advice: Draw a chart or diagram detailing the various price reductions for each 30 days.

Getting to the Answer:

Date	% of Most Recent Price	Resulting Price
Jan. 15	100 – 25% = 75%	$1,500 × 0.75 = $1,125
Feb. 15	100 – 10% = 90%	$1,125 × 0.9 = $1,012.50
Mar. 15	100 – 10% = 90%	$1,012.50 × 0.9 = $911.25

You can stop here because the refrigerator was sold on April 2, which is not 30 days after March 15. The final selling price was $911.25.

27. A
Difficulty: Hard

Category: Additional Topics in Math / Geometry

Strategic Advice: Organize information as you read the question. Here, you'll definitely want to draw and label a sketch.

Getting to the Answer:

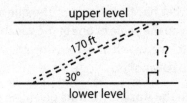

The lower level, the vertical distance between levels, and the diagonal elevator track form a 30-60-90 triangle, where the elevator track is the hypotenuse. The vertical distance is opposite the 30° angle so it is the shortest leg. The rules for 30-60-90 triangles state that the shortest leg is half the length of the hypotenuse, so the vertical distance between levels is approximately $170 \div 2 = 85$ feet.

28. Any value greater than 16.25, but less than 22.5.

Difficulty: Easy

Category: Heart of Algebra / Inequalities

Strategic Advice: Choose the best strategy to answer the question. Here, the fractions make it look more complicated than it really is, so start by clearing the fractions by multiplying everything by 20.

Getting to the Answer: You don't need to separate this compound inequality into pieces. Just remember, whatever you do to one piece, you must do to all three pieces. Don't forget to flip the inequality symbols if you multiply or divide by a negative number.

$$20\left(-\frac{3}{2}\right) < 20\left(3 - \frac{a}{5}\right) < 20\left(-\frac{1}{4}\right)$$
$$-30 < 60 - 4a < -5$$
$$-30 - 60 < 60 - 60 - 4a < -5 - 60$$
$$-90 < -4a < -65$$
$$\frac{-90}{-4} > \frac{-4a}{-4} > \frac{-65}{-4}$$
$$22.5 > a > 16.25$$
$$16.25 < a < 22.5$$

29. 88

Difficulty: Hard

Category: Passport to Advanced Math / Exponents

Strategic Advice: When you're asked to solve an equation that has two variables, the question usually gives you the value of one of the variables. Read carefully to see which variable is given and which one you're solving for.

Getting to the Answer: You are given the diameter (0.12), so substitute this value for d in the equation and then solve for the other variable, h. Before dealing with the radical, divide both sides of the equation by 0.015.

$$0.12 = 0.015 \times \sqrt{h - 24}$$
$$8 = \sqrt{h - 24}$$
$$8^2 = \left(\sqrt{h - 24}\right)^2$$
$$64 = h - 24$$
$$88 = h$$

30. 252

Difficulty: Medium

Category: Problem Solving and Data Analysis / Rates, Ratios, Proportions, and Percentages

Strategic Advice: Break the question into steps. First, find how long it took Daniel to spray one lawn, and then use that amount to find how long it took him to spray all the lawns.

Getting to the Answer: According to the figure, he started the first house at 9:00 and the sixth house at 10:00, so it took him 1 hour, or 60 minutes, to spray 5 houses. This gives a unit rate of $60 \div 5 = 12$ minutes per house. Count the houses in the figure—there are 21. Multiply the unit rate by the number of houses to get $12 \times 21 = 252$ minutes to spray all the lawns.

31. 4

Difficulty: Hard

Category: Problem Solving and Data Analysis / Rates, Ratios, Proportions, and Percentages

Strategic Advice: This part of the question contains several steps. Think about the units given in the question and what you need to convert so that you can get to the answer.

Getting to the Answer: The total acreage of all the lawns in the neighborhood is $21 \times 0.2 = 4.2$ acres. This is equivalent to $4.2 \times 43,560 = 182,952$ square feet. Each gallon of spray covers 2,500 square feet so divide to find that Daniel needs $182,952 \div 2,500 = 73.1808$ gallons to spray all the lawns. The spray rig holds 20 gallons, so Daniel will need to fill it 4 times. After he fills it the fourth time and finishes all the lawns, there will be some spray left over.

PART FIVE

Answers & Explanations

CHAPTER 1

PREPARE

1. A

Difficulty: Easy

Category: Heart of Algebra / Linear Equations

Strategic Advice: Look for a way to make the algebra manipulations easier (and quicker).

Getting to the Answer: Begin by multiplying both sides by 6 to eliminate the fractions. Then distribute the resultant 3 on the left. Combine like terms and solve for x to reveal that $x = -61$, which is (A).

2. D

Difficulty: Easy

Category: Heart of Algebra / Linear Equations

Strategic Advice: Straightforward math works well on simple equations like this one.

Getting to the Answer: Start by distributing the 2 on the left. Then combine like terms and divide by 2 on both sides to isolate x. You should find that $x = \frac{11}{2}$, which is (D).

3. D

Difficulty: Medium

Category: Heart of Algebra / Linear Equations

Strategic Advice: Working with unwieldy fractions will be inefficient. Because the answer choices are decimals, you can convert the fractions to decimals to save time.

Getting to the Answer: First, multiply both sides by 7 to eliminate the fraction outside the parentheses, and convert all fractions to decimal form: $8(x - 0.46) + 28(x + 0.89) = 266$.

Distribute where necessary, then combine like terms to reveal that $x = 6.8$, (D).

4. C

Difficulty: Easy

Category: Heart of Algebra / Linear Equations

Strategic Advice: Wordy problems call for the Kaplan Strategy for Translating English into Math.

Getting to the Answer: "k can be determined" becomes "$k =$"; "multiply m by 2, add $3n$ to the result" is translated into "$2m + 3n$"; and "subtract $(4m - 5n)$ from this sum" becomes "$-(4m - 5n)$." Put the pieces together into an equation: $k = 2m + 3n - (4m - 5n)$. Simplifying yields $k = -2m + 8n$, which matches (C).

5. A

Difficulty: Easy

Category: Heart of Algebra / Linear Equations

Strategic Advice: No real math acrobatics here, but the Kaplan Method for Math will still prove useful.

Getting to the Answer: You're asked to determine the graph that corresponds to $y = 4x + 7$. Therefore, you need a line with a positive (up and to the right) slope and a y-intercept of 7. This eliminates all choices except (A), the correct answer.

6. C

Difficulty: Medium

Category: Heart of Algebra / Linear Equations

Strategic Advice: Don't get bogged down by the prose; zero in on what you need to answer the question posed.

Getting to the Answer: Temperature (T) is the independent variable on the x-axis, and volume (V) is the dependent variable on the y-axis. Therefore, the skeleton of the equation you're looking for is $V = mT + b$. Because each answer choice has a different y-intercept, finding this is enough to get you to the right answer; no need to determine the slope. Although the graph is not centered like you're used to, you can still find the y-intercept. In this case, it's 1. This eliminates every answer choice except (C), which is correct.

7. C
Difficulty: Easy

Category: Heart of Algebra / Linear Equations

Strategic Advice: As with question 6, don't waste time on the words. Track down the question asked.

Getting to the Answer: You need to find the slope of the trend lines before and after the college's policy change, but you need not do any calculations if you notice the differences among the answer choices. According to the graph, you're looking for a negative slope before the policy change, which eliminates B and D. The line after the policy change has a positive slope, eliminating A and leaving the correct answer, (C).

PRACTICE

8. C
Difficulty: Easy

Category: Heart of Algebra / Linear Equations

Strategic Advice: The Kaplan Strategy for Translating English into Math will work well here. Watch out for extra information that's meant to confuse you.

Getting to the Answer: Let a be the average of Test One (92); b, the average of Test Two (77); c, the average of Test Three (what you need to find); and d, the overall test average (84). The average is the sum of terms divided by the

number of terms: $\frac{(a+b+c)}{3} = d$. Plugging in the values you know yields $\frac{(92+77+c)}{3} = 84$. Solving for c gives 83, which corresponds to (C).

9. D
Difficulty: Medium

Category: Heart of Algebra / Linear Equations

Strategic Advice: This is another question suited for the Kaplan Strategy for Translating English into Math.

Getting to the Answer: Let b represent the total number of candies in the box. Then write each candy quantity as a fraction of b.

Putting the pieces together in an equation gives $\frac{1}{4}b + \frac{1}{6}b + \frac{1}{3}b + 9 = b$. From here you can find a common denominator, but multiplying through with a common multiple (like 12) will be easier. Solving for b yields 36, but you're not done yet. Plug 36 back into the expressions for peppermints (12) and chocolates (9), then multiply together to get 108, which is (D).

PERFORM

10. C
Difficulty: Medium

Category: Heart of Algebra / Linear Equations

Strategic Advice: The question is only asking for the equation. You don't need to plug anything in, but you certainly could to verify that your selected answer is correct.

Getting to the Answer: You know there will be a flat fee of $50, and for text messages you'll be looking for 0.1t. This eliminates answer choice D. If you're stuck on the data plan cost, plug in some numbers. For $g = 2$, we wouldn't expect there to be an additional fee. For $g = 3$, we'd expect to see an $8 charge, and for $g = 4$, we'd expect to see a $16 charge. The only answer choice that reflects this is (C).

11. 1/3
Difficulty: Medium

Category: Heart of Algebra / Linear Equations

Strategic Advice: $(n - 2)$ is in both equations. Find that first and plug it into the second equation.

Getting to the Answer: First determine the value of $(n - 2)$ by dividing both sides of $3(n - 2) = 6$ by 3. Now you know that $n - 2 = 2$, so plug 2 into the numerator of the second equation. To tackle the denominator, continue simplifying the first equation to find that $n = 4$. Plug 4 into $(n + 2)$, which leaves $\frac{2}{(4 + 2)} = \frac{2}{6} = \frac{1}{3}$. Grid in $\frac{1}{3}$ and move on to the next question.

12. B
Difficulty: Medium

Category: Heart of Algebra / Linear Equations

Strategic Advice: Follow the Kaplan Strategy for Translating English into Math. $D =$ die-hard package, $P =$ personal package, and $V =$ number of visits.

Getting to the Answer: Assemble equations and set them equal to each other.

$$D = 250 \text{ and } P = 130 + 4V$$
$$250 = 130 + 4V$$
$$120 = 4V$$
$$30 = V$$

This is an exact match for (B).

Be careful! Trap answer choices will often correspond to other variables. Choose logical names to ensure you're always solving for the right one.

EXTRA PRACTICE

1. C

Difficulty: Easy

Category: Heart of Algebra / Linear Equations

Strategic Advice: For the equations, look at the exponents on the variables, and consider whether the equation could be written in the form $y = mx + b$. For the graph, recall that the slope of a linear equation is constant or, in other words, does not change. For the table, compare the changes in x to the changes in y from one row to the next.

Getting to the Answer: The graph in (C) does not represent a linear relationship because the slope on the left side of the y-axis is negative (the graph is decreasing) while the slope on the right side of the y-axis is positive (the graph is increasing). The graph of a linear relationship does not change direction. Choice (C) is correct.

2. D

Difficulty: Easy

Category: Heart of Algebra / Linear Equations

Strategic Advice: Quickly examine the numbers in the equation, and choose the best strategy to answer the question. Distributing the $\frac{2}{3}$ will result in messy calculations, so clear the fraction instead.

Getting to the Answer: To make the numbers easier to work with, clear the fraction by multiplying both sides of the equation by the reciprocal of $\frac{2}{3}$, which is $\frac{3}{2}$.

$$\frac{3}{2} \times \frac{2}{3}(x-1) = 12 \times \frac{3}{2}$$
$$x - 1 = 18$$
$$x = 19$$

You could also clear the fraction by multiplying both sides of the equation by the denominator (3) and then using the distributive property, but this is not the most time-efficient strategy.

3. B

Difficulty: Easy

Category: Heart of Algebra / Linear Equations

Strategic Advice: Write the equation in words first, then translate from English to math.

Getting to the Answer: The total cost, c, is the weight of the watermelon in pounds, p, multiplied by the sale price since the purchase is made on Monday: $\$0.60 \times 80\% = 0.6 \times 0.8 = 0.48$. This gives the first part of the expression: $0.48p$. Now add the cost of four sweet potatoes, $0.79 \times 4 = 3.16$, to get the equation $c = 0.48p + 3.16$.

You could also use the Picking Numbers strategy: Pick a number for the weight of the watermelon and calculate how much it would cost (on sale). Then add the cost of four sweet potatoes. Finally, find the equation that gives the same amount.

4. C

Difficulty: Easy

Category: Heart of Algebra / Linear Equations

Strategic Advice: When writing a linear equation, a flat rate is a constant while a unit rate is always multiplied by the independent variable. You can identify the unit rate by looking for words like *per* or *for each*.

Getting to the Answer: Because the amount Sandy gets paid per day, $70, is a flat rate that doesn't depend on the number of tires she sells, it should be the constant in the equation. The clue "for each" tells you to multiply $14 by the number of tires she sells, so the equation is *pay* = 14 × *number of tires* + 70, or $y = 14x + 70$.

5. D

Difficulty: Easy

Category: Heart of Algebra / Linear Equations

Strategic Advice: Think about whether 0.02 is a constant in the equation or a coefficient that is multiplied by the independent variable.

Getting to the Answer: The total bill consists of a flat tax and a percentage of annual income. The flat per capita tax is a one-time fee that does not depend on the taxpayer's income and therefore should not be multiplied by i. This means that 25 is the per capita tax. The other expression in the equation, $0.02i$, represents the percentage income tax times the annual income (which the question tells you is i.) Therefore, 0.02 must represent the amount of the income tax as a percentage.

6. C

Difficulty: Easy

Category: Heart of Algebra / Linear Equations

Strategic Advice: Ask yourself whether 27,000 is a constant in the equation that represents an initial amount or a rate of change.

Getting to the Answer: It is reasonable to assume that the value of the car is determined by multiplying the depreciation rate by the number of years the car is owned, which is given in the equation as $0.15x$, and subtracting it from the car's initial value. This means 27,000, which is the constant in the equation, is the value of the car when the number of years is 0, or in other words, the purchase price of the car.

7. A

Difficulty: Easy

Category: Heart of Algebra / Linear Equations

Strategic Advice: To find the slope of a line from a graph, look for two points on the line that hit the intersection of two grid lines. Then count the rise (or the fall if the line is decreasing) and the run as you move from one point to the next (always left to right). The slope is the rise over the run.

Getting to the Answer: Put your pencil on the y-intercept, (0, 6), and move to the point (3, 1). The line moves down 5 units and to the right 3 units, so the slope is $-\dfrac{5}{3}$.

You could also substitute the two points, (0, 6) and (3, 1), into the slope formula $\left(m = \dfrac{y_2 - y_1}{x_2 - x_1} \right)$ to find the slope of the line.

8. A

Difficulty: Easy

Category: Heart of Algebra / Linear Equations

Strategic Advice: Read the axis labels carefully. The y-intercept is the point at which $x = 0$, which means the number of rides is 0.

Getting to the Answer: The y-intercept is (0, 8). This means the cost is $8 before riding any rides, and therefore 8 most likely represents a flat entrance fee.

9. C

Difficulty: Medium

Category: Heart of Algebra / Linear Equations

Strategic Advice: When a linear equation has no solution, the variables cancel out, and the resulting equation is two numbers that are not equal to each other.

Getting to the Answer: Start by simplifying the left side of the equation.

$$36 + 3(4x - 9) = c(2x + 1) + 25$$
$$36 + 12x - 27 = c(2x + 1) + 25$$

Because the variable terms must cancel, the right side of the equation must also have a 12x, so try $c = 6$. Solve the equation to make sure it results in no solution.

$$36 + 3(4x - 9) = 6(2x + 1) + 25$$
$$36 + 12x - 27 = 12x + 6 + 25$$
$$9 + 12x = 12x + 31$$
$$9 \neq 31$$

10. A

Difficulty: Medium

Category: Heart of Algebra / Linear Equations

Strategic Advice: Simplify the numerators first and then go from there.

Getting to the Answer: Simplify the numerators, cross-multiply, and then solve for n using inverse operations. Don't forget to distribute the negative to both terms inside the parentheses on the right side of the equation.

$$\frac{7(n-3)+11}{6} = \frac{18-(6+2n)}{8}$$
$$\frac{7n-21+11}{6} = \frac{18-6-2n}{8}$$
$$\frac{7n-10}{6} = \frac{12-2n}{8}$$
$$8(7n-10) = 6(12-2n)$$
$$56n-80 = 72-12n$$
$$68n = 152$$
$$n = \frac{152}{68} = \frac{38}{17}$$

11. B

Difficulty: Medium

Category: Heart of Algebra / Linear Equations

Strategic Advice: Don't look at the answer choices right away. Use the information in the question to write your own equation, then look for the answer choice that matches. Simplify your equation only if you don't find a match.

Getting to the Answer: Start with the cost, not including tax or the environmental impact fee. If Jenna rents a car for d days at a daily rate of $54.95, the untaxed total is $54.95d$. There is a 6% tax on this amount, so multiply by 1.06 to get $1.06(54.95d)$. The $10.00 environmental impact fee is *not* taxed, so simply add 10 to your expression. The total cost is $c = 1.06(54.95d) + 10$, which matches (B), so you do not need to simplify.

12. A

Difficulty: Medium

Category: Heart of Algebra / Linear Equations

Strategic Advice: The answer choices are given in slope-intercept form, so start by finding the slope.

Getting to the Answer: Find the slope by substituting two pairs of values from the table into the slope formula, $m = \frac{y_2 - y_1}{x_2 - x_1}$. Keep in mind that the projected number of cans sold *depends* on the price, so the price is the independent variable (x) and the projected number is the dependent variable (y). Using the points (0.75, 10,000) and (1.0, 5,000), the slope is:

$$m = \frac{5,000 - 10,000}{1.00 - 0.75}$$
$$m = \frac{-5,000}{0.25}$$
$$m = -20,000$$

This means that (A) must be correct because it is the only one that has a slope of –20,000. Don't let D fool you—the projected number of cans sold goes *down* as the price goes *up*, so there is an inverse relationship, and the slope must be negative.

13. A

Difficulty: Medium

Category: Heart of Algebra / Linear Equations

Strategic Advice: In this scenario, both the rental fee for the room and the per person rate are fixed amounts (determined by the hotel), while the number of people attending the conference is likely to be a variable amount.

Getting to the Answer: The total cost is the dependent variable and is calculated by multiplying the per person rate by the number of people attending and then adding the room rental fee. Therefore, the total cost is represented by *y*. Because the room rental fee and the per person rate are fixed amounts, they should be represented by numbers in the equation—325 and 15, respectively. The total cost depends on the number of people attending, so the number of people is the independent variable and is represented by *x*.

14. B

Difficulty: Medium

Category: Heart of Algebra / Linear Equations

Strategic Advice: There is not a lot of information to go on here, so start by determining the relationship between the number given in the problem, 3,600 bolts per day, and the number in the equation, 150.

Getting to the Answer: Because 3,600 ÷ 150 = 24 and there are 24 hours in a day, 150 is the number of bolts the machine can produce in 1 hour. If the machine can produce 150 in 1 hour, then it can produce 150 times *x* in *x* hours. This means the equation $y = 150x$ represents the number of bolts the machine can produce in *x* hours.

15. C

Difficulty: Medium

Category: Heart of Algebra / Linear Equations

Strategic Advice: Quickly scan the answer choices—they are written as inequalities, so you'll need to translate them into something that makes more sense to you. Use the fact that "< 0" means *negative* and "> 0" means *positive*.

Getting to the Answer: When a linear equation is written in the form $y = mx + b$, the variable *m* represents the slope of the line, and *b* represents the *y*-intercept of the line. Look at the graph—the line is increasing (going up from left to right), so the slope is positive ($m > 0$). This means you can eliminate A and B. Now look at the *y*-intercept—it is below the *x*-axis and is therefore negative ($b < 0$), which means (C) is correct.

16. B

Difficulty: Medium

Category: Heart of Algebra / Linear Equations

Strategic Advice: Don't look at the answer choices right away. Use the graph to identify the *y*-intercept and the slope of the line. Then write an equation in slope-intercept form, $y = mx + b$. Once you have your equation, look for the answer choice that matches.

Getting to the Answer: The line crosses the *y*-axis at (0, 6), so the *y*-intercept (*b*) is 6. The line falls vertically 1 unit for every 2 units that it runs to the right, so the slope (*m*) is $-\frac{1}{2}$. The equation of the line is $y = -\frac{1}{2}x + 6$, which matches (B).

Resist the temptation to graph each answer choice on your calculator—such a strategy is too time consuming for the PSAT.

17. B

Difficulty: Medium

Category: Heart of Algebra / Linear Equations

Strategic Advice: The slope-intercept form of a linear equation is $y = mx + b$, where m represents the slope. If the slope is 0, that means $m = 0$.

Getting to the Answer: Substitute 0 for m and simplify $y = mx + b$.

$$y = (0)x + b$$
$$y = b$$

The only answer that matches this form is (B), $y = 2$. You could also memorize that $x = a$ represents a vertical line with an undefined slope, and $y = b$ represents a horizontal line with a 0 slope.

18. B

Difficulty: Medium

Category: Heart of Algebra / Linear Equations

Strategic Advice: You could find the unit rate by calculating the slope of the line using two of the points shown on the graph, but it may be quicker to simply read the answer from the graph.

Getting to the Answer: The x-axis represents the number of golf balls, so find 1 on the x-axis and trace up to where it meets the graph of the line. The y-value is somewhere between $1 and $2, so the only possible correct answer choice is $1.67.

Finding the slope should result in the same answer—the graph rises 5 units and runs 3 units from one point to the next, so the slope is $\frac{5}{3}$, or 1.67.

19. A

Difficulty: Medium

Category: Heart of Algebra / Linear Equations

Strategic Advice: Quickly skim the answer choices to get the right context. Because the number of bacteria *depends* on the temperature of the room, the temperature would be graphed on the x-axis and the number of bacteria on the y-axis. Add these labels to the graph. Then describe what you see using your labels.

Getting to the Answer: Looking at the graph, notice that as the temperature increases, the number of bacteria also increases. Unfortunately, this is not one of the answer choices, so think of the scenario in terms of the type of relationship between the variables: There is a direct variation between them, or in other words, when one goes up, the other goes up. This can also be stated as when one goes down, the other goes down; when the temperature decreases, the number of bacteria decreases, and (A) is correct. Don't let D fool you—the *change* in the number of bacteria is constant, but the actual number of bacteria is not constant.

20. D

Difficulty: Hard

Category: Heart of Algebra / Linear Equations

Strategic Advice: A linear equation can have one solution, no solutions, or infinitely many solutions. If both a positive value of x and a negative value of x satisfy the equation, then it must have infinitely many solutions.

Getting to the Answer: When solving a linear equation that has infinitely many solutions, the variable terms will all cancel out, leaving a number that is equal to itself. Start by looking for an equation that, when simplified, has the same variable term on the left side of the equation as on the right side. Choice (D) is correct because:

$$8\left(\frac{3}{4}x - 5\right) = -2(20 - 3x)$$
$$6x - 40 = -40 + 6x$$
$$-40 = -40$$

21. C
Difficulty: Hard

Category: Heart of Algebra / Linear Equations

Strategic Advice: Look for a way to make the math easier, such as clearing the fractions first.

Getting to the Answer: Clear the fractions first by multiplying both sides of the equation by 6. Then solve for h using inverse operations.

$$6\left[\frac{2}{3}(3h)\right] - 6\left[\frac{5}{2}(h-1)\right] = 6\left[-\frac{1}{3}\left(\frac{3}{2}h\right)\right] + 6[8]$$
$$4(3h) - 15(h-1) = -2\left(\frac{3}{2}h\right) + 48$$
$$12h - 15h + 15 = -3h + 48$$
$$-3h + 15 = -3h + 48$$
$$15 \neq 48$$

Because the variable terms in the equation cancel out, and 15 does not equal 48, the equation has no solution. In other words, there is no value of x that satisfies the equation.

22. C
Difficulty: Hard

Category: Heart of Algebra / Linear Equations

Strategic Advice: The key to answering this question is to determine how many arrows hit each circle. If there are 12 arrows total and a hit the inner circle, the rest, or $12 - a$, must hit the outer circle.

Getting to the Answer: Try writing the expression in words first: points per inner circle (8) times number of arrows in inner circle (a) plus points per outer circle (4) times number of arrows in outer circle ($12 - a$). Now translate the words

into numbers, variables, and operations: $8a + 4(12 - a)$. This is not one of the answer choices, so simplify the expression by distributing the 4 and then combining like terms: $8a + 4(12 - a) = 8a + 48 - 4a = 4a + 48$, so the equation is $p = 4a + 48$.

23. A
Difficulty: Hard

Category: Heart of Algebra / Linear Equations

Strategic Advice: Always pay careful attention to units of measure. In many questions, they can guide you to the correct answer.

Getting to the Answer: The units change from hours to days. The mouse receives one pellet every 2.5 *hours*, which is equivalent to $\frac{24}{2.5}$ pellets per *day*. Over the course of d full days, the mouse will be fed $\frac{24d}{2.5}$ pellets.

24. D
Difficulty: Hard

Category: Heart of Algebra / Linear Equations

Strategic Advice: Write an equation in words first, then translate from English to math. Finally, rearrange your equation to find what you're interested in, which is the initial amount.

Getting to the Answer: Call the initial amount A. After you've written your equation, solve for A.

Amount now (x) = initial amount (A) minus y plus 6.

$$x = A - y + 6$$
$$x + y - 6 = A$$

This is the same as $y + x - 6$, so (D) is correct.

You could also use Picking Numbers to solve this question.

25. B

Difficulty: Hard

Category: Heart of Algebra / Linear Equations

Strategic Advice: This question sounds more difficult than it is. Try to match each number or term in the expression with a piece of information given in the question.

Getting to the Answer: Start with 2*f*: You are given that 2 is the number of points earned for fish with a purple dot and that Karla catches *f* of these fish, so 2*f* is the total number of points she earns for fish with purple dots. Move on to the second term, 5(8 − *f*). You are given that 5 is the number of points earned for fish with a green dot. If Karla catches *f* fish with a purple dot, then she must catch (the number of attempts − *f*) fish with a green dot. Because the term in parentheses is 8 − *f*, Karla must have made a total of 8 attempts. Each attempt costs 50 cents, so she spent $0.50(8) = $4 playing the game.

26. A

Difficulty: Hard

Category: Heart of Algebra / Linear Equations

Strategic Advice: There is not a lot of information to go on, so put the equation in slope-intercept form, and see what conclusions you can draw.

Getting to the Answer:

$$ax + by = c$$
$$by = -ax + c$$
$$y = -\frac{a}{b}x + \frac{c}{b}$$

The slope $\left(-\dfrac{a}{b}\right)$ is negative, so the line is decreasing (going down) from left to right. This means you can eliminate C and D because those lines are increasing. The *y*-intercept $\left(\dfrac{c}{b}\right)$ is positive, but this doesn't help because the *y*-intercepts in A and B are both positive. But don't forget, you are given that $c = b$, so rewrite the *y*-intercept as $\dfrac{c}{b} = \dfrac{b}{b} = 1$. The *y*-intercept is 1, so (A) is correct.

27. D

Difficulty: Hard

Category: Heart of Algebra / Linear Equations

Strategic Advice: Be careful! The question says the *x*-intercept is negative, not the *y*-intercept.

Getting to the Answer: The graph is increasing, so the slope must be positive. This means you should put each of the answer choices in slope-intercept form and check the sign of the slope. However, you can eliminate some of the answer choices fairly quickly using the other piece of information—the graph has a negative *x*-intercept, so when *y* = 0, the resulting value of *x* is negative. Quickly check each equation. You don't need to find the exact value of *x*, simply whether it is positive or negative.

Choice A: $4x + 3(0) = 1 \rightarrow 4x = 1$ so *x* is +
Choice B: $-x + 2(0) = -8 \rightarrow -x = -8$ so *x* is +
Choice C: $2x + 3(0) = -9 \rightarrow 2x = -9$ so *x* is −
Choice D: $3x - 5(0) = -10 \rightarrow 3x = -10$ so *x* is −

Eliminate A and B and write C in slope-intercept form.

$$2x + 3y = -9$$
$$3y = -2x - 9$$
$$y = -\frac{2}{3}x - 3$$

Eliminate choice C because it is decreasing (has a negative slope). Choice (D) must be correct.

28. A
Difficulty: Hard

Category: Heart of Algebra / Linear Equations

Strategic Advice: Sometimes drawing a diagram is the quickest way to answer a question. Sketch a quick graph of any linear equation. Change the signs of the slope and the y-intercept, then sketch the new graph on the same coordinate plane.

Getting to the Answer: Pick a simple equation that you can sketch quickly, like $y = -2x + 3$, and then change the signs of m and b. The new equation is $y = 2x - 3$. Sketch both graphs. The second graph is a perfect reflection of the first graph across the x-axis. If you're not convinced, try another pair of equations.

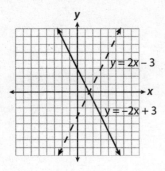

You could also graph your equations in a graphing calculator and compare them.

29. C
Difficulty: Hard

Category: Heart of Algebra / Linear Equations

Getting to the Answer: The birth rate starts high on the y-axis, while the gross domestic product (indicating wealth) starts low on the x-axis. At the other end of the graph, the birth rate is lower, while the gross domestic product is higher. This tells you that there is an inverse relationship between birth rate and wealth. In other words, as one variable increases, the other variable decreases. The only answer choice that describes this type of inverse relationship is (C).

30. D
Difficulty: Hard

Category: Heart of Algebra / Linear Equations

Strategic Advice: In a real-world scenario, the y-intercept of a graph usually represents a flat fee or an initial value. The slope of the line represents a unit rate, such as the cost per pound.

Getting to the Answer: The y-intercept of the graph is 12, so the flat fee is $12. To find the cost per pound (the unit rate), substitute two points from the graph into the slope formula. Using the points (0, 12) and (2, 17), the unit rate is $\frac{17-12}{2-0} = \frac{5}{2} = 2.5$, which means $2.50 per pound will be added to the cost. The total cost to ship a 25-pound box is $12 + 2.50(25) = 12 + 62.50 = 74.50$.

31. 14
Difficulty: Medium

Category: Heart of Algebra / Linear Equations

Strategic Advice: Eliminate the fractions to simplify the math.

Getting to the Answer: Clear the fractions first by multiplying both sides of the equation by 4. Then solve for y using inverse operations.

$$4\left[\frac{9}{4}(y-8)\right] = 4\left[\frac{27}{2}\right]$$
$$9(y-8) = 54$$
$$9y - 72 = 54$$
$$9y = 126$$
$$y = 14$$

32. 24

Difficulty: Medium

Category: Heart of Algebra / Linear Equations

Strategic Advice: The place where the line crosses the y-axis is the y-intercept, or b when the equation is written in slope-intercept form ($y = mx + b$).

Getting to the Answer: Rewrite the equation in slope-intercept form using inverse operations.

$$4x - \frac{1}{2}y = -12$$

$$-\frac{1}{2}y = -4x - 12$$

$$-2\left(-\frac{1}{2}y\right) = -2(-4x - 12)$$

$$y = 8x + 24$$

The y-intercept is 24.

Because the y-intercept of a graph is always of the form $(0, y)$, you could also substitute 0 for x and solve for y.

CHAPTER 2

PREPARE

1. C
Difficulty: Easy

Category: Heart of Algebra / Linear Equations

Strategic Advice: Don't just use substitution! Find a way to strategically use the second equation by writing the first equation to take advantage of that.

Getting to the Answer: Rewrite the first equation so that $(r + s)$ is a component. First, express $3r$ as $r + 2r$. Then factor a 2 out of the left-hand side to get $r + 2(r + s) = 24$. Now you can substitute 12 in for $(r + s)$, simplify, and solve for r. Be careful. The question is asking for $r + 6$, so A is a trap corresponding to the value of r alone. Instead, (C) is correct.

2. B
Difficulty: Medium

Category: Heart of Algebra / Linear Equations

Strategic Advice: Beware of math autopilot with this one. The question states that there are infinitely many solutions; use that to your advantage.

Getting to the Answer: A system of equations with infinitely many solutions means that when the equations are in the same arrangement (as they are here), you can manipulate one to get the other. Examining the right sides of the equations, you see that $40 \times 40 = 1,600$; therefore, multiplying the top equation by 40 will get you 1,600 on the right: $5q + 8s = 1,600$. The first equation is now identical to the second equation, meaning z must be 5, which is (B).

3. B
Difficulty: Easy

Category: Heart of Algebra / Linear Equations

Strategic Advice: Substitution will get you the answer, but there's a faster route.

Getting to the Answer: Looking at the coefficients of the two equations, you'll notice that multiplying the second equation by -3 will allow you to eliminate b:

$$\begin{array}{r} 6a + 6b = 30 \\ + \ -9a - 6b = -42 \\ \hline -3a + 0b = -12 \end{array}$$

Simplifying gives $a = 4$. (B) is the only choice that contains this value, so it is correct.

4. D
Difficulty: Easy

Category: Heart of Algebra / Linear Equations

Strategic Advice: Read the question carefully to determine what you need to find.

Getting to the Answer: The question asks for $b + c$, so don't waste your time finding the variables individually. After rearranging the equations so that variables and constants are aligned, you can add them together:

$$\begin{array}{r} -2b + 5c = 15 \\ + \ 3b - 4c = 12 \\ \hline b + c = 27 \end{array}$$

This matches (D).

5. D

Difficulty: Medium

Category: Heart of Algebra / Linear Equations

Strategic Advice: Another wordy question means another chance to use the Kaplan Strategy for Translating English into Math.

Getting to the Answer: First, define your variables logically: d for hot dogs, b for hamburgers. You're given the cost of each, as well as the number of snacks sold and the total revenue generated. Next, write the system of equations that represents the information given:

$$d + b = 27$$
$$3.5d + 5b = 118.5$$

Multiplying the top equation by -5 allows you to solve for d by combination:

$$+\quad\begin{array}{r} -5d - 5b = -135 \\ 3.5d + 5b = 118.5 \\ \hline -1.5d + 0b = -16.5 \end{array}$$

Solving for d gives 11, which eliminates choices A and B. Plugging this value back into the first equation allows you to find b, which equals 16. This matches (D).

6. C

Difficulty: Medium

Category: Heart of Algebra / Linear Equations

Strategic Advice: Take advantage of questions like this that do not require you to actually solve a system of equations. Instead, construct the appropriate equations as quickly as possible.

Getting to the Answer: Because you're given the variables, the only thing left for you to do here is figure out how they relate to one another. There will be two equations: one involving the total number of aircraft that landed and one involving the total amount of landing fees collected. Add together both aircraft to get the former: $p + c = 312$. Think carefully about which type of plane should be associated with which fee to get the latter. Commercial airliners are much more expensive; hence, your second equation should be $281c + 31p = 47,848$. Only (C) contains both of those equations.

PRACTICE

7. A

Difficulty: Medium

Category: Heart of Algebra / Linear Equations

Strategic Advice: Use the Kaplan Strategy for Translating English into Math to make sense of the prose.

Getting to the Answer: First, define your variables: t for texts and p for pictures are good choices. Breaking apart the question, you know this student sent a total of 75 texts and pictures. You're also told each text costs $0.10 and each picture is $0.15, as well as the fact that the bill is $8.90. You'll have two equations: one relating the number of texts and pictures and a second relating the costs associated with each.

$$t + p = 75$$
$$0.1t + 0.15p = 8.9$$

Multiplying the top equation by -0.1 allows you to solve for p by combination:

$$+\quad\begin{array}{r} -0.1t - 0.1p = -7.5 \\ 0.1t + 0.15p = 8.9 \\ \hline 0t + 0.05p = 1.4 \end{array}$$

You'll find $p = 28$. But you're not done yet; you're asked for the difference between the text and picture count. Plug 28 in for p in the first equation and then solve for t to get $t = 47$. Subtracting 28 from 47 yields 19, which is (A).

8. 51

Difficulty: Medium

Category: Heart of Algebra / Linear Equations

Strategic Advice: This question only looks harder than others you've seen. In fact, the same methods you've used for other systems of equations will still work here.

Getting to the Answer: As mentioned, creativity is key to getting the right answer. Instead of multiplying just one equation by a factor, you'll need to multiply both by a factor. Which factors do you pick? It depends on which variable you want to eliminate. Suppose you want to eliminate x. The coefficients on the x terms are 2 and 5, so you need to multiply the equations by numbers that will give you −10 and 10 as your new x term coefficients. To do this, use −5 for the first equation and 2 for the second:

$$-5(2x + 5y = 49)$$
$$2(5x + 3y = 94)$$

Combine as usual:

$$-10x - 25y = -245$$
$$+ \quad 10x + 6y = 188$$
$$\overline{\quad 0x - 19y = -57}$$

Solving for y gives you 3. Next, plug 3 back in for y in either equation and solve for x, which equals 17. Multiplying x and y together gives you 51, the correct answer.

PERFORM

9. A

Difficulty: Hard

Category: Heart of Algebra / Linear Equations

Strategic Advice: Remember, a system of equations with no solution should describe two parallel lines. The coefficients in front of the

variables should be the same. Only the constant should be different.

Getting to the Answer: The easiest way to make the constants the same is to look at the second equation. Clearly, multiplying it by 40 would make the coefficients in front of x the same: $8x + 40zy = 20$. Now equate the coefficients in front of y: $4y = 40zy$. Solve for z, to reveal that $z = \dfrac{1}{10}$, (A).

10. 14

Difficulty: Medium

Category: Heart of Algebra / Linear Equations

Strategic Advice: Resist the urge to use substitution by default; there's an easier route.

Getting to the Answer: Using combination will make life easier. First, add both equations together:

$$x + 6 = 17$$
$$+ \quad y + 9 = 12$$
$$\overline{\quad x + y + 15 = 29}$$

Further simplification reveals:

$$x + y + 15 = 29$$
$$x + y = 14$$

Because x and y are both integers, that means the value of $x + y$ is 14. Grid in a 14 and move on to the next problem.

11. C

Difficulty: Medium

Category: Heart of Algebra / Linear Equations

Strategic Advice: Use the Kaplan Strategy for Word Problems to extract what you need.

Getting to the Answer: First, define the variables using letters that make sense. Let's assign children the variable c and adults the variable a. Now you can break the word problem into shorter phrases: Children's tickets sold for $8; adults' tickets sold for $12; 60 people attended the concert; $624 was collected in ticket money. Translating each phrase into a math expression will get us the components of our system of equations.

Children's tickets cost $8 → $8c$

Adult tickets cost $12 → $12a$

60 people attended the concert →
$c + a = 60$

$624 was collected in ticket money →
Total $ = 624

Putting the expressions together gets your system of equations.

$$c + a = 60$$
$$8c + 12a = 624$$

Solving for the variables using combination or substitution gives $a = 36$ and $c = 24$. Remember, the question asks you for the product of the number of children and the number of adults: $36 \times 24 = 864$, which corresponds to (C).

EXTRA PRACTICE

1. C
Difficulty: Easy

Category: Heart of Algebra / Systems of Linear Equations

Strategic Advice: Translate from English to math. One equation should represent the total *number* of meals ordered, while the other equation should represent the *cost* of the meals.

Getting to the Answer: The number of people who ordered chicken plus the number who ordered vegetarian equals the total number of people, 62, so one equation is $c + v = 62$. This means you can eliminate A. Now write the cost equation: Cost per chicken dish (12.75) times number of dishes (c) plus cost per vegetarian dish (9.5) times number of dishes (v) equals the total bill (725.25). The cost equation is $12.75c + 9.5v = 725.25$. Together, these two equations form the system in (C).

2. A
Difficulty: Easy

Category: Heart of Algebra / Systems of Linear Equations

Strategic Advice: Quickly compare the two equations. The system is already set up perfectly to solve using elimination. Be careful! Before you select your answer, check that you answered the right question (the y-coordinate of the solution).

Getting to the Answer: Add the two equations to cancel $-4y$ and $4y$. Then solve the resulting equation for x. Remember, the question asks for the y-coordinate of the solution, so you will need to substitute x back into one of the original equations and solve for y.

$$
\begin{array}{ll}
2x - 4y = 14 & 2(5) - 4y = 14 \\
5x + 4y = 21 & 10 - 4y = 14 \\
\hline
7x = 35 & -4y = 4 \\
x = 5 & y = -1
\end{array}
$$

3. C
Difficulty: Easy

Category: Heart of Algebra / Systems of Linear Equations

Strategic Advice: Graphically, the solution to a system of linear equations is the point where the lines intersect. Be careful! Before you select your answer, check that you answered the right question (the sum of $x + y$).

Getting to the Answer: Jot down the coordinates of the point on the graph where the two lines intersect, $(-1, 2)$. The question asks for the sum of $x + y$, so add the coordinates to get $-1 + 2 = 1$.

4. D
Difficulty: Medium

Category: Heart of Algebra / Systems of Linear Equations

Strategic Advice: Because x has a coefficient of 1 in the second equation, solve the system using substitution. Before you select your answer, check that you answered the right question (what is the difference of x and y).

Getting to the Answer: First, solve the second equation for x. Then substitute that value for x into the first equation and solve for y.

$$x = 6y + 10$$
$$2(6y + 10) + 3y = 8 - y$$
$$12y + 20 + 3y = 8 - y$$
$$15y + 20 = 8 - y$$
$$16y = -12$$
$$y = -\frac{3}{4}$$

Next, substitute this value back into $x = 6y + 10$ and simplify.

$$x = 6\left(-\frac{3}{4}\right) + 10$$
$$= -\frac{9}{2} + \frac{20}{2}$$
$$= \frac{11}{2}$$

Finally, subtract $x - y$ to find the difference.

$$\frac{11}{2} - \left(-\frac{3}{4}\right) = \frac{22}{4} + \frac{3}{4} = \frac{25}{4}$$

5. A

Difficulty: Medium

Category: Heart of Algebra / Systems of Linear Equations

Strategic Advice: Write a system of equations with r being the cost of the radio in dollars and t equaling the cost of the television in dollars.

Getting to the Answer: Translate English into math to write two equations: A television costs $25 less than twice the cost of the radio, or $t = 2r - 25$; together, a radio and a television cost $200, so $r + t = 200$.

The system is:

$$t = 2r - 25$$
$$r + t = 200$$

The top equation is already solved for t, so substitute $2r - 25$ into the second equation for t.

$$r + 2r - 25 = 200$$
$$3r - 25 = 200$$
$$3r = 225$$
$$r = 75$$

The radio costs $75, so the television costs $2(75) - 25 = 150 - 25 = \$125$. This means the television costs $125 - 75 = $50 more than the radio.

6. C

Difficulty: Medium

Category: Heart of Algebra / Systems of Linear Equations

Strategic Advice: Write a system of equations with t being the cost of a turkey burger and w equaling the cost of a bottle of water. Before you choose your answer, check that you answered the right question.

Getting to the Answer: Translate English into math to write two equations: The first statement is translated as $2t + w = \$3.25$ and the second as $3t + w = \$4.50$. The system is:

$$2t + w = 3.25$$
$$3t + w = 4.50$$

You could solve the system using substitution, but elimination is quicker in this question because subtracting the first equation from the second eliminates w and you can solve for t:

$$3t + w = 4.50$$
$$\underline{-(2t + w = 3.25)}$$
$$t = 1.25$$

Substitute this value for t in the first equation and solve for w:

$$2(1.25) + w = 3.25$$
$$2.50 + w = 3.25$$
$$w = 0.75$$

Two bottles of water would cost $2 \times \$0.75 = \$1.50$.

7. A

Difficulty: Hard

Category: Heart of Algebra / Systems of Linear Equations

Strategic Advice: The easiest way to answer this question is to think about the graphs of the equations. Graphically, a system of linear equations that has no solution indicates two parallel lines or, in other words, two lines that have the same slope. Write each of the equations in slope-intercept form ($y = mx + b$), and set their slopes (m) equal to each other to solve for w.

Getting to the Answer:

First equation:

$$3x - 4y = 10$$
$$-4y = -3x + 10$$
$$y = \frac{3}{4}x - \frac{5}{2}$$

Second equation:

$$6x + wy = 16$$
$$wy = -6x + 16$$
$$y = -\frac{6}{w}x + \frac{16}{w}$$

Set the slopes equal:

$$\frac{3}{4} = -\frac{6}{w}$$
$$3w = -24$$
$$w = -8$$

8. B

Difficulty: Hard

Category: Heart of Algebra / Systems of Linear Equations

Strategic Advice: A system of linear equations has infinitely many solutions if both lines in the system have the same slope and the same y-intercept (in other words, they are the same line).

Getting to the Answer: Write each of the equations in slope-intercept form ($y = mx + b$). Their slopes should be the same. To find c, set the y-intercepts (b) equal to each other and solve.

Before rewriting the equations, multiply the first equation by 6 to make it easier to manipulate.

First equation:

$$6 \bullet \left[\frac{1}{2}x - \frac{2}{3}y = c \right]$$
$$3x - 4y = 6c$$
$$-4y = -3x + 6c$$
$$y = \frac{3}{4}x - \frac{3}{2}c$$

Second equation:

$$6x - 8y = -1$$
$$-8y = -6x - 1$$
$$y = \frac{3}{4}x + \frac{1}{8}$$

Set the y-intercepts equal:

$$-\frac{3}{2}c = \frac{1}{8}$$
$$-24c = 2$$
$$c = -\frac{1}{12}$$

9. C

Difficulty: Hard

Category: Heart of Algebra / Systems of Linear Equations

Strategic Advice: Create a system of two linear equations where x represents tables with 2 chairs and y represents tables with 4 chairs.

Getting to the Answer: The first equation should represent the total number of *tables*, each with 2 or 4 chairs, or $x + y = 25$. The second equation should represent the total number of *chairs*. Because x represents tables with 2 chairs and y represents tables with 4 chairs, the second equation should be $2x + 4y = 86$. Now solve the system using substitution. Solve the first equation for either variable, and substitute the result into the second equation.

$$x + y = 25$$
$$x = 25 - y$$

$$2(25 - y) + 4y = 86$$
$$50 - 2y + 4y = 86$$
$$2y = 36$$
$$y = 18$$

There are 18 tables with 4 chairs each. This is what the question asks for. Thus, you don't need to find the value of x.

CHAPTER 3

PREPARE

1. A
Difficulty: Easy

Category: Problem Solving / Data Analysis / Rates, Ratios, Proportions, Percentages

Strategic Advice: Map out your route from starting units to end units, being mindful of the fact that you have area units.

Getting to the Answer: Your starting quantity is in ft^2, and your desired quantity should be in yd^2. The lone conversion factor you need is 3 ft = 1 yd. Setting up your route to yd^2, you get $\frac{81\ ft^2}{1} \times \frac{1\ yd}{3\ ft} \times \frac{1\ yd}{3\ ft} = \frac{81}{9} yd^2 = 9\ yd^2$, which matches (A).

2. 27
Difficulty: Easy

Category: Problem Solving / Data Analysis / Rates, Ratios, Proportions, Percentages / Extended Thinking

Strategic Advice: Keep in mind what you're being asked, resisting the urge to get every piece of information involved in the first step if you don't need them all.

Getting to the Answer: Mr. Black begins his journey to New York at 7:00 AM ET and arrives at 8:15 AM ET, meaning his time in transit is 75 minutes. Using the DIRT equation, you can find Ms. Weiss's travel time: 20 mi = 25 mi/h × t. Simplifying gives $t = 0.8$ h = 48 min. Taking the difference yields 75 − 48 = 27 minutes.

3. 5.7
Difficulty: Medium

Strategic Advice: Remember to account for all discrepancies that will alter the final answer.

Getting to the Answer: The question supplies Dr. Grey's distance traveled and flight speed, making this a great time to use the DIRT equation again. Plugging in what you know, you see 830 mi = 332 mi/h × t. Solving for t yields $t = 2.5$ h = 2 h 30 min. Now add this to the delay-adjusted departure time, 9:15 AM CT, to get 11:45 AM CT. Tack on an extra hour for the time zone change to yield 12:45 PM ET. You know from part 1 that Ms. Weiss spends 48 minutes in transit; adding this figure to her 6:15 AM ET departure time gives 7:03 AM ET. Determine the difference between this time and Dr. Grey's arrival time; you'll get 5 h 42 min. Converting to hours gives your answer, 5.7 h.

4. D
Difficulty: Medium

Category: Problem Solving / Data Analysis Rates, Ratios, Proportions, Percentages

Strategic Advice: Look for a way to consolidate the two given ratios into one, and ensure you provide the ratio requested.

Getting to the Answer: The dioxane:water ratio is 7:3, and the water:methanol ratio is 5:2. They cannot be combined as they are, so you need a common factor to link them. Water is the term common to both ratios; look for the least common multiple of the water components, 3 and 5. Using 15 as the common multiple, determine factors that, when multiplied by the ratios, turn the water components into 15. For dioxane:water, the calculation is 5 × (7:3) = 35:15. Repeating for water:methanol, you get 3 × (5:2) = 15:6. The combined ratio dioxane:water:methanol becomes 35:15:6, making dioxane:methanol 35:6. The question asks for the ratio of methanol to dioxane, so flip your ratio to get 6:35, which is (D).

5. C

Difficulty: Easy

Category: Problem Solving / Data Analysis / Rates, Ratios, Proportions, Percentages

Strategic Advice: Use the percentage three-part formula to find what you need.

Getting to the Answer: Starting with the 14-gallon tank, plug your known values into the three-part formula: 15% × 14 = ? → 0.15 × 14 = 2.1 gal ethanol. Repeat for the smaller tank: 6% × 10 = ? → 0.06 × 10 = 0.6 gal ethanol. The question asks how many times more ethanol is in the larger tank, so divide the quantities: $\frac{2.1}{0.6} = 3.5$. This matches (C).

6. 24.9

Difficulty: Easy

Category: Problem Solving / Data Analysis / Rates, Ratios, Proportions, Percentages/ Extended Thinking

Strategic Advice: When you're asked to find the percent of something, think three-part formula.

Getting to the Answer: First, find the annual interest earned by each account. The regular account equation is 0.0025 × 5,000 = 12.5; the student's is 0.0042 × 1,000 = 4.2. Multiplying each number by 3 gives $37.50 in interest for the regular account and $12.60 for the student account. Taking the difference gives $37.50 – $12.60 = $24.90. Grid in as 24.9.

7. 2976

Difficulty: Hard

Strategic Advice: Setting up a system of equations will be very helpful here.

Getting to the Answer: An account's interest earned depends on the balance, so assemble an equation for each scenario. The regular account can be represented by $y = 0.0025x$ where $x \geq 5,000$, and the student account is shown by the equation $y = 0.0042x$ where $x \geq 1,000$. You know the annual interest on the regular account from part 1 ($12.50); all that's left is to find at what value of x will y equal 12.5. Plugging in 12.5 for y, you get 12.5 = 0.0042x. Solving for x gives 2,976.19, which, rounded to the nearest dollar, becomes 2976.

PRACTICE

8. D

Difficulty: Easy

Category: Problem Solving / Data Analysis / Rates, Ratios, Proportions, Percentages

Strategic Advice: The unit "mpg" (miles per gallon) is a rate, so use the DIRT equation.

Getting to the Answer: Determine the fuel used during each leg of Jack's trip. Plugging in values for the first leg, you get 180 mi = 40 mi/gal × t → t = 4.5 gal. The second leg: 105 mi = 35 mi/gal × t → t = 3 gal. Added together, you get 7.5 gal fuel used, which matches (D).

9. B

Difficulty: Medium

Category: Problem Solving / Data Analysis / Rates, Ratios, Proportions, Percentages

Strategic Advice: Remember to avoid merely adding the percentages together. Tackle each change individually.

Getting to the Answer: You're not given a concrete share count in the question, so assume the client starts with 100. To save a step with each change, calculate the shares left instead of the shares gained or lost. The first change is –25%; the number of shares left is 75% × 100 = ? → 0.75 × 100 = 75. The second change is +10%, which corresponds to 110% × 75 = ? → 1.1 × 75 = 82.5 shares. The final change is +50%, which means there are now 150% × 82.5 = ? → 1.5 × 82.5 = 123.75 shares. The percent change is $\frac{23.75}{100} \times 100 = 23.75\%$; rounded to the nearest percent, you get 24%, which is (B).

10. 432

Difficulty: Medium

Category: Problem Solving / Data Analysis / Rates, Ratios, Proportions, Percentages / Extended Thinking

Strategic Advice: Determine the number of times the pattern repeats, and then find the corresponding number of green tiles.

Getting to the Answer: The question states that the ratio of green to blue tiles is 5:3 and that the pattern appears once per square foot. There are 12 × 18 or 216 square feet in the mosaic, meaning there are 5 × 216 or 1,080 green tiles and 3 × 216 or 648 blue tiles. Taking the difference gives 1,080 – 648 = 432 more green tiles than blue.

11. 324

Difficulty: Medium

Strategic Advice: Use the blue tile count from the previous question to determine the new green tile count.

Getting to the Answer: The green tile count changes in part 2, so determine that first. The blue tile count stays constant, so you can just

multiply 2 × 216 to get 432 green tiles needed with the new pattern. The ratio of red to green tiles should be 3:4; you can use this in conjunction with the new green tile count in a proportion to find the number of red tiles needed: $\frac{red}{green} = \frac{3}{4} = \frac{r}{432}$. Cross-multiplication gives 1,296 = 4r; solving for r yields 324 red tiles.

PERFORM

12. A

Difficulty: Medium

Category: Problem Solving / Data Analysis / Rates, Ratios, Proportions, Percentages

Strategic Advice: Draw diagrams to make sense of the given situation and aid with solving.

Getting to the Answer: Your diagram should look similar to what's shown:

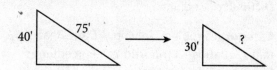

You'll notice you have a pair of similar triangles, which means you can use a proportion to answer the question. First, find the correct height by taking 25% of 40, which is 10, and deducting that from 40 to give 30. Keeping the heights on the left of your proportion and hypotenuses on the right, you have $\frac{30}{40} = \frac{x}{75}$. Reduce the left to get $\frac{3}{4} = \frac{x}{75}$, then cross-multiply to eliminate the fractions: 225 = 4x. Solving for x yields 56.25. But don't stop yet: The question asks for the difference in escalator length, not the corrected length. Subtract 56.25 from 75 to get 18.75, which matches (A).

$$z^2 + 8z - 20 = 0$$

$$(z + 10)(z - 2) = 0$$

Keep in mind that while z is equal to -10 and 2, the problem only asks for the positive value, which is (A).

11. B
Difficulty: Hard

Category: Passport to Advanced Math / Quadratics

Strategic Advice: Consider Picking Numbers to quickly get to the answer.

Getting to the Answer: Because you have variables, you might think to pick numbers. Unless you coincidentally pick the "right" numbers, you won't actually get an answer choice, but you'll be able to confirm what happens with those numbers. Given the rules of the problem, you might pick $a = -2$ and $b = 3$. Setting up the binomials and performing FOIL, you get:

$$(x + 2)(x - 3) = x^2 - x - 6$$

Many choices look similar. What makes this hard is that when you naturally set up the binomials, you assume the parabola is opening up. If you multiply the entire function by -1, it reflects about the x-axis, but because the solutions are on the x-axis, they will stay the same. The correct answer is (B).

12. 0
Difficulty: Easy

Category: Passport to Advanced Math / Quadratics

Strategic Advice: Stick to your tools for quadratics based on what you are given.

Getting to the Answer: All the problem is really asking you to do is solve for the zeros and subtract them.

$$g(x) = -2x^2 + 16x - 32$$

$$0 = -2x^2 + 16x - 32$$

$$0 = x^2 - 8x + 16$$

$$0 = (x - 4)(x - 4)$$

The quadratic only has one unique solution, so the positive difference between the two is actually 0.

13. C
Difficulty: Medium

Category: Passport to Advanced Math / Quadratics

Strategic Advice: You know that an axis of symmetry splits the parabola in half and travels through the vertex.

Getting to the Answer: All you need to do is solve for the x-coordinate of the vertex, which can be accomplished using the formula for h:

$$h = \frac{-b}{2a} = \frac{-4}{2(2)} = \frac{-4}{4} = -1$$

Thus, the answer is (C).

EXTRA PRACTICE

1. C

Difficulty: Easy

Category: Passport to Advanced Math / Quadratics

Strategic Advice: Taking the square root is the inverse operation of squaring, and both sides of this equation are already perfect squares, so take their square roots. Then solve the resulting equations. Remember, there will be two equations to solve.

Getting to the Answer:

$$(x+1)^2 = \frac{1}{25}$$

$$\sqrt{(x+1)^2} = \frac{\sqrt{1}}{\sqrt{25}}$$

$$x+1 = \pm\frac{1}{5}$$

$$x = -1 \pm \frac{1}{5}$$

Now simplify each equation: $x = -1 + \frac{1}{5} = -\frac{5}{5} + \frac{1}{5} = -\frac{4}{5}$ and $x = -1 - \frac{1}{5} = -\frac{5}{5} - \frac{1}{5} = -\frac{6}{5}$.

2. B

Difficulty: Easy

Category: Passport to Advanced Math / Quadratics

Strategic Advice: Use the factored form to find the x-intercepts and the standard form to find the y-intercept.

Getting to the Answer: From the factored form of the equation, you can see that the values of –2 and 7 would make y equal 0, so the x-intercepts are –2 and 7. This means you can eliminate A and C. From the standard form of the equation, you can see that the y-intercept is –14 because $0^2 - 2(0) - 14 = -14$, so (B) is correct.

3. D

Difficulty: Easy

Category: Passport to Advanced Math / Quadratics

Strategic Advice: Quadratic equations can be written in several forms, each of which reveals something special about the graph. For example, the vertex form of a quadratic equation $(y = a(x - h)^2 + k)$ gives the minimum or maximum value of the function (it's k), while the standard form $(y = ax^2 + bx + c)$ reveals the y-intercept (it's c).

Getting to the Answer: The factored form of a quadratic equation reveals the solutions to the equation, which graphically represent the x-intercepts. Choice (D) is the only equation written in factored form and therefore must be correct. You can set each factor equal to 0 and quickly solve to find that the x-intercepts of the graph are $x = -\frac{4}{3}$ and $x = 2$, which agree with the graph.

4. B

Difficulty: Medium

Category: Passport to Advanced Math / Quadratics

Strategic Advice: When finding solutions to a quadratic equation, always start by rewriting the equation to make it equal 0 (unless both sides of the equation are already perfect squares). Then take a peek at the answer choices—if they are all nice numbers, then factoring is probably the quickest method for solving the equation. If the answers include messy fractions or square roots, then using the quadratic formula may be a better choice.

Getting to the Answer: To make the equation equal 0, subtract 48 from both sides to get $x^2 + 8x - 48 = 0$. The answer choices are all integers, so factor the equation. Look for two numbers whose product is −48 and whose sum is 8. The two numbers are −4 and 12, so the factors are $(x − 4)$ and $(x + 12)$. Set each factor equal to 0 and solve to find that $x = 4$ and $x = −12$. The question states that $x > 0$, so x must equal 4. Before selecting an answer, don't forget to check that you answered the right question—the question asks for the value of $x − 5$, not just x, so the correct answer is $4 − 5 = −1$.

If this question appeared in the Calculator section of the test, you could also graph the equation in your graphing calculator and use the "zero" function to find the solutions.

5. B
Difficulty: Medium

Category: Passport to Advanced Math / Quadratics

Strategic Advice: Examine the graph—there are no grid lines and no numbers along the axes. This means that arriving at the correct answer will require some thought.

Getting to the Answer: According to the graph, one x-intercept is to the left of the y-axis, and the other is to the right. This tells you that one value of x is positive, while the other is negative, so you can immediately eliminate choices A and C (both factors have the same sign). To choose between choices B and D, find the x-intercepts by setting each factor equal to 0 and solving for x. In choice B, the x-intercepts are 7 and −3. In choice D, the x-intercepts are 1 and −10. Choice (B) is correct because the x-intercepts are exactly 10 units apart, while the x-intercepts in choice D are 11 units apart.

6. B
Difficulty: Medium

Category: Passport to Advanced Math / Quadratics

Strategic Advice: There are no coefficients (numbers) in the equation, so you'll need to think about how the values of a, b, and c affect the graph. You'll also need to recall certain vocabulary. For example, *increasing* means rising from left to right while *decreasing* means falling from left to right, and *zero* is another way of saying x-intercept.

Getting to the Answer: Compare each statement to the graph to determine whether it is true, eliminating choices as you go. Remember, you are looking for the statement that is *not* true. The parabola opens downward, so the value of a must be negative, which means you can eliminate A. When a quadratic equation is written in standard form, c is the y-intercept of the parabola. According to the graph, the y-intercept is above the x-axis and is therefore positive, so the statement in (B) is false, making it the correct answer. Move on to the next question. (Choice C is true because the graph rises from left to right until you get to $x = 3$, and then it falls. Choice D is true because the zeros are the same as the x-intercepts, and the graph does intersect the x-axis at −2 and 8.)

7. C
Difficulty: Medium

Category: Passport to Advanced Math / Quadratics

Strategic Advice: When a quadratic equation is written in vertex form, $y = a(x − h)^2 + k$, the minimum value (or the maximum value if $a < 0$) is given by k, and the axis of symmetry is given by the equation $x = h$.

Getting to the Answer: The question states that the minimum of the parabola is −3, so look for an equation where k is −3. You can eliminate choices A and B because k is +2 in both equations. The question also states that the axis of symmetry is 2, so h must be 2. Be careful—this is tricky. The equation in choice D is not correct because the vertex form of a parabola has a negative before the h, so $(x + 2)$ actually means $(x – (–2))$, and the axis of symmetry would be –2. This means (C) is correct.

You could also graph each equation in your graphing calculator to see which one matches the criteria given in the question, but this is likely to use up valuable time on Test Day.

8. C

Difficulty: Medium

Category: Passport to Advanced Math / Quadratics

Strategic Advice: Equations that are equivalent have the same solutions, so you are looking for the equation that is simply written in a different form. You could expand each of the equations in the answer choices, but unless you get lucky, this will use up quite a bit of time.

Getting to the Answer: The answer choices are written in vertex form, so use the method of completing the square to make the equation given in the question match. First, subtract the constant, 17, from both sides of the equation. To complete the square on the right-hand side, find $\left(\dfrac{b}{2}\right)^2 = \left(\dfrac{6}{2}\right)^2 = 3^2 = 9$, and add the result to both sides of the equation.

$$y = x^2 + 6x + 17$$

$$y - 17 = x^2 + 6x$$

$$y - 17 + 9 = x^2 + 6x + 9$$

$$y - 8 = x^2 + 6x + 9$$

Next, factor the right-hand side of the equation (which should be a perfect square trinomial), and rewrite it as a square.

$$y - 8 = (x + 3)(x + 3)$$

$$y - 8 = (x + 3)^2$$

Finally, solve for y.

$$y = (x + 3)^2 + 8$$

9. A

Difficulty: Medium

Category: Passport to Advanced Math / Quadratics

Strategic Advice: When a quadratic equation is written in vertex form, $y = a(x - h)^2 + k$, the axis of symmetry is given by the equation $x = h$.

Getting to the Answer: Don't let the different letters in the equation confuse you. The letter p is simply being used in place of h. Because the h (in the vertex form of a quadratic) has a negative in front of it, the value of h is the opposite sign of the operation performed on h. Here, h (and therefore p) is –5 because $(x - (–5)) = (x + 5)$. So the axis of symmetry is $x = –5$.

10. B

Difficulty: Medium

Category: Passport to Advanced Math / Quadratics

Strategic Advice: Even though one of the equations in this system is not linear, you can still solve the system using substitution.

Getting to the Answer: You already know that y is equal to $3x$, so substitute $3x$ for y in the second equation. Don't forget that when you square $3x$, you must square both the coefficient and the variable.

$$x^2 - y^2 = -288$$

$$x^2 - (3x)^2 = -288$$

$$x^2 - 9x^2 = -288$$

$$-8x^2 = -288$$

$$x^2 = 36$$

The question asks for the value of x^2, not x, so there is no need to take the square root of 36 to find the value of x.

11. A

Difficulty: Medium

Category: Passport to Advanced Math / Quadratics

Strategic Advice: The roots of an equation are the same as its solutions. Take a peek at the answer choices—they contain radicals, so you can either complete the square or solve the equation using the quadratic formula, whichever you are more comfortable using.

Getting to the Answer: The equation is already written in the form $y = ax^2 + bx + c$ and the coefficients are fairly small, so using the quadratic formula is probably the quickest method. Jot down the values that you'll need: $a = 1$, $b = 8$, and $c = -3$. Then substitute these values into the formula and simplify:

$$x = \frac{-b \pm \sqrt{b^2 - 4ac}}{2a}$$
$$= \frac{-(8) \pm \sqrt{(8)^2 - 4(1)(-3)}}{2(1)}$$
$$= \frac{-8 \pm \sqrt{64 + 12}}{2}$$
$$= \frac{-8 \pm \sqrt{76}}{2}$$

This is not one of the answer choices, which tells you that you'll need to simplify the radical, but before you do, you can eliminate C and D because $\frac{-8}{2}$ is -4. To simplify the radical, look for a perfect square that divides into 76 and take its square root.

$$x = \frac{-8 \pm \sqrt{4 \times 19}}{2}$$
$$= \frac{-8 \pm 2\sqrt{19}}{2}$$
$$= -4 \pm \sqrt{19}$$

12. D

Difficulty: Hard

Category: Passport to Advanced Math / Quadratics

Strategic Advice: Look for an equation that has a maximum value that is less than the one shown in the graph (because Meagan's ball did not go as high). You do not need to graph the equations to determine this. In fact, this question is likely to be in the non-calculator section of the test, so becoming familiar with the vertex form of a quadratic equation will you serve you well on Test Day.

Getting to the Answer: The maximum value shown in the graph is about 31 feet. When a quadratic equation is written in vertex form, $y = a(x - h)^2 + k$, the maximum value is given by k, so check C and D first because they will be the easiest to compare to the graph. In C, k is 35, which is greater than 31 and therefore not correct. In (D), k is 28, which is less than 31 and therefore the correct answer. You do not need to examine the other two equations. Note: If all of the answer choices had been given in standard form, you would have needed to convert each one to vertex form, or you could have substituted the result of finding $\frac{-b}{2a}$ into each equation to find the maximum value.

13. A

Difficulty: Hard

Category: Passport to Advanced Math / Quadratics

Strategic Advice: This is a challenging question, so save it for last on Test Day. To get a picture of what is going on, you could draw a quick sketch using the information given in the question and what you know about quadratic equations. If you can identify the solutions (zeros) and one other point on the graph, you'll be able to work out the equation.

Getting to the Answer: First, determine the solutions of the equation by thinking about where the x-intercepts, or the zeros, of its graph would be. Because the lead ball is thrown from ground level, the graph would begin at the origin, so one solution is 0. The ball returns to the ground, or has a height of 0 again, at 150 feet, so the other solution is 150. Write the solutions as factors: $x - 0$ and $x - 150$. Then write the equation as the product of the two factors and use the distributive property (or FOIL) to multiply them together: $y = (x - 0)(x - 150) = x(x - 150) = x^2 - 150x$. The general equation is $y = a(x^2 - 150x)$. To find the value of a, use another point that satisfies the equation or, in other words, lies on its graph. Because the graph of a parabola is symmetrical, the ball reaches its maximum height, 45 feet, exactly halfway between the two zeros, 0 and 150, which is 75. Therefore, another point on the graph is (75, 45). Substitute the x- and y-values into the equation and solve for a.

$$y = a(x^2 - 150x)$$

$$45 = a(75^2 - 150(75))$$

$$45 = a(5,625 - 11,250)$$

$$45 = -5,625a$$

$$-0.008 = a$$

The equation is $y = -0.008(x^2 - 150x)$ or $y = -0.008x^2 + 1.2x$.

If you have time, you could also graph each equation in your graphing calculator and find the one that has a maximum value of 45. Choice (A) is the only equation for which this is true.

14. A

Difficulty: Hard

Category: Passport to Advanced Math / Quadratics

Strategic Advice: To answer this question, you need to recall just about everything you've learned about quadratic graphs. The equation is given in vertex form ($y = a(x - h)^2 + k$), which reveals the vertex (h, k), the direction in which the parabola opens (upward when $a > 0$ and downward when $a < 0$), the axis of symmetry ($x = h$), and the minimum/maximum value of the function (k).

Getting to the Answer: Start by comparing each answer choice to the equation, $y = -2(x - 6)^2 + 5$. The only choice that you cannot immediately compare is A because vertex form does not readily reveal the y-intercept, so start with B. Don't forget, you are looking for the statement that is *not* true. Choice B: The axis of symmetry is given by $x = h$, and h is 6, so this statement is true and therefore *not* correct. Choice C: The vertex is given by (h, k), so the vertex is indeed (6, 5) and this choice is not correct. Choice D: The value of a is -2, which indicates that the parabola opens downward, so this choice is also not correct. That means (A) must be the correct answer. To confirm, you could substitute 0 for x in the equation to find the y-intercept.

$$y = -2(x - 6)^2 + 5$$

$$= -2(0 - 6)^2 + 5$$

$$= -2(-6)^2 + 5$$

$$= -2(36) + 5$$

$$= -72 + 5$$

$$= -67$$

The y-intercept is (0, -67), not (0, 5), so the statement is false.

15. D

Difficulty: Hard

Category: Passport to Advanced Math / Quadratics

Strategic Advice: Trying to answer this question algebraically would take entirely too much time. You are not expected to solve each system. Instead, think about it graphically. The solution to a system of equations is the point(s) where their graphs intersect, so graph each pair of equations in your graphing calculator, and look for the ones that intersect at $x = -8$ and $x = -3$.

Getting to the Answer: The graphs of the equations in A don't intersect at all, so you can eliminate A right away. The graphs in B and C intersect, but one of the points of intersection for each pair is positive, which means (D) must be correct. The graph looks like the following:

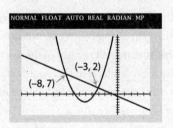

way, don't forget that you must first set the whole equation equal to 0.

$$x + 1 = \frac{1}{2}x^2 - x - \frac{3}{2}$$
$$2(x + 1) = 2\left(\frac{1}{2}x^2 - x - \frac{3}{2}\right)$$
$$2x + 2 = x^2 - 2x - 3$$
$$0 = x^2 - 4x - 5$$
$$0 = (x + 1)(x - 5)$$

Now set each factor equal to 0 and solve to find that $x = -1$ and $x = 5$. The question only asks for a, which is the x-coordinate of the solution, so you do not need to substitute x back into an equation and solve for y. The two possible values of a are -1 and 5. Because the question specifies that $a > 0$, the answer must be 5.

16. 5

Difficulty: Hard

Category: Passport to Advanced Math / Quadratics

Strategic Advice: Unfortunately, this is a non-calculator question, so you'll need to solve the system using substitution. There is a bit of work involved, but take your time and you'll arrive at the correct answer.

Getting to the Answer: Substitute the first equation for y into the second. Before you solve for x, multiply the whole equation by 2 to remove the fractions. If you factor along the

CHAPTER 7

PREPARE

1. B
Difficulty: Easy

Category: Reading / Global

Strategic Advice: When you're asked for the main purpose of a passage, look at the passage as a whole.

Getting to the Answer: Choices A and D are way outside of the scope of the passage. Choice C may be tempting, but talk of the disadvantages of traditional grocery stores constitutes only half of the passage. The passage's purpose is really to show the advantages that supermarkets have over traditional grocery stores. Choice (B) is correct.

PRACTICE

The following passage is excerpted from a study of modern architecture.

Fallingwater, a small country house constructed in 1936, stands as perhaps the greatest residential building achievement of the American architect
Line Frank Lloyd Wright. In designing the dwelling
5 for the Pittsburgh millionaire Edgar J. Kaufmann, Wright was confronted with an unusually challenging site, beside a waterfall deep in a Pennsylvania ravine. However, Wright viewed this difficult location not as an obstacle, but as a unique opportunity to put
10 his architectural ideas into concrete form. In the end, Wright was able to turn Fallingwater into an artistic link between untamed nature and domestic tranquil-

thesis →

ity, and a masterpiece in his brilliant career.
Edgar J. Kaufmann had originally planned for
15 his house to sit at the bottom of the waterfall, where there was ample flat land on which to build. But Wright proposed a more daring response to the site. The architect convinced Kaufmann to build his house at the top of the waterfall, on a small stone
20 precipice. Wright further proposed extending the living room of the house out over the rushing water and making use of modern building techniques so that no vertical supports would be needed to hold up the room. Rather than allowing the environment
25 to determine the placement and shape of the house, Wright sought to construct a home that actually confronted and interacted with the landscape.

Wright = more daring

In one sense, Fallingwater can be viewed as a showcase for unconventional building tactics. In
30 designing the living room, for example, Wright made brilliant use of a technique called the "cantilever," in which steel rods are laid inside a shelf of concrete, eliminating the need for external supports. But Fallingwater also contains a great many traditional
35 and natural building materials. The boulders that form the foundation for the house also extend up through the floor and form part of the fireplace. A staircase in the living room extends down to an enclosed bathing pool at the top of the waterfall. To
40 Wright, the ideal dwelling in this spot was not simply a modern extravaganza or a direct extension of natural surroundings; rather, it was a little of both.

construction

opinion: Wright

Critics have taken a wide range of approaches to understanding this unique building. Some have
45 postulated that the house exalts the artist's triumph over untamed nature. Others have compared Wright's building to a cave, providing a psychological and physical safe haven from a harsh, violent world. Edgar Kaufmann, Jr., the patron's son, may have summed
50 up Fallingwater best when he said, "Wright understood that people were creatures of nature; hence, an architecture which conformed to nature would conform to what was basic in people . . . Sociability and privacy are both available, as are the comforts of
55 home and the adventures of the seasons." This, then, is Frank Lloyd Wright's achievement in Fallingwater, a home that connects the human and the natural for the invigoration and exaltation of both.

one critical opinion (triumph)

another critical opinion (psych)

opinion/ quote = EK Jr.

2. D

Difficulty: Easy

Category: Reading / Global

Strategic Advice: Answers to questions that ask about the primary purpose of a passage should relate to the thesis and themes that run throughout the passage.

Getting to the Answer: The answer should incorporate the running theme of the passage—the relationship of the house to the natural setting. Choice A is too broad. The author discusses Wright's "tactics and techniques" only in the design of one specific building, Fallingwater, which this choice does not specify. Choice B is a distortion; although Kaufmann and Wright had different ideas about the ideal location for the house, "describing their relationship" is not the purpose of the passage. The author never discusses Fallingwater's place in "architectural history," eliminating C. Therefore, (D) is correct.

3. A

Difficulty: Medium

Category: Reading / Inference

Strategic Advice: When a question does not provide a line reference, use your Passage Map to find the part of the passage that the question refers to.

Getting to the Answer: Kaufmann's original plans for the house are discussed only at the beginning of paragraph 2. Kaufmann had originally planned to put the house on a flat place near the bottom of the waterfall, but Wright convinced him to accept the "more daring" (line 17) response of building the house right over the waterfall. The author implies that Kaufmann's original plans were less daring, less risky, or, as (A) has it, more "conservative."

PERFORM

For four months in the fall of 1940, citizens of the Puget Sound area of Washington used one of the most illustrious, and most dangerous, suspension bridges
Line ever built. The Tacoma Narrows Bridge, or "Galloping
5 Gertie," enjoyed a relatively short life compared to similar structures in the United States. But in its short career, "Gertie" taught important lessons on what to do—and what not to do—when building a suspension bridge.

State officials in Washington saw a need for a bridge
10 across Puget Sound to connect the city of Tacoma, on the mainland, with the Olympic Peninsula on the other side. The closest point was the Tacoma Narrows, a windy 2,800-foot gap that, at the time, appeared to be the ideal place for a suspension bridge. Construction
15 began in November of 1938, and the bridge was officially opened on July 1, 1940. Spanning the length of the Narrows, the Tacoma Narrows Bridge was the third largest span in the world at the time and was hailed by the public as a triumph of engineering.
20 In accordance with the architectural trends of the period, the Tacoma Narrows Bridge emphasized slim, streamlined forms and slender structures. The towers were sleek and tall, and its pencil-thin roadway appeared to float delicately above the water, hanging
25 gracefully from the light, airy cables. The engineers saw a bridge that was light, beautiful, and sturdy—one that would stand the test of time.

Even during construction, though, the bridge acquired its ominous nickname. Although they knew
30 about form and structure, the bridge's engineers failed to take its aerodynamics into account, particularly the gusts of the Narrows and their effect on the roadway. Because the road bed was made of solid, stiffening plate girders, it could not absorb the winds of the Sound.
35 Instead, the road acted like a giant sail, collecting the force of the gusts. The narrowness of the bridge—it was only two lanes wide—made it extremely flexible. Therefore, on any windy day, the roadway buckled and contorted, or "galloped"—hence, its nickname. The un-
40 dulation became so severe that the bridge was eventually closed to traffic.

Margin notes:
topic = TNB = dangerous

tone = factual

why TNB was built

const. details

TNB appearance

engineers' opinion

purpose = history of TNB & why it didn't last

4. C

Difficulty: Medium

Category: Reading / Rhetoric

Strategic Advice: Read around the cited lines and make a prediction.

Getting to the Answer: The engineers thought that the bridge would "stand the test of time," but in reality the bridge was so bad that it had to be closed. The author's reason for including the engineers' opinion must have been to show how wrong it was. That's (C).

5. A

Difficulty: Easy

Category: Reading / Detail

Strategic Advice: Even though there are no line references, the answer is still in the passage.

Getting to the Answer: Figure out which paragraph alludes to the bridge's nickname: paragraph 1 and the beginning of paragraph 4. The fourth paragraph says in lines 38-39 that the bridge "galloped" because of the wind. Find an answer that matches this. Choice (A) is correct.

EXTRA PRACTICE

Civil War: worth it?

The American Civil War was an enormous tragedy in the history of the United States. To prevent secession by the Southern states, the American public found itself fighting its own people rather than foreign invaders. Sparked in 1861, this terrible war included many bloody battles with severe casualties. In fact, the body count was so high that the South had started running out of manpower when the war finally ended four years later in 1865. While the war did unite America, was it truly worth the price?

negative effects

There are many reasons that both historians and laymen have stated that the American Civil War was "not worth it." Of these, the three most commonly cited reasons are the lasting racial legacy, the high death toll, and the destruction visited upon the South. In the case of the first, legal freedom for African Americans did not translate into actual societal advancement or increased rights. Moreover, the death toll of hundreds of thousands of Americans seems too steep for any cause. Finally, the economic and social devastation wrought upon half the nation had a profound impact that wasn't alleviated until the Second World War.

didn't solve oppression

The most common argument for those who believe that the war was necessary is that President Abraham Lincoln freed the slaves. In reality, at the conclusion of the Civil War, the Emancipation Proclamation still allowed the ownership of slaves in areas that had not seceded or otherwise rebelled against the Union. (It was only with the passing of the 13th Amendment, not the Appomattox Armistice, that slavery became outlawed in the United States.) This continued subjugation of the Southern states served as a rallying cry for Southern agitators who expressed their dissatisfaction by conducting acts of violence against African Americans and their Northern supporters. During Reconstruction, political and social groups, such as the Ku Klux Klan and the White League, were formed to affirm white supremacy, oppress blacks, and enact laws that codified inequality. Thus, the use of force to exact the end of slavery perversely fueled the very mechanisms—such as Jim Crow laws and poll taxes—that perpetuated racial inequality until the Civil Rights Era.

This extreme level of racial hostility was nothing new. After all, differing opinions over the rights of African Americans are what provoked the South to secede in the first place. The South refused to yield power to a pro-abolitionist government that would only bolster the powers of the national government, while many in the North were intolerant of the South's "peculiar institution." With the North and South so firmly entrenched in their positions,

terrible losses

it is no wonder that the Civil War was so long and the body count was so high. Neither side, however, could have predicted the unprecedented violence at battles such as Shiloh, Antietam, and Gettysburg that shocked citizens and international observers alike. An estimated 620,000 men—roughly 2 percent of the population—lost their lives in the line of duty over the course of four years.

Spurred in part by anger over mounting casualties, the Union war effort from 1864–1865 increasingly included efforts to, as William T. Sherman said, make "the South howl." President Lincoln knew that he had to leave no doubt that the North had defeated the South to claim victory in the Civil War.

The Union armies marched through the region confiscating whatever they desired and destroying everything else. Aside from the high number of casualties that the South endured, the emancipation further reduced the workforce. Moreover, many of the farm animals that had not been confiscated by the Union died from disease or famine, further restricting the food supply and labor. In the aftermath, the region lay in ruins and the South was locked into a cycle of poverty. Despite attempts at Reconstruction, it took over a century for the

South destroyed → poverty

South to recover from the destruction wrought by the Union armies.

Outfitted with more men and material to fight the war, the North overpowered the Confederacy 85 and claimed victory in the end. However, the win came at far too high a price. Racial oppression, an astonishing body count, and the crippling of half of the nation's economy are difficult points to overcome. With the nation in tatters, it would take 90 generations before Americans would agree that the Union had been preserved.

auth: not worth it

1. B
Difficulty: Medium

Category: Reading / Rhetoric

Strategic Advice: Make sure you have a sound understanding of the author's overall point of view and central idea.

Getting to the Answer: The author's overall purpose in writing the passage is to suggest that the Civil War was not worth its high casualties and aftermath. This is particularly supported by the author's statement "The win came at too high a price" (lines 85–86). The correct answer is (B).

2. D
Difficulty: Easy

Category: Reading / Command of Evidence

Strategic Advice: Look for the lines of the passage that best summarize the correct answer choice for the previous question.

Getting to the Answer: As determined by the answer to the previous question, the author devotes the entire passage to asserting that the Civil War was not worth its high casualties and aftermath. This opinion is particularly explicit in the final paragraph, which (D) belongs to.

3. A
Difficulty: Hard

Category: Reading / Vocab-in-Context

Strategic Advice: Identify the closest synonym for the word in question. Context is important here, so be careful to avoid near synonyms.

Getting to the Answer: In the sentence in which "alleviated" appears, the author is making the point that the South didn't recover from the effects of the Civil War until World War II. Choice (A) is correct.

4. C
Difficulty: Medium

Category: Reading / Global

Strategic Advice: Carefully read the cited section and choose the answer that best summarizes the author's argument about how African Americans were affected by the conflict.

Getting to the Answer: The author devotes this section to debunking the idea that African Americans were better off after the Civil War. The correct answer is (C).

5. A
Difficulty: Medium

Category: Reading / Command of Evidence

Strategic Advice: Look for the answer choice that best summarizes the author's attitude toward the topic addressed in the section cited in the previous question.

Getting to the Answer: The author argues that while slavery was abolished after the war, the backlash from Southern whites was so severe that African Americans never improved in status until the mid-twentieth century. The selection that best conveys this position is (A).

6. A

Difficulty: Medium

Category: Reading / Rhetoric

Strategic Advice: Choose the answer that correctly describes the author's intent.

Getting to the Answer: Choice (A) is correct because the author is using this segment as a bridge between previous arguments and the argument that the North deliberately laid waste to portions of the South. This eventually supports the main point that the North's victory was a hollow one.

7. C

Difficulty: Medium

Category: Reading / Vocab-in-Context

Strategic Advice: Identify the closest synonym for the word in question. Pay attention to the author's use of the word in the sentence and the point being made in the section.

Getting to the Answer: Choice (C) is the correct answer because the author is explaining the motives of the North and the South. The North's "intolerance" toward slavery and its spread was an inciting cause for Northern supporters.

8. D

Difficulty: Medium

Category: Reading / Detail

Strategic Advice: Read not only the lines cited by a question stem but also the lines surrounding the citation.

Getting to the Answer: Choice (D) is the correct answer because the author explains that the Emancipation Proclamation did not free all slaves: It "still allowed the ownership of slaves in areas that had not seceded" (lines 28-29). This implies that states that did secede were the territories affected by the proclamation.

9. B

Difficulty: Easy

Category: Reading / Rhetoric

Strategic Advice: The author repeatedly asserts that the number of casualties from the war was unacceptably high. Choose the answer choice that most clearly summarizes the reason the author would do this.

Getting to the Answer: By strongly emphasizing the fact that "An estimated 620,000 men—roughly 2% of the population—lost their lives in the line of duty over the course of four years" (lines 60-62), the author is giving supporting facts to the overall thesis that the war was "too high of a price" (line 86). Choice (B) is the correct answer because it summarizes the author's reasoning.

10. B

Difficulty: Easy

Category: Reading / Detail

Strategic Advice: When a question asks you to find the exception to the statement in the question stem, try to find evidence in the passage that supports each answer. The answer you cannot find evidence for is correct.

Getting to the Answer: Throughout the passage, the author cites three main reasons why the Civil War was not worth the price paid by Americans: the "lasting racial legacy, the high death toll, and the destruction visited upon the South" (lines 14-16). While the author does mention legal freedom for African Americans in line 17, this was not listed as one of the reasons why the war wasn't worth the cost. Indeed, legal freedom for African Americans in southern states is one of the positive outcomes of the war, not a resultant problem, like those listed in A, C, and D. Therefore, (B) is correct.

CHAPTER 8

PREPARE

1. B

Difficulty: Medium

Category: Reading / Global

Strategic Advice: When asked for a description of a character in a U.S. and World Literature passage, use your Passage Map to gather an overall sense of the character.

Getting to the Answer: The author's tone is generally negative when referring to and describing Mr. Elliot, so look for the answer choice that is fully negative. Watch out for answer choices that have only one negative adjective. Both adjectives must apply for the answer to be correct. While A also contains negative adjectives, there is no indication that Mr. Elliot is "monotonous," even though the suburbs are boring. Choice (B) is correct.

2. A

Difficulty: Medium

Category: Reading / Detail

Strategic Advice: Active Reading means always searching for the author's opinion about what is being described.

Getting to the Answer: Look for hints that reveal the author's opinion. The phrases "filmy heavens" (line 3) and "gray monotony" (line 8) are negative. The author also says "there was no necessity for this—it was only rather convenient to his father" (lines 9-10). Choice (A) captures the negative tone of the passage and its emphasis on the convenience of Mr. Elliot.

3. D

Difficulty: Medium

Category: Reading / Command of Evidence

Strategic Advice: Always use the Kaplan Strategy for Command of Evidence questions.

Getting to the Answer: In answering the previous question, you established that the Elliot family's experience in the suburbs was negative and all for the convenience of Mr. Elliot. The sentence in (D) supports this.

PRACTICE

Paleontology is the study of life from prehistoric or geological times through the use of fossils. The following is adapted from a magazine article written by a paleontologist for a general interest magazine.

Of the thousands of different kinds of rocks on Earth's surface, the sedimentary, or "water-made," rocks hold the most information for paleontologists
Line and other fossil collectors, since water plays such
5 an important role in the making of fossils. Because water-made rocks are common and fossils are easy to find and extract in many locations, many people overlook these fascinating objects. This is quite a shame since fossils can act as windows into the past
10 for the informed observer.

Sandstone, limestone, and shale are three of the most common water-made rocks, and they all can play a role in fossil creation. Shale is composed of mud—often distinct layers that have dried
15 together—and usually is formed by erosion from landmasses. By contrast, sandstone and limestone often come from the ocean bottom. Sandstone is made up of grains of sand that, with the help of water, have adhered to one another over time, often
20 trapping and fossilizing simple sea creatures and plants in the process. Limestone is a more complex category. Sometimes, the lime that occurs naturally in water settles to the bottom of a body of water and hardens into rock. Of more interest to fossil hunters
25 is the limestone that forms when the shells of water animals, like crab or shrimp, pile up on the bottom

water-made rocks = lots of info

fossils from water-made rocks; lots of info but ignored

3 of most common water-made rocks

shale

sandstone

limestone

of a body of water and eventually become a layer of stone. Limestone formed through such accretion is actually a composite of myriad fossilized shells.

creation of fossils in shale

30 Unlike the slow but inevitable creation of fossilized limestone on the ocean floor, the creation of fossils in shale requires a rather incredible sequence of circumstances. Consider the fossilized footprint of a dinosaur. It starts when a dinosaur steps in semisoft

example of dino footprint

35 mud. In mud that is too soft, the footprint will simply disappear as the mud levels out, while mud that is too dry will not take a print at all. Under the right circumstances, however, the print will be captured in the drying dirt when the sun comes out. In the

40 meantime, the print can easily be ruined or obscured by the tracks of other animals or even the delicate touch of a fallen leaf or branch. If the print somehow survives these dangers, a reasonably dry environment will eventually harden the mud to form rock. Incred-

45 ibly, many such fragile offerings have been produced through this process and found by paleontologists.

use of fossils

Fossils in any form of sedimentary rock act as a vital source of information about animals, insects, and plants from long ago. Many parts of Earth's surface are

50 dominated by metamorphic or volcanic rocks rather than sedimentary rocks, and so have a dearth of fossils. Such places, blank slates to the paleontologist, serve to remind us of the gift of the water-made rock and our good fortune in having so much of it on our planet.

4. D
Difficulty: Easy

Category: Reading / Global

Strategic Advice: Summarize the central idea of the passage even when you can't make a specific prediction.

Getting to the Answer: It's tough to make a specific prediction before looking at the answer choices, but you do know that the author thinks

fossils are great. Choice (D) makes sense; fossils are important because they provide "windows into the past" (line 9) and are a "vital source of information about animals, insects, and plants from long ago" (lines 47-49).

5. D
Difficulty: Hard

Category: Reading / Detail

Strategic Advice: Beware of details that are true but not relevant to the question at hand.

Getting to the Answer: After making this statement, the author asserts that limestone can be formed when lime settles to the bottom of the ocean or when the shells of sea creatures collect. It's complex because it can be created in a variety of ways. Choice (D) matches this and is, therefore, correct.

6. B
Difficulty: Easy

Category: Reading / Command of Evidence

Strategic Advice: Even if you don't use specific lines of text to answer the question preceding a Command of Evidence question, start looking for the answer in the general portion of the passage that led you to your previous answer.

Getting to the Answer: In answering the previous question, you established that limestone can be created in different ways. Choice (B) details these different ways and is correct.

PERFORM

This passage, about the decline of the Norse colonies that once existed in Greenland, is from a comprehensive research report examining this anthropological mystery.

In 1721, the Norwegian missionary Hans Egede discovered that the two known Norse settlements on Greenland were completely deserted. Ever since, the reasons behind the decline and eventual disappearance of these people have been greatly debated. Greenland, established by the charismatic outlaw Eric the Red in about 986 CE, was a colony of Norway by 1000, complete with a church hierarchy and trading community. After several relatively prosperous centuries, the colony had fallen on hard times and was not heard from in Europe, but it wasn't until Egede's discovery that the complete downfall of the settlement was confirmed.

Throughout the nineteenth century, researchers attributed the demise of the Norse colonies to war between the colonies and Inuit groups. This is based largely on evidence from the work *Description of Greenland*, written by Norse settler Ivar Bardarson around 1364, which describes strained relationships between the Norse settlers and the Inuits who had recently come to Greenland. However, because there is no archeological evidence of a war or a massacre, and the extensive body of Inuit oral history tells of no such event, modern scholars give little credence to these theories.

New theories about the reason for the decline of the Norse colonies are being proposed partially because the amount of information available is rapidly increasing. Advances in paleoclimatology, for example, have increased the breadth and clarity of our picture of the region. Most notably, recent analyses of the central Greenland ice core, coupled with data obtained from plant material and sea sediments, have indicated severe climate changes in the region that some are now calling a "mini ice age." Such studies point toward a particularly warm period for Greenland that occurred between the years 800 and 1300, which was then followed—unfortunately for those inhabiting even the most temperate portions of the island—by a steady decline in overall temperatures that lasted for nearly 600 years. The rise and fall of the Norse colonies in Greenland, not surpris-

ingly, roughly mirrors this climate-based chronology. Researchers have also found useful data in a most surprising place—fly remains. The insect, not native to the island, was brought over inadvertently on Norse ships. Flies survived in the warm and less than sanitary conditions of the Norse dwellings and barns and died out when these were no longer inhabited. By carbon dating the fly remains, researchers have tracked the occupation of the settlements and confirmed that the human population began to decline around 1350.

Changing economic conditions likely also conspired against the settlers. The colonies had founded a moderately successful trading economy based on exporting whale ivory, especially important given their need for the imported wood and iron that were in short supply on the island. Unfortunately, inexpensive and plentiful Asian and African elephant ivory flooded the European market during the fourteenth century, destroying Greenland's standing in the European economy. At the same time, the trading fleet of the German Hanseatic League supplanted the previously dominant Norwegian shipping fleets. Since the German merchants had little interest in the Norse colonists, Greenland soon found itself visited by fewer and fewer ships each year until its inhabitants were completely isolated by 1480.

Cultural and sociologic factors may have also contributed to the demise of the Norse settlements. The Inuit tribes, while recent immigrants to Greenland, had come from nearby areas to the west and had time-tested strategies to cope with the severe environment. The Norse settlers, however, seem to have viewed themselves as fundamentally European and did not adopt Inuit techniques. Inuit apparel, for example, was far more appropriate for the cold, damp environment; the remains from even the last surviving Norse settlements indicate a costume that was undeniably European in design. Likewise, the Norse settlers failed to adopt Inuit hunting techniques and tools, such as the toggle harpoon, which made it possible to capture calorie-rich

Line 5

10

15

20

25

30

35

40

45

50

55

60

65

70

75

Margin notes:
Norse colonies disappeared; reason unclear

theory proposed; no arch. evidence

new theories based on climate

increasing amt. of info.

warm → mini ice age

fly as evidence

carbon dating

economy changed

trade

cultural factors

Norse settlers' view of themselves

clothing

hunting

farming

80 seal meat. Instead, the Norse relied on the farming styles that had been so successful for their European ancestors, albeit in a radically different climate. It seems likely that this stubborn cultural inflexibility prevented the Norse civilization in Greenland from adapting to increasingly severe environmental and economic conditions

7. A

Difficulty: Medium

Category: Reading / Global

Strategic Advice: After reading a passage, you should be able to predict a general purpose for the passage. Be careful not to make your prediction overly specific.

Getting to the Answer: The author discusses the disappearance of a group of Norse settlers and offers a number of explanations for this occurrence; he does not seem to advocate any one explanation over another. Predict that the main purpose is to explain possible reasons. Choice (A) matches this prediction.

8. A

Difficulty: Medium

Category: Reading / Detail

Strategic Advice: This question requires you to put together details from different parts of the passage.

Getting to the Answer: The author writes, "a particularly warm period for Greenland . . . occurred between the years 800 and 1300" (lines 33-35). The beginning of the passage states that the colony was founded around the year 1000, right in the middle of the warm period. Choice (A) works. The "mild," warm weather was uncharacteristic of the usually cold, harsh climate.

9. B

Difficulty: Medium

Category: Reading / Command of Evidence

Strategic Advice: If you used a line reference to answer the previous question, start by seeing if that line reference is one of the answer choices.

Getting to the Answer: In answering the previous question, you determined that the climate during the initial founding of the Norse settlements was "uncharacteristically mild." This strange, mild weather is detailed in lines 33-35, (B).

EXTRA PRACTICE

In the following excerpt from a novella, Rosemary, an elderly woman, reminisces about her childhood as she waits for her grandson to wake up.

[margin note: R: keep mind active]

Rosemary sat at her kitchen table, working a crossword puzzle. Crosswords were nice; they filled the time, and kept the mind active. She needed just
Line one word to complete this morning's puzzle; the
5 clue was "a Swiss river," and the first of its three letters was "A." Unfortunately, Rosemary had no idea what the name of the river was, and could not look it up. Her atlas was on her desk, and the desk was in the guest room, currently being occupied by her
10 grandson Victor. Looking up over the tops of her bifocals, Rosemary glanced at the kitchen clock: It was almost 10 AM. *Land sakes!* Did the boy intend to sleep all day? She noticed that the arthritis in her wrist was throbbing, and put down her pen. At 87

[margin note: R: treasure all as you get old]

15 years of age, she was glad she could still write at all. She had decided long ago that growing old was like slowly turning to stone; you couldn't take anything for granted. She stood up slowly, painfully, and started walking to the guest room.
20 The trip, though only a distance of about 25 feet, seemed to take a long while. Late in her ninth decade now, Rosemary often experienced an expanded sense of time, with present and past tense intermingling in her mind. One minute she
25 was padding in her slippers across the living room carpet, the next she was back on the farm where she'd grown up, a sturdy little girl treading the path behind the barn just before dawn. In her mind's eye, she could still pick her way among the stones in the

[margin note: past & present mingled]

30 darkness, more than 70 years later. . . . Rosemary arrived at the door to the guest room. It stood slightly ajar, and she peered through the opening. Victor lay sleeping on his side, his arms bent, his expression slightly pained. *Get up, lazy bones,* she

[margin note: R always early riser]

35 wanted to say. Even in childhood, Rosemary had never slept past 4 AM; there were too many chores to do. How different things were for Victor's generation! Her youngest grandson behaved as if he had never done a chore in his life. Twenty-one years old,

[margin note: R: V is lazy]

40 he had driven down to Florida to visit Rosemary in his shiny new car, a gift from his doting parents. Victor would finish college soon, and his future appeared bright—if he ever got out of bed, that is.
Something Victor had said last night over dinner
45 had disturbed her. Now what was it? Oh yes; he had been talking about one of his college courses—a

[margin note: V: easy class]

"gut," he had called it. When she had asked him to explain the term, Victor had said it was a course that you took simply because it was easy to pass.
50 Rosemary, who had not even had a high school education, found the term repellent. If she had been allowed to continue her studies, she would never have taken a "gut" . . . The memory flooded back then, still painful as an open wound all these years

[margin note: memories of HS]

55 later. It was the first day of high school. She had graduated from grammar school the previous year, but her father had forbidden her to go on to high school that fall, saying she was needed on the farm. After much tearful pleading, she had gotten him to
60 promise that next year, she could start high school. She had endured a whole year of chores instead of books, with animals and rough farmhands for company instead of people her own age. Now, at

[margin note: desperate to go to HS]

last, the glorious day was at hand. She had put on
65 her best dress (she owned two), her heart racing in anticipation.
But her father was waiting for her as she came downstairs.
"Where do you think you're going?" he asked.

[margin note: R's dad: no way!]

70 "To high school, Papa."
"No you're not. Take that thing off and get back to work."
"But Papa, you promised!"
"Do as I say!" he thundered.
75 There was no arguing with Papa when he spoke that way. Tearfully, she had trudged upstairs to change clothes. Rosemary still wondered what her life would have been like if her father had not been

waiting at the bottom of the stairs that day, or if
80 somehow she had found the strength to defy him. . . .

(Suddenly,) Victor stirred, without waking, and mumbled something unintelligible. Jarred from her reverie, Rosemary stared at Victor. She wondered if he were having a nightmare.

1. A

Difficulty: Medium

Category: Reading / Rhetoric

Strategic Advice: Look for the answer choice that best paraphrases Rosemary's attitude toward aging.

Getting to the Answer: The last three sentences of the first paragraph (lines 14-19) discuss Rosemary's attitude toward old age: "At 87 years of age, she was glad she could still write at all. She had decided long ago that growing old was like slowly turning to stone; you couldn't take anything for granted." This attitude is best summarized by (A).

2. D

Difficulty: Easy

Category: Reading / Detail

Strategic Advice: Identify the answer choice that describes the explicit meaning of the selection mentioned in the question.

Getting to the Answer: When you read the lines around the cited text, you see that the trip, though short, "seemed to take a long while" (line 21) and that Rosemary "often experienced an expanded sense of time" (lines 22-23). Choice (D) restates this perfectly, because "elastic" means to be able to expand and contract.

3. D

Difficulty: Easy

Category: Reading / Inference

Strategic Advice: Reread the section of the passage that describes Rosemary's first day of high school to develop a firm understanding of her memory of that day.

Getting to the Answer: The question refers to Rosemary on that "glorious" day when she was going to high school, which is found near the end of paragraph 3. She gets up, puts on her "best dress . . . , her heart racing in anticipation" (lines 65-66). This points to (D) as the correct answer.

4. C

Difficulty: Medium

Category: Reading / Command of Evidence

Strategic Advice: Identify the answer choice that is the best supporting evidence for the idea expressed in the answer to the previous question.

Getting to the Answer: The correct answer to the previous question established that Rosemary was eager to start high school and continue her education. Choice (C) most clearly demonstrates that by describing how she had begged her father for permission to continue her studies.

5. C

Difficulty: Hard

Category: Reading / Rhetoric

Strategic Advice: When you see the words "in order to" in a question stem, rephrase that question as a "Why" question. For example: Why did the author include Rosemary's thoughts regarding her grandson in lines 38-43?

Getting to the Answer: Choice (C) details why the author includes Rosemary's thoughts on her grandson: These musings set the stage for her memories of her own educational frustrations as a child, which is quite different from her perception of Victor's life as easy. While B is tempting, it is presented as a fact; it may be true that Victor does not appreciate how fortunate it is, but you cannot know this for sure, as the passage is filtered through Rosemary's perspective. Choice (C) is correct.

6. C

Difficulty: Hard

Category: Reading / Command of Evidence

Strategic Advice: Review how you answered the previous question to answer Command of Evidence questions.

Getting to the Answer: Choice (C) continues where the passage cited in the previous question left off. In the lines cited by (C), the author makes the juxtaposition between Victor and Rosemary's experiences more explicit.

7. B

Difficulty: Medium

Category: Reading / Vocab-in-Context

Strategic Advice: Identify the closest synonym for the word in question, while making sure your selection also makes sense in context of the passage.

Getting to the Answer: Given that this section of the passage alludes to Rosemary's childhood growing up on a farm and that the theme of farm labor runs throughout the passage, (B) is closest in meaning to "sturdy."

8. C

Difficulty: Medium

Category: Reading / Inference

Strategic Advice: Reread the cited line to develop a firm grasp of the author's underlying point.

Getting to the Answer: Rosemary refers to Victor as a "lazy bones" who has been given every advantage by his "doting parents . . . his future appeared bright—if he ever got out of bed, that is" (lines 41-43). Choice (C) matches this.

9. D

Difficulty: Medium

Category: Reading / Global

Strategic Advice: Identify the answer choice that most directly addresses the central theme and narrative direction of the passage.

Getting to the Answer: Though Victor is important in this passage, his real role is to awaken thoughts in Rosemary about her past. Most of the passage is about Rosemary and her life. Choice (D) addresses this.

CHAPTER 9

PREPARE

1. A

Difficulty: Medium

Category: Reading / Vocab-in-Context

Strategic Advice: When you see the phrase "most nearly means" and a cited line, pretend the word or phrase is a blank.

Getting to the Answer: Read the sentence without "exercised" and ask what the author did. Predict: She utilized her rights. Choice (A) matches.

2. D

Difficulty: Medium

Category: Reading / Inference

Strategic Advice: When the question describes part of a Cause-and-Effect relationship, ask how things will turn out.

Getting to the Answer: The word "without" in the question stem is a Cause-and-Effect clue. Look at your Passage Map: Where does the author discuss how things turn out? Paragraph 4. Although the author doesn't state it directly, she implies that without the right to vote, women cannot consent to the government. Therefore, (D) is correct.

3. B

Difficulty: Easy

Category: Reading / Inference

Strategic Advice: The phrase, "Which of the following is . . ." indicates that a relationship is present. Figure out what that relationship is.

Getting to the Answer: The question stem implies that something is necessary "in order" to "secure the blessings of liberty." Check your Passage Map. Paragraph 3 links securing liberty to voting. Choice (B) is correct.

PRACTICE

When I had somewhat collected my senses, I realized that in a large back room into which the main room opened, there was a young fellow sing- *Line* ing a song, accompanied on the piano by a short,
5 thickset young man. After each verse, he did some dance steps, which brought forth great applause and a shower of small coins at his feet. After the singer had responded to a rousing encore, the stout man at the piano began to run his fingers up and down the
10 keyboard. This he did in a manner which indicated that he was a master of a good deal of technique. Then he began to play; and such playing! I stopped talking to listen. It was music of a kind I had never heard before. It was music that demanded physi-
15 cal response, patting of the feet, drumming of the fingers, or nodding of the head in time with the beat. The dissonant harmonies, the audacious reso- lutions, often consisting of an abrupt jump from one key to another, the intricate rhythms in which
20 the accents fell in the most unexpected places, but in which the beat was never lost, produced a most curious effect . . .

This was rag-time music, then a novelty in New York, and just growing to be a rage, which has not
25 yet subsided. It was originated in the questionable resorts about Memphis and St. Louis by black piano players who knew no more of the theory of music than they did of the theory of the universe, but were guided by natural musical instinct and
30 talent. It made its way to Chicago, where it was popular some time before it reached New York. These players often improvised simple and, at times, vulgar words to fit the melodies. This was the beginning of the rag-time song . . .
35 American musicians, instead of investigating rag-time, attempt to ignore it, or dismiss it with a contemptuous word. But that has always been the course of scholasticism in every branch of

Margin notes:
Music

good player

New kind of music

good

RTM

history

beginning

AM mus don't like RTM

art. Whatever new thing the *people* like is pooh-
poohed; whatever is *popular* is spoken of as not
worth the while. The fact is, nothing great or
enduring, especially in music, has ever sprung
full-fledged and unprecedented from the brain of
any master; the best that he gives to the world he
45 gathers from the hearts of the people, and runs
it through the alembic* of his genius. In spite of
the bans which musicians and music teachers
have placed upon it, the people still demand and
enjoy rag-time. One thing cannot be denied; it is
50 music which possesses at least one strong element
of (greatness) it appeals universally; not only the
American, but the English, the French, and even
the German people find delight in it. In fact, there
is not a corner of the civilized world in which it is
55 not known, and this proves its originality; for if it
were an imitation, the people of Europe, anyhow,
would not have found it a novelty . . .

I became so interested in both the music and
the player that I left the table where I was sitting,
60 and made my way through the hall into the back
room, where I could see as well as hear. I talked to
the piano player between the musical numbers and
found out that he was just a natural musician, never
having taken a lesson in his life. Not only could he
65 play almost anything he heard, but he could accompany singers in songs he had never heard. He
had, by (ear alone,) composed some pieces, several
of which he played over for me; each of them was
properly proportioned and balanced. I began to
70 wonder what this man with such a lavish natural
endowment would have done had he been trained.
Perhaps he wouldn't have done anything at all; he
might have become, at best, a mediocre imitator of
the great masters in what they have already done
75 to a finish, or one of the modern innovators who
strive after originality by seeing how cleverly they
can dodge about through the rules of harmony and
at the same time avoid melody. It is (certain) that
he would not have been so delightful as he was in
80 ragtime.

*alembic: scientific apparatus used in the process
of distillation

Margin notes (left column):

people like = scholars don't like

great = hearts + genius

popular all over

no training

play by ear

write by ear

need train-ing?

Opinion: better without

4. C

Difficulty: Medium

Category: Reading / Vocab-in-Context

Strategic Advice: Remember to avoid common meanings when answering Vocab-in-Context questions.

Getting to the Answer: Read the sentence without "intricate" and ask what the author is trying to communicate. Predict: The rhythm had complicated parts. Choice (C) matches.

5. A

Difficulty: Medium

Category: Reading / Inference

Strategic Advice: The phrase "According to the author," and the relationship clue word "effect" indicate that you should ask how items are related.

Getting to the Answer: The question stem cites the result and asks for the cause. Read around the cited lines. Just before, the author lists the elements of the music that produced the "curious effect." This matches (A).

6. B

Difficulty: Hard

Category: Reading / Inference

Strategic Advice: When only one part of a rela-tionship is presented, look for the other part in the answer choices.

Getting to the Answer: The question asks about the basis for author's opinion. Ask why the author thinks that the piano player is "a natural musician" (line 63). Go to the cited line and look for the reasons that the author gives: He used his "ear." Therefore, (B) is correct.

PERFORM

Baby needs lang

For an infant just beginning to interact with the surrounding world, it is imperative that he quickly become proficient in his native language.

Line While developing a vocabulary and the ability to

first steps:
5 communicate using it are obviously important steps in this process, an infant must (first) be able to learn from the various streams of audible communication around him. To that end, during the course of even the first few months of development, an infant will begin to

absorb
10 (absorb) the rhythmic patterns and sequences of sounds that characterize his language, and will begin to

differenti-ate
(differentiate) between the meanings of various pitch and stress changes.

However, it is important to recognize that such
15 learning does not take place in a vacuum. Infants must

many voices
confront these language acquisition challenges in an environment where, quite frequently, several streams of communication or noise are occurring simultaneously. In other words, infants must (not only) learn how to seg-
20 ment individual speech streams into their component

need to tell apart
words (but) they must also be able to distinguish between concurrent streams of sound.

example
Consider, (for example,) an infant being spoken to by his mother. (Before) he can learn from the nuances of
25 his mother's speech, he must first separate that speech

diff/com-peting sounds
from the sounds of the dishwasher, the family dog, the bus stopping on the street outside, and, quite possibly, background noise in the form of speech: a newscaster on the television down the hall or siblings playing in an
30 adjacent room.

setup
(How) exactly do infants wade through such a murky conglomeration of audible stimuli? (While) most in-fants are capable of separating out two different voices

can hear two
(despite) the presence of additional, competing streams of
35 sound, this capability is predicated upon several specific conditions.

explain solution
(First,) infants are better able to learn from a particular speech stream when that voice is louder than any of the competing streams of background speech; when two

40 voices are of equal amplitude, infants typically dem-onstrate little preference for one stream over the other.

louder

Most likely, equally loud competing voice streams, for the infant, become combined into a single stream that necessarily contains unfamiliar patterns and sounds that
45 can quite easily induce confusion. (Secondly,) an infant is more likely to attend to a particular voice stream if

more familiar

it is perceived as more familiar than another stream. When an infant, for example, is presented with a voice stream spoken by his mother and a background stream
50 delivered by an unfamiliar voice, usually he can eas-ily separate out her voice from the distraction of the background stream. (By) using these simple yet important cues an infant can become quite adept at concentrating on a single stream of communication and, (therefore,)

single stream = learns faster

55 capable of more quickly learning the invaluable charac-teristics and rules of his native language.

7. D
Difficulty: Easy

Category: Reading / Inference

Strategic Advice: "Whether . . . whether" indicates that you should look for what needs to happen to produce a specific outcome.

Getting to the Answer: Refer to your Passage Map for paragraph 5. This paragraph describes how an infant can tell two voices apart when one of the voices is louder or more familiar. Because loud is not an answer choice, (D) must be correct.

8. D
Difficulty: Hard

Category: Reading / Vocab-in-Context

Strategic Advice: Be wary of answer choices that sound or look like the word or phrase in question.

Getting to the Answer: This question is hard for two reasons. First, the word "predicated" is used infrequently; second, the context you need is in the following paragraph. Your Passage Map notes that the author asks a "how" question in the fourth paragraph and answers the question in the next paragraph by informing you of how different conditions produce different results. Predict that the "capability" is "altered by" the conditions. Choice (D) matches.

9. C

Difficulty: Medium

Category: Reading / Inference

Strategic Advice: When you see the phrase "which choice best describes" and the question provides both sides of the relationship, look for the answer choice that joins the sides correctly, even if the author doesn't state it directly.

Getting to the Answer: Because describing this relationship is why the author wrote the passage, check the first and last paragraphs for clues. In the first paragraph, the author suggests that learning the language is important. In the last paragraph, the author asserts that concentrating on a single stream speeds up the process. Choice (C) matches.

10. C

Difficulty: Medium

Category: Reading / Vocab-in-Context

Strategic Advice: Be careful when a Vocab-in-Context question asks about a phrase that includes a preposition. Make sure your answer uses the correct word and preposition.

Getting to the Answer: Read the sentence without "attend to" and ask what the author is trying to communicate. Because the paragraph is about choosing between two speakers, predict: "pay attention." Choice (C) is correct.

EXTRA PRACTICE

This passage is an excerpt adapted from the novel You Can't Go Home Again *by Thomas Wolfe. (©1934, 1937, 1938, 1939, 1940 by Maxwell Perkins as Executor of the Estate of Thomas Wolfe. Reprinted by permission of HarperCollins Publishers.)*

out of it at dusk

It was late afternoon and the shadows were slant-
ing swiftly eastward when George Webber came
to his senses somewhere in the wilds of the upper
Bronx. . . . All he could remember was that suddenly
5 he felt hungry and stopped and looked about him
and realized where he was. His dazed look gave way
to one of amazement and incredulity, and his mouth
began to stretch into a broad grin. In his hand he still
held the rectangular slip of crisp yellow paper. . . .

success!

10 It was a check for five hundred dollars. His book
had been accepted, and this was an advance against
his royalties.

So he was happier than he had ever been in all
his life. Fame, at last, was knocking at his door and

fame coming

15 wooing him with her sweet blandishments. . . . The
next weeks and months were filled with the excitement of the impending event. The book would not
be published till the fall, but meanwhile there was
much work to do. Foxhall Edwards had made some

pre-pub tasks

20 suggestions for cutting and revising the manuscript,
and, although George at first objected, he surprised
himself in the end by agreeing with Edwards. . . .

George had called his novel *Home to Our
Mountains,* and in it he had packed everything he

book = his youth

25 knew about his home town in Old Catawba. . . . He
had distilled every line of it out of his own experience of life. And, now that the issue was decided,
he sometimes trembled when he thought that it
would only be a matter of months before the whole
30 world knew what he had written. He loathed the

fam & friends might get mad

thought of giving pain to anyone, and that he
might do so had never occurred to him until now.
. . . Of course it was fiction, but it was made as all
honest fiction must be, from the stuff of human

"fiction," but...

35 life. Some people might recognize themselves and
be offended, and then what would he do? Would
he have to go around in smoked glasses and false

whiskers? He comforted himself with the hope that
his characterizations were not so true as, in another

might get away with it

40 mood, he liked to think they were, and he thought
that perhaps no one would notice anything.

Rodney's Magazine, too, had become interested
in the young author and was going to publish a
story, a chapter from the book. . . . This news added

excited abt mag.

45 immensely to his excitement. He was eager to see
his name in print, and in the happy interval of
expectancy he felt like a kind of universal Don Juan,
for he literally loved everybody—his fellow instruc-
tors at the school, his drab students, the little shop-

deliriously happy

50 keepers in all the stores, even the nameless hordes
that thronged the streets. *Rodney's,* of course, was
the greatest and finest publishing house in all the
world, and Foxhall Edwards was the greatest editor
and the finest man that ever was. George had liked

self-respect

55 him instinctively from the first, and now, like an old
and intimate friend, he was calling him Fox. George
knew that Fox believed in him, and the editor's faith
and confidence . . . restored his self-respect and
charged him with energy for new work.

dreads next book

60 Already his next novel was begun and was
beginning to take shape within him. . . . He dreaded
the prospect of buckling down in earnest to write
it, for he knew the agony of it. . . . While the fury of
creation was upon him, it meant sixty cigarettes a
65 day, twenty cups of coffee, meals snatched anyhow
and anywhere and at whatever time of day or night
he happened to remember he was hungry. It meant

painful process

sleeplessness, and miles of walking to bring on the
physical fatigue without which he could not sleep,
70 then nightmares, nerves, and exhaustion in the
morning. As he said to Fox:

owns his process

"There are better ways to write a book, but this,
God help me, is mine, and you'll have to learn to
put up with it."

75   When *Rodney's Magazine* came out with the
story, George fully expected convulsions of the
earth, falling meteors, suspension of traffic in the
streets, and a general strike. But nothing happened.
A few of his friends mentioned it, but that was all.
80 For several days he felt let down, but then his common sense reassured him that people couldn't really
tell much about a new author from a short piece
in a magazine. The book would show them who
he was and what he could do. . . . He could afford
85 to wait a little longer for the fame which he was
certain would soon be his.

no reac. to mag??

1. B

Difficulty: Medium

Category: Reading / Global

Strategic Advice: You need to develop a firm grasp of the passage as a whole to be able to accurately summarize central ideas and characters.

Getting to the Answer: Choice (B) is correct. Over the course of the passage, the author describes George's experiencing a wide range of emotions, including joy over his recent publication, fear over how people in his hometown will feel, and disappointment over how his story in *Rodney's* is received.

2. A

Difficulty: Medium

Category: Reading / Global

Strategic Advice: Remember that your approach to reading U.S. and World Literature passages should include keeping a running tally of a character's traits.

Getting to the Answer: Choice (A) is correct because the main character, George Webber, is hungry for fame and recognition. This is alluded to throughout the passage and is addressed clearly in lines 13-15 ("So he was happier than he had ever been in all his life. Fame, at last, was knocking at his door").

3. B

Difficulty: Medium

Category: Reading / Detail

Strategic Advice: Look at your notes for the paragraph that introduces and discusses the subtopic mentioned in the question stem. Once you have a firm grasp on the details, select the answer choice that best summarizes the subtopic.

Getting to the Answer: In the fourth paragraph, the author explains that George's new book is a "novel" (line 23) and that it is based on his hometown of Old Catawba (line 25). Choice (B) is correct.

4. C

Difficulty: Easy

Category: Reading / Command of Evidence

Strategic Advice: The correct answer choice should explicitly address the subtopic discussed in the previous question.

Getting to the Answer: Choice (C) is correct because it is in these lines that the author explicitly addresses that George's new book is a novel based on his experiences in his hometown of Old Catawba.

5. A

Difficulty: Hard

Category: Reading / Vocab-in-Context

Strategic Advice: Pay attention to the author's use of the word in the sentence and the point being made in that section of the passage.

Getting to the Answer: Choice (A) is correct because in lines 4-8 ("All he could remember . . . broad grin"), the author describes George's transition from confusion to remembrance and then reacceptance of his recent success at getting his book published. George is described as feeling "incredulity" because he still has trouble believing his good fortune.

6. C

Difficulty: Medium

Category: Reading / Inference

Strategic Advice: Develop a firm grasp of the author's intent in the section cited in the question stem. Choose the answer that best describes what is implied by the text.

Getting to the Answer: In this section, George seems nervous that people from his hometown "might recognize themselves" in characters from his new book and "be offended" (lines 35-36). The reader can infer that the book is closely based on details of real events and people in Old Catawba. The correct answer is (C).

7. D

Difficulty: Medium

Category: Reading / Detail

Strategic Advice: Review your notes for the section that discusses George's writing process.

Getting to the Answer: In lines 60-74 ("Already . . . 'put up with it'"), the author describes George's tumultuous creative periods. It is made explicit that the writing process takes a toll on George's body and mind. Choice (D) is correct.

8. B

Difficulty: Medium

Category: Reading / Command of Evidence

Strategic Advice: Identify the answer choice that provides the best evidence for the correct answer to the previous question.

Getting to the Answer: In the previous question, you looked at lines 60-74, which detail George's writing process. These lines are featured in (B), which is correct.

9. B

Difficulty: Medium

Category: Reading / Vocab-in-Context

Strategic Advice: Choose the closest synonym for the questioned word in context.

Getting to the Answer: Choice (B) is correct, as agitation is the best synonym of "fury" in this particular context. The definitions of "fury" that imply indignation or animosity are not valid to describe George's creative process.

CHAPTER 10

PREPARE

1. A

Difficulty: Medium

Category: Reading / Rhetoric

Strategic Advice: When you see the phrase "main purpose of" and a cited section, ask what role this section plays in the passage.

Getting to the Answer: When you read the passage, notice that the author explains a standard theory first and then calls it into question. Choice (A) matches.

2. A

Difficulty: Medium

Category: Reading / Rhetoric

Strategic Advice: When the question asks you to describe the author's stance, determine how the author sees things.

Getting to the Answer: The author refers to "Homo sapiens" in the introduction and the conclusion. Your Passage Map suggests that the author is skeptical of the position humans hold in the grand scheme of things. Predict that the author doesn't agree with a standard interpretation. Choice (A) is correct.

3. C

Difficulty: Easy

Category: Reading / Rhetoric

Strategic Advice: "Meant to convey" is a signal that the question is asking about the author's purpose.

Getting to the Answer: Because the author wants to question Darwin and his conclusions, it is important that the author communicates how important Darwin is. Without Darwin's importance, the passage loses its power to persuade. Choice (C) is correct.

PRACTICE

The following is adapted from two excerpts from a 1926 diary of a resident of Moscow, Russia. At that time, Russia, as part of the Soviet Union, was ruled by a dictatorial government and was experiencing a severe economic depression.

   Late afternoon, blustery and gray.

   It has been many years since I have attended a performance of a play. My black fox fur is quite tat-
Line tered, but I have spent the last two evenings before
5 the fire mending it. Before the children were born, we went to the theater at least once a week. I wished later, during the upheaval, that we had not given it up. Once it was gone, truly gone, I missed it so.

   I did not expect to be this nervous. It's as if I've
10 never been to a proper theater, and I can scarcely remember a time when I've so fussed over the state of my hair. I'm wondering if I will remember how to behave. In truth, the cause of my nervous condi-tion is this feeling that the whole of Moscow has
15 contrived to engage in a rebellious act. Will we be putting ourselves in danger tonight? It's hard to believe we will not. Perhaps only a handful of people will attend.

   Later the same night, very cold.

20   I certainly had no need to fret over the con-dition of my fox fur. Others even attended the performance with tattered bits of sweaters wrapped around their necks, but people were not judged for the state of their clothing. Triumph Square was
25 abuzz with energy and anticipation. Once among the throng, all of my fears of punishment evapo-rated. Moscow was united tonight in support of its theater. The play was by Gogol and of course I've seen it many times, but never like this. The direc-
30 tor was a man whose name I had almost forgotten,

going to a play

mending

memory

misses plays

emotions small con-cerns

real concern danger

small concerns gone

big crowd feels safe

description of play

Vsevolod Meyerhold. The pace of the show was breathtaking. I found that I could scarcely keep up—it's very lucky I'm familiar with the script. The audience was quite bowled over. At the curtain call,
35 much of the audience rose to their feet. The roar of the crowd was a mix of jeering and applause. I

big emotions

was so overwhelmed with emotion, I found myself on my feet clapping loudly—until I realized that the figures on stage for the curtain call were only

feels foolish 40 papier-mâché* dummies, rather than the actors from the performance. I even felt momentarily foolish for being taken in by the ruse. I wonder if this was why others in the crowd were scoffing, or if they were indeed unhappy with the entire
45 production. I did not stop to ask anyone—the paper

is no longer cold

tomorrow morning will tell me. I rushed home, not bothered by the cold.

a material made of paper pulp and glue

4. D

Difficulty: Hard

Category: Reading / Rhetoric

Strategic Advice: When you see the phrase "main rhetorical effect" and a cited line, ask how the cited section influences your understanding of the passage as a whole.

Getting to the Answer: Read the sentence and paraphrase what the narrator is trying to communicate. She is afraid and lives in a dictatorship. Just going to the play could get everyone into trouble. Choice (D) matches.

5. D

Difficulty: Medium

Category: Reading / Rhetoric

Strategic Advice: "Stance" indicates that the question is about point of view.

Getting to the Answer: The italicized introduction describes the government as a dictatorship. The passage describes the lead-up and

the event. From the narrator's point of view, even the simple act of going to a play could be trouble. At the end of the second paragraph, the narrator expresses worry about how many people will attend, and the last paragraph suggests that many people joined the narrator in going to the play despite the danger. This matches (D).

6. A

Difficulty: Hard

Category: Reading / Rhetoric

Strategic Advice: When you see the phrase "main purpose of" and a cited section, ask what role this section plays in the passage.

Getting to the Answer: Here, the question asks about the second paragraph. A quick review of your Passage Map shows that the paragraph starts out with small concerns and then, over its course, reveals the true nature of the narrator's worries. Choice (A) is correct.

PERFORM

The following passage is excerpted from a popular journal of archeology.

About fifty miles west of Stonehenge, buried in the peat bogs of the Somerset flatlands in southwestern England, lies the oldest road known
Line to humanity. Dubbed the "Sweet Track" after its
5 discoverer, Raymond Sweet, this painstakingly constructed 1,800-meter road dates back to the early Neolithic period, some 6,000 years ago. Thanks primarily to the overlying layer of acidic peat, which has kept the wood moist, inhibited the growth of
10 decay bacteria, and discouraged the curiosity of animal life, the road is remarkably well-preserved. Examination of its remains has provided extensive information about the people who constructed it.

The design of the Sweet Track indicates that its
15 builders possessed extraordinary engineering skills. In constructing the road, they first hammered pegs

Sweet Track

well preserved

lots of info

6. B

Difficulty: Medium

Category: Writing & Language / Usage

Strategic Advice: The correct preposition can often only be determined in the context of the sentence.

Getting to the Answer: This sentence states that the Hudson River School was suited to the task of competing with Europe. The job of the prepositional phrase is to explain how that was accomplished. Choice (B) conveys this precisely.

7. C

Difficulty: Hard

Category: Writing & Language / Usage

Strategic Advice: If you can't identify who or what a pronoun refers to, the pronoun's antecedent is unclear.

Getting to the Answer: Because the paragraph mentions only Europe and not Europeans, eliminate D. In the previous sentences, the passage discusses "writers" and their interest in the influence of "wilderness" on their "nationality." Choice (C) is correct.

8. A

Difficulty: Easy

Category: Writing & Language / Usage

Strategic Advice: Look for clues that indicate when something is being compared to something else. Then, check to make sure that the comparison is logical, parallel, and properly phrased.

Getting to the Answer: At the beginning of the sentence, the phrase "Unlike European painters" tells you that the writer is comparing "European painters" to something else. Logically, that something else must also be painters. Choice (A) logically compares painters to painters.

PERFORM

9. C

Difficulty: Easy

Category: Writing & Language / Usage

Strategic Advice: Adjectives in the comparative form compare only two items or people. Use the superlative form to compare three or more items or people.

Getting to the Answer: In context, it is clear that many "financial panics" have occurred in United States history. As a result, the superlative form must be used when comparing them. Because the superlative of "bad" is "worst," there is no need to add "most" to indicate the comparison. Choice (C) is correct.

10. A

Difficulty: Medium

Category: Writing & Language / Usage

Strategic Advice: When nouns in a sentence relate to each other, they need to agree in number.

Getting to the Answer: The sentence discusses "types of gadgets" and gives two examples. Each of the examples must match the plural nouns "types" and "gadgets." Choice (A) makes all the related nouns plural. While D uses the plural forms, it uses an improper connection between the two nouns.

11. B

Difficulty: Hard

Category: Writing & Language / Usage

Strategic Advice: Remember that a pronoun and its antecedent may not be close to each other.

Getting to the Answer: The possessive pronoun correctly indicates the owner of the loan as "investor," but does not match in number. Because the gender of the investor is not specified, be careful not to use a gendered pronoun. Choice (B) is correct.

12. D
Difficulty: Easy

Category: Writing & Language / Usage

Strategic Advice: Remember that *barely*, *hardly*, and *scarcely* imply a negative and when paired with explicitly negative words, create a double negative, which is grammatically incorrect.

Getting to the Answer: Adding the word "hardly" when the predicate contains "could not" creates a double negative and is incorrect. Choice (D) corrects the error by eliminating "hardly."

13. C
Difficulty: Medium

Category: Writing & Language / Usage

Strategic Advice: A pronoun is ambiguous when its antecedent is either missing or unclear.

Getting to the Answer: To find the antecedent for the underlined pronoun, read the previous sentence and think about the focus of the passage. Although the previous sentence has more than one possible antecedent, in the context of the passage, (C) is the clearest and most relevant.

14. B
Difficulty: Medium

Category: Writing & Language / Usage

Strategic Advice: The pronoun "which" may be used only to refer to things or animals. "Who" and "whom" may be used only to refer to people.

Getting to the Answer: In this sentence, the pronoun "which" is used incorrectly to refer to "investors," who are people. To determine if "who" or "whom" is correct, substitute the appropriate third-person pronoun for "who" or "whom," and read the sentence. Choice (B) is correct.

15. C
Difficulty: Hard

Category: Writing & Language / Usage

Strategic Advice: Idiom questions often hinge on correct preposition usage. The correct preposition must convey the correct meaning.

Getting to the Answer: Read the sentence carefully to understand the meaning that the preposition must convey. The "pressure" was on the "market," not "on everyone." Choice (C) conveys the sense that the sellers were the source of the pressure.

16. A
Difficulty: Medium

Category: Writing & Language / Usage

Strategic Advice: Subjects and verbs must agree in person and number. Singular third-person subjects take singular third-person verbs, and plural third-person subjects take plural third-person verbs.

Getting to the Answer: Although many things and people make up a market, the noun is singular and requires a singular verb. Because the market is a thing being spoken about, it takes the third-person verb. The verb *to start* is a regular verb, and its third-person singular form is "starts." Choice (A) provides the third-person singular verb.

EXTRA PRACTICE

1. A
Difficulty: Medium

Category: Writing & Language / Effective Language Use

Strategic Advice: When a single word is underlined, make sure that it is the word that best conveys the author's intended meaning in the context of both the sentence and paragraph.

Getting to the Answer: No change is necessary. One of the definitions of "propagate" is "to cause to spread out" over a great area or population. This sense of the word is correct in the context of this sentence and paragraph. Choice (A) is correct.

2. D
Difficulty: Medium

Category: Writing & Language / Punctuation

Strategic Advice: When an underlined sentence fragment includes a parenthetical remark, look for the answer that shows the correct way to punctuate that clause.

Getting to the Answer: Choice (D) is correct. "Such as murder" is a parenthetical remark because it is not necessary for the sentence to be complete. It is best set aside by two commas.

3. B
Difficulty: Easy

Category: Writing & Language / Punctuation

Strategic Advice: An underlined section that includes punctuation requires an assessment of the current punctuation. Choose the answer that provides the correct punctuation for the sentence and context.

Getting to the Answer: Choice (B) is correct. The sentence cannot be correctly combined with the following sentence using a semicolon, so a question mark is the only appropriate option to follow the word "child."

4. A
Difficulty: Medium

Category: Writing & Language / Organization

Strategic Advice: Make sure sentences are presented in the most logical order for the clarity of the passage.

Getting to the Answer: Choice (A) is correct, as the current placement is the correct one for this paragraph. Before sentence 1 would be confusing for the reader, and later in the paragraph would interfere with the author's transition to the next paragraph.

5. A
Difficulty: Hard

Category: Writing & Language / Development

Strategic Advice: Determine if the underlined sentence is effective and correct in its current form, or if one of the other options more clearly develops the author's ideas.

Getting to the Answer: No change is necessary. The current sentence covers all of the points it needs to in order to address the questions posed in the previous paragraph. It also serves as an introduction to the new paragraph. Choice (A) is correct.

6. C
Difficulty: Medium

Category: Writing & Language / Effective Language Use

Strategic Advice: Pay attention to the construction of the sentence (its syntax). Choose the option that correctly and effectively conveys the author's narrative intent, while also preserving additional points the author is trying to make.

Getting to the Answer: Choice (C) is correct because it uses a more effective and clear active voice sentence structure. Choice D is also active voice, but it leaves out the author's additional point about the exchange being "one of the most terrifying conversations in all literature."

7. B

Difficulty: Medium

Category: Writing & Language / Effective Language Use

Strategic Advice: Determine if the underlined sentence is effective in its current form. Pay attention to word choice and precision of language.

Getting to the Answer: In this case, the original sentence is not grammatically incorrect, but there are less wordy options that get the point across clearly. Choice (B) is the best option, as its language is precise and helpful to the overall narrative.

8. D

Difficulty: Medium

Category: Writing & Language / Development

Strategic Advice: For the first sentence of a paragraph, look for the answer choice that embodies the main idea of the paragraph while also serving as an effective connection to, or transition from, the previous paragraph.

Getting to the Answer: Choice (D) is correct because it serves as a logical and effective transition from the previous paragraph. Here, the author is shifting from describing the unsavory aspects of fairy tales to explaining a theory for why they evolved to be that way.

9. A

Difficulty: Medium

Category: Writing & Language / Effective Language Use

Strategic Advice: When a single word is underlined, make sure that it is the word that best conveys the author's intended meaning in the context of both the sentence and paragraph.

Getting to the Answer: No change is necessary because "fantastic" is the best option for this context; the author is creating a parallel between "realistic" threats in the real world with the unrealistic elements of fairy tales. Choice (A) is correct.

10. B

Difficulty: Medium

Category: Writing & Language / Sentence Formation

Strategic Advice: When an underlined section includes the connection between two sentences, consider if the two sentences should remain separate. If they should be joined, choose the best option for doing so.

Getting to the Answer: Choice (B) is correct because these two sentences need to be combined, and a comma is the correct way to do so in this instance. If kept separate, the second sentence is actually a sentence fragment.

11. C

Difficulty: Medium

Category: Writing & Language / Development

Strategic Advice: The final sentence serves the important dual function of concluding the paragraph and the passage. Choose the option that is true to the author's intent for both.

Getting to the Answer: Choice (C) is correct, as it accurately and effectively summarizes the author's central idea that fairy tales should not be thrown into the same category as modern entertainment industry products and that fairy tales possibly helped children navigate the dangers of real life.